READINGS FOR AN INTRODUCTION TO PSYCHOLOGY

READINGS FOR AN INTRODUCTION TO PSYCHOLOGY

SECOND EDITION

Edited by

RICHARD A. KING

University of North Carolina
Chapel Hill, N. C.

McGraw-Hill Book Company

NEW YORK   ST. LOUIS   SAN FRANCISCO

TORONTO   LONDON   SYDNEY

PREFACE
TO THE
FIRST
EDITION

The editor of a readings book is always faced with the problem of establishing criteria for the selection of material from the plethora which faces him. This problem has not been fully resolved, but here are some of the guidelines which were used in assembling these readings:

1. The excerpts should be largely empirical, as opposed to speculative or theoretical. This book is intended for college students who are being exposed to psychology as a formal science for the first time, and it is impossible for anyone to evaluate theory without some facts. A theoretical article may be included if its author has substantiated his ideas with observations. It is hoped that the inclusion of such articles will help to correct the stereotyped misconception held by some students that psychology is a nonempirical, or "talking," discipline.

2. Psychological jargon should be at a minimum. The articles should be in language that most college students can understand— with some effort and appropriate aids, for example, dictionaries. Some excerpting can be done to aid the student.

3. Insofar as possible, a good many classics should be included. It is difficult to define a "classic," but for practical purposes, let us say that this term, as used here and as applied by a substantial majority of psychologists, means a book or an article of definitive historical importance. The inclusion of some classics in this book will be of help, both in the small school with limited library facilities and in the university with very large sections of the introductory class.

4. The articles should have some intrinsic interest for the student. Of necessity, some articles meet this criterion much better than others.

5. Finally, the selection of material should be guided by the fact that this book is primarily intended to accompany the third edition of Introduction to Psychology *by Clifford Morgan and Richard King. The articles should enlarge upon points in the text, but the choice*

should not be so narrow as to limit the scope and value of the readings as a whole. The selections should cover enough common ground to fit in with any standard general psychology text.

All the articles do not, of course, meet all the requirements, but a sufficient number meet most of them to make the book useful in all introductory psychology courses, and especially useful (1) as a stimulus in discussion sections, (2) for the 5 to 10 per cent of students who become psychology majors (exposure to the material presented here should give them a head start), and (3) in colleges with small libraries, or in universities with large sections of the introductory class.

The editor is especially grateful to the authors whose works have been reprinted here. He also wishes to thank the American Psychological Association, Science, and the McGraw-Hill Book Company, Inc., for permission to reprint many excerpts. His colleagues at the University of North Carolina, especially Samuel Fillenbaum, Eugene R. Long, Harold G. McCurdy, and John W. Thibaut, gave valuable suggestions.

RICHARD A. KING
Editor

PREFACE TO THE SECOND EDITION

Nothing has changed with respect to the criteria for article selection. But colleagues and students have found certain articles more suitable than others in the actual use of the first edition; these articles have been retained.

In addition, new articles have been added so that the total number is now 64. Many new articles have been added to the sections on learning and the physiological bases of behavior.

The editor is very grateful to the authors who have so graciously allowed reprinting of their work in both this and the first edition. The final preparation of this book was materially aided by the skillful secretarial work of Margaret S. King and Ruth Boyce.

RICHARD A. KING
Editor

CONTENTS

SECTION SEVEN
EMOTION

SECTION EIGHT
SENSORY PROCESSES AND VISION

SECTION NINE
HEARING AND THE OTHER SENSES

SECTION TEN
PERCEPTION

SECTION ELEVEN
PSYCHOLOGICAL MEASUREMENT

THE
SCIENCE
OF
PSYCHOLOGY

Psychologists have many occupations. This article takes up four major areas of endeavor: statistics and measurement, experimental and theoretical psychology, clinical psychology, and social psychology. The psychologists in these areas are interested, from different points of view, in describing or explaining behavior. Within each area there are many subareas to which you will be introduced during your psychology course.

Some of the humor in the following article is professional in nature. You may not understand it all, but you should finish this reading with a more or less correct impression of the major current fields of psychology.

POINTS TO GUIDE YOUR STUDY *(1) Try to understand as many of the professional jokes as possible. Consult your text for help. (2) On what "continents" would you find the subfields of psychology mentioned in your text?*

1: PSYCHOLOGY IN SPACE—A METAPHOR

Thomas G. Andrews, University of Maryland

American psychologists have traveled in many countries over the world, have crossed both oceans several times, and have been behind the iron curtain. Most of these visits have been brief, and some countries we have seen only from the van-

This article is, with minor modifications, the Presidential address delivered to the Maryland Psychological Association in 1958.

T. G. Andrews. Psychology in space—a metaphor. *Amer. Psychologist,* 1959, **14**, 684–686. Copyright © 1959 by the American Psychological Association. Reprinted here with permission from the author and the American Psychological Association.

tage point of the bar at the airport or by listening to the people in a conference room or a night club. We know that brief visits as tourists tend nevertheless to make us *experts* on the land and the people of foreign countries, however brief our visits and biased our sources of information.

I ask that you go on such a trip with me—a space trip to the planet *Psychology.* We will touch down at a few places, have a few conversations, drink with the natives, admire their scenery, and in this way be

1

able to do the superficial expertizing of the typical American tourist. In the interests of time we will not be able to explore very deeply but will gather large sweeping impressions like true tourists.

Our travel folders tell us that the economic geography of this planet *Psychology* is especially interesting to interdisciplinary space travelers. This world contains four major continents. They are named in turn: *Sigma, Lab, Klinikos,* and *Socio.* The inhabitants of this planet look very much alike, so we will have to be very careful in addressing the natives for fear we insult them by misplacing their places of origin and primary loyalties.

As we tour these four continents we will visit briefly a few selected countries and try to get a quick picture of their fauna, resources, politics, and power centers. As we go from one place to another we will naturally find some underdeveloped lands, some places that are even deliciously dangerous, and of course we may expect certain difficulties with some of the immigration officers who may give us trouble over our visas. Even with these expected irritations of foreign travel, I hope that you will find the trip interesting and will want to revisit some of the out-of-the-way places again, not as tourists but as explorers.

We land first on the continent *Sigma.* This is a land of quantitative enterprise. Our guidebook shows that there are three major nations on this continent: *Statistics, Personnel,* and *Measurement.* The continent has tremendous natural resources, and these are exported rather freely and with great pride of craftsmanship. An embargo is placed on the best exports, however, unless the consumer countries guarantee to maintain certain standards in their use and to order the materials properly with careful advance planning.

In the big production centers we find many launching pads for cargo spaceships to travel even to other planets in the delivery of loads of tests, equations, and personnel assessment systems. The people of

this continent *Sigma* seem to travel rather widely in their own continent and very often go to other continents for long periods. Some of them never return, and it is felt in the government circles that these technicians have defected or have been captured and become slaves in other continents, forced to work on local endeavors.

The government soon learned that this technique made for a good economic balance, and so visitors from the distant planet *Math* sometimes find themselves lured into traps by the fascinating and seductive charms of the local endeavors on *Sigma.* These slaves are happy and contented people, but they are carefully guarded. There are even some legendary captives about whom ballads are sung, such as Spearman, Thurstone, and Mosier.

It is not difficult to obtain a visa to enjoy the countries of *Statistics* and *Measurement,* but it is very difficult to get a work permit in either. There is a rumor that for anyone from elsewhere on the planet to get a work permit he has to be brainwashed to forget all of the Psychology he might have learned. This is not really true, although it is very easy to understand how the rumor got started on the planet. If such brainwashing were true, then of course about all these people could do would be to become department chairmen or deans.

The nation of *Personnel* has no immigration officers, and visitors often find such comforts in its pleasant climate and lush gardens that they stay for long periods. Some of them retire there—early in life. Occasionally the natives will drift across the border to *Measurement* to refreshen certain of their supplies. The economy in *Personnel* is rather an unstable one because it imports much more than it exports, and the port authorities have permitted large stocks of useless merchandise to pile up in the warehouses. In the old days the nation *Personnel* depended for its imports on its neighboring countries on the same continent *Sigma.* It has more recently found great use for imports from the continents of *Socio* and *Klinikos*. There is an occasional fear expressed that the country has run up such a debt to these sources that *Socio* and *Klinikos* may swallow it up in their axis.

Our time is too short to push back into the underdeveloped areas on this continent of *Sigma*. Also we run the risk of losing some of our tour members who may be brainwashed and become statisticians or fall into the traps of the test builders. Of course, this is just rumor, but one cannot be too careful.

We will leave our spaceship behind and take a regularly scheduled flight to the next continent on our itinerary—*Lab*. This is a very intriguing continent, made up loosely of a large number of countries or baronial states of Experimental and Theoretical Psychology. This is the oldest inhabited continent on the planet, and it takes its seniority very seriously. It has a central government that is a very strong oligarchy. A new central government palace is being planned, and the leaders are reported to be in great debate over the style of architecture to be employed. Some are demanding that it be in the classical shape of an Ivory Tower, but there is a rapidly growing faction that is holding out for a Skinner Box.

As we debark on the continent *Lab* we are met by some rather suspicious immigration officers who check our visas very carefully. Those of us who are allowed to go on further find certain delights in this place. The people are all very busy, and they seem somewhat preoccupied and detached. In one of the states we find animals dominating the activity of automated recording systems. There are large supplies of II and VIII nerves lying about. In one place we find the natives working mainly with chalk boards and reams of paper. These latter are theoreticians and are catered to as high priests.

Only a few of the natives seem much interested in the large planetary affairs.

However, there is a real spirit of cohesiveness and common purpose among these indigenous people. We learn that this spirit is especially noticeable when there is a planetary congress. The representatives from this continent *Lab* prefer a separate area for their own affairs at which they cavort with glee. There is a persistent but false rumor that the continent has expressed a desire to secede from the planetary congress. The trade of this continent is very active. There is no embargo on exports, and there is a great deal of pride on the part of the artisans in the way in which they shape their products for sheer beauty, although less for utility. Imports are from other planets of *Math*, *Physics*, and *Physiology* and some from the continent *Sigma*. The younger generation here is learning to check the lists of available stock from the continents of *Socio* and *Klinikos*. When they are able to smuggle a good hypothesis in from these continents, they develop it well; but the old guard tends to frown on this smuggling activity. Some of the younger generation have been taking extended excursions into other lands, where they are always in demand; and they have no trouble getting visas and work permits wherever they go.

As we leave the brassy shores of the continent *Lab* we start out for the next continent *Klinikos*, a very great distance away. We have time to study our guidebooks, and we find that this continent is the largest one on the planet. It is made up of several nations: *Clinical, Counseling, Child, Developmental,* and *School Psychology,* and *Personality*. Even in these highly civilized nations, there are very large areas of undeveloped land. The natives greet us with warmth and friendship. They seem to be exceedingly interested in us as individuals, although they seem to disagree markedly in their interpretations of our behavior.

The history of this continent is particularly interesting. It has developed very rapidly, and its rate of population increase has been amazing compared to the other continents on the planet. There is some concern on the part of the other continents that its representation in the planetary congress is growing too rapidly. There are occasional interplanetary skirmishes that are engaged in by war lords on this continent of *Klinikos,* especially with the continent *Psyche* on the neighboring planet *Medic.* The planetary congress on *Psychology* devotes considerable time to strategy and tactics in helping this continent *Klinikos* in these battles. In recent years the production centers on *Klinikos* have dredged great stores of gold from the mines in the areas of *Hew* and *Usphus* to develop their natural resources, and in general the natives fare rather well with their conditions of life.

The boundaries between the separate states on this continent are not well marked, and often it is difficult for visitors and natives alike to tell just exactly where they are. The fields are green, and the flowers are sweet smelling, however, so getting lost here is not at all unpleasant— except possibly for a few visitors from *Lab* who come over on brief inspection trips and on occasional political skirmishes. Some of these visitors are attracted to stay, however, and they find that they can lead very productive lives here.

Our time is running out, and we have one continent left. This is the continent *Socio.* Our visit there must be very brief for us to get back on schedule. On arrival here we are met by natives in groups. They are very pleasant and helpful, but we cannot seem to learn as much about them as we would like in the short time we have. They are very busy and seem to be involved in activities that require them to work together a great deal. The continent here is rather unified, and there are no boundaries and so no problems with visas

and work permits. They import freely from the other three continents and also other planets. Some of the local continents have expressed the wish that the continent *Socio* would buy more locally. We get the impression that our traveling group is being studied rather carefully by the natives, and so we stay on our best behavior even while we are partaking of their fruits and beverages. As good space travelers, we asked the natives of *Socio* to take us to their leader. This threw them into confusion and provoked a long discussion of the meaning of the term. We concluded that they did not have any real leaders because they all disagreed on what the term means. We apologize for the necessity of our very brief stay and return to our spaceship pad to blast off for *Earth.*

As we rise slowly on our first-stage power we look back at the planet *Psychology* and see it revolving slowly as it recedes from us, much like the over-all impression one gets from flying away from the island of Bermuda and looking back to see the spaces of land and waterways all at once. Our earlier impression is confirmed: that the oceans between the continents on this planet *Psychology* are far too big and, also, that the underdeveloped parts of all of the four continents stretch out in tremendous size, beckoning for explorers.

Our trip has been very brief, but like American tourists we have gathered snatches of impressions here and there and are now experts on matters pertaining to the planet we have seen and walked on so briefly. I leave it to you to judge whether the impressions I have related are all superficial ones made in the role of a typical American tourist or whether any of them gets close to reality. If your collective leg has been pulled by this travelog, just how much?

In psychology, theory is a scientific shorthand, a predictor, and a guide to research. Theories which have these three characteristics are sometimes called hypothetico-deductive theories, and they have been quite useful in physics. Such theories start with some general guesses as to the laws relating independent and dependent variables. (You should know what these are by now.) Such guesses are the postulates of the theory, or the axioms. From the postulates, one then deduces the consequences according to certain "guessed-at" rules. Finally, the theorist can become an experimenter or observer and can look, do experiments, or make observations to see if the consequences are those that are predicted by the theory. If they are, he has more assurance that the original "guessed-at" postulates and rules of derivation are correct. This selection is from the opening chapter of a book that presents a hypothetico-deductive theory of behavior.

C. L. Hull has been an influential figure in American psychology. He might be classed by some as a functionalist, but he belongs more nearly to the behaviorist offshoot of functionalism. He is sometimes said to be a member, along with K. W. Spence and B. F. Skinner, of the neobehaviorist school, the behaviorists who followed J. B. Watson. His emphasis on hypothetico-deductive theory in psychology, and the apparent rigor of his theories, made him quite appealing to the more "tough-minded" psychologists of the 1930s and 1940s.

POINTS TO GUIDE YOUR STUDY   *(1) How does the discussion of the spherical nature of planets illustrate the hypothetico-deductive method?   (2) What are some other examples of hypothetico-deductive theories in other sciences?*

2: PRINCIPLES OF BEHAVIOR

C. L. Hull

The two aspects of science: empirical and explanatory

Men are ever engaged in the dual activity of making observations and then seeking explanations of the resulting revelations. All normal men in all times have observed the rising and setting of the sun and the several phases of the moon. The more thoughtful among them have then proceeded to ask the question, "Why? Why does the moon wax and wane? Why does the sun rise and set, and where does it go when it sets?" Here we have the two essential elements of modern science: the making of observations constitutes the empirical or factual component, and the systematic attempt to explain these facts constitutes the theoretical component. As science has developed, specialization, or division of labor, has occurred; some men have devoted their time mainly to the making of observations, while a smaller number have occupied themselves largely with the problems of explanation.

During the infancy of science, observations are for the most part casual and qualitative—the sun rises, beats down strongly at midday, and sets; the moon grows from the crescent to full and then diminishes. Later observations, usually

C. L. Hull. *Principles of behavior.* New York: D. Appleton-Century Co., Inc., 1943. Copyright © 1943 by D. Appleton-Century Co., Inc. Excerpts reprinted here by permission of Appleton-Century-Crofts, a Division of the Meredith Publishing Company.

motivated by practical considerations of one kind or another, tend to become quantitative and precise—the number of days in the moon's monthly cycle are counted accurately, and the duration of the sun's yearly course is determined with precision. As the need for more exact observations increases, special tools and instruments, such as graduated measuring sticks, protractors, clocks, telescopes, and microscopes, are devised to facilitate the labor. Kindred tools relating to a given field of science are frequently assembled under a single roof for convenience of use; such an assemblage becomes a laboratory.

As scientific investigations become more and more searching it is discovered that the spontaneous happenings of nature are not adequate to permit the necessary observations. This leads to the setting up of special conditions which will bring about the desired events under circumstances favorable for such observations; thus experiments originate. But even in deliberate experiment it is often extraordinarily difficult to determine with which among a complex of antecedent conditions a given consequence is primarily associated; in this way arise a complex maze of control experiments and other technical procedures, the general principles of which are common to all sciences but the details of which are peculiar to each. Thus in brief review we see the characteristic technical development of the empirical or factual aspect of science.

Complex and difficult as are some of the problems of empirical science, those of scientific theory are perhaps even more difficult of solution and are subject to a greater hazard of error. It is not a matter of chance that the waxing and waning of the moon was observed for countless millennia before the comparatively recent times when it was at last successfully explained on the basis of the Copernican hypothesis. Closely paralleling the development of the technical aids employed by empirical science, there have also grown up in the field of scientific theory a complex array of tools and special procedures, mostly mathematical and logical in nature, designed to aid in coping with these difficulties. Because of the elementary nature of the present treatise, very little explicit discussion of the use of such tools will be given.

The deductive nature of scientific theory and explanation

The term *theory* in the behavioral or "social" sciences has a variety of current meanings. As understood in the present work, a theory is a systematic deductive derivation of the secondary principles of observable phenomena from a relatively small number of primary principles or postulates, much as the secondary principles or theorems of geometry are all ultimately derived as a logical hierarchy from a few original definitions and primary principles called axioms. In science an observed event is said to be explained when the proposition expressing it has been logically derived from a set of definitions and postulates coupled with certain observed conditions antecedent to the event. This, in brief, is the nature of scientific theory and explanation as generally understood and accepted in the physical sciences after centuries of successful development.

The preceding summary statement of the nature of scientific theory and explanation needs considerable elaboration and exemplification. Unfortunately the finding of generally intelligible examples presents serious difficulties; because of the extreme youth of systematic behavior theory as here understood, it is impossible safely to assume that the reader possesses any considerable familiarity with it. For this reason it will be necessary to choose all the examples from such physical sciences as are now commonly taught in the schools.

We can best begin the detailed consideration of the nature of scientific explanation by distinguishing it from something often confused with it. Suppose a naïve person with a moderate-sized telescope has observed Venus, Mars, Jupiter, and Saturn, together with numerous moons (including our own), and found them all to be round in contour and presumably spherical in form. He might proceed to formulate his observations in a statement such as, "All heavenly bodies are spherical," even though this statement goes far beyond the observations, since he has examined only a small sample of these bodies. Suppose, next, he secures a better telescope; he is now able to observe Uranus and Neptune, and finds both round in contour also. He may, in a manner of speaking, be said to explain the sphericity of Neptune by subsuming it under the category of heavenly bodies and then applying his previous empirical generalization. Indeed, he could have predicted the spherical nature of Neptune by this procedure before it was observed at all:

All heavenly bodies are spherical.
Neptune is a heavenly body,
Therefore Neptune is spherical.

Much of what is loosely called explanation in the field of behavior is of this nature. The fighting propensities of a chicken are explained by the fact that he is a game cock and game cocks are empirically known to be pugnacious. The gregariousness of a group of animals is explained by the fact that the animals in question are dogs, and dogs are empirically known to be gregarious. As we have seen, it is possible to make concrete predictions of a sort on the basis of such generalizations, and so they have significance. Nevertheless this kind of procedure—the subsumption of a particular set of conditions under a category involved in a previously made empirical generalization—is not exactly which is regarded here as a scientific theoretical explanation.

For one thing, a theoretical explanation as here understood grows out of a problem, e.g., "What must be the shape of the heavenly bodies?" Secondly, it sets out from certain propositions or statements. These propositions are of two rather different kinds. Propositions of the first type required by an explanation are those stating the relevant initial or *antecedent conditions.* For example, an explanation of the shape of heavenly bodies might require the preliminary assumption of the existence of (1) a large mass of (2) more or less plastic, (3) more or less homogeneous matter, (4) initially of any shape at all, (5) the whole located in otherwise empty space. But a statement of the antecedent conditions is not enough; there must also be available a set of statements of *general principles* or rules of action relevant to the situation. Moreover, the particular principles to be utilized in a given explanation must be chosen from the set of principles generally employed by the theorist in explanations of this class of phenomena, the choice to be made strictly on the basis of the nature of the question or problem under consideration taken in conjunction with the observed or assumed conditions. For example, in the case of the shape of the heavenly bodies the chief principle employed is the Newtonian law of gravitation, namely, that every particle of matter attracts every other particle to a degree proportional to the product of their masses and inversely proportional to the square of the distances separating them. These principles are apt themselves to be verbal formulations of empirical generalizations, but may be merely happy conjectures or guesses found by a certain amount of antecedent trial-and-error to agree with observed fact. At all events they originate in one way or another in empirical observation.

The concluding phase of a scientific explanation is the derivation of the answer to the motivating question from the conditions and the principles, taken jointly, by a process of inference or reasoning. For example, it follows from the principle of gravitation that empty spaces which might at any time have existed within the mass of a heavenly body would at once be closed. Moreover, if at any point on the surface there were an elevation and adjacent to it a depression or valley, the sum of the gravitational pressures of the particles of matter in the elevation acting on the plastic material beneath would exert substantially the same pressure laterally as toward the center of gravity. But since there would be no equal lateral pressure originating in the valley to oppose the pressure originating in the elevation, the matter contained in the elevation would flow into the valley, thus eliminating both. This means that in the course of time all the matter in the mass under consideration would be arranged about its center of gravity with no elevations or depressions; i.e., the radius of the body at all points would be the same. In other words, if the assumed mass were not already spherical it would in the course of time automatically become so. It follows that all heavenly bodies, including Neptune, must be spherical in form.

The significance of the existence of these two methods of arriving at a verbal formulation of the shape of the planet Neptune may now be stated. The critical characteristic of scientific theoretical explanation is that it reaches independently through a process of reasoning the same outcome with respect to (secondary) principles as is attained through the process of empirical generalization. Thus scientific theory may arrive at the general proposition, "All heavenly bodies of sufficient size, density, plasticity, and homogeneity are spherical," as a theorem, simply by means of a process of inference or deduction without any moons or planets having been observed at all. The fact that, in certain fields at least, practically the same statements or propositions can be attained quite independently by empirical methods as by theoretical procedures is of enormous importance for the development of science. For one thing, it makes possible the checking of results

obtained by one method against those obtained by the other. It is a general assumption in scientific methodology that if everything entering into both procedures is correct, the statements yielded by them will never be in genuine conflict.

Summary

Modern science has two inseparable components—the empirical and the theoretical. The empirical component is concerned primarily with observation; the theoretical component is concerned with the interpretation and explanation of observation. A natural event is explained when it can be derived as a theorem by a process of reasoning from (1) a knowledge of the relevant natural conditions antedating it, and (2) one or more relevant principles called postulates. Clusters or families of theorems are generated, and theorems are often employed in the derivation of other theorems; thus is developed a logical hierarchy resembling that found in ordinary geometry. A hierarchy of interrelated families of theorems, all derived from the same set of consistent postulates, constitutes a scientific system.

Scientific theory resembles argumentation in being logical in nature but differs radically in that the objective of argument is to convince. In scientific theory logic is employed in conjunction with observation as a means of inquiry. Indeed, theoretical procedures are indispensable in the establishment of natural laws. The range of validity of a given supposed law can be determined only by trying it out empirically under a wide range of conditions where it will operate in simultaneous conjunction with the greatest variety and combination of other natural laws. But the only way the scientist can tell from the outcome of such an empirical procedure whether a given hypothetical law has acted in the postulated manner is first to deduce by a logical process what the outcome of the investigation *should* be if the hypothesis really holds. This deductive process is the essence of scientific theory.

The typical procedure in science is to adopt a postulate tentatively, deduce one or more of its logical implications concerning observable phenomena, and then check the validity of the deductions by observation. If the deduction is in genuine disagreement with observation, the postulate must be either abandoned or so modified that it implies no such conflicting statement. If, however, the deductions and the observations agree, the postulate gains in dependability. By successive agreements under a very wide variety of conditions it may attain a high degree of justified credibility, but never absolute certainty.

Not all psychologists hold that hypothetico-deductive theories are useful—quite the contrary. Some would even say that, while in the advanced sciences such theories may be useful, not enough data have been collected in psychology to justify theorizing. Psychologists of this type often point to the painful accumulation of data which took place before the great theories in the physical sciences were formulated. These psychologists, therefore, study the phenomena of behavior for their own sake and let their observations lead them. (This is perhaps more in the tradition of the biological sciences.) One experimental outcome suggests the next experiment; the outcome of this experiment suggests the next and so on. The following article shows that this can be a fruitful strategy.

B. F. Skinner is the founder of a neobehavioristic school which puts special emphasis on the collection of data and the control of the behavior of individual organisms. The observations of this school have given rise to methodologies for assessing the effects of drugs on behavior, or psychopharmacology, and a method of teaching school subjects which utilizes "teaching machines." It is currently a vigorous movement in psychology.

POINTS TO GUIDE YOUR STUDY *(1) Contrast Skinner's approach with that of Hull. (2) One of the important reasons for doing experiments is that the control of variables is possible. In what ways has Skinner attempted to achieve such control?*

3: A CASE HISTORY IN SCIENTIFIC METHOD

B. F. Skinner, Harvard University

It has been said that college teaching is the only profession for which there is no

Address of the President at the Eastern Psychological Association meetings in Philadelphia, April, 1955.

B. F. Skinner. A case history in scientific method. *Amer. Psychologist,* 1956, 11, 221–233. Copyright © 1956 by the American Psychological Association. Reprinted here with permission from the author and the American Psychological Association.

(Some of the investigators mentioned in this article are now working at laboratories other than those indicated. *Ed.*)

professional training, and it is commonly argued that this is because our graduate schools train scholars and scientists rather than teachers. We are more concerned with the discovery of knowledge than with its dissemination. But can we justify ourselves quite so easily? It is a bold thing to say that we know how to train a man to be a scientist. Scientific thinking is the most complex and probably the most subtle of all human activities. Do we actually know how to shape up such behavior, or do we simply mean that some of the people who attend our graduate schools eventually become scientists?

Except for a laboratory course which acquaints the student with standard apparatus and standard procedures, the only explicit training in scientific method generally received by a young psychologist is a course in statistics—not the introductory course, which is often required of so many kinds of students that it is scarcely scientific at all, but an advanced course which includes "model building," "theory construction," and "experimental design." But it is a mistake to identify scientific practice with the formalized constructions of statistics and scientific method. These disciplines have their place, but it does not coincide with the place of scientific research. They offer *a* method of science but not, as is so often implied, *the* method. As formal disciplines they arose very late in the history of science, and most of the facts of science have been discovered without their aid. It takes a great deal of skill to fit Faraday with his wires and magnets into the picture which statistics gives us of scientific thinking. And most current scientific practice would be equally refractory, especially in the important initial stages. It is no wonder that the laboratory scientist is puzzled and often dismayed when he discovers how his behavior has been reconstructed in the formal analyses of scientific method. He is likely to protest that this is not at all a fair representation of what he does.

But his protest is not likely to be heard. For the prestige of statistics and scientific methodology is enormous. Much of it is borrowed from the high repute of mathematics and logic, but much of it derives from the flourishing state of the art itself. Some statisticians are professional people employed by scientific and commercial en-

terprises. Some are teachers and pure researchers who give their colleagues the same kind of service for nothing—or at most a note of acknowledgment. Many are zealous people who, with the best of intentions, are anxious to show the nonstatistical scientist how he can do his job more efficiently and assess his results more accurately. There are strong professional societies devoted to the advancement of statistics, and hundreds of technical books and journals are published annually.

Against this, the practicing scientist has very little to offer. He cannot refer the young psychologist to a book which will tell him how to find out all there is to know about a subject matter, how to have the good hunch which will lead him to devise a suitable piece of apparatus, how to develop an efficient experimental routine, how to abandon an unprofitable line of attack, how to move on most rapidly to later stages of his research. The work habits which have become second nature to him have not been formalized by anyone, and he may feel that they possibly never will be. As Richter (5) has pointed out, "Some of the most important discoveries have been made without any plan of research," and "there are researchers who do not work on a verbal plane, who cannot put into words what they are doing."

If we are interested in perpetuating the practices responsible for the present corpus of scientific knowledge, we must keep in mind that some very important parts of the scientific process do not now lend themselves to mathematical, logical, or any other formal treatment. We do not know enough about human behavior to know how the scientist does what he does. Although statisticians and methodologists may seem to tell us, or at least imply, how the mind works—how problems arise, how hypotheses are formed, deductions made, and crucial experiments designed—we as psychologists are in a position to remind them that they do not have methods appropriate to the empirical observation or the functional analysis of such data. These are aspects of human behavior, and no one knows better than we how little can at the moment be said about them.

Some day we shall be better able to express the distinction between empirical analysis and formal reconstruction, for we shall have an alternative account of the behavior of Man Thinking. Such an account will not only plausibly reconstruct what a particular scientist did in any given case, it will permit us to evaluate practices and, I believe, to teach scientific thinking. But that day is some little distance in the future. Meanwhile we can only fall back on examples.

Some time ago the director of Project A of the American Psychological Association asked me to describe my activities as a research psychologist. I went through a trunkful of old notes and records and, for my pains, reread some of my earlier publications. This has made me all the more aware of the contrast between the reconstructions of formalized scientific method and at least one case of actual practice. Instead of amplifying the points I have just made by resorting to a generalized account which is not available, I should like to discuss a case history. It is not one of the case histories we should most like to have, but what it lacks in importance is perhaps somewhat offset by accessibility. I therefore ask you to imagine that you are all clinical psychologists—a task which becomes easier and easier as the years go by—while I sit across the desk from you or stretch out upon this comfortable leather couch.

The first thing I can remember happened when I was only twenty-two years old. Shortly after I had graduated from college Bertrand Russell published a series of articles in the old *Dial* magazine on the epistemology of John B. Watson's Behaviorism. I had had no psychology as an undergraduate, but I had had a lot of biology, and two of the books which my biology professor had put into my hands were Loeb's *Physiology of the Brain* and the newly published Oxford edition of Pavlov's *Conditioned Reflexes*. And now here was Russell extrapolating the principles of an objective formulation of behavior to the problem of knowledge! Many years later when I told Lord Russell that his articles were responsible for my interest in behavior, he could only exclaim, "Good Heavens! I had always supposed that those articles had demolished Behaviorism!" But at any rate he had taken Watson seriously, and so did I.

When I arrived at Harvard for graduate study, the air was not exactly full of behavior, but Walter Hunter was coming in once a week from Clark University to give a seminar, and Fred Keller, also a graduate student, was an expert in both the technical details and the sophistry of Behaviorism. Many a time he saved me as I sank into the quicksands of an amateurish discussion of "What is an image?" or "Where is red?" I soon came into contact with W. J. Crozier, who had studied under Loeb. It had been said of Loeb, and might have been said of Crozier, that he "resented the nervous system." Whether this was true or not, the fact was that both these men talked about animal behavior without mentioning the nervous system and with surprising success. So far as I was concerned, they cancelled out the physiological theorizing of Pavlov and Sherrington and thus clarified what remained of the work of these men as the beginnings of an independent science of behavior. My doctoral thesis was in part an operational analysis of Sherrington's synapse, in which behavioral laws were substituted for supposed states of the central nervous system.

But the part of my thesis at issue here was experimental. So far as I can see, I began simply by looking for lawful processes in the behavior of the intact organism. Pavlov had shown the way; but I could not then, as I cannot now, move without a jolt from salivary reflexes to the important business of the organism in everyday life. Sherrington and Magnus had found order in surgical segments of the organism. Could not something of the same sort be found, to use Loeb's phrase, in "the organism as a whole?" I had the clue from Pavlov: control your conditions and you will see order.

It is not surprising that my first gadget was a silent release box, operated by compressed air and designed to eliminate disturbances when introducing a rat into an apparatus. I used this first in studying the way a rat adapted to a novel stimulus. I built a soundproof box containing a specially structured space. A rat was released, pneumatically, at the far end of a darkened tunnel from which it emerged in exploratory fashion into a well-lighted area. To accentuate its progress and to facilitate recording, the tunnel was placed at the top of a flight of steps, something like a functional Parthenon (Figure 1). The rat would peek out from the tunnel, perhaps glancing suspiciously at the one-way window through which I was watching it, then stretch itself cautiously down the steps. A soft click (carefully calibrated, of course) would cause it to pull back into the tunnel and remain there for some time. But repeated clicks had less and less of an effect. I recorded the rat's advances and retreats

FIGURE 1.

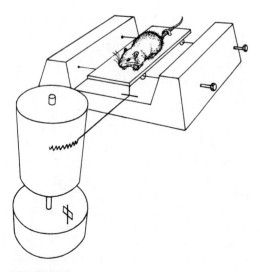

FIGURE 2.

by moving a pen back and forth across a moving paper tape.

The major result of this experiment was that some of my rats had babies. I began to watch young rats. I saw them right themselves and crawl about very much like the decerebrate or thalamic cats and rabbits of Magnus. So I set about studying the postural reflexes of young rats. Here was a first principle not formally recognized by scientific methodologists: When you run onto something interesting, drop everything else and study it. I tore up the Parthenon and started over.

If you hold a young rat in one hand and pull it gently by the tail, it will resist you by pulling forward and then, with a sudden sharp spring which usually disengages its tail, it will leap out into space. I decided to study this behavior quantitatively. I built a light platform covered with cloth and mounted it on tightly stretched piano wires (Figure 2). Here was a version of Sherrington's torsion-wire myograph, originally designed to record the isometric contraction of the *tibialis anticus* of a cat, but here adapted to the response of a whole organism. When the tail of the young rat was gently pulled, the rat clung to the cloth floor and tugged forward. By amplifying the fine movements of the platform, it was possible to get a good kymograph record of the tremor in this motion and then, as the pull against the tail was increased, of the desperate spring into the air (Figure 3).

Now, baby rats have very little future, except as adult rats. Their behavior is literally infantile and cannot be usefully extrapolated to everyday life. But if this technique would work with a baby, why not try it on a mature rat? To avoid attaching anything to the rat, it should be possible to record, not a pull against the substrate, but the ballistic thrust exerted as the rat runs forward or suddenly stops in response to my calibrated click. So, invoking the first principle of scientific practice again, I threw away the piano-wire platform, and built a runway, eight feet long. This was constructed of light wood, in the form of a girder, mounted rigidly on vertical glass plates, the elasticity of which permitted a very slight longitudinal movement (Figure 4). The runway became the

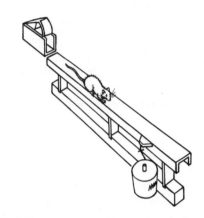

FIGURE 4.

floor of a long tunnel, not shown, at one end of which I placed my soundless release box and at the other end myself, prepared to reinforce the rat for coming down the runway by giving it a bit of wet mash, to sound a click from time to time when it had reached the middle of the runway, and to harvest kymograph records of the vibrations of the substrate.

Now for a second unformalized principle of scientific practice: Some ways of doing research are easier than others. I got tired of carrying the rat back to the other end of the runway. A back alley was therefore

FIGURE 3.

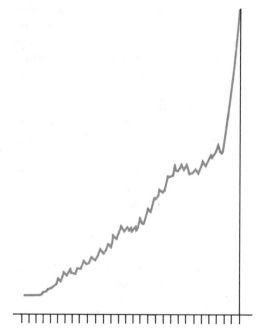

FIGURE 5.

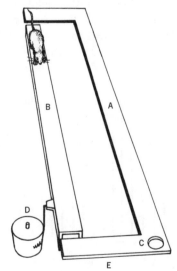

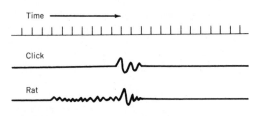

FIGURE 6.

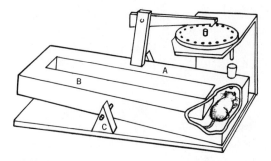

FIGURE 8.

added (Figure 5). Now the rat could eat a bit of mash at point C, go down the back alley A, around the end as shown, and back home by runway B. The experimenter at E could collect records from the kymograph at D in comfort. In this way a great many records were made of the forces exerted against the substratum as rats ran down the alley and occasionally stopped dead in their tracks as a click sounded (Figure 6).

There was one annoying detail, however. The rat would often wait an inordinately long time at C before starting down the back alley on the next run. There seemed to be no explanation for this. When I timed these delays with a stop watch, however, and plotted them, they seemed to show orderly changes (Figure 7). This was, of course, the kind of thing I was looking for. I forgot all about the movements of the substratum and began to run rats for the sake of the delay measurements alone. But there was now no reason why the runway had to be eight feet long and, as the second principle came into

FIGURE 7.

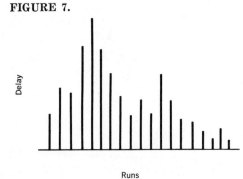

Runs

play again, I saw no reason why the rat could not deliver its own reinforcement.

A new apparatus was built. In Figure 8, we see the rat eating a piece of food just after completing a run. It produced the food by its own action. As it ran down the back alley A to the far end of the rectangular runway, its weight caused the whole runway to tilt slightly on the axis C and this movement turned the wooden disc D, permitting a piece of food in one of the holes around its perimeter to drop through a funnel into a food dish. The food was pearl barley, the only kind I could find in the grocery stores in reasonably uniform pieces. The rat had only to complete its journey by coming down the home stretch B to enjoy its reward. The experimenter was able to enjoy *his* reward at the same time, for he had only to load the magazine, put in a rat, and relax. Each tilt was recorded on a slowly moving kymograph.

A third unformalized principle of scientific practice: Some people are lucky. The disc of wood from which I had fashioned the food magazine was taken from a storeroom of discarded apparatus. It happened to have a central spindle, which fortunately I had not bothered to cut off. One day it occurred to me that if I wound a string around the spindle and allowed it to unwind as the magazine was emptied (Figure 9), I would get a different kind of record. Instead of a mere report of the up-and-down movement of the runway, as a series of pips as in a polygraph, I would

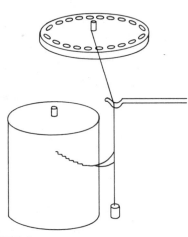

FIGURE 9.

get a *curve*. And I knew that science made great use of curves, although, so far as I could discover, very little of pips on a polygram. The difference between the old type of record at A (Figure 10) and the new at B may not seem great, but as it turned out the curve revealed things in the rate of responding, and in changes in that rate, which would certainly otherwise have been missed. By allowing the string to unwind rather than to wind, I had got my curve in an awkward Cartesian quadrant, but that was easily remedied. Psychologists have adopted cumulative curves only very slowly, but I think it is fair to say that they have become an indispensable tool for certain purposes of analysis.

Eventually, of course, the runway was seen to be unnecessary. The rat could simply reach into a covered tray for pieces of food, and each movement of the cover

could operate a solenoid to move a pen one step in a cumulative curve. The first major change in rate observed in this way was due to ingestion. Curves showing how the rate of eating declined with the time of eating comprised the other part of my thesis. But a refinement was needed. The behavior of the rat in pushing open the door was not a normal part of the ingestive behavior of *Rattus rattus*. The act was obviously learned but its status as part of the final performance was not clear. It seemed wise to add an initial conditioned response connected with ingestion in a quite arbitrary way. I chose the first device which came to hand—a horizontal bar or lever placed where it could be conveniently depressed by the rat to close a switch which operated a magnetic magazine. Ingestion curves obtained with this initial response in the chain were found to have the same properties as those without it.

Now, as soon as you begin to complicate an apparatus you necessarily invoke a fourth principle of scientific practice: Apparatuses sometimes break down. I had only to wait for the food magazine to jam to get an extinction curve. At first I treated this as a defect and hastened to remedy the difficulty. But eventually, of course, I deliberately disconnected the magazine. I can easily recall the excitement of that first complete extinction curve (Figure 11). I had made contact with Pavlov at last! Here was a curve uncorrupted by the physiological process of ingestion. It was an orderly change due to nothing more

FIGURE 10.

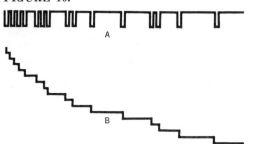

A

B

FIGURE 11.

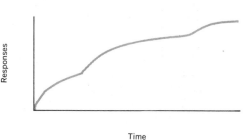

Responses

Time

than a special contingency of reinforcement. It was pure behavior! I am not saying that I would not have got around to extinction curves without a breakdown in the apparatus; Pavlov had given too strong a lead in that direction. But it is still no exaggeration to say that some of the most interesting and surprising results have turned up first because of similar accidents. Foolproof apparatus is no doubt highly desirable, but Charles Ferster and I in recently reviewing the data from a five-year program of research found many occasions to congratulate ourselves on the fallibility of relays and vacuum tubes.

I then built four soundproof ventilated boxes, each containing a lever and a food magazine and supplied with a cumulative recorder, and was on my way to an intensive study of conditioned reflexes in skeletal behavior. I would reinforce every response for several days and then extinguish for a day or two, varying the number of reinforcements, the amount of previous magazine training, and so on.

At this point I made my first use of the deductive method. I had long since given up pearl barley as too unbalanced a diet for steady use. A neighborhood druggist had shown me his pill machine, and I had had one made along the same line (Figure 12). It consisted of a fluted brass bed across which one laid a long cylinder of stiff paste (in my case a MacCollum formula for an adequate rat diet). A similarly fluted cutter was then lowered onto the cylinder and rolled slowly back and forth,

FIGURE 12.

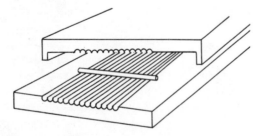

converting the paste into about a dozen spherical pellets. These were dried for a day or so before use. The procedure was painstaking and laborious. Eight rats eating a hundred pellets each per day could easily keep up with production. One pleasant Saturday afternoon I surveyed my supply of dry pellets, and, appealing to certain elemental theorems in arithmetic, deduced that unless I spent the rest of that afternoon and evening at the pill machine, the supply would be exhausted by ten-thirty Monday morning.

Since I do not wish to deprecate the hypothetico-deductive method, I am glad to testify here to its usefulness. It led me to apply our second principle of unformalized scientific method and to ask myself why *every* press of the lever had to be reinforced. I was not then aware of what had happened at the Brown laboratories, as Harold Schlosberg later told the story. A graduate student had been given the task of running a cat through a difficult discrimination experiment. One Sunday the student found the supply of cat food exhausted. The stores were closed and so, with a beautiful faith in the frequency-theory of learning, he ran the cat as usual and took it back to its living cage unrewarded. Schlosberg reports that the cat howled its protest continuously for nearly forty-eight hours. Unaware of this I decided to reinforce a response only once every minute and to allow all other responses to go unreinforced. There were two results: (a) my supply of pellets lasted almost indefinitely and (b) each rat stabilized at a fairly constant rate of responding.

Now, a steady state was something I was familiar with from physical chemistry, and I therefore embarked upon the study of periodic reinforcement. I soon found that the constant rate at which the rat stabilized depended upon how hungry it was. Hungry rat, high rate; less hungry rat, lower rate. At that time I was bothered by the practical problem of controlling food deprivation. I was working half time at the Medical School (on chronaxie of subordination!) and could not maintain a good schedule in working with the rats. The rate of responding under periodic reinforcement suggested a scheme for keeping a rat at a constant level of deprivation. The argument went like this: Suppose you reinforce the rat, not at the end of a given period, but when it has completed the number of responses ordinarily emitted in that period. And suppose you use substantial pellets of food and give the rat continuous access to the lever. Then, except for periods when the rat sleeps, it should operate the lever at a constant rate around the clock. For, whenever it grows slightly hungrier, it will work faster, get food faster, and become less hungry, while whenever it grows slightly less hungry, it will respond at a lower rate, get less food, and grow hungrier. By setting the reinforcement at a given number of responses it should even be possible to hold the rat at any given level of deprivation. I visualized a machine with a dial which one could set to make available, at any time of day or night, a rat in a given state of deprivation. Of course, nothing of the sort happens. This is "fixed-ratio" rather than "fixed-interval" reinforcement and, as I soon found out, it produces a very different type of performance. This is an example of a fifth unformalized principle of scientific practice, but one which has at least been named. Walter Cannon described it with a word invented by Horace Walpole: *serendipity*—the art of finding one thing while looking for something else.

This account of my scientific behavior up to the point at which I published my results in a book called *The Behavior of Organisms* is as exact in letter and spirit as I can now make it. The notes, data, and publications which I have examined do not show that I ever behaved in the manner of Man Thinking as described by John Stuart Mill or John Dewey or in reconstructions of scientific behavior by other philosophers of science. I never faced a Problem which was more than the eternal problem of finding order. I never attacked a problem by constructing a Hypothesis. I never deduced Theorems or submitted them to Experimental Check. So far as I can see, I had no preconceived Model of Behavior—certainly not a physiological or mentalistic one, and, I believe, not a conceptual one. The "reflex reserve" was an abortive, though operational, concept which was retracted a year or so after publication in a paper at the Philadelphia meeting of the APA. It lived up to my opinion of theories in general by proving utterly worthless in suggesting further experiments. Of course, I was working on a basic Assumption—that there was order in behavior if I could only discover it—but such an assumption is not to be confused with the hypotheses of deductive theory. It is also true that I exercised a certain Selection of Facts but not because of relevance to theory but because one fact was more orderly than another. If I engaged in Experimental Design at all, it was simply to complete or extend some evidence of order already observed.

Most of the experiments described in *The Behavior of Organisms* were done with groups of four rats. A fairly common reaction to the book was that such groups were too small. How did I know that other groups of four rats would do the same thing? Keller, in defending the book, countered with the charge that groups of four were too *big*. Unfortunately, however, I allowed myself to be persuaded of the contrary. This was due in part to my association at the University of Minnesota with W. T. Heron. Through him I came into close contact for the first time with traditional animal psychology. Heron was interested in inherited maze behavior, inherited activity, and certain drugs—the effects of which could then be detected only through the use of fairly large groups. We did an experiment together on the effect of starvation on the rate of pressing a lever and started the new era with a group of sixteen rats. But we had only four boxes, and this was so inconvenient that Heron applied for a grant and built a battery of twenty-four lever-boxes and cumulative recorders. I supplied an attachment which would record, not only the mean performance of all twenty-four rats in a single averaged curve, but mean curves for four subgroups of twelve rats each and four subgroups of six rats each (3). We thus provided for the design of experiments according to the principles of R. A. Fisher, which were then coming into vogue. We had, so to speak, mechanized the latin square.

With this apparatus Heron and I published a study of extinction in maze-bright and maze-dull rats using *ninety-five* subjects. Later I published mean extinction curves for groups of twenty-four, and W. K. Estes and I did our work on anxiety with groups of the same size. But although Heron and I could properly voice the hope that "the possibility of using large groups of animals greatly improves upon the method as previously reported, since tests of significance are provided for and properties of behavior not apparent in single cases may be more easily detected," in actual practice that is not what happened. The experiments I have just mentioned are almost all we have to show for this elaborate battery of boxes. Undoubtedly more work could be done with it and would have its place, but something had happened to the natural growth of the method. You cannot easily make a change in the conditions of an experiment when twenty-four apparatuses have to be altered. Any gain in rigor is more than matched by a loss in flexibility. We were forced to confine ourselves to processes which could be studied with the baselines already developed in earlier work. We could not move on to the

discovery of other processes or even to a more refined analysis of those we were working with. No matter how significant might be the relations we actually demonstrated, our statistical Leviathan had swum aground. The art of the method had stuck at a particular stage of its development.

Another accident rescued me from mechanized statistics and brought me back to an even more intensive concentration on the single case. In essence, I suddenly found myself face to face with the engineering problem of the animal trainer. When you have the responsibility of making absolutely sure that a given organism will engage in a given sort of behavior at a given time, you quickly grow impatient with theories of learning. Principles, hypotheses, theorems, satisfactory proof at the .05 level of significance that behavior at a choice point shows the effect of secondary reinforcement—nothing could be more irrelevant. No one goes to the circus to see the average dog jump through a hoop significantly oftener than untrained dogs raised under the same circumstances, or to see an elephant demonstrate a principle of behavior.

Perhaps I can illustrate this without giving aid and comfort to the enemy by describing a Russian device which the Germans found quite formidable. The Russians used dogs to blow up tanks. A dog was trained to hide behind a tree or wall in low brush or other cover. As a tank approached and passed, the dog ran swiftly alongside it, and a small magnetic mine attached to the dog's back was sufficient to cripple the tank or set it afire. The dog, of course, had to be replaced.

Now I ask you to consider some of the technical problems which the psychologist faces in preparing a dog for such an act of unintentional heroism. The dog must wait behind the tree for an indefinite length of time. Very well, it must therefore be intermittently reinforced for waiting. But what schedule will achieve the highest probability of waiting? If the reinforcement is to be food, what is the absolutely optimal schedule of deprivation consistent with the health of the dog? The dog must run to the tank—that can be arranged by reinforcing it with a practice tank—but it must start instantly if it is to overtake a swift tank, and how do you differentially reinforce short reaction times, especially in counteracting the reinforcement for sitting and waiting? The dog must react only to tanks, not to a refugee driving his oxcart along the road, but what are the defining properties of a tank so far as a dog is concerned?

I think it can be said that a functional analysis proved adequate in its technological application. Manipulation of environmental conditions alone made possible a wholly unexpected practical control. Behavior could be shaped up according to specifications and maintained indefinitely almost at will. One behavioral technologist who worked with me at the time (Keller Breland) is now specializing in the production of behavior as a salable commodity and has described this new profession in the *American Psychologist* (2).

There are many useful applications within psychology itself. Ratliff and Blough have recently conditioned pigeons to serve as psychophysical observers. In their experiment a pigeon may adjust one of two spots of light until the two are equally bright or it may hold a spot of light at the absolute threshold during dark adaptation. The techniques which they have developed to induce pigeons to do this are only indirectly related to the point of their experiments and hence exemplify the application of a behavioral science (4). The field in which a better technology of behavior is perhaps most urgently needed is education. I cannot describe here the applications which are now possible, but perhaps I can indicate my enthusiasm by hazarding the guess that educational techniques at all age levels are on the threshold of revolutionary changes.

The effect of a behavioral technology on scientific practice is the issue here. Faced with practical problems in behavior, you necessarily emphasize the refinement of *experimental* variables. As a result, some of the standard procedures of statistics appear to be circumvented. Let me illustrate. Suppose that measurements have been made on two groups of subjects differing in some detail of experimental treatment. Means and standard deviations for the two groups are determined, and any difference due to the treatment is evaluated. If the difference is in the expected direction but is not statistically significant, the almost universal recommendation would be to study larger groups. But our experience with practical control suggests that we may reduce the troublesome variability by changing the conditions of the experiment. By discovering, elaborating, and fully exploiting every relevant variable, we may eliminate *in advance of measurement* the individual differences which obscure the difference under analysis. This will achieve the same result as increasing the size of groups, and it will almost certainly yield a bonus in the discovery of new variables which would not have been identified in the statistical treatment.

The same may be said of smooth curves. In our study of anxiety, Estes and I published several curves, the reasonable smoothness of which was obtained by averaging the performances of 12 rats for each curve. The individual curves published at that time show that the mean curves do not faithfully represent the behavior of any one rat. They show a certain tendency toward a change in slope which supported the point we were making, and they may have appeared to justify averaging for that reason.

But an alternative method would have been to explore the individual case until an equally smooth curve could be obtained. This would have meant, not only rejecting the temptation to produce smoothness by averaging cases, but manipulating all relevant conditions as we later learned to manipulate them for practical purposes. The individual curves which we published at that time do not point to the need for larger groups but for improvement in experimental technique. Here, for example, is a curve the smoothness of which is characteristic of current practice. Such curves were shown in the making in a demonstration which Ferster and I arranged at the Cleveland meeting of the American Psychological Association (Figure 13). Here, in a single organism, three different schedules of reinforcement are yielding corresponding performances with great uniformity under appropriate stimuli alternating at random. One does not reach this kind of order through the application of statistical methods.

In *The Behavior of Organisms* I was content to deal with the over-all slopes and curvature of cumulative curves and could make only a rough classification of the properties of behavior shown by the finer grain. The grain has now been improved. The resolving power of the micro-

FIGURE 13.

scope has been increased manyfold, and we can see fundamental processes of behavior in sharper and sharper detail. In choosing rate of responding as a basic datum and in recording this conveniently in a cumulative curve, we make important temporal aspects of behavior *visible*. Once this has happened, our scientific practice is reduced to simple looking. A new world is opened to inspection. We use such curves as we use a microscope, X-ray camera, or telescope. This is well exemplified by recent extensions of the method. These are no longer part of my case history, but perhaps you will permit me to consult you about what some critics have described as a *folie à deux* or group neurosis.

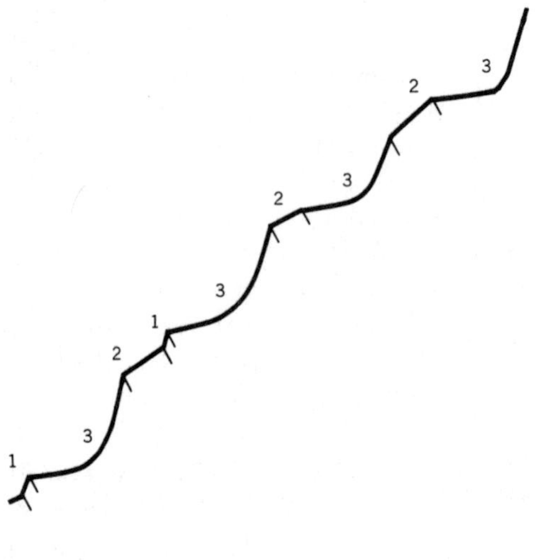

An early application of the method to the behavior of avoidance and escape was made by Keller in studying the light aversion of the rat. This was brilliantly extended by Murray Sidman in his shock-avoidance experiments. It is no longer necessary to describe avoidance and escape by appeal to "principles," for we may *watch* the behavior develop when we have arranged the proper contingencies of reinforcement, as we later watch it change as these contingencies are changed.

Hunt and Brady have extended the use of a stable rate in the study of anxiety-producing stimuli and have shown that the depression in rate is eliminated by electroconvulsive shock and by other measures which are effective in reducing anxiety in human patients. O. R. Lindsley has found the same thing for dogs, using insulin-shock therapy and sedatives. Brady has refined the method by exploring the relevance of various schedules of reinforcement in tracing the return of the conditioned depression after treatment. In these experiments you *see* the effect of a treatment as directly as you see the constriction of a capillary under the microscope.

Early work with rats on caffeine and Benzedrine has been extended by Lindsley with dogs. A special technique for evaluating several effects of a drug in a single short experimental period yields a record of behavior which can be read as a specialist reads an electrocardiogram. Dr. Peter Dews of the Department of Pharmacology at the Harvard Medical School is investigating dose-response curves and the types and effects of various drugs, using pigeons as subjects. In the Psychological Laboratories at Harvard additional work on drugs is being carried out by Morse, Herrnstein, and Marshall, and the technique is being adopted by drug manufacturers. There could scarcely be a better demonstration of the experimental treatment of variability. In a *single* experimental session with a *single* organism one observes the onset, duration, and decline of the effects of a drug.

The direct observation of *defective* behavior is particularly important. Clinical or experimental damage to an organism is characteristically unique. Hence the value of a method which permits the direct observation of the behavior of the individual. Lindsley has studied the effects of near-lethal irradiation, and the effects of prolonged anesthesia and anoxia are currently being examined by Thomas Lohr in cooperation with Dr. Henry Beecher of the Massachusetts General Hospital. The technique is being applied to neurological variables in the monkey by Dr. Karl Pribram at the Hartford Institute. The pattern of such research is simple: establish the behavior in which you are interested, submit the organism to a particular treatment, and then look again at the behavior. An excellent example of the use of experimental control in the study of *motivation* is some work on obesity by J. E. Anliker in collaboration with Dr. Jean Mayer of the Harvard School of Public Health, where abnormalities of ingestive behavior in several types of obese mice can be compared by direct inspection.

There is perhaps no field in which be-

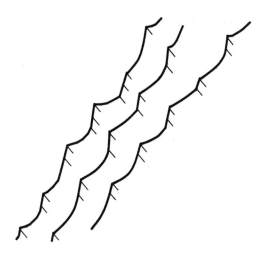

FIGURE 14.

havior is customarily described more indirectly than psychiatry. In an experiment at the Massachusetts State Hospital, under the sponsorship of Dr. Harry Solomon and myself, O. R. Lindsley is carrying out an extensive program which might be characterized as a quantitative study of the temporal properties of psychotic behavior. Here again it is a question of making certain characteristics of the behavior visible.

The extent to which we can eliminate sources of variability before measurement is shown by a result which has an unexpected significance for comparative psychology and the study of individual differences. Figure 14 shows tracings of three curves which report behavior in response to a multiple fixed-interval fixed-ratio schedule. The hatches mark reinforcements. Separating them in some cases are short, steep lines showing a high constant rate on a fixed-ratio schedule and, in others, somewhat longer "scallops" showing a smooth acceleration as the organism shifts from a very low rate just after reinforcement to a higher rate at the end of the fixed interval. The values of the intervals and ratios, the states of deprivation, and the exposures to the schedules were different in the three cases, but except for these details the curves are quite similar. Now, one of them was made by a *pigeon* in some experiments by Ferster and me, one was made by a *rat* in an experiment on anoxia by Lohr, and the third was made by a *monkey* in Karl Pribram's laboratory at the Hartford Institute. Pigeon, rat, monkey, which is which? It doesn't matter. Of course, these three species have behavioral repertoires which are as different as their anatomies. But once you have allowed for differences in the ways in which they make contact with the environment, and in the ways in which they act upon the environment, what remains of their behavior shows astonishingly similar properties. Mice, cats, dogs, and human children could have added other curves to this figure. And when organisms which differ as widely as this nevertheless show similar properties of behavior, differences between members of the same species may be viewed more hopefully. Difficult problems of idiosyncrasy or individuality will always arise as products of biological and cultural processes, but it is the very business of the experimental analysis of behavior to devise techniques which reduce their effects except when they are explicitly under investigation.

We are within reach of a science of the individual. This will be achieved, not by resorting to some special theory of knowledge in which intuition or understanding takes the place of observation and analysis, but through an increasing grasp of relevant conditions to produce order in the individual case.

A second consequence of an improved technology is the effect upon behavior theory. As I have pointed out elsewhere, it is the function of learning theory to create an imaginary world of law and order and thus to console us for the disorder we observe in behavior itself. Scores on a T maze or jumping stand hop about from trial to trial almost capriciously. Therefore we argue that if learning is, as

we hope, a continuous and orderly process, it must be occurring in some other system of dimensions—perhaps in the nervous system, or in the mind, or in a conceptual model of behavior. Both the statistical treatment of group means and the averaging of curves encourage the belief that we are somehow going behind the individual case to an otherwise inaccessible, but more fundamental, process. The whole tenor of our paper on anxiety, for example, was to imply that the change we observed was not necessarily a property of behavior, but of some theoretical state of the organism ("anxiety") which was merely *reflected* in a slight modification of performance.

When we have achieved a practical control over the organism, theories of behavior lose their point. In representing and managing relevant variables, a conceptual model is useless; we come to grips with behavior itself. When behavior shows order and consistency, we are much less likely to be concerned with physiological or mentalistic causes. A datum emerges which takes the place of theoretical fantasy. In the experimental analysis of behavior we address ourselves to a subject matter which is not only manifestly the behavior of an individual and hence accessible without the usual statistical aids but also "objective" and "actual" without recourse to deductive theorizing.

Statistical techniques serve a useful function, but they have acquired a purely honorific status which may be troublesome. Their presence or absence has become a shibboleth to be used in distinguishing between good and bad work. Because measures of behavior have been highly variable, we have come to trust only results obtained from large numbers of subjects. Because some workers have intentionally or unconsciously reported only selected favorable instances, we have come to put a high value on research which is planned in advance and reported in its entirety. Because measures have behaved capriciously, we have come to value skill-ful deductive theories which restore order. But although large groups, planned experi-ments, and valid theorizing are associated with significant scientific results, it does not follow that nothing can be achieved in their absence. Here are two brief examples of the choice before us.

How can we determine the course of dark adaptation in a pigeon? We move a pigeon from a bright light to a dark room. What happens? Presumably the bird is able to see fainter and fainter patches of light as the process of adaptation takes place, but how can we follow this process? One way would be to set up a discrimina-tion apparatus in which choices would be made at specific intervals after the begin-ning of dark adaptation. The test patches of light could be varied over a wide range, and the percentages of correct choices at each value would enable us eventually to locate the threshold fairly accurately. But hundreds of observations would be needed to establish only a few points on the curve and to prove that these show an actual change in sensitivity. In the experiment by Blough already mentioned, the pigeon holds a spot of light close to the threshold throughout the experimental period. A single curve, such as the one sketched in Figure 15, yields as much information as hundreds of readings, together with the means and standard deviations derived from them. The information is more accu-rate because it applies to a single organism in a single experimental session. Yet many psychologists who would accept the first as a finished experiment because of the tables of means and standard deviations would boggle at the second or call it a preliminary study. The direct evidence of one's senses in observing a process of be-havior is not trusted.

As another example, consider the behav-ior of several types of obese mice. Do they all suffer from a single abnormality in their eating behavior or are there differences?

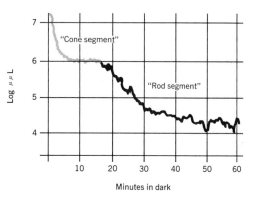

FIGURE 15.

One might attempt to answer this with some such measure of hunger as an ob-struction apparatus. The numbers of cross-ings of a grid to get to food, counted after different periods of free access to food, would be the data. Large numbers of read-ings would be needed, and the resulting mean values would possibly not describe the behavior of any one mouse in any ex-perimental period. A much better picture may be obtained with one mouse of each kind in single experimental sessions, as Anliker has shown (1). In an experiment reported roughly in Figure 16, each mouse was reinforced with a small piece of food after completing a short "ratio" of re-sponses. The hypothalamic-obese mouse shows an exaggerated but otherwise nor-mal ingestion curve. The hereditary-obese mouse eats slowly but for an indefinite

FIGURE 16.

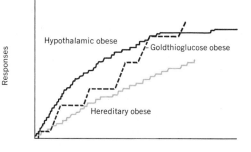

length of time and with little change in rate. The gold-poisoned obese mouse shows a sharp oscillation between periods of very rapid responding and no responding at all. These three individual curves contain more information than could probably ever be generated with measures requiring statistical treatment, yet they will be viewed with suspicion by many psychologists because they are single cases.

It is perhaps natural that psychologists should awaken only slowly to the possibility that behavioral processes may be directly observed, or that they should only gradually put the older statistical and theoretical techniques in their proper perspective. But it is time to insist that science does not progress by carefully designed steps called "experiments" each of which has a well-defined beginning and end. Science is a continuous and often a disorderly and accidental process. We shall not do the young psychologist any favor if we agree to reconstruct our practices to fit the pattern demanded by current scientific methodology. What the statistician means by the design of experiments is design which yields the kind of data to which *his* techniques are applicable. He does not mean the behavior of the scientist in his laboratory devising research for his own immediate and possibly inscrutable purposes.

The organism whose behavior is most extensively modified and most completely

FIGURE 17.

controlled in research of the sort I have described is the experimenter himself. The point was well made by a cartoonist in the Columbia *Jester* (Figure 17). The caption read: "Boy, have I got this guy conditioned! Everytime I press the bar down he drops in a piece of food." The subjects we study reinforce us much more effectively than we reinforce them. I have been telling you simply how I have been conditioned to behave. And of course it is a mistake to argue too much from one case history. My behavior would not have been shaped as it was were it not for personal characteristics which all psychologists fortunately do not share. Freud has had something to say about the motivation of scientists and has given us some insight into the type of person who achieves the fullest satisfaction from precise experimental design and the intricacies of deductive systems. Such a person tends to be more concerned with his success as a scientist than with his subject matter, as is shown by the fact that he often assumes the role of a roving ambassador. If this seems unfair, let me hasten to characterize my own motivation in equally unflattering terms. Several years ago I spent a pleasant summer writing a novel called *Walden Two*. One of the characters, Frazier, said many things which I was not yet ready to say myself. Among them was this:

I have only one important characteristic, Burris. I'm stubborn. I've had only one idea in my life—a true *idée fixe* . . . to put it as bluntly as possible, the idea of having my own way. "Control" expresses it, I think. The control of human behavior, Burris. In my early experimental days it was a frenzied, selfish desire to dominate. I remember the rage I used to feel when a prediction went awry. I could have shouted at the subjects of my experiments, "Behave, damn you, behave as you ought!" Eventually I realized that the subjects were always right. They always behaved as they ought. It was I who was wrong. I had made a bad prediction.

(In fairness to Frazier and the rest of myself, I want to add his next remark: "And what a strange discovery for a would-be tyrant, that the only effective technique of control is unselfish." Frazier means, of course, positive reinforcement.)

We have no more reason to say that all psychologists should behave as I have behaved than that they should all behave like R. A. Fisher. The scientist, like any organism, is the product of a unique history. The practices which he finds most appropriate will depend in part upon this history. Fortunately, personal idiosyncrasies usually leave a negligible mark on science as public property. They are important only when we are concerned with the encouragement of scientists and the prosecution of research. When we have at last an adequate empirical account of the behavior of Man Thinking, we shall understand all this. Until then, it may be best not to try to fit all scientists into any single mold.

References

1. Anliker, J. E. Personal communication.
2. Breland, K., and Breland, Marion. A field of applied animal psychology. *Amer. Psychologist,* 1951, **6,** 202–204.
3. Heron, W. T., and Skinner, B. F. An apparatus for the study of behavior. *Psychol. Rec.,* 1939, **3,** 166–176.
4. Ratliff, F., and Blough, D. S. Behavioral studies of visual processes in the pigeon. Report of Contract N5ori-07663, Psychological Laboratories, Harvard University, September 1954.
5. Richter, C. P. Free research versus design research. *Science,* 1953, **118,** 91–93.

One crucial point of the following article is that discussions of scientific method, theories, and other formal properties of science must be tempered by a very simple fact: Science is made by men. Thus psychological processes shape the fads and currents of thought in the sciences at all points in their development.

What is the nature of creative thought in the sciences? What are the personality characteristics of creative scientists? These two questions about the scientific process have an immediate relevance to psychology.

A POINT TO GUIDE YOUR STUDY *Are you "science-minded"? If so, how accurately does the description of the creative scientist fit you?*

GLOSSARY **Taxonomy:** *the science of classification and the search for lawful relationships between events or objects; the term is applied especially to the classification of the many species of animals and plants.* **Cognition:** *a thought or idea.* **Ego:** *the system of personality structure concerned with realistic thought and behavior.* **Superego:** *as it is used here, the term refers to an individual's conscience—the system within the personality structure that forbids certain thoughts and actions.*

4: THE PSYCHOLOGY OF THE SCIENTIST

Anne Roe, Harvard University

Science is the creation of scientists, and every scientific advance bears somehow the mark of the man who made it. The artist exposes himself in his work; the scientist seems rather to hide in his, but he is there. Surely the historian of science must understand the man if he is fully to understand the progress of science, and he must have some comprehension of the science if he is to understand the men who make it.

The general *public* image of the scientist has not been and indeed is not now a flattering one, and at best it certainly is not an endearing one. Characterizations of scientists almost always emphasize the objectivity of their work and describe their cold, detached, impassive, unconcerned observation of phenomena which have no emotional meaning for them. This could hardly be further from the truth. The scientist as a person is a nonparticipating observer in only a very limited sense. He does not *interact* with what he is observing, but he does participate as a person. It is, perhaps, this fact—that the scientist does not expect, indeed does not want, the things that he is concerned with to be equally concerned with him—that has given others this impression of coldness, remoteness, and objectivity. (The social scientist is in a remarkably difficult position since the "objects with which he is concerned" are people, and both they and he may be more than a little ambivalent about this matter of interaction. But this is a special problem which I will by-pass here, noting only that in many ways the social scientist dif-

fers from the natural scientist in terms of personality and motivations.)

The truth of the matter is that the creative scientist, whatever his field, is very deeply involved emotionally and personally in his work, and that he himself is his own most essential tool. We must consider both the subjectivity of science and what kinds of people scientists are.

The personal factor

But first we must consider the processes of science. Suppose we take the scientist at the time when he has asked a question, or has set up a hypothesis which he wants to test. *He* must decide what observations to make. It is simply not possible to observe everything that goes on under a given set of conditions; he must choose what to observe, what measurements to make, how fine these measurements are to be, how to record them. These choices are never dictated entirely by the question or hypothesis (and anyway, that too bears his own particular stamp). One has only to consider how differently several of his colleagues would go about testing the same hypothesis to see that personal choice enters in here.

But this is just the beginning. Having decided what is to be observed, and having set up the techniques for observing, the scientist comes to the point of making the actual observations, and of recording these observations. All the complex apparatus of modern science is only a means of extending the range of man's sensory and perceptual capacities, and all the information derived through such extensions must eventually be reduced to some form in which man, with his biological limitations, can receive it. Here, too, in spite of all precautions and in spite of complete hon-

The author is Lecturer on Education in the Graduate School of Education, Harvard University, Cambridge, Mass. This article is adapted from a lecture presented December 28, 1960, before the History of Science Society at the annual meeting of the AAAS in New York.

Anne Roe. The psychology of the scientist. *Science*, 1961, 134, 456–459. Copyright © 1961 by the American Association for the Advancement of Science. Reprinted here with permission from the author and the American Association for the Advancement of Science.

esty, the personal factor enters in. The records of two observers will not dovetail exactly, even when they read figures from a dial. Errors may creep in, and the direction of the error is more likely than not to be associated with the observer's interest in how the findings come out. Perhaps the clearest evidence on this point comes from research on extrasensory perception. A scientist who is deeply committed to a hypothesis is well advised to have a neutral observer if the import of an observation is immediately apparent. Often, of course, such errors are minor, but they can be important, not only to the immediate problem but to society. I have wondered to what extent the disparity in figures on radioactive fallout may reflect such factors. Very few scientists, including psychologists, who have demonstrated selective perception as a laboratory exercise, take account of the phenomenon in their own work.

Once the observations are recorded, other questions are asked: When is the evidence sufficient to be conclusive, one way or the other? How important are discrepancies? What degree of generalization is permissible? Here, again, we may expect personally slanted answers. Taxonomy offers a very clear illustration of the effect of personality: One biologist may classify a given set of specimens into a few species, and another may classify them into many species. Whether the specimens are seen as representing a few or many groups depends largely on whether one looks for similarities or for differences, on whether one looks at the forest or the trees. A "lumper" may honestly find it impossible to understand how a "splitter" arrives at such an obviously incorrect solution, and vice versa. Such differences cannot be resolved by appeal to the "facts"—there are no facts which cannot be perceived in different ways. This is not to say that the facts are necessarily distorted. The problem of the criterion exists in all science,

although some scientists are more aware of it than others.

The matter of personal commitment to a hypothesis is one that deserves more consideration than it usually receives. Any man who has gone through the emotional process of developing a new idea, of constructing a new hypothesis, is to some extent, and usually to a large extent, committed to that hypothesis in a very real sense. It is his baby. It is as much his creation as a painting is the personal creation of the painter. True, in the long run it stands or falls, is accepted or rejected, on its own merits, but its creator has a personal stake in it. The scientist has more at stake than the artist, for data which may support or invalidate his hypothesis are in the public domain in a sense in which art criticism never is. It may even be because of this that scientists customarily check their hypotheses as far as they can before they state them publicly. And, indeed, the experienced scientist continues to check, hoping that if errors are to be found, it will be he who finds them, so that he will have a chance to make revisions, or even to discard the hypothesis, should that prove necessary. He finds it less difficult to discard his hypothesis, if, in his efforts at checking, he has been able to come up with another one.

The extent of personal commitment to a hypothesis is a prominent factor in the historical interplay between scientists. The degree of this commitment varies in an individual with different hypotheses, and varies between individuals. One very important factor here is the scientist's productivity. If he has many new ideas he will be less disturbed (and less defensive) if one fails to pan out. If he has very few ideas, an error is much harder to take, and there are many historical instances of errors which the author of the idea has never been able to see himself. I think many scientists are genuinely unaware of the extent, or even of the fact, of this personal involvement, and themselves accept the myth of impersonal objectivity. This is really very unfortunate. It is true that only a man who is passionately involved in his work is likely to make important contributions, but the committed man who knows he is committed and can come to terms with this fact has a good chance of getting beyond his commitment and of learning how to disassociate himself from his idea when this is necessary. There is little in the traditional education of scientists to prepare them for this necessity, and there are many who are still unaware of it. The extent of a scientist's personal involvement in a theory can now be a matter of grave public concern. Scientists who become advisers on political or other policy have an extraordinarily heavy responsibility for achieving some detachment from their own theories. How many of them realize this?

But once one hypothesis is found acceptable, this is not the end of it. One hypothesis inevitably leads to another; answering one question makes it possible to ask other, hopefully more precise ones. And so a new hypothesis or a new theory is offered. How is this new theory arrived at? This is one expression of the creative process, and it is a completely personal process. It is personal regardless of whether one or more individuals is involved, for in every advance made by a group, the person contributing at the moment has had to assimilate the contributions of the others and order them in his own personal way.

The creative process

There have been many millions of words written about the creative process, few of them very illuminating. The reason is not hard to find. The process is intimate and personal and characteristically takes place not at the level of full consciousness but at subconscious or preconscious levels. It has been inaccessible to study largely because

we have not yet found any means for controlling it. Many effective scientists and artists have learned a few techniques which may reduce interference with it, but no one to my knowledge has discovered any means by which he can set it in motion at will.

It is probable that the fundamentals of the creative process are the same in all fields, but in those fields in which an advance in knowledge is sought, there is an additional requirement—or rather, one requirement receives particular emphasis. This is the need for a large store of knowledge and experience. The broader the scientist's experience and the more extensive his stock of knowledge, the greater the possibility of a real breakthrough.

The creative process involves a scanning or searching through stocks of stored memories. There seems to be a rather sharp limit to the possibility of very significant advance through voluntary, logical scanning of these stores. For one thing, they vary enormously in their accessibility to conscious recall and in the specificity of their connections, so that reliance upon conscious, orderly, logical thinking is not likely to produce many results at this stage, however essential such procedures become later in verification. This scanning is typically for patterns and complex associations rather than for isolated units. It may be, however, that a small unit acts as a sort of key to a pattern. What seems to happen, in creative efforts in science as well as in every other field, is that the individual enters a state in which logical thinking is submerged and in which thought is prelogical. Such thought is described as random largely because it typically tries seemingly illogical and distantly related materials, and it often makes major advances in just this way. It is not fully random, however, because it is goal-directed and because even in this preconscious work there is appropriate selection and rejection of available connections. This stage of the creative process is accompanied by generally confused or vague states of preoccupation of varying degrees of depth; it is well described as "stewing." It is this stage which apparently cannot be hurried or controlled.

Although termination of this stage (finding a solution, or "getting insight," as it is often called) quite frequently occurs in a moment of dispersed attention, it apparently does not help to induce a state of dispersed attention in the hope of provoking a quicker end to the process. It should be added that, while insights do frequently occur "in a flash," they need not do so, and that the process is the same whether or not the insight turns out to have validity.

To acquire the necessary store of knowledge requires long and difficult application, and as science advances, the amount of information to be assimilated becomes greater and greater, despite increasing generalization in the organizing of the data. Obviously, as more experience is stored and as the interconnections become better established and more numerous, the scanning becomes more effective. Such interconnections develop more and more readily as the process of acquiring experience takes on significance in the light of theory. This process requires not only the basic capacity to assimilate experiences but very strong motivation to persist in the effort. Strong motivation is also required if one is to continue with a search which may for a long time be unproductive. Motivation of this kind and strength derives from the needs and structure of the personality. Its sources are rarely obvious, although they can sometimes be traced. They do not necessarily derive from "neurotic problems," although they frequently do. It is no cause for dismay when they do. The ability of the human being to find in a personal problem motivation for a search for truth is one of the major accomplishments of the species.

If past experiences have brought about a compartmentalization of the storage areas, so that some portions are partially or wholly inaccessible, obviously the scientist is limited in his search. Compartmentalization of particular areas may result from personal experiences of a sort that lead to neurotic structures generally, or it may result from specific cultural restrictions, such as political or religious indoctrination. The extent to which such indoctrination will inhibit creative effort, however, depends upon how close the inaccessible areas are in content to the problems at issue. We have fairly conclusive evidence that political indoctrination need not interfere with inquiry into mathematical and physical science. Religious indoctrination can interfere strongly at any point, as history has documented very fully for us. The conclusion is no different from the basic principle of therapy: the more areas of experience there are accessible to conscious and preconscious thought, the better are the prospects for creativity.

Once an apparent answer to the scientist's question has been found, there is still a long process of pursuing and checking to be gone through. Not every man who can produce new ideas is also good at the business of checking them, and of course the reverse is also true. It is in the utilization of such personal differences as these that a "team approach" can make sense.

The creative scientist

This, then, is a brief review of what little we know of the process of creation. What do we know of the characteristics of scientists who can use this process effectively? Many lines of inquiry have demonstrated that the range of characteristics that are associated with creative productivity in a human being is very wide. These characteristics fall into almost all categories into which personal traits have been divided for purposes of study—abilities, interests, drives, temperament, and so on.

To limit our discussion to scientific productivity, it is clear to start with that there are great variations in the amount of curiosity possessed by different people. Curiosity appears to be a basic drive. I suspect it may vary consistently with sex, on either a biological or a cultural basis, but we have as yet no idea how to measure such drives. No one becomes a scientist without a better-than-average amount of curiosity, regardless of whether he was born with it, was brought up in a stimulating environment, or just did not have it severely inhibited.

Intelligence and creativity are not identical, but intelligence does play a role in scientific creativity—rather more than it may play in some other forms of creativity. In general, one may summarize by saying that the minimum intelligence required for creative production in science is considerably better than average, but that, given this, other variables contribute more to variance in performance. It must also be noted that special abilities (numerical, spatial, verbal, and so on) play somewhat different roles in different scientific fields, but that ability must in no case be below average. A cultural anthropologist, for example, has little need for great facility with numbers. An experimental physicist, on the other hand, does require facility with numbers, although he need not have great facility with words.

Personality patterns

A number of studies have contributed to the picture of the personality patterns of productive scientists, and it is rather striking that quite different kinds of investigations have produced closely similar results. These can be briefly summarized in six different groups, as follows:

1. Truly creative scientists seek experience and action and are independent and self-sufficient with regard to perception, cognition, and behavior. These findings have been expressed in various studies in such terms as the following: they are more observant than others and value this quality; they are more independent with respect to cognition and value judgments; they have high dominance; they have high autonomy; they are Bohemian or radical; they are not subject to group standards and control; they are highly egocentric.

2. They have a preference for apparent but resolvable disorder and for an esthetic ordering of forms of experience. They have high tolerance for ambiguity, but they also like to put an end to it in their own way —and in their own time.

3. They have strong egos (whether this derives from or is responsible for their independence and their tolerance for ambiguity is a moot question). This ego strength permits them to regress to preconscious states with certainty that they will return from these states. They have less compulsive superegos than others. They are capable of disciplined management of means leading to significant experience. They have no feeling of guilt about the independence of thought and action mentioned above. They have strong control of their impulses.

4. Their interpersonal relations are generally of low intensity. They are reported to be ungregarious, not talkative (this does not apply to social scientists), and rather asocial. There is an apparent tendency to femininity in highly original men, and to masculinity in highly original women, but this may be a cultural interpretation of the generally increased sensitivity of the men and the intellectual capacity and interests of the women. They dislike interpersonal controversy in any form and are especially sensitive to interpersonal aggression.

5. They show much stronger preoccupation with things and ideas than with people. They dislike introversive and affect-associated preoccupations except in connection with their own research.

6. They like to take the calculated risk, but it must involve nature, not people, and must not depend on simple luck.

Conclusions

How do these personality characteristics relate to the creative process in science as I have discussed it? An open attitude toward experience makes possible accumulation of experience with relatively little compartmentalization; independence of perception, cognition, and behavior permit greater than average reordering of this accumulated experience (the behavioral eccentricities so often noted are consistent with this). The strong liking for turning disorder into order carries such individuals through the searching period which their tolerance for ambiguity permits them to enter. The strong egos, as noted, permit regression to prelogical forms of thought without serious fear of failure to get back to logical ones. Preoccupation with things and ideas rather than with people is obvi-

ously characteristic of natural scientists, and even of some social scientists. This characteristic is not directly related to creativity, I think, but rather to the content of it.

I need not add that such statements as these are generalizations and that any individual case may be an exception. We may go farther, however, and generalize differences among men who follow different branches of science. That a man chooses to become a scientist and succeeds means that he has the temperament and personality as well as the ability and opportunity to do so. The branch of science he chooses, even the specific problems he chooses and the way he works on them, are intimately related to what he is and to his deepest needs. The more deeply engaged he is, the more profoundly is this true. To understand what he does, one must try to know what his work means to him. The chances are that he does not know or care to know. Indeed, he does not need to know. We do.

Graduate work is necessary for a professional career in psychology —that is the main point of the next selection. But undergraduate training in psychology may be valuable in other lines of work.

A POINT TO GUIDE YOUR STUDY *From what you know about psychology already, can you think of any aspects of undergraduate psychological training which would be valuable for an executive trainee?*

5: JOB OPPORTUNITIES FOR UNDERGRADUATE PSYCHOLOGY MAJORS

Margaret Skeel King, University of North Carolina at Chapel Hill, and Gregory A. Kimble, Duke University

When he is considering an undergraduate major, the college student sometimes rules

psychology out on grounds expressed something like this: "Well, psychology is

This research was carried out under multiple auspices. The senior author used the data reported here for a paper in a course in educational and occupational information taught by Robert M. Colver, Department of Education, Duke University. The initial suggestion for conducting the survey came from the Duke University Psychology Club. Members of the club assisted in the clerical aspects of the study. Preliminary results were reported in May 1957 to the North Carolina Psychological Association.

M. S. King and G. A. Kimble. Job opportunities for undergraduate psychology majors. *Amer. Psychologist*, 1958, **13**, 23–27. Copyright © 1958 by the American Psychological Association. Reprinted here with permission from the authors and the American Psychological Association.

very interesting, but what can you do with it after you graduate?" The answer to this question, of course, is that you can do with a psychology major exactly what you can with a major in any other liberal arts subject: compete with other college graduates for the jobs available to all such individuals. However, such a response, although it is honest and factually correct, is less than completely satisfying to a student who is beginning to think in terms of a career. He is apt to feel that the selection of a major involves a decision with long-term implications for his future success and happiness and that such an answer does an injustice to the seriousness of the matter.

Largely on this basis, we undertook a survey of job opportunities for undergraduate majors in psychology. Our assumption was that, even if the results did not alter our conception of the situation at all, having concrete and contemporary data on this problem would be valuable, particularly in advising undergraduate students. It is even possible that such advice would contribute a little to a reversal of the alarming trend toward decreasing numbers of psychology majors recently described in the pages of this journal (2).

To obtain information about job opportunities for undergraduate psychology majors, questionnaires were sent to 540 organizations in the following major groups: business and industry, 385; education, schools, and universities, 51; government, 34; and social service, 70. The sample is probably not representative of the American economic scene in that the organizations selected were engaged in activities which were likely to appeal to a psychology major. Accordingly, about half of the sample of organizations came from the *1955 APA Directory*. Every fourth page was examined and a list compiled of companies and other (mainly nonacademic) organizations employing psychologists. The rest of the sample came from

organizations listed in the *College Placement Directory* (4), the card files of the Duke University Appointments Office, the stock exchange listings of the Sunday *New York Times,* and advertisements from several issues of *Scientific American, Saturday Evening Post* and the *Handbook of Measurement and Control* (1). Of the 540 organizations sampled, 278 (51%) returned the questionnaires. The various subgroups returned the following percentages of the questionnaires distributed: business and industry, 50% (193); education, schools, and universities, 47% (24); government, 100% (34); and social service, 36% (25). As evidence of the seriousness with which the questionnaire was taken, two of the organizations (a West Coast refinery and a national distiller) ran IBM analyses of their entire personnel (some 10,000 individuals) to obtain answers to our questions. One governmental agency duplicated the questionnaire and sent it to a number of subsidiary projects.

The materials sent to the organizations sampled were a letter, signed by the junior author as Director of Undergraduate Studies in Psychology at Duke University, and the questionnaire. The letter described the purpose of the study in terms very similar to those in the first paragraph of this paper. It outlined the preparation of the typical Duke undergraduate psychology major, mentioning the experimental emphasis of the Duke curriculum, and stressed the fact that undergraduate training does not prepare a person for professional work in psychology. The specific statement on this point was:

First of all he is not a psychologist. Rather, he is a student with a broad, liberal arts education. He has a well-rounded background highlighted by certain of the outlooks and a few of the rudimentary skills of the psychologist.

The questionnaire covered three main topics: (a) the kinds of jobs available to undergraduate psychology majors, (b) salary and opportunities for advancement, and (c) special training and other factors which employers consider in hiring individuals.

Job opportunities

As an initial step in analyzing the results of the survey, the questionnaires were divided into two groups: (a) "positive" responses (about 65% of the questionnaires returned[1]), which mentioned one or more jobs for which the psychology major described in our letter would be qualified, and (b) "negative" responses (about 35%), which mentioned no such jobs. By far the most common reason offered by organizations responding negatively was that their needs were for individuals with more specialized training (psychological or otherwise) than the undergraduate major provides.

For example, one governmental agency indicated that:

Undergraduate majors are not hired as psychologists.

The Department of Education in a large city replied:

I interpret your questionnaire to concern only those students who have completed a Bachelor's degree. To be eligible for employment in the field of social service or psychology, we are requiring a Master's degree.

And a social service worker wrote:

My present feeling is that *all* jobs wherein the activities are defined as applied psychology and the person is called psychologist require broader and more extensive training than can be gotten at the undergraduate level. . . . Your program would seem to pro-

vide an excellent foundation for advanced study.

The following two replies are representative of a number where the employers' needs were for special training in fields other than psychology:

This is a public relations firm and as such the openings that might occur here are more or less limited to individuals who have had considerable writing experience such as newspaper, wire service, and the like. [And] At the present time we are primarily seeking engineering graduates.

Another point made in a few of the replies was that psychological work, to which our students presumably would be attracted, is often available in the larger organizations in a certain field and not in the small ones. As an illustration, a small southern advertising firm noted:

A psychology major would be of help in certain research—establishing motivations, etc.— but only large agencies have such departments.

Many of the negative responses indicated that the respondent had not understood (in spite of our strong statement on the point) that we were not representing the undergraduate major as a competent psychologist. For example:

As a publisher, we do not specifically require psychology majors in our job openings here. [Or] We are not hiring psychology majors at this time. Therefore we feel it would not be appropriate for us to complete your questionnaire. [Or] We do not employ at the professional psychology level.

In analyzing the positive responses to the questionnaire, a tally was made of the positions which our respondents mentioned as ones in their organizations which a psychology major might fill. The results of this analysis appear in Table 1, which gives the frequency with which various

[1] The numbers in Tables 1 and 3 are based on positive replies as follows: business and industry, 134; education, 9; government, 20; social service, 13; and total, 176. Note that one reply may be responsible for more than one entry in these tables.

TABLE 1   *Positions for which undergraduate psychology majors could qualify in various types of organizations*

CATEGORY	BUSINESS AND INDUSTRY	EDUCATION	GOVERNMENT	SOCIAL SERVICE	TOTAL
Personnel, interviewing, industrial relations, counseling	110	1	10	2	123
Management development trainee, supervisor	39	0	2	5	46
Research, experimental psychologist	11	5	6	3	25
Psychometrist, statistical analyst	10	4	8	0	22
Sales	21	0	0	0	21
Clerical	14	4	1	0	19
Manufacturing, production	14	0	0	1	15
Technician, job analyst	9	0	5	0	14
Psychologist (assistant), psychologist in training	3	0	3	5	11
Social service	0	1	3	6	10
Writing, reporting, editing	7	0	0	0	7
Miscellaneous	3	0	0	0	3
Total	241	15	38	22	316

positions were mentioned. Clearly, psychology is regarded as something which is most appropriate to the general field of personnel work. At the same time, several of the replies mentioned that it was not the psychology major per se that counted and that more importance attaches to personal characteristics and the fact that the individual has a bachelor's degree. A personnel manager in a photographic corporation declared:

There are plenty of opportunities for young people, but not *because* of their psychological training. There are several positions in training and personnel in which persons with some psychological training would be useful but, at present, such requirements are not part of the job descriptions.

Another personnel supervisor replied:

The man is of more importance than the major as to qualifications for consideration in the company. . . . If a man has the personal characteristics we look for, indicating management potential, and has at least an under-graduate degree from a qualified institution of learning such as Duke, we are interested in that man. Of great importance, too, is the man's interest in us—namely the type of work he seeks. . . . Your undergraduate psychology majors would qualify for consideration in the company in almost every activity of a non-technical nature. The activities would include some of the following: Sales, Production, Advertising, Purchasing, Personnel Administration, and Public Relations.

Salaries and prospects for promotion

The median starting salary for newly graduated male AB's in psychology estimated from the present sample is $365.00 per month.[2] This is close to the value which has figured in recent articles in the popular press. For example, the average starting salary for liberal arts majors with bachelor's degrees reported recently in *U. S. News and World Report* (3) is $350-$400 per month. A more detailed break-

[2] Remember that this article was written in 1957. (*Ed.*)

down appears in Table 2. Obviously there are marked differences among the various occupations in starting salaries. Table 2, however, certainly presents far too low a value for the field of education, since the teaching profession is not represented (see the categories in Table 1). Teaching requires certification and, therefore, special training in all states. For this reason, the ordinary psychology major does not qualify for such positions. This leaves secretarial and training positions (for example, graduate assistant) as the main jobs reflected in the data presented in Table 2 for education. Such positions, of course, pay less than those covered in the other categories.

The median starting salary for women estimated from this sample is $305.00 per month. There were 25 organizations answering who had no opportunities for women with undergraduate psychology training, while only 8 organizations had no opportunities for men. Of those which gave specific salary information, 50 organizations paid men and women the same starting salaries, but the salary was lower for women in 35 organizations. Some of this difference in starting salary is attributable to the fact that clerical jobs were mentioned more often for women. But even in the cases where the tasks are identical, equal pay for equal work is still not universal.

The question about opportunities for promotion elicited routinely optimistic replies from most of the respondents. The

exceptions were confined almost completely to the clerical jobs in the educational and social service organizations. One social science research project indicated that "To date we have had 'jobs' rather than 'positions.' When the job is over, no position exists."

Those who elaborated on this question in a more positive vein were most often representatives of the business and industry category. Two themes seemed to characterize their points. One was that firsthand experience in a business is important, not only in developing knowledge about the functioning of the organization, but also in more subtle attitudinal areas.

Operating experience, i.e., doing or supervising activities which are closely related to the main objectives of a particular business—early in one's career, builds relationships, attitudes, and background helpful in advancing anywhere in the business.

The other point stressed frequently was a statement of a promotion-from-within policy. Apparently many organizations explicitly plan to draw high level executive personnel from the ranks. Many of them couple this with a policy of promoting the man as rapidly as his development warrants.

Related training

Table 3 presents a summary of data on business skills and related course work. The questionnaire listed the training presented in the table and asked the respondent to check off those which were desirable. The numbers in Table 3 are the numbers of times each item was checked. As regards business skills, it was interesting to note that these abilities were regarded as important at all levels—not just for clerical workers. In the case of related courses, there is a clear preference for mathematics and economics. The latter of these stresses is, to a large degree, a reflection of the

TABLE 2 *Median starting salary per month for men and women*

CATEGORY	MEN	WOMEN
Business and industry	$385	$308
Education	200	206
Government	331	317
Social service	285	285
Overall median	$365	$305

TABLE 3   *Business skills and areas of related course work which were checked as being desirable in various types of organizations*

	BUSINESS AND INDUSTRY	EDU-CATION	GOVERN-MENT	SOCIAL SERVICE	TOTAL
Business skills					
Computing machines	55	4	11	6	76
Office machines	47	1	11	3	62
Shorthand	54	1	4	4	63
Typing	61	5	11	6	83
Related course work					
Biological science	17	5	3	3	28
Economics	72	2	5	1	80
Mathematics	67	5	15	6	93
Physical science	47	2	7	3	59
Political science	18	4	4	1	27
Social science	48	9	9	3	69

heavy preponderance of business and industrial organizations in the sample. The stress on mathematics is more nearly characteristic of all the areas. In addition to the skills and courses listed in Table 3, the respondents were asked to mention others which they thought would be especially useful. Replies to this question were heterogeneous and often reflected the specialty of the organization represented by the individual filling out the questionnaire. There were, however, two trends which stood out. One was a recognition of the importance of training in statistics. This, no doubt, is related to the value placed upon mathematics. The second stress was on communication skills: English grammar, composition, and report writing.

The overview

It was evident from the responses to the questionnaire that psychology has an established acceptance in the economic world as a valuable major subject. Contrary to what the prospective major is apt to think, he is under no handicap by comparison with students in other liberal arts fields either as regards his chances of getting a good job or in terms of salary. There are courses which the student can take to better his chances of getting the job he wants; these include English, mathematics, economics, and statistics. But these could be recommended to a major in any subject. For it must be emphasized that a psychology major does not prepare a student for a particular position. The majority of jobs mentioned—personnel, management training, and sales—are ones in which a psychology major might be happy, but training in psychology, such as is usually provided by an undergraduate major, is not a prerequisite.

In fact, business and industry apparently recognize the strengths and weaknesses of the liberal arts training more clearly than those of us in the academic world sometimes give them credit for. Most large organizations have their own in-training programs and have specifically assumed the responsibility for providing the practical experience which is missing in the undergraduate liberal arts program. Moreover there seems to be a considerable sentiment to the effect that this is as it should be. Comments emphasized the importance of a broad liberal arts background, rather than the particular field of major study. Almost all employers want persons with a well-rounded education— those who have not only excelled in school, but who have participated in extracurricular activities and have displayed initiative and responsibility. Specific training is of distinctly secondary importance. One governmental organization expressed it this way: "We look for bright people even though they are not fully trained." A corporation personnel manager summed up much current emphasis very well: "If you will educate them, we will train them."

References

1. Behar, M. S. (Ed.) *Handbook of measurement and control.* (2nd ed.) Pittsburgh: Instruments Publishing Company, 1954.
2. Recktenwald, L. N. The drop in undergraduate degrees. *Amer. Psychologist,* 1957, **12,** 229–230.
3. *U. S. News and World Report.* 1957, May 17, pp. 45–49.
4. Zimmerman, O. T. *College placement directory.* (2nd ed.) Dover, New Hampshire: Industrial Research Service, 1955.

SECTION TWO

MATURATION AND DEVELOPMENT

A child will benefit from training only after sufficient maturation, or growth, has taken place. Another relationship between experience and maturation is also possible. In some species, and perhaps in humans too, very rapid behavioral changes can take place only during a very short time span which is the critical period. One type of such rapid change is called imprinting.

The etologists, that is, the zoologists concerned with species-specific behavior, were the first to study the phenomenon. They studied it in the field, but, although the method had its advantages, it was not until laboratory investigations were made that some important variables were uncovered. This, of course, is one of the major strengths of the laboratory method.

POINTS TO GUIDE YOUR STUDY *(1) The first two paragraphs give the basic orientation for this article. (2) Make sure you understand the two graphs and the table in this article.*

6: IMPRINTING

Eckhard H. Hess, University of Chicago

Students of behavior generally agree that the early experiences of animals (including man) have a profound effect on their adult behavior. Some psychologists go so far as to state that the effect of early experience upon adult behavior is inversely correlated with age. This may be an over-

E. H. Hess. Imprinting. *Science*, 1959, **130**, 133–141. Copyright © 1959 by the American Association for the Advancement of Science. Excerpts reprinted here with permission from the author and the American Association for the Advancement of Science. The table is renumbered. Reference 24 completed; was in press. (*Ed.*)

simplification, but in general it appears to hold true. Thus, the problem of the investigator is not so much to find out *whether* early experience determines adult behavior as to discover *how* it determines adult behavior.

Three statements are usually made about the effects of early experience. The first is that early habits are very persistent and may prevent the formation of new ones. This, of course, refers not only to the experimental study of animals but also to the rearing of children. The second statement is that early perceptions deeply affect all future learning. This concept leads to the difficult question whether basic perceptions—the way we have of seeing the world about us—are inherited or acquired. The third statement is simply that early social contacts determine the character of adult social behavior. This is the phenomenon of imprinting.

At the turn of the century, Craig (1), experimenting with wild pigeons, found that in order to cross two different species it was first necessary to rear the young of one species under the adults of the other. Upon reaching maturity the birds so reared preferred mates of the same species as their foster parents. Other interspecies sexual fixations have been observed in birds and fishes.

Heinroth (2,3) and his wife successfully reared by hand the young of almost every species of European birds. They found that many of the social responses of these birds were transferred to their human caretaker. Lorenz (4) extended these experiments, dealing especially with greylag geese.

Lorenz was the first to call this phenomenon "imprinting," although earlier workers had observed this effect. He was also the first to point out that it appeared to occur at a critical period early in the life of an animal. He postulated that the first object to elicit a social response later released not only that response but also related responses such as sexual behavior. Imprinting, then, was related not only to the problem of behavior but also to the general biological problem of evolution and speciation.

Although imprinting has been studied mainly in birds, it also has been observed to occur in other animals. Instances of imprinting have been reported in insects (5), in fish (6), and in some mammals. Those mammals in which the phenomenon has been found—sheep (7), deer (8), and buffalo (8a)—are all animals in which the young are mobile almost immediately after birth. Controlled experimental work with mammals, however, has just begun.

The first systematic investigations of imprinting were published in 1951. Simultaneously in this country and in Europe, the work of Ramsay (9) and Fabricius (10) gave the first indication of some of the important variables of the process. Ramsay worked with several species of ducks and a variety of breeds of chickens. He noticed the importance of the auditory component in the imprinting experiment and the effect of changes in coloring on parental recognition as well as on recognition of the parents by the young. His findings also showed that color is an essential element in recognition, while size or form seemed to be of less importance. Most of Ramsay's experiments dealt with exchange of parents and young and did not involve the use of models or decoys as imprinting objects, although he also imprinted some waterfowl on such objects as a football or a green box.

Fabricius carried on experiments with several species of ducklings and was able to determine approximately the critical age at which imprinting was most successful in several species of ducks. In some laboratory experiments he found it impossible to do imprinting in ducklings with a silent decoy—something which my co-workers and I were easily able to do a few years later in our Maryland laboratory. After the appearance of this pioneer work by Ramsay and by Fabricius, no relevant papers appeared until 1954. At that time Ramsay and Hess (11) published a paper on a laboratory approach to the study of imprinting. The basic technique was modified slightly the following the year and then was continued in the form described below. Papers in 1956 by Margaret Nice (12) and by Hinde, Thorpe, and Vince (13) include most of the pertinent materials published up to 1956 since Lorenz's classic statement of the problem.

Since 1956, however, there has been an

increasing number of papers on imprinting in a variety of journals. However, most investigators report experiments which are primarily designed to look for ways in which imprinting can be likened to associative learning and are not primarily carried out to investigate the phenomenon itself. Later we shall return to a consideration of these experiments; for the present we shall concern ourselves mainly with the program carried out since 1951 at McDonogh and at Lake Farm Laboratory, Maryland, and at our laboratories at the University of Chicago (14).

Experimental studies

Our laboratory in Maryland had access to a small duck pond in which we kept relatively wild mallards. The birds laid their eggs in nesting boxes, so the eggs could be collected regularly. After storage for a few days, the eggs were incubated in a dark, forced-air incubator. About two days before hatching, the eggs were transferred to a hatching incubator. Precautions were taken to place the newly hatched bird into a small cardboard box (5 by 4 by 4 inches) in such a way that it could see very little in the dim light used to carry out the procedure.

Each bird was given a number, which was recorded on the box itself as well as in our permanent records. The box containing the bird was then placed in a still-air incubator, used as a brooder, and kept there until the bird was to be imprinted. After the young bird had undergone the imprinting procedure, it was automatically returned to the box, and the box was then transferred to a fourth incubator, also used as a brooder, and kept there until the bird was to be tested. Only after testing was completed was the duckling placed in daylight and given food and water.

The apparatus we constructed to be used in the imprinting procedure consisted of a circular runway about 5 feet in diameter. This runway was 12 inches wide and 12½

feet in circumference at the center. Boundaries were formed by walls of Plexiglas 12 inches high. A mallard duck decoy, suspended from an elevated arm radiating from the center of the apparatus, was fitted internally with a loud-speaker and a heating element. It was held about 2 inches above the center of the runway. The arms suspending the decoy could be rotated by either of two variable-speed motors. The speed of rotating and intermittent movement could be regulated from the control panel located behind a one-way screen about 5 feet from the apparatus. The number of rotations of both the decoy and the animal were recorded automatically. Tape recorders with continuous tapes provided the sound that was played through the speaker inside the decoy. A trap door in the runway, operated from the control panel, returned the duckling to its box.

IMPRINTING PROCEDURE The young mallard, at a certain number of hours after hatching, was taken in its box from the incubator and placed in the runway of the apparatus (Figure 1). The decoy at this time was situated about 1 foot way. By means of a cord, pulley, and clip arrangement, the observer released the bird and removed the box. As the bird was released,

FIGURE 1 *The apparatus used in the study of imprinting consists primarily of a circular runway around which a decoy duck can be moved. In this drawing a duckling follows the decoy. The controls of the apparatus are in the foreground.*

the sound was turned on in the decoy model, and after a short interval the decoy began to move about the circular runway. The sound we used in the imprinting of the mallard ducklings was an arbitrarily chosen human rendition of *"gock,* gock, gock, gock, gock." The decoy emitted this call continually during the imprinting process. The duckling was allowed to remain in the apparatus for a specified amount of time while making a certain number of turns in the runway. At the end of the imprinting period, which was usually less than 1 hour, the duckling was automatically returned to its box and placed in an incubator until it was tested for imprinting strength at a later hour.

TESTING FOR IMPRINTING Each duckling to be tested was mechanically released from its box halfway between two duck models placed 4 feet apart. One of these was the male mallard model upon which it had been imprinted; the other was a female model which differed from the male only in its coloration. One minute was allowed for the duckling to make a decisive response to the silent models. At the end of this time, regardless of the nature of the duckling's response, sound was turned on

simultaneously for each of the models. The male model made the "gock" call upon which the duckling had been imprinted, while the female model gave the call of a real mallard female calling her young.

Four test conditions followed each other in immediate succession in the testing procedure. They were: (i) both models stationary and silent; (ii) both models stationary and calling; (iii) the male stationary and the female calling; (iv) the male stationary and silent and the female moving and calling. We estimated these four tests to be in order of increasing difficulty. The time of response and the character of the call note (pleasure tones or distress notes) were recorded. Scores in percentage of positive responses were then recorded for each animal. If the duckling gave a positive response to the imprinting object (the male decoy) in all four tests, imprinting was regarded as complete, or 100 percent.

Determination of the "critical period"

To determine the age at which an imprinting experience was most effective we imprinted our ducklings at various ages after hatching. In this series of experiments the imprinting experience was standard. It consisted in having the duckling follow the model 150 to 200 feet around the runway during a period of 10 minutes. Figure 2 shows the scores made by ducklings in the different age groups. It appears that some imprinting occurs immediately after hatching, but a maximum score is consistently made only by those ducklings imprinted in the 13- to 16-hour-old group. This result is indicated in Figure 3, which shows the percentage of animals in each age group that made perfect imprinting scores.

FIGURE 2 *The critical age at which ducklings are most effectively imprinted is depicted by this curve, which shows the average test score of ducklings imprinted at each age group.*

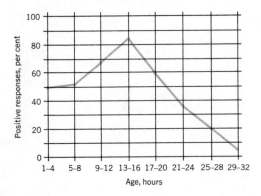

SOCIAL FACILITATION IN IMPRINTING In order to find whether imprinting would occur in those ducklings which were past the critical age for imprinting—that is, over 24 hours of age—we attempted to imprint these older ducklings in the presence of another duckling which had received an intensive imprinting experience. Ducklings ranging in age from 24 to 52 hours were given 100 feet of following experience during a period of 30 minutes. The average score for the ducklings was 50 percent; this shows that some imprinting can occur as a result of social facilitation. Two conclusions can be drawn. (i) Social facilitation will extend the critical age for imprinting. (ii) The strength of imprinting in these older ducklings is significantly less than that when the animal is imprinted alone at the critical age under the same time and distance conditions; under the latter circumstances the average score made is between 80 and 90 percent. A further indication of this dissipation of imprintability with increasing age is obtained when we average the scores for those animals which were between 24 and 32 hours old. The average score for these animals was 60 percent, while the score made by older animals ranging in age from 36 to 52 hours was 43 percent. One last item points to the difference; even when the time and distance were increased during imprinting of the older ducklings there were no perfect scores. With such a large amount of distance to travel during the imprinting period, approximately 40 percent of the animals would be expected to make perfect scores if they were imprinted during the critical period.

Genetic studies

We have also considered the genetic side of imprinting. We kept ducklings which were highly imprintable and bred them separately from ducklings which showed very little imprinting response. We thus had two groups of offspring, those produced by "imprinters" and those produced by "non-imprinters." There was a clear

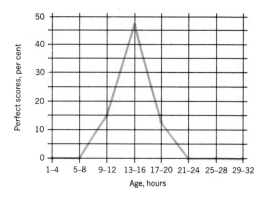

FIGURE 3 *Another way of showing the critical age is by plotting the percentage of animals in each age group that made scores of 100 per cent in testing.*

and significant difference in the imprinting behavior of the two groups, even in the first generation. The offspring of imprintable parents were easily imprinted; those of less imprintable parents were difficult to imprint. The "imprinter" ducklings had imprinting test scores more than three times better than those of the "non-imprinter" ducklings. Similar results were also obtained in a study of bantam chicks. We are also following up those animals which have had experimental imprinting experiences to determine what influence, if any, these experiences have on their behavior as adults. So far the results are inconclusive, but they do suggest that experimental imprinting of mallards affects their behavior as adults, particularly with respect to courtship patterns.

Birds of various species show differing degrees of imprintability. Domestic fowl do show imprinting responses, but the results are not as clear as for wild birds. We have had good success in imprinting some breeds of chicks, and the best imprinters among them are the Vantress broilers. Leghorns, on the other hand, appear to be too highly domesticated to give clear results. Other animals we have used in our experimentation are two kinds of geese, black ducks, wood ducks, turkeys, pheasants, quail, Peking ducks, and Rouens. The various breeds we have so far used in our work and the degree of imprintability found in each are shown in Table 1.

TABLE 1 *Number and imprintability of different experimental animals. Most of the animals were imprinted in runway and mallard decoy situations. Some of the Vantress broilers were imprinted on colored spheres, and the sheep were imprinted on human beings.*

ANIMAL	NO.*	IMPRINT-ABILITY†
Ducks		
Wild mallard	3,500	E+
Domesticated mallard	150	E
Peking	200	G
Rouen	100	F
Wood	50	P
Black	50	G
Total	4,050	
Geese		
Canada	30	E+
Pilgrim	50	G
Total	80	
Chickens		
Jungle fowl	100	G
Cochin bantam	300	G
New Hampshire Red	100	G
Rhode Island Red	100	G
Barred Rock	200	G
Vantress broiler	500	G+
White Rock	100	F
Leghorn	200	P
Total	1,600	
Other fowl		
Pheasant	100	P
Eastern bobwhite quail	50	G
California valley quail	20	E
Turkey	30	F
Total	200	
Mammals		
Sheep	2	G
Guinea pig	12	G
Total	14	
Total	5,944	

* Estimated for fowl, actual for mammals.
† E, excellent; G, good; F, fair; P, poor.

Imprinting in mammals

The guinea pig is similar to the chick and the duckling in that it is mobile and reasonably self-sufficient soon after birth. For this reason we used it in exploratory work. We first developed a method of obtaining the young from the mother with minimal parental contact. This was done by Caesarean section. However, further work showed that it was sufficient to obtain the young within an hour after they were born, and for the moment we are doing this. Guinea pigs imprint on human beings and follow them about as do the fowl with which we have been working. The maximum effectiveness of the imprinting experience seems to be over by the second day. So far, in using our imprinting apparatus with our usual duck decoy we have obtained best results sometime before the end of the first day of age. Work is being continued so that we can have a more standardized procedure before beginning a major program in this area.

Imprinting and learning

The supposed irreversibility of imprinting has been particularly singled out by some investigators to show that imprinting is nothing but "simple learning"—whatever that is. We do have some isolated instances which point to a long-range effect, but systematic work is just now beginning in our laboratories. Canada goslings, imprinted on human beings for a period of a week or two, will from that time on respond to their former caretaker with the typical "greeting ceremony," as well as accept food out of his hand. This occurs in spite of the fact that they normally associate entirely with the Canada geese on our duck pond. A more striking case is that of a jungle fowl cock which was imprinted by me and kept away from his own species for the first month. This animal, even after

5 years—much of that time in association with his own species—courts human beings with typical behavior, but not females of his own species. This certainly is a far-reaching effect and is similar to the finding of Räber (21), who reported on a male turkey whose behavior toward human beings was similar. An increased amount of homosexual courtship in mallards has been observed with some of our laboratory imprinted animals, which, while not a statistically valuable finding, perhaps points also to long-range, irreversible effects.

Imprinting is currently receiving much attention, and papers on the subject are being published at an impressive rate. Unfortunately, most experimenters appear to be certain that imprinting is identical with simple association learning and design their experiments as studies in association learning. In many instances the animals are too old when used in the experiments to fall within the critical age for imprinting, with the result that only association learning can occur. Papers falling into this category are those of Jaynes (22), Moltz (23), and James (24).

Our own experiments on the relation between association learning with food as a reward and imprinting during the critical period show four distinct differences.

In the first place, learning a visual discrimination problem is quicker and more stable when practice trials are spaced by interspersing time periods between trials than when practice trials are massed by omitting such intervening time periods. With imprinting, however, massed practice is more effective than spaced practice, as shown by our law of effort. Secondly, *recency* in experience is maximally effective in learning a discrimination; in imprinting, *primacy* of experience is the maximally effective factor. The second difference is illustrated by the following experiment. Two groups of 11 ducklings each were imprinted on two different imprinting objects. Group 1 was first imprinted on a male mallard model and then on a female model. Group 2, on the other hand, was first imprinted on a female model and subsequently on a male model. Fourteen of the 22 ducklings, when tested with both models present, preferred the model to which they first had been imprinted, showing primacy. Only five preferred the model to which they had been imprinted last, showing recency, and three showed no preference at all.

In addition, it has been found that the administration of punishment or painful stimulation increases the effectiveness of the imprinting experience, whereas such aversive stimulation results in avoidance of the associated stimulus in the case of visual discrimination learning.

Finally, chicks and ducklings under the influence of meprobamate are able to learn a color discrimination problem just as well as, or better than, they normally do, whereas the administration of this drug reduces imprintability to almost zero.

Imprinting, then, is an obviously interesting phenomenon, and the proper way to approach it is to make no assumptions. To find out its characteristics, to explore its occurrence in different organisms, and to follow its effects would seem a worth-while program of study.

What can we say in conclusion about the general nature of imprinting? Our best guess to date is that it is a rigid form of learning, differing in several ways from the usual association learning which comes into play immediately after the peak of imprintability. In other words, imprinting in our experiments results in the animal learning the rough, generalized characteristics of the imprinting object. Its detailed appreciation of the *specific* object comes as a result of normal conditioning—a process which in the case of these animals takes a much longer time and is possible days after the critical period for imprinting has passed. It is an exciting new field and is certainly worthy of study.

References and notes

1. W. Craig, *Am. J. Sociol.* 14, 86 (1908).
2. O. Heinroth, *Verhandl. 5th Intern. Ornithol. Kong.* 589–702 (1910).
3. ——— and M. Heinroth, *Die Vögel Mitteleuropas* (Lichterfelde, Berlin, 1924–33).
4. K. Lorenz, *J. Ornithol.* 83, 137, 289 (1935).
5. W. H. Thorpe, *Proc. Linnean Soc. London.* 156, 70 (1944).
6. G. P. Baerends and J. M. Baerends-van Roon, *Behaviour,* Suppl. 1, 1 (1950).
7. U. Grabowski, Z. *Tierpsychol.* 4, 326 (1941).
8. F. F. Darling, *Wild Country* (Cambridge Univ. Press, London, 1938).
8a. H. Hediger, *Wild Animals in Captivity* (Butterworths, London, 1938).
9. A. O. Ramsay, *Auk.* 68, 1 (1951).
10. E. Fabricius, *Acta Zool. Fennica.* 68, 1 (1951).
11. A. O. Ramsay and E. H. Hess, *Wilson Bull.* 66, 196 (1954).
12. M. M. Nice, *Condor.* 55, 33 (1953).
13. R. A. Hinde, W. H. Thorpe, M. A. Vince, *Behaviour.* 9, 214 (1956).
14. The work described in this article was supported in part by grant No. M-776 of the National Institutes of Health, Public Health Service, Department of Health, Education, and Welfare, Bethesda, Md.; by the Wallace C. and Clara A. Abbott Memorial Fund, of the University of Chicago, Chicago, Ill.; and by the Wallace Laboratories, New Brunswick, N.J.
15–20a omitted.
21. H. Räber, *Behaviour.* 1, 237 (1948).
22. J. Jaynes, *J. Comp. and Physiol. Psychol.* 49, 201 (1956); *ibid.* 50, 6 (1957); *ibid.* 51, 234, 238 (1958).
23. H. Moltz and L. A. Rosenblum, *ibid.* 51, 580 (1958).
24. H. James, *Can. J. Psychol.* 13, 59 (1959).

Studies on imprinting seem to show that critical periods during which early experience is effective do exist. In addition, and apart from the idea of sharply defined critical periods, experiments have shown that early experience is necessary for the full development of behavioral capacities. For instance, it has been shown that visual perception is very much dependent upon early exposure to patterned light stimulation. Similarly, as this article demonstrates, the development of pain perception is dependent upon early stimulation.

POINTS TO GUIDE YOUR STUDY   *(1) The* t *values and levels of significance are simply statistical ways of stating that the average differences between conditions are not due to chance alone. If a difference is significant at the .001 level, there is a probability of 1 out of 1,000 that the difference is not a real one and is due to chance alone. Thus, since the probability of the difference being due to chance alone is so small, the statistical inference is that the difference between the groups is a real one. (See also the introduction to the article by Braun and Geiselhart in Section Three, Principles of Learning.)   (2) Note that a restricted early environment seems to affect the "meaning" of pain, not the sensation itself.*

7: THE EFFECTS OF EARLY EXPERIENCE ON THE RESPONSE TO PAIN

Ronald Melzack, McGill University, and T. H. Scott

There has recently been an increase of theoretical interest in the effects of early experience on behavior, together with an increasing number of experimental studies (1). In one area, however, there is a marked discrepancy between theoretical emphasis and amount of empirical investigation: the area of avoidance behavior and pain.

Earlier clinical and theoretical formulations of the problem of early experience by Freud and his followers (4, and others there cited) have not led to any experimental studies relevant to pain perception and response, although the importance of early experience as a determinant of adult behavior was fully recognized. More recently, Scott and his associates (12) have arrived at a new hypothesis of the effects of early experience. They maintain that during the development of the organism there are specific critical periods after which sufficient maturation has occurred for various types of experience to have lasting effects on adult behavior. Although Fuller (3) has provided evidence for a critical period in the dog for the acquisition of conditioned responses to pain, there is no direct evidence which relates early pain experience with the behavior of the mature organism.

Hebb's (5) distinction between pain perception as a neurophysiological event and the overt response to pain, such as avoidance, has important implications for any attempt to relate early experience and pain perception in the mature organism. Hebb conceives of pain as a disruption of spatially and temporally organized activity in the cerebrum, this disruption per se constituting the physiological basis of pain. Since aggregates of neurons are assumed to develop their particular spatio-temporal organization as a result of prolonged, patterned sensory stimulation in early life, the theory thus suggests that the degree of pain perceived is, in part at least, dependent on the earlier experience of the organism. Pain, then, in the context of Hebb's theory, is not an elementary sensation, but a complex perceptual process in which a major role is played by all kinds of earlier perceptual learning, including both specific and nonspecific experience involving all the senses. Furthermore, as a result of direct experience with noxious stimuli, the organism tends to repeat and thus acquire any responses which decrease the cerebral disruption (i.e., pain).

That early experience does indeed play an important role in perceiving and responding to pain is strongly suggested by the study of a chimpanzee deprived of normal somesthetic stimulation during infancy and early maturity (11). After removal from somesthetic restriction, the chimpanzee appeared to have a heightened pain threshold, since "he 'panted' as chimpanzees do when they are being tickled" (11, p. 502) when his legs or lower ventral trunk was poked with a sharp pencil point or pin. Furthermore, the animal was found to be strikingly poor in localizing sites of noxious stimulation on its body.

The method of sensory deprivation or

Part of the results reported in this paper are contained in a thesis submitted by the senior author in partial fulfillment of the requirements of the Ph.D. degree at McGill University. The authors gratefully acknowledge the advice and guidance of Dr. D. O. Hebb throughout this study and the technical assistance of Dr. Peter Milner. This experiment was supported by grants from the Foundations Fund for Research in Psychiatry, the Rockefeller Foundation, and a Fellowship stipend given to the senior author by the National Research Council of Canada.

Ronald Melzack and T. H. Scott. The effects of early experience on the response to pain. *J. comp. physiol. Psychol.*, 1957, **50**, 155–161. Copyright © 1957 by the American Psychological Association. Reprinted here with permission from the authors and the American Psychological Association.

restriction has proved successful in ascertaining the effects of early perceptual experience on adult behavior (7, 14). The present experiment, then, is an attempt to study the effects of early sensory restriction, with special emphasis on the restriction of pain experience, on the adult response to noxious stimuli.

Subjects

Six litters of an inbred Scottish terrier strain were used. Each litter was randomly divided into two groups. One group, containing a total of 10 dogs, was placed in restriction cages. The 12 dogs which comprised the "free environment" or control group were raised normally as pets in private homes and in the laboratory.

Each restricted dog used in the present study was reared in isolation from puppyhood to maturity in a cage which was specially designed to prevent the dogs from seeing outside, although daylight was permitted to enter through a large air vent at the top of each cage. Each cage contained two compartments, and when the sliding partition between them was opened once a day, the dog was allowed to enter a freshly cleaned compartment. In this way the dogs were deprived of normal sensory and social experience from the time that weaning was completed at the age of four weeks until they were removed at about eight months of age. After the restricted dogs were released from their cages, they received the same opportunities for social and sensory stimulation as their normally reared littermates.

Testing of the dogs began about three to five weeks after the restricted animals were released. Two of the restricted dogs were tested a second time about two years after their release. Since the litters used in this study were born at different times over a three-year period, it was impossible to use all the dogs for all the tests.

Experiment I.
Response to electric shock

METHOD *Subjects.* The Ss were seven restricted and nine free-environment dogs.

Apparatus. A toy car that could be maneuvered by hand through a battery and steering mechanism was connected to a variable electric shock source provided by a variac and transformer circuit. The dogs were tested with the car on a 6-ft. by 3-ft. sheet-metal floor surrounded by a 2-ft.-high wire-mesh enclosure.

Procedure. The toy car was used to pursue the dogs and deliver a 1500-v., 6-ma. shock when it hit them. Each shock was of 1-sec. duration, although the dogs could escape the full shock by moving away rapidly. The car, which had a constant speed, was kept in waiting about 2 ft. from S. If S were sitting, E moved the car directly toward S. If S were moving, however, E moved the car into S's path and pursued S up to one of the far sides of the enclosure.

The E tried to hit each dog ten times during a testing period. However, if at some time during testing, the dog made five successive avoidances of the approaching car without being hit and shocked, testing was discontinued for that period, and the total number of shocks received by the dog up to that time was recorded. A dog reached the *criterion* of successful avoidance learning when it received no shock during a testing period.

RESULTS The restricted dogs received a mean of 24.7 shocks (range: 10 to 40) from the toy car, while the free-environment dogs received a mean of 6 shocks (range: 2 to 11). This difference between the two groups provided a t value of 4.4, which is significant at the .001 level. By the end of the fourth test period all the free-environment dogs had reached criterion. Three of the seven restricted dogs, however, had not yet done so; and two of these had received the full 40 shocks and gave no sign of learning to avoid the toy car. Testing was therefore discontinued at this time. The mean number of shocks received by the restricted dogs, then, would probably be considerably higher than it is if the restricted dogs were tested until all had reached criterion.

Characteristic differences in the behavior of the two groups were striking. The normal dogs were found to show smooth, precise movements which were oriented directly toward the toy car. They often sat looking at the car, swaying from side to side as it moved toward them, and only at the last moment, when the car was inches away from them, did they jump up and trot out of the way. Although these dogs were excited at first, their behavior after the first few shocks showed little excitement, and they made only minimal, unhurried avoidance movements of a leg or the tail to avoid being hit.

This behavior stands in marked contrast with the wild, aimless activity first shown by the restricted dogs. Their typical behavior consisted of running around in a circular path with excessive, exaggerated movements of the whole body. They often avoided being hit only by virtue of the remarkable rapidity of their action. But there was no difficulty in hitting them if the car were moved into the circular path. They then ran right into it. At other times, they stood up at the side of the testing enclosure, in an attempt to climb out, and received the full ten shocks in this position.

Two years after restriction. Two restricted dogs were tested two years after they had been released from restriction and still showed the same exaggerated behavior. While one learned after 9 shocks, the other received 23 shocks before it began to avoid successfully. This gave a mean of 16 shocks, which differs significantly from the mean of 6 shocks for the normal animals at the .01 level ($t = 3.5$).

Experiment II. Avoidance training

METHOD *Subjects.* The Ss were 7 restricted and 12 free-environment dogs.

Apparatus. A 6-ft. by 3-ft. testing enclosure, bounded by wire mesh 2 ft. high, was divided lengthwise into two halves by a 3-in.-high barrier. The steel grid floor was connected to a variable electric shock source provided by a variac and transformer circuit.

Procedure. The threshold levels at which the dogs responded to electric shock in the apparatus were first determined by raising the voltage stepwise. The voltmeter reading at which an animal first showed signs of startle or slight jumping was recorded as the threshold value. The behavior of the animals to this value of shock was then observed for two test periods during which each dog received about ten shocks on both sides of the barrier.

For the avoidance training which followed, the side which was to be "hot" for a particular animal was the one to which it moved and which it seemed to "prefer" when placed in the apparatus. The first shock on the training days was given 1 min. after the dog was placed on the "hot" side, and a shock was given every 60 sec. thereafter, as long as the dog stayed on the "hot" side, until S had received a total of ten shocks. However, when a dog jumped to the safe side during avoidance training, it was placed back on the "hot" side, and E waited 60 sec. before shock was again presented. If a dog made three successive jumps from the "hot" to the safe side without receiving shock, testing was discontinued for that period for the animal, and the number of shocks received up to that time was recorded. The shock was of 1-sec. duration, and 1500 v., 6 ma., which was about three times the mean threshold value measured by the voltmeter. The *criteria* for successful avoidance learning were: (a) two successive days with no more than one shock on each day or (b) a training day on which a dog went to the safe side immediately and received no shock.

RESULTS No significant difference in the thresholds at which the two groups first responded to electric shock was obtained in this experiment. Furthermore, no behavioral differences between the two groups were observed with these minimal values of shock, either in degree of responsiveness or type of response made.

During avoidance training with 1500 v., however, differences in the behavior of the two groups were obvious. By the end of the third testing period, only 2 of the 12 free-environment dogs had not reached criterion; 5 of the 7 restricted dogs, however, had not reached criterion at this stage, and 3 of these 5 had received the full 30 shocks and gave no sign of learning. Because of the obvious differences between the two groups, and the clearly unpleasant nature of the electric shock used, testing was discontinued at this point. Thus no dog received more than 30 shocks during avoidance training.

While the free-environment dogs received a mean of 5 shocks (range: 1 to 22), the restricted dogs received a mean of 20.3 shocks (range: 1 to 30) during avoidance training. The t score of the difference between the means, 5.07, is significant at the .001 level.

The three dogs that received the full 30 shocks showed stereotyped forms of behavior to the shock. One dog whirled around violently in narrow circles on the "hot" side immediately after getting the first shock in the enclosure and continued to do so until it was removed after getting 10 shocks. The second dog always ran to a particular corner on the "hot" side after the first shock, and sat in a peculiar, awkward position, getting shock after shock without moving. The third dog learned a partial response to the shock, consisting of placing its forelegs on the barrier, while its hindquarters were on the "hot" side, in

this way getting repeated shocks without learning the entire response.

Two years after restriction. Two dogs that had been out of restriction for two years, and were reared normally in the laboratory during that time, nevertheless received a mean of 19 shocks during the three testing periods, which differed significantly from the free-environment dogs' mean of 5 shocks at the .02 level of significance ($t = 2.78$). One of these dogs received 25 shocks, and S still maintained the same awkward, "frozen" position in the corner that it had assumed when first tested two years previously, giving little sign of learning permanently to make the appropriate response of stepping over the 3-in. barrier to the safe side.

Experiment III. Response to burning

METHOD *Subjects.* The Ss were ten restricted and eight free-environment dogs.

Apparatus. A box of safety matches.

Procedure. Each dog was allowed to roam the testing room freely for 1 min., and the amount of time S spent near E in an area which had been demarcated previously by a chalk line was recorded. The S was then called by E to this area. A safety match was struck, and E attempted to push the flame into the dog's nose at least three times. Although the dog was held forcibly by E, S was able to avoid being burned by moving or turning its head away rapidly from the match. The dog was then allowed to move to any part of the room, and the time spent near E in the area of the source of burning was recorded during a 2-min. period. The percentages of time S spent near E before and after presentation of the flame were then compared.

RESULTS Of the eight free-environment dogs tested, six spent less time near E after he tried to burn them than before. Of the ten restricted dogs, however, nine spent *more* time in the area near E *after* nose-burning than before. While the restricted dogs spent 27.9 per cent of the time near E before stimulation, they spent 51.2 per cent of the time in that area following presentation of the match. The amount of time spent by the free-environment dogs near E decreased from 45.1 per cent before to 32.8 per cent after presentation of the match. The nonparametric sign test (9) provided a chi-square value of 5.40 with Yates' correction, which is significant at the .02 level of confidence.

One of the most remarkable features of the restricted dogs was their behavior during and following presentation of the flame. To the astonishment of the observers, seven of the ten restricted dogs made no attempt to get away from E *during* stimulation, and it was not even necessary to hold them. The sequence of behavior observed was almost identical for all seven dogs: they moved their noses into the flame as soon as it was presented, after which the head or whole body jerked away, as though reflexively; but then they came right back to their original position and hovered excitedly near the flame. Three of them repeatedly poked their noses into the flame and sniffed at it as long as it was present. If they snuffed it out, another match was struck, and the same sequence of events occurred. The other four did not sniff at the match, but offered no resistance nor made any attempt to get away after the first contact, and E was able to touch the dogs' noses with the flame as often as he wished. Only three of the restricted dogs squealed on making contact with the flame and tried subsequently to avoid it by moving their heads. Two of these, however, made no attempt to get away from E after stimulation had stopped.

In contrast, the normal dogs moved their heads so rapidly that it was often impossible to hit their noses with the flame. The E tried to move the match in from unexpected angles or to distract the Ss in order to hit them with the flame. But the normal dogs moved their heads slightly and usually successfully, receiving only one or two very brief contacts with the flame; and they then struggled to escape from E's grasp at their sides.

Experiment IV. Response to pin-prick

METHOD   *Subjects.* The Ss were eight restricted and nine free-environment dogs.

Apparatus. A large, sharp dissecting needle.

Procedure. The procedure in this experiment is the same as that used in Exp. III, except that the dogs were pin-pricked rather than burned. While the dog was held at the neck, a long dissecting needle was jabbed into the skin at the sides and hind thighs about three or four times.

RESULTS   Of the eight restricted dogs, six spent more time near E after pin-pricking than before. These dogs increased the time spent in the demarcated area from 50.8 per cent before to 58.4 per cent after pin-pricking. The normal dogs, on the other hand, spent a mean of only 8.9 per cent of the time after pin-pricking near E, compared with 42.2 per cent before. Of the nine normally reared dogs, eight spent less time near E after pin-pricking than before. The sign test provided a chi-square value of 4.74, which is significant at the .05 level.

The behavior of the restricted dogs in response to pin-prick was almost identical with that observed with the flame: they appeared unaware that they were being stimulated *by something in the environment.* Four of the restricted dogs made no response whatever apart from localized reflexive twitches at the side or leg when they were pricked. The E was often able to pierce the skin of these dogs completely so that the needle was lodged in it without eliciting withdrawal or any behavioral indication that pain was being "felt" or responded to other than spasmodic, reflexive jerks. The remaining four restricted dogs pulled their bodies aside a few inches or yipped to *some* of the pin-pricks, but when released two of them stayed right next to *E,* who was able to repeat the procedure and jab them with the needle as often as he wished. The noxious stimulation received was apparently not "perceived" as coming from *E,* and their behavior subsequently was not oriented or organized in terms of the noxious stimulus in any noticeable way.

The free-environment dogs, however, provided an unmistakable index of perceived pain. They tried to jump aside to escape the pin-prick, yelped, and often struggled for release after two or three pin-pricks. They would then dash away from *E*'s hand and take up a position in the farthest corner of the testing room.

Supplementary observations. The behavior of the restricted dogs in the four experiments just described is entirely consistent with everyday observations of their behavior. It was noted, for example, that their aimless activity resulted in some of them frequently striking their heads against water pipes that ran along the walls just above the floor of the testing room. One dog, by actual count, struck his head against these pipes more than 30 times in a single hour. This was never observed once in the normal dogs. Similarly, the rapid movement of the restricted dogs and their unpredictability as to direction resulted a number of times in the dogs' having a paw or the tail stepped on. Often there was no sign that the dogs "felt" pain when this happened, though the procedure would have elicited a howl from a normal dog, and the restricted *S* made no attempt to withdraw from the place where injury was received.

Discussion

The outstanding feature of the behavior of the restricted dogs was their inability to respond adaptively and intelligently to the variety of stimuli which were presented to them. There can be little doubt that the restricted dogs "felt" electric shock: their disturbance by it was marked and unmistakable. Similarly, the behavior of at least three of the restricted dogs indicates that pin-prick and contact with fire were "felt" in some way. Nevertheless, it was obvious that the restricted dogs did not know how to make the proper avoidance responses which would have prevented further stimulation. The results permit the conclusion, then, that early experience plays an essential role in the emergence of such basic behavior as avoidance of noxious stimuli.

Sherrington has defined pain as "the psychical adjunct of an imperative protective reflex" (13, p. 286). And many psychologists since then (2, 8, 10) have interpreted pain in terms of imperative reflex responses. Such a view, however, is not consistent with the observations reported here. Most of the restricted dogs did indeed show localized reflex responses to the stimulation, yet their behavior was clearly inadequate to cope with the intense electric shocks or such grossly injurious stimuli as contact with fire or piercing of the skin. In comparison, their littermates which had been reared normally in a free environment exhibited the ability to avoid prolonged contact with injurious stimuli, and they were able to learn with great rapidity to make highly organized, ambiently oriented responses to every form of noxious stimulus that was presented. However, the capacity of the restricted dogs to acquire good, adaptive behavior to noxious stimulation was notably limited after release from restriction, even with the adequate opportunity that was provided for them to gain varied, normal perceptual experience. Maladaptive behavior like freezing and whirling also developed, and they were observed as consistent responses as long as two years after release. Thus, it appears that the requisite experience must come at the correct time in the young organism's life. During later stages of development, the experience necessary for adaptive, well-organized responses to pain may never be properly acquired.

The inability of the restricted dogs to cope intelligently with noxious stimuli, however, cannot be attributed to inadequate response mechanisms alone. Their reflexive jerks and movements during pin-prick and contact with fire suggest that they may have "felt something" during stimulation; but the *lack* of any observable emotional disturbance apart from these reflex movements in at least four of the dogs following pin-prick and in seven of them after nose-burning indicates that their *perception* of the event was highly abnormal in comparison with the behavior of the normally reared control dogs. Livingston (6) has made the observation that experience with pain in childhood is an important determinant of the manner in which the adult perceives and responds to pain; that is, the "meaning" involved in a perception such as pain, and the attitudes of the individual in situations involving pain, are largely a function of the earlier, related experiences of that individual. The results reported here are consistent with observations such as this and can be interpreted in a similar manner.

The isolation of the restricted dogs prevented them from acquiring experience early in life with severe skin-damage and fire. It is evident, then, that the flame and pin-prick could not have evoked the neural "phase sequences" (memories) acquired during earlier pain experiences (5) that might have been aroused in the normal dogs. The results strongly suggest that the restricted dogs lacked awareness of a necessary aspect of normal pain perception: the "meaning" of physical damage or at least *threat* to the physical well-being that is inherent in the normal organism's perception of pain. The observations of the restricted dogs' poking their noses into fire, or permitting *E* to cause bodily damage by

fire and pin-prick without emotional disturbance apart from localized reflexes, indicates that an interpretation such as this is valid. Indeed, to say that these restricted dogs perceived fire and pin-prick as *threatening,* or even painful in any *normal* sense, would be anthropomorphism rather than inference from observed behavior.

The results which have been reported here then, make it difficult to treat behavior related to pain simply in terms of frequency and intensity of stimulations or in terms of imperative reflex responses alone (2, 8, 10) without regard to the earlier perceptual experience of the organism. The behavior of the restricted dogs suggests that perceiving and responding to pain, which is so fundamental to normal adult behavior and presumably so important for the survival of an individual or species, requires a background of early, prolonged, perceptual experience.

Summary

1. Ten dogs were reared in isolation from puppyhood to maturity in specially constructed cages which drastically restricted their sensory experience. Twelve control littermates were raised normally as pets in private homes and in the laboratory.
2. In two tests using strong electric shock, the restricted dogs required significantly more shocks before they learned to make the proper avoidance responses than their free-environment littermates.
3. In tests using nose-burining and pin-pricking, the behavior of the restricted dogs was found to be strikingly different in capacity to perceive pain and respond to it when compared to their normal littermates.
4. It is concluded that early perceptual experience determines, in part at least, (a) the emergence of overt responses such as avoidance to noxious stimulation, and (b) the actual capacity to perceive pain normally.

References

1. Beach, F. A., and Jaynes, J. Effects of early experience upon the behavior of animals. *Psychol. Bull.*, 1954, 51, 239–263.

2. Estes, W. K. An experimental study of punishment. *Psychol. Monogr.*, 1944, 57, No. 3 (Whole No. 263).

3. Fuller, J. L., Easler, C A., and Banks, E. M. Formation of conditioned avoidance responses in young puppies. *Amer. J. Physiol.*, 1950, 160, 462–466.

4. Greenacre, P. The biological economy of birth. In O. Fenichel (Ed.), *The psychoanalytic study of the child.* New York: International Universities Press, 1945.

5. Hebb, D. O. *The organization of behavior.* New York: John Wiley and Sons, Inc., 1949.

6. Livingston, W. K. What is pain? *Sci. Amer.*, 1953, 188, 59–66.

7. Melzack, R. The genesis of emotional behavior: an experimental study of the dog. *J. comp. Physiol. Psychol.*, 1954, 47, 166–168.

8. Miller, N. E. Learnable drives and rewards. In S. S. Stevens (Ed.), *Handbook of experimental psychology.* New York: John Wiley and Sons, Inc., 1951.

9. Moses, L. E. Non-parametric statistics for psychological research. *Psychol. Bull.*, 1952, 49, 122–143.

10. Mowrer, O. H. *Learning theory and personality dynamics.* New York: Ronald Press, 1950.

11. Nissen, H. W., Chow, K. L., and Semmes, Josephine. Effects of restricted opportunity for tactual, kinesthetic, and manipulative experience on the behavior of a chimpanzee. *Amer. J. Psychol.*, 1951, 64, 485–507.

12. Scott, J. P., Fredricson, E., and Fuller, J. L. Experimental exploration of the critical period hypothesis. *Personality,* 1951, 1, 162–183.

13. Sherrington, C. S. *Man on his nature.* New York: Macmillan, 1941.

14. Thompson, W. R., and Heron, W. The effects of restricting early experience on the problem solving capacity of dogs. *Canad. J. Psychol.*, 1954, 8, 17–31.

The necessity of early experience in normal development is dramatically illustrated in this article. Early experience with a mother, and the early opportunity to play with others of the individual's own age group, are among the most important factors in the development of normal patterns of social behavior in monkeys. It seems likely that similar types of social contact are important and necessary for development in the human species also.

A POINT TO GUIDE YOUR STUDY   *Maternal and sexual behaviors of monkeys are stressed in this article because these are some of the most important social behaviors of monkeys—and humans too. Other social behaviors of monkeys—and of humans—discussed are clinging and affiliation, aggression, and rough-and-tumble play.*

8: THE EFFECT OF REARING CONDITIONS ON BEHAVIOR

Harry F. Harlow and Margaret K. Harlow, University of Wisconsin

A wealth of clinical evidence shows that human children who have never had ade-

H. F. Harlow and Margaret K. Harlow. The effect of rearing conditions on behavior. *Bull. Menninger Clinic,* 1962, **26**, 213–224. Copyright © 1962 by The Menninger Foundation. Reprinted here with permission from the *Bulletin of the Menninger Clinic,* vol. **26**, pp. 213–224, and the senior author.

quate maternal care or who have been separated from adequate maternal care within some critical stage, suffer disturbance and delay or even irreparable damage in terms of subsequent personal-social development. The importance of maternal ministrations in the child's development is further supported by many clinical investigations and by some limited experimental data.

Personality malfunctions that have been attributed to maternal inadequacy include such syndromes as marasmus, hospitalism, infantile autism, feeble-mindedness, inadequate maternal responsiveness, and deviant or depressed heterosexuality. If these disorders are the results of maternal inadequacy, only research with human subjects can establish the conditions and kinds of maternal behavior that produce them. Unfortunately, experiments critical to the resolution of these problems cannot be done with human subjects. We cannot rear babies in illuminated black boxes during the first half-year, year, or two years of their lives. We cannot have mothers rear their children in isolation from other children and from adults for the first two, four, or eight years. We dare not have human children reared with either no mothers or inadequate mothers while providing them with maximal opportunity to interact with age-mates, either identically reared or differentially reared. Yet these are the kinds of experiments which are required if we are to assess the effects of maternal variables unconfounded with other experiential variables on the child's personal-social development.

Most clinical investigations have given primary attention to the effects of maternal privation, defined as absence or inadequacy of maternal responsiveness, or to maternal deprivation, defined as infant separation after the infant has established profound, or at least adequate, maternal attachments. Relatively little attention has been given to the effects of the absence or inadequacy of opportunity for the child to interact with other children and to form adequate affectional patterns with and for them. We know that it is important for the child to form effective infant-mother affectional patterns, but it also is likely that he

must form effective child-child affectional patterns if he is to attain normal personal-social, sexual, and parental patterns. Obviously these affectional systems are not independent. It is possible, but by no means a certainty, that at the human level, normal child-child affection requires previous affectional bonds between mother or mother-figure and child. It is certain that the mother plays an important role in the formation of peer affections by providing for and encouraging associations between infants or children, or by preventing or discouraging such associations. Human mothers may also markedly influence the nature and course of child-child relationships.

Psychoanalytic theory, which looks for temporal reduction and temporal primacy, will ascribe primary importance to the earliest causes and conditions whether or not these are of greatest importance. Initial traumas have a false clarity as causative agents since they are not confounded by preceding events, whereas the role of all subsequent events is confounded by the role of these events operating during previous experience. Yet primacy in time need not, and often should not, be equated with primacy in importance.

Effects of total social deprivation on monkeys

Six years ago we took two newborn rhesus monkeys, one male and one female, and subjected them to total social deprivation for the first two years of life. Each was placed in a solid, illuminated cage such that it never saw any other animal—monkey or human—even though it was tested for food responsiveness and learning by remote-control techniques. During isolation these monkeys adapted to solid food slowly and learned with great difficulty, but they were found to have normal weight and good coats when removed—there were no signs of marasmus. At the conclusion of the two years' isolation, they were tested for social responsiveness to each other and to normal monkeys smaller and younger than themselves. They did not respond to each other and either froze or huddled in a corner when abused by the younger animals. Placed together in a cage in a room with many caged monkeys, they showed withdrawal from this new external world, and in the more than two years they lived together, they remained abnormally frightened, showed minimal interaction, and engaged in no sex activities. In follow-up social tests at four years of age with smaller and weaker monkeys, they made no effort to defend themselves except for one brief episode with one of the pair, after which it curled into a ball and passively accepted abuse. The potential for social behaviors in these animals had apparently been obliterated.

We have preliminary, incomplete data on the effects of such total social deprivation confined to a six-month period and are obtaining other data on the effects of such deprivation over a twelve-month period. The results to date indicate severe but not complete withdrawal from external environmental stimulation. Repeated testing in our playroom situation, shown in Figure 1, reveals that one of these monkeys is almost totally unresponsive socially and the other only occasionally engages in brief, infantile-type social interactions. Normally, the playroom is a highly stimulating situation for monkeys. It is 8 feet high with 36 square feet of floor space, and it contains multiple stationary and mobile toys and tools, flying rings, a rotating wheel, an artificial tree, a wire-mesh climbing ramp, and a high, wide ledge, offering opportunities to explore and play in a three-dimensional world.

We also have data on eight monkeys subjected to total social isolation from other monkeys during the first 80 days of life. Although they neither saw nor contacted nor heard other monkeys, they did see and contact human experimenters, who removed them from their isolation boxes and tested them repeatedly on learning problems after the second week of life. A year later these animals appear to be normally responsive to external environmental stimulation and they are socially responsive to each other when tested in the

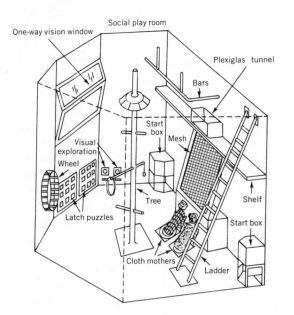

FIGURE 1.

playroom. This social responsiveness as measured by the appearance of increasingly complex play patterns has become qualitatively normal, but probably it is depressed somewhat quantitatively. Whether there will be subsequent effects on heterosexual and maternal behavior remains for future observation.

If we assume a rough developmental ratio of four to one for monkey to man, the results of these eight monkeys are not completely in accord with human clinical data, which at best are only roughly comparable to our experimental situation. Social isolation up to eight or ten months of age is reported to endanger or impair the personal-social development of human infants. It may be that the stimulation and handling of the monkeys in the learning experiments played a positive role in preparing them for subsequent exposure to a monkey environment, thus minimizing the isolation effects. It is also possible that the human infant is more susceptible than the monkey infant to damage from social isolation.

Effects of early partial social deprivation

We have data on various groups of monkeys raised from the day of their birth without their mothers and without any monkey companionship at least through the first half-year. One group of 56, now ranging in age from five to eight years, was raised in individual bare wire cages where they could see and hear other monkeys, but not touch them. A group of four was similarly housed for up to five years, but had access to a single wire surrogate[1] during the first half-year of life. A third group of over 100 monkeys was raised identically except for access to a cloth surrogate[2] or

to both a cloth surrogate and a wire surrogate during at least six months of the first year.[3] Approximately half of these animals have been housed after six months or one year of age with another monkey of like age and like or unlike sex for part or all the time since.

Although there may be differences in the personal-social behaviors of the monkeys comprising these groups, we cannot be sure at the present time, and for this reason we group them together. Many members of all three groups have developed what appear to be abnormal behaviors, including sitting and staring fixedly into space, repetitive stereotyped circling movements about the cage, clasping the head in the hands and arms while engaging in rocking, autistic-type movements, and intrapunitive responses of grasping a foot, hand, arm, or leg and chewing or tearing at it with the teeth to the point of injury.

The sex behavior of the six oldest wire-cage-raised monkeys was first measured by Mason[4] in 1960 and compared with that of rhesus monkeys of equal age which had lived in the wild during most of the first year of life. All the wild-raised monkeys, male and female, showed normal sex behavior, characterized in the male by dorsoventral mounting, clasping the legs of the female by the feet, and holding the buttocks by the hands. The females in turn sexually presented themselves by elevating their buttocks and tails, lowering their heads, and frequently looking backward without threatening. No laboratory-raised male or female showed normal sex behavior. Attempted mounting by the male was random in regard to body part, and the most frequent pattern was grasping a side of the female's body and thrusting laterally. The female's patterns were totally

---

[1] A wire surrogate mother is a bare, welded wire cylindrical form surmounted by a wooden head with a crude face and supported semiupright in a wooden frame.
[2] A cloth surrogate differs from the wire surrogate in that the wire cylinder is cushioned with a sheathing of terry cloth.

[3] Harlow, H. F.: The Nature of Love. *Amer. Psychologist*, 1958, **13**, 673–685. Harlow, H. F.: Love in Infant Monkeys. *Sci. Amer.*, 1959, **200**, 68–74.
[4] Mason, W. A.: The Effects of Social Restriction on the Behavior of Rhesus Monkeys: I. Free Social Behavior. *J. Comp. Physiol. Psychol.*, 1960, **53**, 582–589.

disordered and often involved sitting down and staring aimlessly into space. Although none of these animals was sexually mature, heterosexual positioning in both male and female normally develops during the second year.

Attempts to breed the cage-raised monkeys approximately two years later also ended in complete failure. When the oldest wire-cage-raised females were between five and seven years of age and the oldest surrogate-raised females were between three and five years, repeated attempts were made to breed 11 of the wire-cage-raised females and four of the cloth-surrogate-raised females with highly selected males from our breeding colony. The females were placed in the large breeding cages during estrus, and if no fighting ensued within 15 minutes, they were left overnight. Eventually one wire-cage-raised female and three cloth-surrogate females became pregnant. Although observation did not reveal clear-cut differences in the behavior of these two groups, the differences in pregnancy approach significance in spite of—or possibly because of—the greater immaturity of the cloth-surrogate-raised females. Actually, no female, impregnated or not, demonstrated a normal pattern of sexual behavior. Many females tried to avoid the males; some actually threatened the males and would probably have been injured had our males not been carefully screened. When the males approached and positioned the females, the females usually collapsed and fell flat on the floor. Impregnation of the four females was achieved only through the patience, persistence, knowledgeability, and motor skill of the breeding males.

We have subsequently tested many wire-cage- and surrogate-mother-raised males and females with experienced breeding females and experienced breeding males, respectively, in a large 8-foot by 8-foot by 8-foot room especially designed for breeding studies. All the males have continued to show the disorganized and inappropriately oriented sexual responsiveness which we have already described, and no male has ever appropriately mounted our experienced and cooperative breeding-stock females, let alone achieved intromission.

With a single exception we have never seen normal, appropriate sexual posturing in our wire-cage- or surrogate-raised females. The females do not approach the males, nor do they groom or present. One cloth-surrogate-raised female was not impregnated throughout six mating sessions, and during this time she began to respond positively and appropriately to the males and eventually developed a normal, full-blown pattern of sexual presentation and sexual posturing during copulation.

Effects of maternal conditions

Direct comparison of the effects of being raised by real monkey mothers and cloth surrogate mothers on subsequent personal-social development has been measured by the use of our playpen test situation. In two playpen situations babies were housed with their real mothers, and in a third setup the babies were housed with cloth mothers. The playpen, whose floor plan is given in Figure 2, consists of large living cages each housing a mother and an infant and adjoining a compartment of the playpen. A small opening in each living cage restrains the mother, but gives the infant continuous access to the adjoining playpen compartment. During two daily test sessions, each an hour in length, the screens between playpen compartments were raised, permitting the infant monkeys to interact as pairs during the first six months and as both pairs and groups of four during the second six months. Two experimenters independently observed and recorded the behavior exhibited during test sessions.

The infants raised by real monkey

mothers were more socially responsive to each other than were the infants raised by the cloth surrogates. They showed a wider range of facial expressions, and, probably of paramount importance, they developed simple interactive play patterns earlier than the surrogate-raised monkeys and achieved a level of complex play patterns not achieved by the surrogate-raised monkeys during an 18-month test period.

All the male mother-raised infants have at one time or another responded sexually toward the mother with pelvic thrusting and in at least two cases by dorsoventral mounting. In three cases pelvic thrusting to a female was observed before 50 days of age and in a fourth case, before 100 days of age. Only two (one male and one female) cloth-surrogate-raised monkeys were observed to show pelvic thrusting to the surrogate, and this occurred initially at approximately 100 days of age. Frequency of this sexual play was much higher toward real mothers than toward surrogates. In both situations maximal frequency occurred at about five months and then declined, apparently being superseded by thrusting directed toward other infants.

Surrogate babies and mothered babies showed no significant differences in first-observed, infant-directed thrusting, but the actual mean score of the surrogate group was lower. The frequency of sexual play was higher for the real-mothered babies than for the surrogate babies. Finally, seven of eight mother-raised monkeys showed appropriate adult-form sex behaviors during the first 18 months, including ankle clasp by the males, whereas adult-oriented sex behavior was not observed in the cloth-surrogate-raised babies.

There is every reason to believe that normal mothering facilitates the development of heterosexual behavior in rhesus monkeys. This may be in part the result of direct contacts with the mother growing out of the intimate bonds between

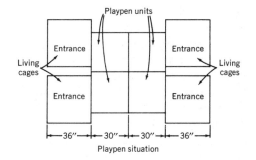

FIGURE 2.

mother and child. One must not, however, underestimate the importance of the role which the real mother apparently plays, indirect though it is, in stimulating the infants to associate with other infants. This is accomplished from the third month on by discouraging the infant from constant clinging as it matures. From time to time the mother restrains the infant's approaches or cuffs it if it nips her or pulls her hair. The chastised infant seeks the companionship of other babies until the storm subsides—the other mothers by this time generally reject all but their own babies—and in the infant-infant interchanges, strong affectional bonds develop along with behaviors, sexual and nonsexual, appropriate to the sexes.

In the present study, as in all ordinary human situations, there is confounding in the roles played by the mother-infant affectional systems and the infant-infant and peer-peer affectional systems in determining later behavior. We expect to resolve this in part by raising two groups of monkey babies with real mothers, but denying them any opportunity to interact with other infants for six months in the one group and 12 months in the other before subjecting them to social testing.

Some information is supplied by another experiment involving eight rhesus babies raised on cloth surrogate mothers, but tested 20 minutes a day in the playroom, which is a more stimulating environment than that afforded by the relatively cramped and bare confines of the play compartments of the playpen situation. These surrogate-mothered babies showed excellent and appropriately timed play behaviors and very early came to assume both sexual and nonsexual behaviors appropriate to males and females. The males threatened, the females did not; the males initiated rough-and-tumble play, but not the females. Males chased males and males chased females, but females practically never chased males and seldom chased females. By a year of age considerable appropriate male and female sex behavior had occurred, and full and complete copulation, other than insemination, was repeatedly observed in the two males and two females on which observations were continued during the second year of life.

It is obvious that we must not underestimate the importance and role of the infant-infant affectional system as a determiner of adolescent and adult adjustments. It is more than possible that this system is essential if the animal is to respond positively to sheer physical contact with a peer, and it is through the operation of this system, probably both in monkey and man, that sexual roles become identified and, usually, acceptable.

The role of the mother in the formation of the adult personality is obviously important, but the exact mechanics are open for experimentation. The most tender and intimate associations occur at a stage in which the monkey infant and human infant can to a considerable extent be molded. Monkey and human mothers both have the obligation of gradually dissolving the intense physical bonds which characterize the early mother-child relationship. For the monkey mother it is easy and natural—when the infant becomes mature enough and strong enough to become bothersome, she rejects or punishes it and the baby retreats for a time. Subsequently, she welcomes the baby back. Independence is gradually established. For the human

mother, with her more complicated motivational systems and her complex culture, it may be difficult to achieve this gradual separation. The overprotective mother is a well-known clinical extreme in the human problem of weaning the infant and child emotionally. Probably the surrogate monkey mother is a parallel of the overprotective human mother, failing usually to equal the normal mother in rearing socially and sexually adjusted monkeys because, at least in part, she is ever available to provide comfort and security. She never discourages contact and thereby never encourages independence in her infant and affectional relationships with other infants and children. The normal state of complete dependency necessary in early infancy is prolonged until it hinders normal personal-social development.

As we have already pointed out, four of our laboratory-raised females never had real mothers of their own, one being raised in a bare wire cage and three with cloth surrogates. The first week after the birth of the baby to the wire-cage-raised female, the mother sat fixedly at one side of the cage staring into space, almost unaware of her infant or of human beings, even when they barked at and threatened the baby. There was no sign of maternal responses, and when the infant approached and attempted contact, the mother rebuffed it, often with vigor, as shown in Figure 3.

The next two unmothered mothers constantly rebuffed the approaches of their infants, but, in addition, frequently engaged in cruel and unprovoked attacks. They struck and beat their babies, mouthed them roughly, and pushed their faces into the wire-mesh floor. These attacks seemed to be exaggerated in the presence of human beings, and for this reason all formal testing was abandoned for three days for the third unmothered mother because we feared for the life of the infant. The fourth unmothered mother ignored and rejected her infant but did not exhibit excessive cruelty.

In strong contrast to the frailty of the maternal affectional system was the vigor and persistence of the infants' bondage to the mother—time after time, hour after hour, the infants returned, contacted, and clasped the mother in spite of being hit, kicked, and scraped unceremoniously off the mother's body, as shown in Figure 4. The physical punishment which these infants took or sought for the privilege of brief contact even to the back or side of the mother's body testified to the fact that, even in infants, attachment to the mother may be prepotent over pain and suffering. One could not help but be reminded of children, removed from indifferent or cruel, indigent, and alcoholic parents, whose primary insistent wish is to return home.

The degree to which monkey data are generalizable to the human being will remain an unsolved dilemma. Nevertheless, we are so struck by the many apparent analogies that we are tempted to say the

FIGURE 3.

FIGURE 4.

monkey experiments give us faith in the human clinical observations.

Summary

Infant rhesus monkeys have been reared starting on the first day of life in a variety of situations, including total isolation; partial isolation, either in individual bare wire cages in a colony room for two years or longer, or in individual wire cages with access to one or two mother surrogates for at least the first six months; and in situations with real or surrogate mothers plus contact with other infants for the first year or two of life.

Total isolation for two years resulted in failure to display social or sexual behavior in the next two years, spent in a joint living cage. Results on six months of such isolation are still being gathered and suggest severe, but not complete, social deficits. Only mild effects have been observed thus far in monkeys isolated through the first 80 days of life.

Partial isolation has produced behavioral aberrations in many monkeys and sexual inadequacy in all males and in all but one female. Four females were impregnated, in spite of inadequate posturing, and proved to be completely inadequate mothers.·

Infants raised by live mothers were more advanced in social and sexual behavior than infants raised by surrogate mothers in a controlled playpen situation. The mother's role is not entirely clear, however, because in a more stimulating playroom situation, surrogate-mothered babies have shown normal social and sexual behavior.

Over all, it appears that the longer and the more complete the social deprivation, the more devastating are the behavioral effects. Further research is needed to evaluate the relative contributions of live mothers and infant companions to later adjustment.

The developmental schedule for the behaviors mentioned in this article is largely genetically determined. A picture of the sequence of development in the first year of life is presented here.

A POINT TO GUIDE YOUR STUDY   *Note that the graph is rather unusual.*

9: A DEVELOPMENTAL GRAPH FOR THE FIRST YEAR OF LIFE

C. Anderson Aldrich, M.D., and Mildred A. Norval, M.D.

This developmental graph is presented in the hope that it will help physicians to follow, with the minimal expenditure of time and effort, the neuromuscular growth of infants under their care and that these steps may be used as an index of the child's maturity.

Since growth follows a regular pattern, the sequence of the steps is established and progressive. This enables one to demonstrate to the mother, each time she comes for advice, what her child will be doing next in his progress.

While the sequence is rigid, each child has his own rate of growth, which reflects his own individuality as well as his maturity. However, the appearance of these emerging abilities may be modified somewhat by the effects of environment.

We followed the development of 215 normal infants from birth to the early part of their second year. The parents of these infants came from all strata of society in Rochester, Minn., which, however, has a larger proportion of professional people than is usual.

We explained to each mother how her infant's behavior would follow the sequence of growth and advised her to encourage her baby to use each ability as it appeared. Since we were to record the time of onset of these various accomplishments, this information was obtained by testing the infants at monthly intervals and in-

From the Rochester Child Health Project, and the Section on Pediatrics, Mayo Clinic.

C. A. Aldrich and M. A. Norval. A developmental graph for the first year of life. *J. Pediat.*, 1946, **29**, 304–308. Copyright © 1946 by The C. V. Mosby Company. Reprinted here with permission from The C. V. Mosby Company and Dr. M. A. Norval for the authors.

structing the mothers to watch for the achievements not so easily elicited in the clinic. The latter method is subject to the inaccuracy of lay observation but does allow the infant to be observed in his natural environment by an interested person.

The more evident steps in neuromuscular growth were chosen. Some of these have been used previously (1) to make parents conscious of the stereotyped progress of growth. The selected steps were:

1. Smile—the baby begins to smile in response to an adult or to his voice.

2. Vocal—the infant utters such sounds as "ah," "eh," and "uh" spontaneously or on stimulation.

3. Head control—when the infant is lifted by his hands from the supine to the sitting position, the head does not lag but is supported by the anterior muscles of the neck.

4. Hand control—when a toy is dangled in the midline above his chest, the infant is able to close in on the toy with one or both hands and to grasp it.

5. Roll—the baby makes a complete roll from back to abdomen.

6. Sit—the baby sits alone for several moments.

7. Crawl—the baby is able to move across the room or pen toward some distant object; this may be accomplished by rolling over and over, pushing himself along on his stomach or back, or by any individual modification of progression.

8. Prehension—this is the bringing together of the thumb and index finger to pick up a small object. This can be tested with a bright-colored button.

9. Pull up—the infant pulls himself to a standing position.

10. Walk with support—the infant walks by holding to his playpen, a piece of furniture, or an adult.

11. Stand alone—without any support, the infant stands for several moments.

12. Walk alone—the infant takes several steps alone.

While our records aimed to record the onset of these achievements in infancy, many of the statements in the literature indicate the age of achievement of the perfected act; hence, they will record a somewhat later age. In previous reports there is a wide variation in the number of infants observed, their selection, the methods of testing them, and the definition of the various levels of development.

It is generally stated that the first voluntary behavior is smiling in response to the mother's voice, which occurred in our series at the average age of 0.9 month. Chaillé (2) stated that after 3 weeks of age many babies begin to smile. Preyer (3) observed a smile on his son's face during the fourth week (0.9 month). Sixty per cent of babies smile socially at one month of age according to Linfert and Hierholzer (4), while others have recorded this as an accomplishment at 1.4 months (5, 6) and at 2 months (7-10).

Morgan and Morgan (9) found that one-half of the babies were cooing at 6 weeks (1.4 months), as was also found by Gesell, Thompson, and Amatruda (6), and Bayley (5). The average infant in our group uttered sounds, such as "uh" and "ah," at 1.7 months. Other authors (3, 7, 8, 11) have reported vocalization at 2 months.

When the infant is raised from the supine to the sitting position, the head will lag slightly at 12 weeks (2.8 months) according to Gesell and associates and at 16 weeks (3.7 months) according to Amatruda (12). We found, on the average, the baby was able to control his head at 2.9 months. Other authors have stated that the head could be held erect and steady at 3 months (2, 11), and at 4 months (4).

Bühler (7) expressed the belief that the ability of the infant to reach for and grasp a toy is the best index of normal activity in a 4-month-old child. This is the age at which our average infant attained this achievement. Gesell (13) and Hetzer and

Wolf (8) have observed reaching movements in infants at this age and stated that the infants may close in on the object and grasp it, while some (10, 14, 15) have seen this achievement first during the fifth month.

In our series the mothers first observed their infants to roll from back to stomach at an average age of 5.1 months, while Shinn (10) saw her niece do this at 24 weeks (5.5 months). Gesell (16) stated that a few infants may roll from back to stomach as early as 4 months but that this is a usual feat at 6 months. Bühler reported this ability at 6 months, Shirley (15) at 29 weeks (6.7 months), and Hetzer and Wolf at 7 months.

The average infant in our grasp was sitting alone for several minutes at 6.2 months. Sitting alone, at least briefly, has been reported at 25 weeks (5.8 months) (10), 6 months (2, 14), and 7 months (13, 15).

By many diverse means our average infant began "going places" on the floor at 7.3 months. Bühler (7) and others (2, 8) reported that infants are able to move toward a desired object at 7 months, while some consider crawling at 8 months (13) and 8.5 months (15) an achievement.

Our infants started to pick up objects with thumb and forefinger at an average age of 8.1 months. Gesell (13) stated that the 9-month-old infant can bring the thumb and forefinger together deftly in a plucking movement and that this movement is highly characteristic of that age. Bayley listed this as an accomplishment at 9.3 months.

Shinn reported that her niece pulled herself to a standing position at 33 weeks (7.6 months) and Bühler observed the first attempts of an infant to raise himself to a standing position at 8 months, while our infants did this at the average age of 8.7 months. Others have reported this at 9 months (2, 13) and 10 months (8, 15).

Infants have been seen to walk with help at 9 months (6, 7), 42 weeks (9.7 months) (15), and 49 weeks (11.3 months) (3), but Gesell (13) listed this as an achievement for those 12 months of age. The average child in our series walked with help at 9.5 months.

Shinn's niece stood alone on the three hundred and sixteenth day (10.4 months). Our average child was observed to stand alone for several moments at 10.7 months, but Gesell and Thompson have this as a momentary achievement in their age group at 56 weeks (12.9 months).

Our average child as well as Shinn's niece and Chaillé's group of children succeeded in walking alone at 12 months of age. Shirley expressed the belief that this may occur between 11.5 and 17.5 months, while 77 per cent of McGraw's (17) series were walking independently by 14 months and the median child of Gesell's (13) group walked at 15 months.

The average ages of these developmental steps are shown in Fig. 1. There was no difference between the rate of the boys and that of the girls. The course of the

FIGURE 1 *A developmental graph for the first year of life shows the average age for the achievements selected and the zone in which 95 per cent of the infants' developmental graphs fell.*

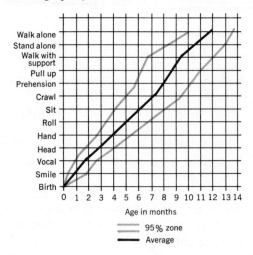

Age in months

95% zone
Average

more rapidly developing infants and of the slower ones followed the average graph but at earlier and later ages, respectively.

Our results in this study show the age of walking alone to be accelerated about two months as compared with the generally accepted standards. Inasmuch as our group forms a fairly representative sampling of an average American city we find it hard to account for this discrepancy. It may be due to the fact that our mothers were instructed to foster rather than to oppose the steps of growth. Possibly the emotional freedom thus produced had an influence on the early postural achievements of the group.

Summary

Twelve developmental steps of neuromuscular growth were chosen for study in an unselected group of 215 infants observed at a well baby clinic. Observations of the age of attainment of these steps were made and a graph depicting the average curve and the variation is presented. In our group walking alone appeared accelerated somewhat as compared with the generally accepted standard time.

References

1. Aldrich, C. A.: *J. Pediat.* **20**: 272, 1942.
2. Chaillé, S. E.: *New Orleans M. & S. J.* **14**: 893, 1886–1887.
3. Preyer, W.: Mental Development in the Child (Translated by H. W. Brown), New York, 1893, D. Appleton and Company.
4. Linfert, H. E., and Hierholzer, H. M.: *Stud. Psychol. & Psychiat.* **1**: 1, 1926–1928.
5. Bayley, N.: Mental Growth During the First Three Years, In Barker, R. G. Kounin, J. S., and Wright, H. F.: Child Behavior and Development; a Course of Representative Studies, ed. 1, New York, 1943, McGraw-Hill Book Company, Inc., chap. 6, pp. 87–105.
6. Gesell, A., Thompson, H., and Amatruda, C. S.: The Psychology of Early Growth; Including Norms of Infant Behavior and a Method of Genetic Analysis, New York, 1938, The Macmillan Company.
7. Bühler, C.: The first year of life (Translated by Pearl Greenberg and Rowena Ripin), New York, 1930, The John Day Company, Inc.
8. Hetzer, H., and Wolf, K.: *Ztschr. f. Psychol. u. Physiol. d. Sinnesorg.* (Abt. 1) **107**: 62, 1928.
9. Morgan, S. S., and Morgan, J. J. B.: *J. Pediat.* **25**: 168, 1944.
10. Shinn, M. W.: Notes on the Development of a Child, vol. 1, Berkeley, 1899, University of California Press, pts. 3–4.
11. Cattell, P.: The Measurement of Intelligence of Infants and Young Children, New York, 1940, The Psychological Corporation.
12. Amatruda, C. S.: *J. Pediat.* **20**: 265, 1942.
13. Gesell, A.: Infancy and Human Growth, New York, 1928, The Macmillan Company.
14. Halverson, H. M.: The Development of Prehension in Infants, In Barker, R. G., Kounin, J. S., and Wright, H. F.: Child Behavior and Development; a Course of Representative Studies, ed. 1, New York, 1943, McGraw-Hill Book Company, Inc., chap. 4, pp. 49–65.
15. Shirley, M. M.: The First Two Years: A Study of Twenty-five Babies, Volume I: Postural and Locomotor Development, Minneapolis, 1931, The University of Minnesota Press.
16. Gesell, A. L.: The Mental Growth of a Pre-school Child; a Psychological Outline of Normal Development from Birth to the Sixth Year, Including a System of Developmental Diagnosis, New York, 1925, The Macmillan Company.
17. McGraw, M. B.: *J. Pediat.* **17**: 747, 1940.

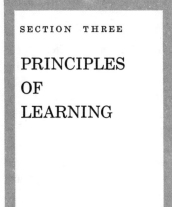

PRINCIPLES OF LEARNING

This classic statement from William James's Principles of Psychology *deals with the importance of habit. The older psychologists, philosophers themselves, or at least being very close to philosophy, were much more concerned with ethical questions than are present-day psychologists. James's interest in the training of character stems from this orientation toward ethics.*

10: "DISCUSSION OF HABIT" FROM THE PRINCIPLES OF PSYCHOLOGY
William James

This brings us by a very natural transition to the *ethical implications of the law of habit.* They are numerous and momentous. Dr. Carpenter, from whose "Mental Physiology" we have quoted, has so prominently enforced the principle that our organs grow to the way in which they have been exercised, and dwelt upon its consequences, that his book almost deserves to be called a work of edification, on this account alone. We need make no apology, then, for tracing a few of these consequences ourselves:

"Habit a second nature! Habit is ten times nature," the Duke of Wellington is said to have exclaimed; and the degree to which this is true no one can probably appreciate as well as one who is a veteran soldier himself. The daily drill and the years of discipline end by fashioning a man completely over again, as to most of the possibilities of his conduct.

There is a story, which is credible enough, though it may not be true, of a practical joker, who, seeing a discharged veteran carrying home his dinner, suddenly called out, "Attention!" whereupon the man instantly brought his hands down, and lost his mutton and potatoes in the gutter. The drill had been thorough, and its effects had become embodied in the man's nervous structure.[1]

Riderless cavalry-horses, at many a battle, have been seen to come together and go through their customary evolutions

William James. *The principles of psychology.* vol. I. New York: Holt, 1890. Copyright © 1890 by Henry Holt and Company. Excerpt reprinted here with permission from Holt, Rinehart and Winston, Inc.

[1] Huxley's "Elementary Lessons in Physiology," lesson XII.

at the sound of the bugle-call. Most trained domestic animals, dogs and oxen, and omnibus- and carhorses, seem to be machines almost pure and simple, undoubtingly, unhesitatingly doing from minute to minute the duties they have been taught, and giving no sign that the possibility of alternative ever suggests itself to their mind. Men grown old in prison have asked to be readmitted after being once set free. In a railroad accident to a travelling menagerie in the United States some time in 1884, a tiger, whose cage had broken open, is said to have emerged, but presently crept back again, as if too much bewildered by his new responsibilities, so that he was without difficulty secured.

Habit is thus the enormous fly-wheel of society, its most precious conservative agent. It alone is what keeps us all within the bounds of ordinance, and saves the children of fortune from the envious uprisings of the poor. It alone prevents the hardest and most repulsive walks of life from being deserted by those brought up to tread therein. It keeps the fisherman and the deck-hand at sea through the winter; it holds the miner in his darkness, and nails the countryman to his log-cabin and his lonely farm through all the months of snow; it protects us from invasion by the natives of the desert and the frozen zone. It dooms us all to fight out the battle of life upon the lines of our nurture or our early choice, and to make the best of a pursuit that disagrees, because there is no other for which we are fitted, and it is too late to begin again. It keeps different social strata from mixing. Already at the age of twenty-five you see the professional mannerism settling down on the young commercial traveler, on the young doctor, on the young minister, on the young counsellor-at-law. You see the little lines of cleavage running through the character, the tricks of thought, the prejudices, the ways of the "shop," in a word, from which the man can by-and-by no more escape than

his coat-sleeve can suddenly fall into a new set of folds. On the whole, it is best he should not escape. It is well for the world that in most of us, by the age of thirty, the character has set like plaster, and will never soften again.

If the period between twenty and thirty is the critical one in the formation of intellectual and professional habits, the period below twenty is more important still for the fixing of *personal* habits, properly so called, such as vocalization and pronunciation, gesture, motion, and address. Hardly ever is a language learned after twenty spoken without a foreign accent; hardly ever can a youth transferred to the society of his betters unlearn the nasality and other vices of speech bred in him by the associations of his growing years. Hardly ever, indeed, no matter how much money there be in his pocket, can he even learn to *dress* like a gentleman-born. The merchants offer their wares as eagerly to him as to the veriest "swell," but he simply *cannot* buy the right things. An invisible law, as strong as gravitation, keeps him within his orbit, arrayed this year as he was the last; and how his better-bred acquaintances contrive to get the things they wear will be for him a mystery till his dying day.

The great thing, then, in all education, is to *make our nervous system our ally instead of our enemy*. It is to fund and capitalize our acquisitions, and live at ease upon the interest of the fund. *For this we must make automatic and habitual, as early as possible, as many useful actions as we can*, and guard against the growing into ways that are likely to be disadvantageous to us, as we should guard against the plague. The more of the details of our daily life we can hand over to the effortless custody of automatism, the more our higher powers of mind will be set free for their own proper work. There is no more miserable human being than one in whom nothing is habitual but indecision, and for whom the lighting of every cigar, the drinking of every cup, the time of rising and going to bed every day, and the beginning of every bit of work, are subjects of express volitional deliberation. Full half the time of such a man goes to the deciding, or regretting, of matters which ought to be so ingrained in him as practically not to exist for his consciousness at all. If there be such daily duties not yet ingrained in any one of my readers, let him begin this very hour to set the matter right.

In Professor Bain's chapter on "The Moral Habits" there are some admirable practical remarks laid down. Two great maxims emerge from his treatment. The first is that in the acquisition of a new habit, or the leaving off of an old one, *we must take care to launch ourselves with as strong and decided an initiative as possible.* Accumulate all the possible circumstances which shall re-enforce the right motives; put yourself assiduously in conditions that encourage the new way; make engagements incompatible with the old; take a public pledge, if the case allows; in short, envelop your resolution with every aid you know. This will give your new beginning such a momentum that the temptation to break down will not occur as soon as it otherwise might; and every day during which a breakdown is postponed adds to the chances of its not occurring at all.

The second maxim is: *Never suffer an exception to occur till the new habit is securely rooted in your life.* Each lapse is like the letting fall of a ball of string which one is carefully winding up; a single slip undoes more than a great many turns will wind again. *Continuity* of training is the great means of making the nervous system act infallibly right. As Professor Bain says:

The peculiarity of the moral habits, contradistinguishing them from the intellectual acquisitions, is the presence of two hostile powers, one to be gradually raised into the ascendant over the other. It is necessary, above all things, in such a situation, never to lose a battle. Every gain on the wrong side undoes the effect of many conquests on the right. The essential precaution, therefore, is so to regulate the two opposing powers that the one may have a series of uninterrupted successes, until repetition has fortified it to such a degree as to enable it to cope with the opposition, under any circumstances. This is the theoretically best career of mental progress.

The need of securing success at the *outset* is imperative. Failure at first is apt to dampen the energy of all future attempts, whereas past experience of success nerves one to future vigor. Goethe says to a man who consulted him about an enterprise but mistrusted his own powers: "Ach! you need only blow on your hands!" And the remark illustrates the effect on Goethe's spirits of his own habitually successful career. Prof. Baumann, from whom I borrow the anecdote,[2] says that the collapse of barbarian nations when Europeans come among them is due to their despair of ever succeeding as the newcomers do in the larger tasks of life. Old ways are broken and new ones not formed.

The question of "tapering-off," in abandoning such habits as drink and opium-indulgence, comes in here, and is a question about which experts differ within certain limits, and in regard to what may be best for an individual case. In the main, however, all expert opinion would agree that abrupt acquisition of the new habit is the best way, *if there be a real possibility of carrying it out.* We must be careful not to give the will so stiff a task as to insure its defeat at the very outset; but, *provided one can stand it,* a sharp period of suffering, and then a free time, is the best thing to aim at, whether in giving up a habit like that of opium, or in simply changing one's hours of rising or of work. It is sur-

[2] See the admirable passage about success at the outset, in his *Handbuch der Moral* (1878), pp. 38–43.

prising how soon a desire will die of inanition if it be never fed.

One must first learn, unmoved, looking neither to the right nor left, to walk firmly on the straight and narrow path, before one can begin "to make one's self over again." He who every day makes a fresh resolve is like one who, arriving at the edge of the ditch he is to leap, forever stops and returns for a fresh run. Without *unbroken* advance there is no such thing as *accumulation* of the ethical forces possible, and to make this possible, and to exercise us and habituate us in it, is the sovereign blessing of regular work.[3]

A third maxim may be added to the preceding pair: *Seize the very first possible opportunity to act on every resolution you make, and on every emotional prompting you may experience in the direction of the habits you aspire to gain.* It is not in the moment of their forming, but in the moment of their producing *motor effects,* that resolves and aspirations communicate the new "set" to the brain. As the author last quoted remarks:

The actual presence of the practical opportunity alone furnishes the fulcrum upon which the lever can rest, by means of which the moral will may multiply its strength, and raise itself aloft. He who has no solid ground to press against will never get beyond the stage of empty gesture-making.

No matter how full a reservoir of *maxims* one may possess, and no matter how good one's *sentiments* may be, if one have not taken advantage of every concrete opportunity to *act,* one's character may remain entirely unaffected for the better. With mere good intentions, hell is proverbially paved. And this is an obvious consequence of the principles we have laid down. A "character," as J. S. Mill says, "is a completely fashioned will"; and a will, in the sense in which he means it, is an aggregate of tendencies to act in a firm and prompt

[3] J. Bahnsen: "Beiträge zu Charakterologie" (1867), vol. I p. 209.

and definite way upon all the principal emergencies of life. A tendency to act only becomes effectively ingrained in us in proportion to the uninterrupted frequency with which the actions actually occur, and the brain "grows" to their use. Every time a resolve or a fine glow of feeling evaporates without bearing practical fruit is worse than a chance lost; it works so as positively to hinder future resolutions and emotions from taking the normal path of discharge. There is no more contemptible type of human character than that of the nerveless sentimentalist and dreamer, who spends his life in a weltering sea of sensibility and emotion, but who never does a manly concrete deed. Rousseau, inflaming all the mothers of France, by his eloquence, to follow Nature and nurse their babies themselves, while he sends his own children to the foundling hospital, is the classical example of what I mean. But every one of us in his measure, whenever, after glowing for an abstractly formulated Good, he practically ignores some actual case, among the squalid "other particulars" of which that same Good lurks disguised, treads straight on Rousseau's path. All Goods are disguised by the vulgarity of their concomitants, in this work-a-day world; but woe to him who can only recognize them when he thinks them in their pure and abstract form! The habit of excessive novel-reading and theatre-going will produce true monsters in this line. The weeping of a Russian lady over the fictitious personages in the play, while her coachman is freezing to death on his seat outside, is the sort of thing that everywhere happens on a less glaring scale. Even the habit of excessive indulgence in music, for those who are neither performers themselves nor musically gifted enough to take it in a purely intellectual way, has probably a relaxing effect upon the character. One becomes filled with emotions which habitually pass without prompting to any deed, and so the inertly sentimental condition is kept up. The remedy would be, never to suffer one's self to have an emotion at a concert, without expressing it afterward in some active way.[4] Let the expression be the least thing in the world— speaking genially to one's aunt, or giving up one's seat in a horsecar, if nothing more heroic offers—but let it not fail to take place.

These latter cases make us aware that it is not simply *particular lines* of discharge, but also *general forms* of discharge, that seem to be grooved out by habit in the brain. Just as, if we let our emotions evaporate, they get into a way of evaporating; so there is reason to suppose that if we often flinch from making an effort, before we know it the effort-making capacity will be gone; and that, if we suffer the wandering of our attention, presently it will wander all the time. Attention and effort are, as we shall see later, but two names for the same psychic fact. To what brain-processes they correspond we do not know. The strongest reason for believing that they do depend on brain-processes at all, and are not pure acts of the spirit, is just this fact, that they seem in some degree subject to the law of habit, which is a material law. As a final practical maxim, relative to these habits of the will, we may, then, offer something like this: *Keep the faculty of effort alive in you by a little gratuitous exercise every day.* That is, be systematically ascetic or heroic in little unnecessary points, do every day or two something for no other reason than that you would rather not do it, so that when the hour of dire need draws nigh, it may find you not unnerved and untrained to stand the test. Asceticism of this sort is like the insurance which a man pays on his house and goods. The tax does him no good at the time, and possibly may never bring him a return. But if the fire *does* come, his having paid

it will be his salvation from ruin. So with the man who has daily inured himself to habits of concentrated attention, energetic volition, and self-denial in unnecessary things. He will stand like a tower when everything rocks around him, and when his softer fellow-mortals are winnowed like chaff in the blast.

The physiological study of mental conditions is thus the most powerful ally of hortatory ethics. The hell to be endured hereafter, of which theology tells, is no worse than the hell we make for ourselves in this world by habitually fashioning our characters in the wrong way. Could the young but realize how soon they will become mere walking bundles of habits, they would give more heed to their conduct while in the plastic state. We are spinning our own fates, good or evil, and never to be undone. Every smallest stroke of virtue or of vice leaves its never so little scar. The drunken Rip Van Winkle, in Jefferson's play, excuses himself for every fresh dereliction by saying, "I won't count this time!" Well! he may not count it, and a kind Heaven may not count it; but it is being counted none the less. Down among his nerve-cells and fibres the molecules are counting it, registering and storing it up to be used against him when the next temptation comes. Nothing we ever do is, in strict scientific literalness, wiped out. Of course, this has its good side as well as its bad one. As we become permanent drunkards by so many separate drinks, so we become saints in the moral, and authorities and experts in the practical and scientific spheres, by so many separate acts and hours of work. Let no youth have anxiety about the upshot of his education, whatever the line of it may be. If he keep faithfully busy each hour of the working day, he may safely leave the final result to itself. He can with perfect certainty count on waking up some fine morning, to find himself one of the competent ones of his generation, in whatever pursuit he may

[4] See for remarks on this subject a readable article by Miss V. Scudder on "Musical Devotees and Morals," in the Andover Review for January 1887.

have singled out. Silently, between all the details of his business, the *power of judging* in all that class of matter will have built itself up within him as a possession that will never pass away. Young people should know this truth in advance. The ignorance of it has probably engendered more discouragement and faint-heartedness in youths embarking on arduous careers than all other causes put together.

This experiment illustrates classical conditioning. The conditioned stimulus—the CS—is an increase in the illumination of a disc; the unconditioned stimulus—the US (or UCS)—is a puff of air delivered to the corner of the eye; the unconditioned response—the UR—is a reflex blink to the puff of air. Conditioned responses—CRs— were established in acquisition by pairing the increase in illumination with the puff of air. Soon, as a result of this pairing, conditioned responses—blinks—to the light alone appeared. These conditioned responses occurred in the ½-second (500 msec) interval between the beginning of the change in illumination and the puff. Thus, conditioned responses were those responses which came after the onset of the light and before the puff; they anticipated the puff.

In addition to illustrating the use of anticipatory responses in classical conditioning, this article shows that older people condition very poorly. Several ideas about the reasons for this fact are presented in the discussion.

POINTS TO GUIDE YOUR STUDY   *(1) Note that Figure 1 shows a learning curve: Performance is plotted on the ordinate (vertical axis of the graph) and number of learning trials are plotted on the abscissa (horizontal axis of the graph). When performance in a learning situation is plotted against trials or time, the resulting curve is called a learning curve. Figure 1 shows performance in conditioning, that is, during acquisition of the conditioned response, when the CS and US (UCS) are paired; it also shows performance in extinction. (2) The results have been evaluated by statistical techniques and tests; the Mann-Whitney U test is one such. The p values and levels of significance, the .002 level, for instance, may be interpreted as follows: These are the odds that a difference as big as that obtained in the experiment might be obtained by chance alone if the groups were not really different. Thus, the .002 level of significance means that there are two chances in 1,000 that the difference between the children and old adults shown in Figure 1 is simply a chance difference which does not represent a real difference in conditioned performance between the two groups.   (3) Many courses in psychology require the writing of experimental reports and your instructor may ask that they be done in "APA (American Psychological Association) journal style"; this article is a good model of such a format. The method of citing references, and the arrangement of topics, are in the approved form for the writing of most psychological reports.*

GLOSSARY   S: *subject of the experiment.* **msec:** *milliseconds, or thousandths of a second.* **Negatively accelerated curve:** *one in which the rate of change constantly decreases.* **Positively accelerated curve:** *one in which the rate of change constantly increases.*

11: AGE DIFFERENCES IN THE ACQUISITION AND EXTINCTION OF THE CONDITIONED EYELID RESPONSE

Harry W. Braun and Richard Geiselhart, Wright-Patterson AFB

This study was stimulated in part by a report of Gakkel and Zinina (1953) that Ss over 60 years of age required a longer period for conditioning of the eyeblink and also for its extinction. It was also performed to provide systematic information on the conditioning and extinction performance of children, young adults, and old adults under the same controlled conditions. Apparently this problem has been hitherto unexplored.

Method

SUBJECTS   These were 15 boys in the age range 8–10 yr., with a mean age of 9.36 yr.; 15 male young adults (college students) aged 18–25 yr. whose mean age was 20.63 yr.; and 13 male adults whose mean age was 70.5 yr., range 62–84 yr. The old adults were noninstitutionalized and were either employed full time or part time, or retired. All Ss were volunteers and some of the elderly group were compensated for their services.

APPARATUS AND METHOD OF RECORDING The equipment for recording the eyelid closure and for presenting the CS and UCS was similar to that used by Spence (1953), and will not be described here.

This investigation was supported in part by a research grant, M-1365, from the National Institute of Mental Health, U.S. Public Health Service.

H. W. Braun and R. Geiselhart. Age differences in the acquisition and extinction of the conditioned eyelid response. *J. exp. Psychol.,* 1959, **57,** 386–388. Copyright © 1959 by the American Psychological Association. Reprinted here with permission of the junior author and the American Psychological Association.

The S sat in a dental chair in a darkened room adjoining that in which the stimulus controls and recording apparatus were located. He was instructed to blink on receiving a ready signal, and then to fixate on a 6-cm. circular milk glass disc placed at a distance at 125 cm.

The CS was an increase in the brightness of this disc from 0.05 to 1.5 apparent ft.-candles. The duration of the CS on each trial was 1 sec. The UCS was a puff of air with an intensity of 2.0 lb./sq. in. delivered to the right eye, with a duration of 500 msec. The CS-UCS interval was 500 msec. All Ss were given 80 conditioning trials, on each of which the light and air puff were paired. Intertrial intervals of 10, 15, and 20 sec. were used according to a prearranged schedule. Following the last conditioning trial, 20 extinction trials were given, in which both light and air puff were paired, but in which the CS-UCS interval was lengthened to 1500 msec. Only those CR's whose latency was 300 msec. or more were included in the data. No Ss were excluded as voluntary responders, i.e., Ss who gave at least half of their CR's with a latency of less than 300 msec.

Results

Curves of acquisition of the CR for the three age groups are shown in Fig. 1 in terms of the percentage of CR's in each block of 10 trials. Through the 60th conditioning trial, the curve for the children is consistently above that of the young adults, and it is above that of the elderly

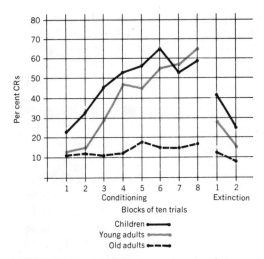

FIGURE 1 *Conditioning and extinction as a function of age.*

group throughout the entire 80 trials. The conditioning performance of the young and old adults is similar through the first 20 trials after which the young group improves markedly and the elderly group only slightly. The conditioning curve of the children is negatively accelerated, that of the young adult group is positively accelerated, while the curve of the old adults is flat. At the start of conditioning, the performance level of the children is relatively high and/or the rate of conditioning is high. On the other hand, the performance level of the other two age groups at the beginning of conditioning is relatively low and/or the rate of conditioning is slow.

Statistical evaluation of these results was made by the Mann-Whitney test. The difference between the number of CR's made by the children and the old adults was significant beyond the .002 level for a two-tailed test ($U = 23$) and the difference between the number of CR's made by the young adults and the old adults was also significant beyond the same level of confidence ($U = 25$). The children and young adults did not differ significantly in the number of CR's ($U = 89$).

Curves of latency of the CR's in blocks of 20 trials for the three age groups appear

in Fig. 2. These data, which are measures of latency of CR to the onset of the CS on the 80 acquisition trials, show that during the first 60 trials, the CR's of the children are slower than those of the other two groups. During the last 20 conditioning trials, however, the three age groups do not appreciably differ on this measure. The sharp decrease in latency shown by the elderly group in the third block of twenty trials was caused by two new responders.

The use of the Mann-Whitney test showed that the children made significantly more CR's during extinction than the elderly adults ($U = 27$; $P < .002$) as did the young adults ($U = 49$, $P = .05$). The two younger groups did not differ significantly in this respect. However, after analysis of covariance, age differences in extinction were not significant.

Discussion

The main and striking finding of this study is the relative inability of the elderly Ss to acquire the conditioned eyeblink response. Of the 13 Ss in this group, four Ss gave no CR's during the 80 conditioning trials, seven gave from one to eight CR's,

FIGURE 2 *Latency of CR as a function of age.*

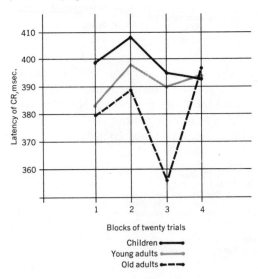

while 37 and 75 CR's were given by the other two Ss. There were no instances of failure to condition in the two younger groups. This result confirms the report of Gakkel and Zinina (1953) although in their study data on the conditioning performance of younger Ss were not included. To account for the failure of older Ss to acquire CR's, Gakkel and Zinina quote Pavlov as coming to the conclusion that "liveliness of the nerve processes suffer(s) from the development of senile changes." They also invoke the construct of "inertia" of the stimulating process at senile age.

However, several considerations indicate that this hypothesis may not be entirely satisfactory. The latency of the CR's of the elderly group are not longer than those of the other groups. It is admitted that these are tenuous data since they involve only a very small number of responses. However, Weiss (1956) has shown that the latency of the retina as reflected in the retinogram does not change with age. His Ss were 15 males aged 66 to 76 yr. and 10 between the ages of 18 to 37 yr. Similarly, Kumnick has reported that "the efficiency of the pupillary mechanism in relation to similar original diameter in the response to light stimuli did not decrease with increasing age" (Kumnick, 1956, p. 160). Thus, activation time of at least these aspects of the visual organ seems to be unchanged with age. It would be premature to conclude that the latencies of all simple involuntary responses or reflexes do not change with age. Magladery, Teasdall, and Norris (1958) have shown that the latencies of plantar flexor responses and superficial abdominal reflexes are markedly slower in elderly Ss and children than in young adults.

The authors suggest the consideration of an adaptation hypothesis to account for the relative unconditionability of elderly Ss. Both MacDonald (1946) and Taylor (1956) have reported that Ss who were adapted to the UCS (air puff) show a significantly lower level of conditioned eye-lid responses than Ss who were not given preadaptation trials. It is proposed that in the course of many years of living, the eyelid response as well as probably other responses have been "adapted out" and thus less susceptible to subsequent conditioning. Research is under way to study several consequences of this hypothesis: that both frequency and amplitude of blink are reduced as a function of age. The procedures employed in the present study did not provide data on these variables.

Summary

This study investigated eyelid conditioning and extinction of children, young adults, and old adults under the same controlled conditions. All Ss were given 80 conditioning trials and 20 extinction trials. The children and young adults gave significantly more conditioned responses than the old adults. Elderly Ss were relatively unable to acquire the conditioned eyeblink response. Latency of response and extinction were not related to age.

References

Gakkel, L. B., & Zinina, N. V. Changes of higher nerve function in people over 60 years of age. *Fiziolog. Zhurnal.,* 1953, **39,** 533–539.

Kumnick, L. S. Aging and the efficiency of the pupillary mechanism. *J. Geront.,* 1956, **11,** 160–164.

MacDonald, A. The effect of adaptation to the unconditioned stimulus upon the formation of conditioned avoidance responses. *J. exp. Psychol.,* 1946, **36,** 1–12.

Magladery, J. W., Teasdall, R. D., & Norris, A. N. Effect of aging on plantar flexor and superficial abdominal reflexes in man—a clinical and electromyographic study. *J. Geront.,* 1958, **13,** 282–288.

Spence, K. W. Learning and performance in eyelid conditioning as a function of the intensity of the UCS. *J. exp. Psychol.,* 1953, **45,** 57–63.

Taylor, J. A. Level of conditioning and intensity of the adaptation stimulus. *J. exp. Psychol.,* 1956, **51,** 127–130.

Weiss, A. D. The relation of A-wave latency of the electroretinogram to human aging. *J. Geront.,* 1956, **11,** 448. (Abstract).

Instrumental, or operant, conditioning is the focus of this article which gives a rather practical demonstration of the way in which children's responses may be modified by the appropriate use of reinforcers—attention from a teacher in this case.

In instrumental (operant) conditioning, the attainment of a reinforcing situation is made to depend upon the performance of a particular response. If the response no longer produces reinforcement, the response gradually becomes less likely—that is to say, it extinguishes. In this experiment, the extinction of operant crying was studied; operant crying responses were extinguished by the withholding of social reinforcement for such responses.

The experiment proceded as follows: First, a baseline was established—the frequency of operant crying was observed before any intentional manipulation of reinforcement was done. Next, extinction began and social reinforcement was withheld for operant crying responses; then, the operant crying response was reestablished by introducing reinforcement for it once more. Finally, the response was extinguished again.

The results indicate that behavior was quite sensitive to the reinforcement conditions. Thus, by the appropriate use of reinforcers, the behavior of the boys was controlled and crying could be made a weak or strong response in terms of its likelihood of occurrence. The implications of such studies for the practical control of behavior are, perhaps, obvious.

A POINT TO GUIDE YOUR STUDY   *The curves presented in Figures 1 and 2 are cumulative curves. Time is represented along the horizontal axis, while responses are represented in the vertical direction. Each time a response is made, the curve moves up a little; thus, the rate of response, as time runs on, is indicated by the slope of the curve. High response rates result in curves with steep slopes; low response rates result in curves with shallow slopes. When no responses are made, as is the case after complete extinction, the curve does not rise at all—no more responses are being made to be added to it—and the curve is a horizontal line. On such a cumulative record, we might say that the rate of response over time is being plotted.*

12:   EFFECTS OF SOCIAL REINFORCEMENT ON OPERANT CRYING

Betty M. Hart, K. Eileen Allen, Joan S. Buell, Florence R. Harris, and Montrose M. Wolf, University of Washington and University of Kansas

Two preschool boys who showed a high frequency of operant crying were helped to develop more effective responses to mild frustrations. Teachers systematically applied reinforcement procedures: gave no attention to outcries, unless the child was actually hurt, and gave immediate approving attention to

The authors acknowledge their indebtedness to Sidney W. Bijou, Donald M. Baer, and Jay S. Birnbrauer for frequent consultation and ready assistance with technical and procedural problems.

This investigation was supported in part by Public Health Service Research Grant MH-02232, from the National Institute of Mental Health.

Betty M. Hart, K. Eileen Allen, Joan S. Buell, Flor-

every more appropriate response to mildly distressful situations. Within a week, operant crying had practically disappeared in each case.

Reversal of procedures reinstated operant crying responses in Subject 1. Return to original procedures quickly reduced operant crying to a very low level, which was maintained during the rest of the year. With Subject 2, reversal of procedures raised the operant crying level for a few days. Then suddenly the crying dropped out. When the crying rate remained at practically zero for several more days, all procedures were dropped. Shortly, operant crying again rose. The original procedures were again applied. Operant crying quickly dropped and remained negligible during the rest of the school year.

The studies indicated that frequent crying may be largely a function of adult attention.

The application of reinforcement principles as a preschool guidance technique under field conditions has recently come under study (Allen *et al.*, 1964; Harris *et al.*, 1964, Johnston *et al.*, 1963). Other applications made under field conditions in hospital situations include Wolf's treatment of autism in a child (Wolf *et al.*, 1964) and Ayllon's work with psychotic patients (Ayllon and Haughton, 1962). The present paper deals with the application of reinforcement principles to two cases of "operant crying."

Two classes of crying behavior seem readily discriminable on an "intuitive" basis by almost every teacher and parent: respondent crying and operant crying. Criteria for each class can be defined in terms of its dependent variables. Respondent crying occurs in response to a sudden unexpected and/or painful stimulus event. In general, preschool teachers assume crying to be respondent if the child has a hard or sudden fall; if he falls in an awkward position or is caught in equipment; if he is forced down and pummeled by a larger child; or if he has just faced a dire, unexpected event, such as a near accident.

Teachers attend at once to respondent crying. Operant crying, on the other hand, is emitted and/or maintained depending upon its effects on the social environment. In general, the most clear-cut indication that a crying episode is operant rather than respondent is that the child looks around momentarily and makes eye-contact with an adult before he begins to cry. An increase in the volume and intensity of the child's cry when an adult fails to attend immediately, together with the child's neither calling nor coming for help, provide other criteria for operant crying. Crying that is initially respondent may readily become operant.

Since by 3 years of age children vary widely in their patterns of response to pain-fear situations, any reasonably exact discrimination between respondent and operant crying of an individual child can be made only on the basis of close daily observation of his crying behavior.

This paper presents two studies of the systematic use of positive social reinforcement to help children showing a high rate of operant crying to acquire more effective behavior in mildly distressful situations. Although the studies were conducted at different times, procedures and recording methods were the same in each.

Method

SUBJECTS Both subjects were enrolled in the Laboratory Preschool at the University of Washington. Both were in the same group, which included eight boys and eight girls of similar age (4–4½), socio-economic level (upper middle class), and intelligence (above average). All children attended school five mornings a week for approximately 2½ hours.

Subject 1. The first subject, Bill, was 4 years and 1 month old when he entered school. He was a tall, healthy, handsome child with well-developed verbal, social, and motor skills. Outdoors he ran, climbed, and rode a tricycle with energy and agility; indoors, he made use of all the available materials, though he appeared to prefer construction materials such as blocks, or imaginative play in the housekeeping corner, to activities such as painting or working with clay. His verbalizations to both teachers and children were characterized by persuasive and accurate use of vocabulary, and frequently demonstrated unusually sophisticated conceptualizations. He and many of the other children who entered nursery school at the same time had been together in a group situation the previous year and were thus fairly well acquainted. His former teachers had described Bill as a child eagerly sought by other children as a playmate. His capability and desirability as a playmate were immediately evident at the beginning of the second year. He moved almost directly into play with two other boys, and with his many good ideas structured one play situation after another with them, situations which often lasted an entire morning. Bill was frequently observed arbitrating differences of opinion between his playmates, insisting on his own way of doing things, or defending his own rights and ideas; nearly always, he did so verbally rather than physically.

In the first few days of school, teachers noted that in spite of Bill's sophisticated techniques for dealing with children, he cried more often during the morning than any other child in school. If he stubbed his toe while running or bumped his elbow on a piece of furniture, he cried until a teacher went to him. If he fell down, or if he was frustrated or threatened with any kind of physical attack by another child, he screamed and cried; all play, his and his companions', stopped until Bill had had several minutes of comfort from a teacher. In view of his advanced verbal and social skills, teachers questioned whether his crying was due to actual injury or maintained by adult attention.

Subject 2. The second subject, Alan, lacked 2 weeks of being 4 years old when he entered the Preschool. He was enrolled in the same 4-year-old group as Bill. Unlike Bill, however, Alan was new to the group and therefore had had no previous acquaintance with any of the children. He spent most of the first month of school exploring with vigor all the equipment, materials, and social situations the school had to offer. He climbed, rode trikes, swung and dug, with skill and application. His use of creative materials was free and imaginative; his block-buildings were complex, intricately balanced structures. With children and adults he spoke confidently and assertively, often demanding that they listen to a lengthy story or fulfill his requests immediately. He defended himself both verbally and physically, holding on tenaciously to a possession, or saying "Don't!" over and over. Sometimes he forcibly appropriated an object from another child, calling names when the child resisted; but though he was the physical equal or superior of most of the others, he rarely attacked another child. He was attractive and vicacious as well as skillful. By the end of the first 6 weeks of school he was playing as an integral member of one or more groups of children every morning.

Though he did not cry quite as often as Bill, Alan cried equally as hard over much the same kinds of bumps and falls. Like Bill, he screamed and cried whenever another child succeeded in appropriating an object in his possession. He was observed to endure shoving and even hitting by a child smaller than he but to cry vociferously at a push by a child equal to him in size and strength. Though Alan's crying was noted from the beginning of school, the staff thought that Alan should fully adapt to the school situation and develop in play skills before any procedures were undertaken to deal directly with his crying behavior.

In dealing with both Alan and Bill, a distinction was made between respondent and operant crying. Teachers had observed that neither was unjustifiably aggressive; both could defend themselves, were physically strong and large relative to the group, and had better than average physical, verbal, and social skills. Neither had injured himself or been injured by another child in the group. Both were often observed to make momentary eye-contact with a teacher before beginning to cry, and the cries of both rapidly increased in volume until a teacher attended to them. Teachers agreed that both children would benefit if the frequency of crying episodes could be decreased and if more appropriate responses to mild pain and frustration could be developed.

RECORDING OF CRYING EPISODES In both cases the operant crying behavior was recorded by a teacher using a pocket counter. She depressed the lever on the counter once for each crying episode. A crying episode was defined as a cry (a) loud enough to be heard at least 50 feet away and (b) of 5 seconds or more duration. At the end of the day the total number of crying episodes was recorded and plotted on a cumulative graph.

PROCEDURES FOR PRESENTING AND WITHDRAWING REINFORCERS For 10 days before initiating reinforcement-extinction procedures, the number of Bill's operant crying episodes per morning was to be recorded in order to obtain a baseline record of the operant level of the behavior. This was done at the end of his first month of school. A baseline record of Alan's daily crying episodes was similarly planned several months later, after Alan had attended school for 3 months.

For each child, extinction of operant crying was to be instituted immediately after these data had been secured. Teachers were to ignore each child's operant cries, neither going to him, speaking to him, nor looking at him while he was crying, except for an initial glance in order

to assess the situation. If he was in close proximity to a teacher when he began to cry, she was to turn her back or walk away to be busy with another child. However, every time that either child responded in a more appropriate manner after a fall, scrape, push, or dispossession, however minor, he was immediately to be given much teacher attention and approval.

In order to substantiate the hypothesis that the operant crying of these children was truly a function of adult reinforcement, it was judged necessary, if the extinction process was successful, to reinstate the behavior. At first teachers were to give attention to every approximation to a cry, such as whimpering and sulking; then, if and when the behavior was re-established in strength, they were to go to the child immediately every time he began to cry and give him solicitous attention for several minutes.

If and when operant crying had again reached a level similar to that of the baseline period, it was again to be extinguished. The procedures of the first extinction period were to be re-instituted, teachers ignoring all operant cries by turning away or focusing their attention elsewhere. At the same time, they were to reinforce the boys for all verbal responses emitted during mild pain or frustration. As the second extinction progressed, teachers were gradually to refine the criteria for reinforcement to "appropriate" verbal responses, and differentially reinforce more socially acceptable verbal behavior evoked by minor injuries and frustrations. Threats and name-calling were to be ignored, and attention given only for such verbalizations as "Stop that," "That hurts," "Ouch!" or explanation of prior possession.

Results

Subject 1. As can be seen in the baseline period for Bill (see Fig. 1), at the beginning of the study he was crying 5–10 times every morning at school. Within 5

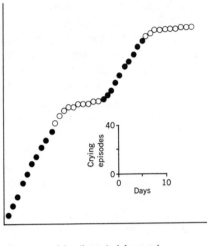
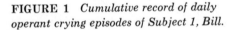

● Baseline and reinforcement
○ Extinction

FIGURE 1 *Cumulative record of daily operant crying episodes of Subject 1, Bill.*

days after introduction of extinction procedures his operant crying decreased to between 0 and 2 episodes per day. When continuous adult attention was again given to all operant cries and approximations to cries, the baseline rate of crying episodes was soon re-established. Then, 4 days after re-introduction of extinction for operant crying, the behavior was practically eliminated.

Subject 2. Alan's rate of operant crying during the baseline period (see Fig. 2) averaged about 5 episodes per morning. As with Bill, Alan's crying episodes decreased to 2 or fewer per day within 5 days after the introduction of extinction procedures. The behavior again reached a level nearly as high as baseline 4 days after reinforcement of operant crying was re-instituted, and maintained approximately this level for 6 days. On the eleventh day of reinstatement of operant crying, the behavior suddenly decreased to one or fewer episodes per day (day 28, Fig. 2). After continuing reinforcement procedures for 7 more days, teachers decided that, though their attention may have initially reinstated the behavior, other uncontrolled factors in the environment had apparently

led to its cessation. Therefore, systematic reinforcement techniques were discontinued (after day 35 on Fig. 2). However, very soon the behavior reappeared and gradually increased in frequency until on the 50th day it had reached a frequency almost double that of the baseline period. Extinction procedures were again introduced (on day 51, Fig. 2). The rate of operant crying dropped much more gradually this time than had Bill's: there was a burst on the 56th day, and it was not until 10 days later that operant crying episodes stabilized at one or fewer per day.

Discussion

During the extinction periods for both Bill and Alan, teachers noticed no unexpected side-effects. They had anticipated that play would become more rewarding to both children once the frequent interruptions for crying episodes were eliminated. Each of the children, during the extinction periods, sustained a cooperative, sometimes directing, role in play. Each appeared to become more constructively absorbed in such play, often to the point of appearing oblivious to persons outside the realm of the imaginative play situation.

Subject 1. After Bill's operant crying was reinstated and his play was again being interrupted six or seven times a morning for operant crying episodes, teachers began to notice occasional signs of impatience on his part. Even as teachers comforted him and he continued to shriek, he sometimes turned away from their comfort, though he did not leave. Also, the extent of the interruption of his play seemed more noticeable than it had during the baseline period. At that time his companions had often ignored, or retreated from, his crying episodes. During the reinstatement period they usually remained near Bill, watching him throughout the episode. Teachers thought that the powerful reinforcement that Bill obtained from play with his companions greatly contrib-

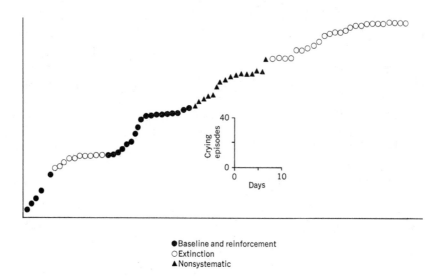

Baseline and reinforcement
Extinction
Nonsystematic

FIGURE 2   *Cumulative record of daily operant crying episodes of Subject 2, Alan.*

uted to the rapidity of the second extinction process.

Subject 2. After Alan's operant crying had risen during the reinstatement period to a rate equal to that of the baseline period, the sudden disappearance of the behavior was completely unexpected. Teachers continued to reinforce all cries and approximations to cries for 7 more days before deciding that some other factor in the environment had apparently decreased Alan's operant crying. Only after reinforcement procedures had been discontinued and the behavior had begun to reappear did teachers reflect on the possible significance of particular behaviors they had observed during the reinstatement period. At that time they had noticed that Alan often screwed up his face as though about to emit a loud cry when he was in close proximity to them. In accordance with the reinforcement procedures in effect, they immediately offered him comfort, and frequently he did not actually cry (only audible cries were counted in the data). One day, for example, Alan was climbing on an iron frame, a teacher watching him. As he climbed down from the frame he screwed up his face and

clutched his ankle. The teacher approached at once, asked what had happened and comforted him. Alan explained that he had bumped his ankle, and then said, "I'm going to do that [climb the frame] again." As he descended the frame a second time, Alan bumped his leg and, looking at the teacher, emitted a low whimper. The teacher immediately comforted him, whereupon he again climbed the frame, and again bumped himself descending. On none of these occasions did Alan actually cry. It appeared, upon subsequent reflection, that Alan did not need to cry: he had apparently effectively "shaped up" a teacher to give him comfort and attention whenever he merely looked as if he were about to cry.

When systematic reinforcement procedures were discontinued and Alan's "looking as if he were about to cry" was no longer given immediate adult attention and comfort, full-scale operant crying reappeared and was apparently reinforced in the period that followed, on some sort of unsystematic intermittent schedule. The rate of operant crying increased irregularly; the decline in rate after several days of a rise in rate might possibly be correlated with (a) teachers' having inadvertently put the behavior on extinction for a time after it became aversive to them, and (b) such frequent interruptions in Alan's play that his playmates moved away from him and into other activities. These intervals of extinction, if such they were, were not, however, planned procedures.

After systematic extinction procedures were reinstated, Alan's operant crying behavior extinguished much more gradually than had Bill's. A possible cause was the preceding unsystematic intermittent schedule of reinforcement in Alan's case. In the literature (e.g., Ferster and Skinner, 1957) it has been well demonstrated that extinction after a continuous schedule of reinforcement is more rapid than after an intermittent schedule.

Though many of the findings concerning Alan's operant crying are still conjectural, the data from the studies seem to demonstrate that frequent crying may be largely a function of social reinforcement. The implications for parents and teachers in helping children to behave more appropriately appear evident.

References

Allen, K. Eileen, Hart, Betty, Buell, Joan S., Harris, Florence R., and Wolf, M. M. Effects of social reinforcement on isolate behavior of a nursery school child. *Child Develpm.*, 1964, 35, 511–518.

Ayllon, T., and Haughton, E. Control of the behavior of schizophrenic patients by food. *J. exp. anal. Behav.*, 1962, 5, 343–352.

Ferster, C. B., and Skinner, B. F. *Schedules of reinforcement.* New York: Appleton-Century-Crofts, 1957.

Harris, Florence R., Johnston, Margaret S., Kelley, C. Susan, and Wolf, M. M. Effects of positive social reinforcement on regressed crawling in a preschool child. *J. ed. Psychol.*, 1964, 55, 35–41.

Johnston, Margaret S., Kelley, C. Susan, Buell, Joan S., Harris, Florence R., and Wolf, M. M. Effects of positive social reinforcement on isolate behavior of a nursery child. Unpublished manuscript, 1963.

Wolf, M., Mees, H., and Risley, T. Application of operant conditioning procedures to the behavior problems of an autistic child. *Behav. Res. Ther.*, 1964, 2, 305–312.

The pigeons in this study were trained by instrumental, or operant, techniques, and this report shows that behavior can be controlled rather precisely. Such control is sometimes spoken of as the stimulus control of behavior. After control has been achieved by operant training, the organism will respond under one set of stimulus conditions and not under another set, or the organism will respond in one way under one set of stimulus conditions and in another way under another set. Many of the same processes are probably at work in the natural socialization and "shaping" of children's behavior.

A POINT TO GUIDE YOUR STUDY   *How were the pigeons trained to peck some stimuli and not others?*

13: PIGEONS IN A PELICAN

B. F. Skinner, Harvard University

This is the history of a crackpot idea, born on the wrong side of the tracks intellectu-

B. F. Skinner. Pigeons in a pelican. *Amer. Psychologist*, 1960, 15, 28–37. Copyright © 1960 by the American Psychological Association. Reprinted here with permission from the author and the American Psychological Association.

ally speaking, but eventually vindicated in a sort of middle class respectability. It is the story of a proposal to use living organisms to guide missiles—of a research program during World War II called "Project Pigeon" and a peacetime continuation at the Naval Research Laboratory called "ORCON," from the words "organic control." Both of these programs have now been declassified.

Man has always made use of the sensory capacities of animals, either because they are more acute than his own or more convenient. The watchdog probably hears better than his master and in any case listens while his master sleeps. As a detecting system the dog's ear comes supplied with an alarm (the dog need not be taught to announce the presence of an intruder), but special forms of reporting are sometimes set up. The tracking behavior of the bloodhound and the pointing of the hunting dog are usually modified to make them more useful. Training is sometimes quite explicit. It is said that sea gulls were used to detect submarines in the English Channel during World War I. The British sent their own submarines through the Channel releasing food to the surface. Gulls could see the submarines from the air and learned to follow them, whether they were British or German. A flock of gulls, spotted from the shore, took on special significance. In the seeing-eye dog the repertoire of artificial signaling responses is so elaborate that it has the conventional character of the verbal interchange between man and man.

The detecting and signaling systems of lower organisms have a special advantage when used with explosive devices which can be guided toward the objects they are to destroy, whether by land, sea, or air. Homing systems for guided missiles have now been developed which sense and signal the position of a target by responding to visible or invisible radiation, noise, radar reflections, and so on. These have not always been available, and in any case a living organism has certain advantages. It is almost certainly cheaper and more compact and, in particular, is especially good at responding to patterns and those classes of patterns called "concepts." The lower organism is used not because it is more sensitive than man—after all, the kamikaze did very well—but because it is readily expendable.

Project Pelican

The ethical question of our right to convert a lower creature into an unwitting hero is a peacetime luxury. There were bigger questions to be answered in the late thirties. A group of men had come into power who promised, and eventually accomplished, the greatest mass murder in history. In 1939 the city of Warsaw was laid waste in an unprovoked bombing, and the airplane emerged as a new and horrible instrument of war against which only the feeblest defenses were available. Project Pigeon was conceived against that background. It began as a search for a homing device to be used in a surface-to-air guided missile as a defense against aircraft. As the balance between offensive and defensive weapons shifted, the direction was reversed, and the system was to be tested first in an air-to-ground missile called the "Pelican." Its name is a useful reminder of the state of the missile art in America at that time. Its detecting and servomechanisms took up so much space that there was no room for explosives: hence the resemblance to the pelican "whose beak can hold more than its belly can." My title is perhaps now clear. Figure 1

FIGURE 1 *Thirty-two pigeons, jacketed for testing.*

FIGURE 2 *Nose of the pelican, showing lenses.*

shows the pigeons, jacketed for duty. Figure 2 shows the beak of the Pelican.

At the University of Minnesota in the spring of 1940 the capacity of the pigeon to steer toward a target was tested with a moving hoist. The pigeon, held in a jacket and harnessed to a block, was immobilized except for its neck and head. It could eat grain from a dish and operate a control system by moving its head in appropriate directions. Movement of the head operated the motors of the hoist. The bird could ascend by lifting its head, descend by lowering it, and travel from side to side by moving appropriately. The whole system, mounted on wheels, was pushed across a room toward a bull's-eye on the far wall. During the approach the pigeon raised or lowered itself and moved from side to side in such a way as to reach the wall in position to eat grain from the center of the bull's-eye. The pigeon learned to reach any target within reach of the hoist, no matter what the starting position and during fairly rapid approaches.

The experiment was shown to John T. Tate, a physicist, then Dean of the Graduate School at the University of Minnesota, who brought it to the attention of R. C. Tolman, one of a group of scientists engaged in early defense activities. The result was the first of a long series of rejections. The proposal "did not warrant further development at the time." The project was accordingly allowed to lapse.

On December 7, 1941 the situation was suddenly restructured; and, on the following day, with the help of Keller Breland, then a graduate student at Minnesota, further work was planned. A simpler harnessing system could be used if the bomb were to rotate slowly during its descent, when the pigeon would need to steer in only one dimension: from side to side. We built an apparatus in which a harnessed pigeon was lowered toward a large revolving turntable across which a target was driven according to contacts made by the bird during its descent. It was not difficult to train a pigeon to "hit" small ship models during fairly rapid descents. We made a demonstration film showing hits on various kinds of targets, and two psychologists then engaged in the war effort in Washington, Charles Bray and Leonard Carmichael, undertook to look for government support. Tolman, then at the Office of Scientific Research and Development, again felt that the project did not warrant support, in part because the United States had at that time no missile capable of being guided toward a target. Commander (now Admiral) Luis de Florez, then in the Special Devices Section of the Navy, took a sympathetic view. He dismissed the objection that there was no available vehicle by suggesting that the pigeon be connected with an automatic pilot mounted in a small plane loaded with explosives. But he was unable to take on the project because of other commitments and because, as he explained, he had recently bet on one or two other equally long shots which had not come in.

The project lapsed again and would probably have been abandoned if it had not been for a young man whose last name I have ungratefully forgotten, but whose first name—Victor—we hailed as a propitious sign. His subsequent history led us to refer to him as Vanquished; and this, as it turned out, was a more reliable omen. Victor walked into the Department of Psychology at Minnesota one day in the summer of 1942 looking for an animal psychologist. He had a scheme for installing dogs in antisubmarine torpedoes. The dogs were to respond to faint acoustic signals from the submarine and to steer the torpedo toward its goal. He wanted a statement from an animal psychologist as to its feasibility. He was understandably surprised to learn of our work with pigeons but seized upon it eagerly, and citing it in support of his contention that dogs could be trained to steer torpedoes he went to a number of companies in Minneapolis. His project was rejected by everyone he approached; but one company, General Mills, Inc., asked for more information about our work with pigeons. We described the project and presented the available data to Arthur D. Hyde, Vice-President in Charge of Research. The company was not looking for new products, but Hyde thought that it might, as a public service, develop the pigeon system to the point at which a governmental agency could be persuaded to take over.

Breland and I moved into the top floor of a flour mill in Minneapolis and with the help of Norman Guttman, who had joined the project, set to work on further improvements. It had been difficult to induce the pigeon to respond to the small angular displacement of a distant target. It would start working dangerously late in the descent. Its natural pursuit behavior was not appropriate to the characteristics of a likely missile. A new system was therefore designed. An image of the target was projected on a translucent screen as in a camera obscura. The pigeon, held near the screen, was reinforced for pecking at the image on the screen. The guiding signal was to be picked up from the point of contact of screen and beak.

In an early arrangement the screen was a translucent plastic plate forming the larger end of a truncated cone bearing a lens at the smaller end. The cone was mounted, lens down, in a gimbal bearing. An object within range threw its image on the translucent screen; and the pigeon, held vertically just above the plate, pecked the image. When a target was moved about within range of the lens, the cone continued to point to it. In another apparatus a translucent disk, free to tilt slightly on gimbal bearings, closed contacts operating motors which altered the position of a large field beneath the apparatus. Small cutouts of ships and other objects were placed on the field. The field was constantly in motion, and a target would go out of range unless the pigeon continued to control it. With this apparatus we began to study the pigeon's reactions to various patterns and to develop sustained steady rates of responding through the use of appropriate schedules of reinforcement, the reinforcement being a few grains occasionally released onto the plate. By building up large extinction curves a target could be tracked continuously for a matter of minutes without reinforcement. We trained pigeons to follow a variety of land and sea targets, to neglect large patches intended to represent clouds or flak, to concentrate on one target while another was in view, and so on. We found that a pigeon could hold the missile on a particular street intersection in an aerial map of a city. The map which came most easily to hand was of a city which, in the interests of international relations, need not be identified. Through appropriate schedules of reinforcement it was possible to maintain longer uninterrupted runs than could conceivably be required by a missile.

We also undertook a more serious study of the pigeon's behavior, with the help of W. K. Estes and Marion Breland who joined the project at this time. We ascertained optimal conditions of deprivation, investigated other kinds of deprivations, studied the effect of special reinforcements (for example, pigeons were said to find hemp seed particularly delectable), tested the effects of energizing drugs and increased oxygen pressures, and so on. We differentially reinforced the force of the pecking response and found that pigeons could be induced to peck so energetically that the base of the beak became inflamed. We investigated the effects of extremes of temperature, of changes in atmospheric pressure, of accelerations produced by an improvised centrifuge, of increased carbon dioxide pressure, of increased and prolonged vibration, and of noises such as pistol shots. (The birds could, of course, have been deafened to eliminate auditory distractions, but we found it easy to maintain steady behavior in spite of intense noises and many other distracting conditions using the simple process of adaptation.) We investigated optimal conditions for the quick development of discriminations and began to study the pigeon's reactions to patterns, testing for induction from a test figure to the same figure inverted, to figures of different sizes and colors, and to figures against different grounds. A simple device using carbon paper to record the points at which a pigeon pecks a figure showed a promise which has never been properly exploited.

We made another demonstration film and renewed our contact with the Office of Scientific Research and Development. An observer was sent to Minneapolis, and on the strength of his report we were given an opportunity to present our case in Washington in February 1943. At that time we were offering a homing device capable of reporting with an on-off signal the orientation of a missile toward various visual patterns. The capacity to respond to pattern was, we felt, our strongest argument, but the fact that the device used only visible radiation (the same form of information available to the human bombardier) made it superior to the radio-controlled missiles then under development because it was resistant to jamming. Our film had some effect. Other observers were sent to Minneapolis to see the demonstration itself. The pigeons, as usual, behaved beautifully. One

of them held the supposed missile on a particular intersection of streets in the aerial map for five minutes although the target would have been lost if the pigeon had paused for a second or two. The observers returned to Washington, and two weeks later we were asked to supply data on (a) the population of pigeons in the United States (fortunately, the census bureau had some figures) and (b) the accuracy with which pigeons struck a point on a plate. There were many arbitrary conditions to be taken into account in measuring the latter, but we supplied possibly relevant data. At long last, in June 1943, the Office of Scientific Research and Development awarded a modest contract to General Mills, Inc. to "develop a homing device."

At that time we were given some information about the missile the pigeons were to steer. The Pelican was a wing-steered glider, still under development and not yet successfully steered by any homing device. It was being tested on a target in New Jersey consisting of a stirrup shaped pattern bulldozed out of the sandy soil near the coast. The white lines of the target stood out clearly against brown and green cover. Colored photographs were taken from various distances and at various angles, and the verisimilitude of the reproduction was checked by flying over the target and looking at its image in a portable camera obscura.

Because of security restrictions we were given only very rough specifications of the signal to be supplied to the controlling system in the Pelican. It was no longer to be simply on-off; if the missile was badly off target, an especially strong correcting signal was needed. This meant that the quadrant-contact system would no longer suffice. But further requirements were left mainly to our imagination. The General Mills engineers were equal to this difficult assignment. With what now seems like unbelievable speed, they designed and constructed a pneumatic pickup system giving a graded signal. A lens in the nose of the missile threw an image on a translucent plate within reach of the pigeon in a pressure sealed chamber. Four air valves resting against the edges of the plate were jarred open momentarily as the pigeon pecked. The valves at the right and left admitted air to chambers on opposite sides of one tambour, while the valves at the top and bottom admitted air to opposite sides of another. Air on all sides was exhausted by a Venturi cone on the side of the missile. When the missile was on target, the pigeon pecked the center of the plate, all valves admitted equal amounts of air, and the tambours remained in neutral positions. But if the image moved as little as a quarter of an inch off-center, corresponding to a very small angular displacement of the target, more air was admitted by the valves on one side, and the resulting displacement of the tambours sent appropriate correcting orders directly to the servosystem.

The device required no materials in short supply, was relatively foolproof, and delivered a graded signal. It had another advantage. By this time we had begun to realize that a pigeon was more easily controlled than a physical scientist serving on a committee. It was very difficult to convince the latter that the former was an orderly system. We therefore multiplied the probability of success by designing a multiple bird unit. There was adequate space in the nose of the Pelican for three pigeons each with its own lens and plate. A net signal could easily be generated. The majority vote of three pigeons offered an excellent guarantee against momentary pauses and aberrations. (We later worked out a system in which the majority took on a more characteristically democratic function. When a missile is falling toward *two* ships at sea, for example, there is no guarantee that all three pigeons will steer toward the same ship. But at least two

must agree, and the third can then be punished for his minority opinion. Under proper contingencies of reinforcement a punished bird will shift immediately to the majority view. When all three are working on one ship, any defection is immediately punished and corrected.)

The arrangement in the nose of the Pelican is shown in Figure 3. Three systems of lenses and mirrors, shown at the left, throw images of the target area on the three translucent plates shown in the center. The ballistic valves resting against the edges of these plates and the tubes connecting them with the manifolds leading to the controlling tambours may be seen. A pigeon is being placed in the pressurized chamber at the right.

The General Mills engineers also built a simulator (Figure 4)—a sort of Link trainer for pigeons—designed to have the steering characteristics of the Pelican, in so far as these had been communicated to us. Like the wing-steered Pelican, the simulator tilted and turned from side to side. When the three-bird nose was attached to it, the pigeons could be put in full control—the "loop could be closed"— and the adequacy of the signal tested under pursuit conditions. Targets were moved back and forth across the far wall of a room at prescribed speeds and in

FIGURE 3 *Demonstration model of the three-pigeon guidance system.*

FIGURE 4 *Simulator for testing the adequacy of the pigeon signal.*

given patterns of oscillation, and the tracking response of the whole unit was studied quantitatively.

Meanwhile we continued our intensive study of the behavior of the pigeon. Looking ahead to combat use we designed methods for the mass production of trained birds and for handling large groups of trained subjects. We were proposing to train certain birds for certain *classes* of targets, such as ships at sea, while special squads were to be trained on special targets, photographs of which were to be obtained through reconnaissance. A large crew of pigeons would then be waiting for assignment, but we developed harnessing and training techniques which should have solved such problems quite easily.

A multiple unit trainer is shown in Figure 5. Each box contains a jacketed pigeon

held at an angle of 45° to the horizontal and perpendicular to an 8″ x 8″ translucent screen. A target area is projected on each screen. Two beams of light intersect at the point to be struck. All on-target responses of the pigeon are reported by the interruption of the crossed beams and by contact with the translucent screen. Only a four-inch, disc-shaped portion of the field is visible to the pigeon at any time, but the boxes move slowly about the field, giving the pigeon an opportunity to respond to the target in all positions. The positions of all reinforcements are recorded to reveal any weak areas. A variable-ratio schedule is used to build sustained, rapid responding.

By December 1943, less than six months after the contract was awarded, we were ready to report to the Office of Scientific

Research and Development. Observers visited the laboratory and watched the simulator follow a target about a room under the control of a team of three birds. They also reviewed our tracking data. The only questions which arose were the inevitable consequence of our lack of information about the signal required to steer the Pelican. For example, we had had to make certain arbitrary decisions in compromising between sensitivity of signal and its integration or smoothness. A high vacuum produced quick, rather erratic movements of the tambours, while a lower vacuum gave a sluggish but smooth signal. As it turned out, we had not chosen the best values in collecting our data, and in January 1944 the Office of Scientific Research and Development refused to extend the General Mills contract. The reasons given seemed to be due to misunderstandings or, rather, to lack of communication. We had already collected further data with new settings of the instruments, and these were submitted in a request for reconsideration.

We were given one more chance. We took our new data to the radiation lab at the Massachusetts Institute of Technology where they were examined by the servo-specialists working on the Pelican controls. To our surprise the scientist whose task it was to predict the usefulness of the pigeon signal argued that our data were inconsistent with respect to phase lag and certain other characteristics of the signal. According to his equations, our device could not possibly yield the signals we reported. We knew, of course, that it had done so. We examined the supposed inconsistency and traced it, or so we thought, to a certain nonlinearity in our system. In pecking an image near the edge of the plate, the pigeon strikes a more glancing blow; hence the air admitted at the valves is not linearly proportional to the displacement of the target. This could be corrected in several ways: for example, by using a lens to distort radial distances. It was our under-

standing that in any case the signal was adequate to control the Pelican. Indeed, one servo-authority, upon looking at graphs of the performance of the simulator, exclaimed: "This is better than radar!"

Two days later, encouraged by our meeting at MIT, we reached the summit. We were to present our case briefly to a committee of the country's top scientists. The hearing began with a brief report by the scientist who had discovered the "inconsistency" in our data, and to our surprise he still regarded it as unresolved. He predicted that the signal we reported would cause the missile to "hunt" wildly and lose the target. But his prediction should have applied as well to the closed loop simulator. Fortunately another scientist was present who had seen the simulator performing under excellent control and who could confirm our report of the facts. But reality was no match for mathematics.

The basic difficulty, of course, lay in convincing a dozen distinguished physical scientists that the behavior of a pigeon could be adequately controlled. We had hoped to score on this point by bringing with us a demonstration. A small black box had a round translucent window in one end. A slide projector placed some distance away threw on the window an image of the New Jersey target. In the box, of course, was a pigeon—which, incidentally, had at that time been harnessed for 35 hours. Our intention was to let each

FIGURE 5   *A trainer for four pigeons.*

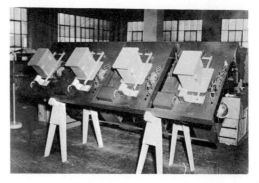

member of the committee observe the response to the target by looking down a small tube; but time was not available for individual observation, and we were asked to take the top off the box. The translucent screen was flooded with so much light that the target was barely visible, and the peering scientists offered conditions much more unfamiliar and threatening than those likely to be encountered in a missile. In spite of this the pigeon behaved perfectly, pecking steadily and energetically at the image of the target as it moved about on the plate. One scientist with an experimental turn of mind intercepted the beam from the projector. The pigeon stopped instantly. When the image again appeared, pecking began within a fraction of a second and continued at a steady rate.

It was a perfect performance, but it had just the wrong effect. One can talk about phase lag in pursuit behavior and discuss mathematical predictions of hunting without reflecting too closely upon what is inside the black box. But the spectacle of a living pigeon carrying out its assignment, no matter how beautifully, simply reminded the committee of how utterly fantastic our proposal was. I will not say that the meeting was marked by unrestrained merriment, for the merriment was restrained. But it was there, and it was obvious that our case was lost.

Hyde closed our presentation with a brief summary: we were offering a homing device, unusually resistant to jamming, capable of reacting to a wide variety of target patterns, requiring no materials in short supply, and so simple to build that production could be started in 30 days. He thanked the committee, and we left. As the door closed behind us, he said to me: "Why don't you go out and get drunk!"

Official word soon came: "Further prosecution of this project would seriously delay others which in the minds of the Division would have more immediate promise of combat application." Possibly the reference was to a particular combat applica-

tion at Hiroshima a year and a half later, when it looked for a while as if the need for accurate bombing had been eliminated for all time. In any case we had to show, for all our trouble, only a loftful of curiously useless equipment and a few dozen pigeons with a strange interest in a feature of the New Jersey coast. The equipment was scrapped, but 30 of the pigeons were kept to see how long they would retain the appropriate behavior.

In the years which followed there were faint signs of life. Winston Churchill's personal scientific advisor, Lord Cherwell, learned of the project and "regretted its demise." A scientist who had had some contact with the project during the war, and who evidently assumed that its classified status was not to be taken seriously, made a good story out of it for the *Atlantic Monthly,* names being changed to protect the innocent. Other uses of animals began to be described. The author of the *Atlantic Monthly* story also published an account of the "incendiary bats." Thousands of bats were to be released over an enemy city, each carrying a small incendiary time bomb. The bats would take refuge, as is their custom, under eaves and in other out-of-the-way places; and shortly afterwards thousands of small fires would break out practically simultaneously. The scheme was never used because it was feared that it would be mistaken for germ warfare and might lead to retaliation in kind.

Another story circulating at the time told how the Russians trained dogs to blow up tanks. I have described the technique elsewhere [Skinner, 1956]. A Swedish proposal to use seals to achieve the same end with submarines was not successful. The seals were to be trained to approach submarines to obtain fish attached to the sides. They were then to be released carrying magnetic mines in the vicinity of hostile submarines. The required training was apparently never achieved. I cannot vouch for the authenticity of probably the most fantastic story of this sort, but it ought to be recorded. The Russians were said to have trained sea lions to cut mine cables. A complicated device attached to the sea lion included a motor-driven cable-cutter, a tank full of small fish, and a device which released a few fish into a muzzle covering the sea lion's head. In order to eat, the sea lion had to find a mine cable and swim along side it so that the cutter was automatically triggered, at which point a few fish were released from the tank into the muzzle. When a given number of cables had been cut, both the energy of the cutting mechanism and the supply of fish were exhausted, and the sea lion received a special stimulus upon which it returned to its home base for special reinforcement and reloading.

Orcon

The story of our own venture has a happy ending. With the discovery of German accomplishments in the field of guided missiles, feasible homing systems suddenly became very important. Franklin V. Taylor of the Naval Research Laboratory in Washington, D. C. heard about our project and asked for further details. As a psychologist Taylor appreciated the special capacity of living organisms to respond to visual patterns and was aware of recent advances in the control of behavior. More important, he was a skillful practitioner in a kind of control which our project had conspicuously lacked: he knew how to approach the people who determine the direction of research. He showed our demonstration film so often that it was completely worn out—but to good effect, for support was eventually found for a thorough investigation of "organic control" under the general title ORCON. Taylor also enlisted the support of engineers in obtaining a more effective report of the pigeon's behavior. The translucent plate upon which the image of the target was thrown had a semiconducting surface, and the tip of the bird's beak was covered with a gold electrode. A single contact with the plate sent an immediate report of the location of the target to the controlling mechanism. The work which went into this system contributed to the so-called Pick-off Display Converter developed as part of the Naval Data Handling System for human observers. It is no longer necessary for the radar operator to give a verbal report of the location of a pip on the screen. Like the pigeon, he has only to touch the pip with a special contact. (He holds the contact in his hand.)

At the Naval Research Laboratory in Washington the responses of pigeons were studied in detail. Average peck rate, average error rate, average hit rate, and so on were recorded under various conditions. The tracking behavior of the pigeon was analyzed with methods similar to those employed with human operators (Figure 6). Pattern perception was studied, including generalization from one pattern to another. A simulator was constructed in which the pigeon controlled an image projected by a moving-picture film of an actual target: for example, a ship at sea as seen from a plane approaching at 600 miles per hour. A few frames of a moving picture of the pigeon controlling the orientation toward a ship during an approach are shown in Figure 7.

The publications from the Naval Research Laboratory which report this work (Chernikoff & Newlin, 1951; Conklin,

FIGURE 6 *Arrangement for studying pursuit movements.*

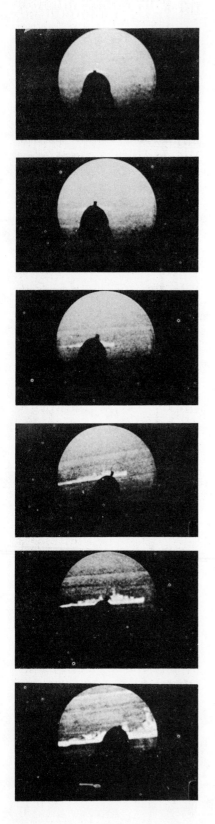

Newlin, Taylor, & Tipton, 1953; Searle & Stafford, 1950; Taylor, 1949; White, 1952) provide a serious evaluation of the possibilities of organic control. Although in simulated tests a single pigeon occasionally loses a target, its tracking characteristics are surprisingly good. A three- or seven-bird unit with the same individual consistency should yield a signal with a reliability which is at least of the order of magnitude shown by other phases of guided missiles in their present stage of development. Moreover, in the seven years which have followed the last of these reports, a great deal of relevant information has been acquired. The color vision of the pigeon is now thoroughly understood; its generalization along single properties of a stimulus has been recorded and analyzed; and the maintenance of behavior through scheduling of reinforcement has been drastically improved, particularly in the development of techniques for pacing responses for less erratic and steadier signals (Skinner, 1957). Tests made with the birds salvaged from the old Project Pigeon showed that even after six years of inactivity a pigeon will immediately and correctly strike a target to which it has been conditioned and will continue to respond for some time without reinforcement.

The use of living organisms in guiding missiles is, it seems fair to say, no longer a crackpot idea. A pigeon is an extraordinarily subtle and complex mechanism capable of performances which at the moment can be equalled by electronic equipment only of vastly greater weight and size, and it can be put to reliable use through the principles which have emerged from an experimental analysis of its behavior. But this vindication of our original proposal is perhaps the least important result. Something happened during the brief life of Project Pigeon which it has

FIGURE 7 *Frames from a simulated approach.*

taken a long time to appreciate. The practical task before us created a new attitude toward the behavior of organisms. We had to maximize the probability that a given form of behavior would occur at a given time. We could not enjoy the luxury of observing one variable while allowing others to change in what we hoped was a random fashion. We had to discover all relevant variables and submit them to experimental control whenever possible. We were no doubt under exceptional pressure, but vigorous scientific research usually makes comparable demands. Psychologists have too often yielded to the temptation to be content with hypothetical processes and intervening variables rather than press for rigorous experimental control. It is often intellectual laziness rather than necessity which recommends the *a posteriori* statistical treatment of variation. Our task forced us to emphasize prior experimental control, and its success in revealing orderly processes gave us an exciting glimpse of the superiority of laboratory practice over verbal (including some kinds of mathematical) explanation.

The crackpot idea

If I were to conclude that crackpot ideas are to be encouraged, I should probably be told that psychology has already had more than its share of them. If it has, they have been entertained by the wrong people. Reacting against the excesses of psychological quackery, psychologists have developed an enormous concern for scientific respectability. They constantly warn their students against questionable facts and unsupported theories. As a result the usual PhD thesis is a model of compulsive cautiousness, advancing only the most timid conclusions thoroughly hedged about with qualifications. But it is just the man capable of displaying such admirable caution who needs a touch of uncontrolled speculation. Possibly a generous exposure

to psychological science fiction would help. Project Pigeon might be said to support that view. Except with respect to its avowed goal, it was, as I see it, highly productive; and this was in large measure because my colleagues and I knew that, in the eyes of the world, we were crazy.

One virtue in crackpot ideas is that they breed rapidly and their progeny show extraordinary mutations. Everyone is talking about teaching machines nowadays, but Sidney Pressey can tell you what it was like to have a crackpot idea in that field 40 years ago. His self-testing devices and self-scoring test forms now need no defense, and psychomotor training devices have also achieved a substantial respectability. This did not, however, prepare the way for devices to be used in verbal instruction—that is, in the kinds of teaching which are the principal concern of our schools and colleges. Even five short years ago that kind of instruction by machine was still in the crackpot category. (I can quote official opinion to that effect from high places.) Now, there is a direct genetic connection between teaching machines and Project Pigeon. We had been forced to consider the mass education of pigeons. True, the scrap of wisdom we imparted to each was indeed small, but the required changes in behavior were similar to those which must be brought about in vaster quantities in human students. The techniques of shaping behavior and of bringing it under stimulus control which can be traced, as I have suggested elsewhere (Skinner, 1958), to a memorable episode on the top floor of that flour mill in Minneapolis needed only a detailed reformulation of verbal behavior to be directly applicable to education.

I am sure there is more to come. In the year which followed the termination of Project Pigeon I wrote *Walden Two* (Skinner, 1948), a utopian picture of a properly engineered society. Some psychotherapists might argue that I was suffering from personal rejection and simply retreated to a fantasied world where everything went according to plan, where there never was heard a discouraging word. But another explanation is, I think, equally plausible. That piece of science fiction was a declaration of confidence in a technology of behavior. Call it a crackpot idea if you will; it is one in which I have never lost faith. I still believe that the same kind of wide-ranging speculation about human affairs, supported by studies of compensating rigor, will make a substantial contribution toward that world of the future in which, among other things, there will be no need for guided missiles.

References

Chernikoff, R., and Newlin, E. P. ORCON. Part III. Investigations of target acquisition by the pigeon. *Naval Res. Lab. lett., Rep.,* 1951, No. S–3600–629a/51 (Sept. 10).

Conklin, J. E., Newlin, E. P., Jr., Taylor, F. V., and Tipton, C. L. ORCON. Part IV. Simulated flight tests. *Naval Res. Lab. Rep.,* 1953, No. 4105.

Searle, L. V., and Stafford, B. H. ORCON. Part II. Report of phase I research and bandpass study. *Naval Res. Lab. lett. Rep.,* 1950, No. S–3600–157/50 (May 1).

Skinner, B. F. *Walden Two.* New York: Macmillan, 1948.

Skinner, B. F. A case history in scientific method. *Amer. Psychologist,* 1956, **11**, 221–233.

Skinner, B. F. The experimental analysis of behavior. *Amer. Scient.,* 1957, **45**, 343–371.

Skinner, B. F. Reinforcement today. *Amer. Psychologist,* 1958, **13**, 94–99.

Taylor, F. V. ORCON. Part I. Outline of proposed research. *Naval Res. Lab. lett. Rep.,* 1949, No. S–3600–157/50 (June 17).

White, C. F. Development of the NRL ORCON tactile missile simulator. *Naval Res. Lab. Rep.,* 1952, No. 3917.

Neutral stimuli which are paired with primary reinforcement will themselves become reinforcers, that is, secondary reinforcers, *as this experiment demonstrates. Thus the range of the primary reinforcers is considerably extended.*

POINTS TO GUIDE YOUR STUDY   *(1) Make sure that the four conditions of this experiment are clear. Also note the two types of comparisons that are made in the results section.   (2) The decimals on the right in Table 1 give the chances in one hundred that the differences obtained are due to chance alone. For instance, the probability that the difference between the means of groups 2 and 3, 9.0 and 10.7 respectively, is due to chance alone is 2/100. Psychologists usually consider probabilities of 5/100, the .05 level, good enough to conclude that the difference is not due to chance. Sigma (the standard deviation) in Table 1 is a measure of the variation of the scores.*

GLOSSARY   **Kinesthetic:** *stimulation from movements of the body.*

14: MAZE LEARNING IN THE ABSENCE OF PRIMARY REINFORCEMENT: A STUDY OF SECONDARY REINFORCEMENT

Irving J. Saltzman, Indiana University

For many years experimenters have been successfully using food as an incentive to promote the learning of hungry animals. When an incentive, such as food, is used to

A dissertation submitted in 1948 to the Board of University Studies of The Johns Hopkins University in conformity with the requirements for the degree of Doctor of Philosophy. The writer is indebted to Dr. W. R. Garner and Dr. S. B. Williams, under whose guidance this research was carried out.

I. J. Saltzman. Maze learning in the absence of primary reinforcement: A study of secondary reinforcement. *J. comp. physiol. Psychol.,* 1949, **42**, 161–173. Copyright © 1949 by the American Psychological Association. Excerpts reprinted here with permission from the author and the American Psychological Association.

promote learning through satisfying a primary drive, like hunger, it is often said to possess primary reward value, and it is called a primary reinforcing agent, or more simply, a primary reward. Any stimuli which occur consistently and repeatedly along with a primary reward may, themselves, soon come to act like a primary reward in promoting learning. Such stimuli are called secondary reinforcing agents; they are said to possess secondary or acquired reward value.

Maze learning without primary reward

STATEMENT OF PROBLEM The primary purpose of this investigation was to devise a technique for showing that rats are able to learn a simple maze under conditions of secondary reward. If this aim could be realized, it was felt that a systematic study of the variables affecting the acquisition and the persistence of secondary reward value could be carried out.

Probably the greatest difficulty in showing learning in the absence of primary reward is that the acquired reward value is rapidly lost during the learning trials. If the acquired reward value is small to begin with, and if the task to be learned is very difficult, the reward value will be lost before any learning occurs, or at least before any learning that can be measured occurs. If the learning task is a simple one, however, the chances of getting a measure of learning are better. Therefore, a small, single choice maze was used as the learning task. Also, three different methods for building up the reward value were used, in the hope that at least one of them would result in a measurable indication of learning.

EXPERIMENTAL PROCEDURE *Subjects.* Forty-eight naïve, hooded, female rats, from the Johns Hopkins Psychology Department colony, were divided into four equal groups of twelve. At the start of the investigation the rats averaged 179 grams in weight, and ranged in age from 85 to 130 days.

Apparatus. The apparatus (Figures 1 and 2) consisted of a closed runway, a single choice, closed U-maze, six goal boxes and one starting box. The boxes could be used with either the runway or the maze. All the apparatus was made of heavy five-ply wood and was painted grey with the exception of four of the goal boxes, two of which were painted black, and two, white. Each piece of apparatus, except the two

FIGURE 1 *Floor plan of maze and runway. S = starting box; G = goal box.*

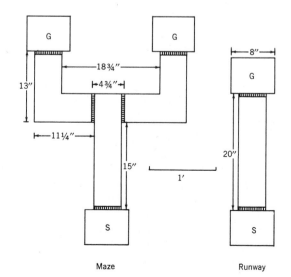

Maze   Runway

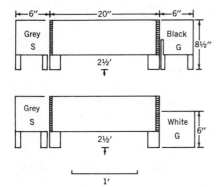

FIGURE 2 *Side view of runway showing positions of black and white goal boxes. S = starting box; G = goal box.*

white goal boxes, was raised from the table on which it was located, by small legs. The tops of all the apparatus were made of wire mesh and were removable.

Runway. At each end of the runway vertically sliding doors were located. These doors could be manipulated by the experimenter from the starting position by means of attached strings. When the starting box was placed adjacent to the runway, a rat could proceed directly from the box into the runway, as soon as the starting door was raised. The black goal boxes each had a hurdle 2.5 inches high on the open side. The hurdle had to be climbed by the rats in entering the box from the runway. To enter the white goal boxes, which were not raised on legs, the rats had to jump down from the runway.

Maze. The maze consisted of a straight alley leading into a U-shaped alley. Vertically sliding doors, which could be controlled from the starting position, were located at the beginning of the straight alley and at the ends of the U-shaped alley. An additional pair of doors was located at the junction of the two alleys to prevent retracing after a choice had been made. The goal boxes could not be seen by the rats until after a choice had been made. The grey goal boxes were exactly like the starting box, and were used on the

maze during the test for position preference. The other goal boxes were used on the maze in the same manner as they were used on the runway.

Establishment of feeding rhythm. At the start of the experiment the rats were removed from the colony and housed in individual cages. At the same time of day, for six consecutive days, they were allowed to eat moist Purina (Growena) chicken mash from small metal containers for one half hour. The animals received no other food during this period; water was available at all times. The feeding was omitted on the seventh day.

Preliminary training. Of the four groups of rats, three were experimental secondary reward groups, and one was a comparison, primary reward group. A different technique was used with each of the experimental groups during the preliminary training.

Group 1: Consecutive reinforcement group: On day eight, at the usual feeding time, the rats in this group received the following treatment. A rat was placed into the grey starting box. After a 10-second delay, the door leading into the runway was raised. When the rat moved into the runway, the door was lowered behind it. The door at the goal box was already raised. When the rat entered the goal box, this door was lowered, and the rat was given a metal cup containing wet mash, and was allowed to eat for two minutes. The rat was then removed to its home cage. Five such runway trials were given each of the rats, each trial separated from the preceding one by approximately five minutes. Following the fifth runway trial, each animal was allowed to eat in the goal box for 20 minutes. In this manner, each rat received his daily ration of food in the goal box. For one half of the animals in this group, the goal box used was the black box with the hurdle; for the other half, the white box without legs was used.

This procedure was repeated for five consecutive days, at the end of which time each rat had received 25 rewarded runs to its particular box. On the last day of runway experience, between the second and third trials, the position habits of the rats were tested in the maze. The two grey goal boxes were used as the goal. Thirty seconds after the rat had entered a goal box, it was removed from the box. A choice of one side two out of three times was the measure of side preference used. Following the tests, the rewarded runway trials were resumed.

Group 2: Alternate reinforcement group: The rats in this group received the same treatment as those in Group 1 on the first day of runway experience. From the second day on, the rats in this group, in addition to the five rewarded runs per day, received several non-rewarded trials. A rewarded trial always preceded and always followed a non-rewarded trial. The first non-rewarded run was given after the second rewarded run, on the second day of runway trials. In all, 14 non-rewarded runs were given each of the rats in addition to the 25 rewarded runs. Three were given on the second and on the fifth day of the runway trials, and four each on the third and fourth days. On the fifth day the position habit test was given, instead of the second non-rewarded run of the day. The same kind of goal box was used with a given rat for both the rewarded and non-rewarded runs.

Group 3: Differential reinforcement group: The rats in this group received the same treatment as those in Group 2, with the exception that on the non-rewarded trials, the goal box was not the same one that was used for the rewarded trials. The rats receiving food in the black goal box found the white goal box at the end of the runway on the non-rewarded runs, and those receiving food in the white box found the black box on the non-rewarded runs.

Group C: The rats in Group C, the comparison primary reward group, received exactly the same treatment as the rats in Group 1.

Learning trials. Groups 1, 2, and 3: The learning trials were conducted on the day following the last day of runway trials. All three experimental groups of rats received the same treatment. The goal box, either black or white, in which the rats had received food on the runway, was located in the goal position on the nonpreferred side. The other goal box was placed in the goal position of the preferred side. All the doors in the maze, except the one at the starting box, were raised. The non-correction technique was used. The rat was first placed in the starting box. After a 10-second delay, the door was raised. When the rat entered the straight alley of the maze, the door was lowered behind it. After the rat had made its choice of path, the door at the choice point was lowered to prevent retracing. As soon as the rat entered the goal box located at the end of the arm of the U, the final door was lowered, and 30 seconds later, the rat was removed to its home cage. Fifteen such trials in the maze were given each rat. Each trial was separated from the preceding one by a period of from 5 to 15 minutes. Food was never presented to any of the animals in the maze regardless of the choice that had been made.

Group C: When the rats of Group C were run on the maze, both of the goal boxes were identical, and both were different from the goal box in which the rats had received food on the runway. When a rat which had been fed in a black box on the runway was run in the maze, white goal boxes were placed in each of the goal positions of the maze, and vice versa. Following correct choices in the maze, the rats in this group were offered a cup of food from which they were allowed to eat for 30 seconds. A correct choice was a choice of the non-preferred side, as determined by the position habit test. Food was not presented to the animals when incorrect choices were made. In such instances, the rats were merely removed from the goal box after 30 seconds. Fifteen maze trials were given, regardless of the choices that had been made.

RESULTS   The main purpose of the study was to find out whether it could be shown that rats can learn a simple maze in the absence of primary reward. The test of learning consisted merely of 15 runs in the maze with a secondary reinforcing agent serving as the only source of reinforcement. If learning occurred under these conditions, it could be said that secondary reinforcement learning of a maze is possible. Since a comparison group of rats which received primary reinforcement on the maze was also run, two indices of learning were available: (1) Comparison of the maze choices of the secondary reward groups with chance expectancy, and (2) Comparison of the maze choices of the secondary reward groups with the choices of the primary reward group.

Comparison with chance expectancy. If the goal boxes in which the rats had been fed on the runway had *not* acquired any secondary reward value, it might be expected that the average number of choices of the correct alley out of a possible 15 would be approximately seven and one half or less, since the rats were run against their position habits. On the other hand, if the box *had* acquired reward value, it might be expected that the path leading to that box in the maze would be selected more often than the other path. The number of correct choices was used, therefore, as the measure of the effectiveness of the secondary reinforcing agent, and at the same time, as a measure of learning. If the mean number of correct choices was significantly greater than chance, then learning was said to have occurred.

Comparison with primary reinforcement group. In order to use the results of the primary reinforcement group in getting an index of learning, one assumption has to be made. It has to be assumed that the mean number of correct choices made by

this group is the number of correct choices that ought to occur if the maze were being learned. In other words, it was assumed that the rats in this group were learning the maze. Then a comparison of the mean number of correct choices made by this group with the means of the other groups tells us something about the learning of the other groups. We have a measure of the relative effectiveness of primary and secondary rewards. In addition, this comparison serves as a check of our first index of learning.

The mean number of correct choices out of a possible 15 for each of the experimental groups, as well as for the comparison group, is indicated in Table 1, along with the standard deviations of the means. The table also shows the probabilities with which the differences which were obtained between the means of the groups and 7.5 could be obtained purely by chance. Included, too, are the probabilities with which the differences between the several group means could occur by chance. The mean number of correct choices for Groups 1, 2, and 3 are 8.3, 9.0, and 10.7 respectively. The comparison group, Group C, has a mean of 10.0 correct choices.

Each of the means is different from chance (7.5) at the 1 percent level of confidence, except for Group 1. The difference which exists between the mean of Group 1 (8.3) and chance would occur 4 times in 100 by chance factors alone. If the criterion of significance adopted to indicate statistical significance is the 1 percent level of confidence, then it can be said that Groups 2 and 3 learned the maze, and that Group 1 did not.

The differences between the mean of Group C, the primary reward group, and the means of Groups 2 and 3, are not significant statistically. This indicates that the secondary reward value built up with either of these two methods is probably as effective in influencing the choices that were made in the maze as is a primary reward. The difference between the means

TABLE 1 *Means, sigmas, and probabilities of differences from chance and between means*

	MEAN NUMBER CORRECT CHOICES	SIGMA	CHANCE (7.5)	PROBABILITIES		
GROUPS*				GROUP C	GROUP 1	GROUP 2
C	10.0	2.16	.01	—	—	—
1	8.3	1.25	.04	.04	—	—
2	9.0	1.73	.01	.25	.29	—
3	10.7	1.31	.01	.95	.01	.02

* Groups 1, 2, and 3 ran the maze under conditions of secondary reward, and Group C under primary reward.

of Group 1 and Group C would occur on the basis of pure chance factors only 4 times in 100, suggesting that a real difference may exist between the two means. In 15 learning trials, the rats in Group 1 did not learn to the same extent as did those of Group C.

SUMMARY AND CONCLUSION The experiment establishes the ability of the rat to learn a simple maze when correct choices are followed only by stimuli previously associated with food, and probably enhances the possibilities of secondary reinforcement as a general principle of learning. Inasmuch as the distinctive aspects of the goal boxes were at least several, including kinesthetic as well as visual components, it is impossible to say which of them was the most effective. Taken together, however, they were at least as effective, or slightly more effective than food. This last fact challenges a re-interpretation of the whole problem of the relative effectiveness of rewards in learning.

References

1. Anderson, E. E.: The externalization of drive: III. Maze learning by non-rewarded and by satiated rats. *J. genet. Psychol.*, 1941, 59, 397–426.

2. Cowles, J. T.: Food-tokens as incentives for learning by chimpanzees. *Comp. Psychol. Monogr.*, 1937, 14, No. 5.

3. Denny, M. R.: Differential end boxes in a simple T-maze. *Amer. Psychologist*, 1946, 1, 245.

4. Ellson, D. G.: The acquisition of a token-reward habit in dogs. *J. comp. Psychol.*, 1937, 24, 505–522.

5. Grindley, G. C.: Experiments on the influence of the amount of reward on learning in young chickens. *Brit. J. Psychol.*, 1929, 20, 173–180.

6. Hull, C. L.: *Principles of behavior*. New York: Appleton Century Co., 1943.

7. Humphreys, L. G.: The strength of a Thorndikian response as a function of the number of practice trials. *J. comp. Psychol.*, 1943, 35, 101–110.

8. McCulloch, T. L.: The use of the "comfort" drive as motivation in visual discrimination by the infant chimpanzee. *Psychol. Bull.*, 1937, 34, 540.

9. Miller, N. E.: Studies of fear as an acquirable drive: I. Fear as motivation and fear-reduction as reinforcement in the learning of new responses. *J. exp. Psychol.*, 1948, 38, 89–101.

10. Mote, F. A. and Finger, F. W.: Exploratory drive and secondary reinforcement in the acquisition and extinction of a simple running response. *J. exp. Psychol.*, 1942, 31, 57–68.

11. Mowrer, O. H. and Jones, H.: Habit strength as a function of the pattern of reinforcement. *J. exp. Psychol.*, 1945, 35, 293–310.

12. Nissen, N. W. and Crawford, M. P.: A preliminary study of food-sharing behavior in young chimpanzees. *J. comp. Psychol.*, 1936, 22, 383–419.

13. Skinner, B. F.: *The behavior of organisms*. New York: Appleton Century Co., 1938.

14. Spence, K. W.: The role of secondary reinforcement in delayed reward learning. *Psychol. Rev.*, 1947, 54, 1–8.

15. Williams, Katherine A.: The reward value of a conditioned stimulus. *Univ. Calif. Publ. Psychol.*, 1929, 4, 31–55.

16. Wolfe, J. B.: Effectiveness of token-rewards for chimpanzees. *Comp. Psychol. Monogr.*, 1936, 12, No. 60.

The experiments which are mentioned in this article provide some of the strongest support for perceptual learning.

A POINT TO GUIDE YOUR STUDY   *What types of experiments does Dr. Tolman use to support his belief in perceptual, or cognitive, learning? How do they support this view?*

15: COGNITIVE MAPS IN RATS AND MEN

Edward C. Tolman

I shall devote the body of this paper to a description of experiments with rats. But I shall also attempt in a few words at the close to indicate the significance of these findings on rats for the clinical behavior of men. Most of the rat investigations, which I shall report, were carried out in the Berkeley laboratory. But I shall also include, occasionally, accounts of the behavior of non-Berkeley rats who obviously have misspent their lives in out-of-State laboratories. Furthermore, in reporting our Berkeley experiments I shall have to omit a very great many. The ones I *shall* talk about were carried out by graduate students (or underpaid research assistants) who, supposedly, got some of their ideas from me. And a few, though a very few, were even carried out by me myself.

Let me begin by presenting diagrams for a couple of typical mazes, an alley maze and an elevated maze. In the typical experiment a hungry rat is put at the entrance of the maze (alley or elevated), and wanders about through the various true path segments and blind alleys until he finally comes to the food box and eats. This is repeated (again in the typical experiment) one trial every 24 hours and

the animal tends to make fewer and fewer errors (that is, blind-alley entrances) and to take less and less time between start and goal-box until finally he is entering no blinds at all and running in a very few seconds from start to goal. The results are usually presented in the form of average curves of blind-entrances, or of seconds from start to finish, for groups of rats.

All students agree as to the facts. They disagree, however, on theory and explanation.

1. First, there is a school of animal psychologists which believes that the maze behavior of rats is a matter of mere simple stimulus-response connections. Learning, according to them, consists in the strengthening of some of these connections and in the weakening of others. According to this "stimulus-response" school the rat in progressing down the maze is helplessly responding to a succession of external stimuli —sights, sounds, smells, pressures, etc., impinging upon his external sense organs— plus internal stimuli coming from the viscera and from the skeletal muscles. These external and internal stimuli call out the walkings, runnings, turnings, retracings, smellings, rearings, and the like which appear. The rat's central nervous system, according to this view, may be likened to a complicated telephone switchboard. There are the incoming calls from sense-organs and there are the outgoing messages to muscles. Before the learning of a specific maze, the connecting switches (synapses according to the physiologist)

34th Annual Faculty Research Lecture, delivered at the University of California, Berkeley, March 17, 1947. Presented also on March 26, 1947, as one in a series of lectures in Dynamic Psychology sponsored by the division of psychology of Western Reserve University, Cleveland, Ohio.

E. C. Tolman. Cognitive maps in rats and men. *Psychol. Rev.*, 1948, **55**, 189–208. Copyright © 1948 by the American Psychological Association. Reprinted here with permission from the American Psychological Association.

14–unit T–alley maze

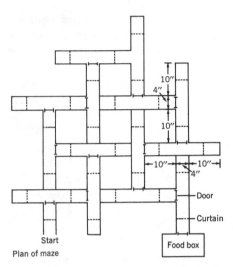

Start
Plan of maze

FIGURE 1   *Plan of maze; 14-unit T-alley maze. (From M. H. Elliott. The effect of change of reward on the maze performance of rats.* Univ. Calif. Publ. Psychol., *1928, 4, p. 20.)*

are closed in one set of ways and produce the primarily exploratory responses which appear in the early trials. *Learning,* according to this view, consists in the respective strengthening and weakening of various of these connections; those connections which result in the animal's going down the true path become relatively more open to the passage of nervous impulses, whereas those which lead him into the blinds become relatively less open.

It must be noted in addition, however, that this stimulus-response school divides further into two subgroups.

a.   There is a subgroup which holds that the mere mechanics involved in the running of a maze is such that the crucial stimuli from the maze get presented simultaneously with the correct responses more frequently than they do with any of the incorrect responses. Hence, just on a basis of this greater frequency, the neural connections between the crucial stimuli and the correct responses will tend, it is said,

to get strengthened at the expense of the incorrect connections.

b.   There is a second subgroup in this stimulus-response school which holds that the reason the appropriate connections get strengthened relatively to the inappropriate ones is, rather, the fact that the responses resulting from the correct connections are followed more closely in time by need-reductions. Thus a hungry rat in a maze tends to get to food and have his hunger reduced *sooner* as a result of the true path responses than as a result of the blind alley responses. And such immediately following need-reductions or, to use another term, such "positive reinforcements" tend somehow, it is said, to strengthen the connections which have most closely preceded them. Thus it is as if—although this is certainly not the way this subgroup would themselves state it— the satisfaction-receiving part of the rat telephoned back to Central and said to the girl: "Hold that connection; it was good;

FIGURE 2   *Fourteen-unit T-elevated mazes. These were two identical mazes placed side by side in the same room. (From C. H. Honzik. The sensory basis of maze learning in rats.* Compar. Psychol. Monogr., *1936, 13, No. 4, p. 4.)*

14–unit T–elevated mazes

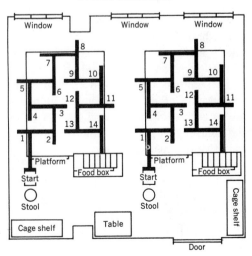

and see to it that you blankety-blank well use it again the next time these same stimuli come in." These theorists also assume (at least some of them do some of the time) that, if bad results—'annoyances,' 'negative reinforcements'—follow, then this same satisfaction- and annoyance-receiving part of the rat will telephone back and say, "Break that connection and don't you dare use it next time either."

So much for a brief summary of the two subvarieties of the 'stimulus-response,' or telephone switchboard school.

2. Let us turn now to the second main school. This group (and I belong to them) may be called the field theorists. We believe that in the course of learning something like a field map of the environment gets established in the rat's brain. We agree with the other school that the rat in running a maze is exposed to stimuli and is finally led as a result of these stimuli to the responses which actually occur. We feel, however, that the intervening brain processes are more complicated, more patterned and often, pragmatically speaking, more autonomous than do the stimulus-response psychologists. Although we admit that the rat is bombarded by stimuli, we hold that his nervous system is surprisingly selective as to which of these stimuli it will let in at any given time.

Secondly, we assert that the central office itself is far more like a map control room than it is like an old-fashioned telephone exchange. The stimuli, which are allowed in, are not connected by just simple one-to-one switches to the outgoing responses. Rather, the incoming impulses are usually worked over and elaborated in the central control room into a tentative, cognitive-like map of the environment. And it is this tentative map, indicating routes and paths and environmental relationships, which finally determines what responses, if any, the animal will finally release.

Finally, I, personally, would hold further that it is also important to discover

in how far these maps are relatively narrow and strip-like or relatively broad and comprehensive. Both strip-maps and comprehensive-maps may be either correct or incorrect in the sense that they may (or may not), when acted upon, lead successfully to the animal's goal. The differences between such strip maps and such comprehensive maps will appear only when the rat is later presented with some change within the given environment. Then, the narrower and more strip-like the original map, the less will it carry over successfully to the new problem; whereas, the wider and the more comprehensive it was, the more adequately it will serve in the new set-up. In a strip-map the given position of the animal is connected by only a relatively simple and single path to the position of the goal. In a comprehensive-map a wider arc of the environment is represented, so that, if the starting position of the animal be changed or variations in the specific routes be introduced, this wider

FIGURE 3   *Error curves for four groups, 36 rats. A maze identical with the alley maze shown in Figure 1 was used. (From E. C. Tolman and C. H. Honzik. Degrees of hunger, reward and non-reward, and maze learning in rats. Univ. Calif. Publ. Psychol., 1930, 4, No. 16, p. 246.)*

Error curves for four groups, 36 rats

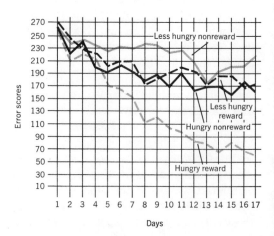

map will allow the animal still to behave relatively correctly and to choose the appropriate new route.

But let us turn, now, to the actual experiments. The ones, out of many, which I have selected to report are simply ones which seem especially important in reinforcing the theoretical position I have been presenting. This position, I repeat, contains two assumptions: First, that learning consists not in stimulus-response connections but in the building up in the nervous system of sets which function like cognitive maps and second, that such cognitive maps may be usefully characterized as varying from a narrow strip variety to a broader comprehensive variety.

The experiments fall under five heads: (1) "latent learning," (2) "vicarious trial and error" or "VTE," (3) "searching for the stimulus," (4) "hypotheses" and (5) "spatial orientation."

1. "LATENT LEARNING" EXPERIMENTS The first of the latent learning experiments was performed at Berkeley by Blodgett. It was published in 1929. Blodgett not only performed the experiments, he also originated the concept. He ran three groups of rats through a six-unit alley maze, shown in Figure 4. He had a control group and two experimental groups. The error curves for these groups appear in Figure 5. The solid line shows the error curve for Group I, the control group. These animals were run in orthodox fashion. That is, they were run one trial a day and found food in the goal-box at the end of each trial. Groups II and III were the experimental groups. The animals of Group II, the dash line, were not fed in the maze for the first six days but only in their home cages some two hours later. On the seventh day (indicated by the small cross) the rats found food at the end of the maze for the first time and continued to find it on subsequent days. The animals of Group III were treated similarly except that they first found food

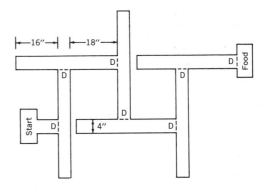

6–unit alley T–maze

FIGURE 4 *Six-unit T-alley maze. (From H. C. Blodgett. The effect of the introduction of reward upon the maze performance of rats.* Univ. Calif. Publ. Psychol., *1929, 4, No. 8, p. 117.)*

at the end of the maze on the third day and continued to find it there on subsequent days. It will be observed that the experimental groups as long as they were not finding food did not appear to learn much. (Their error curves did not drop.) But on the days immediately succeeding their first finding of the food their error curves did drop astoundingly. It appeared,

FIGURE 5 *(From H. B. Blodgett. The effect of the introduction of reward upon the maze performance of rats.* Univ. Calif. Publ. Psychol., *1929, 4, No. 8, p. 120.)*

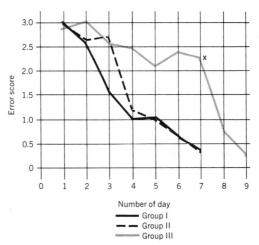

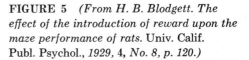

in short, that during the non-rewarded trials these animals had been learning much more than they had exhibited. This learning, which did not manifest itself until after the food had been introduced, Blodgett called "latent learning." Interpreting these results anthropomorphically, we would say that as long as the animals were not getting any food at the end of the maze they continued to take their time in going through it—they continued to enter many blinds. Once, however, they knew they were to get food, they demonstrated that during these preceding non-rewarded trials they had learned where many of the blinds were. They had been building up a "map," and could utilize the latter as soon as they were motivated to do so.

Honzik and myself repeated the experiments (or rather he did and I got some of the credit) with the 14-unit T-mazes shown in Figure 1, and with larger groups of animals, and got similar results. The resulting curves are shown in Figure 6. We used two control groups—one that never found food in the maze (HNR) and one that found it throughout (HR). The experimental group (HNR-R) found food

FIGURE 6 *Error curves for HR, HNR, and HNR-R. (From E. C. Tolman and C. H. Honzik. Introduction and removal of reward, and maze performance in rats. Univ. Calif. Publ. Psychol., 1930, 4, No. 19, p. 267.)*

Error curves for HR, HNR, and HNR-R

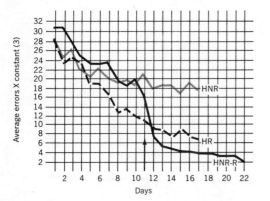

Ground plan of the apparatus

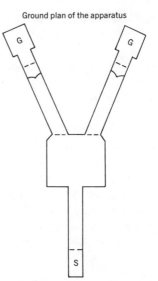

FIGURE 7 *Ground plan of the apparatus. (Taken from K. W. Spence and R. Lippitt. An experimental test of the sign-gestalt theory of trial and error learning. J. exp. Psychol., 1946, 36, p. 494. In this article they were describing another experiment but used the same maze.)*

at the end of the maze from the 11th day on and showed the same sort of a sudden drop.

But probably the best experiment demonstrating latent learning was, unfortunately, done not in Berkeley but at the University of Iowa, by Spence and Lippitt. Only an abstract of this experiment has as yet been published. However, Spence has sent a preliminary manuscript from which the following account is summarized. A simple Y-maze (see Figure 7) with two goal-boxes was used. Water was at the end of the right arm of the Y and food at the end of the left arm. During the training period the rats were run neither hungry nor thirsty. They were satiated for both food and water before each day's trials. However, they were willing to run because after each run they were taken out of whichever end box they had got to and put into a living cage, with other animals in it. They were given four trials a day in this fashion for seven days, two trials to the right and two to the left.

In the crucial test the animals were divided into two subgroups, one made solely hungry and one solely thirsty. It was then found that on the first trial the hungry group went at once to the left, where the food had been, statistically more frequently than to the right; and the thirsty group went to the right, where the water had been, statistically more frequently than to the left. These results indicated that under the previous non-differential and very mild rewarding conditions of merely being returned to the home cages the animals had nevertheless been learning where the water was and where the food was. In short, they had acquired a cognitive map to the effect that food was to the left and water to the right, although during the acquisition of this map they had not exhibited any stimulus-response propensities to go more to the side which became later the side of the appropriate goal.

There have been numerous other latent learning experiments done in the Berkeley laboratory and elsewhere. In general, they have for the most part all confirmed the above sort of findings.

Let us turn now to the second group of experiments.

2. "VICARIOUS TRIAL AND ERROR" OR "VTE"

The term Vicarious Trial and Error (abbreviated as VTE) was invented by Prof. Muenzinger at Colorado[1] to designate the hesitating, looking-back-and-forth sort of behavior which rats can often be observed to indulge in at a choice-point before actually going one way or the other.

Quite a number of experiments upon VTEing have been carried out in our laboratory. I shall report only a few. In most of them what is called a discrimination

set-up has been used. In one characteristic type of visual discrimination apparatus designed by Lashley (shown in Figure 8) the animal is put on a jumping stand and faced with two doors which differ in some visual property, say, as here shown, vertical stripes vs. horizontal stripes.

One of each such pair of visual stimuli is made always correct and the other wrong; and the two are interchanged from side to side in random fashion. The animal is required to learn, say, that the vertically striped door is always the correct one. If he jumps to it, the door falls open and he gets to food on a platform behind. If on the other hand, he jumps incorrectly, he finds the door locked and falls into a net some two feet below from which he is picked up and started over again.

Using a similar set-up (see Figure 9),

FIGURE 8 *Apparatus used for testing discrimination of visual patterns.*
(From K. S. Lashley, The mechanism of vision. I. A method for rapid analyses of pattern-vision in the rat. J. genet. Psychol., 1930, 37, p. 44.)

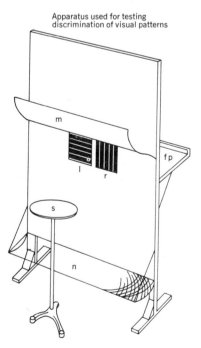

Apparatus used for testing discrimination of visual patterns

---

[1] Vide: K. F. Muenzinger, Vicarious trial and error at a point of choice: I. A general survey of its relation to learning efficiency. *J. genet. Psychol.*, 1938, **53**, 75–86.

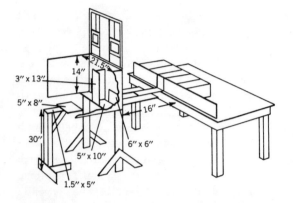

FIGURE 9   *(From E. C. Tolman.
Prediction of vicarious trial and error
by means of the schematic sowbug.*
Psychol. Rev., *1939,* **46,** *p. 319.)*

but with landing platforms in front of the doors so that if the rat chose incorrectly he could jump back again and start over, I found that when the choice was an easy one, say between a white door and a black door, the animals not only learned sooner but also did more VTEing than when the choice was difficult, say between a white door and a gray door (see Figure 10). It appeared further (see Figure 11) that the VTEing began to appear just as (or just before) the rats began to learn. After the learning had become established, however, the VTE's began to go down. Further, in a study of individual differences by myself, Geier and Levin[2] (actually done by Geier and Levin) using this same visual discrimination apparatus, it was found that

[2] F. M. Geier, M. Levin & E. C. Tolman, Individual differences in emotionality, hypothesis formation, vicarious trial and error and visual discrimination learning in rats. *Comp. Psychol. Monogr.*, 1941, 17, No. 3.

with one and the same difficulty of problem the smarter animal did the more VTEing.

To sum up, in *visual discrimination* experiments the better the learning, the more the VTE's. But this seems contrary to what we would perhaps have expected. We ourselves would expect to do more VTEing, more sampling of the two stimuli, when it is difficult to choose between them than when it is easy.

What is the explanation? The answer lies, I believe, in the fact that the manner in which we set the visual discrimination problems for the rats and the manner in which we set similar problems for ourselves are different. We already have our "instructions." We know beforehand what it is we are to do. We are told, or we tell ourselves, that it is the lighter of the two grays, the heavier of the two weights, or

Learning curves, average number
of correct runs per day

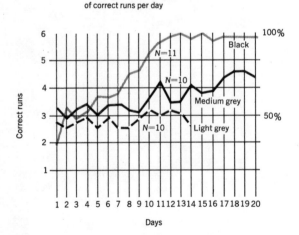

Days

FIGURE 10   *(From E. C. Tolman.
Prediction of vicarious trial and error
by means of the schematic sowbug.*
Psychol. Rev. *1939,* **46,** *p. 319.)*

the like, which is to be chosen. In such a setting we do more sampling, more VTE-ing, when the stimulus-difference is small. But for the rats the usual problem in a discrimination apparatus is quite different. They do not know what is wanted of them. The major part of their learning in most such experiments seems to consist in their discovering the instructions. The rats have to discover that it is the differences in visual brightness, not the differences between left and right, which they are to pay attention to. Their VTEing appears when they begin to "catch on." The greater the difference between the two stimuli the more the animals are attracted by this difference. Hence the sooner they catch on, and during this catching on, the more they VTE.

That this is a reasonable interpretation appeared further, from an experiment by myself and Minium (the actual work done, of course, by Minium) in which a group of six rats was first taught a white vs. black discrimination, then two successively more difficult gray vs. black discriminations. For each difficulty the rats were given a long series of further trials beyond the points at which they had learned. Comparing the beginning of each of these three difficulties the results were that the rats did more VTEing for the easy discriminations than for the more difficult ones. When, however, it came to a comparison of amounts of VTEing during the final performance after each learning had reached a plateau, the

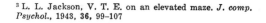

Average number of VTE's per day

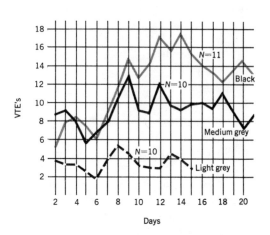

Days

FIGURE 11   *(From E. C. Tolman. Prediction of vicarious trial and error by means of the schematic sowbug.* Psychol. Rev., *1939,* **46,** *p. 320.)*

opposite results were obtained. In other words, after the rats had finally divined their instruction, then they, like human beings, did more VTEing, more sampling, the more difficult the discrimination.

Finally, now let us note that it was also found at Berkeley by Jackson[3] that in a maze the difficult maze units produce more VTEing and also that the more stupid rats do the more VTEing. The explanation, as I see it, is that, in the case of mazes, rats know their instructions. For them it is natural to expect that the same

[3] L. L. Jackson, V. T. E. on an elevated maze. *J. comp. Psychol.,* 1943, **36,** 99–107

FIGURE 12   *(From E. C. Tolman and E. Minium. VTE in rats: overlearning and difficulty of discrimination.* J. comp. Psychol., *1942, 34, p. 303.)*

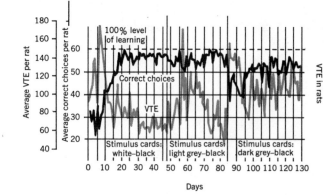

Days

spatial path will always lead to the same outcome. Rats in mazes don't have to be told.

But what, now, is the final significance of all the VTEing? How do these facts about VTEing affect our theoretical argument? My answer is that these facts lend further support to the doctrine of a building up of maps. VTEing, as I see it, is evidence that in the critical stages—whether in the first picking up of the instructions or in the later making sure of which stimulus is which—the animal's activity is not just one of responding passively to discrete stimuli, but rather one of the active selecting and comparing of stimuli. This brings me then to the third type of experiment.

3. "SEARCHING FOR THE STIMULUS" I refer to a recent, and it seems to me extremely important experiment, done for a Ph.D. dissertation by Hudson. Hudson was first interested in the question of whether or not rats could learn an avoidance reaction in one trial. His animals were tested one at a time in a living cage (see Figure 13) with a small striped visual pattern at

FIGURE 13 *(From Bradford Hudson. Ph.D. Thesis: One trial learning: A study of the avoidance behavior of the rat. On deposit in the Library of the University of California, Berkeley, Calif.)*

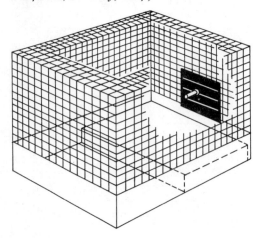

the end, on which was mounted a food cup. The hungry rat approached this food cup and ate. An electrical arrangement was provided so that when the rat touched the cup he could be given an electric shock. And one such shock did appear to be enough. For when the rat was replaced in this same cage days or even weeks afterwards, he usually demonstrated immediately strong avoidance reactions to the visual pattern. The animal withdrew from that end of the cage, or piled up sawdust and covered the pattern, or showed various other amusing responses all of which were in the nature of withdrawing from the pattern or making it disappear.

But the particular finding which I am interested in now appeared as a result of a modification of this standard procedure. Hudson noticed that the animals, anthropomorphically speaking, often seemed to look around *after* the shock to see what it was that had hit them. Hence it occurred to him that, if the pattern were made to disappear the instant the shock occurred, the rats might not establish association. And this indeed is what happened in the case of many individuals. Hudson added further electrical connections so that when the shock was received during the eating, the lights went out, the pattern and the food cup dropped out of sight, and the lights came on again all within the matter of a second. When such animals were again put in the cage 24 hours later, a large percentage showed no avoidance of the pattern. Or to quote Hudson's own words:

Learning what object to avoid . . . may occur exclusively during the period *after* the shock. For if the object from which the shock was actually received is removed at the moment of the shock, a significant number of animals fail to learn to avoid it, some selecting other features in the environment for avoidance, and others avoiding nothing.

In other words, I feel that this experiment reinforces the notion of the largely

active selective character in the rat's building up of his cognitive map. He often has
to look actively for the significant stimuli
in order to form his map and does not
merely passively receive and react to all
the stimuli which are physically present.
Turn now to the fourth type of experiment.

4. THE "HYPOTHESIS" EXPERIMENTS Both
the notion of hypotheses in rats and the
design of the experiments to demonstrate
such hypotheses are to be credited to
Krech. Krech used a four-compartment
discrimination-box. In such a four-choice
box the correct door at each choice-point
may be determined by the experimenter in
terms of its being lighted or dark, left or
right, or various combinations of these. If
all possibilities are randomized for the 40
choices made in 10 runs of each day's test,
the problem could be made insoluble.

When this was done, Krech found that
the individual rat went through a succession of systematic choices. That is, the
individual animal might perhaps begin
by choosing practically all right-hand
doors, then he might give this up for
choosing practically all left-hand doors,
and then, for choosing all dark doors, and
so on. These relatively persistent, and well-
above-chance systematic types of choice
Krech called "hypotheses." In using this
term he obviously did not mean to imply
verbal processes in the rat but merely referred to what I have been calling cognitive
maps, which, it appears from his experiments, get set up in a tentative fashion to
be tried out first one and then another
until, if possible, one is found which works.

Finally, it is to be noted that these
hypothesis experiments, like the latent
learning, VTE, and "looking for the stimulus" experiments, do not, as such, throw
light upon the widths of the maps which
are picked up but do indicate the generally
map-like and self-initiated character of
learning.

For the beginning of an attack upon the

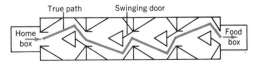

FIGURE 14   *(From I. Krechevsky (now
D. Krech). The genesis of "hypotheses"
in rats.* Univ. Calif. Publ. Psychol.,
1932, **6,** *No. 4, p. 46.)*

problem of the width of the maps let me
turn to the last group of experiments.

5. "SPATIAL ORIENTATION" EXPERIMENTS
As early as 1929, Lashley reported incidentally the case of a couple of his rats
who, after having learned an alley maze,
pushed back the cover near the starting
box, climbed out and ran directly across
the top to the goal-box where they climbed
down in again and ate. Other investigators
have reported related findings. All such
observations suggest that rats really develop wider spatial maps which include
more than the mere trained-on specific
paths. In the experiments now to be reported this possibility has been subjected
to further examination.

In the first experiment, Tolman, Ritchie,
and Kalish (actually Ritchie and Kalish)
used the set-up shown in Figure 15.

This was an elevated maze. The animals ran from A across the open circular
table through CD (which had alley walls)
and finally to G, the food box. H was a
light which shone directly down the path
from G to F. After four nights, three trials
per night, in which the rats learned to run
directly and without hesitation from A to
G, the apparatus was changed to the sun-
burst shown in Figure 16. The starting
path and the table remained the same but
a series of radiating paths was added.

The animals were again started at A and
ran across the circular table into the alley
and found themselves blocked. They then
returned onto the table and began exploring practically all the radiating paths.
After going out a few inches only on any

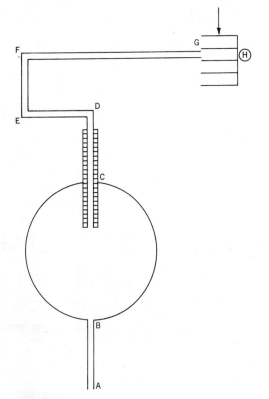

FIGURE 15 *Apparatus used in preliminary training. (From E. C. Tolman. B. F. Ritchie and D. Kalish, Studies in spatial learning. I. Orientation and the short-cut. J. exp. Psychol., 1946, 36, p. 16.)*

one path, each rat finally chose to run all the way out on one. The percentages of rats finally choosing each of the long paths from 1 to 12 are shown in Figure 17. It appears that there was a preponderant tendency to choose path No. 6 which ran to a point some four inches in front of where the entrance to the food-box had been. The only other path chosen with any appreciable frequency was No. 1—that is, the path which pointed perpendicularly to the food-side of the room.

These results seem to indicate that the rats in this experiment had learned not only to run rapidly down the original roundabout route but also, when this was blocked and radiating paths presented, to select one pointing rather directly towards

the point where the food had been or else at least to select a path running perpendicularly to the food-side of the room.

As a result of their original training, the rats had, it would seem, acquired not merely a strip-map to the effect that the original specifically trained-on path led to food but, rather, a wider comprehensive map to the effect that food was located in such and such a direction in the room.

Consider now a further experiment done by Ritchie alone. This experiment tested still further the breadth of the spatial map which is acquired. In this further experiment the rats were again run across the table—this time to the arms of a simple T. (See Figure 18.)

Twenty-five animals were trained for seven days, 20 trials in all, to find food at F_1; and twenty-five animals were trained to find it at F_2. The L's in the diagram indicate lights. On the eighth day the starting path and table top were rotated through 180 degrees so that they were now in the position shown in Figure 19. The dotted lines represent the old position. And a series of radiating paths was

FIGURE 16 *Apparatus used in the test trial. (From E. C. Tolman, B. F. Ritchie and D. Kalish. Studies in spatial learning. I. Orientation and the short-cut. J. exp. Psychol., 1946, 36, p. 17.)*

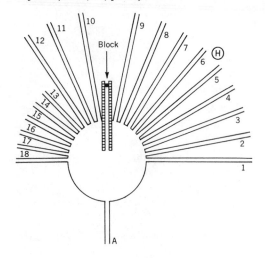

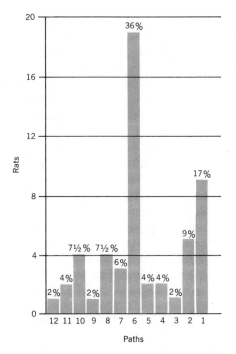

FIGURE 17 *Number of rats which chose each of the paths. (From E. C. Tolman, B. F. Ritchie and D. Kalish. Studies in spatial learning. I. Orientation and the short-cut. J. exp. Psychol., 1946, 36, p. 19.)*

added. What happened? Again the rats ran across the table into the central alley. When, however, they found themselves blocked, they turned back onto the table and this time also spent many seconds touching and trying out for only a few steps practically all the paths. Finally, however, within seven minutes, 42 of the 50 rats chose one path and ran all the way out on it. The paths finally chosen by the 19 of these animals that had been fed at F_1 and by the 23 that had been fed at F_2 are shown in Figure 20.

This time the rats tended to choose, not the paths which pointed directly to the spots where the food had been, but rather paths which ran perpendicularly to the corresponding sides of the room. The spatial maps of these rats, when the animals were started from the opposite side of the room, were thus not completely adequate

to the precise goal positions but were adequate as to the correct sides of the room. The maps of these animals were, in short, not altogether strip-like and narrow.

This completes my report of experiments. There were the *latent learning experiments, the VTE experiments, the searching for the stimulus experiment, the hypothesis experiments,* and these last *spatial orientation experiments.*

And now, at last, I come to the humanly significant and exciting problem: namely, what are the conditions which favor narrow strip-maps and what are those which tend to favor broad comprehensive maps not only in rats but also in men?

There is considerable evidence scattered throughout the literature bearing on this question both for rats and for men. Some of this evidence was obtained in Berkeley and some of it elsewhere. I have not time to present it in any detail. I can merely summarize it by saying that narrow strip

FIGURE 18 *(From B. F. Ritchie. Ph.D. Thesis: Spatial learning in rats. On deposit in the Library of the University of California, Berkeley, Calif.)*

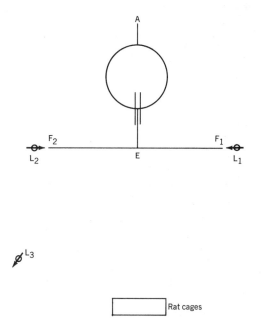

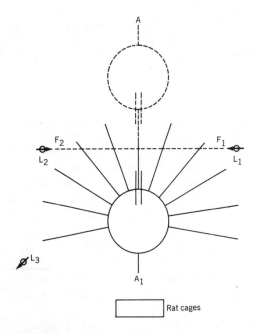

FIGURE 19   *(From B. F. Ritchie, Ph.D.*
Thesis: Spatial learning in rats. On
deposit in the Library of the University
of California, Berkeley, Calif.)

maps rather than broad comprehensive
maps seem to be induced: (1) by a dam-
aged brain, (2) by an inadequate array of
environmentally presented cues, (3) by an
overdose of repetitions on the original
trained-on path and (4) by the presence
of too strongly motivational or of too
strongly frustrating conditions.

It is this fourth factor which I wish to
elaborate upon briefly in my concluding
remarks. For it is going to be my contention that some, at least, of the so-called
"psychological mechanisms" which the
clinical psychologists and the other students of personality have uncovered as the
devils underlying many of our individual
and social maladjustments can be interpreted as narrowings of our cognitive maps
due to too strong motivations or to too
intense frustration.

My argument will be brief, cavalier, and
dogmatic. For I am not myself a clinician
or a social psychologist. What I am going

to say must be considered, therefore, simply as in the nature of a *rat* psychologist's
*rat*iocinations offered free. By way of illustration, let me suggest that at least the
three dynamisms called, respectively, "regression," "fixation," and "displacement of
aggression onto outgroups" are expressions
of cognitive maps which are too narrow
and which get built up in us as a result of
too violent motivation or of too intense
frustration.

a. Consider *regression*. This is the term
used for those cases in which an individual, in the face of too difficult a problem,
returns to earlier more childish ways of behaving. Thus, to take an example, the over-
protected middle-aged woman (reported a
couple of years ago in *Time Magazine*)
who, after losing her husband, regressed
(much to the distress of her growing daughters) into dressing in too youthful a fashion and into competing for their beaux and
then finally into behaving like a child requiring continuous care, would be an illustration of regression. I would not wish you
to put too much confidence in the repor-
torial accuracy of *Time,* but such an extreme case is not too different from many
actually to be found in our mental hospitals or even sometimes in ourselves. In
all such instances my argument would be
(1) that such regression results from too
strong a present emotional situation and
(2) that it consists in going back to too
narrow an earlier map, itself due to too
much frustration or motivation in early
childhood. *Time's* middle-aged woman was
presented by too frustrating an emotional
situation at her husband's death and she
regressed, I would wager, to too narrow
adolescent and childhood maps since these
latter had been originally excessively impressed because of over-stressful experiences at the time she was growing up.

b. Consider *fixation*. Regression and
fixation tend to go hand in hand. For another way of stating the fact of the undue
persistence of early maps is to say that

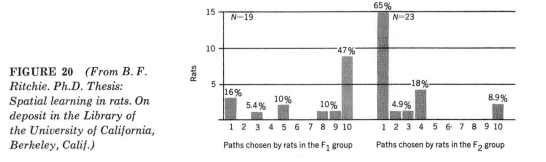

FIGURE 20   *(From B. F. Ritchie. Ph.D. Thesis: Spatial learning in rats. On deposit in the Library of the University of California, Berkeley, Calif.)*

they were fixated. This has even been demonstrated in rats. If rats are too strongly motivated in their original learning, they find it very difficult to relearn when the original path is no longer correct. Also after they have relearned, if they are given an electric shock they, like *Time's* woman, tend to regress back again to choosing the earlier path.

c. Finally, consider the *"displacement of aggressions onto outgroups."* Adherence to one's own group is an ever-present tendency among primates. It is found in chimpanzees and monkeys as strongly as in men. We primates operate in groups. And each individual in such a group tends to identify with his whole group in the sense that the group's goals become his goals, the group's life and immortality, his life and immortality. Furthermore, each individual soon learns that, when as an individual he is frustrated, he must not take out his aggressions on the other members of his own group. He learns instead to displace his aggressions onto outgroups. Such a displacement of aggression I would claim is also a narrowing of the cognitive map. The individual comes no longer to distinguish the true locus of the cause of his frustration. The poor Southern whites, who take it out on the Negroes, are displacing their aggressions from the landlords, the southern economic system, the northern capitalists, or wherever the true cause of their frustrations may lie, onto a more convenient outgroup. The physicists on the Faculty who criticize the humanities, or we psychologists who criticize all

the other departments, or the University as a whole which criticizes the Secondary School system or, vice versa, the Secondary School system which criticizes the University or—on a still larger and far more dangerous scene—we Americans who criticize the Russians and the Russians who criticize us, are also engaging, at least in part, in nothing more than such irrational displacements of our aggressions onto outgroups.

I do not mean to imply that there may not be some true interferences by the one group with the goals of the other and hence that the aggressions of the members of the one group against the members of the other are necessarily *wholly* and *merely* displaced aggressions. But I do assert that often and in large part they are such mere displacements.

Over and over again men are blinded by too violent motivations and too intense frustrations into blind and unintelligent and in the end desperately dangerous hates of outsiders. And the expression of these their displaced hates ranges all the way from discrimination against minorities to world conflagrations.

What in the name of Heaven and Psychology can we do about it? My only answer is to preach again the virtues of reason—of, that is, broad cognitive maps. And to suggest that the child-trainers and the world-planners of the future can only, if at all, bring about the presence of the required rationality (i.e., comprehensive maps) if they see to it that nobody's children are too over-motivated or too frustrated. Only then can these children learn to look before and after, learn to see that there are often round-about and safer paths to their quite proper goals—learn, that is, to realize that the well-being of White and of Negro, of Catholic and of Protestant, of Christian and of Jew, of American and of Russian (and even of males and females) are mutually inter-dependent.

We dare not let ourselves or others become so over-emotional, so hungry, so ill-clad, so over-motivated that only narrow strip-maps will be developed. All of us in Europe as well as in America, in the Orient as well as in the Occident, must be made calm enough and well-fed enough to be able to develop truly comprehensive maps, or, as Freud would have put it, to be able to learn to live according to the Reality Principle rather than according to the too narrow and too immediate Pleasure Principle.

We must, in short, subject our children and ourselves (as the kindly experimenter would his rats) to the optimal conditions of moderate motivation and of absence of unnecessary frustrations, whenever we put them and ourselves before that great God-given maze which is our human world. I cannot predict whether or not we will be able, or be allowed, to do this; but I *can* say that, only insofar as we *are* able and *are* allowed, have we cause for hope.

Can learning take place without the reinforcement of particular responses? Can associations be made between stimuli as well as between stimuli and responses? Is perceptual learning possible? This experiment seems to demonstrate that animals can learn the route through a maze simply by being pulled through it. They apparently learn to associate stimuli in the maze until they build up a "cognitive map."

GLOSSARY   **Water maze:** *a maze in which the animal swims instead of walks.* **S:** *the subject in an experiment.* **Hullian theory:** *a relatively sophisticated stimulus-response learning theory which can sometimes be extended to account for some types of apparent perceptual learning.*

16:   LEARNING WITHOUT SWIMMING IN A WATER MAZE

P. C. Dodwell and D. E. Bessant, Queen's University, Kingston, Ontario, Canada

Thorndike has outlined a program of experiments designed to establish or refute the validity of expectancy-type theories of learning (Thorndike, 1946). The experi-

P. C. Dodwell and D. E. Bessant. Learning without swimming in a water maze. *J. comp. physiol. Psychol.,* 1960, **53,** 422–425. Copyright © 1960 by the American Psychological Association. Reprinted here with permission from the authors and the American Psychological Association.

ments suggested by Thorndike are such that the subjects (animals) should, according to any expectancy theory, learn without actually performing any instrumental responses; he implies that, in his view, such experiments would yield negative results. One of his suggestions is:

Put the rat, in a little wire car, in the entrance chamber of a maze, run it through the correct path of a simple maze and into the food compartment. Release it there and let it eat the morsel provided. Repeat ten to a hundred times according to the difficulty of the maze under ordinary conditions. The rat has had an opportunity to form expectancies that presence in the food compartment is followed by food, that the last correct turn is followed by the food chamber, and so on. Then put it in the entrance chamber free to go wherever it is inclined and observe what it does. Compare the behavior of such rats with that of rats run in the customary manner (p. 278).

Several experiments (Bugelski, 1958; Gleitman, 1955; McNamara, Long, & Wike, 1956) have aimed at establishing whether learning can occur under conditions similar to those suggested in the above quotation. Gleitman investigated preferences of groups of rats for places at which previously (1) shock was started, (2) no shock was received, and (3) shock was terminated. He demonstrated a significant preference for (3) over (1) but not for (3) over (2) or for (2) over (1). Bugelski's results (not published in detail) were inconclusive, and those of McNamara, Long, and Wike demonstrated learning of an elevated T maze without performance, but only when extra-maze cues are present.

The two studies which yielded positive results are restricted to relatively simple situations. No demonstration has yet been given of the formation of "expectancies" in more complex mazes, where one might expect that "curiosity" drive could enter as an important variable (MacCorquodale & Meehl, 1954). In the absence of precise definition of the situations in which expectancies are supposed to be formed by rats, one could argue two possibilities: first, that expectancies are only formed in relatively simple choice situations, or secondly, that simple situations yield such rapid learning anyway that a very sensitive measure would be needed to show differences between "expectation" and "no expectation"

groups. Taking the first position, one would predict no learning without performance in a complex maze, and taking the second, that any effect of expectancies (provided they can be formed in complex choice situations) should be more easily measurable in a complex situation than in a simple one. It seemed worth investigating whether in fact learning without performance of instrumental responses could be demonstrated in a complex maze.

Method

APPARATUS A water maze with eight choice points was used (see Fig. 1). It appears that there is, generally, a rather sharp increase in maze difficulty for rats when eight choice points or more are present (Munn, 1950). The walls of the alleys (12 in. high) and the depth of water (5½ in.) were such that the rats could neither stand in an alley, nor jump out of it, with

FIGURE 1 *Diagram of the apparatus.*

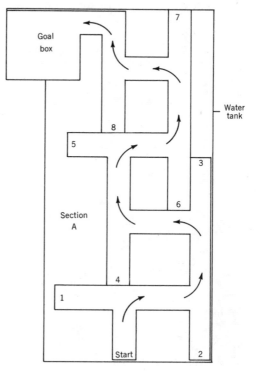

ease. A wooden trolley was constructed, 4½ in. long, 2¾ in. wide, and 5¾ in. high, with casters fixed to its underside, so that its upper surface was ¼ in. above the water when placed in the maze. It could be propelled through the maze with a long wooden handle (see Fig. 2).

SUBJECTS   The Ss were 16 male hooded rats of two different strains, which had previously been used in discrimination experiments with a Lashley-type jumping stand. The strains were Long-Evans, and an unknown strain from a local breeder; both types of rat were present in both experimental conditions, and there were no differences in the performances of the two strains.

PROCEDURE   The Ss were randomly assigned to two groups, experimental (E) and control (C). The control animals swam through the maze to a criterion of 3 errorless trials. Five trials were given in the first day of training, and the remaining trials on the second day. Intertrial inter-

vals within days were short; the animal was left for about a minute in the goal box after swimming the maze, and then replaced at the start. The experimental animals were propelled through the maze on the trolley, at approximately the swimming speed of a rat, for the mean number of trials required by the control group to learn the maze, i.e., 10. They then learned the maze by swimming through it in the ordinary way. Five trials riding the trolley were given on the first day, the second 5 riding trials and all swimming trials on the second day. Intertrial intervals and time in goal box were the same for riding as for swimming trials. The number of swimming trials required to reach the criterion, and the number of errors made, were recorded. Before learning the maze, Group C rats were run back and forth on the trolley in Section A of the maze (see Figure 1) 50 times, to ensure that both groups had approximately equal familiarity with the close proximity of water on the first swimming trials. In a preliminary test (with different rats) it had been established that

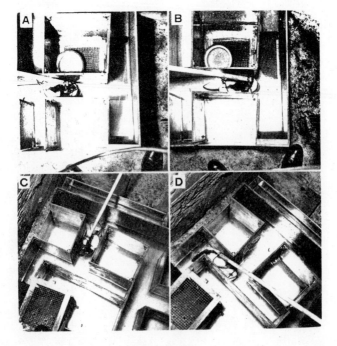

FIGURE 2.

rats prefer to sit on a raft rather than swim in 5½ in. of water. This does not mean that Group E was as well motivated to learn the maze as Group C, but it indicates that they were motivated to avoid being in the maze, which is further demonstrated by the fact that they invariably left the trolley on arrival at the goal box.

Results

The learning of Group E was superior to that of Group C, both in terms of number of trials and of errors. The mean numbers of trials for the C and E groups were 9.6 (range, 8 to 11) and 5.6 (range, 4 to 7), respectively, and the mean number of errors 96.4 (range 55 to 130) and 18.9 (range, 10 to 45), respectively. Since the distributions are mutually exclusive in both cases no statistical test of the significance of this result was deemed necessary.

The behavior of the two groups differed considerably, especially in the first two or three swims through the maze. Whereas Group C rats swam through the maze vigorously from the start, Group E showed characteristic "startle" behavior, remaining still for long periods and then moving jerkily through the maze. They also tended to jump out of the maze much more frequently than control rats; no correlation was found between learning scores and number of jumps out of the maze in Group E, so it appears unlikely that this was an important factor in the over-all superiority of the experimental group. Jumps out of the maze are included as errors in the numbers cited above. If they were not included, the error score would differentiate the two groups even more sharply, since jumps out of the maze were very infrequent in Group C (less than 1 per rat, compared with a mean of 8.3 per rat in Group E).

The behavior of Group E rats on the trolley was interesting. After the first three or four trials they showed definite anticipation of the next correct turn in the maze. Not only did they very frequently turn their heads in the correct direction at, or just before, each choice point, but also this behavior became more marked as the goal box was approached: the rats moved up to the front of the trolley, and in some cases jumped off the trolley into the water just before the goal box was reached. Figure 2, A through D, illustrates this behavior. No quantitative measure of the number of correct anticipations was made, but the phenomenon is very striking, and was found in all rats in Group E.

Discussion

Clearly the Group E rats were making responses while on the trolley, so it is arguable that learning without performance has not been demonstrated. However, these responses were not instrumental, and since the experimental design satisfies Thorndike's paradigm, we may assert that performance (of instrumental responses) is not a necessary condition of learning the maze, and that "expectancies" can be formed in their absence. The head-turning and subsequent rapid learning of the maze both support this assertion. The rats used in this experiment were experimentally sophisticated and had been trained in visual discrimination. This may have induced more searching for visual cues than would be found in naïve animals. However, theories of expectancy learning make no specific requirements vis-a-vis sophistication, and a Hullian-type theory would require performance for learning to occur, no matter how sophisticated the *S*s. It should be noted that, in a sense, the head-turning was a performance which was (fortuitously) reinforced, hence a Hullian might argue that the findings here reported could in fact be predicted from Hull's theory. The logical fallacies involved in this sort of argument have been exposed by Deutsch (1956).

No attempt was made to eliminate extra-maze cues; this may be an important factor, and undoubtedly the nature of the anticipations formed would be better understood if some control over such cues had been exercised. By far the most frequently entered blind alley for Group E was Number 5, which indicates that apart from being able to make specific anticipations at a choice point, they also had a "general notion" of the position of the goal box. It also indicates that the findings cannot be explained in terms of a "curiosity" drive; if faster learning were due simply to lack of curiosity about blind alleys already inspected from the trolley, there should be no differential tendency to enter some blind alleys rather than others. It is concluded, therefore, that rats previously trained in visual discriminations can subsequently form "expectancies" in a moderately complex maze when no instrumental responses are elicited, and that these "expectancies" significantly affect the speed with which the correct maze path can be learned. The writers have not, as yet, attempted to demonstrate the phenomenon with naïve rats.

Summary

An experiment was performed with two groups of rats, one of which was allowed to learn a moderately complex maze by swimming through it in the ordinary way, the other being run through the maze on a trolley before learning to swim through. The number of runs through on the trolley for each rat in the second group was equal to the mean number of trials required to learn the maze by the first group. On subsequently learning to swim through the maze, the second group showed significantly better performance than the first, both in terms of the number of trials needed and the number of errors made. This finding is held to support the contention that learning can occur, by the formation of "expectancies," without the elicitation of instrumental responses.

References

Bugelski, B. R. Psychology of learning. New York: Holt, 1958.

Deutsch, J. A. The inadequacy of the Hullian derivations of reasoning and latent learning. Psychol. Rev., 1956, 63, 389–399.

Gleitman, H. Place learning without prior performance. J. comp. physiol. Psychol., 1955, 48, 77–79.

Hilgard, E. R. Theories of learning. New York: Appleton-Century-Crofts, 1956.

McNamara, H. J., Long, J. B., & Wike, E. L. Place learning without performance. J. comp. physiol. Psychol., 1956, 49, 477–480.

MacCorquodale, K., & Meehl, P. E. Edward C. Tolman. In W. K. Estes, K. MacCorquodale, P. E. Meehl, C. G. Mueller, Jr., W. N. Schoenfeld, & W. S. Verplanck (Eds.), Modern learning theory. New York: Appleton-Century-Crofts, 1954.

Munn, N. L. Handbook of psychological research on the rat. New York: Houghton Mifflin, 1950.

Thorndike, E. K. Expectation. Psychol. Rev., 1946, 53, 277–281.

Learning sets are interesting phenomena which may provide a stimulus-response explanation for some of the results of experiments on insight. One indication of insight is a sudden decrease in the number of errors made on a problem. In the learning set, or learning-to-learn situation, after enough problems have been presented, a sharp decrease in the number of errors also occurs. Compare the curve for problems 1 to 8 with that for problems 257 to 312 in Figure 2. Suppose that, unknown to us, we had a subject who had had a good deal of preliminary practice. If we put him in a situation where this learning could transfer, he would soon be doing perfectly. In other words, he would seem to show insight.

A POINT TO GUIDE YOUR STUDY   *Note that most of the figures have "problems" rather than "trials" plotted on the abscissa. These figures always have "per cent correct responses" plotted on the ordinate. When "problems" are plotted on the abscissa, the ordinate "per cent correct responses" usually means correct responses on trial 2, or trials 2 to 6, of a problem. If the subject has learned that "this is a discrimination problem," i.e., that one of the objects is correct and the other incorrect, he may make a mistake on the first trial of a problem because he does not yet know which is correct and which is incorrect. On trials 2 to 6, however, he will switch to the other response if he has the learning set and if he made an incorrect response on trial 1. If he has the learning set and is correct on trial 1, he will persist in that response on trials 2 to 6. Thus, if the subject has the learning set, all responses on trials 2 to 6 should be correct.*

17: THE FORMATION OF LEARNING SETS

Harry F. Harlow, University of Wisconsin

In most psychological ivory towers there will be found an animal laboratory. The scientists who live there think of themselves as theoretical psychologists, since they obviously have no other rationalization to explain their extravagantly paid and idyllic sinecures. These theoretical psychologists have one great advantage over those psychological citizens who study men and women. The theoreticians can subject their subhuman animals, be they rats, dogs, or monkeys, to more rigorous controls than can ordinarily be exerted over human beings. The obligation of the theoretical psychologist is to discover general laws of behavior applicable to mice, monkeys, and men. In this obligation the theoretical psychologist has often failed. His deductions frequently have had no

generality beyond the species which he has studied, and his laws have been so limited that attempts to apply them to man have resulted in confusion rather than clarification.

One limitation of many experiments on subhuman animals is the brief period of time the subjects have been studied. In the typical problem, 48 rats are arranged in groups to test the effect of three different intensities of stimulation operating in conjunction with two different motivational conditions upon the formation of *an isolated* conditioned response. A brilliant Blitzkrieg research is effected—the controls are perfect, the results are important, and the rats are dead.

If this *do and die* technique were applied widely in investigations with human subjects, the results would be appalling. But of equal concern to the psychologist should be the fact that the derived general laws would be extremely limited in their application. There are experiments in which the use of naïve subjects is justified, but the psychological compulsion to follow this

This paper was presented as the presidential address of the Midwestern Psychological Association meetings in St. Paul, May 7, 1948. The researches described were supported in part by grants from the Special Research Fund of the University of Wisconsin for 1944–48.

H. F. Harlow. The formation of learning sets. *Psychol. Rev.*, 1949, **56**, 51–65. Copyright © 1949 by the American Psychological Association. Reprinted here with permission from the author and the American Psychological Association.

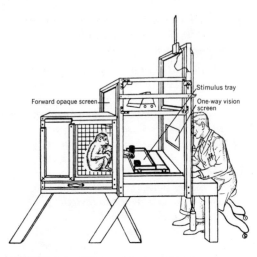

FIGURE 1 *Wisconsin general test apparatus.*

design indicates that frequently the naïve animals are to be found on both sides of the one-way vision screen.

The variety of learning situations that play an important rôle in determining our basic personality characteristics and in changing some of us into thinking animals are repeated many times in similar form. The behavior of the human being is not to be understood in terms of the results of single learning situations but rather in terms of the changes which are affected through multiple, though comparable, learning problems. Our emotional, personal, and intellectual characteristics are not the mere algebraic summation of a near infinity of stimulus-response bonds. The learning of primary importance to the primates, at least, is the formation of learning sets; it is the *learning how to learn efficiently* in the situations the animal frequently encounters. This learning to learn transforms the organism from a creature that adapts to a changing environment by trial and error to one that adapts by seeming hypothesis and insight.

The rat psychologists have largely ignored this fundamental aspect of learning and, as a result, this theoretical domain remains a *terra incognita*. If learning

sets are the mechanisms which, in part, transform the organism from a conditioned response robot to a reasonably rational creature, it may be thought that the mechanisms are too intangible for proper quantification. Any such presupposition is false. It is the purpose of this paper to demonstrate the extremely orderly and quantifiable nature of the development of certain learning sets and, more broadly, to indicate the importance of learning sets to the development of intellectual organization and personality structure.

The apparatus used throughout the studies subsequently referred to is illustrated in Figure 1. The monkey responds by displacing one of two stimulus-objects covering the food-wells in the tray before him. An opaque screen is interposed between the monkey and the stimulus situation between trials and a one-way vision screen separates monkey and man during trials.

The first problem chosen for the investigation of learning sets was the object-quality discrimination learning problem. The monkey was required to choose the rewarded one of two objects differing in multiple characteristics and shifting in the left-right positions in a predetermined balanced order. A series of 344 such problems using 344 different pairs of stimuli was run on a group of eight monkeys. Each of the first 32 problems was run for 50 trials; the next 200 problems for six trials; and the last 112 problems for an average of nine trials.

In Figure 2 are presented learning curves which show the per cent of correct responses on the first six trials of these discriminations. The data for the first 32 discriminations are grouped for blocks of eight problems, and the remaining discriminations are arranged in blocks of 100, 100, 56, and 56 problems. The data indicate that the subjects progressively improve in their ability to learn object-quality discrimination problems. The monkeys *learn how to learn* individual problems with a minimum of errors. It is this *learning how to learn a kind of problem* that we designate by the term *learning set.*

The very form of the learning curve changes as learning sets become more efficient. The form of the learning curve for the first eight discrimination problems appears S-shaped: it could be described as a curve of "trial-and-error" learning. The curve for the last 56 problems approaches linearity after Trial 2. Curves of similar form have been described as indicators of "insightful" learning.

We wish to emphasize that this *learning to learn,* this *transfer from problem to problem* which we call the formation of a learning set, is a highly *predictable, orderly* process which can be demonstrated as long as controls are maintained over the subjects' experience and the difficulty of the problems. Our subjects, when they started these researches, had no previous laboratory learning experience. Their entire discrimination learning set history was obtained in this study. The stimulus pairs employed had been arranged and their serial order determined from tables of random numbers. Like nonsense syllables, the stimulus pairs were equated for difficulty. It is unlikely that any group of problems differed significantly in intrinsic difficulty from any other group.

In a conventional learning curve we plot change of performance over a series of *trials;* in a learning set curve we plot change in performance over a series of *problems.* It is important to remember that *we measure learning set in terms of problems* just as *we measure habit in terms of trials.*

Figure 3 presents a discrimination learning set curve showing a progressive increase in the per cent of correct responses on Trials 2–6 on successive blocks of problems. This curve appears to be negatively accelerated or possibly linear.

Discrimination learning set curves ob-

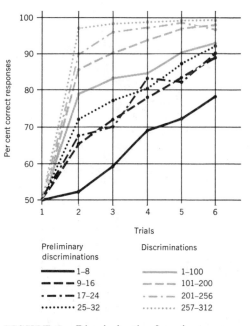

FIGURE 2 *Discrimination learning curves on successive blocks of problems.*

tained on four additional naïve normal monkeys and eight naïve monkeys with extensive unilateral cortical lesions, are shown in Figure 4. Brain-injured as well as normal monkeys are seen to form effective discrimination learning sets, although the partial hemidecorticate monkeys are less efficient than the normal subjects. Im-

FIGURE 3 *Discrimination learning set curve based on Trial 2–6 responses.*

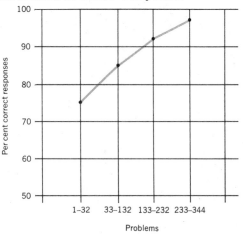

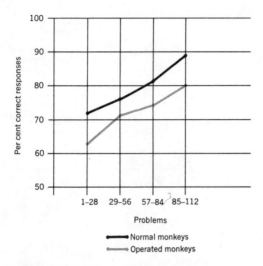

FIGURE 4 *Discrimination learning set curves based on Trial 2–6 responses: normal and operated monkeys.*

provement for both groups is progressive and the fluctuations that occur may be attributed to the small number of subjects and the relatively small number of problems, 14, included in each of the problem blocks presented on the abscissa.

Through the courtesy of Dr. Margaret Kuenne we have discrimination learning set data on another primate species. These animals were also run on a series of six-trial discrimination problems but under slightly different conditions. Macaroni beads and toys were substituted for food rewards, and the subjects were tested sans iron-barred cages. The data for these 17 children, whose ages range from two to five years and whose intelligence quotients range from 109 to 151, are presented in Figure 5. Learning set curves are plotted for groups of children attaining a predetermined learning criterion within differing numbers of problem blocks. In spite of the small number of cases and the behavioral vagaries that are known to characterize this primate species, the learning set curves are orderly and lawful and show progressive increase in per cent of correct responses.

Learning set curves, like learning curves, can be plotted in terms of correct responses or errors on any trial or total trials. A measure which we have frequently used is per cent of correct Trial 2 responses—the behavioral measure of the amount learned on Trial 1.

Figure 6 shows learning set curves measured in terms of the per cent correct Trial 2 responses for the 344-problem series. The data from the first 32 preliminary discriminations and the 312 subsequent discriminations have been plotted separately. As one might expect, these learning set curves are similar to those that have been previously

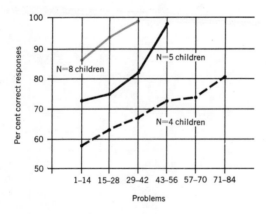

FIGURE 5 *Discrimination learning set curves based on Trial 2–6 responses: children*

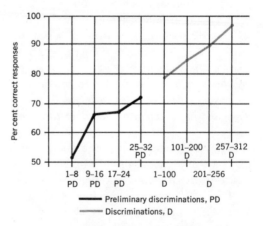

FIGURE 6 *Discrimination learning set curve based on Trial 2 responses.*

presented. What the curves show with especial clarity is the almost unbelievable change which has taken place in the *effectiveness of the first training trial.* In the initial eight discriminations, this single paired stimulus presentation brings the Trial 2 performance of the monkeys to a level less than three per cent above chance; in the last 56 discriminations, this first training trial brings the performance of the monkeys to a level *less than three per cent* short of perfection. Before the formation of a discrimination learning set, a single training trial produces negligible gain; after the formation of a discrimination learning set, *a single training trial constitutes problem solution.* These data clearly show that *animals can gradually learn insight.*

In the final phase of our discrimination series with monkeys there were subjects that solved from 20 to 30 consecutive problems with no errors whatsoever following the first blind trial—and many of the children, after the first day or two of training, did as well or better.

These data indicate the function of a learning set in converting a problem which is initially difficult for a subject into a problem which is so simple as to be immediately solvable. The learning set is the mechanism that changes the problem from an intellectual tribulation into an intellectual triviality and leaves the organism free to attack problems of another hierarchy of difficulty.

For the analysis of learning sets in monkeys on a problem that is ostensibly at a more complex level than the discrimination problem, we choose the discrimination reversal problem. The procedure was to run the monkeys on a discrimination problem for 7, 9, or 11 trials and then to reverse the reward value of the stimuli for eight trials; that is to say, the stimulus previously correct was made incorrect and the stimulus previously incorrect became correct.

The eight monkeys previously trained

on discrimination learning were tested on a series of 112 discrimination reversal problems. Discrimination reversal learning curves for successive blocks of 28 problems are shown in Figure 7. The measure used is per cent of correct responses on Reversal Trials 2 to 6. Figure 8 presents data on the formation of the discrimination reversal learning set in terms of the per cent of correct responses on Reversal Trial 2 for successive blocks of 14 problems. Reversal Trial 2 is the first trial following the "informing" trial, i.e., the initial trial reversing the reward value of the stimuli. Reversal Trial 2 is the measure of the effectiveness with which the single informing trial leads the subject to abandon a reaction pattern which has proved correct for 7 to 11 trials, and to initiate a new reaction pattern to the stimulus pair. On the last 42 discrimination reversal problems the monkeys were responding as efficiently on Reversal Trial 2 as they were on complementary Discrimination Trial 2, i.e., they were making over 97 per cent correct responses on both aspects of the prob-

FIGURE 7 *Discrimination reversal learning curves on successive blocks of problems.*

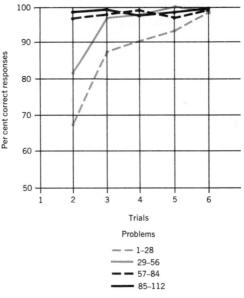

Trials

Problems
- - - 1–28
——— 29–56
▬ ▬ 57–84
▬▬▬ 85–112

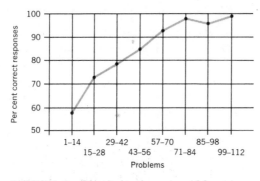

FIGURE 8 *Discrimination reversal learning set curve based on Trial 2 responses.*

lems. The eight monkeys made from 12 to 57 successive correct second trial reversal responses. Thus it becomes perfectly obvious that at the end of this problem the monkeys possessed sets both to learn and to reverse a reaction tendency, and that this behavior could be consistently and immediately elicited with hypothesis-like efficiency.

This terminal performance level is likely to focus undue attention on the one-trial learning at the expense of the earlier, less efficient performance levels. It should be kept in mind that this one-trial learning

FIGURE 9 *Discrimination reversal and discrimination learning set curves based on Trial 2 responses.*

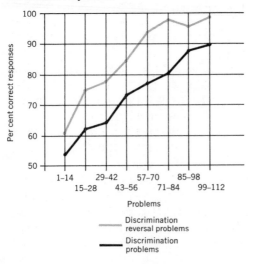

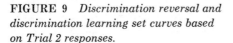

appeared only as the end result of an orderly and progressive learning process; insofar as these subjects are concerned, the insights are only to be understood in an historical perspective.

Although the discrimination reversal problems might be expected to be more difficult for the monkeys than discrimination problems, the data of Figure 9 indicate that the discrimination reversal learning set was formed more rapidly than the previously acquired discrimination learning set. The explanation probably lies in the nature of the transfer of training from the discrimination learning to the discrimination reversal problems. A detailed analysis of the discrimination learning data indicates the operation throughout the learning series of certain error-producing factors, but with each successive block of problems the frequencies of errors attributable to these factors are progressively decreased, although at different rates and to different degrees. The process might be conceived of as a learning of response tendencies that counteract the error-producing factors. A description of the reduction of the error-producing factors is beyond the scope of this paper, even though we are of the opinion that this type of analysis is basic to an adequate theory of discrimination learning.

Suffice it to say that there is reason to believe that there is a large degree of transfer from the discrimination series to the reversal series, of the learned response tendencies counteracting the operation of two of the three primary error-producing factors thus far identified.

The combined discrimination and discrimination reversal data show clearly how the learning set delivers the animal from Thorndikian bondage. By the time the monkey has run 232 discriminations and followed these by 112 discriminations and reversals, he does not possess 344 or 456 specific habits, bonds, connections or associations. We doubt if our monkeys at this time could respond with much more than chance efficiency on the first trial of any series of the previously learned problems. But the monkey does have a generalized ability to learn *any* discrimination problem or *any* discrimination reversal problem with the greatest of ease. Training on several hundred specific problems has not turned the monkey into an automaton exhibiting forced, stereotyped, reflex responses to specific stimuli. These several hundred habits have, instead, made the monkey an adjustable creature with an *increased capacity* to adapt to the ever-changing demands of a psychology laboratory environment.

We believe that other learning sets acquired in and appropriate to the monkey's natural environment would enable him to adapt better to the changing conditions there. We are certain, moreover, that learning sets acquired by man in and appropriate to his environment have accounted for his ability to adapt and survive.

Before leaving the problem of discrimination reversal learning we submit one additional set of data that we feel merits attention. Nine of the children previously referred to were also subjected to a series of discrimination reversal problems. The outcome is partially indicated in Figure 10 which shows the per cent of correct Reversal Trial 2 responses made on successive blocks of 14 problems. It can be seen that these three- to five-year-old children clearly bested the monkeys in performance on this series of problems. Trial 2 responses approach perfection in the second block of 14 discrimination reversal problems. Actually, over half of the total Trial 2 errors were made by one child.

These discrimination reversal data on the children are the perfect illustration of set formation and transfer producing adaptable abilities rather than specific bonds. Without benefit of the monkey's discrimination reversal set learning curves we might be tempted to assume that the

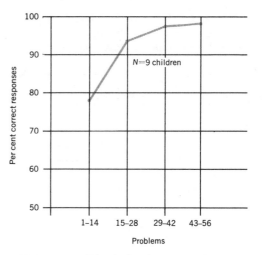

FIGURE 10 *Discrimination reversal learning set curve based on Trial 2 responses: children.*

children's data indicate a gulf between human and subhuman learning. But the *extremely rapid* learning on the part of the children is not unlike the *rapid* learning on the part of the monkeys, and analysis of the error-producing factors shows that the same basic mechanisms are operating in both species.

Following the discrimination reversal problem the eight monkeys were presented a new series of 56 problems designed to elicit alternation of unequivocally antagonistic response patterns. The first 7, 9, or 11 trials of each problem were simple object-quality discrimination trials. These were followed immediately by ten right-position discrimination trials with the same stimuli continuing to shift in the right-left positions in predetermined orders. In the first 7 to 11 trials, a particular object was correct regardless of its position. In the subsequent 10 trials, a particular position—the experimenter's right position—was correct, regardless of the object placed there. Thus to solve the problem the animal had to respond to object-quality cues and disregard position cues in the first 7 to 11 trials and, following the failure of reward of the previously rewarded

FIGURE 11 *Learning set curves for problem requiring shift from object-quality discrimination to right-position discrimination.*

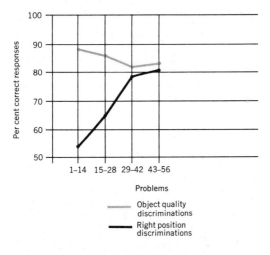

Problems

Object quality discriminations

Right position discriminations

object, he had to disregard object-quality cues and respond to position cues.

The learning data on these two antagonistic tasks are presented in Figure 11. It is to be noted that the object-quality curve, which is based on Trials 1 to 7, begins at a very high level of accuracy, whereas the position curve, plotted for Trials 1 to 10, begins at a level little above chance. This no doubt reflects the operation of the

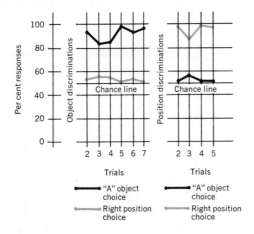

Trials   Trials

"A" object choice   "A" object choice

Right position choice   Right position choice

FIGURE 12 *Object and position choices following initial errors on both phases of object-position shift series, based on Problems 42–56.*

previously well-established object-quality discrimination learning set. As the series continues, the object-quality curve shows a drop until the last block of problems, while the position curve rises progressively. In the evaluation of these data, it should be noted that chance performance is 50 per cent correct responses for the object-quality discriminations and 45 per cent for the position discriminations, since each sequence of 10 position trials includes an error "informing" trial. It would appear that the learning of the right-position discriminations interferes with the learning of the object-quality discriminations to some extent. In spite of this decrement in object-quality discrimination performance for a time, the subjects were functioning at levels far beyond chance on the antagonistic parts of the problems during the last half of the series. We believe that this behavior reflects the formation of a right-position learning set which operates at a high degree of independence of the previously established object-quality discrimination learning set.

The precision of the independent operation of these learning sets throughout the last 14 problems is indicated in Figure 12. Since the right-position part of the problem was almost invariably initiated by an error trial, these data are limited to those problems on which the first trial object-quality discrimination response was incorrect. The per cent of correct Trial 7 responses to the "A" object, the correct stimulus for the object-quality discriminations, is 98. The initiating error trial which occurs when the problem shifts without warning to a right-position problem, drops this per cent response to the "A" object to 52—a level barely above chance. The per cent of Trial 7 responses to the right position during the object-quality discriminations is 52. The single error trial initiating the shift of the problem to a right-position discrimination is followed by 97 per cent right-position responses on the next trial.

In other words, *it is as though* the outcome of a single *push of an object* is adequate to switch off the "A"-object choice reaction tendency and to switch on the right-position choice reaction tendency.

The cue afforded by a single trial produces at this point almost complete discontinuity of the learning process. The only question now left unsettled in the controversy over hypotheses in subhuman animals is whether or not to use this term to describe the behavior of a species incapable of verbalization.

Again, it should be remembered that both the object-quality discrimination learning set and the right-position discrimination learning set developed in a gradual and orderly manner. Only after the learning sets are formed do these phenomena of discontinuity in learned behavior appear.

Further evidence for the integrity of learning sets is presented in an additional experiment. Six monkeys with object-quality discrimination learning experience, but without training on reversal problems or position discriminations, were given seven blocks of 14 problems each, starting with a block of 25-trial object-quality discriminations, followed by a block of 14 25-trial positional discriminations composed of right-position and left-position problems presented alternately. The remaining five blocks of problems continued the alternate presentation of 14 object-quality discrimination problems and 14 right-left positional discrimination problems. Figure 13 presents curves showing the per cent of correct responses on total trials on these alternate blocks of antagonistic discriminations. The complex positional discrimination learning set curve shows progressive improvement throughout the series, whereas the object-quality discrimination curve begins at a high level of accuracy, shows decrement on the second block, and subsequently recovers. By the end of the experiment the two basically

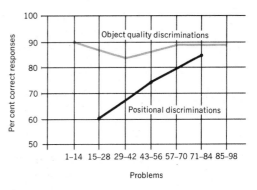

FIGURE 13 *Learning set curves for problem series with alternating object-quality and positional discriminations, based on total trial responses.*

antagonistic learning sets had "learned" to live together with a minimum of conflict. These data are the more striking if it is recalled that between each two blocks of object-quality discriminations there were 350 trials in which no object was differentially rewarded, and between each two blocks of 14 positional discriminations there were 350 trials in which no position was differentially rewarded.

In Figure 14 we present additional total-trial data on the formation of the positional learning set. These data show the change in performance on the first and

FIGURE 14 *Right-left positional discrimination learning set curve based on total trial responses. (Data on antagonistic object-quality discrimination problems omitted.)*

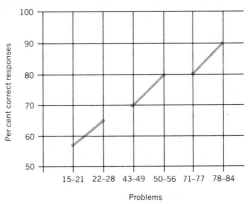

last seven positional discriminations in each of the three separate blocks of positional discriminations. The interposed object-quality discrimination problems clearly produced interference, but they did not prevent the orderly development of the positional learning sets, nor the final attainment of a high level of performance on these problems.

We have data which suggest that the educated man can face arteriosclerosis with confidence, if the results on brain-injured animals are applicable to men. Figure 15 shows discrimination learning set curves for the previously described groups of four normal monkeys and eight monkeys with very extensive unilateral cortical injury. The upper curves show total errors on an initial series of 112 six-trial discriminations. The lower curves show total errors on an additional group of 56 discriminations presented one year later. In both situations the full-brained monkeys make significantly better scores, but one should note that the educated hemidecorticate animals are superior to the uneducated unoperated monkeys. Such data suggest that half a brain is better than one if you compare the individuals

FIGURE 15 *Discrimination learning set curves based on total error responses: normal and operated monkeys.*

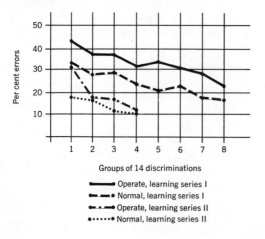

having appropriate learning sets with the individuals lacking them.

More seriously, these data may indicate why educated people show less apparent deterioration with advancing age than uneducated individuals, and the data lend support to the clinical observation that our fields of greatest proficiency are the last to suffer gross deterioration.

Although our objective data are limited to the formation of learning sets which operate to give efficient performance on intellectual problems, we have observational data of a qualitative nature on social-emotional changes in our animals. When the monkeys come to us they are wild and intractable but within a few years they have acquired, from the experimenter's point of view, good personalities. Actually we believe that one of the very important factors in the development of the good personalities of our monkeys is the formation of social-emotional learning sets organized in a manner comparable with the intellectual learning sets we have previously described. Each contact the monkey has with a human being represents a single specific learning trial. Each person represents a separate problem. Learning to react favorably to one person is followed by learning favorable reactions more rapidly to the next person to whom the monkey is socially introduced. Experience with additional individuals enables the monkey to learn further how to behave with human beings, and eventually the monkey's favorable reactions to new people are acquired so rapidly as to appear almost instantaneous.

The formation of social-emotional learning sets is not to be confused with mere stimulus generalization, a construct applied in this field with undue freedom. Actually a learning set once formed determines in large part the nature and direction of stimulus generalization. In the classic study in which Watson conditioned fear in Albert, the child developed a fear of the rat and generalized this fear, but failed to develop or generalize fear to Watson, even though Watson must have been the more conspicuous stimulus. Apparently Albert had already formed an affectional social-emotional learning set to people, which inhibited both learning and simple Pavlovian generalization.

Our observations on the formation of social-emotional learning sets have been entirely qualitative and informal, but there would appear to be no reason why they could not be studied experimentally.

The emphasis throughout this paper has been on the role of the historical or experience variable in learning behavior—the forgotten variable in current learning theory and research. Hull's Neo-behaviorists have constantly emphasized the necessity for an historical approach to learning, yet they have not exploited it fully. Their experimental manipulation of the experience variable has been largely limited to the development of isolated habits and their generalization. Their failure to find the phenomenon of discontinuity in learning may stem from their study of individual as opposed to repetitive learning situations.

The field theorists, unlike the Neo-behaviorists, have stressed insight and hypothesis in their description of learning. The impression these theorists give is that these phenomena are properties of the innate organization of the individual. If such phenomena appear independently of a gradual learning history, we have not found them in the primate order.

Psychologists working with human subjects have long believed in the phenomenon of learning sets and have even used sets as explanatory principles to account for perceptual selection and incidental learning. These psychologists have not, however, investigated the nature of these learning sets which their subjects bring to the experimental situation. The determining experiential variables of these learning sets lie buried in the subjects' pasts, but the development of such sets can be studied in the laboratory as long as the human race continues to reproduce its kind. Actually, detailed knowledge of the nature of the formation of learning sets could be of such importance to educational theory and practice as to justify prolonged and systematic investigation.

In the animal laboratory where the experiential factor can be easily controlled, we have carried out studies that outline the development and operation of specific learning sets. We believe that the construct of learning sets is of importance in the understanding of adaptive behavior. Since this is our faith, it is our hope that our limited data will be extended by those brave souls who study *real* men and *real* women.

HUMAN LEARNING, REMEMBERING, AND FORGETTING

Psychologists would not be nearly so interested in instrumental, or operant, conditioning if the principles involved did not apply to important human learning. In this experiment, behavior is manipulated by reinforcement. The subject is reinforced for a certain type of statement. The frequency of the reinforced response, as measured by an attitude scale, rises as one would expect if the word "good" were actually working as a reinforcer.

POINTS TO GUIDE YOUR STUDY (1) Can you think of applied situations, other than those in interviewing, where instrumental conditioning principles similar to those mentioned here might be at work? What about psychotherapy? (2) Note that the reinforcements used are of the sort usually called "secondary." What is "secondary reinforcement"? How did the word "good" acquire such properties? (3) Why do you think the experimenters selected an attitude which was not strongly held? Does this indicate that these principles will not work with strongly held attitudes?

18: VERBAL REINFORCEMENT AND INTERVIEWER BIAS

Donald C. Hildum, Oakland University, Rochester, Michigan, and Roger W. Brown, Harvard University

In several recent studies verbal behavior has been manipulated by means of selective reinforcement. These studies have very disturbing implications for the clin-ical and public-opinion interview. In the initial experiment Greenspoon (2) asked college students to voice nouns *ad libitum.* For one group of Ss, E murmured "Mm-hmm" whenever a plural noun was produced, while for a control group he said nothing at all. The reinforced Ss used more plural nouns than the control Ss. A somewhat different technique was developed by Taffel (4) and also employed by

This study was supported by the Laboratory of Social Relations, Harvard University.

D. C. Hildum and R. W. Brown. Verbal reinforcement and interviewer bias. *J. abnorm. soc. Psychol.*, 1956, **53**, 108–111. Copyright © 1956 by the American Psychological Association. Reprinted here with permission from the authors and the American Psychological Association.

Cohen *et al.* (1). They required S to form a sentence when given a verb and a choice of one of six personal pronouns to be used in starting the sentence. It proved to be possible to affect the frequency with which S used the various pronouns by saying "Good" in a flat unemotional tone after sentences employing the desired pronoun subject. Finally, Greenspoon has reported (3) the successful use of two nonverbal stimuli (a red light and a 190-c.p.s. tone) to increase the frequency of plural and also of nonplural responses. In all of these studies S said that he had not been conscious of any connection between his own behavior and the reactions of E. This is learning without awareness.

In these experiments reinforcement seems to act like the moon on the tides with inevitable and uncontingent effect. For those interested in such things there appears a glittering new prospect for human manipulation; for others only the quiet pleasure to be found in any new proof of human stupidity. The verbal-reinforcement data will confirm many in their suspicion of the methods of clinical and social psychology. The therapist who believes in the importance of the Oedipus complex could elicit Oedipal content by means of selective reinforcement. Perhaps a patient could even be brought to an appearance of mental health through the encouragement of "healthy" utterances. Is not "Mm-hmm" the very hallmark of a therapeutic school? In an opinion interview the S might be infected with the opinions of the interviewer by means of patterned reinforcement. Perhaps verbal reinforcement is a mechanism of interviewer bias.

It can be answered to these alarms that neither interviewers nor therapists wish to influence their Ss and consequently they would not use verbal reinforcement. There is no comfort in this answer. Anyone who has worked with verbal reinforcement knows that our "Mm-hmm" and "Good" are ordinarily unconscious and automatic.

They can only be controlled after some practice. It follows that an interviewer might influence his S in all innocence and we know from the experiments that an S might unwittingly accept the influence. Here is powerful social influence operating outside the awareness of everybody concerned.

Two important differences between the laboratory studies and actual interviews should however be noted: (a) Greenspoon and the other experimenters have taken as their response units particular words or word types. Interviewers are not ordinarily pleased either by plural nouns or by the use of the first person singular. If they are moved to agree or disagree it is likely to be with reference to a line of thought or an expressed attitude. In short, interviewers would be likely to reinforce content categories rather than specific verbalizations. (b) In a face-to-face conversation there are many ways of communicating agreement or disagreement—smiles, nods, averted eyes. In the laboratory studies of verbal reinforcement E sometimes placed himself behind the S and sometimes faced him but endeavored to avoid giving visual cues. These efforts at isolating the independent variable may not have succeeded. In any case they must have created a rather strange social atmosphere unlike the usual interviewing situation.

We undertook an experiment intended to correct these two laboratory artificialities. The experiment took the form of an attitude survey conducted by telephone. The interviewer asked questions concerning the Harvard philosophy of General Education. He revealed a bias for or against the philosophy by his reactions to the answers of the interviewee. In effect, he played the role of one who favored or of one who opposed General Education. However, the role-play was limited to the single matter of verbal reinforcement. The S could discover E's bias from his first few reactions and might then provide more of the kind of content that was reinforced.

Administering the questionnaire by telephone created a situation in which vocal reaction was the only kind possible and so the independent variable was isolated in a natural way.

Method

THE QUESTIONNAIRE   In order to maximize the likelihood of obtaining a verbal reinforcement effect, a topic (General Education) was selected on which Ss were not expected to have very strong opinions and so were expected to be open to influence. Also, though E might be expected to have an opinion, there was no obvious stereotype to tell S what that opinion should be. In the questionnaire there were 15 questions, with 4 possible responses to each: Agree strongly, agree slightly, disagree slightly, disagree strongly. The statements were worded so that agreement with some statements represented an attitude favorable to General Education while agreement with other statements represented an unfavorable attitude. Consequently the interviewer reinforced an attitude rather than a particular response. To make sure that the favorable or unfavorable nature of each statement was clear, we originally wrote 40 statements intended to sound unlike but really covering much the same ground. From these we selected 15 which on pretest proved to constitute a maximally redundant subset. It is generally possible to predict from the answer to one of these questions the answers to all the others. In addition the questionnaire was prefaced with a brief statement defining the philosophy of General Education so as to make sure that the S would understand which statements favored the philosophy and which were opposed.

SUBJECTS   Forty male students, graduate and undergraduate, were sampled from those in the Harvard Summer School who listed Cambridge telephone numbers and home addresses in the United States. Ten Ss were assigned at random to each of four experimental groups.

PROCEDURE   The same E conducted all the interviews. He identified himself as a member of the Social Relations Department and said that the survey was designed to compare summer-school opinion with that of the rest of the student body. He then administered the questionnaire.

For two groups the reinforcement was "Mm-hmm," pronounced after pro General Education answers for one group, and after anti answers for the other group. For the remaining two groups the reinforcement was "Good," again with one group rewarded for favorable responses and the other for unfavorable responses. Both reactions were fed back immediately following an approved answer in a neutrally-toned, rising inflection. The E (a trained linguist) carefully equated the intonation used in reading questions and responding to Ss in all groups.

At the close of the interview S was asked to guess E's opinion on General Education and also to say whether he thought there was any bias in the questionnaire or in its administration. If S thought there was bias or felt that he knew E's opinion he was then asked whether his answers were influenced by these conditions.

Results

THE REINFORCEMENT EFFECT   Each answer was scored from 1 to 4: 1 when an answer was strongly in favor of General Education, 2 when slightly favorable, 3 when slightly unfavorable, and 4 when strongly unfavorable. Refusals to answer (12 of 600 responses) were scored 2.5. The total score for an S had a possible range from 15 to 60. The actual range for all Ss was from 15 to 39.5. The Ss tended to favor the General Education philosophy.

In Table 1 appear the mean attitude scores for the four experimental groups and in Table 2 are the t scores and proba-

TABLE 1 *Mean attitude scores for four experimental groups*

GROUP	MEAN	SD
"Good"—pro	24.95	5.10
"Good"—anti	31.75	3.46
"Mm-hmm"—pro	29.8	3.96
"Mm-hmm"—anti	27.1	4.06

bilities for the crucial comparisons among these means. Reinforcement with "Good" was effective while reinforcement with "Mm-hmm" was not effective. In fact, with "Mm-hmm" the obtained difference was in the opposite direction to that predicted from the reinforcement scheme. With the same pattern of reinforcement "Good" was more effective than "Mm-hmm."

AWARENESS OF REINFORCEMENT Eight of 20 Ss noticed that the interviewer said "Good" but only 1 of these assumed that it indicated approval. Only 1 of 20 Ss noticed that E said "Mm-hmm." He thought it might have meant approval. All Ss rejected the notion that their answers had been influenced by the interviewer's reactions.

Of 24 Ss who were willing to guess at E's opinion all but one said that E favored General Education. Apparently they based

TABLE 2 *t scores and probabilities for crucial comparisons among the four experimental groups*

COMPARISON*	t SCORE	p
"Good"—pro vs. "Good"—anti	3.31	.01
"Mm-hmm"—anti vs. "Mm-hmm"—pro	1.43	.20
"Good"—pro vs. "Mm-hmm"—pro	2.25	.05
"Mm-hmm—anti vs. "Good"—anti	2.62	.02

* First member of comparison has score more favorable to General Education.

this guess on the assumption that someone surveying opinions on General Education would himself favor the principle, rather than on the pattern of reinforcement.

REPLICATION OF THE EXPERIMENT The essential design was repeated by members of an undergraduate tutorial group with 25 Ss. The results were like those of the initial study. The mean "Good"—pro score was lower than the mean "Good"—anti score with $p < .05$, while the mean scores for the two groups reinforced with "Mm-hmm" were not significantly different. The mean "Good"—pro score was lower than the mean "Mm-hmm"—pro score with $p < .01$. The mean "Good"—anti and "Mm-hmm"—anti scores did not differ significantly. This study involved new interviewers and Ss enrolled for the regular academic year at Harvard rather than in summer school.

Discussion

In the present interview situation "Good" is a reinforcer while "Mm-hmm" is not. This result conflicts with Greenspoon's finding that "Mm-hmm" affects the frequency of plural nouns. If conscious learning were involved, an explanation for the discrepancy would be available. When an S free-associates aloud for 25 minutes, he may be expected to search rather desperately for some indication from E as to the purpose of the task and the proper direction to take. In these circumstances he will notice "Mm-hmm" or even a red light or a tone of 190 c.p.s. and be guided by them. When S is asked to give his opinion of a set of statements, he is engaged in a task that makes sense as presented, and consequently he will not attend so closely to E's reactions. In this situation the muttered "Mm-hmm" should have no effect. The difficulty is, of course, that Ss in our experiment and in Greenspoon's nearly all said they had been quite unaware of E's

"Mm-hmm." In other words the two sets of data give no indication of differential attention to *E*'s reactions and so do not support our explanation. Still, the explanation may be correct and our measures of awareness insufficiently sensitive.

There are many questions one might ask to test *S*'s awareness. Does he know the purpose of the experiment? Did he notice anything about *E*'s behavior? Did he notice that *E* said "Mm-hmm?" Does he realize that these "Mm-hmms" have influenced his behavior? All of the studies so far find that *S*s usually do not attain to this last level of awareness. It is not clear from the experimental descriptions which other questions were asked nor what the answers were. It is possible, therefore, that reinforcers are more effective on the higher levels of awareness than on the lower levels and that these levels have not been adequately distinguished in the studies reported.

We did ask our *S*s several questions before inquiring whether they knew about *E*'s influence on their behavior. Eight *S*s were aware that *E* had said "Good" while only one *S* noticed "Mm-hmm." Evidently "Good" is more "visible" in the interviewer's role than is "Mm-hmm." Probably this is because saying "Good" very nearly violates the prescribed nondirective character of that role. This is a difference of awareness that may help to account for the effectiveness in our study of "Good" and the ineffectiveness of "Mm-hmm." We also asked our *S*s to guess at *E*'s opinion of General Education. We thought it quite possible that while *S* usually fails to notice *E*'s responses he might react to them in forming a conception of *E*'s opinions and this conception might be verbalizable when its behavioral sources were not. This measure disappointed us in the present case, in that all but one *S* thought *E* favored General Education. However, there is a tendency for the *S*s who were reinforced for anti-General Education answers to attribute to *E* a somewhat less favorable attitude than do the *S*s reinforced for pro-responses. Furthermore the *S*s whose conceptions of *E*'s attitude show more sensitivity to the pattern of reinforcement received are also the *S*s whose own attitude scores seem to have been most influenced by *E*'s reactions. While all of these trends fall short of significance in the present study, they do open the possibility that levels of awareness will help to account for differences in the effectiveness of selectively interpolated experimenter reactions.

There is a further point of contrast between our results and those of Greenspoon. Since a light and a tone have been used as reinforcers it would seem that semantics plays no necessary part in this phenomenon. Yet we find "Good" effective and "Mm-hmm" ineffective, and we are inclined to think that this may be partly due to the fact that "Good" has a more clearly favorable meaning than "Mm-hmm." The meaning of "Mm-hmm" is altogether dependent on the intonation pattern. As a sequence of segmental phonemes, as a printed word, its meaning is ambiguous. It may be a neutral indication that one is listening or it may even be questioning or disapproving. "Good" is somewhat less dependent on intonation. It is more reliably a favorable sign. This semantic difference may help to account for the superior effectiveness of "Good."

Our experimental procedure has brought the verbal reinforcement experiment nearer the interview situation. It may eventually prove to be necessary to train interviewers to control their specific reactions to the content received from an informant. Some of these reactions (smiles, averted eyes, etc.) may not be susceptible of control. It may be wiser, in a study of public opinion, to use interviewers of opposed bias, letting their reinforcing reactions operate freely but hoping the effects will cancel one another in the total sample. Pollsters might even learn much about opinion stability by having interviewers deliberately take different sides for different *S*s.

In any case, there is much to be learned about the reinforcement of verbal behavior before worrying unduly about its effects in the interview. It has not yet been shown, for instance, that a reaction like "Mm-hmm" is selectively used to express approval in ordinary conversations or interviews. The reactions *can* be selectively interpolated by an experimenter but *is* it selectively interpolated outside the laboratory? Can one predict the naïve speaker's use of "Mm-hmm" from knowledge of his attitudes? Even if this be possible, it does not follow that the usage of either the clinician or the opinion interviewer is similarly predictable. Their efforts to play a nondirective role may well change the ordinary usage of "Mm-hmm." Actual interviewer behavior needs to be studied before deciding on the importance of the studies of verbal reinforcement for the interview.

Summary

A questionnaire was administered by telephone and the interviewer attempted to influence his *S*s through the selective interpolation of two reactions—"Good" and "Mm-hmm." "Good" proved to bias the results obtained while "Mm-hmm" did not. The study was repeated and the same result obtained. These results were compared with those obtained by other experiments. The implications of the verbal reinforcement phenomenon for the clinical and opinion interview are discussed.

References

1. Cohen, B. D., Kalish, H. I., Thurston, J. R., and Cohen, E. Experimental manipulation of verbal behavior. *J. exp. Psychol.*, 1954, 47, 106–110.

2. Greenspoon, J. The effect of verbal and non-verbal stimuli on the frequency of members of two verbal response classes. Unpublished doctor's dissertation, Indiana Univer., 1951.

3. Greenspoon, J. The effect of two nonverbal stimuli on the frequency of members of two verbal response classes. *Amer. Psychologist*, 1954, 9, 384. (Abstract)

4. Taffel, C. Conditioning of verbal behavior in an institutionalized population and its relation to "anxiety level." Unpublished doctor's dissertation, Indiana Univer., 1952.

The question of learning during sleep comes up with some frequency. Many psychologists have concluded that learning during true sleep is unlikely, a conclusion based upon studies similar to the one presented here. Learning during the drowsy state before sleep seems possible, but, as these authors point out, there are disadvantages, such as decreased efficiency, to learning in this state. On the other hand, the utilization of this drowsy state might be somewhat efficient in that it adds a few minutes to a busy person's day. In the main, however, this is not "the royal road to learning." Learning is still hard work.

POINTS TO GUIDE YOUR STUDY   *(1) Note the care taken to control the group differences which might spuriously affect the results.*
(2) Your text provides more material on the EEG. In general, the EEG correlates with the state of sleep or arousal. Some of these correlations are given in Table 1. The alpha rhythm *mentioned in Table 1 is the normal resting frequency of the EEG with the eyes shut—about 8 to 13 cycles per second. In this experiment, the characteristics of the EEG are used as an index of the depth of sleep.*

19: RESPONSES TO MATERIAL PRESENTED DURING VARIOUS LEVELS OF SLEEP

Charles W. Simon, Hughes Aircraft Co., and William H. Emmons

Recently, there has been an increased interest in the possibility of learning during sleep. A critical review of the few scientific studies in this field to date leads to the conclusion that the evidence supporting claims of learning during actual sleep is inconclusive. The chief criticism against the existing studies is their failure to continuously determine the sleep state of Ss during the stimulus input period (16).

After considerable exploratory work (15), the present experiment was designed to study the effect of presenting material at different levels between wakefulness and deep sleep on the ability of Ss (a) to respond to it immediately, and (b) to recall it later upon awakening. It was hypothesized that learning during sleep was improbable.

Method

SUBJECTS   Twenty-one male experimental Ss were used. In order to facilitate the detection of gradual changes which occur in the EEG between wakefulness and light sleep, it was necessary to use only Ss having a persistent occipital alpha rhythm when awake and relaxed with their eyes closed. Ten Ss were junior college students, nine were scientists, and two were policemen. Results from students and policemen were combined since they were similar on critical variables. Means and SD's of descriptive variables for the experimental subgroups were determined. For the scientist group, these values were: age, 30.6 yr. ± 5.0; IQ, 122.6 ± 6.0; items correct on pretest, 11.7 ± 3.4. For the college men and policemen combined, these values were: age, 23.2 yr. ± 6.3; IQ, 108.6 ± 4.7; items correct on pretest, 6.8 ± 3.0.

Forty junior college males and 24 male scientists acted as a control group without regard for their alpha rhythm. These Ss were used to obtain an estimate of the probability of correct answers being chosen on a multiple-choice test, since it seemed unlikely that educated Ss would select their answers to unknown questions solely by chance. This control group was first given a pretest to determine the number of test questions known without training and before seeing the multiple-choice alternatives. With no intervening training and after items correct on the pretest were removed, the pretest significantly predicted scores on the multiple-choice test. This prediction was not significantly improved when IQ or age was added in a multiple-regression equation.

Control and experimental subgroups were matched on means and variances of their IQ, age, and pretest scores. Only the variances of the age and IQ of the college subgroups were unmatched.[1]

APPARATUS   The Ss slept in clean comfortable beds in three separate soundproof, air conditioned, electrically-shielded booths. EEG electrodes were applied to the right occipital area, the vertex, and the left mastoid process. The electrode wires were arranged to allow relatively free

The authors wish to acknowledge the valuable assistance of Louie W. Mason, Jr., and James L. Barnes in the analysis of the data in this study. Appreciation is expressed to the faculty and students of Santa Monica City College, to the Santa Monica Police Department, and to the volunteer Ss within the RAND Corporation for their cooperation throughout the project.

[1] Supporting and additional statistics along with data by S have been deposited with the American Documentation Institute. Order Document No. 4738, remitting $1.25 for 35-mm. microfilm or $1.25 for 6 x 8 in. photocopies.

movement and comfort during sleep. Two monopolar EEG recordings (right occipital and vertex) were made from each S using a six-channel Offner electroencephalograph and Dynograph inkwriter. A marker pen mounted on the inkwriter automatically marked the exact time an auditory stimulus was presented to S. The learning material was recorded on magnetic tape and played through loudspeakers placed inside the booths. A two-way intercommunication system allowed Es to communicate with Ss.

PROCEDURE *Pretesting period.* Several hours before retiring, Ss were pretested to discover what information they knew in order to have a base from which to evaluate how much had been learned following "sleep-training" on the same material. They were encouraged to guess answers to as many questions as they could, since a chance guess might be the correct one. No time limit was imposed.

Ninety-six general information questions were culled from various books on the basis of the following criteria: (a) the information was not generally known; (b) the answers required were not outside the verbal experience of the Ss; (c) questions could be answered in short phrases or single words. These same 96 questions and their answers were recorded on tape at 5-min. intervals for presentation during the sleep period. The answer was presented as a restatement of the question with the critical information near the end. For example, Question: "In what kind of store did Ulysses S. Grant work before the war?" Answer: "Before the war, Ulysses S. Grant worked in a hardware store."

Preliminary period. Following the pretest, Ss prepared for bed and the EEG electrodes were applied. Three Ss were run simultaneously. Since it was not possible to adjust the auditory intensity of the stimulus material in each booth individually, it was necessary to find a level satisfactory to all three. "Satisfactory" was defined as the point at which the training material could be heard clearly by the waking S, yet not be loud enough to materially disturb him once he was asleep. As Ss lay in their booths, practice verbal material was played at approximately the same loudness as the experimental stimulus material was to be played. This loudness level was adjusted after a number of tests so that the S with the highest threshold was able to hear the words clearly.

Before turning out the lights and allowing Ss to go to sleep, the following instructions were given: (a) if they awakened during the night at any time, they were to call out their name and booth number as soon as possible and to say that they were awake; (b) if they heard the answer to any of the question-answer combinations during the night, they were to wait until the answer was completed, and then call out their name and booth number. In order to impress these instructions on S, each was asked to repeat them back to E.

Training period. Within 5 min. after S retired, the tape recorder was turned on and the question-answer combinations were played into the booths at approximately 5-min. intervals. A pen automatically marked the EEG record whenever a question or answer was played. The Es marked on the record whether or not S stated he heard the answer. Records of any other pertinent information were kept, e.g., if S awoke, his remarks, and so forth.

Posttest period. Shortly after the last question and answer was played, Ss were awakened (if they were not already so), permitted to dress, and wash their face and hands. The same questions which they received on the pretest and during the training were again presented for them to answer; as before, Ss were encouraged to guess. This unaided recall was followed by a multiple-choice test in which five alternative answers (including the correct one) were provided with the questions.

Control group testing. All members of the control groups were given the 96 questions and asked to answer them by guessing whenever they were not certain. Following a brief rest and no training, they were given the questions along with the multiple-choice answers and retested.

Intelligence testing. Following the completion of the experiment, both experimental and control groups were given the 30-min. Otis Self-Administering Test of Mental Ability, Form D.

Results

The basic data available for analysis were: (a) the levels of sleep during the training period as indicated by EEG records, (b) the frequencies with which *S*s immediately reported they had heard an answer, and (c) the frequencies with which *S*s correctly recalled an answer, both unaided

and by recognizing the correct multiple-choice alternative.

SLEEP LEVELS   Those portions of the EEG record occurring simultaneously with the presentation of the answers were categorized into 22 distinguishable patterns. These 22 EEG patterns were divided into eight groups, or sleep levels, which were ordered on their proportion of visually observable cyclical activity within the alpha frequency range (8-13 cps) and on their amplitude, frequency, and the effects of stimulation when alpha frequencies were no longer present. This order corresponds to *S's* state of consciousness between wakefulness and deep sleep and is described in Table 1.

IMMEDIATE RESPONSE AND UNAIDED RECALL The "immediate response" or "reported heard" analysis was based on 1,827 items;

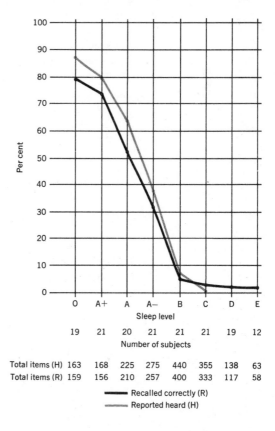

FIGURE 1 *The percentage of items reported heard during the stimulation at varying levels along the wake-sleep continuum and the percentage subsequently recalled correctly unaided. The number of Ss contributing to each level and the number of items from which each percentage was computed are shown.*

	O	A+	A	A−	B	C	D	E
Number of subjects	19	21	20	21	21	21	19	12
Total items (H)	163	168	225	275	440	355	138	63
Total items (R)	159	156	210	257	400	333	117	58

Sleep level

━━━ Recalled correctly (R)
━━━ Reported heard (H)

TABLE 1   *EEG and psychological conditions along the sleep-wakefulness continuum*

LEVEL	% ITEMS	% Ss	ELECTROENCEPHALOGRAM	PSYCHOLOGICAL CONDITION
0	8	90	Continuous or nearly continuous alpha of maximum amplitude and frequency of not more than 1 cps slower than the S's normal alpha frequency. Frequency and amplitude are slightly less after sleeping than before.	Awake. Relaxed with eyes closed. Responsive to external stimulation.
A+	9	100	More than 50% of the scoring period contains alpha. Also low level, random activity characteristic of an alpha block may be present with alpha disappearing at the onset of stimulation and returning shortly after its cessation.	Drowsy.
A	12	95	Less than 50% alpha but scoring period contains at least three cycles of activity having the same frequency as the 0 level. The alpha amplitude may be the same as or considerably lower than before.	Attention wanders; reverie. Increased reaction time.
A−	14	100	Contains cyclical activity having a frequency more than 1 cps slower than the Level 0 record. May include waves of mixed duration with periods between .12 and .08 sec. with no one period being dominant. Also includes records showing no alpha rhythm during stimulation, but with alpha occurring within 30 sec. prior to stimulation or following but not both.	Partial awareness.
B	22	100	Absence of alpha during the stimulus period and the adjacent 30 sec. of record. Stimulus effects may occur consisting of low level fast activity or an increase in activity containing both high and low frequency components, with some waves having periods within the alpha range. Low-level delta activity is present in the absence of stimulus effects.	Transition. Dreamlike state. Infrequent responses to external stimulation. Onset of sleep. Easily awakened.
C	18	100	Absence of alpha with an increase of delta and the appearance of sleep spindles (14 cps). This state is characterized by stimulus effects such as increases in amplitude of delta waves with the onset of the stimulus. Types of effects vary with individuals.	Light sleep. No behavioral responses to external stimulation (unless stimulus awakens). Dreams sometimes remembered.
D	7	90	A further increase in delta amplitude with a reduction in frequency and diminution of stimulus effects and sleep spindles. Amplitude of delta almost at maximum.	Deep sleep. No memory for dreams. Difficult to awaken.
E	3	57	Absence of sleep spindles and stimulus effects. Very large delta activity with smooth waves of .5- to 1.5-sec. duration.	Very deep sleep.

items were removed when the EEG was obscured by artifacts and when it was impossible to determine which of the three *S*s running simultaneously had responded. The "unaided recall" analysis was based on 1,690 items; items were removed when the EEG was obscured by artifacts and when the items were known on the pretraining test.

The percentage of items reported heard at time of presentation and the percentage correctly recalled unaided, upon awakening, are shown in Figure 1. These percentages in Figure 1, based on the combined data for all *S*s and items occurring at each level, decrease as the amount of alpha decreases and delta appears, that is, as the sleep level deepens.

RECOGNITION TEST Figure 2 shows the percentage of items recalled correctly for all *S*s when multiple-choice answers were provided, along with the standard error of these percentages. As in Figure 1, with a

decrease in alpha frequencies at the time of presentation, there was a corresponding decrease in the number of items recalled later. Unlike the others, however, the recall curve from this recognition test leveled off around 23% instead of dropping to zero.

Since it was possible for *S*s to answer correctly solely by chance on the multiple-choice test, it was necessary to compare the percentages obtained by the experimental groups with an empirical estimate of what the theoretical percentage would be. Although 20% was chance expectancy for this test, the difficulty of making a perfect multiple-choice test with answers equal in selectivity caused the *E*s to use scores of a control group as the basis for estimating the expected value.

It was found that the scientist control subgroup answered 26% correctly without training and the college control subgroup answered 22% correctly. The expected percentages shown in Figure 2 were based on

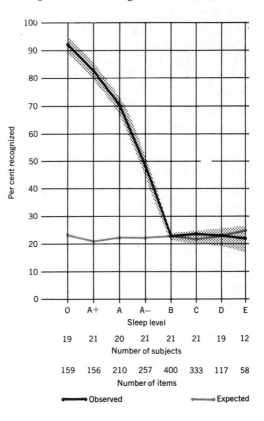

FIGURE 2 *The percentage of answers recognized on the multiple-choice test after being presented at varying levels along the continuum between a waking and deep sleep state. The shaded portion represents plus and minus one standard error of the percentage. The expected value was that obtained from an untrained control group of comparable ability answering the same items.*

empirical values from the control groups weighted according to the items contributed by the scientist and college-police experimental groups in each sleep level.

Thus, from Figure 2, it can be seen that the expected values remain essentially the same for all sleep levels, while the values observed from the experimental group changed. In Levels 0 through A−, the experimental Ss showed a considerably higher percentage correct, while in Levels B through E, the percentage correct for the experimental group was essentially equal to (within $\pm.5\sigma\%$) and in most cases less than the mean expected value.

Discussion

The results support the hypothesis that learning during sleep is unlikely. Although a few items were answered correctly unaided, with the easier recognition test (13) no more items were answered in Levels B through E by the experimental group than would be expected from the performance of the untrained control group. Since it is generally conceded that sleep occurs somewhere during Level B, then it appears that learning was slight, if any, at this point or below. There appears some basis for assuming that many of these atypical cases were artifacts and not true sleep-learning.

What had been done in the present sleep-learning study that had not been done adequately in any previous studies (16) was the careful monitoring of Ss during the presentation period so that their levels of sleep during training were always known. The use of the EEG for this purpose proved most adequate.

Although it appears that learning during real sleep is not feasible, the practical utilization of the drowsy state for training is still open to speculation. The results in this study show that approximately 30% of the simple and highly organized material presented in the period just prior to sleep was recalled. Just how efficient learning in this state is has not been suf-

ficiently evaluated experimentally. Anderson (1) found that the amount of recall decreases when training follows sleep closely. One must weigh the advantages of limited learning against the possible harmful effects from loss of sleep as well as against the time demanded to learn in the subnormal receptive state. It may be that in the drowsy state preceding sleep, the individual is more susceptible to suggestions; perhaps one's attitudes or habits can be modified during this presleep period when criticalness is minimized (8). Perhaps the future development of new and unknown techniques will permit someone to learn complex material while he sleeps, but for the present, sleep-learning is not the simple matter that some Es and commercial firms, which sell equipment for this purpose, would lead us to believe.

References

1. Anderson, D. V. The effect of relaxation on the recall of nonsense syllables, words, and poetry. Unpublished doctor's dissertation, Univ. of California, Los Angeles, 1953.

2. Coyne, M. L. Some problems and parameters of sleep learning. Unpublished honors' thesis, Wesleyan Univ., 1953.

3. Davis, H., Davis, P. A., Loomis, A. L., Harvey, E. N., and Hobart, G. Human brain potential during the onset of sleep. J. Neurophysiol., 1938, 1, 24–38.

4. Emmons, W. H., and Simon, C. W. The non-recall of material presented during sleep. Santa Monica, Calif.: The RAND Corp., Paper No. 619, 1955.

5. Gibbs, F. A., and Gibbs, E. L. Atlas of electroencephalography. Cambridge, Mass.: Lew A. Cummings Co., 1941.

6. Hovland, C. I. Human learning and retention. In S. S. Stevens (Ed.), Handbook of experimental psychology. New York: Wiley, 1951. Pp. 613–689.

7. Hoyt, W. G. The effect of learning of auditory material presented during sleep. Unpublished master's thesis, George Washington Univ., 1953.

8. LeShan, L. The breaking of a habit by suggestion during sleep. J. abnorm. soc. Psychol., 1942, 37, 406–408.

9. Lindsley, D. B. Electroencephalography. In J. McV. Hunt (Ed.), Personality and behavior disorders, Vol. II. New York: Ronald, 1944. Pp. 1033–1103.

10. Lindsley, D. B. Emotion. In S. S. Stevens (Ed.), *Handbook of experimental psychology*. New York: Wiley, 1951. Pp. 473–516.

11. Lindsley, D. B. Psychological phenomena and the electroencephalogram. *EEG clin. Neurophysiol.*, 1952, **4**, 443–456.

12. Loomis, A. L., Harvey, E. N., and Hobart, G. A. Cerebral states during sleep, as studied by human brain potentials. *J. exp. Psychol.*, 1937, **21**, 127–144.

13. Luh, C. W. The conditions of retention. *Psychol. Monogr.*, 1922, **31**, No. 3 (Whole No. 142).

14. Moruzzi, G., and Magoun, H. W. Brain stem reticular formation and activation of the EEG. *EEG clin. Neurophysiol.*, 1949, **1**, 455–473.

15. Simon, C. W., and Emmons, W. H. Considerations for research in a sleep-learning program. Santa Monica, Calif.: The RAND Corp., Paper No. 565, 1954.

16. Simon, C. W., and Emmons, W. H. Learning during sleep? *Psychol. Bull.*, 1955, **52**, 328–342.

17. Stampfl, T. The effect of frequency of repetition on the retention of auditory material presented during sleep. Unpublished master's thesis, Loyola Univ., Chicago, 1953.

This classical paper in the area of transfer of training was among the first to make an analysis of transfer in terms of the stimulus (S) and response (R) components of a task. It was also one of the first investigations of the effect of the similarity of the S and R components on transfer of training. Although there have been a good many refinements, the conclusions derived from this study have held up.

POINTS TO GUIDE YOUR STUDY *(1) This experiment uses the paired-associates method of rote learning. Can you describe this method? (2) State the conclusions of this paper in your own words. Try to make up a memory scheme for remembering them, e.g., "O-N-N," old stimulus–new response–negative transfer. (3) Note that some of these conclusions depend upon a rigorous definition of what is and what is not similar to something else. In other words, the conclusions depend upon the specification of a dimension of similarity. (4) Note that this article is written in a style different from more recent ones. If you become a psychologist or, much more likely, if you write reports of your own experiments, you will want to follow one of the more current styles. (See the article by Braun and Geiselhart in Section Three.)*

20: CONDITIONS OF TRANSFER OF TRAINING

Robert Wallace Bruce, Wabash College

Introduction

This study is an investigation of some of the conditions of transfer of training. We shall seek to answer these questions:

I. What is the relation of the following conditions of learning to transfer:

   A. Learning to make a new response to an old stimulus?

   B. Learning to make an old response to a new stimulus?

   C. Learning to make a new response to a new stimulus?

II. What is the relation of the degree of integration of the initial learning to transfer in

From the Psychological Laboratory of the University of Chicago. The writer wishes to acknowledge his indebtedness to Professors Edward S. Robinson and Arthur G. Bills for assistance in planning and completing the study.

A. Learning to make a new response to an old stimulus?

B. Learning to make an old response to a new stimulus?

III. What is the relation of certain similarities between the $S_1R_1S_2R_2$ terms of the initial and subsequent learning material to transfer in

A. Learning to make a new response to an old stimulus?

B. Learning to make an old response to a new stimulus?

In most of the previous studies of learning transfer, the stimulus-response terms are undifferentiated. The usual procedure is to learn task *A*, then task *B*, check and compare the two results, and ascribe the difference to transfer. As a consequence, results have been obtained which give positive, zero, and negative transfer. Since the previous experiments have not been made for the purpose of reconciling these diverse results, we are attempting such a reconciliation by discovering some of the conditions of transfer.

Technique

1. LEARNING TERMS DEFINED   Learning transfer relates to the effect of initial upon subsequent learning. In this investigation, the initial and subsequent learning are further differentiated into stimulus and response terms, which are designated initial stimulus, initial response, subsequent stimulus, subsequent response, $S_1R_1S_2R_2$.

2. GENERAL NATURE OF THE LEARNING MATERIAL   The learning material in these studies consists of nonsense syllables. The syllables may be similar, different, or identical; by arbitrary definition, 'similar' syllables are syllables which vary only in respect to the final letter, such as var, vam.

3. DESCRIPTION OF THE CONDITIONS, RELATIVE TO (a) *identities between certain of*

the $S_1R_1S_2R_2$ *terms*. The relation of identity of the $S_1R_1S_2R_2$ terms is varied. In condition IX, the terms are all different. In conditions I, II, III, IV, the S_1 and S_2 are identical, which means that the subjects are required to learn a new response to an old stimulus. In conditions V, VI, VII, VIII, the R_1 and R_2 are identical, which means that the subjects are required to learn to make an old response to a new stimulus.

(b) *Similarities between certain of the* $S_1R_1S_2R_2$ *terms*. In conditions I, V, IX, no similarities are present. In conditions II and VI, the initial stimulus and initial response are similar. In conditions III and VII, the subsequent stimulus and subsequent response are similar. In condition IV, the initial response and subsequent response are similar, and in condition VIII, the initial stimulus and the subsequent stimulus are similar.

(c) *Integration of the initial learning*. In each of the nine conditions, an initial list of syllables is presented to the subject either 0, 2, 6 or 12 times, regardless of the number of repetitions required to learn the initial list. By means of this variation, situations are provided in which the original material may be entirely unlearned, slightly learned, almost learned, completely learned, or overlearned. A subsequent list is then repeatedly presented until it is learned. It is assumed that a list is learned when the subject can correctly anticipate the second member of each pair before it actually appears. The last repetition therefore is not counted. The following table is a partial summary of the conditions.

4. RATE OF PRESENTATION   A 2-second interval is given per successive exposure.

5. METHOD OF PRESENTATION   In all of the conditions, a variation of the paired-associates method is used, in which the subject is presented first with a given syllable,

Summary of conditions and illustration of identities and similarities between terms in the different conditions

	INITIAL LEARNING		SUBSEQUENT LEARNING		
CONDITION	STIMULUS S_1	RESPONSE R_1	STIMULUS S_2	RESPONSE R_2	RELATION OF INITIAL TO SUBSEQUENT MATERIAL
I	req	kiv	req	zam	S_1S_2 identical
II	bij	bic	bij	tab	S_1S_2 identical, S_1R_1 similar
III	mir	ped	mir	miy	S_1S_2 identical, S_2R_2 similar
IV	tec	zox	tec	zop	S_1S_2 identical, R_1R_2 similar
V	lan	qip	fis	qip	R_1R_2 identical
VI	soj	soy	nel	soy	R_1R_2 identical, S_1R_1 similar
VII	zaf	qer	qec	qer	R_1R_2 identical, S_2R_2 similar
VIII	bes	yor	bef	yor	R_1R_2 identical, S_1S_2 similar
IX	xal	pom	cam	lup	All terms different

then with the syllable and its associate, and so forth. An illustrative list of syllables follows:

Initial S_1R_1 list (S_1 with R_1)		Subsequent S_2R_2 list (S_2 with R_2)	
req		fiz	
req	kiy	fiz	sej
taw		mip	
taw	rif	mip	boc
qix		bul	
qix	lep	bul	puw
wam		nic	
wam	bos	nic	git
zed		caj	
zed	dib	caj	lim

6. LENGTH OF THE LISTS   It was necessary, in arranging the length of the lists for the various conditions, to make certain that they were long enough, in all cases, to require several repetitions in the learning. Conditions III and VII permitted more rapid learning than the other conditions, and hence longer lists were employed in these two conditions. Therefore, the length of the lists, as determined by pre-experimentation, is 5 syllables in conditions I, II, IV, V, VI, VIII, IX, and 7 syllables in conditions III and VII.

7. DIFFERENT GROUPINGS OF THE PAIRS OF SYLLABLES   The members of each pair of syllables remain invariably together, but the order of the pairs in the list is varied in an irregular manner from trial to trial. This arrangement, which provides for four different groupings of the pairs per list, follows:

REPETITION OF LIST	SEQUENCE OF PRESENTATION OF THE SYLLABLES PER LIST				
1st	1	2	3	4	5
2d	4	1	5	3	2
3d	5	4	2	1	3
4th	2	5	1	3	4
5th, etc.	1	2	3	4	5

8. PRACTICE EFFECTS EQUALIZED   The conditions of integration are regularly shifted per subject per cycle in a manner calculated to equalize the benefits to be derived from practice. The sequence is so adjusted that every subject studies each of the four conditions of integration under each of the four successive learning periods of the cycle.

9. DIFFERENCES IN DIFFICULTY OF LISTS ADJUSTED   The syllable lists are given in a

sequence per subject per condition calculated to equalize their difficulty in learning. The sequence is so adjusted that each syllable list is learned 2 or more times under each of the conditions of integration, and under each of the four successive learning periods of a cycle group.

10. THE SUBJECTS   Eighty-one college students served as subjects; nine are used in each condition, and each one is tested individually. Each subject is tested under each of the four conditions of integration, and this is repeated for four cycles. Thus sixteen periods of experimentation are required of each person, and as far as possible, these periods of experimentation are given one at a time, at the rate of one per day.

11. APPARATUS   The apparatus used in this study consists of a metronome, some adding machine paper, and a 12 x 12 inch cardboard in the center of which are two parallel 4½-inch slits ⅝ inches apart.

The metronome is used to provide 2-second intervals.

The adding machine paper is used as a convenient medium for presenting type-written lists of syllables. In order to present four different groupings of lists of pairs, and in order to provide at least double spacing between successive items, rolls of approximately 36 inches in length are used.

The 12 x 12 inch cardboard is used in lieu of a memory drum. The syllable roll, concealed beneath the cardboard except for the small portion exposed between the two parallel slits, is pulled forward by the experimenter at regular intervals of 2 seconds per exposure item.

Results

I. Relation of the following types of learning to transfer:

A. Learning to make a new response to an old stimulus.

B. Learning to make an old response to a new stimulus.

C. Learning to make a new response to a new stimulus.

The data of Table I indicate that learning to make a new response to an old stimulus is not benefited by the initial learning of 12 repetitions; in fact the number of repetitions required increases from

TABLE I*   *Relation to transfer of learning to make a new response to an old stimulus, an old response to a new stimulus, a new response to a new stimulus*

CONDITION	MEAN REPETITIONS REQUIRED IN THE SUBSEQUENT LEARNING UNDER CONDITIONS OF 0 AND 12 REPETITIONS OF INITIAL LEARNING		MEAN VALUES LETTING THE CONDITION 0 VALUE = 100	
	0	12	0	12
I	10.3	11.2	100	109
V	14.4	9.0	100	63
IX	9.9	8.3	100	84

* Each mean value in this and the following tables is an average of 36 measures.

The probable errors are omitted from the tables, chiefly for reasons of convenience. The P.E. of the difference of given means is stated in the discussion, in a few crucial instances; the subsequent findings hinge upon these values.

The great differences between the 0 integration values in this and the following tables are not of any particular significance inasmuch as

    a. different persons serve as subjects in each of the nine conditions of the study,

    b. different lists of memory material are used in each of the nine conditions of the study,

    c. longer lists of memory material are used under some of the conditions than under others,

    d. learning is easier under some of the conditions than under others, since the pairs of syllables are similar in some conditions and different in others.

10.3 to 11.2 indicating a negative transfer of 100:109, although the difference of 0.9 repetitions is statistically insignificant.

Learning to make an old response to a new stimulus is materially benefited by the initial learning; the number of repetitions required decreases from 14.4 to 9.0 indicating a positive transfer of 100:63. The difference of 5.4 repetitions is statistically significant since it is more than three times the P.E. of the difference, 1.5.

Learning to make a new response to a new stimulus is slightly benefited by the initial learning; the number of repetitions required decreases from 9.9 to 8.3 indicating a positive transfer of 100:84. The difference of 1.6 repetitions is too small to be of much significance since the P.E. of the difference is 1.5.

In general the data indicate that there is a marked positive transfer in learning to make an old response to a new stimulus (100:63), a slight positive transfer in learning to make a new response to a new stimulus (100:84), and a slight negative transfer in learning to make a new response to an old stimulus (100:109).

II. Relation of the degree of integration of the initial learning to transfer in

A. Learning to make a new response to an old stimulus.

B. Learning to make an old response to a new stimulus.

In learning to make a new response to an old stimulus, the number of repetitions required varies with the degree of integration of the initial learning: 2 repetitions causes a negative transfer of 100:117; 6 repetitions causes a negative transfer of 100:116; and 12 repetitions causes a negative transfer of 100:109.

In learning to make an old response to a new stimulus, 2 repetitions of the initial learning causes a negative transfer of 100:115; 6 repetitions causes a positive transfer of 100:83; and 12 repetitions causes a positive transfer of 100:63.

In learning to make a new response to a new stimulus, 2 repetitions of the initial learning causes a zero transfer; 6 repetitions causes a negative transfer of 100:108; and 12 repetitions causes a positive transfer of 100:84.

The difficulty of the learning tends to decrease, as the amount of the initial learning is increased from 2 to 6 to 12 repetitions (compare 117 with 116 with 109; also 115 with 83 with 63; also 100 with 108 with 84); this is true, moreover, regardless of whether or not similarities are present (see Tables III and IV, and compare also 101,90,90; 127,123,102; 102, 101,80; 103,81,77; 66,56,40; 84,64,44); the decreased difficulty may show itself in terms of a decreasing negative transfer (117,116,109), or in terms of a shift from negative to positive transfer (115,83,63),

TABLE II *Influence of the degree of integration (0, 2, 6, 12 repetitions) of the initial learning upon the subsequent learning, relative to learning to make a new response to an old stimulus, an old response to a new stimulus, a new response to a new stimulus.*

CON-DITION	MEAN REPETITIONS REQUIRED IN THE SUB-SEQUENT LEARNING UNDER CONDITIONS OF 0, 2, 6, 12 REPETITIONS OF INITIAL LEARNING				MEAN VALUES LETTING THE CONDITION 0 VALUE = 100			
	0	2	6	12	0	2	6	12
I	10.3	12.1	11.9	11.2	100	117	116	109
V	14.4	16.6	12.0	9.0	100	115	83	63
IX	9.9	9.9	10.7	8.3	100	100	108	84

TABLE III *Influence of similarity of terms involved in initial and subsequent material upon the subsequent learning when learning to make a new response to an old stimulus*

CON-DITION	MEAN REPETITIONS REQUIRED IN THE SUBSEQUENT LEARNING UNDER CONDITIONS OF 0, 2, 6, 12 REPETITIONS OF INITIAL LEARNING				MEAN VALUES LETTING THE CONDITION 0 VALUE = 100			
	0	2	6	12	0	2	6	12
I	10.3	12.1	11.9	11.2	100	117	116	109
II	11.1	11.2	10.0	10.0	100	101	90	90
III	8.2	10.4	10.1	8.4	100	127	123	102
IV	9.6	9.8	9.7	7.7	100	102	101	80

or in terms of an increasing positive transfer, if similarities are involved (see Table IV, 84,64,44).

III. Relation of the similarity between the $S_1R_1S_2R_2$ terms of the initial and subsequent material, to transfer in

A. Learning to make a new response to an old stimulus.

B. Learning to make an old response to a new stimulus.

Learning to make a new response to an old stimulus when no similarities are present, is slightly hindered by 12 repetitions of initial learning, 100:109. If the stimulus and response terms of the subsequent learning are similar, transfer is practically zero, 100:102. If the stimulus and response terms of the initial learning are similar, a slight positive transfer occurs, 100:90. If the response terms of the initial and subsequent learning are similar, a further

slight increment of positive transfer is added, 100:80. In general, the learning is least facilitated when no similarities are present (compare 109 with 90,102,80), and most facilitated when the initial and subsequent responses are related (compare 80 with 109,90,102); the first gives a slight degree of negative transfer, the latter a moderate degree of positive transfer. The relative effectiveness of the four conditions of experimentation varies irregularly with the degree of integration of the initial learning. Under the best conditions, a slight positive transfer occurs; under the poorest conditions, a slight negative transfer occurs.

Learning to make an old response to a new stimulus when no similarities are present is materially aided by an initial learning of 12 repetitions; the repetitions required decrease from 14.4 to 9.0, a positive transfer of 100:63. If the stimulus and

TABLE IV *Influence of similarity of terms involved in initial and subsequent material upon the subsequent learning when learning to make an old response to a new stimulus*

CON-DITION	MEAN REPETITIONS REQUIRED IN THE SUBSEQUENT LEARNING UNDER CONDITIONS OF 0, 2, 6, 12 REPETITIONS OF INITIAL LEARNING				MEAN VALUES LETTING THE CONDITION 0 VALUE = 100			
	0	2	6	12	0	2	6	12
V	14.4	16.6	12.0	9.0	100	115	83	63
VI	12.8	13.2	10.4	9.8	100	103	81	77
VII	13.1	8.7	7.3	5.3	100	66	56	40
VIII	13.5	11.4	8.7	5.9	100	84	64	44

response terms of the initial learning are similar, the amount of positive transfer slightly decreases, 100:77. If the stimulus and response terms of the subsequent learning are similar, the amount of positive transfer is greatly increased, 100:40; so also, if the initial stimulus and the subsequent stimulus are similar, 100:44. In general, the positive transfer is greatest when the subsequent stimulus is similar either to the subsequent response, 100:40, or to the initial stimulus, 100:44. The positive transfer is least when the similarities are restricted to the terms of the initial learning, 100:77; in this latter case, the similarity is even a disadvantage; compare 100:77 with 100:63.

IV. Summary of results, concerning the conditions of transfer of training:

1. Learning to make an old response to a new stimulus almost invariably gives marked positive transfer, whereas learning to make a new response to an old stimulus usually results in a slight degree of negative transfer; this is true regardless of whether the

integration is controlled and the similarity controlled

integration is varied and the similarity controlled

integration is controlled and the similarity varied

integration is varied and the similarity varied.

2. The difficulty of subsequent learning tends to decrease as the amount of the initial learning is increased from 2 to 6 to 12 repetitions, regardless of whether learning to make a new response to an old stimulus, or learning to make an old response to a new stimulus; this decrease may be in terms of a decreasing negative transfer, in terms of a shift from negative to positive transfer, or in terms of an increasing positive transfer.

3. The effects of similarity vary as follows:

a. When learning to make a new response to an old stimulus, the learning is least facilitated when no similarities are present, and most facilitated when the initial and subsequent response are similar; when least facilitated, a slight degree of negative transfer occurs, and when most facilitated, a moderate degree of positive transfer occurs.

b. When learning to make an old response to a new stimulus, the learning is most facilitated when the subsequent stimulus is similar either to the subsequent response or to the initial stimulus, and least facilitated when the similarities are restricted to the factors of the initial learning; in this latter case, the similarity is even a disadvantage. But in all cases, marked positive transfer occurs.

Interpretation

Laws concerning the conditions of transfer of training:

1. Learning to make an old response to a new stimulus results in a marked degree of positive transfer.

2. Learning to make a new response to a new stimulus results in a slight degree of positive transfer.

3. Learning to make a new response to an old stimulus results in a slight degree of negative transfer.

4. Introducing similarities between two or more of the $S_1R_1S_2R_2$ terms increases positive transfer, and decreases negative transfer.

5. With increasing degrees of integration of the initial learning, there is an increase in the amount of positive transfer, and a decrease in the amount of negative transfer; where the amount of negative transfer is slight, it shifts to positive transfer.

*We are surrounded by a rich world that we take in through the senses:
The question is, how much is taken in at a time? We also retain
some of the information in immediate memory: The question is, how
much can be held in immediate memory at a time? This article
discusses the capacities of people to process information and some
answers to these questions are suggested.*

*This study has two rather separate aspects. First, the question of the
amount of information handled at a time is raised. From the data
presented, it would seem that the amount of information which
can be processed at a time has a rather definite limit. The second
main theme concerns memory. The author tries to show that there is
a limit on the number of items which can be retained in immediate
memory. In both cases, "the magic number seven" crops up: With
information input, the greatest number of inputs, on a unidimensional
scale, which can be identified without error, is about seven; in
immediate memory, the greatest number of items which can be held
in temporary storage is about seven. However, to some extent we
can break out of these limits: By adding dimensions to the stimulus
input, more information can be handled at a time; by recoding
information in memory, we can greatly extend the number of items
held in immediate storage.*

A POINT TO GUIDE YOUR STUDY   *The author is careful to define the
terms* channel, capacity, *and* bit *in the first few pages. An
understanding of these terms is essential for comprehension
of the article.*

21: THE MAGICAL NUMBER SEVEN, PLUS OR MINUS TWO: SOME LIMITS ON OUR CAPACITY FOR PROCESSING INFORMATION

George A. Miller, Harvard University

My problem is that I have been persecuted by an integer. For seven years this number has followed me around, has intruded in my most private data, and has assaulted me from the pages of our most public journals. This number assumes a variety of disguises, being sometimes a little larger and sometimes a little smaller than usual, but never changing so much as to be un-recognizable. The persistence with which this number plagues me is far more than a random accident. There is, to quote a famous senator, a design behind it, some pattern governing its appearances. Either there really is something unusual about the number or else I am suffering from delusions of persecution.

I shall begin my case history by telling you about some experiments that tested how accurately people can assign numbers to the magnitudes of various aspects of a stimulus. In the traditional language of psychology these would be called experiments in absolute judgment. Historical accident, however, has decreed that they should have another name. We now call them experiments on the capacity of people to transmit information. Since these

This paper was first read as an Invited Address before the Eastern Psychological Association in Philadelphia on April 15, 1955. Preparation of the paper was supported by the Harvard Psycho-Acoustic Laboratory under Contract N5ori-76 between Harvard University and the Office of Naval Research, U. S. Navy (Project NR142-201, Report PNR-174). Reproduction for any purpose of the U. S. Government is permitted.
    G. A. Miller. The magical number seven, plus or minus two: Some limits on our capacity for processing information. *Psychol. Rev.*, 1956, 53, 81-97. Copyright © 1956 by the American Psychological Association. Reprinted here with permission from the author and the American Psychological Association.

experiments would not have been done without the appearance of information theory on the psychological scene, and since the results are analyzed in terms of the concepts of information theory, I shall have to preface my discussion with a few remarks about this theory.

Information measurement

The "amount of information" is exactly the same concept that we have talked about for years under the name of "variance." The equations are different, but if we hold tight to the idea that anything that increases the variance also increases the amount of information we cannot go far astray.

The advantages of this new way of talking about variance are simple enough. Variance is always stated in terms of the unit of measurement—inches, pounds, volts, etc.—whereas the amount of information is a dimensionless quantity. Since the information in a discrete statistical distribution does not depend upon the unit of measurement, we can extend the concept to situations where we have no metric and we would not ordinarily think of using the variance. And it also enables us to compare results obtained in quite different experimental situations where it would be meaningless to compare variances based on different metrics. So there are some good reasons for adopting the newer concept.

The similarity of variance and amount of information might be explained this way: When we have a large variance, we are very ignorant about what is going to happen. If we are very ignorant, then when we make the observation it gives us a lot of information. On the other hand, if the variance is very small, we know in advance how our observation must come out, so we get little information from making the observation.

If you will now imagine a communication system, you will realize that there is a great deal of variability about what goes into the system and also a great deal of variability about what comes out. The input and the output can therefore be described in terms of their variance (or their information). If it is a good communication system, however, there must be some systematic relation between what goes in and what comes out. That is to say, the output will depend upon the input, or will be correlated with the input. If we measure this correlation, then we can say how much of the output variance is attributable to the input and how much is due to random fluctuations or "noise" introduced by the system during transmission. So we see that the measure of transmitted information is simply a measure of the input-output correlation.

There are two simple rules to follow. Whenever I refer to "amount of information," you will understand "variance." And whenever I refer to "amount of transmitted information," you will understand "covariance" or "correlation."

The situation can be described graphically by two partially overlapping circles. Then the left circle can be taken to represent the variance of the input, the right circle the variance of the output, and the overlap the covariance of input and output. I shall speak of the left circle as the amount of input information, the right circle as the amount of output information, and the overlap as the amount of transmitted information.

In the experiments on absolute judgment, the observer is considered to be a communication channel. Then the left circle would represent the amount of information in the stimuli, the right circle the amount of information in his responses, and the overlap the stimulus-response correlation as measured by the amount of transmitted information. The experimental problem is to increase the amount of input information and to measure the amount of transmitted information. If the observer's absolute judgments are quite accurate, then nearly all of the input information will be transmitted and will be recoverable from his responses. If he makes errors, then the transmitted information may be considerably less than the input. We expect that, as we increase the amount of input information, the observer will begin to make more and more errors; we can test the limits of accuracy of his absolute judgments. If the human observer is a reasonable kind of communication system, then when we increase the amount of input information the transmitted information will increase at first and will eventually level off at some asymptotic value. This asymptotic value we take to be the *channel capacity* of the observer: it represents the greatest amount of information that he can give us about the stimulus on the basis of an absolute judgment. The channel capacity is the upper limit on the extent to which the observer can match his responses to the stimuli we give him.

Now just a brief word about the *bit* and we can begin to look at some data. One bit of information is the amount of information that we need to make a decision between two equally likely alternatives. If we must decide whether a man is less than six feet tall or more than six feet tall and if we know that the chances are 50–50, then we need one bit of information. Notice that this unit of information does not refer in any way to the unit of length that we use—feet, inches, centimeters, etc. However you measure the man's height, we still need just one bit of information.

Two bits of information enable us to decide among four equally likely alternatives. Three bits of information enable us to decide among eight equally likely alternatives. Four bits of information decide among 16 alternatives, five among 32, and so on. That is to say, if there are 32 equally likely alternatives, we must make five successive binary decisions, worth one bit each, before we know which alternative

is correct. So the general rule is simple: every time the number of alternatives is increased by a factor of two, one bit of information is added.

There are two ways we might increase the amount of input information. We could increase the rate at which we give information to the observer, so that the amount of information per unit time would increase. Or we could ignore the time variable completely and increase the amount of input information by increasing the number of alternative stimuli. In the absolute judgment experiment we are interested in the second alternative. We give the observer as much time as he wants to make his response; we simply increase the number of alternative stimuli among which he must discriminate and look to see where confusions begin to occur. Confusions will appear near the point that we are calling his "channel capacity."

Absolute judgments
of unidimensional stimuli

Now let us consider what happens when we make absolute judgments of tones. Pollack (17) asked listeners to identify tones by assigning numerals to them. The tones were different with respect to frequency, and covered the range from 100 to 8000 cps in equal logarithmic steps. A tone was sounded and the listener responded by giving a numeral. After the listener had made his response he was told the correct identification of the tone.

When only two or three tones were used the listeners never confused them. With four different tones confusions were quite rare, but with five or more tones confusions were frequent. With fourteen different tones the listeners made many mistakes.

These data are plotted in Fig. 1. Along the bottom is the amount of input information in bits per stimulus. As the number of alternative tones was increased from 2 to 14, the input information increased from 1 to 3.8 bits. On the ordinate is plotted the amount of transmitted information. The amount of transmitted information behaves in much the way we would expect a communication channel to behave; the transmitted information increases linearly up to about 2 bits and then bends off toward an asymptote at about 2.5 bits. This value, 2.5 bits, therefore, is what we are calling the channel capacity of the listener for absolute judgments of pitch.

So now we have the number 2.5 bits. What does it mean? First, note that 2.5 bits corresponds to about six equally likely alternatives. The result means that we cannot pick more than six different pitches that the listener will never confuse. Or, stated slightly differently, no matter how many alternative tones we ask him to judge, the best we can expect him to do is to assign them to about six different classes without error. Or, again, if we know that there were N alternative stimuli, then his judgment enables us to narrow down the particular stimulus to one out of $N/6$.

Most people are surprised that the number is as small as six. Of course, there is evidence that a musically sophisticated person with absolute pitch can identify accurately any one of 50 or 60 different pitches. Fortunately, I do not have time to discuss these remarkable exceptions. I say it is fortunate because I do not know how to explain their superior performance. So I shall stick to the more pedestrian fact that most of us can identify about one out of only five or six pitches before we begin to get confused.

It is interesting to consider that psychologists have been using seven-point rating scales for a long time, on the intuitive basis that trying to rate into finer categories does not really add much to the usefulness of the ratings. Pollack's results indicate that, at least for pitches, this intuition is fairly sound.

Next you can ask how reproducible this

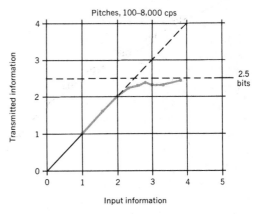

FIGURE 1 *Data from Pollack (17,18) on the amount of information that is transmitted by listeners who make absolute judgments of auditory pitch. As the amount of input information is increased by increasing from 2 to 14 the number of different pitches to be judged, the amount of transmitted information approaches as its upper limit a channel capacity of about 2.5 bits per judgment.*

result is. Does it depend on the spacing of the tones or the various conditions of judgment? Pollack varied these conditions in a number of ways. The range of frequencies can be changed by a factor of about 20 without changing the amount of information transmitted more than a small percentage. Different groupings of the pitches decreased the transmission, but the loss was small. For example, if you can discriminate five high-pitched tones in one series and five low-pitched tones in another series, it is reasonable to expect that you could combine all ten into a single series and still tell them all apart without error. When you try it, however, it does not work. The channel capacity for pitch seems to be about six and that is the best you can do.

While we are on tones, let us look next at Garner's (7) work on loudness. Garner's data for loudness are summarized in Fig. 2. Garner went to some trouble to get the best possible spacing of his tones over the intensity range from 15 to 110 db. He used

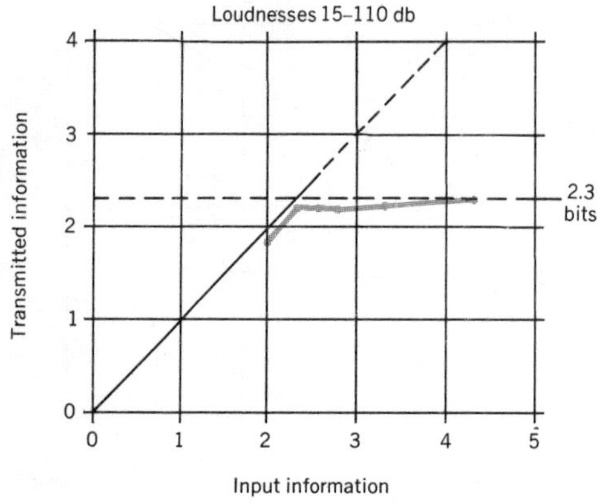

Loudnesses 15–110 db

2.3 bits

FIGURE 2 *Data from Garner (7) on the channel capacity for absolute judgments of auditory loudness.*

4, 5, 6, 7, 10, and 20 different stimulus intensities. The results shown in Fig. 2 take into account the differences among subjects and the sequential influence of the immediately preceding judgment. Again we find that there seems to be a limit. The channel capacity for absolute judgments of loudness is 2.3 bits, or about five perfectly discriminable alternatives.

Since these two studies were done in different laboratories with slightly different techniques and methods of analysis,

FIGURE 3 *Data from Beebe-Center, Rogers, and O'Connell (1) on the channel capacity for absolute judgments of saltiness.*

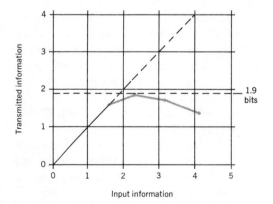

Tastes, judgments of saline concentration

1.9 bits

we are not in a good position to argue whether five loudnesses is significantly different from six pitches. Probably the difference is in the right direction, and absolute judgments of pitch are slightly more accurate than absolute judgments of loudness. The important point, however, is that the two answers are of the same order of magnitude.

The experiment has also been done for taste intensities. In Fig. 3 are the results obtained by Beebe-Center, Rogers, and O'Connell (1) for absolute judgments of the concentration of salt solutions. The concentrations ranged from 0.3 to 34.7 gm. NaCl per 100 cc. tap water in equal subjective steps. They used 3, 5, 9, and 17 different concentrations. The channel capacity is 1.9 bits, which is about four distinct concentrations. Thus taste intensities seem a little less distinctive than auditory stimuli, but again the order of magnitude is not far off.

On the other hand, the channel capacity for judgments of visual position seems to be significantly larger. Hake and Garner (8) asked observers to interpolate visually between two scale markers. Their results are shown in Fig. 4. They did the experiment in two ways. In one version they let the observer use any number between zero and 100 to describe the position, although they presented stimuli at only 5, 10, 20, or 50 different positions. The results with this unlimited response technique are shown by the filled circles on the graph. In the other version the observers were limited in their responses to reporting just those stimulus values that were possible. That is to say, in the second version the number of different responses that the observer could make was exactly the same as the number of different stimuli that the experimenter might present. The results with this limited response technique are shown by the open circles on the graph. The two functions are so similar that it seems fair to conclude that the number of

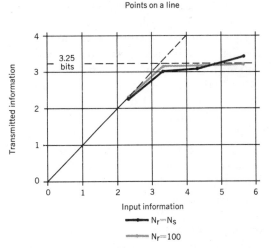

Points on a line

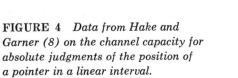

FIGURE 4 *Data from Hake and Garner (8) on the channel capacity for absolute judgments of the position of a pointer in a linear interval.*

responses available to the observer had nothing to do with the channel capacity of 3.25 bits.

The Hake-Garner experiment has been repeated by Coonan and Klemmer. Although they have not yet published their results, they have given me permission to say that they obtained channel capacities ranging from 3.2 bits for very short exposures of the pointer position to 3.9 bits for longer exposures. These values are slightly higher than Hake and Garner's, so we must conclude that there are between 10 and 15 distinct positions along a linear interval. This is the largest channel capacity that has been measured for any unidimensional variable.

At the present time these four experiments on absolute judgments of simple, unidimensional stimuli are all that have appeared in the psychological journals. However, a great deal of work on other stimulus variables has not yet appeared in the journals. For example, Eriksen and Hake (6) have found that the channel capacity for judging the sizes of squares is 2.2 bits, or about five categories, under a wide range of experimental conditions. In a separate experiment Eriksen (5) found 2.8 bits for size, 3.1 bits for hue, and 2.3 bits for brightness. Geldard has measured the channel capacity for the skin by plac-

ing vibrators on the chest region. A good observer can identify about four intensities, about five durations, and about seven locations.

One of the most active groups in this area has been the Air Force Operational Applications Laboratory. Pollack has been kind enough to furnish me with the results of their measurements for several aspects of visual displays. They made measurements for area and for the curvature, length, and direction of lines. In one set of experiments they used a very short exposure of the stimulus—$\frac{1}{40}$ second—and then they repeated the measurements with a 5-second exposure. For area they got 2.6 bits with the short exposure and 2.7 bits with the long exposure. For the length of a line they got about 2.6 bits with the short exposure and about 3.0 bits with the long exposure. Direction, or angle of inclination, gave 2.8 bits for the short exposure and 3.3 bits for the long exposure. Curvature was apparently harder to judge. When the length of the arc was constant, the result at the short exposure duration was 2.2 bits, but when the length of the chord was constant, the result was only 1.6 bits. This last value is the lowest that anyone has measured to date. I should add, however, that these values are apt to be slightly too low because the data from all subjects were poled before the transmitted information was computed.

Now let us see where we are. First, the channel capacity does seem to be a valid notion for describing human observers. Second, the channel capacities measured for these unidimensional variables range from 1.6 bits for curvature to 3.9 bits for positions in an interval. Although there is no question that the differences among the variables are real and meaningful, the more impressive fact to me is their considerable similarity. If I take the best estimates I can get of the channel capacities for all the stimulus variables I have mentioned, the mean is 2.6 bits and the standard deviation is only 0.6 bit. In terms of distinguishable alternatives, this mean corresponds to about 6.5 categories, one standard deviation includes from 4 to 10 categories, and the total range is from 3 to 15 categories. Considering the wide variety of different variables that have been studied, I find this to be a remarkably narrow range.

There seems to be some limitation built into us either by learning or by the design of our nervous systems, a limit that keeps our channel capacities in this general range. On the basis of the present evidence it seems safe to say that we possess a finite and rather small capacity for making such unidimensional judgments and that this capacity does not vary a great deal from one simple sensory attribute to another.

Absolute judgments of multi-dimensional stimuli

You may have noticed that I have been careful to say that this magical number seven applies to one-dimensional judgments. Everyday experience teaches us that we can identify accurately any one of several hundred faces, any one of several thousand words, any one of several thousand objects, etc. The story certainly would not be complete if we stopped at this point. We must have some understanding of why the one-dimensional variables we judge in the laboratory give results so far out of line with what we do constantly in our behavior outside the laboratory. A possible explanation lies in the number of independently variable attributes of the stimuli that are being judged. Objects, faces, words, and the like differ from one another in many ways, whereas the simple stimuli we have considered thus far differ from one another in only one respect.

Fortunately, there are a few data on what happens when we make absolute judgments of stimuli that differ from one another in several ways. Let us look first at the results Klemmer and Frick (13) have reported for the absolute judgment of the position of a dot in a square. In Fig. 5 we see their results. Now the channel capacity seems to have increased to 4.6 bits, which means that people can identify accurately any one of 24 positions in the square.

The position of a dot in a square is clearly a two-dimensional proposition. Both its horizontal and its vertical position must be identified. Thus it seems natural to compare the 4.6-bit capacity for a square with the 3.25-bit capacity for the position of a point in an interval. The point in the square requires two judgments of the interval type. If we have a capacity of 3.25 bits for estimating intervals and we do this twice, we should get 6.5 bits as our capacity for locating points in a square. Adding the second independent dimension gives us an increase from 3.25 to 4.6, but it falls short of the perfect addition that would give 6.5 bits.

Another example is provided by Beebe-Center, Rogers, and O'Connell. When they asked people to identify both the saltiness and the sweetness of solutions containing various concentrations of salt and sucrose, they found that the channel capacity was 2.3 bits. Since the capacity for salt alone was 1.9, we might expect about 3.8 bits if the two aspects of the compound stimuli were judged independently. As with spatial locations, the second dimension adds a little to the capacity but not as much as it conceivably might.

A third example is provided by Pollack (18), who asked listeners to judge both the loudness and the pitch of pure tones. Since pitch gives 2.5 bits and loudness gives 2.3 bits, we might hope to get as much as 4.8 bits for pitch and loudness together. Pollack obtained 3.1 bits, which again indicates that the second dimension augments the channel capacity but not so much as it might.

A fourth example can be drawn from the work of Halsey and Chapanis (9) on confusions among colors of equal luminance. Although they did not analyze their results in informational terms, they estimate that there are about 11 to 15 identifiable colors, or, in our terms, about 3.6 bits. Since these colors varied in both hue and saturation, it is probably correct to regard this as a two-dimensional judgment. If we compare this with Eriksen's 3.1 bits for hue (which is a questionable comparison to draw), we again have something less than perfect addition when a second dimension is added.

It is still a long way, however, from these two-dimensional examples to the multidimensional stimuli provided by faces, words, etc. To fill this gap we have only one experiment, an auditory study done by Pollack and Ficks (19). They managed to get six different acoustic variables that they could change: frequency, intensity, rate of interruption, on-time fraction, total duration, and spatial location. Each one of these six variables could assume any one of five different values, so altogether there were 5^6, or 15,625 different tones that they could present. The listeners made a separate rating for each one of these six dimensions. Under these conditions the transmitted information was

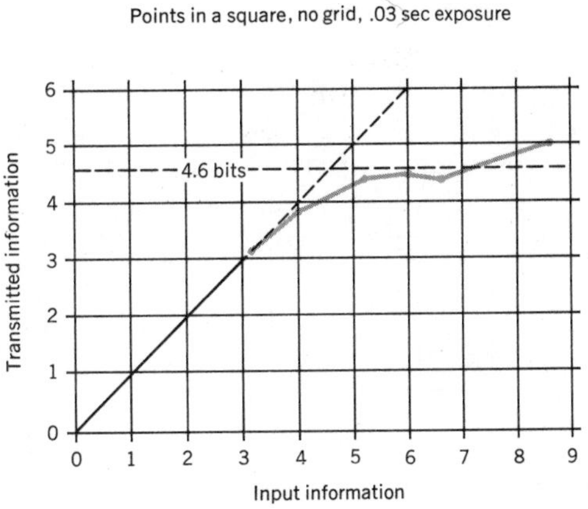

Points in a square, no grid, .03 sec exposure

FIGURE 5 *Data from Klemmer and Frick (13) on the channel capacity for absolute judgments of the position of a dot in a square.*

7.2 bits, which corresponds to about 150 different categories that could be absolutely identified without error. Now we are beginning to get up into the range that ordinary experience would lead us to expect.

Suppose that we plot these data, fragmentary as they are, and make a guess about how the channel capacity changes with the dimensionality of the stimuli. The result is given in Fig. 6. In a moment of considerable daring I sketched the dotted line to indicate roughly the trend that the data seemed to be taking.

Clearly, the addition of independently variable attributes to the stimulus increases the channel capacity, but at a decreasing rate. It is interesting to note that the channel capacity is increased even when the several variables are not independent. Eriksen (5) reports that, when size, brightness, and hue all vary together in perfect correlation, the transmitted information is 4.1 bits as compared with an average of about 2.7 bits when these attributes are varied one at a time. By confounding three attributes, Eriksen increased the dimensionality of the input without increasing the amount of input information; the result was an increase in channel

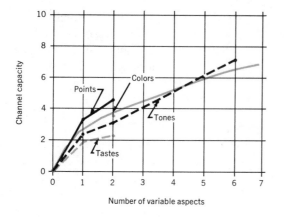

FIGURE 6 *The general form of the relation between channel capacity and the number of independently variable attributes of the stimuli.*

capacity of about the amount that the dotted function in Fig. 6 would lead us to expect.

The point seems to be that, as we add more variables to the display, we increase the total capacity, but we decrease the accuracy for any particular variable. In other words, we can make relatively crude judgments of several things simultaneously.

We might argue that in the course of evolution those organisms were most successful that were responsive to the widest range of stimulus energies in their environment. In order to survive in a constantly fluctuating world, it was better to have a little information about a lot of things than to have a lot of information about a small segment of the environment. If a compromise was necessary, the one we seem to have made is clearly the more adaptive.

Pollack and Ficks's results are very strongly suggestive of an argument that linguists and phoneticians have been making for some time (11). According to the linguistic analysis of the sounds of human speech, there are about eight or ten dimensions—the linguists call them *distinctive features*—that distinguish one phoneme from another. These distinctive features are usually binary, or at most ternary, in nature. For example, a binary distinction is made between vowels and consonants, a binary decision is made between oral and

nasal consonants, a ternary decision is made among front, middle, and back phonemes, etc. This approach gives us quite a different picture of speech perception than we might otherwise obtain from our studies of the speech spectrum and of the ear's ability to discriminate relative differences among pure tones. I am personally much interested in this new approach (15), and I regret that there is not time to discuss it here.

It was probably with this linguistic theory in mind that Pollack and Ficks conducted a test on a set of tonal stimuli that varied in eight dimensions, but required only a binary decision on each dimension. With these tones they measured the transmitted information at 6.9 bits, or about 120 recognizable kinds of sounds. It is an intriguing question, as yet unexplored, whether one can go on adding dimensions indefinitely in this way.

In human speech there is clearly a limit to the number of dimensions that we use. In this instance, however, it is not known whether the limit is imposed by the nature of the perceptual machinery that must recognize the sounds or by the nature of the speech machinery that must produce them. Somebody will have to do the experiment to find out. There is a limit, however, at about eight or nine distinctive features in every language that has been studied, and so when we talk we must resort to still another trick for increasing our channel capacity. Language uses sequences of phonemes, so we make several judgments successively when we listen to words and sentences. That is to say, we use both simultaneous and successive discriminations in order to expand the rather rigid limits imposed by the inaccuracy of our absolute judgments of simple magnitudes.

These multidimensional judgments are strongly reminiscent of the abstraction experiment of Külpe (14). As you may remember, Külpe showed that observers report more accurately on an attribute for which they are set than on attributes for which they are not set. For example, Chapman (4) used three different attributes and compared the results obtained when the observers were instructed before the tachistoscopic presentation with the results obtained when they were not told until after the presentation which one of the three attributes was to be reported. When the instruction was given in advance, the judgments were more accurate. When the instruction was given afterwards, the subjects presumably had to judge all three attributes in order to report on any one of them and the accuracy was correspondingly lower. This is in complete accord with the results we have just been considering, where the accuracy of judgment on each attribute decreased as more dimensions were added. The point is probably obvious, but I shall make it anyhow, that the abstraction experiments did *not* demonstrate that people can judge only one attribute at a time. They merely showed what seems quite reasonable, that people are less accurate if they must judge more than one attribute simultaneously.

Subitizing

I cannot leave this general area without mentioning, however briefly, the experiments conducted at Mount Holyoke College on the discrimination of number (12). In experiments by Kaufman, Lord, Reese, and Volkmann random patterns of dots were flashed on a screen for ⅕ of a second. Anywhere from 1 to more than 200 dots could appear in the pattern. The subject's task was to report how many dots there were.

The first point to note is that on patterns containing up to five or six dots the subjects simply did not make errors. The performance on these small numbers of dots was so different from the performance with more dots that it was given a special name. Below seven the subjects were said to *subitize;* above seven they were said to *estimate.* This is, as you will recognize, what we once optimistically called "the span of attention."

This discontinuity at seven is, of course, suggestive. Is this the same basic process that limits our unidimensional judgments to about seven categories? The generalization is tempting, but not sound in my opinion. The data on number estimates have not been analyzed in informational terms; but on the basis of the published data I would guess that the subjects transmitted something more than four bits of information about the number of dots. Using the same arguments as before, we would conclude that there are about 20 or 30 distinguishable categories of numerousness. This is considerably more information than we would expect to get from a unidimensional display. It is, as a matter of fact, very much like a two-dimensional display. Although the dimensionality of the random dot patterns is not entirely clear, these results are in the same range as Klemmer and Frick's for their two-dimensional display of dots in a square. Perhaps the two dimensions of numerousness are area and density. When the subject can subitize, area and density may not be the significant variables, but when the subject must estimate perhaps they are significant. In any event, the comparison is not so simple as it might seem at first thought.

This is one of the ways in which the magical number seven has persecuted me. Here we have two closely related kinds of experiments, both of which point to the significance of the number seven as a limit on our capacities. And yet when we examine the matter more closely, there seems to be a reasonable suspicion that it is nothing more than a coincidence.

The span of immediate memory

Let me summarize the situation in this way. There is a clear and definite limit to the accuracy with which we can identify absolutely the magnitude of a unidimensional stimulus variable. I would propose to call this limit the *span of absolute judgment,* and I maintain that for unidimensional judgments this span is usually somewhere in the neighborhood of seven. We are not completely at the mercy of this limited span, however, because we have a variety of techniques for getting around it and increasing the accuracy of our judgments. The three most important of these devices are (a) to make relative rather than absolute judgments; or, if that is not possible, (b) to increase the number of dimensions along which the stimuli can differ; or (c) to arrange the task in such a way that we make a sequence of several absolute judgments in a row.

The study of relative judgments is one of the oldest topics in experimental psychology, and I will not pause to review it now. The second device, increasing the dimensionality, we have just considered. It seems that by adding more dimensions and requiring crude, binary, yes-no judgments on each attribute we can extend the span of absolute judgment from seven to at least 150. Judging from our everyday behavior, the limit is probably in the thousands, if indeed there is a limit. In my opinion, we cannot go on compounding dimensions indefinitely. I suspect that

there is also a *span of perceptual dimensionality* and that this span is somewhere in the neighborhood of ten, but I must add at once that there is no objective evidence to support this suspicion. This is a question sadly needing experimental exploration.

Concerning the third device, the use of successive judgments, I have quite a bit to say because this device introduces memory as the handmaiden of discrimination. And, since mnemonic processes are at least as complex as are perceptual processes, we can anticipate that their interactions will not be easily disentangled.

Suppose that we start by simply extending slightly the experimental procedure that we have been using. Up to this point we have presented a single stimulus and asked the observer to name it immediately thereafter. We can extend this procedure by requiring the observer to withhold his response until we have given him several stimuli in succession. At the end of the sequence of stimuli he then makes his response. We will still have the same sort of input-output situation that is required for the measurement of transmitted information. But now we have passed from an experiment on absolute judgment to what is traditionally called an experiment on immediate memory.

Before we look at any data on this topic I feel I must give you a word of warning to help you avoid some obvious associations that can be confusing. Everybody knows that there is a finite span of immediate memory and that for a lot of different kinds of test materials this span is about seven items in length. I have just shown you that there is a span of absolute judgment that can distinguish about seven categories and that there is a span of attention that will encompass about six objects at a glance. What is more natural than to think that all three of these spans are different aspects of a single underlying process? And that is a fundamental mistake, as I shall be at some pains to demonstrate. This mistake is one of the malicious persecutions that the magical number seven has subjected me to.

My mistake went something like this. We have seen that the invariant feature in the span of absolute judgment is the amount of information that the observer can transmit. There is a real operational similarity between the absolute judgment experiment and the immediate memory experiment. If immediate memory is like absolute judgment, then it should follow that the invariant feature in the span of immediate memory is also the amount of information that an observer can retain. If the amount of information in the span of immediate memory is a constant, then the span should be short when the individual items contain a lot of information and the span should be long when the items contain little information. For example, decimal digits are worth 3.3 bits apiece. We can recall about seven of them, for a total of 23 bits of information. Isolated English words are worth about 10 bits apiece. If the total amount of information is to remain constant at 23 bits, then we should be able to remember only two or three words chosen at random. In this way I generated a theory about how the span of immediate memory should vary as a function of the amount of information per item in the test materials.

The measurements of memory span in the literature are suggestive on this question, but not definitive. And so it was necessary to do the experiment to see. Hayes (10) tried it out with five different kinds of test materials: binary digits, decimal digits, letters of the alphabet, letters plus decimal digits, and with 1,000 monosyllabic words. The lists were read aloud at the rate of one item per second and the subjects had as much time as they needed to give their responses. A procedure described by Woodworth (20) was used to score the responses.

The results are shown by the filled circles in Fig. 7. Here the dotted line indicates what the span should have been if the amount of information in the span were constant. The solid curves represent the data. Hayes repeated the experiment using test vocabularies of different sizes but all containing only English monosyllables (open circles in Fig. 7). This more homogeneous test material did not change the picture significantly. With binary items the span is about nine and, although it drops to about five with monosyllabic English words, the difference is far less than the hypothesis of constant information would require.

There is nothing wrong with Hayes's experiment, because Pollack (16) repeated it much more elaborately and got essen-

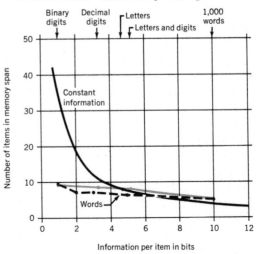

FIGURE 7 *Data from Hayes (10) on the span of immediate memory plotted as a function of the amount of information per item in the test materials.*

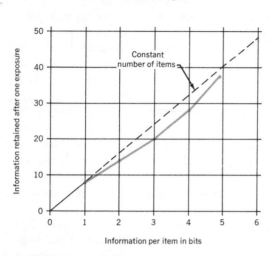

Letters and digits

Information retained after one exposure (y-axis)

Constant
number of items

Information per item in bits (x-axis)

FIGURE 8　*Data from Pollack (16) on
the amount of information retained
after one presentation plotted as a
function of the amount of information
per item in the test materials.*

tially the same result. Pollack took pains to measure the amount of information transmitted and did not rely on the traditional procedure for scoring the responses. His results are plotted in Fig. 8. Here it is clear that the amount of information transmitted is not a constant, but increases almost linearly as the amount of information per item in the input is increased.

And so the outcome is perfectly clear. In spite of the coincidence that the magical number seven appears in both places, the span of absolute judgment and the span of immediate memory are quite different kinds of limitations that are imposed on our ability to process information. Absolute judgment is limited by the amount of information. Immediate memory is limited by the number of items. In order to capture this distinction in somewhat picturesque terms, I have fallen into the custom of distinguishing between *bits* of information and *chunks* of information. Then I can say that the number of bits of information is constant for absolute judgment and the number of chunks of information is constant for immediate memory. The span of immediate memory seems to be almost independent of the number of bits per chunk, at least over the range that has been examined to date.

The contrast of the terms *bit* and *chunk* also serves to highlight the fact that we are not very definite about what constitutes a chunk of information. For example, the memory span of five words that Hayes obtained when each word was drawn at random from a set of 1,000 English monosyllables might just as appropriately have been called a memory span of 15 phonemes, since each word had about three phonemes in it. Intuitively, it is clear that the subjects were recalling five words, not 15 phonemes, but the logical distinction is not immediately apparent. We are dealing here with a process of organizing or grouping the input into familiar units or chunks, and a great deal of learning has gone into the formation of these familiar units.

Recoding

In order to speak more precisely, therefore, we must recognize the importance of grouping or organizing the input sequence into units or chunks. Since the memory span is a fixed number of chunks, we can increase the number of bits of information that it contains simply by building larger and larger chunks, each chunk containing more information than before.

A man just beginning to learn radio-telegraphic code hears each *dit* and *dah* as a separate chunk. Soon he is able to organize these sounds into letters and then he can deal with the letters as chunks. Then the letters organize themselves as words, which are still larger chunks, and he begins to hear whole phrases. I do not mean that each step is a discrete process, or that plateaus must appear in his learning curve, for surely the levels of organization are achieved at different rates and overlap each other during the learning process. I am simply pointing to the obvious fact that the dits and dahs are organized by learning into patterns and that as these larger chunks emerge the amount of message that the operator can remember increases correspondingly. In the terms I am proposing to use, the operator learns to increase the bits per chunk.

In the jargon of communication theory, this process would be called *recoding*. The input is given in a code that contains many chunks with few bits per chunk. The operator recodes the input into another code that contains fewer chunks with more bits per chunk. There are many ways to do this recoding, but probably the simplest is to group the input events, apply a new name to the group, and then remember the new name rather than the original input events.

Since I am convinced that this process is a very general and important one for psychology, I want to tell you about a demonstration experiment that should make perfectly explicit what I am talking about. This experiment was conducted by Sidney Smith and was reported by him before the Eastern Psychological Association in 1954.

Begin with the observed fact that people can repeat back eight decimal digits, but only nine binary digits. Since there is a large discrepancy in the amount of information recalled in these two cases, we suspect at once that a recoding procedure could be used to increase the span of immediate memory for binary digits. In Table 1 a method for grouping and renaming is illustrated. Along the top is a sequence of 18 binary digits, far more than any subject was able to recall after a single presentation. In the next line these same binary digits are grouped by pairs. Four possible pairs can occur: 00 is renamed 0, 01 is renamed 1, 10 is renamed 2, and 11 is renamed 3. That is to say, we recode from a base-two arithmetic to a base-four arithmetic. In the recoded sequence there are now just nine digits to remember, and this is almost within the span of immediate memory. In the next line the same sequence of binary digits is regrouped into chunks of three. There are eight possible sequences of three, so we give each sequence a new name between 0 and 7. Now we have recoded from a sequence of 18

TABLE 1 *Ways of recoding sequences of binary digits*

BINARY DIGITS (BITS)	1 0 1 0 0 0 1 0 0 1 1 1 0 0 1 1 1 0								
2:1 Chunks	10	10	00	10	01	11	00	11	10
Recoding	2	2	0	2	1	3	0	3	2
3:1 Chunks	101	000		100	111		001	110	
Recoding	5	0		4	7		1	6	
4:1 Chunks	1010		0010		0111		0011		10
Recoding	10		2		7		3		
5:1 Chunks	10100		01001			11001			110
Recoding	20		9			25			

binary digits into a sequence of 6 octal digits, and this is well within the span of immediate memory. In the last two lines the binary digits are grouped by fours and by fives and are given decimal-digit names from 0 to 15 and from 0 to 31.

It is reasonably obvious that this kind of recoding increases the bits per chunk, and packages the binary sequence into a form that can be retained within the span of immediate memory. So Smith assembled 20 subjects and measured their spans for binary and octal digits. The spans were 9 for binaries and 7 for octals. Then he gave each recoding scheme to five of the subjects. They studied the recoding until they said they understood it—for about 5 or 10 minutes. Then he tested their span for binary digits again while they tried to use the recoding schemes they had studied.

The recoding schemes increased their span for binary digits in every case. But the increase was not as large as we had expected on the basis of their span for octal digits. Since the discrepancy increased as the recoding ratio increased, we reasoned that the few minutes the subjects had spent learning the recoding schemes had not been sufficient. Apparently the translation from one code to the other

must be almost automatic or the subject will lose part of the next group while he is trying to remember the translation of the last group.

Since the 4:1 and 5:1 ratios require considerable study, Smith decided to imitate Ebbinghaus and do the experiment on himself. With Germanic patience he drilled himself on each recoding successively, and obtained the results shown in Fig. 9. Here the data follow along rather nicely with the results you would predict on the basis of his span for octal digits. He could remember 12 octal digits. With the 2:1 recoding, these 12 chunks were worth 24 binary digits. With the 3:1 recoding they were worth 36 binary digits. With the 4:1 and 5:1 recodings, they were worth about 40 binary digits.

It is a little dramatic to watch a person get 40 binary digits in a row and then repeat them back without error. However, if you think of this merely as a mnemonic trick for extending the memory span, you will miss the more important point that is implicit in nearly all such mnemonic devices. The point is that recoding is an extremely powerful weapon for increasing the amount of information that we can deal with. In one form or another we use recoding constantly in our daily behavior.

One highly practiced subject

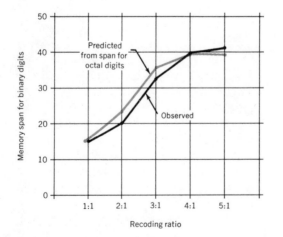

FIGURE 9   *The span of immediate memory for binary digits is plotted as a function of the recoding procedure used. The predicted function is obtained by multiplying the span for octals by 2, 3, and 3.3 for recoding into base 4, base 8, and base 10, respectively.*

In my opinion the most customary kind of recoding that we do all the time is to translate into a verbal code. When there is a story or an argument or an idea that we want to remember, we usually try to re-phrase it "in our own words." When we witness some event we want to remember, we make a verbal description of the event and then remember our verbalization. Upon recall we recreate by secondary elab-oration the details that seem consistent with the particular verbal recoding we happen to have made. The well-known ex-periment by Carmichael, Hogan, and Wal-ter (3) on the influence that names have on the recall of visual figures is one dem-onstration of the process.

The inaccuracy of the testimony of eye-witnesses is well known in legal psychol-ogy, but the distortions of testimony are not random—they follow naturally from the particular recoding that the witness used, and the particular recoding he used depends upon his whole life history. Our language is tremendously useful for re-packaging material into a few chunks rich in information. I suspect that imagery is a form of recoding, too, but images seem much harder to get at operationally and to study experimentally than the more symbolic kinds of recoding.

It seems probable that even memoriza-tion can be studied in these terms. The process of memorizing may be simply the formation of chunks, or groups of items that go together, until there are few enough chunks so that we can recall all the items. The work by Bousfield and Cohen (2) on the occurrence of clustering in the recall of words is especially interesting in this respect.

Summary

I have come to the end of the data that I wanted to present, so I would like now to make some summarizing remarks.

First, the span of absolute judgment and the span of immediate memory impose severe limitations on the amount of infor-mation that we are able to receive, process, and remember. By organizing the stimulus input simultaneously into several dimen-sions and successively into a sequence of chunks, we manage to break (or at least stretch) this informational bottleneck.

Second, the process of recoding is a very important one in human psychology and deserves much more explicit attention than it has received. In particular, the kind of linguistic recoding that people do seems to me to be the very lifeblood of the thought processes. Recoding procedures are a con-stant concern to clinicians, social psycholo-gists, linguists, and anthropologists and yet, probably because recoding is less ac-cessible to experimental manipulation than nonsense syllables or **T** mazes, the tradi-tional experimental psychologist has con-tributed little or nothing to their analysis. Nevertheless, experimental techniques can be used, methods of recoding can be speci-fied, behavioral indicants can be found. And I anticipate that we will find a very orderly set of relations describing what now seems an uncharted wilderness of in-dividual differences.

Third, the concepts and measures pro-vided by the theory of information provide a quantitative way of getting at some of these questions. The theory provides us with a yardstick for calibrating our stimu-lus materials and for measuring the per-formance of our subjects. In the interests of communication I have suppressed the technical details of information measure-ment and have tried to express the ideas in more familiar terms; I hope this para-phrase will not lead you to think they are not useful in research. Informational con-cepts have already proved valuable in the study of discrimination and of language; they promise a great deal in the study of learning and memory; and it has even been proposed that they can be useful in the study of concept formation. A lot of questions that seemed fruitless twenty or thirty years ago may now be worth another look. In fact, I feel that my story here must stop just as it begins to get really interesting.

And finally, what about the magical number seven? What about the seven wonders of the world, the seven seas, the seven deadly sins, the seven daughters of Atlas in the Pleiades, the seven ages of man, the seven levels of hell, the seven primary colors, the seven notes of the musical scale, and the seven days of the week? What about the seven-point rating scale, the seven categories for absolute judgment, the seven objects in the span of attention, and the seven digits in the span of immediate memory? For the present I propose to withhold judgment. Perhaps there is something deep and profound behind all these sevens, something just calling out for us to discover it. But I suspect that it is only a pernicious, Pythagorean coincidence.

References

1. Beebe-Center, J. G., Rogers, M. S., & O'Connell, D. N. Transmission of information about sucrose and saline solutions through the sense of taste. *J. Psychol.,* 1955, 39, 157–160.
2. Bousfield, W. A., & Cohen, B. H. The occurrence of clustering in the recall of randomly arranged words of different frequencies-of-usage. *J. gen. Psychol.,* 1955, 52, 83–95.
3. Carmichael, L., Hogan, H. P., & Walter, A. A. An experimental study of the effect of language on the reproduction of visually perceived form. *J. exp. Psychol.,* 1932, 15, 73–86.
4. Chapman, D. W. Relative effects of determinate and indeterminate *Aufgaben. Amer. J. Psychol.,* 1932, 44, 163–174.
5. Eriksen, C. W. Multidimensional stimulus differences and accuracy of discrimination. *USAF, WADC Tech. Rep.,* 1954, No. 54, 165.

6. Eriksen, C. W., & Hake, H. W. Absolute judgments as a function of the stimulus range and the number of stimulus and response categories. *J. exp. Psychol.,* 1955, 49, 323–332.
7. Garner, W. R. An informational analysis of absolute judgments of loudness. *J. exp. Psychol.,* 1953, 46, 373–380.
8. Hake, H. W., & Garner, W. R. The effect of presenting various numbers of discrete steps on scale reading accuracy. *J. exp. Psychol.,* 1951, 42, 358–366.
9. Halsey, R. M., & Chapanis, A. Chromaticity-confusion contours in a complex viewing situation. *J. Opt. Soc. Amer.,* 1954, 44, 442–454.
10. Hayes, J. R. M. Memory span for several vocabularies as a function of vocabulary size. In *Quarterly Progress Report,* Cambridge, Mass.: Acoustics Laboratory, Massachusetts Institute of Technology, Jan.–June, 1952.
11. Jakobson, R., Fant, C. G. M., & Halle, M. *Preliminaries to speech analysis.* Cambridge, Mass.: Acoustics Laboratory, Massachusetts Institute of Technology, 1952. (Tech. Rep. No. 13.)
12. Kaufman, E. L., Lord, M. W., Reese, T. W., & Volkmann, J. The discrimination of visual number. *Amer. J. Psychol.,* 1949, 62, 498–525.
13. Klemmer, E. T., & Frick, F. C. Assimilation of information from dot and matrix patterns. *J. exp. Psychol.,* 1953, 45, 15–19.
14. Külpe, O. Versuche über Abstraktion. *Ber. ü. d. I Kongr. f. exper. Psychol.,* 1904, 56–68.
15. Miller, G. A., & Nicely, P. E. An analysis of perceptual confusions among some English consonants. *J. Acoust. Soc. Amer.,* 1955, 27, 338–352.
16. Pollack, I. The assimilation of sequentially encoded information. *Amer. J. Psychol.,* 1953, 66, 421–435.
17. Pollack, I. The information of elementary auditory displays. *J. Acoust. Soc. Amer.,* 1952, 24, 745–749.
18. Pollack, I. The information of elementary auditory displays. II. *J. Acoust. Soc. Amer.,* 1953, 25, 765–769.
19. Pollack, I., & Ficks, L. Information of elementary multi-dimensional auditory displays. *J. Acoust. Soc. Amer.,* 1954, 26, 155–158.
20. Woodworth, R. S. *Experimental psychology.* New York: Holt, 1938.

Memory traces seem to get stronger for a short period after exposure to the learning material. In other words, the memory trace seems to "consolidate." As shown in many animal experiments and, as here, in a study with human subjects, the memory trace seems to be rather fragile and easily disrupted immediately after learning. More evidence for the consolidation of memory traces is given in the article on the "Material Basis of Memory" in Section Twenty.

The electroconvulsive shock (ECS) given to patients in this experiment was used as therapy to alleviate behavioral, or mental, symptoms. It is a standard type of therapy with certain types of behavior disorders; when used as therapy, it is usually termed electroconvulsive therapy (ECT). ECS—a large electric current passed through the brain—presumably disrupts the ongoing electrical activity of the brain which carries the short-term memory trace. Presumably this disruption of the brain electrical activity interferes with consolidation.

POINTS TO GUIDE YOUR STUDY   *(1) Of the three groups of the experiment, Group I patients received both drug sedation and ECS; Group II patients were given drug sedation but no ECS; Group III patients received neither sedation nor ECS—thus Group III was a control group. Since patients in both groups I and II received sedation, but only Group I patients received ECS, a comparison between these groups gives information about the memory effects of ECS. A comparison of Groups II and III gives information about the effects of drug sedation alone on memory consolidation.   (2) The values given in Table 1 are: the means, or averages; the standard deviations, or measures of variability (abbreviated s in the table); the differences between the means of scores before and after ECS; and the t values (see below). The differences between the means are most revealing. In Table 2, the differences between the means are systematically arranged and F values (see below) are given. In addition, t values (see below) for comparisons between the groups are given.*

(3) The p values are to be interpreted as in other experiments in which statistical analysis was done. (See the article by Braun and Geiselhart in Section Three.) Just to refresh your memory—in case consolidation has not occurred—the p values give the odds that the obtained differences are due to chance alone. For instance, a p value of .001 means that the difference would be obtained once in 1,000 times by chance alone. Therefore, since the chance odds are so small, we can argue that the obtained difference is a real one and not due to chance. The t values and F values in Tables 1 and 2 are the numbers from which these probability statements can be derived.

22: MEMORY DISTURBANCES AFTER ELECTROCONVULSIVE THERAPY. 4. INFLUENCE OF INTERPOLATED ELECTROCONVULSIVE SHOCK ON RETENTION OF MEMORY MATERIAL

Börje Cronholm, Karolinska Sjukhuset, Stockholm, Sweden, and Lars Molander, Statens Arbetsklinik, Solna, Sweden

Problem

The aim of the present investigation is to study the influence of an electroconvulsive shock (ECS) on retention of memory material learnt one hour before shock. We have also studied the effect in the same respect of a dose of Evipan given one hour after learning.

Earlier investigations

It is well known that memory material learnt some time before an ECS will be forgotten to an abnormal extent. Most of the psychological methods used to study retrograde amnesia after an ECS in man do not seem to be either sensitive or reliable enough to be used to study possible differences between influence on retention by an ECS when induced by different methods, under different conditions or in different groups of individuals.—For a review see *Cronholm & Lagergren* (1959).

A priori it seems just as reasonable to assume that a dose of Evipan given after learning will facilitate or hamper retention. Several investigations have shown the disturbing influence of activity on retention of memory material, and that sleep immediately after learning improves retention [see *Woodworth & Schlosberg* (1954)]. It is thus possible that if sleep (or at least drowsiness) is medically induced shortly after learning, retention will be better than when the patient remains awake. On the other hand, *Leukel* (1957)

found that anesthetization of rats by means of sodium pentothal 1 min. after each trial during maze learning slowed the rate of habit acquisition. Anesthetization 30 min. after learning had no such effect, however. He concludes that sodium pentothal has the effect of attenuating a "consolidation" process following each experimental trial.

GENERAL PROCEDURE   A number of patients for whom electroconvulsive therapy (ECT) was prescribed (or could at least be considered) were examined with two parallel forms of three memory tests on two successive days. (In two cases the interval was two days). Reproduction was studied immediately after learning and six hours later. The two forms of the tests were used alternatively at the first and at the second examination.

Three groups of patients were examined.

In Group I the possible influence on retention of an ECS (in combination with Evipan (hexobarbital sodium), Skopyl (methscopolamine nitrate) and Celocurin (suxamethonium iodide)) was studied.

In Group II the possible influence on retention of Evipan (in combination with Skopyl) was studied.

In Group III the possible influence of repeating the same test procedure on succeeding days was studied. This group served as a control relative to Groups I and II.

MATERIAL   For the investigation we chose in-patients at the Psychiatric Department, Karolinska sjukhuset, with a relatively mild disturbance, which in most cases had a depressive colouring. The patients should be "testable," that is, they should agree to the examination and have a good motiva-

B. Cronholm and L. Molander. Memory disturbances after electroconvulsive therapy. 4. Influence of an inter-polated electroconvulsive shock on retention of memory material. *Acta Psychiat. Neurol. Scand.*, 1961, 36, 83–90. Copyright © 1961 by Munksgaard. Reprinted here with permission from the authors and the publisher.

tion for it. If these criteria were satisfied we found it permissible to include even patients with a mild schizophrenic residual state, alcoholism or abuse of barbiturates. Each group comprised 16 patients, 10 women and 6 men.

In Group I the patients' ages ranged from 26–55 years (M = 39.6 years). The diagnoses were psychoneurosis 9 (in one case with mental deficiency), psychogenic depression 2 (in one case with abuse of barbiturates), mild endogenous depression 3, mild schizophrenic residual state (with abuse of barbiturates) 1 and psychopathic personality 1. 3 of the patients had received ECT earlier, the minimum interval was one year.

In Group II the patients' ages ranged from 27–53 years (M = 38.0 years). The diagnoses were psychoneurosis 6, psychogenic depression 4, mild endogenous depression 4, torticollis spastica 1 and psychopathic personality 2 (in one case with alcoholism). 4 of the patients had received ECT earlier; the minimum interval was one year. 10 patients received ECT after the examination.

In Group III the patients' ages ranged from 26–56 years (M = 40.3 years). The diagnoses were psychoneurosis 8, psychogenic depression 4 (in one case with alcoholism), mild endogenous depression 2, psychopathic personality 1 and neurocirculatory asthenia 1. 5 patients had received ECT earlier; the minimum interval was about eleven months. 9 patients received ECT after the examination.

The groups seem to be fairly equal as regards age and mental state, in spite of the varying clinical diagnoses.

PSYCHOLOGICAL METHODS   The 30 word pair and the 20 figure tests, described by *Cronholm & Molander* (1957), and the 15 letter-symbol pair test, described by *Cronholm & Blomquist* (1959), were used. The method of administration was the same as described in these papers; the

only difference in procedure was that we studied reproduction immediately and six hours after learning instead of immediately and three hours after learning. The reason for this was that in Groups I and II we wished to carry out the second study of reproduction late enough to ensure that the most acute effects of ECS and the Evipan dose had disappeared. The order of the tests was always the same: first the figure, then the word pair and last the letter-symbol pair test.

The learning and the first examination required about 20 min. and the second examination about 10 min.

In all the tests the number of items recalled immediately is denoted immediate reproduction and that recalled six hours later is denoted delayed reproduction. The difference between these two scores is denoted forgetting.

EXPERIMENTAL PROCEDURE   In all groups there was no medical interference between learning and reproduction six hours later on the first day of examination. The results thus served as controls on the results achieved during the second day of examination, where the procedure differed in the different groups.

Group I. On the second day of examination, learning started one hour before an ECS was induced. Siemens Konvulsator III [*v. Braunmühl* (1951)] was used for electroshock treatment. ECS was induced with unidirectional electric impulses, the apparatus was adjusted to gains 7–8 and the current was applied for 1.9–5.4 sec. depending on age. In all cases a major seizure was induced. About forty-five minutes before an ECS was induced the patients received 0.25 mg Skopyl intramuscularly. Immediately before treatment they were given intravenously a dose of Evipan (5 mg/kg body weight) and of Celocurin (in men 1.5 mg and in women 1 mg/kg body weight) [see *Holmberg & Thesleff* (1952)]. At the examination five

TABLE 1   *Test results*

| | GROUP I | | | | | |
| | 1. EXAM. NO MEDICAL IN- TEFERENCE | | 2. EXAM. ECS (+ EVIPAN) 1 HOUR AFTER LEARNING | | DIFFERENCE | |
	MEAN	s	MEAN	s	MEAN	t
The 30 word pair test						
Correct answers immediately (A)	19.1	4.2	18.6	5.2	0.4	–
Correct answers 6 hrs later (B)	12.1	4.1	5.9	4.2	6.2	5.68***
Forgetting (A-B)	6.9	3.5	12.7	4.7	—5.8	4.71***
The 20 figure test[1]						
Correct answers immediately (A)	16.3	2.5	16.1	2.9	0.3	–
Correct answers 6 hrs later (B)	14.4	2.6	9.6	4.6	4.8	4.76***
Forgetting (A-B)	1.9	1.1	6.4	3.5	—4.6	4.58***
The 15 letter-symbol test						
Correct answers immediately (A)	8.2	3.9	9.9	3.2	—1.9	2.10
Correct answers 6 hrs later (B)	3.8	3.2	1.8	1.6	2.1	3.31**
Forgetting (A-B)	4.4	2.3	8.2	2.8	—3.8	5.29***

[1] Without correction for guessing.
** $0.0001 < p < 0.01$.   *** $p \leq 0.001$.

hours after ECS the patients displayed as a rule a slight elevation of mood compared with their emotional state at the first examination. Some of them, however, complained of headache and nausea.

Group II. On the second day of examination the same doses of Skopyl and Evipan were given at the same times relative to learning as in Group I. No ECS was given. It is highly improbable that Skopyl influences memory performances but to be able to compare performances in this group and in Group I we found it desirable to make conditions as similar as possible. As Celocurin causes some discomfort and as it is still more improbable that this drug influences memory performances, we refrained from giving it in this group. After the injection of Evipan the patients became markedly somnolent and some fell asleep for a short while. At the examination five hours later the patients' mental state was the same as before the injections, and many of them expressed their satisfaction with the relaxing effect of the injection.

Group III. In this group there was no medical interference between learning and reproduction six hours later, neither on the first nor on the second day of examination.

STATISTICAL METHODS   To examine whether the mean test results at the first and second day of examination differ significantly we have made use of Fisher's t-test for paired sets of measurements [see *Guilford* (1950) formula 9.41]. To examine whether these mean differences are significantly dissimilar between the groups we have first applied an analysis of variance [see, e.g. *Guilford* (1950) p. 236 ff.]. When the variance ratio F proved significant below the 0.05 level we also made use of Fisher's t-test for uncorrelated means [see *Guilford* (1950) formula 9.39].

RESULTS   The test results in all three groups are seen from Table 1. The results

| GROUP II | | | | | | GROUP III | | | | | |
| 1. EXAM. NO MEDICAL IN-TEFERENCE | | 2. EXAM. EVIPAN 1 HOUR AFTER LEARNING | | DIFFERENCE | | 1. EXAM. NO MEDICAL IN-TEFERENCE | | 2. EXAM. NO MEDICAL IN-TEFERENCE | | DIFFERENCE | |
MEAN	s	MEAN	s	MEAN	t	MEAN	s	MEAN	s	MEAN	t
18.8	5.8	17.5	6.7	1.3	–	17.3	5.3	17.7	5.4	−0.4	–
12.3	6.4	10.8	6.9	1.7	1.74	11.9	6.3	11.6	5.1	0.3	–
6.4	2.4	6.8	3.7	−0.4	–	5.3	3.0	6.1	3.8	−0.8	–
17.4	2.2	16.2	3.2	1.3	–	17.1	3.4	16.1	2.8	0.9	–
14.8	4.3	13.7	3.1	1.1	–	15.3	3.4	13.4	2.9	1.9	3.96**
2.7	2.7	2.5	1.6	0.2	–	1.8	1.5	2.8	2.1	−0.9	–
8.1	3.7	9.3	3.9	−1.1	–	8.2	3.4	8.3	3.2	−0.1	–
4.0	2.8	3.4	3.3	0.6	–	4.3	3.2	3.9	3.3	0.4	–
4.1	2.8	5.8	3.3	−1.7	–	3.9	1.9	4.4	1.9	−0.6	–

of analysis of variance and the t-tests of the differences between the mean group differences in scores at the first and second day of examination are seen from Table 2.

Discussion

It is seen from Table 1 that the test results at the first day of examination are rather similar in the three groups. The pre-treatment level of performance could thus be regarded as uniform in the groups. The scores on immediate reproduction differ only insignificantly at the first and second day of examination in all groups.

In all three tests performances were much worse six hours after learning at the second day of examination in Group I, where an ECS was interpolated one hour after learning. The same holds true of the scores for forgetting. In the other groups there were only small differences between these performances at the first and second day of examination. The only exception is

that delayed reproduction was significantly worse in the figure test at the second day of examination in Group III, where exactly the same procedure was repeated on both days.

It is seen from Table 2 that the change from the first to the second day of examination in scores for delayed reproduction and forgetting differ significantly between Group I and the other groups in the word pair and the figure tests. In the letter-symbol pair test, however, there is a significant difference only as regards forgetting between Groups I and III.

In line with earlier investigations the study has shown that an ECS has a considerable, adverse effect on the retention of recently learnt memory material. When Evipan was given at the same time after learning it had no effect on retention and thus the effect in the group who had an ECS could be ascribed to the ECS itself. A possible source of error is that the impairment of the general state, with head-

TABLE 2 *Statistical analysis of mean group differences (M_d) between test performances at the first and second day of examination. The standard deviations of M_d (s) are given in italics.*

| | ANALYSIS OF VARIANCE | | | | t-VALUES FOR THE DIFFERENCES BETWEEN | | |
| | M_d AND s IN GROUP | | | | M_d IN GROUP | | |
	I	II	III	F	I–II	I–III	II–III
The 30 word pair test							
Correct answers	0.4	1.3	—0.4	0.71	–	–	–
immediately (A)	*3.8*	*4.8*	*3.2*				
Correct answers	6.2	1.7	0.3	6.51**	2.39*	4.18***	0.79
6 hrs. later (B)	*4.2*	*5.9*	*3.5*				
Forgetting (A-B)	—5.8	—0.4	0.8	8.45***	3.51**	3.29**	0.31
	4.7	*3.7*	*3.5*				
The 20 figure test[1]							
Correct answers	0.3	1.3	0.9	0.85	–	–	–
immediately (A)	*2.0*	*2.3*	*2.2*				
Correct answers	4.8	1.1	1.9	6.24**	3.03**	2.59*	0.96
6 hrs. later (B)	*3.9*	*2.7*	*1.8*				
Forgetting (A-B)	—4.6	0.2	0.9	9.64***	3.90***	3.14**	1.15
	3.9	*2.8*	*2.3*				
The 15 letter-symbol test							
Correct answers	—1.9	—1.1	—0.1	1.10	–	–	–
immediately (A)	*3.4*	*3.0*	*2.6*				
Correct answers	2.1	0.6	0.4	1.90	–	–	–
6 hrs. later (B)	*2.4*	*3.6*	*3.2*				
Forgetting (A-B)	3.8	1.7	0.6	4.86*	1.76	3.60**	1.02
	2.8	*3.7*	*2.0*				

[1] Without correction for guessing.
* $0.01 < p \leq 0.05$.　　** $0.001 < p < 0.01$.
*** $p \leq 0.001$.

ache and nausea in some cases, might have influenced the results adversely. However, the patients worked with good motivation and such impairment of the general state was neither marked nor present in all cases. Further, *Cronholm & Molander* (1957) found no impairment in any other tests than memory tests six hours after an ECS. It is thus improbable that this factor is of any importance.

Neither the hypothesis of impaired nor of improved retention after a dose of Evipan could be confirmed. It is still possible that a greater dose, or a dose given sooner after learning, may have some effect, however. The great differences between performances in the word pair and the figure tests when an ECS was interpolated after learning, and when it was not, indicate a high sensitivity of the tests to the influence of an ECS. Thus they could be expected to be useful in studies of possible differences between the influence of an ECS on retention when different methods are used or when conditions differ otherwise.

Summary

In three groups of patients, reproduction of memory material immediately and six hours after learning was studied under different conditions by means of the 30 word pair, the 20 figure and the 15 letter-symbol pair tests. Each group consisted of 16 in-patients at the Psychiatric Department, Karolinska sjukhuset, all with a relatively mild mental disturbance. They were all considered "testable," they agreed to the examination and were well motivated. In one group an ECS in combination with Evipan (hexobarbital sodium), Skopyl (methscopolamine nitrate) and Celocurin (suxamethonium iodide) was given one hour after learning, in another group Evipan was given one hour after learning (in combination with Skopyl). In both groups performances were compared with performances in the same individuals when there was no medical interference between learning and delayed reproduction. In the third group the same procedure with no medical interference was repeated on succeeding days. In the word pair and the figure tests forgetting was much greater when an ECS was given one hour after learning than when there was no medical interference or when Evipan (and Skopyl) only was given. Evipan in itself could not be shown to have any effect on forgetting.

References

von Braunmühl, A. (1951): Ein neues Gerät für die Heilkrampfbehandlung mittels elektrischen Stromes. Fortschr. Neurol. & Psychiat. **19**, 325–332.

Cronholm, B., & L. Molander (1957): Memory disturbances after electroconvulsive therapy. 1. Conditions 6 hours after electroshock treatment. Acta psychiat. scand. **32**, 280–306.

Cronholm, B., & C. Blomquist (1959): Memory disturbances after electroconvulsive therapy. 2. Conditions one week after a series of treatments. Acta. psychiat. scand. **34**, 18–25.

Cronholm, B., & Å. Lagergren (1959): Memory disturbances after electroconvulsive therapy. 3. An experimental study of retrograde amnesia after electroshock treatment. Acta psychiat. scand. **34**, 283–310.

Guilford, J. P. (1950): Fundamental statistics in psychology and education. New York.

Holmberg, G., & S. Thesleff (1952): Succinyl-choline-iodide as a muscular relaxant in electroshock therapy. Am. J. Psychiat. **108**, 842–846.

Leukel, F. (1957): A comparison of the effects of ECS and anesthesia on acquisition of the maze habit. J. Comp. Physiol. Psychol. **50**, 300–306.

Woodworth, R. S., & H. Schlosberg (1954): Experimental Psychology. New York, Holt.

Most psychologists agree that interference is the most important cause of forgetting. Two major varieties of interference have been proposed—retroactive interference and proactive interference. In retroactive interference, material learned after the originally learned material interferes with the retention of the originally learned material. In proactive interference, material learned before other material interferes with the retention of the newly-learned material. It is the contention of this article, and evidence is cited to support it, that most forgetting in some of the classical laboratory experiments on forgetting—for instance, those of Ebbinghaus—was due to proactive interference.

A POINT TO GUIDE YOUR STUDY   *With the importance of proactive interference well established, some of the major variables affecting forgetting are analyzed again at the conclusion of this paper.*

23: INTERFERENCE AND FORGETTING

Benton J. Underwood, Northwestern University

I know of no one who seriously maintains that interference among tasks is of no consequence in the production of forgetting. Whether forgetting is conceptualized at a strict psychological level or at a neural level (e.g., neural memory trace), some provision is made for interference to account for at least some of the measured forgetting. The many studies on retroactive inhibition are probably responsible for this general agreement that interference among tasks must produce a sizable proportion of forgetting. By introducing an interpolated interfering task very marked decrements in recall can be produced in a few minutes in the laboratory. But there is a second generalization which has resulted from these studies, namely, that most forgetting must be a function of the learning of tasks which interfere with that which has already been learned (19). Thus, if a single task is learned in the laboratory and retention measured after a week, the loss has been attributed to the interference from activities learned outside the laboratory during the week. It is this generalization with which I am concerned in the initial portions of this paper.

Now, I cannot deny the data which show large amounts of forgetting produced by an interpolated list in a few minutes in the laboratory. Nor do I deny that this loss may be attributed to interference. But I will try to show that use of retroactive inhibition as a paradigm of forgetting (via interference) may be seriously questioned.

Address of the president, Midwestern Psychological Association, St. Louis, Missouri, May, 1956.

Most of the data from my own research referred to in this paper were obtained from work done under Contract N7 onr-45008, Project NR 154-057, between Northwestern University and The Office of Naval Research.

B. J. Underwood. Interference and forgetting. *Psychol. Rev.*, 1957, **64**, 49–60. Copyright © 1957 by the American Psychological Association. Reprinted here with permission from the author and the American Psychological Association.

To be more specific: if a subject learns a single task, such as a list of words, and retention of this task is measured after a day, a week, or a month, I will try to show that very little of the forgetting can be attributed to an interfering task learned outside the laboratory during the retention interval. Before pursuing this further, I must make some general comments by way of preparation.

Whether we like it or not, the experimental study of forgetting has been largely dominated by the Ebbinghaus tradition, both in terms of methods and materials used. I do not think this is due to sheer perversity on the part of several generations of scientists interested in forgetting. It may be noted that much of our elementary knowledge can be obtained only by rote learning. To work with rote learning does not mean that we are thereby not concerning ourselves with phenomena that have no counterparts outside the laboratory. Furthermore, the investigation of these phenomena can be handled by methods which are acceptable to a science. As is well known, there are periodic verbal revolts against the Ebbinghaus tradition (e.g., 2, 15, 22). But for some reason nothing much ever happens in the laboratory as a consequence of these revolts. I mention these matters neither by way of apology nor of justification for having done some research in rote learning, but for two other reasons. First, it may very well be true, as some have suggested (e.g., 22), that studies of memory in the Ebbinghaus tradition are not getting at all of the important phenomena of memory. I think the same statement—that research has not got at all of the important processes—could be made about all areas in psychology; so that the criticism (even if just) should not be indigenous to the study of memory. Science does not deal at will with all natural events. Science deals with natural events only when ingenuity in developing methods and techniques of measurement allow these events to be brought within the scope of science. If, therefore, the studies of memory which meet scientific acceptability do not tap all-important memorial processes, all I can say is that this is the state of the science in the area at the moment. Secondly, because the bulk of the systematic data on forgetting has been obtained on rote-learned tasks, I must of necessity use such data in discussing interference and forgetting.

Returning to the experimental situation, let me again put in concrete form the problem with which I first wish to deal. A subject learns a single task, such as a list of syllables, nouns, or adjectives. After an interval of time, say, 24 hours, his retention of this list is measured. The explanatory problem is what is responsible for the forgetting which commonly occurs over the 24 hours. As indicated earlier, the studies of retroactive inhibition led to the theoretical generalization that this forgetting was due largely to interference from other tasks learned during the 24-hour retention interval. McGeoch (20) came to this conclusion, his last such statement being made in 1942. I would, therefore, like to look at the data which were available to McGeoch and others interested in this matter. I must repeat that the kind of data with which I am concerned is the retention of a list without formal interpolated learning introduced. The interval of retention with which I am going to deal in this, and several subsequent analyses, is 24 hours.

First, of course, Ebbinghaus' data were available and in a sense served as the reference point for many subsequent investigations. In terms of percentage saved in relearning, Ebbinghaus showed about 65 per cent loss over 24 hours (7). In terms of recall after 24 hours, the following studies are representative of the amount

forgotten: Youtz, 88 per cent loss (37); Luh, 82 per cent (18); Krueger, 74 per cent (16); Hovland, 78 per cent (11); Cheng, 65 per cent and 84 per cent (6); Lester, 65 per cent (17). Let us assume as a rough average of these studies that 75 per cent forgetting was measured over 24 hours. In all of these studies the list was learned to one perfect trial. The percentage values were derived by dividing the total number of items in the list into the number lost and changing to a percentage. Thus, on the average in these studies, if the subject learned a 12-item list and recalled three of these items after 24 hours, 9 items (75 per cent) were forgotten.

The theory of interference as advanced by McGeoch, and so far as I know never seriously challenged, was that during the 24-hour interval subjects learned something outside the laboratory which interfered with the list learned in the laboratory. Most of the materials involved in the investigations cited above were nonsense syllables and the subjects were college students. While realizing that I am viewing these results in the light of data which McGeoch and others did not have available, it seems to me to be an incredible stretch of an interference hypothesis to hold that this 75 per cent forgetting was caused by something which the subjects learned outside the laboratory during the 24-hour interval. Even if we agree with some educators that much of what we teach our students in college is nonsense, it does not seem to be the kind of learning that would interfere with nonsense syllables.

If, however, this forgetting was not due to interference from tasks learned outside the laboratory during the retention interval, to what was it due? I shall try to show that most of this forgetting was indeed produced by interference—not from tasks learned outside the laboratory, but from tasks learned previously in the laboratory. Following this I will show that when interference from laboratory tasks is removed, the amount of forgetting which occurs is relatively quite small. It then becomes more plausible that this amount could be produced by interference from tasks learned outside the laboratory, although, as I shall also point out, the interference very likely comes from prior, not interpolated, learning.

In 1950 a study was published by Mrs. Greenberg and myself (10) on retention as a function of stage of practice. The orientation for this study was crassly empirical; we simply wanted to know if subjects learn how to recall in the same sense that they learn how to learn. In the conditions with which I am concerned, naïve subjects learned a list of ten paired adjectives to a criterion of eight out of ten correct on a single trial. Forty-eight hours later this list was recalled. On the following day, these same subjects learned a new list to the same criterion and recalled it after 48 hours. This continued for two additional lists, so that the subjects had learned and recalled four lists, but the learning and recall of each list was complete before another list was learned. There was low similarity among these lists as far as conventional symptoms of similarity are concerned. No words were repeated and no

obvious similarities existed, except for the fact that they were all adjectives and a certain amount of similarity among prefixes, suffixes, and so on must inevitably occur. The recall of these four successive lists is shown in Fig. 1.

As can be seen, the more lists that are learned, the poorer the recall, from 69 per cent recall of the first list to 25 per cent recall of the fourth list. In examining errors at recall, we found a sufficient number of intrusion responses from previous lists to lead us to suggest that the increasing decrements in recall were a function of proactive interference from previous lists. And, while we pointed out that these results had implications for the design of experiments on retention, the relevance to an interference theory of forgetting was not mentioned.

Dr. E. J. Archer has made available to me certain data from an experiment which still is in progress and which deals with this issue. Subjects learned lists of 12 serial adjectives to one perfect trial and recalled them after 24 hours. The recall of a list always took place prior to learning the next list. The results for nine successive lists are shown in Fig. 2. Let me say again that there is no laboratory activity during the 24-hour interval; the subject learns a list, is dismissed from the laboratory, and returns after 24 hours to recall the list. The percentage of recall falls from 71 per cent for the first list to 27 per cent for the ninth.

In summarizing the more classical data on retention above, I indicated that a rough estimate showed that after 24 hours 75 per cent forgetting took place, or recall was about 25 per cent correct. In viewing these values in the light of Greenberg's and Archer's findings, the conclusion seemed inescapable that the classical studies must have been dealing with subjects who had learned many lists. That is to say, the subjects must have served in many conditions by use of counterbalancing and re-

FIGURE 1   *Recall of paired adjectives as a function of number of previous lists learned (10).*

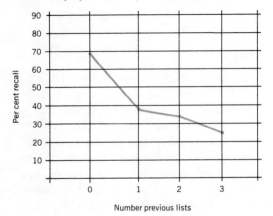

Number previous lists

peated cycles. To check on this I have made a search of the literature on the studies of retention to see if systematic data could be compiled on this matter. Preliminary work led me to establish certain criteria for inclusion in the summary to be presented. First, because degree of learning is such an important variable, I have included only those studies in which degree of learning was one perfect recitation of the list. Second, I have included only studies in which retention was measured after 24 hours. Third, I have included only studies in which recall measures were given. (Relearning measures add complexities with which I do not wish to deal in this paper.) Fourth, the summary includes only material learned by relatively massed practice. Finally, if an investigator had two or more conditions which met these criteria, I averaged the values for presentation in this paper. Except for these restrictions, I have used all studies I found (with an exception to be noted later), although I do not pretend to have made an exhaustive search. From each of these studies I got two facts: first, the percentage recall after 24 hours, and second, the average number of previous lists the subjects had learned before learning the list on which recall after 24 hours was taken. Thus, if a subject had served in five experimental conditions via counterbal-

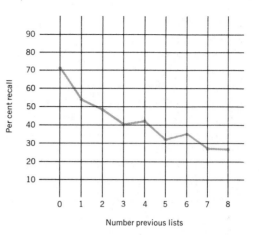

FIGURE 2 *Recall of serial adjective lists as a function of number of previous lists learned. (Unpublished data, courtesy of Dr. E. J. Archer.)*

ancing, and had been given two practice lists, the average number of lists learned before learning the list for which I tabulated the recall was four. This does not take into account any previous experiments in rote learning in which the subject might have served.

For each of these studies the two facts, average number of previous lists learned and percentage of recall, are related as in Fig. 3. For example, consider the study by Youtz. This study was concerned with Jost's law, and had several degrees of learning, several lengths of retention inter-

FIGURE 3 *Recall as a function of number of previous lists learned as determined from a number of studies. From left to right: Weiss and Margolius (35), Gibson (9), Belmont and Birch (3), Underwood and Richardson (33), Williams (36), Underwood (27, 28, 29, 30), Lester (17), Johnson (14), Krueger (16), Cheng (6), Hovland (11), Luh (18), Youtz (37).*

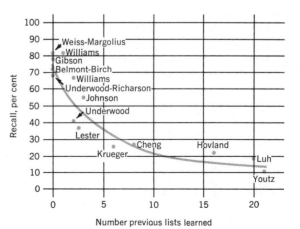

val, and the subjects served in two cycles. Actually, there were 15 experimental conditions and each subject was given each condition twice. Also, each subject learned six practice lists before starting the experimental conditions. Among the 15 conditions was one in which the learning of the syllables was carried to one perfect recitation and recall was taken after 24 hours. It is this particular condition in which I am interested. On the average, this condition would have been given at the time when the subject had learned six practice lists and 15 experimental lists, for a total of 21 previous lists.

The studies included in Fig. 3 have several different kinds of materals, from geometric forms to nonsense syllables to nouns; they include both paired-associate and serial presentation, with different speeds of presentation and different lengths of lists. But I think the general relationship is clear. The greater the number of previous lists learned the greater the forgetting. I interpret this to mean that the greater number of previous lists the greater the *proactive* interference. We know this to be true (26) for a formal proactive-inhibition paradigm; it seems a reasonable interpretation for the data of Fig. 3. That there are minor sources of variance still involved I do not deny. Some of the variation can be rationalized, but that is not the purpose of this report. The point I wish to make is the obvious one of the relationship between number of previous lists learned—lists which presumably had no intentionally built-in similarity—and amount of forgetting. If you like to think in correlational terms, the rank-order correlation between the two variables is −.91 for the 14 points of Fig. 3.

It may be of interest to the historian that, of the studies published before 1942 which met the criteria I imposed, I did not find a single one in which subjects had not been given at least one practice task before starting experimental conditions, and in most cases the subjects had several practice lists and several experimental conditions. Gibson's study (1942) was the first I found in which subjects served in only one condition and were not given practice tasks. I think it is apparent that the design proclivities of the 1920s and 1930s have been largely responsible for the exaggerated picture we have had of the rate of forgetting of rote-learned materials. On the basis of studies performed during the 1920s and 1930s, I have given a rough estimate of forgetting as being 75 per cent over 24 hours, recall being 25 per cent. On the basis of modern studies in which the subject has learned no previous lists— where there is no proactive inhibition from previous laboratory tasks—a rough estimate would be that forgetting is 25 per cent; recall is 75 per cent. The values are reversed. (If in the above and subsequent discussion my use of percentage values as if I were dealing with a cardinal or extensive scale is disturbing, I will say only that it makes the picture easier to grasp, and in my opinion no critical distortion results.)

Before taking the next major step, I would like to point out a few other observations which serve to support my general point that proactive inhibition from laboratory tasks has been the major cause of forgetting in the more classical studies. The first illustration I shall give exemplifies the point that when subjects have served in several conditions, forgetting after relatively short periods of time is greater than after 24 hours if the subject has served in only one condition. In the Youtz study to which I have already referred, other conditions were employed in which recall was taken after short intervals. After 20 minutes recall was 74 per cent, about what it is after 24 hours if the subject has not served in a series of conditions. After two hours recall was 32 per cent. In Ward's (34) well-known reminiscence experiment, subjects who on the average had learned ten previous lists showed a recall of only 64 per cent after 20 minutes.

In the famous Jenkins-Dallenbach (13) study on retention following sleep and following waking, two subjects were used. One subject learned a total of 61 lists and the other 62 in addition to several practice lists. Roughly, then, if the order of the conditions was randomized, approximately 30 lists had been learned prior to the learning of a list for a given experimental condition. Recall after eight waking hours for one subject was 4 per cent and for the other 14 per cent. Even after sleeping for eight hours the recall was only 55 per cent and 58 per cent.

I have said that an interpolated list can produce severe forgetting. However, in one study (1), using the A-B, A-C paradigm for original and interpolated learning, but using subjects who had never served in any previous conditions, recall of the original list was 46 per cent after 48 hours, and in another comparable study (24), 42 per cent. Thus, the loss is not nearly as great as in the classical studies I have cited where there was no interpolated learning in the laboratory.

My conclusion at this point is that, in terms of the gross analysis I have made, the amount of forgetting which might be attributed to interference from tasks learned outside the laboratory has been "reduced" from 75 per cent to about 25 per cent. I shall proceed in the next section to see if we have grounds for reducing this estimate still more. In passing on to this section, however, let me say that the study of factors which influence proactive inhibition in these counterbalanced studies is a perfectly legitimate and important area of study. I mention this because in the subsequent discussion I am going to deal only with the case where a subject has learned a single list in the laboratory, and I do not want to leave the impression that we

should now and forevermore drop the study of interference produced by previous laboratory tasks. Indeed, as will be seen shortly, it is my opinion that we should increase these studies for the simple reason that the proactive paradigm provides a more realistic one than does the retroactive paradigm.

When the subject learns and recalls a single list in the laboratory, I have given an estimate of 25 per cent as being the amount forgotten over 24 hours. When, as shown above, we calculate percentage forgotten of lists learned to one perfect trial, the assumption is that had the subjects been given an immediate recall trial, the list would have been perfectly recalled. This, of course, is simply not true. The major factor determining how much error is introduced by this criterion-percentage method is probably the difficulty of the task. In general, the overestimation of forgetting by the percentage method will be directly related to the difficulty of the task. Thus, the more slowly the learning approaches a given criterion, the greater the drop on the trial immediately after the criterion trial. Data from a study by Runquist (24), using eight paired adjectives (a comparatively easy task), shows that amount of forgetting is overestimated by about 10 per cent. In a study (32) using very difficult consonant syllables, the overestimation was approximately 20 per cent. To be conservative, assume that on the average the percentage method of reporting recall overestimates the amount forgotten by 10 per cent. If we subtract this from the 25 per cent assumed above, the forgetting is now re-estimated as being 15 per cent over 24 hours. That is to say, an interference theory, or any other form of theory, has to account for a very small amount of forgetting as compared with the amount traditionally cited.

What are the implications of so greatly "reducing" the amount of forgetting? There are at least three implications which

I feel are worth pointing out. First, if one wishes to hold to an interference theory of forgetting (as I do), it seems plausible to assert that this amount of forgetting could be produced from learning which has taken place outside of the laboratory. Furthermore, it seems likely that such interference must result primarily from proactive interference. This seems likely on a simple probability basis. A 20-year-old college student will more likely have learned something during his 20 years prior to coming to the laboratory that will interfere with his retention than he will during the 24 hours between the learning and retention test. However, the longer the retention interval the more important will retroactive interference become relative to proactive interferences.

The second implication is that these data may suggest greater homogeneity or continuity in memorial processes than hitherto supposed. Although no one has adequately solved the measurement problem of how to make comparisons of retention among conditioned responses, prose material, motor tasks, concept learning, and rote-learned tasks, the gross comparisons have indicated that rote-learned tasks were forgotten much more rapidly than these other tasks. But the rote-learning data used for comparison have been those derived with the classical design in which the forgetting over 24 hours is approximately 75 per cent. If we take the revised estimate of 15 per cent, the discrepanices among tasks become considerably less.

The third implication of the revised estimate of rate of forgetting is that the number of variables which appreciably influence rate of forgetting must be sharply limited. While this statement does not inevitably follow from the analyses I have made, the current evidence strongly supports the statement. I want to turn to the final section of this paper which will consist of a review of the influence of some of the variables which are or have been

thought to be related to rate of forgetting. In considering these variables, it is well to keep in mind that a variable which produces only a small difference in forgetting is important if one is interested in accounting for the 15 per cent assumed now as the loss over 24 hours. If appropriate for a given variable, I will indicate where it fits into an interference theory, although in no case will I endeavor to handle the details of such a theory.

Time. Passage of time between learning and recall is the critical defining variable for forgetting. Manipulation of this variable provides the basic data for which a theory must account. Previously, our conception of rate of forgetting as a function of time has been tied to the Ebbinghaus curve. If the analysis made earlier is correct, this curve does not give us the basic data we need. In short we must start all over and derive a retention curve over time when the subjects have learned no previous materials in the laboratory. It is apparent that I expect the fall in this curve over time to be relatively small.

In conjunction with time as an independent variable, we must, in explanations of forgetting, consider why sleep retards the processes responsible for forgetting. My conception, which does not really explain anything, is that since forgetting is largely produced by proactive interference, the amount of time which a subject spends in sleep is simply to be subtracted from the total retention interval when predicting the amount to be forgotten. It is known that proactive interference increases with passage of time (5); sleep, I believe, brings to a standstill whatever these processes are which produce this increase.

Degree of learning. We usually say that the better or stronger the learning the more or better the retention. Yet, we do not know whether or not the *rate* of forgetting differs for items of different strength. The experimental problem is a difficult one. What we need is to have a subject learn a single association and measure its decline in strength over time. But this is difficult to carry out with verbal material, since almost of necessity we must have the subject learn a series of associations, to make it a reasonable task. And, when a series of associations is learned, complications arise from interaction effects among associations of different strength. Nevertheless, we may expect, on the basis of evidence from a wide variety of studies, that given a constant degree of similarity, the effective interference varies as some function of the strength of associations.

Distribution of practice. It is a fact that distribution of practice during acquisition influences retention of verbal materials. The facts of the case seem to be as follows. If the subject has not learned previous lists in the laboratory, massed practice gives equal or better retention than does distributed practice. If, on the other hand, the subject has learned a number of previous lists, distributed practice will facilitate retention (32). We do not have the theoretical solution to these facts. The point I wish to make here is that whether or not distribution of learning inhibits or facilitates retention depends upon the amount of interference from previous learning. It is reasonable to expect, therefore, that the solution to the problem will come via principles handling interference in general. I might also say that a theoretical solution to this problem will also provide a solution for Jost's laws.

Similarity. Amount of interference from other tasks is closely tied to similarity. This similarity must be conceived of as similarity among materials as such and also situational similarity (4). When we turn to similarity within a task, the situation is not quite so clear. Empirically and theoretically (8) one would expect that intratask similarity would be a very relevant variable in forgetting. As discussed elsewhere (31), however, variation in intratask similarity almost inevitably leads to variations in intertask similarity. We do know from a recent study (33) that with material of low meaningfulness forgetting is significantly greater with high intralist similarity than with low. While the difference in magnitude is only about 8 per cent, when we are trying to account for a total loss of 15 per cent, this amount becomes a major matter.

Meaningfulness. The belief has long been held that the more meaningful the material the better the retention—the less the forgetting. Osgood (21) has pointed out that if this is true it is difficult for an interference theory to handle. So far as I know, the only direct test of the influence of this variable is a recent study in which retention of syllables of 100 per cent association value was compared with that of zero association value (33). There was no difference in the recall of these syllables. Other less precise evidence would support this finding when comparisons are made among syllables, adjectives, and nouns, as plotted in Fig. 3. However, there is some evidence that materials of very low meaningfulness are forgotten more rapidly than nonsense syllables of zero association value. Consonant syllables, both serial (32) and paired associates (unpublished), show about 50 per cent loss over 24 hours. The study using serial lists was the one mentioned earlier as knowingly omitted from Fig. 3. These syllables, being extremely difficult to learn, allow a correction of about 20 per cent due to criterion overestimation, but even with this much correction the forgetting (30 per cent) is still appreciably more than the estimate we have made for other materials. To invoke the interference theory to account for this discrepancy means that we must demonstrate how interference from other activities could be greater for these consonant syllables than for nonsense syllables, nouns, adjectives, and other materials. Our best guess at the present time is that the sequences of letters in consonant syllables are contrary to other well-established language habits. That is to say, letter sequences which commonly occur in our language are largely different from those in consonant syllables. As a consequence, not only are these consonant syllables very difficult to learn, but forgetting is accelerated by proactive interference from previously well-learned letter sequences. If subsequent research cannot demonstrate such a source of interference, or if some other source is not specified, an interference theory for this case will be in some trouble.

Affectivity. Another task dimension which has received extensive attention is the affective tone of the material. I would also include here the studies attaching unpleasant experiences to some items experimentally and not to others, and measuring retention of these two sets of items. Freud is to a large extent responsible for these studies, but he cannot be held responsible for the malformed methodology which characterizes so many of them. What can one say by way of summarizing these studies? The only conclusion that I can reach is a statistical one, namely, that the occasional positive result found among the scores of studies is about as frequent as one would expect by sampling error, using the 5 per cent level of confidence. Until a reliable body of facts is established for this variable and associated variables, no theoretical evaluation is possible.

Other variables. As I indicated earlier, I will not make an exhaustive survey of the variables which may influence rate of forgetting. I have limited myself to variables which have been rather extensively investigated, which have immediate relevance to the interference theory, or for which reliable relationships are available. Nevertheless, I would like to mention briefly some of these other variables. There is the matter of *warm-up* before recall; some investigators find that this reduces forgetting (12); others, under as nearly replicated conditions as is possible to obtain, do not

(23). Some resolution must be found for these flat contradictions. It seems perfectly reasonable, however, that inadequate set or context differences could reduce recall. Indeed, an interference theory would predict this forgetting if the set or context stimuli are appreciably different from those prevailing at the time of learning. In our laboratory we try to reinstate the learning set by careful instructions, and we simply do not find decrements that might be attributed to inadequate set. For example, in a recent study (33) subjects were given a 24-hour recall of a serial list after learning to one perfect trial. I think we would expect that the first item in the list would suffer the greatest decrement due to inadequate set, yet this item showed only .7 per cent loss. But let it be clear that when we are attempting to account for the 15 per cent loss over 24 hours, we should not overlook any possible source for this loss.

Thus far I have not said anything about forgetting as a function of characteristics of the subject, that is, the personality or intellectual characteristics. As far as I have been able to determine, there is not a single valid study which shows that such variables have an appreciable influence on forgetting. Many studies have shown differences in learning as a function of these variables, but not differences in rate of forgetting. Surely there must be some such variables. We do know that if subjects are severely insulted, made to feel stupid, or generally led to believe that they have no justification for continued existence on the earth just before they are asked to recall, they will show losses (e.g., 25, 38), but even the influence of this kind of psychological beating is short lived. Somehow I have never felt that such findings need explanation by a theory used to explain the other facts of forgetting.

Concerning the causes of forgetting, let me sum up in a somewhat more dogmatic fashion than is probably justified. One of the assumptions of science is finite causality. Everything cannot influence everything else. To me, the most important implication of the work on forgetting during the last ten years is that this work has markedly *reduced* the number of variables related to forgetting. Correspondingly, I think the theoretical problem has become simpler. It is my belief that we can narrow down the cause of forgetting to interference from previously learned habits, from habits being currently learned, and from habits we have yet to learn. The amount of this interference is primarily a function of similarity and associative strength, the latter being important because it interacts with similarity.

Summary

This paper deals with issues in the forgetting of rote-learned materials. An analysis of the current evidence suggests that the classical Ebbinghaus curve of forgetting is primarily a function of interference from materials learned previously in the laboratory. When this source of interference is removed, forgetting decreases from about 75 per cent over 24 hours to about 25 per cent. This latter figure can be reduced by at least 10 per cent by other methodological considerations, leaving 15 per cent as an estimate of the forgetting over 24 hours. This estimate will vary somewhat as a function of intratask similarity, distributed practice, and with very low meaningful material. But the over-all evidence suggests that similarity with other material and situational similarity are by far the most critical factors in forgetting. Such evidence is consonant with a general interference theory, although the details of such a theory were not presented here.

References

1. Archer, E. J., & Underwod, B. J. Retroactive inhibition of verbal associations as a multiple function of temporal point of interpolation and degree of interpolated learning. *J. exp. Psychol.*, 1951, **42**, 283–290.

2. Bartlett, F. C. *Remembering: a study in experimental and social psychology.* London: Cambridge Univer. Press, 1932.

3. Belmont, L., & Birch, H. G. Re-individualizing the repression hypothesis. *J. abnorm. soc. Psychol.*, 1951, **46**, 226–235.

4. Bilodeau, I. McD., & Schlosberg, H. Similarity in stimulating conditions as a variable in retroactive inhibition. *J. exp. Psychol.*, 1951, **41**, 199–204.

5. Briggs, G. E. Acquisition, extinction, and recovery functions in retroactive inhibition. *J. exp. Psychol.*, 1954, **47**, 285–293.

6. Cheng, N. Y. Retroactive effect and degree of similarity. *J. exp. Psychol.*, 1929, **12**, 444–458.

7. Ebbinghaus, H. *Memory: a contribution to experimental psychology.* (Trans. by H. A. Ruger, and C. E. Bussenius) New York: Bureau of Publications, Teachers College, Columbia Univer., 1913.

8. Gibson, Eleanor J. A systematic application of the concepts of generalization and differentiation to verbal learning. *Psychol. Rev.*, 1940, **47**, 196–229.

9. Gibson, Eleanor J. Intra-list generalization as a factor in verbal learning. *J. exp. Psychol.*, 1942, **30**, 185–200.

10. Greenberg, R., & Underwood, B. J. Retention as a function of stage of practice. *J. exp. Psychol.*, 1950, **40**, 452–457.

11. Hovland, C. I. Experimental studies in rote-learning theory. VI. Comparison of retention following learning to same criterion by massed and distributed practice. *J. exp. Psychol.*, 1940, **26**, 568–587.

12. Irion, A. L. The relation of "set" to retention. *Psychol. Rev.*, 1948, **55**, 336–341.

13. Jenkins, J. G., & Dallenbach, K. M. Oblivescence during sleep and waking. *Amer. J. Psychol.*, 1924, **35**, 605–612.

14. Johnson, L. M. The relative effect of a time interval upon learning and retention. *J. exp. Psychol.*, 1939, **24**, 169–179.

15. Katona, G. *Organizing and memorizing: studies in the psychology of learning and teaching.* New York: Columbia Univer. Press, 1940.

16. Krueger, W. C. F. The effect of overlearning on retention. *J. exp. Psychol.*, 1929, **12**, 71–78.

17. Lester, O. P. Mental set in relation to retroactive inhibition. *J. exp. Psychol.*, 1932, **15**, 681–699.

18. Luh, C. W. The conditions of retention. *Psychol. Monogr.*, 1922, **31**, No. 3 (Whole No. 142).

19. McGeoch, J. A. Forgetting and the law of disuse. *Psychol. Rev.,* 1932, **39**, 352–370.

20. McGeoch, J. A. *The psychology of human learning.* New York: Longmans, Green, 1942.

21. Osgood, C. E. *Method and theory in experimental psychology.* New York: Oxford Univer. Press, 1953.

22. Rapaport, D. Emotions and memory. *Psychol. Rev.,* 1943, 50, 234–243.

23. Rockway, M. R., & Duncan, C. P. Prerecall warming-up in verbal retention. *J. exp. Psychol.,* 1952, **43**, 305–312.

24. Runquist, W. Retention of verbal associations as a function of interference and strength. Unpublished doctor's dissertation, Northwestern Univer., 1956.

25. Russell, W. A. Retention of verbal material as a function of motivating instructions and experimentally-induced failure. *J. exp. Psychol.,* 1952, **43**, 207–216.

26. Underwood, B. J. The effect of successive interpolations on retroactive and proactive inhibition. *Psychol. Monogr.,* 1945, **59**, No. 3 (Whole No. 273).

27. Underwood, B. J. Studies of distributed practice: VII. Learning and retention of serial nonsense lists as a function of intralist similarity. *J. exp. Psychol.,* 1952, **44**, 80–87.

28. Underwod, B. J. Studies of distributed practice: VIII. Learning and retention of paired nonsense syllables as a function of intralist similarity. *J. exp. Psychol.,* 1953, **45**, 133–142.

29. Underwod, B. J. Studies of distributed practice: IX. Learning and retention of paired adjectives as a function of intralist similarity. *J. exp. Psychol.,* 1953, **45**, 143–149.

30. Underwood, B. J. Studies of distributed practice: X. The influence of intralist similarity on learning and retention of serial adjective lists. *J. exp. Psychol.,* 1953, **45**, 253–259.

31. Underwood, B. J. Intralist similarity in verbal learning and retention. *Psychol. Rev.,* 1954, **3**, 160–166.

32. Underwood, B. J., & Richardson, J. Studies of distributed practice: XIII. Interlist interference and the retention of serial nonsense lists. *J. exp. Psychol.,* 1955, 50, 39–46.

33. Underwood, B. J., & Richardson, J. The influence of meaningfulness, intralist similarity, and serial position on retention. *J. exp. Psychol.,* 1956, **52**, 119–126.

34. Ward, L. B. Reminiscence and rote learning. *Psychol. Monogr.,* 1937, **49**, No. 4 (Whole No. 220).

35. Weiss, W., & Margolius, G. The effect of context stimuli on learning and retention. *J. exp. Psychol.,* 1954, 48, 318–322.

36. Williams, M. The effects of experimentally induced needs upon retention. *J. exp. Psychol.,* 1950, **40**, 139–151.

37. Youtz, Adella C. An experimental evaluation of Jost's laws. *Psychol. Monogr.,* 1941, **53**, No. 1 (Whole No. 238).

38. Zeller, A. F. An experimental analogue of repression: III. The effect of induced failure and success on memory measured by recall. *J. exp. Psychol.,* 1951, **42**, 32–38.

Teaching machines were developed after extensive research with lower animals had shown that behavior can be "shaped" by the appropriate use of rewards (reinforcements). A similar principle can be applied in aiding students to learn.

The teaching machine is not meant to replace the teacher. It is meant to be used as a technological aid to free the teacher from the more routine jobs of teaching and allow him to spend more time with individual students who need special help or an enriched curriculum. The machines may even prove to be more skillful than many teachers in teaching basic material. The trick is in skillful programming.
It should be emphasized that these machines are not just "memory drums"—the use of programmed material is their outstanding feature.

POINTS TO GUIDE YOUR STUDY *(1) What are some of the principles of learning which are incorporated in these machines? (2) What are some of the disadvantages of this technique? What are some of the advantages that are not mentioned in the article?*

24: TEACHING MACHINES

B. F. Skinner, Harvard University

There are more people in the world than ever before, and a far greater part of them want an education. The demand cannot be met simply by building more schools and training more teachers. Education must become more efficient. To this end curricula must be revised and simplified, and textbooks and classroom techniques improved. In any other field a demand for increased production would have led at once to the invention of labor-saving capital equipment. Education has reached this stage very late, possibly through a misconception of its task. Thanks to the advent of television, however, the so-called audiovisual aids are being reexamined. Film projectors, television sets, phonographs, and tape recorders are finding their way into American schools and colleges.

Audio-visual aids supplement and may even supplant lectures, demonstrations, and textbooks. In doing so they serve one function of the teacher: they present material to the student and, when successful, make it so clear and interesting that the student learns. There is another function to which they contribute little or nothing. It is best seen in the productive interchange between teacher and student in the small classroom or tutorial situation. Much of that interchange has already been sacrificed in American education in order to teach large numbers of students. There is a real danger that it will be wholly obscured if use of equipment designed simply to *present* material becomes widespread. The student is becoming more and more a mere passive receiver of instruction.

B. F. Skinner. Teaching machines. *Science*, 1958, **128**, 969–977. Copyright © 1958 by the American Association for the Advancement of Science. Excerpts reprinted here with permission from the author and the American Association for the Advancement of Science.

Pressey's Teaching Machines

There is another kind of capital equipment which will encourage the student to take an active role in the instructional process. The possibility was recognized in the 1920's, when Sidney L. Pressey designed several machines for the automatic testing of intelligence and information. A recent model of one of these is shown in Figure 1. In using the device the student refers to a numbered item in a multiple-choice test. He presses the button corresponding to his first choice of answer. If he is right, the device moves on to the next item; if he is wrong, the error is tallied, and he must continue to make choices until he is right (1). Such machines, Pressey pointed out (2), could not only test and score, they could *teach*. When an examination is corrected and returned after a delay of many

FIGURE 1 *Pressey's self-testing machine. The device directs the student to a particular item in a multiple-choice test. The student presses the key corresponding to his choice of answer. If his choice is correct, the device advances to the next item. Errors are totaled.*

hours or days, the student's behavior is not appreciably modified. The immediate report supplied by a self-scoring device, however, can have an important instructional effect. Pressey also pointed out that such machines would increase efficiency in another way. Even in a small classroom the teacher usually knows that he is moving too slowly for some students and too fast for others. Those who could go faster are penalized, and those who should go slower are poorly taught and unnecessarily punished by criticism and failure. Machine instruction would permit each student to proceed at his own rate.

The "industrial revolution in education" which Pressey envisioned stubbornly refused to come about. In 1932 he expressed his disappointment (3). "The problems of invention are relatively simple," he wrote. "With a little money and engineering resource, a great deal could easily be done. The writer has found from bitter experience that one person alone can accomplish relatively little and he is regretfully dropping further work on these problems. But he hopes that enough may have been done to stimulate other workers, that this fascinating field may be developed."

Pressey's machines succumbed in part to cultural inertia; the world of education was not ready for them. But they also had limitations which probably contributed to their failure. Pressey was working against a background of psychological theory which had not come to grips with the learning process. The study of human learning was dominated by the "memory drum" and similar devices originally designed to study forgetting. Rate of learning was observed, but little was done to change it. Why the subject of such an experiment bothered to learn at all was of little interest. "Frequency" and "recency" theories of learning, and principles of "massed and spaced practice," concerned the conditions under which responses were remembered.

Pressey's machines were designed against this theoretical background. As versions of the memory drum, they were primarily testing devices. They were to be used after some amount of learning had already taken place elsewhere. By confirming correct responses and by weakening responses which should not have been acquired, a self-testing machine does, indeed, teach; but it is not designed primarily for that purpose. Nevertheless, Pressey seems to have been the first to emphasize the importance of immediate feedback in education and to propose a system in which each student could move at his own pace. He saw the need for capital equipment in realizing these objectives. Above all he conceived of a machine which (in contrast with the audio-visual aids which were beginning to be developed) permitted the student to play an active role.

Another kind of machine

The learning process is now much better understood. Much of what we know has come from studying the behavior of lower organisms, but the results hold surprisingly well for human subjects. The emphasis in this research has not been on proving or disproving theories but on discovering and controlling the variables of which learning is a function. This practical orientation has paid off, for a surprising degree of control has been achieved. By arranging appropriate "contingencies of reinforcement," specific forms of behavior can be set up and brought under the control of specific classes of stimuli. The resulting behavior can be maintained in strength for long periods of time. A technology based on this work has already been put to use in neurology, pharmacology, nutrition, psychophysics, psychiatry, and elsewhere (4).

The analysis is also relevant to education. A student is "taught" in the sense that he is induced to engage in new forms of behavior and in specific forms upon specific occasions. It is not merely a matter of teaching him *what* to do; we are as much concerned with the probability that appropriate behavior will, indeed, appear at the proper time—an issue which would be classed traditionally under motivation. In education the behavior to be shaped and maintained is usually verbal, and it is to be brought under the control of both verbal and nonverbal stimuli. Fortunately, the special problems raised by verbal behavior can be submitted to a similar analysis (5).

If our current knowledge of the acquisition and maintenance of verbal behavior is to be applied to education, some sort of teaching machine is needed. Contingencies of reinforcement which change the behavior of lower organisms often cannot be arranged by hand; rather elaborate apparatus is needed. The human organism requires even more subtle instrumentation. An appropriate teaching machine will have several important features. The student must *compose* his response rather than select it from a set of alternatives, as in a multiple-choice self-rater. One reason for this is that we want him to recall rather than recognize—to make a response as well as see that it is right. Another reason is that effective multiple-choice material must contain plausible wrong responses, which are out of place in the delicate process of "shaping" behavior because they strengthen unwanted forms. Although it is much easier to build a machine to score multiple-choice answers than to evaluate a composed response, the technical advantage is outweighed by these and other considerations.

A second requirement of a minimal teaching machine also distinguishes it from earlier versions. In acquiring complex behavior the student must pass through a carefully designed sequence of steps, often of considerable length. Each step must be so small that it can always be taken, yet in taking it the student moves somewhat closer to fully competent behavior. The machine must make sure that these steps are taken in a carefully prescribed order.

Several machines with the required characteristics have been built and tested. Sets of separate presentations or "frames" of visual material are stored on disks, cards, or tapes. One frame is presented at a time, adjacent frames being out of sight. In one type of machine the student composes a response by moving printed figures or letters (6). His setting is compared by the machine with a coded response. If the two correspond, the machine automatically presents the next frame. If they do not, the response is cleared, and another must be composed. The student cannot proceed to a second step until the first has been taken. A machine of this kind is being tested in teaching spelling, arithmetic, and other subjects in the lower grades.

For more advanced students—from junior high school, say, through college—a machine which senses an arrangement of letters or figures is unnecessarily rigid in specifying form of response. Fortunately, such students may be asked to compare their responses with printed material revealed by the machine. In the machine shown in Figure 2, material is printed in 30 radial frames on a 12-inch disk. The student inserts the disk and closes the machine. He cannot proceed until the machine has been locked, and, once he has begun, the machine cannot be unlocked. All but a corner of one frame is visible through a window. The student writes his response on a paper strip exposed through a second opening. By lifting a lever on the front of the machine, he moves what he has written under a transparent cover and uncovers the correct response in the remaining corner of the frame. If the two responses correspond, he moves the lever horizontally. This movement punches a hole in the paper opposite his response, recording the fact that he called it correct, and alters the machine so that the frame

FIGURE 2 *Student at work on a teaching machine. One frame of material is partly visible in the left-hand window. The student writes his response on a strip of paper exposed at the right. He then lifts a lever with his left hand, advancing his written response under a transparent cover and uncovering the correct response in the upper corner of the frame. If he is right, he moves the lever to the right, punching a hole alongside the response he has called right and altering the machine so that that frame will not appear again when he goes through the series a second time. A new frame appears when the lever is returned to its starting position.*

will not appear again when the student works around the disk a second time. Whether the response was correct or not, a second frame appears when the lever is returned to its starting position. The student proceeds in this way until he has responded to all frames. He then works around the disk a second time, but only those frames appear to which he has not correctly responded. When the disk revolves without stopping, the assignment is finished. (The student is asked to repeat each frame until a correct response is made to allow for the fact that, in telling him that a response is wrong, such a machine tells him what is right.)

The machine itself, of course, does not teach. It simply brings the student into contact with the person who composed the material it presents. It is a labor-saving device because it can bring one programmer into contact with an indefinite number of students. This may suggest mass production, but the effect upon each student is surprisingly like that of a private tutor. The comparison holds in several respects. (i) There is a constant interchange between program and students. Unlike lectures, textbooks, and the usual audio-visual aids, the machine induces sustained activity. The student is always alert and busy. (ii) Like a good tutor, the machine insists that a given point be thoroughly understood, either frame by frame or set by set, before the student moves on. Lectures, textbooks, and their mechanized equivalents, on the other hand, proceed without making sure that the student understands and easily leave him behind. (iii) Like a good tutor the machine presents just that material for which the student is ready. It asks him to take only that step which he is at the moment best equipped and most likely to take. (iv) Like a skillful tutor the machine helps the student to come up with the right answer. It does this in part through the orderly construction of the program and in part with techniques of hinting, prompting, suggesting, and so on, derived from an analysis of verbal behavior (5). (v) Lastly, of course, the machine, like the private tutor, reinforces the student for every correct response, using this immediate feedback not only to shape his behavior most efficiently but to maintain it in strength in a manner which the layman would describe as "holding the student's interest."

Programming material

The success of such a machine depends on the material used in it. The task of programming a given subject is at first sight rather formidable. Many helpful techniques can be derived from a general analysis of the relevant behavior processes, verbal and nonverbal. Specific forms of behavior are to be evoked and, through differential reinforcement, brought under the control of specific stimuli.

This is not the place for a systematic review of available techniques, or of the kind of research which may be expected to discover others. However, the machines themselves cannot be adequately described without giving a few examples of programs. We may begin with a set of frames (see Table 1) designed to teach a third- or fourth-grade pupil to spell the word *manufacture*. The six frames are presented in the order shown, and the pupil moves sliders to expose letters in the open squares.

The word to be learned appears in italic in frame 1, with an example and a simple definition. The pupil's first task is simply to copy it. When he does so correctly frame 2 appears. He must now copy selectively: he must identify "fact" as the common part of "manufacture" and "factory." This helps him to spell the word and also to acquire a separable "atomic" verbal operant (5). In frame 3 another root must be copied selectively from "manual." In frame 4 the pupil must for the first time insert letters without copying. Since he is asked to insert the same letter in two places, a wrong response will be doubly conspicuous, and the chance of failure is thereby minimized. The same principle governs frame 5. In frame 6 the pupil spells the word to complete the sentence used as an example in frame 1. Even a poor student is likely to do this correctly because he has just composed or completed the word five times, has made two important root-responses, and has learned that two letters occur in the word twice. He has probably learned to spell the word without having made a mistake.

Teaching spelling is mainly a process of shaping complex forms of behavior. In other subjects—for example, arithmetic—

TABLE 1 *A set of frames designed to teach a third- or fourth-grade pupil to spell the word "manufacture"*

1. *Manufacture* means to make or build. **Chair factories manufacture chairs.** Copy the word here:
   □ □ □ □ □ □ □ □ □ □ □
2. Part of the word is like part of the word *factory*. Both parts come from an old word meaning **make** or **build**.
   m a n u □ □ □ □ u r e
3. Part of the word is like part of the word *manual*. Both parts come from an old word for **hand**. Many things used to be made by hand.
   □ □ □ □ f a c t u r e
4. The same letter goes in both spaces:
   m □ n u f □ c t u r e
5. The same letter goes in both spaces:
   m a n □ f a c t □ r e
6. **Chair factories** □ □ □ □ □ □ □ □ □ □ □ **chairs.**

responses must be brought under the control of appropriate stimuli. Unfortunately the material which has been prepared for teaching arithmetic (7) does not lend itself to excerpting. The numbers 0 through 9 are generated in relation to objects, quantities, and scales. The operations of addition, subtraction, multiplication, and division are thoroughly developed before the number 10 is reached. In the course of this the pupil composes equations and expressions in a great variety of alternative forms. He completes not only $5 + 4 = \square$, but $\square + 4 = 9$, $5 \square 4 = 9$, and so on, aided in most cases by illustrative materials. No appeal is made to rote memorizing, even in the later acquisition of the tables. The student is expected to arrive at $9 \times 7 = 63$, not by memorizing it as he would memorize a line of poetry, but by putting into practice such principles as that nine times a number is the same as ten times the number minus the number (both of these being "obvious" or already well learned), that the digits in a multiple of nine add to nine, that in composing successive multiples of nine one counts backwards (*nine, eight*een, twenty-*seven*, thirty-*six*, and so on), that nine times a single digit is a number beginning with one less than the digit (nine times *six* is *fifty* something), and possibly even that the product of two numbers separated by only one number is equal to the square of the separating number minus one (the square of eight already being familiar from a special series of frames concerned with squares).

Programs of this sort run to great length. With at least five or six frames per word, four grades of spelling may require 20,000 or 25,000 frames, and three or four grades of arithmetic, as many again. If these figures seem large, it is only because we are thinking of the normal contact between teacher and pupil. Admittedly, a teacher cannot supervise 10,000 or 15,000 responses made by each pupil per year. But the pupil's time is not so limited. In any case, surprisingly little time is needed. Fifteen minutes per day on a machine should suffice for each of these programs, the machines being free for other students for the rest of each day. (It is probably because traditional methods are so inefficient that we have been led to suppose that education requires such a prodigious part of a young person's day.)

A simple technique used in programming material at the high-school or college level, by means of the machine shown in Figure 2, is exemplified in teaching a student to recite a poem. The first line is presented with several unimportant letters omitted. The student must read the line "meaningfully" and supply the missing letters. The second, third, and fourth frames present succeeding lines in the same way. In the fifth frame the first line reappears with other letters also missing. Since the student has recently read the line, he can complete it correctly. He does the same for the second, third, and fourth lines. Subsequent frames are increasingly incomplete, and eventually—say, after 20 or 24 frames—the student reproduces all four lines without external help, and quite possibly without having made a wrong response. The technique is similar to that used in teaching spelling: responses are first controlled by a text, but this is slowly reduced (colloquially, "vanished") until the responses can be emitted without a text, each member in a series of responses being now under the "intraverbal" control of other members.

"Vanishing" can be used in teaching other types of verbal behavior. When a student describes the geography of part of the world or the anatomy of part of the body, or names plants and animals from specimens or pictures, verbal responses are controlled by nonverbal stimuli. In setting up such behavior the student is first asked to report features of a fully labeled map, picture, or object, and the labels are then vanished. In teaching a map, for example, the machine asks the student to describe spatial relations among cities, countries, rivers, and so on, as shown on a fully labeled map. He is then asked to do the same with a map in which the names are incomplete or, possibly, lacking. Eventually he is asked to report the same relations with no map at all. If the material has been well programmed, he can do so correctly. Instruction is sometimes concerned not so much with imparting a new repertoire of verbal responses as with getting the student to describe something accurately in any available terms. The machine can "make sure the student understands" a graph, diagram, chart, or picture by asking him to identify and explain its features—correcting him, of course, whenever he is wrong.

In addition to charts, maps, graphs, models, and so on, the student may have access to auditory material. In learning to take dictation in a foreign language, for example, he selects a short passage on an indexing phonograph according to instructions given by the machine. He listens to the passage as often as necessary and then transcribes it. The machine then reveals the correct text. The student may listen to the passage again to discover the sources of any error. The indexing phonograph may also be used with the machine to teach other language skills, as well as telegraphic code, music, speech, parts of literary and dramatic appreciation, and other subjects.

A typical program combines many of these functions. The set of frames shown in Table 2 is designed to induce the student of high-school physics to talk intelligently, and to some extent technically, about the emission of light from an incandescent source. In using the machine the student will write a word or phrase to complete a given item and then uncover the corresponding word or phrase shown here in the column at the right. The reader who wishes to get the "feel" of the material should cover the right-hand column with a card, uncovering each line only after he has completed the corresponding item.

Several programming techniques are exemplified by the set of frames in Table 2. Technical terms are introduced slowly. For example, the familiar term "fine wire" in frame 2 is followed by a definition of the technical term "filament" in frame 4; "filament" is then asked for in the presence of the nonscientific synonym in frame 5 and without the synonym in frame 9. In the same way "glow," "give off light," and "send out light" in early frames are followed by a definition of "emit" with a synonym in frame 7. Various inflected forms of "emit" then follow, and "emit" itself is asked for with a synonym in frame 16. It is asked for without a synonym but in a helpful phrase in frame 30, and "emitted" and "emission" are asked for without help in frames 33 and 34. The relation between temperature and amount and color of light is developed in several frames before a formal statement using the

word "temperature" is asked for in frame 12. "Incandescent" is defined and used in frame 13, is used again in frame 14, and is asked for in frame 15, the student receiving a thematic prompt from the recurring phrase "incandescent source of light." A formal prompt is supplied by "candle." In frame 25 the new response "energy" is easily evoked by the words "form of . . ." because the expression "form of energy" is used earlier in the frame. "Energy" appears again in the next two frames and is finally asked for, without aid, in frame 28. Frames 30 through 35 discuss the limiting temperatures of incandescent objects, while reviewing several kinds of sources. The figure 800 is used in three frames. Two intervening frames then permit some time to pass before the response "800" is asked for.

Unwanted responses are eliminated with special techniques. If, for example, the second sentence in frame 24 were simply "It is a (n) _____ source of light," the two "very's" would frequently lead the student to fill the blank with "strong" or a synonym thereof. This is prevented by inserting the word "powerful" to make a synonym redundant. Similarly, in frame 3 the words "heat and" preempt the response "heat," which would otherwise correctly fill the blank.

The net effect of such material is more than the acquisition of facts and terms. Beginning with a largely unverbalized acquaintance with flashlights, candles, and so on, the student is induced to talk about familiar events, together with a few new facts, with a fairly technical vocabulary. He applies the same terms to facts which he may never before have seen to be similar. The emission of light from an incandescent source takes shape as a topic or field of inquiry. An understanding of the subject emerges which is often quite surprising in view of the fragmentation required in item building.

It is not easy to construct such a pro-

TABLE 2   *Part of a program in high-school physics. The machine presents one item at a time. The student completes the item and then uncovers the corresponding word or phrase shown at the right*

SENTENCE TO BE COMPLETED	WORD TO BE SUPPLIED
1. The important parts of a flashlight are the battery and the bulb. When we "turn on" a flashlight, we close a switch which connects the battery with the_____.	bulb
2. When we turn on a flashlight, an electric current flows through the fine wire in the _____ and causes it to grow hot.	bulb
3. When the hot wire glows brightly, we say that it gives off or sends out heat and _____.	light
4. The fine wire in the bulb is called a filament. The bulb "lights up" when the filament is heated by the passage of a(n) _____ current.	electric
5. When a weak battery produces little current, the fine wire, or _____, does not get very hot.	filament
6. A filament which is *less* hot sends out or gives off _____ light.	less
7. "Emit" means "send out." The amount of light sent out, or "emitted," by a filament depends on how _____ the filament is.	hot
8. The higher the temperature of the filament the _____ the light emitted by it.	brighter, stronger
9. If a flashlight battery is weak, the _____ in the bulb may still glow, but with only a dull red color.	filament
10. The light from a very hot filament is colored yellow or white. The light from a filament which is not very hot is colored _____.	red
11. A blacksmith or other metal worker sometimes makes sure that a bar of iron is heated to a "cherry red" before hammering it into shape. He uses the _____ of the light emitted by the bar to tell how hot it is.	color
12. Both the color and the amount of light depend on the _____ of the emitting filament or bar.	temperature
13. An object which emits light because it is hot is called "incandescent." A flashlight bulb is an incandescent source of _____.	light
14. A neon tube emits light but remains cool. It is, therefore, not an incandescent _____ of light.	source
15. A candle flame is hot. It is a(n) _____ source of light.	incandescent
16. The hot wick of a candle gives off small pieces or particles of carbon which burn in the flame. Before or while burning, the hot particles send out, or _____, light.	emit
17. A long candlewick produces a flame in which oxygen does not reach all the carbon particles. Without oxygen the particles cannot burn. Particles which do not burn rise above the flame as _____.	smoke
18. We can show that there are particles of carbon in a candle flame, even when it is not smoking, by holding a piece of metal in the flame. The metal cools some of the particles before they burn, and the unburned carbon _____ collect on the metal as soot.	particles
19. The particles of carbon in soot or smoke no longer emit light because they are _____ than when they were in the flame.	cooler, colder
20. The reddish part of a candle flame has the same color as the filament in a flashlight with a weak battery. We might guess that the yellow or white parts of a candle flame are _____ than the reddish part.	hotter

SENTENCE TO BE COMPLETED	WORD TO BE SUPPLIED
21. "Putting out" an incandescent electric light means turning off the current so that the filament grows too _____ to emit light.	cold, cool
22. Setting fire to the wick of an oil lamp is called _____ the lamp.	lighting
23. The sun is our principal _____ of light, as well as of heat.	source
24. The sun is not only very bright but very hot. It is a powerful _____ source of light.	incandescent
25. Light is a form of energy. In "emitting light" an object changes, or "converts," one form of _____ into another.	energy
26. The electrical energy supplied by the battery in a flashlight is converted to _____ and _____.	heat, light; light, heat
27. If we leave a flashlight on, all the energy stored in the battery will finally be changed or _____ into heat and light.	converted
28. The light from a candle flame comes from the _____ released by chemical changes as the candle burns.	energy
29. A nearly "dead" battery may make a flashlight bulb warm to the touch, but the filament may still not be warm enough to emit light— in other words, the filament will not be _____ at that temperature.	incandescent
30. Objects, such as a filament, carbon particles, or iron bars, become incandescent when heated to about 800 degrees Celsius. At that temperature they begin to _____ _____.	emit light
31. When raised to any temperature above 800 degrees Celsius, an object such as an iron bar will emit light. Although the bar may melt or vaporize, its particles will be _____ no matter how hot they get.	incandescent
32. About 800 degrees Celsius is the lower limit of the temperature at which particles emit light. There is no upper limit of the _____ at which emission of light occurs.	temperature
33. Sunlight is _____ by very hot gases near the surface of the sun.	emitted
34. Complex changes similar to an atomic explosion generate the great heat which explains the _____ of light by the sun.	emission
35. Below about _____ degrees Celsius an object is not an incandescent source of light.	800

gram. Where a confusing or elliptical passage in a textbook is forgivable because it can be clarified by the teacher, machine material must be self-contained and wholly adequate. There are other reasons why textbooks, lecture outlines, and film scripts are of little help in preparing a program. They are usually not logical or developmental arrangements of material but stratagems which the authors have found successful under existing classroom conditions. The examples they give are more often chosen to hold the student's interest than to clarify terms and principles. In composing material for the machine, the programmer may go directly to the point.

A first step is to define the field. A second is to collect technical terms, facts, laws, principles, and cases. These must then be arranged in a plausible developmental order—linear if possible, branching if necessary. A mechanical arrangement, such as a card filing system, helps. The material is distributed among the frames of a program to achieve an arbitrary density. In the final composition of an item, techniques for strengthening asked-for responses and for transferring control from one variable to another are chosen from a list according to a given schedule in order to prevent the establishment of irrelevant verbal tendencies appropriate to a single technique. When one set of frames has been composed, its terms and facts are seeded mechanically among succeeding sets, where they will again be referred to in composing later items to make sure that the earlier repertoire remains active. Thus, the technical terms, facts, and examples in Table 2 have been distributed for reuse in succeeding sets on reflection, absorption, and transmission, where they are incorporated into items dealing mainly with other matters. Sets of frames for explicit review can, of course, be constructed. Further research will presumably discover other, possibly more effective, techniques. Meanwhile, it must be admitted that a considerable measure of art is needed in composing a successful program.

Whether good programming is to remain an art or to become a scientific technology, it is reassuring to know that there is a final authority—the student. An unexpected advantage of machine instruction has proved to be the feedback to the *programmer*. In the elementary school machine, provision is made for discovering which frames commonly yield wrong responses, and in the high-school and college machine the paper strips bearing written answers are available for analysis. A trial run of the first version of a program quickly reveals frames which need to be altered, or sequences which need to be lengthened. One or two revisions in the light of a few dozen responses work a great improvement. No comparable feedback is available to the lecturer, textbook writer, or maker of films. Although one text or film may seem to be better than another, it is usually impossible to say, for example, that a given sentence on a given page or a particular sequence in a film is causing trouble.

Difficult as programming is, it has its compensations. It is a salutary thing to try to guarantee a right response at every step in the presentation of a subject matter. The programmer will usually find that he has been accustomed to leave much to the student—that he has frequently omitted essential steps and neglected to invoke relevant points. The responses made to his material may reveal surprising ambiguities. Unless he is lucky, he may find that he still has something to learn about his subject. He will almost certainly find that he needs to learn a great deal more about the behavioral changes he is trying to induce in the student. This effect of the machine in confronting the programmer with the full scope of his task may in itself produce a considerable improvement in education.

Conclusion

An analysis of education within the framework of a science of behavior has broad implications. Our schools, in particular our "progressive" schools, are often held responsible for many current problems, including juvenile delinquency and the threat of a more powerful foreign technology. One remedy frequently suggested is a return to older techniques, especially to a greater "discipline" in schools. Presumably this is to be obtained with some form of punishment, to be administered either with certain classical instruments of physical injury—the dried bullock's tail of the Greek teacher or the cane of the English schoolmaster—or as disapproval or failure, the frequency of which is to be increased by "raising standards." This is probably not a feasible solution. Not only education but Western culture as a whole is moving away from aversive practices. We cannot prepare young people for one kind of life in institutions organized on quite different principles. The discipline of the birch rod may facilitate learning, but we must remember that it also breeds followers of dictators and revolutionists.

In the light of our present knowledge a school system must be called a failure if it cannot induce students to learn except by threatening them for not learning. That this has always been the standard pattern simply emphasizes the importance of modern techniques. John Dewey was speaking for his culture and his time when he attacked aversive educational practices and appealed to teachers to turn to positive and humane methods. What he threw out should have been thrown out. Unfortunately he had too little to put in its place. Progressive education has been a temporizing measure which can now be effectively supplemented. Aversive practices can not only be replaced, they can be replaced with far more powerful techniques. The possibilities should be thoroughly explored if we are to build an educational system which will meet the present demand without sacrificing democratic principles.

References and Notes

1. The Navy's "Self-Rater" is a larger version of Pressey's machine. The items are printed on code-punched plastic cards fed by the machine. The time required to answer is taken into account in scoring.
2. S. L. Pressey, *School and Society,* **23,** 586 (1926).
3. ———, *ibid.,* **36,** 934 (1932).
4. B. F. Skinner, The experimental analysis of behavior, *Am. Scientist,* **45,** 4 (1957).
5. ———, *Verbal behavior,* Appleton-Century-Crofts, New York, 1957.
6. ———, The science of learning and the art of teaching, *Harvard Educational Rev.,* **24,** 2 (1954).
7. This material was prepared with the assistance of Susan R. Meyer.

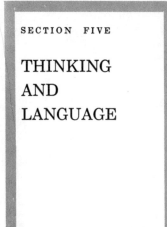

THINKING
AND
LANGUAGE

We are often faced with the problem of abstracting the common properties from large masses of information. In other words, we are often called upon to form concepts. Assuming that we have the required information before us, it is possible to use several strategies, each with certain advantages and disadvantages, in attempting to arrive at the concept. Several of these strategies are described in this selection.

POINTS TO GUIDE YOUR STUDY *(1) Try your friends on a concept formation task similar to that mentioned here—Figure 1 could very well be used. Do your subjects use the strategies mentioned in the selection? (2) Summarize the advantages and disadvantages of each type of strategy.*

25: SELECTION FROM: A STUDY OF THINKING

J. S. Bruner, Harvard University, Jacqueline Goodnow, and G. A. Austin

Ideal selection strategies and their benefits

We concentrate in this chapter on conjunctive concepts. Let us set before a subject all of the instances representing the various combinations of four attributes, each with three values—specifically, all the instances illustrated in Figure 1—an array of 81 cards, each varying in shape of

J. S. Bruner, Jacqueline Goodnow, and G. A. Austin. *A Study of Thinking.* New York: John Wiley and Sons, 1956. Copyright © 1956 by John Wiley and Sons. Excerpts reprinted here with permission from the authors and John Wiley and Sons.

figure, number of figures, color of figure, and number of borders. We explain to the subject what is meant by a conjunctive concept—a set of the cards that share a certain set of attribute values, such as "all red cards," or "all cards containing red squares and two borders"—and for practice ask the subjects to show us all the exemplars of one sample concept. The subject is then told that we have a concept in mind and that certain cards before him illustrate it, others do not, and that it is his task to determine what this concept is. We will always begin by showing him a

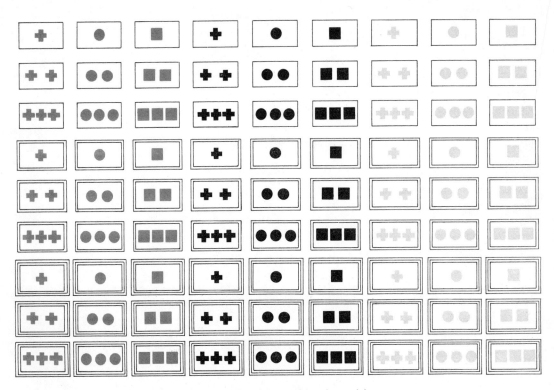

FIGURE 1   *An array of instances comprising combinations of four*
attributes, each exhibiting three values. Green figures are dark gray,
red figures are light gray, and black figures are black.
(Reprinted with permission from John Wiley and Sons.)

card or instance that is illustrative of the concept, a positive instance. His task is to choose cards for testing, one at a time, and after each choice we will tell him whether the card is positive or negative. He may hazard an hypothesis after any choice of a card, but he may not offer more than one hypothesis after any particular choice. If he does not wish to offer an hypothesis, he need not do so. He is asked to arrive at the concept as efficiently as possible. He may select the cards in any order he chooses. That, in essence, is the experimental procedure.

There are four discernible strategies by which a person may proceed in this task. These we label the *simultaneous-scanning strategy,* the *successive-scanning strategy,* the *conservative-focusing strategy,* and the *focus-gambling strategy.* Let us describe

each of these briefly and consider the manner in which each bestows upon its users the three benefits mentioned previously.

SIMULTANEOUS SCANNING   In the present array (Figure 1), composed of instances that may exhibit any of three values of four different attributes, there are 255 possible ways of grouping instances into conjunctive concepts. A first positive card *logically* eliminates 240 of these, and the informational value of any other positive or negative card thereafter presented can similarly be described in terms of the remaining hypotheses that it logically eliminates. Now, simultaneous scanning consists in essence of the person using each instance encountered as an occasion for deducing which hypotheses are tenable and which have been eliminated. This is a highly exacting strategy, for the subject must deal with many independent hypotheses and carry these in memory. Moreover, the deductive process is exacting.

If the subject is able to follow the strategy successfully, his choice of next instances to test will be determined by the objective of eliminating as many hypothetical concepts as possible per instance chosen. Suppose, for example, that a subject in our experiment has narrowed the possible concepts down to three: the concept must either be all *red* cards, all cards with *circles,* or all cards with *red circles.* Prior choices have eliminated all other hypotheses. Since we are dealing with an ideal strategy here, let us also assume an ideal subject: a subject with perfect rationality and perfect discriminative capacities. Such a subject would certainly know how to avoid choosing redundant instances that eliminated no hypotheses. By choosing a card for testing that contained at least one of the two features, circles or red color, he would guarantee that the next instances encountered contained appropriate information. He would have to decide whether to choose an instance containing *one* of the relevant features or *both* of them: the next instance will contain a circle and no other relevant feature, contain red and no other relevant feature, or it will contain red circles. Consider now the consequences of each of these decisions for each of the three possible concepts, as shown in the table below.

Such an analysis of the nine possible outcomes should suggest to the subject that his next choice should contain only one of the relevant attributes; at the least, such a choice will eliminate one hypothetical concept, at best two of them. To choose a card containing both relevant attribute values means that no information will be obtained regardless of what the correct concept is.

Now, if the subject can figure out the nine possible outcomes (and has enough time to do so), he will be able to make a wise decision about how next to proceed. The decision is important, for it will determine whether he will be able to solve the problem with one more choice; if these were expensive experiments rather than simple tests of the status of instances, the difference might be critical. But it is quite obvious that most human beings cannot or will not go through such an elaborate analysis of the situation in order to determine their best next step. Indeed, if there had been ten hypotheses still remaining in our example, the paper and pencil work involved in assessing next moves would have been prohibitive. So we can sum up by remarking that while it is possible in principle for the person using simultaneous scanning to plan the best next step, the task of guaranteeing *maximum* informativeness of a next choice is in practice too difficult to accomplish.

With respect to rendering easier the assimilation and retention of information contained in instances encountered, simultaneous scanning has little to recommend it. After each choice the subject must go through the difficult process of deducing which hypothetical concepts have been eliminated and carrying the result of these deductions in memory. There appears to be no means whereby simultaneous scanning can reduce this heavy load on inference and memory.

Nor does simultaneous scanning provide a way of regulating the riskiness of one's next choices—no practical way, at least. We shall leave the matter at that, hoping that it will become much clearer in a later section. The best one can do is to compute the riskiness of a choice by the method just outlined.

SUCCESSIVE SCANNING This strategy consists in testing a single hypothesis at a time. The subject has the hypothesis that *red* is the feature common to all correct cards, and chooses instances containing red

PROPERTIES OF INSTANCE CHOSEN FOR TESTING	IF CORRECT CONCEPT IS:		
	RED ONLY	CIRCLE ONLY	RED CIRCLE
Red only	Instance positive Eliminates: circle red circle	Instance negative Eliminates: red	Instance negative Eliminates: red
Circle only	Instance negative Eliminates: circle	Instance positive Eliminates: red red circle	Instance negative Eliminates: circle
Red and circle	Instance positive Eliminates: nothing	Instance positive Eliminates: nothing	Instance positive Eliminates: nothing

in order to test whether they are positive instances. He goes on testing hypotheses until he hits the correct concept. The typical successive scanner then *limits his choices to those instances that provide a direct test of his hypothesis.*

Now it is quite apparent that such a technique for choosing instances cannot assure that the person will encounter instances containing the maximum information possible. That is to say, since instances are chosen only to test one hypothesis at a time, one is likely to choose logically redundant cards some feature of which has been used before to test some previous hypothesis. On this point more will be said later, for it is evident that this is much like discontinuity in learning.

It also follows that the strategy has little worth from the point of view of regulating risk. There is little the user can do either to take bigger gambles or lesser gambles in his choice of instances. His only possible maneuver here is a rather far-fetched one, but one that subjects nonetheless indulge in. This consists really of playing a guessing game with the experimenter in choosing an order of hypotheses to test. For example, subjects will often operate on the assumption that the experimenter is out to "trick" them and that, therefore, the correct concept cannot be a "simple" one, namely, that it will not be a single-attribute concept like "red" or "circles." In consequence, users of successive scanning begin, more frequently than would be expected by chance, by "guessing" that the hypothesis is defined by more than one attribute and choose cards to test such multi-attribute hypotheses.

What then is served by the use of successive scanning? The gain is nearly all in the relief of cognitive strain. Limited inference is required and the principal strain on memory is to keep track of what hypotheses have already been tested and found wanting.

A closer examination of the manner in which strain on inference is reduced brings us directly to a most characteristic feature of cognitive activity which we shall encounter on subsequent occasions in analyzing the behavior of subjects in probability situations. It is this. Human subjects—and the same may be true of other species as well—prefer a direct test of any hypothesis they may be working on. To recall the meaning of direct test, a subject is faced with deciding whether a white door or a black door is the correct entrance to a reward chamber and adopts the hypothesis that the white door is correct. There are two ways of testing this hypothesis. The *direct way* is to try the white door. The *indirect way* is to try the black door. In a direct test, as we have noted, the knowledge obtained needs no further transformation for testing the hypothesis. White is either correct or incorrect. The indirect test requires a transformation: if the black door is correct, then the white door was not correct and therefore the hypothesis is wrong; if the black door is wrong then the white door must have been correct and the hypothesis is right. It may be that the reason for the preference for direct test is in the interest of cognitive economy: saving the person from having to transform his knowledge. Another possible explanation, one which does not preclude the first, is that we do not fully accept the possibilities of correctness and incorrectness being mutually exclusive. We have a backlog of experience in which it has not always followed that if white is correct black is wrong or vice versa. We have also experienced situations where more than two alternatives were possible, and only a direct test would be effective.[1]

In any case, when a subject behaves in the typical manner of the successive scanner and limits himself to testing instances directly related to his hypothesis, his behavior appears to follow the principle of direct test. In sum, then, successive scanning has little utility either in guaranteeing maximum informativeness of one's choices or in regulating risk. Its chief benefit is in the reduction of cognitive strain by limiting its user to direct test of hypotheses. As such, its principal utility may be as a procedure that is useful when the cognitive going gets rough or when one has good reason to believe that a particular hypothesis will turn out to be correct.

CONSERVATIVE FOCUSING   In brief, this

[1] It is of interest that the first experiment which drew attention to a preference for direct test—in the form of participant behavior—used a situation where more than two alternatives were possible (Heidbreder, 1924).

strategy may be described as finding a positive instance to use as a focus, then making a sequence of choices each of which alters but one attribute value of the first focus card and testing to see whether the change yields a positive or a negative instance. Those attribute values of the focus card which, when changed, still yield positive instances are *not* part of the concept. Those attribute values of the focus card that yield negative instances when changed *are* features of the concept. Thus, if the first positive card encountered contains three red circles with two borders ($3R\bigcirc2b$), and if the concept is "red circles," the sequence of choices made would be as follows, each choice changing a *single* attribute value of the focus card:

$3R\bigcirc2b$ (+) focus card*
$2R\bigcirc2B$ (+) first choice: eliminate "three figures" as a relevant attribute value
$3G\bigcirc2b$ (−) second choice: retain "red" as a relevant attribute value
$3R+2b$ (−) third choice: retain "circle" as a relevant attribute value
$3R\bigcirc1b$ (+) fourth choice: eliminate "two borders" as a relevant attribute value
Ergo: concept is "red circles."

* The symbol (+) denotes a positive instance; (−) a negative instance.

Note one thing. When a subject has changed an attribute value of the focus card and the new card chosen turns out to be positive, this result logically eliminates the attribute in question from consideration. *No* value of such an attribute can be relevant to the concept. The subject need not sample any further values of it.

Several other features of this strategy are especially noteworthy. From the point of view of guaranteeing that each instance encountered be informative, the strategy does just that. By following it, redundancy can be completely avoided. The strategy guarantees, moreover, that each instance encountered will contain a "safe maximum" of information, as we will see when the risk-regulating property of the strategy is examined below.

The benefits in cognitive economy to be gained by using this strategy are striking. The first of these is that by its use the subject is enabled to disregard completely the bewildering business of eliminating possible hypotheses from the domain of 255 possible concepts in terms of which he may group instances. For in fact, the technique is designed to *test the relevance of attributes*. Given an initial positive card, his choices are designed to consider the four attribute values of the focus card one at a time to see which of these may be eliminated. In the present example there are four single attribute values to be considered, much less than the 15 rather complex hypotheses that would have to be considered in simultaneous scanning . A second contribution of this strategy to cognitive economy is that it guarantees that the relevance of all attribute values in the focus card will be *tested relatively directly*. If a change in an attribute value of the focus instance makes a difference, then that attribute value of the focus is relevant; if not, it is irrelevant. A third benefit is more subtle. By choosing a particular positive instance as a focus, the person *decreases the complexity and abstractness of the task* of keeping track of information he has encountered. All subsequent choices and their outcomes can be referred back to this focus instance much as if it were a score card. The attributes of the focus card are ticked off on the basis of subsequent tests.

There is one notable disadvantage to the strategy from the point of view of cognitive economy. Unless the universe of instances to be tested is arrayed in an orderly fashion so that a particular instance may be easily located on demand, the task of search imposed on the user of conservative focus-ing may become rather severe. We shall see examples of this disadvantage later.

Now for risk regulation. The expression "conservative focusing" has been chosen with good reason. Every choice is safe, safe in the sense that it logically guarantees the presence of information in the instance chosen for testing. This guaranteed information is not the maximum possible. On the other hand, the choice never carries the risk of yielding *no* information. We have already noted that by following the strategy, the subject will never choose a redundant instance, one that carries no new information. To understand fully why it is that a chosen instance almost never contains the maximum amount of information possible, we must turn to a consideration of focus gambling.

FOCUS GAMBLING   The principal feature of this strategy is that the subject uses a positive instance as a focus and then changes *more than one* attribute value at a time. In the present array (Figure 1) from which our examples are drawn, the subject might change two or three attribute values at once. This may not seem very different from conservative focusing, but a closer examination will make clear that it is. In particular, several features of focus gambling are of interest from the point of view of the risk-regulating nature of a strategy, and these we shall consider first.

In most tasks involving concept attainment, whether in the laboratory or in everyday life, one objective is to get the job done in as few choices or tests as possible, particularly if choices or tests are costly. It is always possible, given the use of conservative focusing, to complete the job with only as many tests as there are attributes to be tested. Focus gambling provides a way of attaining the concept in *fewer* trials than this limit. But in doing so it also imposes a risk. The risk is this.

By using the strategy, one *may* succeed in attaining the concept in fewer test choices than required by conservative focusing. But the strategy also *may* require many more test choices than this. If one is in a position to take such a risk—the risk that solution may be very fast, very slow, or in between—then focus gambling is an admirable procedure. Such a position would be one where, presumably, quick solution paid off very handsomely compared to the losses to be suffered by slow solution.

It can readily be seen how the gambling feature is built into this interesting strategy. Again consider an example. Our subject as before takes as his focus the first positive card given him as an example: three red circles with two borders (3R○2b). Rather than change only *one* attribute value of this focus, he will take a flier and change *three* of them. Let us say then that his next choice is 3G+1b. Now, if the change should "make no difference," i.e., if the instance chosen is still positive, then the concept must be that attribute value shared by the positive focus card and the next card chosen (also positive): namely, "three figures." In one fell swoop, the user of this strategy has eliminated three attributes and attained the concept. Similarly, if two attributes of the focus are changed and a positive instance still results, then the two changed attributes are eliminated. So far, the strategy seems riskless enough.

The difficulty arises when a change in more than one attribute of the focus yields a *negative* instance. For when this happens, the only way in which a person can assimilate the information contained in the instance is to revert to the method of simultaneous scanning: to use the instance as an aid to eliminating possible hypotheses. This has the effect, of course, of diminishing drastically the economical nicety of a focus-gambling strategy. It is now no longer possible to proceed by testing *attributes* for their relevance. Instead, one must deal with *hypothesis elimination* by the method described in connection with simultaneous scanning or throw away the potential information contained in negative instances.

From the point of view of guaranteeing that instances chosen contain new information, focus gambling does not have the feature that makes conservative focusing notable. It does not guarantee that redundant instances will be avoided. For in-sofar as the person using this procedure does not use the information contained in negative instances, he is likely to, and frequently does, choose instances in the course of solution that contain the same information that might have been assimilated from such prior negative instances.

Finally, with respect to making the cognitive task of information assimilation easier, the strategy has most of the features of conservative focusing. One does not have to consider the full array of possible hypothetical concepts (unless one wishes to utilize the information of negative instances). It is geared to the testing of attributes in the focus card rather than to hypothesis elimination in the pure sense. It also provides for direct testing of hypotheses about the relevant attributes. As before, it reduces complexity by the use of a focus instance as a "score card." But it is lacking in economical benefits whenever negative instances occur. The user can do nothing with these unless he shifts strategy. And there is a temptation to do just this. Finally, the strategy also has the fault of requiring a considerable amount of search-behavior if one is to find appropriate instances to test.

Set—the tendency to approach a problem in a particular way—often hinders problem solving. Functional fixedness may be thought of as a type of set arising from previous use of the objects and tools needed for problem solving. The three tasks in the following experiment provide an experimental demonstration of the hindering power of functional fixedness. Flexibility—the ability to break set and to see new relationships between objects and events—seems crucial to creative problem-solving proficiency. Thus, functional fixednes and other hindering sets should be avoided.

A POINT TO GUIDE YOUR STUDY   *In this article, as in many of the others, statistical analysis of experimental results is used. The chi-square (χ^2) test and the t-test are used to obtain probability values (p). The probability values have the same meaning as they do in previous articles. (See the article by Braun and Geiselhart, Section Three, for a description of the meaning of the p values.)*

26: FUNCTIONAL FIXEDNESS AS RELATED TO PROBLEM SOLVING: A REPETITION OF THREE EXPERIMENTS

Robert E. Adamson

The study of problem solving and thinking has been retarded by the lack of agreed-upon theoretical concepts supported by adequate data from experiments. As a part of a larger program concerned with these matters, some of the more promising hypotheses have been assembled, and preliminary experiments undertaken to repeat the demonstrations upon which these hypotheses rest.

One inviting hypothesis is that problem solving may in some instances be delayed through the "functional fixedness" of solution objects. That is, owing to his previous use of the object in a function dissimilar to that demanded by the present problem, S is inhibited in discovering the appropriate new use of the object. This hypothesis was proposed by Duncker (3), who designed ingenious experiments to support it, but carried the experiments through with but 14 Ss and under poorly specified experimental conditions. It seemed wise, therefore, to repeat some of his experiments both to substantiate his results, if possible, and to ascertain the efficacy of the problems for use in further investigations. The success of Birch and Rabinowitz (1) in demonstrating functional fixedness in a related experiment encouraged us to hope for positive results.

Procedure

SUBJECTS   All Ss taking part in this study were college students from elementary psychology classes. There were 57 Ss, of whom 35 were men, 22 women. Twenty-nine Ss were assigned to the experimental group, 28 to the control group. All Ss were

This experiment was the first in a series of studies of problem solving being done under Project NR 150–104 and supported by Contract Nonr 225 (02) between Stanford University and the Office of Naval Research. The work was done and the present report prepared under the supervision of Dr. Donald W. Taylor. Work on the contract is under the general direction of Dr. E. R. Hilgard.

R. E. Adamson. Functional fixedness as related to problem solving: A repetition of three experiments. *J. exp. Psychol.*, 1952, 44, 288–291. Copyright © 1952 by the American Psychological Association. Reprinted here with permission from the author and the American Psychological Association.

of proximate ages and had been exposed to little experimentation.

PROBLEMS   Duncker's "box," "gimlet," and "paperclip" problems were presented to each *S* in the order named. In the first of these, the box problem, *S*'s task is to mount three candles vertically on a screen, at a height of about 5 ft., using to accomplish this task any of a large number of objects which are lying before *S* on a table. Among these objects are three pasteboard boxes of varying sizes, five matches, and five thumbtacks, the crucial objects for solution of the problem. The solution is to mount one candle on each box by melting wax on the box and sticking the candle to it, then to tack the boxes to the screen.

The gimlet problem involves suspending three cords from a board attached to an overhead beam. Among the variety of objects available are two screw-hooks and the gimlet itself, the objects from which the cords may be hung.

The paperclip problem consists of first attaching four small black cardboard squares to a large white square, then hanging the large square from an eyelet screwed into the aforementioned beam. Included among the objects lying before *S* on the table are a number of paperclips. These may be used to attach the small squares to the large ones, and one of them, when bent to form a hook, will serve to hang the large square from the eyelet.

DESIGN   The experimental and control groups were given the same problems to solve. For the experimental group, how-ever, at least one of the solution objects was "burdened" with a prior function in each problem. Thus, the candles, matches, and tacks for the box problem were placed in the three boxes before they were given to *S*. Hence, the boxes had for their initial function that of containing, whereas in their solution function they had to be used as supports or platforms. Similarly the gimlet initially had to be used to start holes for the screw-hooks, and in the paperclip problem, the four black squares had to be attached to the white one with paperclips. Duncker referred to the experimental group as the "after pre-utilization" group.

The control group was given the problems without any pre-utilization. In the case of the box problem, the empty boxes were placed on the table at varying distances from the other crucial solution objects. Holes into which the screwhooks and the gimlet could be screwed were already drilled into the beam in the case of the gimlet problem; the four black squares were stapled to the white one in the paperclip problem. Thus, none of the crucial objects was used with a function prior to its use as a solution object.

Solution scores were taken as one possible measure of functional fixedness, and time-to-solution constituted another measure. A maximum time of 20 min. was allowed for solution of each of the problems.

Results

BOX PROBLEM   The results of the box problem, presented in Table 1, confirm

TABLE 1   *Box problem*

GROUP	*n*	NUMBER SOLVING	TIME-TO-SOLUTION*
Exper.	29	12 (41%)	7 (24%)
Control	28	24 (86%)	22 (78%)
		$\chi^2 = 12.0 \; p = .001$	$\chi^2 = 14.8 \; p = .001$

* Number below median of combined group.

Duncker's finding that functional fixed-ness results from pre-utilization. The performance of the experimental group was markedly inferior to that of the control with respect both to the number of solutions obtained and the time required to reach solution. Prior usage of the boxes as containers inhibited their being used as platforms.

The chi-square value comparing the two groups on the time score was obtained by using as a cutting point the median time-to-solution of the combined groups. All cases for which there was no solution were assigned to the above-median category. With 1 *df*, each of the chi squares was highly significant. Since the direction of the difference was predicted, a one-tail test of significance was employed for both this and the following two problems.

GIMLET PROBLEM Since only three *S*s failed to solve this problem, all from the experimental group, the solution score could not demonstrate a difference between the experimental and control groups. Accordingly, only the results from the time measure are given in Table 2. The three *S*s failing to reach solution were not considered in the analysis of the data, thus reducing the total *n* to 54 for this experiment.

TABLE 2 *Gimlet and paperclip problems*

PROBLEM AND GROUP	*n*	MEAN TIME-TO-SOLUTION (SEC.)	SD	*t'*	*p**
Gimlet					
Exper.	26	246.6	124.7	3.71	.001
Control	28	144.0	67.7		
Paperclip					
Exper.	29	107.9	96.0	2.38	.01
Control	28	63.0	31.5		

* Single-tail test.

Since, as shown in Table 2, the variances for the two groups are not homogeneous, the use of *t* as a test of significance was inappropriate. Instead, *t'* was employed.[2] The highly significant difference obtained shows clearly the presence of functional fixedness.

PAPERCLIP PROBLEM The results from the paperclip problem are also shown in Table 2. Since all *S*s were able to solve this problem, only time scores are given. As in the first two problems, pre-utilization of the solution objects with a function different from that demanded by the problem resulted in significantly poorer performance by the experimental group.

RELIABILITY OF INDIVIDUAL PERFORMANCE An analysis was made of the performance of the experimental group to determine whether individual achievement on one of the three problems was significantly related to achievement on either of the other two. Chi square was used to test whether individuals scoring below the median in time-to-solution for one of two problems also showed a significant tendency to score below the median for the other. (Since only 12 of 29 *S*s solved the box problem, a median time-to-solution could not be obtained; instead, the distribution was dichotomized in terms of solution or no-solution.) A relation significant at the .05 level was found between the box problem and the paperclip problem. Neither of the other chi squares was significant. Clearly, achievement on a single problem involving pre-utilization is not a reliable measure of individual susceptibility to functional fixedness.

2 This technique was suggested by Dr. Quinn McNemar. Instead of utilizing one estimate of the population variance, *t'* incorporates the estimated variances from two populations (2). It is, in consequence, useful in such a situation as the present one, replacing *t* which assumes homogeneity of variance.

Discussion

Duncker's study (3), involving these three experiments, used two measures of performance: number of presolutions, and number of solutions. In the present study, the number of presolutions was discarded as a measure, because it was found to be overly dependent upon the subjective judgment of *E.* Number of solutions proved to be a satisfactory measure for only the box problem. Since all *S*s solved the paperclip problem, and all but three solved the gimlet problem, no difference between the experimental and the control groups could be revealed by this measure. It would appear that the *S*s in the present study were more able than those employed by Duncker.

Although the measures previously used by Duncker failed to show functional fixedness in two of the three present experiments, a new measure, time-to-solution, gave positive results in all three experiments. Essentially, then, the present results confirm those obtained by Duncker.

The results of Duncker, of Birch and Rabinowitz, and those obtained in this study afford convincing proof of the existence of functional fixedness. The reality of this phenomenon having been established, two lines of investigation are of immediate interest: (a) determination of those conditions which influence the occurrence of functional fixedness, and (b) exploration of its relation to other kinds of set in problem solving. A study now nearing completion involves both of these lines of experimentation.

Summary

1. Three of Duncker's experiments on functional fixedness were repeated in this study. Fifty-seven *S*s were used, 29 serving as the experimental and 28 as the control group. Both groups were given the "box," "gimlet," and "paperclip" problems in that order. Experimental *S*s were given each problem after first having used the solution objects for that problem in a function dissimilar to that demanded for solution. Control *S*s were given the problems without such pre-utilization.

2. Two measures of performance were used: number of solutions, and time-to-solution. The former measure discriminated between the experimental and control groups on only the box problem; the latter measure gave highly significant differences in the expected direction for all three problems.

3. Functional fixedness was shown to result from the pre-utilization of solution objects. Duncker's results were confirmed in a study using a larger *n* and having more carefully specified experimental conditions.

References

1. Birch, H. G., & Rabinowitz, H. S. The negative effect of previous experience on productive thinking. *J. exp. Psychol.,* 1951, 41, 121–125.

2. Cochran, W. G., & Cox, G. M. *Experimental design.* New York: John Wiley & Sons, 1950.

3. Duncker, K. On problem-solving. *Psychol. Monogr.,* 1945, 58, No. 5 (Whole No. 270).

The solution of a problem often depends, first of all, upon a clear idea of the principle needed for a solution—the "functional" solution—as this article points out. The next step in the solution of the problem is the discovery of a practical way of applying this principle.

A POINT TO GUIDE YOUR STUDY   *Be sure that you try to solve the problems before reading the solutions. Compare your attempts at solution with those which are mentioned.*

27: THE STRUCTURE AND DYNAMICS OF PROBLEM-SOLVING PROCESSES
Karl Duncker

The solution of practical problems

1. INTRODUCTION AND FORMULATION OF THE PROBLEM   A problem arises when a living creature has a goal but does not know how this goal is to be reached. Whenever one cannot go from the given situation to the desired situation simply by action, then there has to be recourse to thinking. (By action we here understand the performance of obvious operations.) Such thinking has the task of devising some action which may mediate between the existing and the desired situations. Thus the "solution" of a practical problem must fulfill two demands: in the first place, its realization[1] must bring about the goal situation, and in the second place one must be able to arrive at it from the given situation simply through action.

The practical problem whose solution was experimentally studied in greatest detail runs as follows: Given a human being with an inoperable stomach tumor, and rays which destroy organic tissue at sufficient intensity, by what procedure can one free him of the tumor by these rays and at the same time avoid destroying the healthy tissue which surrounds it?

Such practical problems, in which one asks, "How shall I attain . . . ?", are related to certain theoretical problems, in which the question is, "How, by what means, shall I comprehend . . . ?" In the former case, a problem situation arises through the fact that a goal has no direct connection with the given reality; in the latter case—in theoretical problems—it arises through the fact that a proposition has no direct connection with what is given in the premises. As an example in the latter field, let us take again the problem with which I experimented in greatest detail: Why is it that all six-place numbers of the type *abcabc,* for example 276276, are divisible by thirteen?

It is common to both types of problems that one seeks the ground for an anticipated consequence; in practical problems, the actual ground is sought; in theoretical problems, the logical ground.[2]

In the present investigation the question is: *How does the solution arise from the problem situation? In what ways is the solution of a problem attained?*

Karl Duncker. On problem-solving. *Psychol. Monogr.,* 1945, 58, no. 5 (whole no. 270). Translated by Lynne S. Lees. Copyright Ⓒ 1945 by the American Psychological Association. Excerpt reprinted here with permission from the American Psychological Association. Footnotes renumbered. References to other parts of the monograph omitted.

[1] [Translator's note: "Realization" is used in the sense of "making real," of "actualization." The terms "embodiment" and "to embody" are used in a closely related sense, which will be clear in context. In the following, all notes of the translator will be given in parentheses. Such notes will add the German terms of the original where entirely satisfactory English terms do not seem to exist.]

[2] Other types of theoretical problems, such as: "What is the essential nature of, or the law of . . .?" or "How are . . . related to each other?", are not investigated here.

2. EXPERIMENTAL PROCEDURE The experiments proceeded as follows: The subjects (Ss), who were mostly students of universities or of colleges, were given various thinking problems, with the request that they think aloud. This instruction, *"Think aloud,"* is not identical with the instruction to introspect which has been common in experiments on thought-processes. While the introspecter makes himself as thinking the object of his attention, the subject who is thinking aloud remains immediately directed to the problem, so to speak allowing his activity to become verbal. When someone, while thinking, says to himself, "One ought to see if this isn't . . .," or, "It would be nice if one could show that . . .," one would hardly call this introspection; yet in such remarks something is revealed which we shall later deal with under the name of 'development of the problem.' The subject (S) was emphatically warned not to leave unspoken even the most fleeting or foolish idea. He was told that where he did not feel completely informed, he might freely question the experimenter, but that no previous specialized knowledge was necessary to solve the problems.

3. A PROTOCOL OF THE RADIATION PROBLEM Let us begin with the radiation problem. Usually the schematic sketch shown in Figure 1 was given with the problem. Thus, it was added, somebody had visualized the situation to begin with (cross-section through the body with the tumor in the middle and the radiation apparatus on the left); but obviously this would not do.

From my records I choose that of a solution-process which was particularly rich in typical hunches and therefore also especially long and involved. The average process vacillated less and could be left to run its own course with considerably less guidance.[3]

[3] Compare the pertinent protocols in my earlier and theoretically much less developed paper, "A qualitative study of productive thinking," *Ped. Sem.,* 1926, v. 33.

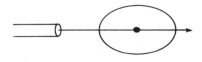

FIGURE 1.

Protocol

1. Send rays through the esophagus.
2. Desensitize the healthy tissues by means of a chemical injection.
3. Expose the tumor by operating.
4. One ought to decrease the intensity of the rays on their way; for example— would this work?—turn the rays on at full strength only after the tumor has been reached. (Experimenter: False analogy; no injection is in question.)
5. One should swallow something inorganic (which would not allow passage of the rays) to protect the healthy stomach-walls. (E: It is not merely the stomach-walls which are to be protected.)
6. Either the rays must enter the body or the tumor must come out. Perhaps one could alter the location of the tumor—but how? Through pressure? No.
7. Introduce a cannula.—(E: What, in general, does one do when, with any agent, one wishes to produce in a specific place an effect which he wishes to avoid on the way to that place?)
8. (Reply): One neutralizes the effect on the way. But that is what I have been attempting all the time.
9. Move the tumor toward the exterior. (Compare 6.) (The E repeats the problem and emphasizes, ". . . which destroy *at sufficient intensity."*)
10. The intensity ought to be variable. (Compare 4.)
11. Adaptation of the healthy tissues by previous weak application of the rays. (E: How can it be brought about that the rays destroy only the region of the tumor?)
12. (Reply:) I see no more than two possibilities: either to protect the body or to make the rays harmless. (E: How could

one decrease the intensity of the rays en route? [Compare 4.])

13. (Reply:) Somehow divert . . . diffuse rays . . . disperse . . . stop! Send a broad and weak bundle of rays through a lens in such a way that the tumor lies at the focal point and thus receives intensive radiation.[4] (Total duration about half an hour.)

4. IMPRACTICABLE "SOLUTIONS"

In the protocol given above, we can discern immediately that the whole process, from the original setting of the problem to the final solution, appears as a series of more or less concrete proposals. Of course, only the last one, or at least its principle, is practicable. All those preceding are in some respect inadequate to the problem, and therefore the process of solution cannot stop there. But however primitive they may be, this one thing is certain, that they cannot be discussed in terms of meaningless, blind, trial-and-error reactions. Let us take for an example the first proposal: "Send rays through the esophagus." Its clear meaning is that the rays should be guided into the stomach by some passage free from tissue. The basis of this proposal is, however, obviously an incorrect representation of the situation inasmuch as the rays are regarded as a sort of fluid, or the esophagus as offering a perfectly straight approach to the stomach, etc. Nevertheless, within the limits of this simplified concept of the situation, the proposal would actually fulfill the demands of the problem. It is therefore genuinely the solution of a problem, although not of the one which was actually presented. With the other proposals, the situation is about the same. The second presupposes that a means—for example, a chemical means—

exists for making organic tissue insensitive to the rays. If such a means existed, then everything would be in order, and the solution-process would have already come to an end. The fourth proposal—that the rays be turned on at full strength only when the tumor has been reached—shows again very clearly its derivation from a false analogy, perhaps that of a syringe which is set in operation only when it has been introduced into the object. The sixth suggestion, finally, treats the body too much as analogous to a rubber ball, which can be deformed without injury. In short, it is evident that such proposals are anything but completely meaningless associations. Merely in the factual situation, they are wrecked on certain components of the situation not yet known or not yet considered by the subject.

Occasionally it is not so much the situation as the demand, whose distortion or simplification makes the proposal practically useless. In the case of the third suggestion, for example ("expose the tumor by operating"), the real reason why radiation was introduced seems to have escaped the subject. An operation is exactly what should be avoided. Similarly in the fifth proposal, the fact is forgotten that not only the healthy stomach-walls must be protected but also all parts of the healthy body which have to be penetrated by the rays.

A remark on principle may here be in order. The psychologist who is investigating, not a store of knowledge, but the genesis of a solution, is not interested primarily in whether a proposal is actually practicable, but only in whether it is formally practicable, that is, practicable in the framework of the subject's given premises. If in planning a project an engineer relies on incorrect formulae or on nonexistent material, his project can nevertheless follow from the false premises as intelligently as another from correct premises. One can be 'psychologically equiva-

---

[4] This solution is closely related to the 'best' solution: *crossing of several weak bundles of rays at the tumor,* so that the intensity necessary for destruction is attained only here. Incidentally, it is quite true that the rays in question are not deflected by ordinary lenses; but this fact is of no consequence from the viewpoint of the psychology of thinking.

lent' to the other. In short, we are interested in knowing how a solution develops out of the system of its subjective premises, and how it is fitted to this system.

5. CLASSIFICATION OF PROPOSALS If one compares the various tentative solutions in the protocol with one another, they fall naturally into certain groups. Proposals 1, 3, 5, 6, 7 and 9 have clearly in common the attempt to *avoid contact between the rays and the healthy tissue.* This goal is attained in quite different ways: in 1 by re-directing the rays over a path naturally free from tissue; in 3 by the removal of the healthy tissue from the original path of the rays by operation; in 5 by interposing a protective wall (which may already have been tacitly implied in 1 and 3); in 6 by translocating the tumor towards the exterior; and in 7, finally, by a combination of 3 and 5. In proposals 2 and 11, the problem is quite differently attacked; the accompanying destruction of healthy tissue is here to be avoided by the *desensitizing or immunizing of this tissue.* A third method is used in 4, pehaps in 8, in 10 and 13: *the reduction of radiation intensity on the way.* As one can see, the process of solution shifts noticeably back and forth among these three methods of approach.

In the interests of clarity, the relationships described are presented graphically below.

6. FUNCTIONAL VALUE AND UNDERSTANDING In this classification, the tentative solutions are grouped according to the manner

in which they try to solve the problem, i.e., according to their "by-means-of-which," their "functional value." Consider the proposal to send rays through the esophagus. The S says nothing at all about avoiding contact, or about a free passage. Nevertheless, the solution-character of the esophagus in this context is due to no other characteristic than that of being a tissue-free path to the stomach. It functions as the embodiment solely of this property (not of the property of being a muscular pipe, or of lying behind the windpipe, or the like). In short, in the context of this problem, the "by-means-of-which," "the functional value" of the esophagus is: a free path to the stomach. The proposals: "direct the rays by a natural approach," "expose by operation," "translocate the tumor toward the exterior," "protective wall," and "cannula" all embody the functional value: no contact between rays and healthy tissue. The functional value of the solution, "concentration of diffuse rays in the tumor," is the characteristic: "less intensity on the way, great intensity in the tumor." The functional value of the lens is the quality: "medium to concentrate rays," and so forth.

The functional value of a solution is indispensable for the understanding of its being a solution. It is exactly what is called the sense, the principle or the point of the solution. The subordinated, more specialized characteristics and properties of a solution embody this principle, applying it to the particular circumstances of the situation. For example, the esophagus is in this way an application of the principle:

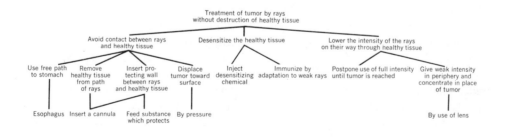

"free passage to the stomach," to the particular circumstances of the human body. To understand the solution as a solution is just the same as to comprehend the solution as embodying its functional value. When someone is asked, "Why is such-and-such a solution?", he necessarily has recourse to the functional value. In all my experiments, aside from two or three unmistakable exceptions, when the E asked about a proposal: "In what way is this a solution of the problem?", the S responded promptly with a statement of its functional value. (In spontaneous statements of the Ss, the functional value was frequently left unmentioned as being too obvious.)

Incidentally, the realization of its functional value mediates understanding of a solution even where there is nothing but an 'unintelligible' (though sufficiently general) relation between the functional value and the demand which it fulfills. Blowing on a weakly glimmering fire, for example, undoubtedly solves the problem of rekindling the fire because in this way fresh oxygen is supplied. In other words, the increase of the oxygen supply is the immediate functional value of blowing on the fire. But why combination with oxygen produces warmth and flame is ultimately not intelligible. Even if the whole of chemistry should be successfully and without a gap derived from the principles of atomic physics, these principles are not in themselves altogether intelligible, i.e., ultimately they must be "accepted as mere facts." Thus, intelligibility frequently means no more than participation in, or derivability from, sufficiently elementary and universal causal relationships. But even if these general laws are not in themselves intelligible, reducibility to such general laws actually mediates a certain type of understanding.

To the same degree to which a solution is understood, it can be transposed, which means that under altered conditions it may be changed correspondingly in such a way

as to preserve its functional value. For, one can transpose a solution only when one has grasped its functional value, its general principle, i.e., the invariants from which, by introduction of changed conditions, the corresponding variations of the solution follow each time.

An example: When, seen from the standpoint of a spectator, someone makes a detour around some obstacle, and yet acts from his own point of view in terms of nothing but, say, "now three yards to the left, then two yards straight ahead, then to the right . . ."—these properties of the solution would certainly satisfy the concrete circumstances of the special situation here and now. But so long as the person in question has not grasped the functional value, the general structure: "detour around an obstacle," he must necessarily fail when meeting a new obstacle which is differently located and of different shape. For to different obstacles correspond different final forms of the solution; but the structure, "detour around an obstacle," remains always the same. Whoever has grasped this structure is able to transpose a detour properly.

7. MEANINGLESS ERRORS AS A SYMPTOM OF DEFICIENT UNDERSTANDING   A solution conceived without functional understanding often betrays itself through nonsensical errors. A good example is supplied by experiments with another thinking problem.

The problem was worded as follows: "You know what a pendulum is, and that a pendulum plays an important rôle in a clock. Now, in order for a clock to go accurately, the swings of the pendulum must be strictly regular. The duration of a pendulum's swing depends, among other things, on its length, and this of course in turn on the temperature. Warming produces expansion and cooling produces contraction, although to a different degree in different materials. Thus every temperature-change would change the length of the pendulum. But the clock should go with absolute regularity. How can this be brought about?—By the way, the length of a pendulum is defined solely by the shortest distance between the point of suspension and the center of gravity. We are concerned only with this length; for the rest, the pendulum may have any appearance at all."

The customary solution of this pendulum problem in actual practice is reproduced in Figure 2. At first this solution will be entirely 'unintelligible' to many a reader.

Let him watch now what takes place when the solution suddenly becomes clear to him. Its functional value is that every expansion in one direction is compensated by an equally great expansion in the opposite direction.

The bars *a* and *a'* (see Figure 3) can expand only downwards; *b* and *b'*, on the other hand, only upwards, since they are fastened below. The bars *b* and *b'* are meant to raise the strip of metal to which *c* is fastened by exactly as much as *a* and *c* together expand downwards. To this end, *b* and *b'* must of course be constructed of a material with a greater coefficient of expansion than *a* and *a'* and *c*.

Only when Figure 3 is grasped as the

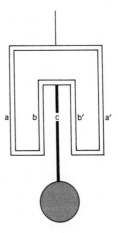

FIGURE 3.

embodiment of this functional value, is it understood as the solution.

Among the many Ss to whom I gave the pendulum problem, there were two who were already vaguely familiar with a pendulum-model, and simply reconstructed it from memory. One was fortunate and did it correctly, while the other drew "just four or five bars like this, from which the weight hung below." (Figure 4.) It is evident that this is a completely meaningless construction, despite all external resemblance to Figure 3, and devoid of any functional understanding (as the S clearly realized and expressed himself). Compare with this the solutions of the problem

FIGURE 2.

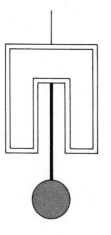

FIGURE 4.

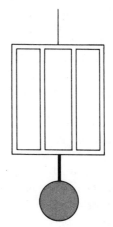

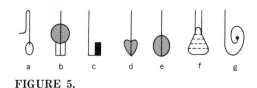

FIGURE 5.

contained in Figure 5, a-g, which, in spite of all external differences, embody the identical functional value and at the same time represent completely new constructions.

In all of them there is compensation in the sense of Figure 3; thus we deal with appropriate transpositions of Figure 3. It is worth mentioning that one S drew the model of Figure 5a, believing that it was the compensation-pendulum dimly familiar from experience. Here it is clear that the reconstruction can have taken place only via the common functional value. Nothing in their form is common to the two pendulums.

"Good" and "stupid" errors in Köhler's sense can be clearly distinguished as follows: In the case of good, intelligent errors, at least the general functional value of the situation is correctly outlined, only the specific manner of its realization is not adequate. For example, an ape stands a box on its corner under the goal object, which hangs high above, because in this way the box comes closer—to be sure, at the price of its stability. In the case of stupid errors, on the other hand, the outward form of an earlier, or an imitated solution is blindly reproduced without functional understanding. For example, an ape jumps into the air from a box—but the goal object is hanging at quite a different spot.

8. THE PROCESS OF SOLUTION AS DEVELOP-MENT OF THE PROBLEM It may already have become clear that the relationship between superordinate and subordinate properties of a solution has *genetic* significance. *The final form of an individual*

solution is, in general, not reached by a single step from the original setting of the problem; on the contrary, the principle, the functional value of the solution, typically arises first, and the final form of the solution in question develops only as this principle becomes successively more and more concrete. In other words, the general or "essential" properties of a solution genetically precede the specific properties; the latter are developed out of the former. The classification given previously presents, thus, a sort of *"family tree"* of the solution of the *radiation* problem.

The finding of a general property of a solution means each time a *reformulation of the original problem.* Consider for example the fourth proposal in the protocol above. Here it is clearly evident that at first there exists only the very general functional value of the solution: "one must decrease the intensity of the radiation on the way." But the decisive reformulation of the original problem is thereby accomplished. No longer, as at the beginning, does the S seek simply a "means to apply rays to the tumor without also destroying healthy tissue," but already—over and above this—a means to decrease the intensity of the radiation on the way. The formulation of the problem has thus been made sharper, more specific—and the proposal not to turn the rays on at full strength until the tumor has been reached, although certainly wrong, arises only as a solution of this new, reformulated problem. From this same reformulation of the problem there arises, at the end of the whole process, the practicable solution, "concentration of diffuse rays in the tumor." With the other proposals in the protocol, the case is similar: the solution-properties found at first, the functional values, *always serve as productive reformulations of the original problem.*

We can accordingly describe a process of solution either as development of the solution or as development of the problem.

Every solution-principle found in the process, which is itself not yet ripe for concrete realization, and which therefore fulfills only the first of the two demands given previously, functions from then on as reformulation, as sharpening of the original setting of the problem. *It is therefore meaningful to say that what is really done in any solution of problems consists in formulating the problem more productively.*

To sum up: *The final form of a solution is typically attained by way of mediating phases of the process, of which each one, in retrospect, possesses the character of a solution, and, in prospect, that of a problem.*

At the same time it is evident that, generally speaking, a process of solution penetrates only by degrees into the more specific circumstances and possibilities of the given situation. In the phase, "avoiding contact between rays and healthy tissue," for example, there is still very little reference to the concrete individuality of the situation. The rays function for the time being as "active agent," the tumor as "the place to be influenced," and the healthy tissue as "surrounding region which must be protected." In the next phase, "redirection of the rays over a tissue-free path to the stomach," at least the possibility of such a displacement of the rays is already made use of. In the search for a free pathway, the situation is then subjected to an even more precise inspection; as a consequence, such a specific component of the situation as the esophagus enters the solution-process and is used in a sensible manner.

To widen our horizon, let us here demonstrate with a mathematical example how a solution-process typically arrives at the final solution by way of mediation problem- or solution-phases. The original problem is to prove that there is an infinite number of prime numbers (to find "something from which follows that there exists . . .").

A step which is quite decisive, although subjectively hardly noted, consists in the solution-phase: "I must prove that for any prime number p there exists a greater one." This reformulation of the problem sounds quite banal and insignificant. Nevertheless I had Ss who never hit on it. And without this step, the final solution cannot be reached.[5]

A further solution-phase would run as follows: "To prove the existence of such a prime number, I must try to construct it." With one of my Ss, I could follow clearly the way in which, to this phase, a further one attached itself as a mere explication: "One must therefore construct a number greater than p which cannot be represented as a product." From here on, clearly directed to "avoiding a product," the S proceeded to construct the product of all numbers from 1 to p and to add 1—incidentally, without having realized that the resultant number need not be itself a prime number, but may merely contain the desired number as a fraction of itself.

9. IMPLICIT SOLUTION-PHASES   Not *all* phases of the various solution-processes are given in a family tree of the kind graphically represented previously: rather, only the more prominent and relatively independent among them are given. Aside from these, there exist phases which are not explicit enough and, above all, too banal ever to appear in a protocol. In the case of the radiation problem, for instance, it is clear to all Ss from the start that, in any case, to find a solution, something must be done, with the actual circumstances concerned, with the rays and the body. As modern Europeans, they do not think of looking for suitable magic for-

[5] The solution consists in the construction of the product of all prime numbers from 1 to p and adding to it 1. The resultant number is either itself a prime number, or it is a product of prime numbers greater than p. For, with the exception of the special case of 1, a prime number less than p cannot be contained in a multiple of itself increased by 1 without a remainder. Thus in any case, a prime number greater than p exists. (Q.E.D.)

mulae; nor would they anticipate that some change in another place would lead to a solution. Similarly in the case of the prime numbers problem, from the beginning there is no doubt that the solution is to be sought in the province of numbers, and not, for example, in the province of physical processes. In short, from the very first, the deliberating and searching is always confined to a province which is relatively narrow as to space and content. Thus preparation is made for the more discrete phases of a solution by certain *approximate regional demarcations,* i.e., by phases in which necessary but not yet sufficient properties of the solution are demanded. Such implicit phases of a solution do not quite fulfill even the first prerequisite of a solution mentioned previously.

This is valid not only for thinking, but also for attempts at solution by action (trial and error). When a layman wishes to adjust the spacing between lines on a typewriter, this much at least of the solution is known to him: "I must screw or press somewhere on the machine." He will not knock on the wall, for instance, nor does he anticipate that any change of the given colors would do. In general, one seeks to achieve mechanical effects by mechanical alterations in the critical object.

One more example, this time from animal psychology. Thorndike set his experimental animals (mostly cats) problems of the following type. They had to learn to bring about the opening of their cage doors by a simple mechanical manipulation—unintelligible to them, to be sure, for they could not survey the connections—and so to escape into freedom. Part of the animals had a whole series of different cage problems to solve. In one cage they had to pull on a loop, in another to lift a bar, or press on a knob, etc. Thorndike made the very interesting observation that generally, in the course of the experiments, "the cat's general tendency to claw at loose objects within the box is strengthened and its tendency to squeeze through holes and bite bars is weakened." Further, "its tendency to pay attention to what it is doing gets strengthened. . . ." It is evident that even animal 'trial and error' is for the most part already under the confining influence of certain demarcations, which, by the way, are not purely instinctive.

10. INSUFFICIENCY OF A PROTOCOL The reader has probably received the impression that the discussions of the preceding paragraphs left the data of the protocol a long way behind. In the case of the very first proposal, for instance, that of the esophagus, there was no mention at all of "redirecting over a tissue-free path," or even of "avoiding contact." That some such thing appeared in other protocols in an analogous place naturally proves nothing about the psychological origin of just this individual proposal.

This is the place in which to say something essential about protocols. One could formulate it thus: A protocol is relatively reliable only for what it positively contains, but not for that which it omits. For even the best-intentioned protocol is only a very scanty record of what actually happens. The reason for this insufficiency of protocols which are based on spoken thoughts must interest us also as characteristic of a solution-process as such. Mediating phases which lead at once to their concrete final realization, and thus are not separated from the solution by clear phase-boundaries, will often not be explicitly mentioned. They blend too thoroughly with their final solutions. On the other hand, mediating phases which must persist as temporary tasks until they find their final 'application' to the situation have a better chance of being explicitly formulated. Furthermore, many superordinate phases do not appear in the protocol, because the situation does not appear to the S promising enough for them. Therefore they are at once suppressed. In other words, they are too fleeting, too provisional, too tentative, occasionally also too 'foolish,' to cross the threshold of the spoken word.

In very many cases, the mediating phases are not mentioned because the S simply does not realize that he has already modified the original demand of the problem. The thing seems to him so self-evident that he does not have at all the feeling of having already taken a step forward.[6] This can go so far that the S deprives himself of freedom of movement to a dangerous degree. By substituting unawares a much narrower problem for the original, he will therefore remain in the framework of this narrower problem, just because he confuses it with the original.

11. "SUGGESTION FROM BELOW" There exist cases in which the final form of a solution is not reached from above, i.e., not by way of its functional value. This is a commonplace of 'familiar' solutions. If the final solution of a problem is familiar to the S, it certainly need no longer be constructed, but can be reproduced as a whole, as soon as the problem is stated.[7]

More interesting cases exist. We must always remember that a solution has, so to speak, two roots, one in that which is sought and one in that which is given. More precisely, *a solution arises from the claim made on that which is given by that which is sought. But these two components vary greatly in the share they have in the genesis of a solution-phase.* A property of a solution is often very definitely demanded (characterized, hinted at) before it is discovered in what is given; but sometimes it is not. An example from the radiation problem: The esophagus may be discovered because a free path to the

stomach is already sought. But it may also happen that, during a relatively vague, planless inspection of what is given in the situation, one 'stumbles on the esophagus.' Then the latter—so to speak, from below—suggests its functional value: "free path to the stomach"; in other words, the concrete realization precedes the functional value. This sort of thing happens not infrequently; for the analysis of the situation is often relatively planless. Nor is this disadvantageous, when the point is to find new ideas. In mathematical problems, this analysis merely of the given situation, the development of consequences from the given data, plays an especially large rôle.

One more example of "suggestion from below." An attractive goal object (for example, a banana) lies out of reach before the cage of a chimpanzee. So long as the solution, "to fish for the banana with a stick," is not very familiar, something like a stick must be in the visual field as a suggesting factor. The stick is not yet *sought* —as embodiment of the previously conceived functional value: "something long and movable"—as it is in later stages; rather it must itself help to suggest this functional value.[8]

The prerequisite for such a suggestion from below is that the 'phase-distance' between what is sought for and what could give the suggestion is not too great.

The following is an example for this influence of the size of the phase distance. Right at the beginning of the radiation problem, the E can speak of "crossing," or can draw a cross, without the S's grasping what that means. (Cf. the solution by crossing a number of weak bundles of rays in the tumor.) If, on the other hand, the

---

[6] Such is especially the case with the demarcation of boundaries.
[7] This of course does not exclude the possibility that the solution is reproduced along with its functional value and as its realization, and that it is thus *understood*.

[8] This suggestion of the functional value from below is even the rule in problems where a number of objects are offered to begin with, with the instruction to choose from among them an appropriate tool for such and such a purpose. Especially when only few objects are concerned, thinking will tend to proceed by looking things over, i.e., it will test the given objects one after another as to their applicability, and no attempt will be made to conceive the appropriate functional value first.

S is already of his own accord directed to "decreasing the intensity on the way," he will understand the suggestion sooner than if his thinking is dominated, for example, by the completely different demand for "a free path for the rays." We can formulate the general proposition that the sooner a suggestion is understood or assimilated, the closer it approaches the genealogical line already under development, and, within this line, the nearer it is to the problem-phase then in operation; in short, the more completely it is already anticipated.

This law is a special case of a more general law, which concerns not suggestions in the narrow sense, but the material of thinking in general. Selz formulated this law as "a general law of anticipation" in the following manner: "An operation succeeds the more quickly, the more the schematic anticipation of the solution approaches a complete anticipation." We shall have more to do with this law.

12. LEARNING FROM MISTAKES (CORRECTIVE PHASES)   As yet we have dealt only with the progress from the superordinate to the subordinate phases (or vice versa), in other words, with progress along a given genealogical line. That this is not the only kind of phase succession is, one should think, sufficiently indicated by the protocol given above. Here the line itself is continually changed, and one way of approach gives way to another. Such a *transition to phases in another line* takes place typically when some tentative solution does not satisfy, or when one makes no further progress in a given direction. *Another* solution, more or less clearly defined, is then looked for. For instance, the first proposal (esophagus) having been recognized as unsatisfactory, quite a radical change in direction takes place. The attempt to avoid contact is completely given up and a means to desensitize tissues is sought in its place. In the third proposal, however,

the S has already returned to old tactics, although with a new variation. And such shifting back and forth occurs frequently.

It will be realized that, in the transition to phases in another line, the thought-process may range more or less widely. Every such transition involves a return to an earlier phase of the problem; an earlier task is set anew; a new branching off from an old point in the family tree occurs. Sometimes an S returns to the original setting of the problem, sometimes just to the immediately preceding phase. An example for the latter case: From the ingenious proposal, to apply the rays in adequate amounts by rotation of the body around the tumor as a center, an S made a prompt transition to the neighboring proposal: "One could also have the radiation apparatus rotate around the body." Another example: The S who has just realized that the proposal of the esophagus is unsatisfactory may look for another natural approach to the stomach. This would be the most "direct" transition, that is, the transition which retrogresses least. Or, renouncing the natural approach to the stomach, he looks for another method of avoiding contact. Or, again, he looks for an altogether different way to avoid the destruction of healthy tissue. Therewith, everything which can be given up at all would have been given up; a "completely different" solution would have to be sought.

In such retrogression, thinking would naturally not be taken back to precisely the point where it had been before. For the failure of a certain solution has at least the result that now one tries *"in another way."* While remaining in the framework of the old *Problemstellung,* one looks for another starting point. Or again, the original setting may itself be altered *in a definite direction,* because there is the newly added demand: from now on, that property of the unsatisfactory solution must be avoided which makes it incompatible with the given conditions. An example: The fully developed form of our radiation problem is naturally preceded by a stage in which the problem runs only as follows: Destroy the tumor with the aid of appropriate rays. The most obvious solution, which consists simply in sending a bundle of sufficiently strong rays through the body into the tumor, appears at once inadequate, since it would clearly have the result of destroying healthy tissue as well. In realization of this, *avoidance of the evil* has to be incorporated *as an additional demand* into the original form of the problem; only in this way does our form of the radiation problem arise (cure . . . without destruction of healthy tissue). One more example: In the pendulum problem, a watchman is often proposed who has the task of keeping the length constant by compensatory changes in the position of the weight. For the most part, Ss realize

spontaneously that this procedure could not possibly be sufficiently precise, and that it would also incessantly interfere with the motion of the clock. Thus the problem: "compensation of the change in length of the pendulum," is enriched by the important addition: "automatically."

Such learning from errors plays as great a rôle in the solution-process as in everyday life.[9] While the simple realization, *that* something does not work, can lead only to some variation of the old method, the realization of *why* it does not work, the recognition of the *ground of the conflict*, results in a correspondingly definite *variation which corrects* the recognized defect.

[9] Life is of course, among other things, a sum total of solution-processes which refer to innumerable problems, great and small. It goes without saying that of these only a small fraction emerge into consciousness. Character, so far as it is shaped by living, is of the type of a resultant solution.

Some aspects of computers as thinkers are discussed here.

A POINT TO GUIDE YOUR STUDY   *This selection was taken from the first part of a book entitled* Computers and Thought; *references to other sections and other articles of the volume appear from time to time.*

28: SELECTION FROM: COMPUTERS AND THOUGHT

E. A. Feigenbaum, University of California, Berkeley, and J. Feldman, University of California, Irvine

What is a computer?
Is it just a "number factory"?

In the popular conception, a computer is a high-speed number calculator. This view is only partly correct. A digital computer is, in fact, a general symbol-processing device, capable of performing any well-

From *Computers and Thought* by E. A. Feigenbaum and J. Feldman. Copyright © 1963 by McGraw-Hill Book Co. Excerpt used by permission of the authors and the McGraw-Hill Book Co.

defined process for the manipulation and transformation of information.

All general-purpose digital computers are basically alike. They have:

1. One or more "input" devices for transforming symbolic information external to the machine into internally usable form. These internal forms are the *symbols* which the machine manipulates. A punched-card reader is an example of an input device.

2. One or more "output" devices for

transforming the internal symbols back into external form. The computer's printer is an example of an output device.

3. One or more "memory" devices capable of storing symbols before, during, and after processing.

4. An "arithmetic unit." One of the possible interpretations that can be given to a computer's symbols is the interpretation as *numbers*. The arithmetic unit is a piece of electronic gear which will operate upon these numbers to produce (under the numerical interpretation) sums, differences, products, etc. Most of the computation described in this volume is nonnumeric. For example, the chess pieces manipulated by the Newell-Shaw-Simon Chess Player are represented and handled as symbols, not numbers.

5. A "control unit." The control unit is the executive of the computer organization. It is wired to understand and obey a repertory of *instructions* (or commands), calling the other units into action when necessary. The instructions are generally elementary processes, *e.g.*, fetch a symbol from a specified place in memory, return a symbol to some place in memory, shift a symbol a certain number of places to the left or right in "working storage."

A very important instruction, "compare and transfer control," enables the computer to make a simple two-choice decision—to take one of two specified courses of action depending on the information found in some cell of the memory. By cascading these simple decisions, highly complex decisions can be fashioned.

Information processes more complicated than those "wired into" the computer can be carried out by means of a sequence of the elementary instructions, called a *program*. The program is the precise statement of the information process that the user desires the machine to carry out. A computer's program is stored in the memory along with all the other problem information and data. One part of a program can call in another part of the program from the memory to the working storage and alter it. The general-purpose digital computer can do any information processing task for which a program can be written. The same computer which one moment is computing a company's payroll may in the next moment be computing aircraft designs or insurance premiums. Any program for a general-purpose computer effectively converts this general-purpose machine into a special-purpose machine for doing that task intended by the user who wrote the program.

Is it possible for computing machines to think?

No—if one defines thinking as an activity peculiarly and exclusively *human*. Any such behavior in machines, therefore, would have to be called thinking-like behavior.

No—if one postulates that there is something in the essence of thinking which is *inscrutable, mysterious, mystical.*

Yes—if one admits that the question is to be answered by *experiment and observation,* comparing the behavior of the computer with that behavior of human beings to which the term "thinking" is generally applied.

We regard the two negative views as unscientifically dogmatic. The positive, or empirical, view is explored with cogency by Turing in an article reprinted in this volume. Armer, in another reprinted article, qualifies the positive view by pointing out that there exists a continuum of intelligent behavior, that the question of how far we can push machines out along that continuum is to be answered by research, not dogma. We might add one further qualification: to assert that thinking machines are possible is not necessarily to assert that thinking machines with human capabilities already exist (or that they will exist in the near future).

The reader of this volume is invited to form a judgment on the matter. The reports reprinted here constitute, we think, the best evidence available on the subject at present.

What, then, is the goal of artificial intelligence research? As we interpret the field, it is this: *to construct computer programs which exhibit behavior that we call "intelligent behavior" when we observe it in human beings.*

Because this research area is still in the formative stage of its development, many different research paths are being explored. Our goal definition may be too ambitious for some researchers, not ambitious enough for others (chiefly because it is tied to human behavior).

Many of the research projects reported in Part 1 achieve this goal within their special problem areas. Shall we call this computer behavior "thinking," or shall we not? Perhaps this is an individual's choice. In our opinion, it is neither an important nor a fruitful topic for debate.

But doesn't a computer do exactly what it is told to do and no more?

Commenting on this familiar question, a well-known researcher in the field had this to say:

This statement—that computers can do only what they are programmed to do—is intuitively obvious, indubitably true, and supports none of the implications that are commonly drawn from it.

A human being can think, learn, and create because the program his biological endowment gives him, together with the changes in that program produced by interaction with his environment after birth, enables him to think, learn, and create. If a computer thinks, learns, and creates, it will be by virtue of a program that endows it with these capacities. Clearly this will not be a program—any more than the human's is—that calls for highly stereotyped and repetitive behavior independent of the stimuli coming from the environ-

ment and the task to be completed. It will be a program that makes the system's behavior highly conditional on the task environment—on the task goals and on the clues extracted from the environment that indicate whether progress is being made toward those goals. It will be a program that analyzes, by some means, its own performance, diagnoses its failures, and makes changes that enhance its future effectiveness (Simon, 1960, p. 25).

Similarly, it is wrong to conclude that a computer can exhibit behavior no more intelligent than its human programmer and that this astute gentleman can accurately predict the behavior of his program. These conclusions ignore the enormous complexity of information processing possible in problem-solving and learning machines. They presume that, because the programmer can write down (as programs) general prescriptions for adaptive behavior in such mechanisms, he can comprehend the remote consequences of these mechanisms after the execution of millions of information processing operations and the interaction of these mechanisms with a task environment. And, more importantly, they presume that he can perform the same complex information processing operations equally well with the device within his skull.

Is it true that a computer will be a chess champion because the computer is so fast that it can examine all possible moves and their consequences?

This view of the problem-solving potential of computers rests on the assumption that, because computers are so fast, they can "think of everything." This kind of computing might be called *brute-force* computing. Brute-force programs generally have a simple structure, employing exhaustive enumeration of possibilities and exhaustive search. Is brute-force computing a general method for handling problems that are usually thought of as having some "intellectual content"?

To answer this question, we must look first at what *a problem* is. A problem exists for a problem-solver when he is faced with the task of choosing one of a set of alternatives placed before him by the problem environment. The problem-solver has no problem if the environment presents him with only one alternative; he must take that alternative. What is troublesome about alternatives is not so much their number as their consequences. Alternatives usually have elaborate consequences, which need to be evaluated before one alternative is chosen. The formal expression of this notion leads us to the so-called *maze model of a problem.* Let us look at this in an example.

Consider the problem of choosing a move at some point in a game of chess. If the position allows the player only one alternative, there is no problem—the move is *forced.* If, however, there is a genuine problem, the decision can be made by examining the immediate and remote consequences of selecting particular alternatives—the moves opened up to the opponent, the possible replies to these moves, etc. This "tree of possibilities" is pictured in Fig. 1.

In principle, this tree can be completely elaborated; the end points can be identified as wins, losses, or draws; and a strategy can be employed to determine the best alternative available at the top of the tree.

Since this procedure can in principle be programmed on modern, high-speed computers, why is chess still an interesting game? Why are computers not unbeatable champions at chess?

The answer is simple: the size of the chess maze is enormous. It has been estimated that there are about 10^{120} different paths through a complete chess maze (give or take, perhaps, many powers of ten). Even under the most generous assumptions about the power of modern computing machinery, now or in the future, it is beyond the limits of plausibility that a computer will ever be able to play "optimum" chess by the exhaustive strategy mentioned above.

Brute-force computing through problem mazes (for any but the most trivial problems) just won't do. Problem-solving by this method is beyond the realm of practical possibility.

How then, are we to construct an intelligent problem-solver?

It appears that the clue to intelligent behavior, whether of men or machines, is *highly selective search,* the drastic pruning of the tree of possibilities explored. *For a computer program to behave intelligently, it must search problem mazes in a highly selective way, exploring paths relatively fertile with solutions and ignoring paths relatively sterile.*

What is a heuristic program?

A *heuristic (heuristic rule, heuristic method)* is a rule of thumb, strategy, trick, simplification, or any other kind of device which drastically limits search for solutions in large problem spaces. Heuristics do not guarantee optimal solutions; in fact, they do not guarantee any solution at all; *all that can be said for a useful heuristic*

FIGURE 1.

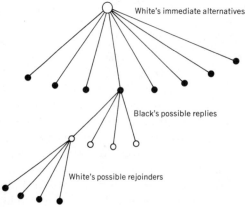

White's immediate alternatives

Black's possible replies

White's possible rejoinders

is that it offers solutions which are good enough most of the time. A *heuristic program* is a program that employs heuristics in solving complex problems.

Heuristic methods have sometimes been contrasted with *algorithmic methods* for finding problem solutions, and a certain amount of intellectual blood has been shed unnecessarily on this battlefield. Without getting into the subtleties of the disagreement, we observe that the term "algorithm" is used with considerable ambiguity in mathematics and logic. Under one commonly held definition, algorithms are decision procedures which are *guaranteed* to produce the solution being sought, given enough time. The brute-force program described above for playing chess is such an algorithm. But algorithms (under this concept) are known, or practical, for only a very small subset of all interesting problems one would like to have computers solve. Over the spectrum of the broader class, heuristic methods seem to offer more general applicability.

The payoff in using heuristics is greatly reduced search and, therefore, practicality. Often, but not always, a price is paid: by drastic search limitations, sometimes the best solution (indeed, *any or all* solutions) may be overlooked.

Heuristics come in at least two varieties: special-purpose and general-purpose. Let us examine these by example:

1. The chess duffer might typically use this rule of thumb: Stop exploring any sequence that puts the queen in immediate danger of being captured. This is a special-purpose chess heuristic. It is useful to the duffer because it keeps him out of one kind of trouble. By using this especially crude search-limiting device, the duffer will never discover those exciting queen-sacrifice combinations which get "!!" annotations in books on chess.

2. In proving theorems, a mathematician usually works backward from the theorem he is trying to prove to known theorems or axioms, instead of working forward from known expressions, using the rules of inference, until he stumbles on the theorem he has to prove. Under certain conditions, "working backward" is a powerful general heuristic for utilizing information in the problem to guide search for the solution.

3. A useful rule of thumb used by human beings in most of their problem-solving is this: Attack a new problem by methods that have solved similar problems in the past. The criteria for "similarity" may themselves be heuristic. If the environment is in a kind of steady state with respect to problem types, this heuristic may be very useful. In environments demanding a high degree of innovative problem-solving, this heuristic will hinder rather than facilitate problem-solving.

4. Two general-purpose heuristic problem-solving methods commonly employed in human reasoning are *means-ends analysis* and *planning*. In means-ends analysis, an initial problem state is transformed into a target state by selecting and applying operations which, step by step, reduce the difference between the states. In the planning method, a simplified statement of the original problem is constructed, and means-ends analysis is applied to this new, simpler problem. The result is a set of plans (guesses at possible operator sequences), hopefully one of which will work, i.e., solve the original problem. Means-ends analysis is discussed in detail in the reprinted article on the General Problem Solver (GPS).

What are some unsolved problems of artificial intelligence research?

In an area so new and exploratory, most of the problems remain unsolved, indeed unattacked. At this stage, it is not easy even to identify and state the problems, except in a very general way. We offer some examples of problems we think are ripe for attack:

1. The learning of heuristics. A puzzling, fascinating, and extremely important question is this: How can computers (and how do people) learn new heuristic methods and rules, both special-purpose and general-purpose? At the moment, our knowledge of learning mechanisms for problem-solving programs is rudimentary. Any significant breakthrough in this area would offer the promise of enabling us to "bootstrap" our way into very much more powerful problem-solving programs.

2. Inductive inference. Artificial intelligence currently is strong on deductive inference, weak on inductive inference. Yet, in the melting pot of everyday intelligence, induction is certainly the more significant ingredient. One way of looking at the problem is that we need programs which will in some sense induce internally stored "models" of external environments —models from which the programs can make valid and useful predictions of future environmental states. Looked at in another way, this is the problem of hypothesis formation by machine. It is the general pattern recognition problem. Today we know very little about this crucial problem.

3. Understanding natural language. A problem of great theoretical and practical interest is that of constructing a program to understand communication in natural language (the word "understand" is here used with its full human connotation). To put it simply, one would like to be able to engage in a dialog with a computer—a dialog in which the computer will hold up its end of the conversation adaptively, intelligently, with understanding. Research on question-answering programs (e.g., the BASEBALL program reprinted in this volume) is a good start. There is much that can be transferred from research on mechanical translation, on information retrieval, on models of human associative memory, and other areas of information science. The problem is ripe for intensive, interdisciplinary study.

What are the limits of artificial intelligence research?

No one can answer this question today.

Perhaps the question has more fascination than importance. In terms of the continuum of intelligence suggested by Armer, the computer programs we have been able to construct are still at the low end. What is important is that we continue to strike out in the direction of the milestone that represents the capabilities of human intelligence. Is there any reason to suppose that we shall never get there? None whatever. Not a single piece of evidence, no logical argument, no proof or theorem has ever been advanced which demonstrates an insurmountable hurdle along the continuum.

Today, despite our ignorance, we can point to that biological milestone, the thinking brain, in the same spirit as the scientists many hundreds of years ago pointed to the bird as a demonstration in nature that mechanisms heavier than air could fly.

SECTION SIX

MOTIVATION

*Plenty of experimental evidence exists to indicate that the list of
"primary" motives should be lengthened to include manipulation and
curiosity for the higher primates. Man seems to have
more than his share of curiosity motivation. In fact, some psychologists
see curiosity motivation as related to man's restlessness, and to a
certain extent, some think it provides the impetus for his creativity.
If you ask a scientist why he spends so much time in his laboratory,
he will probably ultimately not be able to tell you in terms of other
motives. He will, in all likelihood, eventually say that he is curious
to see "what will happen if. . . ." An artist may tell you, eventually,
that he wants to experience a new combination of color or sound.
Indeed, mountain climbers are reputed to climb mountains
"because they are there."*

*The rationale behind the experiment presented below is as follows:
If curiosity, as measured by visual exploration, is a motive, monkeys
should work to satisfy it and this satisfaction should serve as a
reinforcement. For example, it should be possible for a monkey to
learn to go to one color and not to another if he is consistently
reinforced for responding to that color. Here the reinforcement is
visual exploration instead of a more conventional one, e.g., food for a
hungry monkey. In other words, the monkey should be able to
learn a discrimination for visual-exploration reinforcements.*

A POINT TO GUIDE YOUR STUDY   *Notice the care with which the
experiment is described. Such detail makes repetition possible and is
essential in scientific communication.*

GLOSSARY   E: *experimenter.* S: *subject.* .01 **confidence level:** *there is
one chance in one hundred that the differences shown in the
graphs are due to chance alone.*

29: DISCRIMINATION LEARNING BY RHESUS MONKEYS TO VISUAL-EXPLORATION MOTIVATION

Robert A. Butler, University of Chicago

Experiments conducted at the University of Wisconsin Primate Laboratory have demonstrated that rhesus monkeys learn the solution of mechanical puzzles with no other incentive than that provided by the manipulation of the puzzle devices (4, 1, 2) and that these manipulatory responses will persist during prolonged repetitive testing (3). Recently, monkeys have been trained without food or other special incentives to discriminate between differentially colored sets of screw eyes (5). A manipulation drive has been postulated as the motivational basis for this type of behavior, and Harlow postulates that the manipulation drive is "one of a class of externally elicited drives" (3, p. 293).

The present experiments were designed to test the efficacy of another kind of externally elicited motive, that of visual exploration. Monkeys both in their home cages and in test situations continually follow movements of objects and people in their field of vision and persistently explore their environment visually.

Two preliminary experiments were conducted to investigate visually motivated behavior. Experiment I, designed primarily to measure learning, involved testing three monkeys 20 trials a day (an hour or less) for 20 days on a color discrimination, with no other incentive provided than visual exploration. Experiment II, designed primarily to test strength and persistence of visual motivation, involved testing two monkeys 4 hr. a day for 5 days under visual-exploration incentive.

Method

SUBJECTS Three rhesus monkeys, nos. 156, 159, and 167, served as Ss in Experiment I, and two rhesus monkeys, nos. 102 and 147, served as Ss in Experiment II. All animals were adult and had had very extensive previous training on food-rewarded learning problems. Numbers 156, 159, 102, and 147 had been Ss in manipulation-drive studies.

APPARATUS During testing the monkeys were housed in a wire cage 27 by 17 by 26 in. Over this cage E placed a box with front and top made of pressed wood and three sides covered by heavy black cloth. A 25-w. lamp was fastened on the roof of the box to provide illumination within. Two doors measuring 3¾ by 4 in. were fastened, flush, to the front of the box, with their bases 12 in. above the floor and 5 in. apart, center to center. Each door could be locked by a wooden pin, and each locking device contained a leaf switch connected to a 6-v. battery. When the door was pushed, contact was made with the locking device and an electric circuit was completed, illuminating a small signal light mounted on the front of the apparatus. Transparent Lucite plates 3 in. by 3 in. were mounted on the inside face of each door so as to permit differentially colored stimulus cards to be inserted between the Lucite plate and the door. An opaque screen, which could be raised or lowered by E, separated S from the stimulus cards. The apparatus stood on a table

These researches were supported in part by a grant to the University of Wisconsin from the Atomic Energy Commission Contract No. AT(11-1)-64 and in part by the Research Committee of the Graduate School from funds supplied by the Wisconsin Alumni Research Foundation.

R. A. Butler. Discrimination learning by rhesus monkeys to visual-exploration motivation. *J. comp. physiol. Psychol.*, 1953, **46**, 95–98. Copyright © 1953 by the American Psychological Association. Excerpts reprinted here with permission from the author and the American Psychological Association. Figure 2 has been renumbered, and one reference has been completed (was in press).

in the entrance room of the Wisconsin primate laboratory. The temperature in the test room ranged from 70° to 80°F. The temperature within the test box increased 6° to 7°F. above room temperature during the 4-hr. test sessions.

PROCEDURE   *Discrimination training.* In Experiment I the *S*s were tested on a yellow-blue discrimination, blue being the positive stimulus for monkeys 159 and 167, and yellow the positive stimulus for monkey 156. The position of the positive and negative cards followed a predetermined balanced order.

The animals were placed in the apparatus for 5 min. each day before testing began. The *E* initiated each trial by raising the opaque screen, exposing the stimulus cards. If *S* pushed open the door containing the positive stimulus, it was allowed 30 sec. of visual exploration before the screen was lowered. If *S* pushed against the door with the negative card, the door engaged the locking device, illuminating the signal light, and the screen was immediately lowered. The intertrial interval was always 30 sec., during which the stimulus cards were either rearranged or removed and returned to their previous position. A noncorrection technique was used throughout. Each animal received 20 trials a day, 5 days a week, for a total of 20 days. The time of the day for testing was not held constant. The response measures recorded were errors and response latencies, defined as time between *E*'s raising the screen and *S*'s responding to a door. The testing procedures for Experiment II were the same as those described for Experiment I except that the *S*s were tested continuously 4 hr. a day for five days with a day's rest between days 3 and 4 only. The blue card was positive for monkey 102 and the yellow card positive for monkey 147.

During both experiments people were frequently in the test room for a part of each session. When *S* opened the door, *E*, after recording the data for the trial, usu-ally walked around the room, opened cabinets, or stepped outside the building within the 30-sec. period. Thus, the animals ordinarily were provided with a diversified environment in which several activities occurred and which offered auditory as well as visual stimulation. Care was taken to prevent the monkeys from seeing either food or other monkeys during the test sessions.

Results

EXPERIMENT I   The mean percentage of correct responses made by the three monkeys is shown in Figure 1 and clearly demonstrates learning. Animals 156, 159, and 167 attained 17 correct responses in 20 trials (performance significantly better than chance at the .01 confidence level) on days 7, 10, and 12, respectively, and they equaled or exceeded this level on 11, 7, and 2 succeeding days, respectively.

EXPERIMENT II   The individual discrimination-learning curves for the two *S*s of the second experiment are plotted in Figure 2. Number 102 attains and then maintains almost perfect performance; no. 147 performs consistently during the last 600 trials at a level significantly better than chance at the .01 confidence level.

FIGURE 1   *Discrimination learning to visual-exploration incentives.*

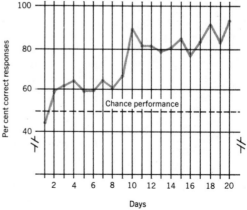

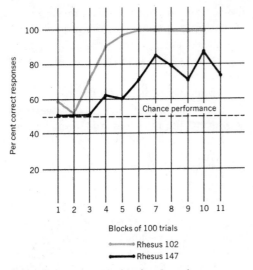

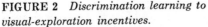

FIGURE 2 *Discrimination learning to visual-exploration incentives.*

Discussion

These experiments demonstrate beyond question that monkeys can learn object discriminations and maintain their performance at a high level of efficiency with visual-exploration reward.

References

1. Davis, R. T., Settlage, P. H., and Harlow, H. F. Performance of normal and brain-operated monkeys on mechanical puzzles with and without food incentive. *J. genet. Psychol.*, 1950, 77, 305–311.
2. Gately, M. J. Manipulation drive in experimentally naïve rhesus monkeys. Unpublished master's thesis, Univer. of Wisconsin, 1950.
3. Harlow, H. F. Learning and satiation of response in intrinsically motivated complex puzzle performance by monkeys. *J. comp. physiol. Psychol.*, 1950, 43, 289–294.
4. Harlow, H. F., Harlow, Margaret K., and Meyer, D. F. Learning motivated by a manipulation drive. *J. exp. Psychol.*, 1950, 40, 228–234.
5. Harlow, H. F., and McClearn, G. E. Object discriminations learned by monkeys on the basis of manipulation motives. *J. comp. physiol. Psychol.*, 1954, 47, 73–76.

Fear is a strong learned, or acquired, drive. This means that, as a result of learning, stimuli which do not originally produce fear can come to do so later. In this experiment, rats were made to fear a white compartment by being shocked while they were in it. This, of course, is an example of classical conditioning. The white box now elicits fear; it did not do this before the shocks had been delivered. Subsequently, rats will learn to make responses which reduce this fear. When this occurs, they are being reinforced by the reduction of fear. In the following case, they learn to turn wheels or push bars which enable them to escape from the white compartment.

This general scheme has been extended greatly by Miller and others of the "Yale school." They maintain that humans, for instance, develop mechanisms or habits which reduce fear. Many symptoms found in cases of combat neuroses (so-called shell-shock) are thought to be fear-reducing mechanisms, for example.

POINTS TO GUIDE YOUR STUDY *(1) The ideas involved in this experiment are general ones. The experiment merely serves to illustrate the general idea that fear can be attached to new cues and that fear-reduction can be a reinforcement for new learning. This is one reason for doing animal experiments. One tries to derive some general rules which will apply to human beings. (2) Two kinds of learning are involved here: classical conditioning of fear and instrumental learning of the fear-reducing response. If you have not yet studied these different types of learning, look them up in your text.*

GLOSSARY *Experimental extinction: this refers to the weakening of a habit when it is not reinforced. Experimental extinction is shown in Figure 3.* t *test: a statistical test of significance. A way of computing the number of times the obtained differences would have occurred by chance alone.*

30: STUDIES OF FEAR AS AN ACQUIRABLE DRIVE: I. FEAR AS MOTIVATION AND FEAR-REDUCTION AS REINFORCEMENT IN THE LEARNING OF NEW RESPONSES

Neal E. Miller, Rockefeller University

An important role in human behavior is played by drives, such as fears, or desires for money, approval, or status, which appear to be learned during the socialization of the individual (1, 12, 16, 17, 18). While some studies have indicated that drives can be learned (2, 8, 15), the systematic experimental investigation of acquired drives has been scarcely begun. A great deal more work has been done on the innate, or primary drives such as hunger, thirst, and sex.

The purpose of the present experiment was to determine whether or not once fear is established as a new response to a given situation, it will exhibit the following functional properties characteristic of primary drives, such as hunger: (a) when present motivate so-called random behavior and (b) when suddenly reduced serve as a reinforcement to produce learning of the immediately preceding response.

This study is part of the research program of the Institute of Human Relations, Yale University. It was first reported as part of a paper at the 1941 meetings of the A.P.A. The author is indebted to Fred D. Sheffield for assistance in the exploratory work involved in establishing the experimental procedure and for criticizing the manuscript.

N. E. Miller. Studies of fear as an acquirable drive: I. Fear as motivation and fear-reduction as reinforcement in the learning of new responses. *J. exp. Psychol.*, 1948, 38, 89–101. Copyright © 1948 by the American Psychological Association. Excerpts reprinted here with permission from the author and the American Psychological Association. Some footnotes have been omitted, the caption of Fig. 1 has been placed in the body of the text, and other figures have been recaptioned. One reference has been completed (was in press).

Apparatus and procedure

The apparatus used in this experiment is illustrated in Figure 1. The left compartment is painted white, the right one black. A shock may be administered through the grid which is the floor of the white compartment. When the animal is placed on the grid which is pivoted at the inside end, it moves down slightly making a contact that starts an electric timer. When the animal performs the correct response, turning the wheel or pressing the bar as the case may be, he stops the clock and actuates a solenoid which allows the door, painted with horizontal black and white

FIGURE 1 *Acquired drive apparatus.*

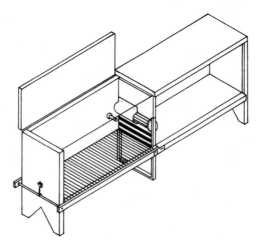

stripes, to drop. The E can also cause the door to drop by pressing a button. The dimensions of each compartment are 18 x 6 x 8½ in.

The procedure involved the following five steps:

1. *Test for initial response to apparatus.* The animals were placed in the apparatus for approximately one min. with the door between the two compartments open and their behavior was observed.

2. *Trials with primary drive of pain produced by electric shock.* The procedure for administering shock was designed to attach the response of fear to as many as possible of the cues in the white compartment instead of merely to the relatively transient stimulus trace of just having been dropped in. This was done so that the animal would remain frightened when he was restrained in the compartment on subsequent non-shock trials. The strength of shock used was 500 volts of 60 cycle AC through a series resistance of 250,000 ohms. The animals were given 10 trials with shock. On the first trial they were allowed to remain in the white compartment for 60 sec. without shock and then given a momentary shock every five sec. for 60 sec. At the end of this period of time the E dropped the door and put a continuous shock on the grid.

As soon as the animal had run into the black compartment, the door was closed behind him and he was allowed to remain there for 30 sec. Then he was taken out and placed in a cage of wire mesh approximately nine in. in diameter and seven in. high for the time between trials. Since the animals were run in rotation in groups of three, the time between trials was that required to run the other two animals, but was never allowed to fall below 60 sec. This procedure was followed on all subsequent trials.

On the second trial the animal was placed into the center of the white compartment facing away from the door, was kept there for 30 sec. without shock, at the

end of which time the shock was turned on and the door opened. On trials 3 through 10 the grid was electrified before the animal was dropped on it and the door was opened before he reached it. On odd numbered trials the animal was dropped at the end of the compartment away from the door and facing it; on even numbered trials he was dropped in the center of the compartment facing away from the door.

3. *Non-shock trials with experimenter dropping door.* The purpose of these trials was to determine whether or not the animals would continue to perform the original habit in the absence of the primary drive of pain from electric shock, and to reduce their tendency to crouch in the white compartment and to draw back in response to the sound and movement of the door dropping in front of them. Each animal was given five of these non-shock trials during which the E dropped the door before the animal reached it. As with the preceding trials the animals were dropped in facing the door on odd numbered trials and facing away from it on even numbered ones; they were allowed to remain in the black compartment for 30 sec. and were kept in the wire mesh cage for at least 60 sec. between trials.

4. *Non-shock trials with door opened by turning the wheel.* The purpose of these trials was to determine whether the continued running without shock was the mere automatic persistence of a simple habit, or whether an acquired drive was involved which could be used to motivate the learning of a new habit. During these trials the E no longer dropped the door. The apparatus was set so that the only way the door could be dropped was by moving the wheel a small fraction of a turn. The bar was present but pressing it would not cause the door to drop. The animals that moved the wheel and caused the door to drop were allowed to remain 30 sec. in the black compartment. Those that did not move the wheel within 100 sec. were picked out of the white compartment at

the end of that time. All animals remained at least 60 sec. between trials in the wire mesh cage. All animals were given 16 trials under these conditions. On each trial the time to move the wheel enough to drop the door was recorded on an electric clock and read to the nearest 10th of a sec.

5. *Non-shock trials with door opened by pressing the bar.* The purpose of these trials was to determine whether or not animals (a) would unlearn the first new habit of turning the wheel if this habit was no longer effective in dropping the door, and (b) would learn a second new habit, pressing the bar, if this would cause the door to drop and allow them to remove themselves from the cues arousing the fear. Animals that had adopted the habit of crouching in the white compartment till the end of the 100-sec. limit and so had not learned to rotate the wheel were excluded from this part of the experiment. These trials were given in exactly the same way as the preceding ones except that the apparatus was set so that turning the wheel would not cause the door to drop but pressing the bar would. During these trials there was no time limit; the animals were allowed to remain in the white compartment until they finally pressed the bar.[1] The time to press the bar was recorded on an electric clock to the nearest 10th of a sec. and the number of revolutions of the wheel was recorded on an electric counter in quarter revolutions.

Results

In the test before the training with electric shock, the animals showed no readily discernible avoidance or preference for either of the two chambers of the apparatus. They explored freely through both of them.

During the trials with primary drive of pain produced by electric shock, all of the animals learned to run rapidly from the white compartment through the door,

[1] One animal which did not hit the bar within 30 min. was finally discarded.

which was dropped in front of them by the *E*, and into the black compartment. On the five trials without shock, and with the *E* still dropping the door, the animals continued to run. The behavior of the animals was markedly different from what it had been before the training with the primary drive of pain from electric shock.

When the procedure of the non-shock trials was changed so that the *E* no longer dropped the door and it could only be opened by moving the wheel, the animals displayed variable behavior which tended to be concentrated in the region of the door. They would stand up in front of it, place their paws upon it, sniff around the edges, bite the bars of the grid they were standing on, run back and forth, etc. They also tended to crouch, urinate, and defecate. In the course of this behavior some of the animals performed responses, such as poking their noses between the bars of the wheel or placing their paws upon it, which caused it to move a fraction of a turn and actuate a contact that caused the door to open. Most of them then ran through into the black compartment almost immediately. A few of them drew back with an exaggerated startle response and crouched. Some of these eventually learned to go through the door; a few seemed to learn to avoid it. Other animals abandoned their trial-and-error behavior before they happened to strike the wheel and persisted in crouching so that they had to be lifted out of the white compartment at the end of the 100 sec. period. In general, the animals that had to be lifted out seemed to crouch sooner and sooner on successive trials.

Thirteen of the 25 animals moved the wheel enough to drop the door on four or more out of their first eight trials. Since, according to theory, a response has to occur before it can be reinforced and learned, the results of these animals were analyzed separately and they were the only ones which were subsequently used in the bar-pressing phase of the experiment. The average speed (reciprocal of time in seconds) with which these animals opened the door by moving the wheel on the 16 successive trials is presented in Figure 2. It can be seen that there is a definite tendency for the animals to learn to turn the wheel more rapidly on successive trials. Eleven out of the 13 individual animals turned the wheel sooner on the 16th than on the first trial, and the two animals which did not show improvement were ones which happened to turn the wheel fairly soon on the first trial and continued this performance throughout. The difference between the average speed on the first and 16th trials is of a magnitude ($t = 3.5$) which would be expected to occur in the direction predicted by theory less than two times in 1000 by chance. Therefore, it must be concluded that those animals that did turn the wheel and run out of the white compartment into the black one definitely learned to perform this new response more rapidly during the 16 trials *without* the primary drive of pain produced by electric shock.

When the setting on the apparatus was changed so that the wheel would not open the door but the bar would, the animals continued to respond to the wheel vigorously for some time. It was obvious that they had learned a strong habit of responding to it. Eventually, however, they stopped reacting to the wheel and began to perform other responses. After longer or shorter periods of variable behavior they finally hit the bar, caused the door to drop, and ran through rapidly into the black compartment. On the first trial the number of complete rotations of the wheel ranged from zero to 530 with a median of 4.75. On successive trials during which turning the wheel did not cause the door to drop, the amount of activity on it progressively dropped till by the tenth trial the range was from 0 to 0.25 rotations with a median of zero. The progressive decrease in the amount of activity on the wheel is shown in Figure 3. It is plotted in medians because of the skewed nature of the distribution. Twelve out of the 13 rats which were used in this part of the experiment gave fewer rotations of the wheel on the tenth than on the first trial. From the binomial expansion it may be calculated that for 12 out of 13 cases to come out in the direction predicted by the theory is an event which would be expected to occur by

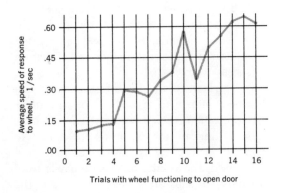

Average speed of response to wheel, 1/sec

Trials with wheel functioning to open door

FIGURE 2 *Learning the first new habit, turning the wheel, during trials without primary drive. With mild pain produced by an electric shock as a primary drive, the animals have learned to run from the white compartment, through the open door, into the black compartment. Then they were given trials without any electric shock during which the door was closed but could be opened by turning a little wheel. Under these conditions, of the 25 animals, the 13 which turned the wheel enough to drop the door on four or more of the first eight trials learned to turn it. This figure shows the progressive increase in the average speed with which these 13 animals ran up to the wheel and turned it enough to drop the door during the 16 non-shock trials.*

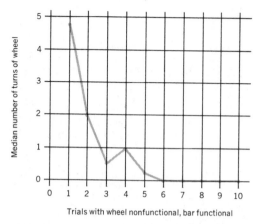

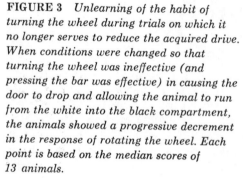

FIGURE 3 *Unlearning of the habit of turning the wheel during trials on which it no longer serves to reduce the acquired drive. When conditions were changed so that turning the wheel was ineffective (and pressing the bar was effective) in causing the door to drop and allowing the animal to run from the white into the black compartment, the animals showed a progressive decrement in the response of rotating the wheel. Each point is based on the median scores of 13 animals.*

chance less than one time in 1000. Thus, it may be concluded that the dropping of the door, which is presumed to have produced a reduction in the strength of fear by allowing the animals to escape from the cues in the white compartment which elicited the fear, was essential to the maintenance of the habit of rotating the wheel.

The results on bar pressing are presented in Figure 4. It can be seen that the speed of bar pressing increased throughout the 10 non-shock trials during which that response caused the door to drop. Since the last trial was faster than the first for 12 out of the 13 animals, the difference was again one which would be expected by chance less than one time in 1000.

Discussion

On preliminary tests conducted before the training with electric shock was begun, the animals showed no noticeable tendency to avoid the white compartment. During training with the primary drive of pain produced by electric shock in the white compartment, the animals learned a strong habit of quickly running out of it, through the open door, and into the black compartment.

On non-shock trials the animals persisted in running from the white compartment through the open door into the black one. On additional non-shock trials during which the door was not automatically dropped in front of the animals, they exhibited so-called random behavior and learned a new response, turning the wheel, which caused the door to drop and allowed them to escape into the black compartment. This trial-and-error learning of a new response demonstrated that the cues in the white compartment had acquired the functional properties of a drive and that escape from the white into the black

FIGURE 4 *Learning a second new habit, bar pressing, under acquired drive. Conditions were changed so that only pressing the bar would cause the door to drop and allow the animals to run from the white compartment where they had been previously shocked, into the black one where they had escaped shock. During non-shock trials under these conditions, the animals learned a second new habit, pressing the bar. Each point is based on the average speed of 13 animals.*

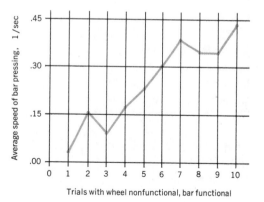

compartment had acquired the functional properties of a reward.

The general pattern of the fear response and its capacity to produce a strong stimulus is determined by the innate structure of the animal. The connection between the pain and the fear is also presumably innate. But the connection between the cues in the white compartment and the fear was learned. Therefore the fear of the white compartment may be called an acquired drive. Because fear can be learned, it may be called acquirable; because it can motivate new learning, it may be called a drive.

Running through the door and into the black compartment removed the animal from the cues in the white compartment which were eliciting the fear and thus produced a reduction in the strength of the fear response and the stimuli which it produced. This reduction in the strength of the intense fear stimuli is presumably what gave the black compartment its acquired reinforcing value.

If the reduction in fear produced by running from the white into the black was the reinforcement for learning the new habit of wheel turning, we would expect this habit to show experimental extinction when that reinforcement was removed. This is exactly what happened. During the first trial on which turning the wheel no longer dropped the door, the animals gradually stopped performing this response and began to exhibit other responses. As would be expected, one of these responses, pressing the bar, which caused the door to drop and allowed the animal to remove himself from the fear-producing cues in the white compartment, was gradually learned in a series of trials during which the wheel turning was progressively crowded out. Thus, it can be seen that the escape from the white compartment, which presumably produced a reduction in the strength of the fear, played a crucial role, similar to that of a primary reward, in the learning and maintenance of the new habits.

References

1. Allport, G. W. *Personality*. New York: Henry Holt, 1937.
2. Anderson, E. E. The externalization of drive: III. Maze learning by non-rewarded and by satiated rats. *J. genet. Psychol.*, 1941, 59, 397–426.
3. Brown, J. S. Generalized approach and avoidance responses in relation to conflict behavior. New Haven: Dissertation, Yale Univ., 1940.
4. Dollard, J. Exploration of morale factors among combat air crewmen. *Memorandum to Experimental Section, Research Branch, Information and Education Division, War Department,* 9 March 1945.
5. Freud, S. *New introductory lectures on psychoanalysis*. New York: Norton, 1933.
6. Freud, S. *The problem of anxiety*. New York: Norton, 1936.
7. May, M. A. Experimentally acquired drives. *J. exp. Psychol.*, 1948, 38, 66–77.
8. Miller, N. E. An experimental investigation of acquired drives. *Psychol. Bull.*, 1941, 38, 534–535.
9. Miller, N. E. Experimental studies of conflict behavior. In: *Personality and the behavior disorders* (Ed. J. McV. Hunt), New York: Ronald Press, 1944, 431–465.
10. Miller, N. E. Theory and experiment relating psychoanalytic displacement to stimulus-response generalization. *J. abnorm. soc. Psychol.*, 1949, 43, 155–178.
11. Miller, N. E. Studies of fear as an acquirable drive: II: Resistance to extinction. In preparation.
12. Miller, N. E., and Dollard, J. *Social learning and imitation*. New Haven: Yale Univ. Press, 1941.
13. Miller, N. E., and Lawrence, D. H. Studies of fear as an acquirable drive: III. Effect of strength of electric shock as a primary drive and of number of trials with the primary drive on the strength of fear. In preparation.
14. Mowrer, O. H. A stimulus-response analysis of its role as a reinforcing agent. *Psychol. Rev.*, 1939, 46, 553–565.
15. Mowrer, O. H., and Lamoreaux, R. R. Fear as an intervening variable in avoidance conditioning. *J. comp. Psychol.*, 1946, 39, 29–50.
16. Shaffer, L. F. *The psychology of adjustment*. Boston: Houghton Mifflin, 1936.
17. Watson, J. B. *Psychology from the standpoint of a behaviorist*. Philadelphia: Lippincott, 1924.
18. Woodworth, R. S. *Dynamic psychology*. New York: Columbia University Press, 1918.

*Complex human motives, such as need for achievement, are
especially interesting. Most psychologists consider them to be the
result of learning, and indeed the present article presents data
to support this view. These complex motives have sometimes been
called secondary motives, but this term is no longer much used because
it implies that they are of secondary importance in human behavior.*

*It seems possible to distinguish three general types of motives.
In the first place, there are the physiological motives proper which
are based on need states of body tissue. In the second place, there
are the motives, such as learned fear, which are modifications of the
physiological motives. Finally, there are the complex motive states,
often somewhat confusingly called needs, which are the result of
prolonged social learning.*

POINTS TO GUIDE YOUR STUDY *(1) What are the experiments and
observations which tie together the successive points of Table 1?
What ties A to B, B to C, and C to D?   (2) Note the lower part of
Table 3, "Analysis of Variance"; the F values are the things to look at.
An F value significant at the 1 or 5 per cent level indicates that
obtained differences were probably* not *due to chance alone. Thus,
the F of 12.21 for religion indicates that the mean ages of expectation
differed so much that the difference could not be explained by
saying it was due to chance. (Don't worry about the "interaction.")
(3) **n** stands for "need" in the following selection.*

31: SOME SOCIAL CONSEQUENCES OF ACHIEVEMENT MOTIVATION
David C. McClelland, Harvard University

Influenced by Hull and other function-alists, many of us for a long time tended to think of motives or drives as if they were functionally interchangeable, like electromotive forces in an equation in physics. From such a point of view it is as ridiculous to ask the question what kind of motive is involved as it is to ask what kind of electromotive force is involved. All motives are functionally equivalent and vary only in intensity. A motive is a motive is a motive is a motive, as Gertrude Stéin might say. It doesn't really matter whether you are working with light-aversion as a drive, or hunger, or thirst, or pain, since they are all functionally equivalent and it is merely a matter of convenience which one you choose to work with. It is also merely a matter of convenience which animal species you choose to work with since again, by assumption, a motive is a motive and it is therefore as useful theoretically to study the hunger drive in the white rat as it is to study the achievement motive in the human being. Today as we have begun to study motivation in its own right, and not just as a convenient construct to explain learning, such a point of view seems painfully inadequate. For one thing, as animal psychologists like Harlow (3) and Nissen (6) have been pointing out, there are major species differences in motivation which must be taken into account if we are to understand animal behavior adequately. For another, and this is the point I intend

D. C. McClelland. Some social consequences of achievement motivation. In M. R. Jones (Ed.), *Nebraska symposium on motivation*, 1955. Lincoln, Neb.: University of Nebraska Press, 1955, pp. 41–65. Copyright © 1955 by the University of Nebraska Press. Excerpts reprinted here with permission from the author and the University of Nebraska Press.

to elaborate here, recent studies of human motivation have demonstrated again and again that knowledge about one particular kind of motivation will enable us to predict varieties of behavior that we could not predict from knowledge of other motives. For example, knowledge of n Achievement scores will enable us to predict how well a group of people will do in a laboratory task (4), but knowledge of n Affiliation scores will not. Knowledge of n Affiliation scores will enable us to predict something about popularity (18) whereas knowledge of n Achievement scores will not. And so on. It is becoming increasingly clear that we must pay attention to the type of motive we are measuring, its particular origins, and its particular consequences for human behavior and society.

As a case in point, let us try to do this for the achievement motive, the human motive about which we know the most at the present time. There is no need to review here the methods we have used for deriving the n Achievement score or the data showing its connections with various types of behavior, since that has been done elsewhere (4) and particularly well by Atkinson at this Symposium last year (1). It will have to suffice here to say that we have developed what appears to be a promising method of measuring the achievement motive by identifying and counting the frequency with which a certain type of imagery appears in the thoughts a person has when he writes a brief story under time pressure. The type of imagery involved, which includes any references to "competition with a standard of excellence," can be identified objectively and reliably and differs in kind from other types of imagery which can be used to identify other motives such as the need for Affiliation, the need for Power, and the like. There are those who argue that what we are identifying in this way are not really motives at all, but something else, perhaps habits (2). I don't want to seem too lighthearted about

psychological theory, but I should hate to see much energy expended in debating the point. If someone can plan and execute a better research by calling these measures habits, so much the better. If, furthermore, it should turn out that all the interesting findings we have turned up are the result of some theoretical "error" in our thinking, I cannot admit to much regret. The fact of the matter is that we know too little about either motives or habits to get into a very useful discussion as to which is which. The important thing is that we accumulate data as rapidly and systematically as we can. Then I believe these theoretical issues will have a way of boiling themselves down to a meaningful level at which they can be settled.

But to return to our main story: we have continued to treat n Achievement as a motive and after hearing where this thinking has led us, you must decide for yourselves whether you want to conceive of it in the same way or in some different way. I want to draw attention now to Winterbottom's very important study (4, 13) on the origins of n Achievement as we measure it. She found, as many of you will remember, that mothers who said they expected their sons to do well on their own at an early age tended to have sons with higher n Achievement scores. That is, mothers who expected their sons to be self-reliant early in life—to make their own friends, to find their own way around their part of town, to do well in competitive sports and the like—tended to have sons with strong achievement motives. Furthermore, this training for self-reliance or independence (11) did not include "care-taking" items such as putting oneself to bed, cutting one's own food, earning one's own spending money, et cetera, a fact which suggested that what was involved here was not rejection by the mother but rather a positive interest in the child's independence, growth, and development. Winterbottom established here a link between a socialization practice, namely independence training, and a motive, namely the desire to do well.

Considered in a social and historical context, this linkage suggested an interesting parallel with Weber's classic description of the nature and characterological consequences of the Protestant Reformation (10). In the first place, he stresses, as others have, that the essence of the Protestant revolt against the Catholic church was a shift from a reliance on an institution to a greater reliance on the self, so far as salvation was concerned. The individual Protestant Lutheran or Calvinist was less dependent on the church as an institution either for its priests or its sacraments or its official dogma. Instead there was to be a "priesthood of all believers," in Luther's words. The Protestant could read and interpret his Bible and find his own way to God without having to rely on the authority of the Church or its official assistance. As Weber describes it, we have here what seems to be an example of a revolution in ideas which should increase the need for independence training. Certainly Protestant parents, if they were to prepare their children adequately for increased self-reliance so far as religious matters were concerned, would tend to stress increasingly often and early the necessity for the child's not depending on adult assistance but seeking his own "salvation." In the second place, Weber's description of the kind of personality type which the Protestant Reformation produced is startlingly similar to the picture we would draw of a person with high achievement motivation. He notes that Protestant working girls seemed to work harder and longer, that they saved their money for long-range goals, that Protestant entrepreneurs seemed to come to the top more often in the business world despite the initial advantages of wealth many Catholic families had, and so forth. In particular, he points out that the early Calvinist business man was pre-

vented by his religious views from enjoying the results of his labors. He could not spend money on himself because of scruples about self-indulgence and display, and so, more often than not, he reinvested his profits in his business, which was one reason he prospered. What then drove him to such prodigious feats of business organization and development? Weber feels that such a man "gets nothing out of his wealth for himself, except the irrational sense of having done his job well" (10, p. 71). This is exactly how we define the achievement motive. So again, the parallel seems clear, although there is not space to give the argument in full here. Is it possible that the Protestant Reformation involves a repetition at a social and historical level of the linkage that Winterbottom found between independence training and *n* Achievement among some mothers and their sons in a small town in Michigan in 1950?

To make such an assumption involves a breath-taking leap of hypothesizing so far as the average psychologist is concerned, who is much more at home with a sample of 30 mothers and 30 sons than he is with major social movements. But the hypothesis seems too fascinating to dismiss without some further study. It can be diagrammed rather simply as in Table 1. In terms of this diagram Weber was chiefly concerned with the linkage between A and

TABLE 1 *Hypothetical series of events relating self-reliance values with economic and technological development*

A Protestantism (self-reliance values)	D Economic and technological development
B Independence training by parents	C *n* Achievement in children

D, with the way in which Protestantism led to a change in the spirit of capitalism in the direction of a speeded-up, high-pressure, competitive business economy. But the manner in which he describes this relationship strongly suggests that the linkage by which these two events are connected involves steps B and C, namely a change in family socialization practices which in turn increased the number of individuals with high achievement motivation. Thus a full statement of the hypothesis would be that Protestantism produced an increased stress on independence training which produced higher achievement motivation which produced more vigorous entrepreneurial activity and rapid economic development. Such a simple statement of the hypothesis obscures many problems, some of which we have only begun to think about. To establish all the links in the chain obviously requires an enormous amount of research, much of which has not been completed. What I have to report today are only some preliminary findings which, however, serve to confirm the hypothesis at several crucial points and, at the very least, dignify it to the point of making it worth very serious investigation.

Let us consider first Weber's general argument about the connection between Protestantism and economic development. Although there has been much discussion among historians, economists, and sociologists of this thesis since it first appeared about 50 years ago, most of it *pro* though some of it *con* (see 9), I could find no simple statistical test of the presumed association such as we would be apt to apply in psychology. Instead the literature seems to consist largely of citing instances which confirm the thesis, drawn chiefly from England, the Scandinavian countries and Holland, or instances which apparently disprove it such as Belgium or pre-Protestant Italy. Having had much experience in my youth with individual rats who

obeyed none of Hull's laws, I wanted to get beyond the battle of instance and counter-instance to see what the general trend looked like. Table 2 shows the results of one such effort. What I tried to do was to get as large a group of Catholic and Protestant countries as I could which were matched roughly for climate and resources.

Then I took the most easily obtainable index of economic or technological development, namely kilowatt hours of electricity consumed as of a given year in a given country, and checked it against the Protestant-Catholic classification of the country, with the result shown in Table 2. A simple rank correlation, a biserial tau, shows that the Protestant character of a country is significantly associated with higher levels of consumption of electrical energy. This may be a crude test of the hypothesis, but the relationship is large and seems not likely to disappear under refinements of techniques for measuring economic development or for equating the natural resources of the two groups of countries. At least it is comforting to a psychologist to have this much statistical backing for a hypothesis before expending a great deal of further energy in trying to study its further implications.

The next step involves tying in our own research findings on the origins of achievement motivation (stages B and C in Table 1). Specifically, we would predict that there should be a connection between A and B in Table 1, that Protestants should favor earlier independence training than Catholics do. The major findings on this point are reproduced in Table 3 from a study by McClelland, Rindlisbacher and deCharms (5). The figures in the table are based on responses to the 13 items in the original Winterbottom independence training questionnaire which she found to be associated with *n* Achievement. A mean age was computed for each parent at which he expected his child to have mastered the items in question. Then averages of these means were computed and cross-classified by sex of parent, by education of parent, and by religious grouping. All three primary sources of variation are significant. Religion makes a significant difference, the Protestants and Jews favoring early independence and the Irish- and Italian-Catholics favoring later independence for their children. The first link of our research with its social context has been established.

The final link in the chain, that between C and D in Table 1, or between high *n* Achievement and economic development, is the one on which we have been working most recently. I want to confess here to doubts we had as to how this would come out. We knew that *n* Achievement as we measured it was significantly correlated with better performance on a wide variety of laboratory tasks (4) and Ricciuti (7) has shown that it is significantly correlated with high school grades with ability level partialed out. But none of this would lead us to predict on the basis of our own work that *n* Achievement would be connected in a peculiar way with more vigorous economic activity. Why not make the simpler assumption that it would be connected with more vigorous activity in any line of endeavor? Wouldn't it be logical to predict on the basis of our task performance or school work data that high *n* Achievement should make a person do better at poetry or politics, law or science, farming or selling real estate? Why pick on business or assume that *n* Achievement would direct people's interests along business lines particularly? Yet the sociological and historical data pointed clearly toward a connection with business activity, at least if we are to take Weber's arguments at all seriously, and continue to entertain the hypothesis sketched in Table 1.

So with some misgivings as to the outcome, we decided to put the hypothesis to the test by seeing whether students with high *n* Achievement were more interested in business occupations than students with

TABLE 2   *Average per capita consumption of electric power in Protestant and Catholic countries beyond the Tropics of Cancer and Capricorn (for the year 1950, in kilowatt-hours.)*

	PROTESTANT	CATHOLIC
Norway	5,310	
Canada	4,120	
Sweden	2,580	
U.S.A.	2,560	
Switzerland	2,230	
New Zealand	1,600	
Australia	1,160	
United Kingdom	1,115	
Finland	1,000	
Belgium		986
Austria		900
Union of South Africa	890	
France		790
Czechoslovakia		730
Holland	725	
Italy		535
Denmark	500	
Poland		375
Hungary		304
Ireland		300
Chile		260
Argentina		255
Spain		225
Uruguay		165
Portugal		110
Mean	1,983	457

Biserial tau = + .45 P <.005

From Woytinski (14).

low *n* Achievement. The null hypothesis is of course that *n* Achievement makes no difference in inclining a person toward one occupation rather than another. To measure occupational interest we simply used the Strong Vocational Interest Blank, which was filled out by a group of college freshmen at the same time that they had been tested for *n* Achievement. To test the hypothesis we simply took the top 20% of the class in *n* Achievement and compared their answers to each of the Strong items with the answers given by the bot-

TABLE 3 *Average ages at which parents expect children to have mastered various independence training items*

	LESS THAN HIGH SCHOOL GRADUATES	HIGH SCHOOL GRADUATE UP TO COLLEGE GRADUATES	COLLEGE GRADUATE OR MORE	MEANS	RELIGIOUS GROUP MEANS
Protestant					6.64
Father	8.04	6.41	6.90	7.12	
Mother	6.56	6.41	5.55	6.17	
Jewish					6.59
Father	7.65	7.12	6.48	7.08	
Mother	5.74	6.66	5.89	6.10	
Irish Catholic					7.66
Father	8.50	7.92	8.26	8.23	
Mother	7.23	7.61	6.40	7.08	
Italian Catholic					8.42
Father	9.05	10.43	6.51	8.66	
Mother	9.68	6.87	8.00	8.18	
Educational level means	7.81	7.43	6.75		
Fathers' mean	7.77				
Mothers' mean	6.88				

Analysis of variance

SOURCE OF VARIATION	SUM OF SQUARES	df.	MEAN SQUARE	F
1. Religion	13.91	3	4.64	12.21*
2. Educational level	4.60	2	2.30	6.05*
3. Sex of parent	4.74	1	4.74	12.47*
4. Interaction‡	11.78	17	.69	1.82†
5. Error		128	.38	

* Significant at the 1% level.
† Significant at the 5% level.
‡ The primary sources of variation interact significantly, a fact which cannot be discussed here as being beyond a preliminary treatment of the results. For this reason it has also been necessary to compute an independent estimate of error based on the actual variation of the individual cases in the various cells following the approximation method described by Walker and Lev (12), pp. 381–382.

tom 20% of the class in *n* Achievement. The results were really startling, at least to us, since we had had so many doubts about the whole enterprise from the beginning. You will recall that on the Strong Test the respondent is asked whether he likes, dislikes, or is indifferent to 100 different occupations on the first part of the test. In Table 4 are listed the only occupations for which consistent and significant differences appeared between the top and bottom fifths of the *n* Achievement distribution. In every case the group high in *n* Achievement likes the occupations listed better than the group low in *n* Achievement. What more striking confirmation of the hypothesis could be expected? The Chi-square for "stockbroker," the most significant single item, was 10.04, P < .01. Shades of Marxist propaganda about the role of "Wall Street" in the capitalist economy!

TABLE 4 *Occupations in the first 100 on the Strong Vocational Interest Blank preferred significantly more by college freshmen with high (top 20%) than with low (bottom 20%) n Achievement scores (listed in order of significance of differences)*

1. Stockbroker
2. Office manager
3. Sales manager
4. Buyer of merchandise
5. Real estate salesman
6. Factory manager

Now some Doubting Thomases among you are sure to point out that in making this many significance tests one ought to come out with about this number of significant differences. We know that, and we are for that reason replicating the study right at this moment, but what are the chances that Lady Luck should hit on these particular occupations when she had so many to pick from, including everything from artist to author to musician to lawyer or electrical repairman? To be more precise, the chances are less than 1 in 4,000, since roughly one-quarter of the occupations might be classified as related to business. Certainly if she did happen to pick on occupations so obviously related to business activity and economic development just by chance, she has played us a dirty trick in getting our scientific hopes aroused. In any case, the evidence does not consist of these items alone. Further item analysis of the rest of the test shows many confirmatory results, although their exact significance will have to await further study and, in particular, a replication.[1]

[1] Subsequent work has shown that this particular result is specific to the group tested, though the general line of reasoning turned out to be correct (*Ed.*). See D. C. McClelland. *The achieving society.* Princeton, N.J.: Van Nostrand, 1961. Chap. 6.

References

1. Atkinson, J. W. Explorations using imaginative thought to assess the strength of human motives. In Marshall Jones (Ed.), *Nebraska Symposium on Motivation,* 1954, 56–112.
2. Farber, I. E. Comments on Professor Atkinson's paper. In Marshall Jones (Ed.), *Nebraska Symposium on Motivation,* 1954, 112–115.
3. Harlow, H. F. Motivation as a factor in the acquisition of new responses. In *Current Theory and Research in Motivation,* Lincoln, Nebraska: University of Nebraska Press, 1953, 24–29.
4. McClelland, D. C., Atkinson, J. W., Clark, R. A., and Lowell, E. L. *The Achievement Motive.* New York: Appleton-Century-Crofts, 1953.
5. McClelland, E. C., Rindlisbacher, A., and deCharms, R. Religious and other sources of parental attitudes toward independence training. In D. C. McClelland (Ed.), *Studies in Motivation.* New York: Appleton-Century-Crofts, 1955.
6. Nissen, H. W. The nature of the drive as innate determinant of behavioral organization. In Marshall Jones (Ed.), *Nebraska Symposium on Motivation,* 1954, 281–321.
7. Ricciuti, H. N., and Sadacca, R. The prediction of academic grades with a projective test of achievement motivation: II. Cross-validation at the high school level. Princeton, N.J.: *Research Bulletin,* Educational Testing Service, 1954.
8. Shipley, T. W., and Veroff, J. A projective measure of need for affiliation. *J. exp. Psychol.,* 1952. 43, 349–356.
9. Tawney, R. H. *Religion and the Rise of Capitalism.* New York: Harcourt, Brace, 1926.
10. Weber, M. *The Protestant Ethic* (translated by Talcott Parsons). New York: Scribner's, 1930.
11. Whiting, J. W. M., and Child, I. L. *Child Training and Personality.* New Haven: Yale Univer. Press. 1953.
12. Walker, H. M., and Lev, J. *Statistical Inference.* New York: Holt, 1953.
13. Winterbottom, M. R. The relation of childhood training in independence to achievement motivation. Unpublished Ph.D. thesis, Univer. of Michigan, 1953. Abstract in Univ. Microfilms, Publication No. 5113.
14. Woytinski, W. S., and Woytinski, E. S. *World Population and Production,* New York: Twentieth Century Fund, 1953.

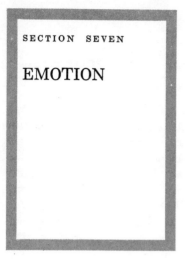

EMOTION

Emotions are characterized by (1) particular experiences, or feelings
and (2) an increase or decrease in the level of arousal. Theories of
emotion have been aimed at accounting for these characteristics.
The James-Lange theory attempts to deal especially with the first
characteristic; another theory, the Cannon-Bard theory, is most
successful in dealing with the second.

The James-Lange theory, as such, is probably not held by very many
psychologists today, but it provides a background for the
understanding of certain contemporary theories of emotion.
(See the next selection.)

William James is perhaps the most famous classical American
psychologist. He set the tone in his Principles of Psychology for much
of the pragmatic, functionalist American psychology which followed.
C. Lange was a Danish physiologist and is known to psychologists
because of his connection with the James-Lange theory.

A POINT TO GUIDE YOUR STUDY The writing style is rather old-
fashioned and flowery, but do not let that bother you. On the contrary,
James is considered a master stylist, and his work has great literary
merit. As someone has said, William James was a psychologist
who wrote like a novelist, while Henry James, his brother,
was a novelist who wrote like a psychologist.

32: SELECTION ON EMOTION FROM: THE PRINCIPLES OF PSYCHOLOGY

William James

Emotion follows upon the bodily expression in the coarser emotions at least

Our natural way of thinking about these coarser emotions is that the mental perception of some fact excites the mental affection called the emotion, and that this latter state of mind gives rise to the bodily expression. My theory, on the contrary, is that *the bodily changes follow directly the perception of the exciting fact, and that our feeling of the same changes as they occur* IS *the emotion.* Common-sense says, we lose our fortune, are sorry and weep; we meet a bear, are frightened and run; we are insulted by a rival, are angry and strike. The hypothesis here to be defended says that this order of sequence is incorrect, that the one mental state is not immediately induced by the other, that the bodily manifestations must first be interposed between, and that the more rational statement is that we feel sorry because we cry, angry because we strike, afraid because we tremble, and not that we cry, strike, or tremble, because we are sorry, angry, or fearful, as the case may be. Without the bodily states following on the perception, the latter would be purely cognitive in form, pale, colorless, destitute of emotional warmth. We might then see the bear, and judge it best to run, receive the insult and deem it right to strike, but we should not actually *feel* afraid or angry.

Stated in this crude way, the hypothesis is pretty sure to meet with immediate disbelief. And yet neither many nor farfetched considerations are required to mitigate its paradoxical character, and possibly to produce conviction of its truth.

William James. *The principles of psychology.* Vol. 2. New York: Holt, 1890. Copyright © 1890 by Henry Holt and Company. Excerpt reprinted here with permission from Holt, Rinehart and Winston, Inc.

To begin with, no reader of the last two chapters will be inclined to doubt the fact that *objects do excite bodily changes* by a preorganized mechanism, or the farther fact that *the changes are so indefinitely numerous and subtle that the entire organism may be called a sounding-board,* which every change of consciousness, however slight, may make reverberate. The various permutations and combinations of which these organic activities are susceptible make it abstractly possible that no shade of emotion, however slight, should be without a bodily reverberation as unique, when taken in its totality, as is the mental mood itself. The immense number of parts modified in each emotion is what makes it so difficult for us to reproduce in cold blood the total and integral expression of any one of them. We may catch the trick with the voluntary muscles, but fail with the skin, glands, heart, and other viscera. Just as an artificially imitated sneeze lacks something of the reality, so the attempt to imitate an emotion in the absence of its normal instigating cause is apt to be rather "hollow."

The next thing to be noticed is this, that *every one of the bodily changes, whatsoever it be, is* FELT, *acutely or obscurely, the moment it occurs.* If the reader has never paid attention to this matter, he will be both interested and astonished to learn how many different local bodily feelings he can detect in himself as characteristic of his various emotional moods. It would be perhaps too much to expect him to arrest the tide of any strong gust of passion for the sake of any such curious analysis as this; but he can observe more tranquil states, and that may be assumed here to be true of the greater which is shown to be true of the less. Our whole cubic capacity is sensibly alive; and each morsel of it contributes its pulsations of feeling, dim or sharp, pleasant, painful, or dubious, to that sense of personality that every one of us unfailingly carries with him. It is surprising what little items give accent to these complexes of sensibility. When worried by any slight trouble, one may find that the focus of one's bodily consciousness is the contraction, often quite inconsiderable, of the eyes and brows. When momentarily embarrassed, it is something in the pharynx that compels either a swallow, a clearing of the throat, or a slight cough; and so on for as many more instances as might be named. Our concern here being with the general view rather than with the details, I will not linger to discuss these, but, assuming the point admitted that every change that occurs must be felt, I will pass on.

I now proceed to urge the vital point of my whole theory, which is this: *If we fancy some strong emotion, and then try to abstract from our consciousness of it all the feelings of its bodily symptoms, we find we have nothing left behind,* no "mind-stuff" out of which the emotion can be constituted, and that a cold and neutral state of intellectual perception is all that remains. It is true that, although most people when asked say that their introspection verifies this statement, some persist in saying theirs does not. Many cannot be made to understand the question. When you beg them to imagine away every feeling of laughter and of tendency to laugh from their consciousness of the ludicrousness of an object, and then to tell you what the feeling of its ludicrousness would be like, whether it be anything more than the perception that the object belongs to the class "funny," they persist in replying that the thing proposed is a physical impossibility, and that they always *must* laugh if they see a funny object. Of course the task proposed is not the practical one of seeing a ludicrous object and annihilating one's tendency to laugh. It is the purely speculative one of subtracting certain elements of

feeling from an emotional state supposed to exist in its fulness, and saying what the residual elements are. I cannot help thinking that all who rightly apprehend this problem will agree with the proposition above laid down. What kind of an emotion of fear would be left if the feeling neither of quickened heart-beats nor of shallow breathing, neither of trembling lips nor of weakened limbs, neither of goose-flesh nor of visceral stirrings, were present, it is quite impossible for me to think. Can one fancy the state of rage and picture no ebullition in the chest, no flushing of the face, no dilatation of the nostrils, no clenching of the teeth, no impulse to vigorous action, but in their stead limp muscles, calm breathing, and a placid face? The present writer, for one, certainly cannot. The rage is as completely evaporated as the sensation of its so-called manifestations, and the only thing that can possibly be supposed to take its place is some cold-blooded and dispassionate judicial sentence, confined entirely to the intellectual realm, to the effect that a certain person or persons merit chastisement for their sins. In like manner of grief: what would it be without its tears, its sobs, its suffocation of the heart, its pang in the breast-bone? A feelingless cognition that certain circumstances are deplorable, and nothing more. Every passion in turn tells the same story. A purely disembodied human emotion is a nonentity. I do not say that it is a contradiction in the nature of things, or that pure spirits are necessarily condemned to cold intellectual lives; but I say that for *us,* emotion dissociated from all bodily feeling is inconceivable. The more closely I scrutinize my states, the more persuaded I become that whatever moods, affections, and passions I have are in very truth constituted by, and made up of, those bodily changes which we ordinarily call their expression or consequence; and the more it seems to me that if I were to become corporeally anaesthetic, I should be excluded from the life of the affections, harsh and tender alike, and drag out an existence of merely cognitive or intellectual form. Such an existence, although it seems to have been the ideal of ancient sages, is too apathetic to be keenly sought after by those born after the revival of the worship of sensibility, a few generations ago.

Schachter and Singer hold that the emotions we feel are due to our interpretations of the stirred-up physiological conditions which are part of emotional activity. Such a theory can easily account for the widely divergent emotional reactions of individuals to substances such as alcohol and the hallucinogenic drugs—LSD-25, for example.

POINTS TO GUIDE YOUR STUDY   *(1) A rather complex experiment is described here. Subjects in different groups were given either a placebo— an ineffective substance—or epinephrine (adrenaline). In addition, the individuals given epinephrine were subject to various conditions: They were told about the effects to be expected from the injection; told nothing about the effects of the injection; or misinformed as to the effects to be expected from the injection. Finally, subjects were put through situations designed to produce either euphoria or anger. Many comparisons are possible among these conditions, and the results of such comparisons enable the authors to draw the conclusions which summarize this selection.   (2) The p values are to be interpreted as follows: $p = .02$, for example, means that there are 2 chances in 100 that the difference being evaluated is due to chance alone and not due to the manipulation of experimental conditions.*

33: COGNITIVE, SOCIAL, AND PHYSIOLOGICAL DETERMINANTS OF EMOTIONAL STATE

Stanley Schachter, Columbia University, and Jerome E. Singer, Pennsylvania State University

The problem of which cues, internal or external, permit a person to label and identify his own emotional state has been with us since the days that James (1890) first tendered his doctrine that "the bodily changes follow directly the perception of the exciting fact, and that our feeling of the same changes as they occur *is* the emotion" (p. 449). Since we are aware of a variety of feeling and emotion states, it should follow from James' proposition that the various emotions will be accompanied

This experiment is part of a program of research on cognitive and physiological determinants of emotional state which is being conducted at the Department of Social Psychology at Columbia University under PHS Research Grant M-2584 from the National Institute of Mental Health, United States Public Health Service. This experiment was conducted at the Laboratory for Research in Social Relations at the University of Minnesota.

The authors wish to thank Jean Carlin and Ruth Hase, the physicians in the study, and Bibb Latané and Leonard Weller who were the paid participants.

S. Schachter and J. Singer. Cognitive, social, and physiological determinants of emotional state. *Psychol. Rev.*, 1962, **69**, 379–399. Copyright © 1962 by the American Psychological Association. Reprinted here with permission from the authors and the American Psychological Association. (Tables corrected.)

by a variety of differentiable bodily states. Following James' pronouncement, a formidable number of studies were undertaken in search of the physiological differentiators of the emotions. The results, in these early days, were almost uniformly negative. All of the emotional states experimentally manipulated were characterized by a general pattern of excitation of the sympathetic nervous system but there appeared to be no clear-cut physiological discriminators of the various emotions. This pattern of results was so consistent from experiment to experiment that Cannon (1929) offered, as one of the crucial criticisms of the James-Lange theory, the fact that "the same visceral changes occur in very different emotional states and in non-emotional states" (p. 351).

More recent work, however, has given some indication that there may be differentiators. Ax (1953) and Schachter (1957) studied fear and anger. On a large number of indices both of these states were characterized by a similarly high level of autonomic activation but on several indices they did differ in the degree of activation. Wolf and Wolff (1947) studied a subject with a gastric fistula and were able to distinguish two patterns in the physiological responses of the stomach wall. It should be noted, though, that for many months they studied their subject during and following a great variety of moods and emotions and were able to distinguish only two patterns.

Whether or not there are physiological distinctions among the various emotional states must be considered an open question. Recent work might be taken to indicate that such differences are at best rather subtle and that the variety of emotion, mood, and feeling states are by no means matched by an equal variety of visceral patterns.

This rather ambiguous situation has led Ruckmick (1936), Hunt, Cole, and Reis (1958), Schachter (1959) and others to suggest that cognitive factors may be major determinants of emotional states. Granted a general pattern of sympathetic excitation as characteristic of emotional states, granted that there may be some differences in pattern from state to state, it is suggested that one labels, interprets, and identifies this stirred-up state in terms of the characteristics of the precipitating situation and one's apperceptive mass. This suggests, then, that an emotional state may be considered a function of a state of physiological arousal[1] and of a cognition appropriate to this state of arousal. The cognition, in a sense, exerts a steering function. Cognitions arising from the immediate situation as interpreted by past experience provide the framework within which one understands and labels his feelings. It is the cognition which determines whether the state of physiological arousal will be labeled as "anger," "joy," "fear," or whatever.

In order to examine the implications of this formulation let us consider the fashion in which these two elements, a state of physiological arousal and cognitive factors, would interact in a variety of situations. In most emotion inducing situations, of course, the two factors are completely interrelated. Imagine a man walking alone down a dark alley, a figure with a gun suddenly appears. The perception-cognition "figure with a gun" in some fashion initiates a state of physiological arousal; this state of arousal is interpreted in terms of knowledge about dark alleys and guns and the state of arousal is labeled "fear." Similarly a student who unexpectedly learns that he has made Phi Beta Kappa may experience a state of arousal which he will label "joy."

[1] Though our experiments are concerned exclusively with the physiological changes produced by the injection of adrenalin, which appear to be primarily the result of sympathetic excitation, the term "physiological arousal" is used in preference to the more specific "excitation of the sympathetic nervous system" because there are indications, to be discussed later, that this formulation is applicable to a variety of bodily states.

Let us now consider circumstances in which these two elements, the physiological and the cognitive, are, to some extent, independent. First, is the state of physiological arousal alone sufficient to induce an emotion? Best evidence indicates that it is not. Marañon[2] (1924), in a fascinating study (which was replicated by Cantril & Hunt, 1932, and Landis & Hunt, 1932), injected 210 of his patients with the sympathomimetic agent adrenalin and then simply asked them to introspect. Seventy-one percent of his subjects simply reported their physical symptoms with no emotional overtones; 29% of the subjects responded in an apparently emotional fashion. Of these the great majority described their feelings in a fashion that Marañon labeled "cold" or "as if" emotions, that is, they made statements such as "I feel *as if* I were afraid" or *"as if* I were awaiting a great happiness." This is a sort of emotional "déjà vu" experience; these subjects are neither happy nor afraid, they feel "as if" they were. Finally a very few cases apparently reported a genuine emotional experience. However, in order to produce this reaction in most of these few cases, Marañon (1924) points out:

One must suggest a memory with strong affective force but not so strong as to produce an emotion in the normal state. For example, in several cases we spoke to our patients before the injection of their sick children or dead parents and they responded calmly to this topic. The same topic presented later, during the adrenal commotion, was sufficient to trigger emotion. This adrenal commotion places the subject in a situation of 'affective imminence.' (Pp. 307–308.)

Apparently, then, to produce a genuinely emotional reaction to adrenalin, Marañon was forced to provide such subjects with an appropriate cognition.

[2] Translated copies of Marañon's (1924) paper may be obtained by writing to the senior author.

Though Marañon (1924) is not explicit on his procedure, it is clear that his subjects knew that they were receiving an injection and in all likelihood knew that they were receiving adrenalin and probably had some order of familiarity with its effects. In short, though they underwent the pattern of sympathetic discharge common to strong emotional states, at the same time they had a completely appropriate cognition or explanation as to why they felt this way. This, we would suggest, is the reason so few of Marañon's subjects reported any emotional experience.

Consider now a person in a state of physiological arousal for which no immediately explanatory or appropriate cognitions are available. Such a state could result were one covertly to inject a subject with adrenalin or, unknown to him, feed the subject a sympathomimetic drug such as ephedrine. Under such conditions a subject would be aware of palpitations, tremor, face flushing, and most of the battery of symptoms associated with a discharge of the sympathetic nervous system. In contrast to Marañon's (1924) subjects he would, at the same time, be utterly unaware of why he felt this way. What would be the consequence of such a state?

Schachter (1959) has suggested that precisely such a state would lead to the arousal of "evaluative needs" (Festinger, 1954), that is, pressures would act on an individual in such a state to understand and label his bodily feelings. His bodily state grossly resembles the condition in which it has been at times of emotional excitement. How would he label his present feelings? It is suggested, of course, that he will label his feelings in terms of his knowledge of the immediate situation.[3] Should he at the time be with a beautiful

[3] This suggestion is not new, for several psychologists have suggested that situational factors should be considered the chief differentiators of the emotions. Hunt, Cole, and Reis (1958) probably make this point most explicitly in their study distinguishing among fear, anger, and sorrow in terms of situational characteristics.

woman he might decide that he was wildly in love or sexually excited. Should he be at a gay party, he might, by comparing himself to others, decide that he was extremely happy and euphoric. Should he be arguing with his wife, he might explode in fury and hatred. Or, should the situation be completely inappropriate he could decide that he was excited about something that had recently happened to him or simply, that he was sick. In any case, it is our basic assumption that emotional states are a function of the interaction of such cognitive factors with a state of physiological arousal.

This line of thought, then, leads to the following propositions:

1. Given a state of physiological arousal for which an individual has no immediate explanation, he will "label" this state and describe his feelings in terms of the cognitions available to him. To the extent that cognitive factors are potent determiners of emotional states, it could be anticipated that precisely the same state of physiological arousal could be labeled "joy" or "fury" or "jealousy" or any of a great diversity of emotional labels depending on the cognitive aspects of the situation.

2. Given a state of physiological arousal for which an individual has a completely appropriate explanation (e.g., "I feel this way because I have just received an injection of adrenalin") no evaluative needs will arise and the individual is unlikely to label his feelings in terms of the alternative cognitions available.

Finally, consider a condition in which emotion-inducing cognitions are present but there is no state of physiological arousal. For example, an individual might be completely aware that he is in great danger but for some reason (drug or surgical) remain in a state of physiological quiescence. Does he experience the emotion "fear"? Our formulation of emotion as a joint function of a state of physiological arousal and an appropriate cognition,

would, of course, suggest that he does not, which leads to our final proposition.

3. Given the same cognitive circumstances, the individual will react emotionally or describe his feelings as emotions only to the extent that he experiences a state of physiological arousal.[4]

Procedure

The experimental test of these propositions requires (a) the experimental manipulation of a state of physiological arousal, (b) the manipulation of the extent to which the subject has an appropriate or proper explanation of his bodily state, and (c) the creation of situations from which explanatory cognitions may be derived.

In order to satisfy the first two experimental requirements, the experiment was cast in the framework of a study of the effects of vitamin supplements on vision. As soon as a subject arrived, he was taken to a private room and told by the experimenter:

In this experiment we would like to make various tests of your vision. We are particularly interested in how certain vitamin compounds and vitamin supplements affect the visual skills. In particular, we want to find out how the vitamin compound called 'Suproxin' affects your vision.

What we would like to do, then, if we can get your permission, is to give you a small injection of Suproxin. The injection itself is mild and harmless; however, since some people do object to being injected we don't want to talk you into anything. Would you mind receiving a Suproxin injection?

If the subject agrees to the injection (and all but 1 of 185 subjects did) the experimenter continues with instructions we shall describe shortly, then leaves the

---

[4] In his critique of the James-Lange theory of emotion, Cannon (1929) also makes the point that sympathectomized animals and patients do seem to manifest emotional behavior. This criticism is, of course, as applicable to the above proposition as it was to the James-Lange formulation. We shall discuss the issues involved in later papers.

room. In a few minutes a physician enters the room, briefly repeats the experimenter's instructions, takes the subject's pulse and then injects him with Suproxin.

Depending upon condition, the subject receives one of two forms of Suproxin—epinephrine or a placebo.

Epinephrine or adrenalin is a sympathomimetic drug whose effects, with minor exceptions, are almost a perfect mimicry of a discharge of the sympathetic nervous system. Shortly after injection systolic blood pressure increases markedly, heart rate increases somewhat, cutaneous blood flow decreases, while muscle and cerebral blood flow increase, blood sugar and lactic acid concentration increase, and respiration rate increases slightly. As far as the subject is concerned the major subjective symptoms are palpitation, tremor, and sometimes a feeling of flushing and accelerated breathing. With a subcutaneous injection (in the dosage administered to our subjects), such effects usually begin within 3–5 minutes of injection and last anywhere from 10 minutes to an hour. For most subjects these effects are dissipated within 15–20 minutes after injection.

Subjects receiving epinephrine received a subcutaneous injection of ½ cubic centimeter of a 1 : 1000 solution of Winthrop Laboratory's Suprarenin, a saline solution of epinephrine bitartrate.

Subjects in the placebo condition received a subcutaneous injection of ½ cubic centimeter of saline solution. This is, of course, completely neutral material with no side effects at all.

MANIPULATING AN APPROPRIATE EXPLANATION By "appropriate" we refer to the extent to which the subject has an authoritative, unequivocal explanation of his bodily condition. Thus, a subject who had been informed by the physician that as a direct consequence of the injection he would feel palpitations, tremor, etc., would be considered to have a completely appro-

priate explanation. A subject who had been informed only that the injection would have no side effects would have no appropriate explanation of his state. This dimension of appropriateness was manipulated in three experimental conditions which shall be called: Epinephrine Informed (Epi Inf), Epinephrine Ignorant (Epi Ign), and Epinephrine Misinformed (Epi Mis).

Immediately after the subject had agreed to the injection and before the physician entered the room, the experimenter's spiel in each of these conditions went as follows:

Epinephrine informed. "I should also tell you that some of our subjects have experienced side effects from the Suproxin. These side effects are transitory, that is, they will only last for about 15 or 20 minutes. What will probably happen is that your hand will start to shake, your heart will start to pound, and your face may get warm and flushed. Again these are side effects lasting about 15 or 20 minutes."

While the physician was giving the injection, she told the subject that the injection was mild and harmless and repeated this description of the symptoms that the subject could expect as a consequence of the shot. In this condition, then, subjects have a completely appropriate explanation of their bodily state. They know precisely what they will feel and why.

Epinephrine ignorant. In this condition, when the subject agreed to the injection, the experimenter said nothing more relevant to side effects and simply left the room. While the physician was giving the injection, she told the subject that the injection was mild and harmless and would have no side effects. In this condition, then, the subject has no experimentally provided explanation for his bodily state.

Epinephrine misinformed. "I should also tell you that some of our subjects have experienced side effects from the Suproxin. These side effects are transitory, that is, they will only last for about 15 or 20 minutes. What will probably happen is that your feet will feel numb, you will have an itching sensation over parts of your body, and you may get a slight headache. Again these are side effects lasting 15 or 20 minutes." And again, the physician repeated these symptoms while injecting the subject.

None of these symptoms, of course, are consequences of an injection of epinephrine and, in effect, these instructions provide the subject with a completely inappropriate explanation of his bodily feelings. This condition was introduced as a control condition of sorts. It seemed possible that the description of side effects in the Epi Inf condition might turn the subject introspective, self-examining, possibly slightly troubled. Differences on the dependent variable between the Epi Inf and Epi Ign conditions might, then, be due to such factors rather than to differences in appropriateness. The false symptoms in the Epi Mis condition should similarly turn the subject introspective, etc., but the instructions in this condition do not provide an appropriate explanation of the subject's state.

Subjects in all of the above conditions were injected with epinephrine. Finally, there was a placebo condition in which subjects, who were injected with saline solution, were given precisely the same treatment as subjects in the Epi Ign condition.

PRODUCING AN EMOTION INDUCING COGNITION Our initial hypothesis has suggested that given a state of physiological arousal for which the individual has no adequate explanation, cognitive factors can lead the individual to describe his feelings with any of a diversity of emotional labels. In order to test this hypothesis, it was decided to manipulate emotional states which can be considered quite different—euphoria and anger.

There are, of course, many ways to induce such states. In our own program of research, we have concentrated on social determinants of emotional states and have been able to demonstrate in other studies that people do evaluate their own feelings by comparing themselves with others around them (Schachter 1959; Wrightsman 1960). In this experiment we have attempted again to manipulate emotional states by social means. In one set of conditions, the subject is placed together with a stooge who has been trained to act euphorically. In a second set of conditions the subject is with a stooge trained to act in an angry fashion.

EUPHORIA Immediately[5] after the subject had been injected, the physician left the room and the experimenter returned with a stooge whom he introduced as another subject, then said:

Both of you have had the Suproxin shot and you'll both be taking the same tests of vision. What I ask you to do now is just wait for 20 minutes. The reason for this is simply that we have to allow 20 minutes for the Suproxin to get from the injection site into the bloodstream. At the end of 20 minutes when we are certain that most of the Suproxin has been absorbed into the bloodstream, we'll begin the tests of vision.

The room in which this was said had been deliberately put into a state of mild disarray. As he was leaving, the experimenter apologetically added:

The only other thing I should do is to apologize for the condition of the room. I just didn't have time to clean it up. So, if you need any scratch paper or rubber bands or pencils, help yourself. I'll be back in 20 minutes to begin the vision tests.

[5] It was, of course, imperative that the sequence with the stooge begin before the subject felt his first symptoms for otherwise the subject would be virtually forced to interpret his feelings in terms of events preceding the stooge's entrance. Pretests had indicated that, for most subjects, epinephrine-caused symptoms began within 3–5 minutes after injection. A deliberate attempt was made then to bring in the stooge within 1 minute after the subject's injection.

As soon as the experimenter had left, the stooge introduced himself again, made a series of standard icebreaker comments, and then launched his routine. For observation purposes, the stooge's act was broken into a series of standard units, demarcated by a change in activity or a standard comment. In sequence, the units of the stooge's routine were the following:

1. Stooge reaches for a piece of paper and starts doodling saying, "They said we could use this for scratch, didn't they?" He doodles a fish for some 30 seconds, then says:

2. "This scrap paper isn't even much good for doodling" and crumples paper and attempts to throw it into wastebasket in far corner of the room. He misses but this leads him into a "basketball game." He crumples up other sheets of paper, shoots a few baskets, says "Two points" occasionally. He gets up and does a jump shot saying, "The old jump shot is really on today."

3. If the subject has not joined in, the stooge throws a paper basketball to the subject saying, "Here, you try it."

4. Stooge continues his game saying. "The trouble with paper basketballs is that you don't really have any control."

5. Stooge continues basketball, then gives it up saying, "This is one of my good days. I feel like a kid again. I think I'll make a plane." He makes a paper airplane saying, "I guess I'll make one of the longer ones."

6. Stooge flies plane. Gets up and retrieves plane. Flies again, etc.

7. Stooge throws plane at subject.

8. Stooge, flying plane, says, "Even when I was a kid, I was never much good at this."

9. Stooge tears off part of plane saying. "Maybe this plane can't fly but at least it's good for something." He wads up paper and making a slingshot of a rubber band begins to shoot the paper.

10. Shooting, the stooge says, "They [paper ammunition] really go better if you make them long. They don't work right if you wad them up."

11. While shooting, stooge notices a sloppy pile of manila folders on a table. He builds a tower of these folders, then goes to the opposite end of the room to shoot at the tower.

12. He misses several times, then hits and cheers as the tower falls. He goes over to pick up the folders.

13. While picking up, he notices, behind a portable blackboard, a pair of hula hoops which have been covered with black tape with a few wires sticking out of the tape. He reaches for these, taking one for himself and putting the other aside but within reaching distance of the subject. The stooge tries the hula hoop, saying, "This isn't as easy as it looks."

14. Stooge twirls hoop wildly on arm, saying, "Hey, look at this—this is great."

15. Stooge replaces the hula hoop and sits down with his feet on the table. Shortly thereafter the experimenter returns to the room.

This routine was completely standard, though its pace, of course, varied depending upon the subject's reaction, the extent to which he entered into this bedlam and the extent to which he initiated activities of his own. The only variations from this standard routine were those forced by the subject. Should the subject originate some nonsense of his own and request the stooge to join in, he would do so. And, he would, of course, respond to any comments initiated by the subject.

Subjects in each of the three "appropriateness" conditions and in the placebo condition were submitted to this setup. The stooge, of course, never knew in which condition any particular subject fell.

ANGER Immediately after the injection, the experimenter brought a stooge into the subject's room, introduced the two and after explaining the necessity for a 20-minute delay for "the Suproxin to get from the injection site into the bloodstream" he continued, "We would like you to use these 20 minutes to answer these questionnaires." Then handing out the questionnaires, he concludes with, "I'll be back in 20 minutes to pick up the questionnaires and begin the tests of vision."

Before looking at the questionnaire, the stooge says to the subject,

I really wanted to come for an experiment today, but I think it's unfair for them to give you shots. At least, they should have told us about the shots when they called us; you hate to refuse, once you're here already.

The questionnaires, five pages long, start off innocently requesting face sheet information and then grow increasingly personal and insulting. The stooge, sitting directly opposite the subject, paces his own answers so that at all times subject and stooge are working on the same question. At regular points in the questionnaire, the stooge makes a series of standardized comments about the questions. His comments start off innocently enough, grow increasingly querulous, and finally he ends up in a rage. In sequence, he makes the following comments.

1. Before answering any items, he leafs quickly through the questionnaire saying, "Boy, this is a long one."

2. Question 7 on the questionnaire requests, "List the foods that you would eat in a typical day." The stooge comments, "Oh for Pete's sake, what did I have for breakfast this morning?"

3. Question 9 asks, "Do you ever hear bells? _____. How often? _____." The stooge remarks, "Look at Question 9. How ridiculous can you get? I hear bells every time I change classes."

4. Question 13 requests, "List the childhood diseases you have had and the age at which you had them" to which the stooge remarks, "I get annoyed at this childhood disease question. I can't remember what childhood diseases I had, and especially at what age. Can you?"

5. Question 17 asks "What is your father's average annual income?" and the stooge says, "This really irritates me. It's none of their business what my father makes. I'm leaving that blank."

6. Question 25 presents a long series of items such as "Does not bathe or wash regularly," "Seems to need psychiatric care," etc., and requests the respondent to write down for which member of his immediate family each item seems most applicable. The question

specifically prohibits the answer "None" and each item must be answered. The stooge says, "I'll be damned if I'll fill out Number 25. 'Does not bathe or wash regularly'—that's a real insult." He then angrily crosses out the entire item.

7. Question 28 reads: "How many times each week do you have sexual intercourse?" 0–1 _____ 2–3 _____ 4–6 _____ 7 and over _____. The stooge bites out, "The hell with it! I don't have to tell them all this."

8. The stooge sits sullenly for a few moments then he rips up his questionnaire, crumples the pieces and hurls them to the floor, saying, "I'm not wasting any more time. I'm getting my books and leaving" and he stamps out of the room.

9. The questionnaire continues for eight more questions ending with: "With how many men (other than your father) has your mother had extramarital relationships?" 4 and under _____: 5–9 _____: 10 and over _____.

Subjects in the Epi Ign, Epi Inf and Placebo conditions were run through this "anger" inducing sequence. The stooge, again, did not know to which condition the subject had been assigned.

In summary, this is a seven condition experiment which, for two different emotional states, allows us (a) to evaluate the effects of "appropriateness" on emotional inducibility and (b) to begin to evaluate the effects of sympathetic activation on emotional inducibility. In schematic form the conditions are the following:

Euphoria	*Anger*
Epi Inf	Epi Inf
Epi Ign	Epi Ign
Epi Mis	Placebo
Placebo	

The Epi Mis condition was not run in the Anger sequence. This was originally conceived as a control condition and it was felt that its inclusion in the Euphoria conditions alone would suffice as a means of evaluating the possible artifactual effect of the Epi Inf instructions.

MEASUREMENT Two types of measures of emotional state were obtained. Standardized observation through a one-way mirror was the technique used to assess the subject's behavior. To what extent did he act euphoric or angry? Such behavior can be considered in a way as a "semiprivate" index of mood, for as far as the subject was concerned, his emotional behavior could be known only to the other person in the room—presumably another student. The second type of measure was self-report in which, on a variety of scales, the subject indicated his mood of the moment. Such measures can be considered "public" indices of mood, for they would, of course, be available to the experimenter and his associates.

OBSERVATION *Euphoria.* For each of the first 14 units of the stooge's standardized routine an observer kept a running chronicle of what the subject did and said. For each unit the observer coded the subject's behavior in one or more of the following categories:

Category 1: Joins in activity. If the subject entered into the stooge's activities, e.g., if he made or flew airplanes, threw paper basketballs, hula hooped, etc., his behavior was coded in this category.

Category 2: Initiates new activity. A subject was so coded if he gave indications of creative euphoria, that is, if, on his own, he initiated behavior outside of the stooge's routine. Instances of such behavior would be the subject who threw open the window and, laughing, hurled paper basketballs at passersby; or, the subject who jumped on a table and spun one hula hoop on his leg and the other on his neck.

Categories 3 and 4: Ignores or watches stooge. Subjects who paid flatly no attention to the stooge or who, with or without comment, simply watched the stooge with-

out joining in his activity were coded in these categories.

For any particular unit of behavior, the subject's behavior was coded in one or more of these categories. To test reliability of coding two observers independently coded two experimental sessions. The observers agreed completely on the coding of 88% of the units.

Anger. For each of the units of stooge behavior, an observer recorded the subject's responses and coded them according to the following category scheme:

Category 1: Agrees. In response to the stooge the subject makes a comment indicating that he agrees with the stooge's standardized comment or that he, too, is irked by a particular item on the questionnaire. For example, a subject who responded to the stooge's comment on the "father's income" question by saying, "I don't like that kind of personal question either" would be so coded (scored $+2$).

Category 2: Disagrees. In responses to the stooge's comment, the subject makes a comment which indicates that he disagrees with the stooge's meaning or mood; e.g., in response to the stooge's comment on the "father's income" question, such a subject might say, "Take it easy, they probably have a good reason for wanting the information" (scored -2).

Category 3: Neutral. A noncommittal or irrelevant response to the stooge's remark (scored 0).

Category 4: Initiates agreement or disagreement. With no instigation by the stooge, a subject, so coded, would have volunteered a remark indicating that he felt the same way or, alternatively, quite differently than the stooge. Examples would be "Boy, I hate this kind of thing" or "I'm enjoying this" (scored $+2$ or -2).

Category 5: Watches. The subject makes no verbal response to the stooge's comment but simply looks directly at him (scored 0).

Category 6: Ignores. The subject makes

no verbal response to the stooge's comment nor does he look at him; the subject, paying no attention at all to the stooge, simply works at his own questionnaire (scored −1).

A subject was scored in one or more of these categories for each unit of stooge behavior. To test reliability, two observers independently coded three experimental sessions. In order to get a behavioral index of anger, observation protocol was scored according to the values presented in parentheses after each of the above definitions of categories. In a unit-by-unit comparison, the two observers agreed completely on the scoring of 71% of the units jointly observed. The scores of the two observers differed by a value of 1 or less for 88% of the units coded and in not a single case did the two observers differ in the direction of their scoring of a unit.

SELF-REPORT OF MOOD AND PHYSICAL CONDITION When the subject's session with the stooge was completed, the experimenter returned to the room, took pulses and said:

Before we proceed with the vision tests, there is one other kind of information which we must have. We have found, as you can probably imagine, that there are many things beside Suproxin that affect how well you see in our tests. How hungry you are, how tired you are, and even the mood you're in at the time—whether you feel happy or irritated at the time of testing will affect how well you see. To understand the data we collect on you, then, we must be able to figure out which effects are due to causes such as these and which are caused by Suproxin.

The only way we can get such information about your physical and emotional state is to have you tell us. I'll hand out these questionnaires and ask you to answer them as accurately as possible. Obviously, our data on the vision tests will only be as accurate as your description of your mental and physical state.

In keeping with this spiel, the questionnaire that the experimenter passed out contained a number of mock questions about hunger, fatigue, etc., as well as questions of more immediate relevance to the experiment. To measure mood or emotional state the following two were the crucial questions:

1. How irritated, angry or annoyed would you say you feel at present?

I don't feel at all irritated or angry (0)	I feel a little irritated and angry (1)	I feel quite irritated and angry (2)	I feel very irritated and angry (3)	I feel extremely irritated and angry (4)

2. How good or happy would you say you feel at present?

I don't feel at all happy or good (0)	I feel a little happy and good (1)	I feel quite happy and good (2)	I feel very happy and good (3)	I feel extremely happy and good (4)

To measure the physical effects of epinephrine and determine whether or not the injection had been successful in producing the necessary bodily state, the following questions were asked:

1. Have you experienced any palpitation (consciousness of your own heart beat)?

Not at all (0)	A slight amount (1)	A moderate amount (2)	An intense amount (3)

2. Did you feel any tremor (involuntary shaking of the hands, arms or legs)?

Not at all (0)	A slight amount (1)	A moderate amount (2)	An intense amount (3)

To measure possible effects of the instructions in the Epi Mis condition, the following questions were asked:

1. Did you feel any numbness in your feet?
2. Did you feel any itching sensation?
3. Did you experience any feeling of headache?

To all three of these questions was attached a four-point scale running from "Not at all" to "An intense amount."

In addition to these scales, the subjects were asked to answer two open-end questions on other physical or emotional sensations they may have experienced during the experimental session. A final measure of bodily state was pulse rate which was taken by the physician or the experimenter at two times—immediately before the injection and immediately after the session with the stooge.

When the subjects had completed these questionnaires, the experimenter announced that the experiment was over, explained the deception and its necessity in detail, answered any questions, and swore the subjects to secrecy. Finally, the subjects answered a brief questionnaire about their experiences, if any, with adrenalin and their previous knowledge or suspicion of the experimental setup. There was no indication that any of the subjects had known about the experiment beforehand but 11 subjects were so extremely suspicious of some crucial feature of the experiment that their data were automatically discarded.

SUBJECTS The subjects were all male, college students taking classes in introductory psychology at the University of Minnesota. Some 90% of the students in these classes volunteer for a subject pool for which they receive two extra points on their final exam for every hour that they serve as experimental subjects. For this study the records of all potential subjects were cleared with the Student Health Service in order to insure that no harmful effects would result from the injections.

EVALUATION OF THE EXPERIMENTAL DESIGN The ideal test of our propositions would require circumstances which our experiment is far from realizing. First, the proposition that: "A state of physiological

arousal for which an individual has no immediate explanation will lead him to label this state in terms of the cognitions available to him" obviously requires conditions under which the subject does not and cannot have a proper explanation of his bodily state. Though we toyed with such fantasies as ventilating the experimental room with vaporized adrenalin, reality forced us to rely on the disguised injection of Suproxin—a technique which was far from ideal for no matter what the experimenter told them, some subjects would inevitably attribute their feelings to the injection. To the extent that subjects did so, differences between the several appropriateness conditions should be attenuated.

Second, the proposition that: "Given the same cognitive circumstances the individual will react emotionally only to the extent that he experiences a state of physiological arousal" requires for its ideal test the manipulation of states of physiological arousal and of physiological quiescence. Though there is no question that epinephrine effectively produces a state of arousal, there is also no question that a placebo does not prevent physiological arousal. To the extent that the experimental situation effectively produces sympathetic stimulation in placebo subjects, the proposition is difficult to test, for such a factor would attenuate differences between epinephrine and placebo subjects.

Both of these factors, then, can be expected to interfere with the test of our several propositions. In presenting the results of this study, we shall first present condition by condition results and then evaluate the effect of these two factors on experimental differences.

Results

EFFECTS OF THE INJECTIONS ON BODILY STATE Let us examine first the success of the injections at producing the bodily state required to examine the propositions at test. Does the injection of epinephrine produce symptoms of sympathetic discharge as compared with the placebo injection? Relevant data are presented in Table 1 where it can be immediately seen that on all items subjects who were in epinephrine conditions show considerably more evidence of sympathetic activation than do subjects in placebo conditions. In all epinephrine conditions pulse rate increases significantly when compared with the decrease characteristic of the placebo conditions. On the scales it is clear that epinephrine subjects experience considerably more palpitation and tremor than do placebo subjects. In all possible comparisons on these symptoms, the mean scores of subjects in any of the epinephrine conditions are greater than the corresponding scores in the placebo conditions at better than the .001 level of significance. Examination of the absolute values of these scores makes it quite clear that subjects in epinephrine conditions were, indeed, in a state of physiological arousal, while most subjects in placebo conditions were in a relative state of physiological quiescence.

The epinephrine injection, of course, did not work with equal effectiveness for all subjects; indeed for a few subjects it did not work at all. Such subjects reported almost no palpitation or tremor, showed no increase in pulse and described no other relevant physical symptoms. Since for such subjects the necessary experimental conditions were not established, they were automatically excluded from the data and all further tabular presentations will not include such subjects. Table 1, however, does include the data of these subjects. There were four such subjects in euphoria conditions and one of them in anger conditions.

In order to evaluate further data on Epi Mis subjects it is necessary to note the results of the "numbness," "itching," and "headache" scales also presented in Table 1. Clearly the subjects in the Epi Mis condition do not differ on these scales from subjects in any of the other experimental conditions.

EFFECTS OF THE MANIPULATIONS ON EMO-TIONAL STATE   *Euphoria.   Self-report.* The effects of the several manipulations on emotional state in the euphoria conditions are presented in Table 2. The scores recorded in this table are derived, for each subject, by subtracting the value of the point he checks on the irritation scale from the value of the point he checks on the happiness scale. Thus, if a subject were to check the point "I feel a little irritated and

TABLE 1   *The effects of the injections on bodily state*

CONDITION	N	PULSE		SELF-RATING OF				
		PRE	POST	PALPITATION	TREMOR	NUMBNESS	ITCHING	HEADACHE
Euphoria								
Epi Inf	27	85.7	88.6	1.20	1.43	0	0.16	0.32
Epi Ign	26	84.6	85.6	1.83	1.76	0.15	0	0.55
Epi Mis	26	82.9	86.0	1.27	2.00	0.06	0.08	0.23
Placebo	26	80.4	77.1	0.29	0.21	0.09	0	0.27
Anger								
Epi Inf	23	85.9	92.4	1.26	1.41	0.17	0	0.11
Epi Ign	23	85.0	96.8	1.44	1.78	0	0.06	0.21
Placebo	23	84.5	79.6	0.59	0.24	0.14	0.06	0.06

angry" on the irritation scale and the point "I feel very happy and good" on the happiness scale, his score would be +2. The higher the positive value, the happier and better the subject reports himself as feeling. Though we employ an index for expositional simplicity, it should be noted that the two components of the index each yield results completely consistent with those obtained by use of this index.

Let us examine first the effects of the appropriateness instructions. Comparison of the scores for the Epi Mis and Epi Inf conditions makes it immediately clear that the experimental differences are not due to artifacts resulting from the informed instructions. In both conditions the subject was warned to expect a variety of symptoms as a consequence of the injection. In the Epi Mis condition, where the symptoms were inappropriate to the subject's bodily state the self-report score is almost twice that in the Epi Inf condition where the symptoms were completely appropriate to the subject's bodily state. It is reasonable, then, to attribute differences between informed subjects and those in other conditions to differences in manipulated appropriateness rather than to artifacts such as introspectiveness or self-examination.

It is clear that, consistent with expectations, subjects were more susceptible to the stooge's mood and consequently more euphoric when they had no explanation of their own bodily states than when they did. The means of both the Epi Ign and Epi Mis conditions are considerably greater than the mean of the Epi Inf condition.

It is of interest to note that Epi Mis subjects are somewhat more euphoric than are Epi Ign subjects. This pattern repeats itself in other data shortly to be presented. We would attribute this difference to differences in the appropriateness dimension. Though, as in the Epi Ign condition, a subject is not provided with an explanation of his bodily state, it is, of course, possible that he will provide one for himself which is not derived from his interaction with the stooge. Most reasonably he could decide for himself that he feels this way because of the injection. To the extent that he does so he should be less susceptible to the stooge. It seems probable that he would be less likely to hit on such an explanation in the Epi Mis condition than in the Epi Ign condition for in the Epi Mis condition both the experimenter and the doctor have told him that the effects of the injection would be quite different from what he actually feels. The effect of such instructions is probably to make it more difficult for the subject himself to hit on the alternative explanation described above. There is some evidence to support this analysis. In open-end questions in which subjects described their own mood and state, 28% of the subjects in the Epi Ign condition made some connection between the injection and their bodily

TABLE 2 *Self-report of emotional state in the euphoria conditions*

CONDI- TION	N	SELF- REPORT SCALES	COMPARISON	p^*
Epi Inf	25	0.98	Epi Inf vs. Epi Mis	<.01
Epi Ign	25	1.78	Epi Inf vs. Epi Ign	.02
Epi Mis	25	1.90	Placebo vs. Epi Mis,	*ns*
Placebo	26	1.61	Ign, or Inf	

* All *p* values reported throughout paper are two-tailed.

state compared with the 16% of subjects in the Epi Mis condition who did so. It could be considered, then, that these three conditions fall along a dimension of appropriateness, with the Epi Inf condition at one extreme and the Epi Mis condition at the other.

Comparing the placebo to the epinephrine conditions, we note a pattern which will repeat itself throughout the data. Placebo subjects are less euphoric than either Epi Mis or Epi Ign subjects but somewhat more euphoric than Epi Inf subjects. These differences are not, however, statistically significant. We shall consider the epinephrine-placebo comparisons in detail in a later section of this paper following the presentation of additional relevant data. For the moment, it is clear that, by self-report manipulating appropriateness has had a very strong effect on euphoria.

Behavior. Let us next examine the extent to which the subject's behavior was affected by the experimental manipulations. To the extent that his mood has been affected, one should expect that the subject will join in the stooge's whirl of manic activity and initiate similar activities of his own. The relevant data are presented in Table 3. The column labeled "Activity index" presents summary figures on the extent to which the subject joined in the stooge's activity. This is a weighted index which reflects both the nature of the activities in which the subject engaged and the amount of time he was active. The index was devised by assigning the following weights to the subject's activities: 5—hula hooping; 4—shooting with slingshot; 3—paper airplanes; 2—paper basketballs; 1—doodling; 0—does nothing. Pretest scaling on 15 college students ordered these activities with respect to the degree of euphoria they represented. Arbitrary weights were assigned so that the wilder the activity, the heavier the weight. These weights are multiplied by an estimate of the amount

TABLE 3 *Behavioral indications of emotional state in the euphoria conditions*

CONDITION	N	ACTIVITY INDEX	MEAN NUMBER OF ACTS INITIATED
Epi Inf	25	12.72	.20
Epi Ign	25	18.28	.56
Epi Mis	25	22.56	.84
Placebo	26	16.00	.54

	p value	
COMPARISON	ACTIVITY INDEX	INITIATES*
Epi Inf vs. Epi Mis	.05	.03
Epi Inf vs. Epi Ign	ns	.08
Plac vs. Epi Mis, Ign, or Inf	ns	ns

* Tested by χ^2 comparison of the proportion of subjects in each condition initiating new acts.

of time the subject spent in each activity and the summed products make up the activity index for each subject. This index may be considered a measure of behavioral euphoria. It should be noted that the same between-condition relationships hold for the two components of this index as for the index itself.

The column labeled "Mean number of acts initiated" presents the data on the extent to which the subject deviates from the stooge's routine and initiates euphoric activities of his own.

On both behavioral indices, we find precisely the same pattern of relationships as those obtained with self-reports. Epi Mis subjects behave somewhat more euphorically than do Epi Ign subjects who in turn behave more euphorically than do Epi Inf subjects. On all measures, then, there is consistent evidence that a subject will take over the stooge's euphoric mood to the extent that he has no other explanation of his bodily state.

Again it should be noted that on these behavioral indices, Epi Ign and Epi Mis subjects are somewhat more euphoric than placebo subjects but not significantly so.

Anger. Self-report. Before presenting data for the anger conditions, one point must be made about the anger manipulation. In the situation devised, anger, if manifested, is most likely to be directed at the experimenter and his annoyingly personal questionnaire. As we subsequently discovered, this was rather unfortunate, for the subjects, who had volunteered for the experiment for extra points on their final exam, simply refused to endanger these points by publicly blowing up, admitting their irritation to the experimenter's face or spoiling the questionnaire. Though as the reader will see, the subjects were quite willing to manifest anger when they were alone with the stooge, they hesitated to do so on material (self-ratings of mood and questionnaire) that the experimenter might see and only after the purposes of the experiment had been revealed were many of these subjects willing to admit to the experimenter that they had been irked or irritated.

This experimentally unfortunate situation pretty much forces us to rely on the behavioral indices derived from observation of the subject's presumably private interaction with the stooge. We do, however, present data on the self-report scales in Table 4. These figures are derived in the same way as the figures presented in Table 2 for the euphoria conditions, that is, the value checked on the irritation scale is subtracted from the value checked on the happiness scale. Though, for the reasons stated above, the absolute magnitude of these figures (all positive) is relatively meaningless, we can, of course, compare condition means within the set of anger conditions. With the happiness-irritation index employed, we should, of course, anticipate precisely the reverse results from those obtained in the euphoria conditions; that is, the Epi Inf subjects in the anger conditions should again be less susceptible to the stooge's mood and should, therefore, describe themselves as in a somewhat happier frame of mind than subjects in the Epi Ign condition. This is the case; the Epi Inf subjects average 1.91 on the self-report scales while the Epi Ign subjects average 1.39.

Evaluating the effects of the injections, we note again that, as anticipated, Epi Ign subjects are somewhat less happy than Placebo subjects but, once more, this is not a significant difference.

Behavior. The subject's responses to the stooge, during the period when both were filling out their questionnaires, were systematically coded to provide a behavioral index of anger. The coding scheme and the numerical values attached to each of the categories have been described in the methodology section. To arrive at an "Anger index" the numerical value assigned to a subject's responses to the stooge is summed together for the several units of stooge behavior. In the coding scheme used, a positive value to this index indicates that the subject agrees with the stooge's comment and is growing angry. A negative value indicates that the subject either disagrees with the stooge or ignores him.

The relevant data are presented in Table 5. For this analysis, the stooge's routine has been divided into two phases —the first two units of his behavior (the

TABLE 4 *Self-report of emotional state in the anger conditions*

CONDITION	N	SELF-REPORT SCALES	COMPARISON	p
Epi Inf	22	1.91	Epi Inf vs. Epi Ign	.08
Epi Ign	23	1.39	Placebo vs. Epi Ign or Inf	ns
Placebo	23	1.63		

"long" questionnaire and "What did I have for breakfast?") are considered essentially neutral revealing nothing of the stooge's mood; all of the following units are considered "angry" units for they begin with an irritated remark about the "bells" question and end with the stooge's fury as he rips up his questionnaire and stomps out of the room. For the neutral units, agreement or disagreement with the stooge's remarks is, of course, meaningless as an index of mood and we should anticipate no difference between conditions. As can be seen in Table 5, this is the case.

For the angry units, we must, of course, anticipate that subjects in the Epi Ign condition will be angrier than subjects in the Epi Inf condition. This is indeed the case. The Anger index for the Epi Ign condition is positive and large, indicating that these subjects have become angry, while in the Epi Inf condition the Anger index is slightly negative in value indicating that these subjects have failed to catch the stooge's mood at all. It seems clear that providing the subject with an appropriate explanation of his bodily state greatly reduces his tendency to interpret his state in terms of the cognitions provided by the stooge's angry behavior.

Finally, on this behavioral index, it can be seen that subjects in the Epi Ign condition are significantly angrier than subjects in the Placebo condition. Behaviorally, at least, the injection of epinephrine appears to have led subjects to an angrier state than comparable subjects who received placebo shots.

CONFORMATION OF DATA TO THEORETICAL EXPECTATIONS   Now that the basic data of this study have been presented, let us examine closely the extent to which they conform to theoretical expectations. If our hypotheses are correct and if this experimental design provided a perfect test for these hypotheses, it should be anticipated that in the euphoria conditions the degree

TABLE 5 *Behavioral indications of emotional state in the anger conditions*

CONDITION	N	NEUTRAL UNITS	ANGER UNITS
Epi Inf	22	+0.07	−0.18
Epi Ign	23	+0.30	+2.28
Placebo	22*	−0.09	+0.79

COMPARISON FOR ANGER UNITS	p
Epi Inf vs. Epi Ign	<.01
Epi Ign vs. Placebo	<.05
Placebo vs. Epi Inf	*ns*

* For one subject in this condition the sound system went dead and the observer could not, of course, code his reactions.

of experimentally produced euphoria should vary in the following fashion:

$$\text{Epi Mis} \geqq \text{Epi Ign} > \text{Epi Inf} = \text{Placebo}$$

And in the anger conditions, anger should conform to the following pattern:

$$\text{Epi Ign} > \text{Epi Inf} = \text{Placebo}$$

In both sets of conditions, it is the case that emotional level in the Epi Mis and Epi Ign conditions is considerably greater than that achieved in the corresponding Epi Inf conditions. The results for the Placebo condition, however, are ambiguous for consistently the Placebo subjects fall between the Epi Ign and the Epi Inf subjects. This is a particularly troubling pattern for it makes it impossible to evaluate unequivocally the effects of the state of physiological arousal and indeed raises serious questions about our entire theoretical structure. Though the emotional level is consistently greater in the Epi Mis and Epi Ign conditions than in the Placebo condition, this difference is significant at acceptable probability levels only in the anger conditions.

In order to explore the problem further, let us examine the experimental factors identified earlier, which might have acted to restrain the emotional level in the Epi

Ign and Epi Mis conditions. As was pointed out earlier, the ideal test of our first two hypotheses requires an experimental setup in which the subject has flatly no way of evaluating his state of physiological arousal other than by means of the experimentally provided cognitions. Had it been possible to physiologically produce a state of sympathetic activation by means other than injection, one could have approached this experimental ideal more closely than in the present setup. As it stands, however, there is always a reasonable alternative cognition available to the aroused subject—he feels the way he does because of the injection. To the extent that the subject seizes on such an explanation of his bodily state, we should expect that he will be uninfluenced by the stooge. Evidence presented in Table 6 for the anger condition and in Table 7 for the euphoria conditions indicates that this is, indeed, the case.

As mentioned earlier, some of the Epi Ign and Epi Mis subjects in their answers to the open-end questions clearly attributed their physical state to the injection, e.g., "the shot gave me the shivers." In Tables 6 and 7 such subjects are labeled "Self-informed." In Table 6 it can be seen that the self-informed subjects are considerably less angry than are the remaining subjects; indeed, they are not angry at all. With these self-informed subjects eliminated the difference between the Epi Ign and the Placebo conditions is significant at the .01 level of significance.

TABLE 6 *The effects of attributing bodily state to the injection on anger in the anger Epi Ign condition*

CONDITION	N	ANGER INDEX
Self-informed subjects	3	−1.67
Others	20	+2.88
Self-informed versus others		$p = .05$

TABLE 7 *The effects of attributing bodily state to the injection on euphoria in the euphoria Epi Ign and Epi Mis conditions*

EPI IGN

	N	ACTIVITY INDEX
Self-informed subjects	8	11.63
Others	17	21.14
Self-informed versus others		$p = .05$

EPI MIS

	N	ACTIVITY INDEX
Self-informed subjects	5	12.40
Others	20	25.10
Self-informed versus others		$p = .10$

Precisely the same pattern is evident in Table 7 for the euphoria conditions. In both the Epi Mis and the Epi Ign conditions, the self-informed subjects have considerably lower activity indices than do the remaining subjects. Eliminating self-informed subjects, comparison of both of these conditions with the Placebo condition yields a difference significant at the .03 level of significance. It should be noted, too, that the self-informed subjects have much the same score on the activity index as do the experimental Epi Inf subjects (Table 3).

It would appear, then, that the experimental procedure of injecting the subjects, by providing an alternative cognition, has, to some extent, obscured the effects of epinephrine. When account is taken of this artifact, the evidence is good that the state of physiological arousal is a necessary component of an emotional experience for when self-informed subjects are removed, epinephrine subjects give consistent indications of greater emotionality than do placebo subjects.

Let us examine next the fact that consistently the emotional level, both reported

Pergament, Mikhail Abramovich.

Зональная стратиграфия и иноцерамы нижней части верхнего мела Тихоокеанского побережья СССР. Москва, Наука, 1966.

81 p. illus., maps. 26 cm. (Академия наук СССР. Геологический институт. Труды, вып. 146)

At head of title: М. А. Пергамент.
Added t. p.: Zonal stratigraphy and inoceramus of the lower-most upper cretaceous on the Pacific coast of the USSR.
Table of contents also in English.
Bibliography: p. 70–74.

(Continued on next card)

72–299315

and behavioral, in Placebo conditions is greater than that in the Epi Inf conditions. Theoretically, of course, it should be expected that the two conditions will be equally low, for by assuming that emotional state is a joint function of a state of physiological arousal and of the appropriateness of a cognition we are, in effect, assuming a multiplicative function, so that if either component is at zero, emotional level is at zero. As noted earlier this expectation should hold if we can be sure that there is no sympathetic activation in the Placebo conditions. This assumption, of course, is completely unrealistic for the injection of placebo does not prevent sympathetic activation. The experimental situations were fairly dramatic and certainly some of the placebo subjects gave indications of physiological arousal. If our general line of reasoning is correct, it should be anticipated that the emotional level of subjects who give indications of sympathetic activity will be greater than that of subjects who do not. The relevant evidence is presented in Tables 8 and 9.

As an index of sympathetic activation we shall use the most direct and unequivocal measure available—change in pulse rate. It can be seen in Table 1 that the predominant pattern in the Placebo condition is a decrease in pulse rate. We shall assume, therefore, that those subjects whose pulse increases or remains the same give indications of sympathetic activity while those subjects whose pulse decreases do not. In Table 8, for the euphoria condition, it is immediately clear that subjects who give indications of sympathetic activity are considerably more euphoric than are subjects who show no sympathetic activity. This relationship is, of course, confounded by the fact that euphoric subjects are considerably more active than noneuphoric subjects—a factor which independent of mood could elevate pulse rate. However, no such factor operates in the anger condition where angry subjects

TABLE 8 *Sympathetic activation and euphoria in the euphoria placebo condition*

SUBJECT WHOSE:	N	ACTIVITY INDEX
Pulse decreased	14	10.67
Pulse increased or remained same	12	23.17
Pulse decreasers versus pulse increasers or same		$p = .02$

are neither more active nor talkative than calm subjects. It can be seen in Table 9 that Placebo subjects who show signs of sympathetic activation give indications of considerably more anger than do subjects who show no such signs. Conforming to expectations, sympathetic activation accompanies an increase in emotional level.

It should be noted, too, that the emotional levels of subjects showing no signs of sympathetic activity are quite comparable to the emotional level of subjects in the parallel Epi Inf conditions (see Tables 3 and 5). The similarity of these sets of scores and their uniformly low level of indicated emotionality would certainly make it appear that both factors are essential to an emotional state. When either the level of sympathetic arousal is low or a completely appropriate cognition is available, the level of emotionality is low.

TABLE 9 *Sympathetic activation and anger in anger placebo condition*

SUBJECTS WHOSE:	N*	ANGER INDEX
Pulse decreased	13	+0.15
Pulse increased or remained same	8	+1.69
Pulse decreasers versus pulse increasers or same		$p = .01$

* N reduced by two cases owing to failure of sound system in one case and experimenter's failure to take pulse in another.

Discussion

Let us summarize the major findings of this experiment and examine the extent to which they support the propositions offered in the introduction of this paper. It has been suggested, first, that given a state of physiological arousal for which an individual has no explanation, he will label this state in terms of the cognitions available to him. This implies, of course, that by manipulating the cognitions of an individual in such a state we can manipulate his feelings in diverse directions. Experimental results support this proposition for following the injection of epinephrine, those subjects who had no explanation for the bodily state thus produced, gave behavioral and self-report indications that they had been readily manipulable into the disparate feeling states of euphoria and anger.

From this first proposition, it must follow that given a state of physiological arousal for which the individual has a completely satisfactory explanation, he will not label this state in terms of the alternative cognitions available. Experimental evidence strongly supports this expectation. In those conditions in which subjects were injected with epinephrine and told precisely what they would feel and why, they proved relatively immune to any effects of the manipulated cognitions. In the anger condition, such subjects did not report or show anger; in the euphoria condition, such subjects reported themselves as far less happy than subjects with an identical bodily state but no adequate knowledge of why they felt the way they did.

Finally, it has been suggested that given constant cognitive circumstances, an individual will react emotionally only to the extent that he experiences a state of physiological arousal. Without taking account of experimental artifacts, the evidence in support of this proposition is consistent but tentative. When the effects of "self-informing" tendencies in epinephrine subjects and of "self-arousing" tendencies in placebo subjects are partialed out, the evidence strongly supports the proposition.

The pattern of data, then, falls neatly in line with theoretical expectations. However, the fact that we were forced, to some extent, to rely on internal analyses in order to partial out the effects of experimental artifacts inevitably makes our conclusions somewhat tentative. In order to further test these propositions on the interaction of cognitive and physiological determinants of emotional state, a series of additional experiments, published elsewhere, was designed to rule out or overcome the operation of these artifacts. In the first of these, Schachter and Wheeler (1962) extended the range of manipulated sympathetic activation by employing three experimental groups—epinephrine, placebo, and a group injected with the sympatholytic agent, chlorpromazine. Laughter at a slapstick movie was the dependent variable and the evidence is good that amusement is a direct function of manipulated sympathetic activation.

In order to make the epinephrine-placebo comparison under conditions which would rule out the operation of any self-informing tendency, two experiments were conducted on rats. In one of these Singer (1961) demonstrated that under fear inducing conditions, manipulated by the simultaneous presentation of a loud bell, a buzzer, and a bright flashing light, rats injected with epinephrine were considerably more frightened than rats injected with a placebo. Epinephrine-injected rats defecated, urinated, and trembled more than did placebo-injected rats. In nonfear control conditions, there were no differences between epinephrine and placebo groups, neither group giving any indication of fear. In another study, Latané and Schachter (1962) demonstrated that rats injected with epinephrine were notably more capable of avoidance learning than were rats injected with a placebo. Using a modified Miller-Mowrer shuttlebox, these investigators found that during an experimental period involving 200 massed trials, 15 rats injected with epinephrine avoided shock an average of 101.2 trials while 15 placebo-injected rats averaged only 37.3 avoidances.

Taken together, this body of studies does give strong support to the propositions which generated these experimental tests. Given a state of sympathetic activation, for which no immediately appropriate explanation is available, human subjects can be readily manipulated into states of euphoria, anger, and amusement. Varying the intensity of sympathetic activation serves to vary the intensity of a variety of emotional states in both rats and human subjects.

Let us examine the implications of these findings and of this line of thought for problems in the general area of the physiology of the emotions. We have noted in the introduction that the numerous studies on physiological differentiators of emotional states have, viewed en masse, yielded quite inconclusive results. Most, though not all, of these studies have indicated no differences among the various emotional states. Since as human beings, rather than as scientists, we have no difficulty identifying, labeling, and distinguishing among our feelings, the results of these studies have long seemed rather puzzling and paradoxical. Perhaps because of this, there has been a persistent tendency to discount such results as due to ignorance or methodological inadequacy and to pay far more attention to the very few studies which demonstrate *some* sort of physiological differences among emotional states than to the very many studies which indicate no differences at all. It is conceivable, however, that these results should be taken at face value and that emotional states may, indeed, be generally characterized by a high level of sympathetic activation with

few if any physiological distinguishers among the many emotional states. If this is correct, the findings of the present study may help to resolve the problem. Obviously this study does *not* rule out the possibility of physiological differences among the emotional states. It is the case, however, that given precisely the same state of epinephrine-induced sympathetic activation, we have, by means of cognitive manipulations, been able to produce in our subjects the very disparate states of euphoria and anger. It may indeed be the case that cognitive factors are major determiners of the emotional labels we apply to a common state of sympathetic arousal.

Let us ask next whether our results are specific to the state of sympathetic activation or if they are generalizable to other states of physiological arousal. It is clear that from our experiments proper, it is impossible to answer the question, for our studies have been concerned largely with the effects of an epinephrine-created state of sympathetic arousal. We would suggest, however, that our conclusions are generalizable to almost any pronounced internal state for which no appropriate explanation is available. This suggestion receives some support from the experiences of Nowlis and Nowlis (1956) in their program of research on the effects of drugs on mood. In their work the Nowlises typically administer a drug to groups of four subjects who are physically in one another's presence and free to interact. The Nowlises describe some of their results with these groups as follows:

At first we used the same drug for all 4 men. In those sessions seconal, when compared with placebo, increased the checking of such words as expansive, forceful, courageous, daring, elated, and impulsive. In our first statistical analysis we were confronted with the stubborn fact that when the same drug is given to all 4 men in a group, the N that has to be entered into the analysis is 1, not 4. This increases the cost of an already expensive experiment by a considerable factor, but it cannot be denied that the effects of these drugs may be and often are quite contagious. Our first attempted solution was to run tests on groups in which each man had a different drug during the same session, such as 1 on seconal, 1 on benzedrine, 1 on dramamine, and 1 on placebo. What does seconal do? Cooped up with, say, the egotistical benzedrine partner, the withdrawn, indifferent dramimine partner, and the slightly bored lactose man, the seconal subject reports that he is distractible, dizzy, drifting, glum, defiant, languid, sluggish, discouraged, dull, gloomy, lazy, and slow! This is not the report of mood that we got when all 4 men were on seconal. It thus appears that the moods of the partners do definitely influence the effect of seconal (p. 350).

It is not completely clear from this description whether this "contagion" of mood is more marked in drug than in placebo groups, but should this be the case, these results would certainly support the suggestion that our findings are generalizable to internal states other than that produced by an injection of epinephrine.

Finally, let us consider the implications of our formulation and data for alternative conceptualizations of emotion. Perhaps the most popular current conception of emotion is in terms of "activation theory" in the sense employed by Lindsley (1951) and Woodworth and Schlosberg (1958). As we understand this theory, it suggests that emotional states should be considered as at one end of a continuum of activation which is defined in terms of degree of autonomic arousal and of electroencephalographic measures of activation. The results of the experiment described in this paper do, of course, suggest that such a formulation is not completely adequate. It is possible to have very high degrees of activation without a subject either appearing to be or describing himself as "emotional." Cognitive factors appear to be indispensable elements in any formulation of emotion.

Summary

It is suggested that emotional states may be considered a function of a state of physiological arousal and of a cognition appropriate to this state of arousal. From this follows these propositions:

1. Given a state of physiological arousal for which an individual has no immediate explanation, he will label this state and describe his feelings in terms of the cognitions available to him. To the extent that cognitive factors are potent determiners of emotional states, it should be anticipated that precisely the same state of physiological arousal could be labeled "joy" or "fury" or "jealousy" or any of a great diversity of emotional labels depending on the cognitive aspects of the situation.

2. Given a state of physiological arousal for which an individual has a completely appropriate explanation, no evaluative needs will arise and the individual is unlikely to label his feelings in terms of the alternative cognitions available.

3. Given the same cognitive circumstances, the individual will react emotionally or describe his feelings as emotions only to the extent that he experiences a state of physiological arousal.

An experiment is described which, together with the results of other studies, supports these propositions.

References

Ax, A. F. Physiological differentiation of emotional states. *Psychosom. Med.*, 1953, 15, 433–442.

Cannon, W. B. *Bodily changes in pain, hunger, fear and rage.* (2nd ed.) New York: Appleton, 1929.

Cantril, H., & Hunt, W. A. Emotional effects produced by the injection of adrenalin. *Amer. J. Psychol.*, 1932, 44, 300–307.

Festinger, L. A theory of social comparison processes. *Hum. Relat.*, 1954, 7, 114–140.

Hunt, J. McV., Cole, M. W., & Reis, E. E. Situational cues distinguishing anger, fear, and sorrow. *Amer. J. Psychol.*, 1958, 71, 136–151.

James, W. *The principles of psychology.* New York: Holt, 1890.

Landis, C., & Hunt, W. A. Adrenalin and emotion. *Psychol. Rev.,* 1932, 39, 467–485.

Latané, B., & Schachter, S. Adrenalin and avoidance learning. *J. comp. physiol. Psychol.,* 1962, 65, 369–372.

Lindsley, D. B. Emotion. In S. S. Stevens (Ed.), *Handbook of experimental psychology.* New York: Wiley, 1951. Pp. 473–516.

Marañon, G. Contribution à l'étude de l'action émotive de l'adrénaline. *Rev. Francaise Endocrinol.,* 1924, 2, 301–325.

Nowlis, V., & Nowlis, H. H. The description and analysis of mood. *Ann. N. Y. Acad. Sci.,* 1956, 65, 345–355.

Ruckmick, C. A. *The psychology of feeling and emotion.* New York: McGraw-Hill, 1936.

Schachter, J. Pain, fear, and anger in hypertensives and normotensives: A psychophysiologic study. *Psychosom. Med.,* 1957, 19, 17–29.

Schachter, S. *The psychology of affiliation.* Stanford, Calif.: Stanford Univer. Press, 1959.

Schachter, S., & Wheeler, L. Epinephrine, chlorpromazine, and amusement. *J. abnorm. soc. Psychol.,* 1962, 65, 121–128.

Singer, J. E. The effects of epinephrine, chlorpromazine and dibenzyline upon the fright responses of rats under stress and non-stress conditions. Unpublished doctoral dissertation, University of Minnesota, 1961.

Wolf, S., & Wolff, H. G. *Human gastric function.* New York: Oxford Univer. Press, 1947.

Woodworth, R. S., & Schlosberg, H. *Experimental psychology.* New York: Holt, 1958.

Wrightsman, L. S. Effects of waiting with others on changes in level of felt anxiety. *J. abnorm. soc. Psychol.,* 1960, 61, 216–222.

*The following excerpts illustrate the concept of absolute threshold
and the change from cone to rod function during dark adaptation.
The change in function, as shown by the "cone-rod break," was
an important piece of evidence used in the duplicity theory, which
postulated separate cone and rod functions. In addition, an ingenious
technique for testing animals is illustrated. It consists of giving
the animal a "language," a way of telling us whether or not he can see
a light. If he can see it, he pecks key A; if not, he pecks key B.*

A POINT TO GUIDE YOUR STUDY   *Take another sensory phenomenon
mentioned in your text and apply this technique to its investigation.
Hint: This technique can be used with differential thresholds
as well as with absolute thresholds.*

GLOSSARY   mL: *an abbreviation of millilambert, one-thousandth of a
lambert. The lambert is a measure of the luminance of a surface. It is
a measure of the physical light energy being reflected from a surface.
The unit of measurement on the ordinate (vertical axis) of Figure 2 is
the $\mu\mu$L, a millionth of a millionth of a lambert.* **Psychophysics:** *this
refers to the study of the relationship between aspects of the physical
stimulus, on the one hand, and experience on the other. For
instance, experienced brightness does not follow increases in physical
light energy, or luminance, in a linear fashion. The determination
of the exact function is the job of psychophysics.* **Photopic:** *refers to
vision under high illumination (day vision).* **Scotopic:** *refers to vision
under low illumination (night vision).*

34: DARK ADAPTATION IN THE PIGEON
Donald S. Blough, Brown University

Information on sensory thresholds is relevant to research topics that range from

discrimination learning to the chemistry
of receptive processes. Unfortunately, ex-

This research was supported, in part, by Contract
N5ori–07663 (Proj. NR140–072) between Harvard University and the Office of Naval Research, directed by
Dr. Floyd Ratliff. It represents part of a thesis submitted to the Department of Psychology, Harvard University, in partial fulfillment of the requirements for
the Ph.D. degree. The writer is indebted to Dr. Ratliff
for his constant interest and helpful advice.

periments on many of these topics involve the use of subhuman species from which few precise psychophysical data have as yet been obtained. In improving this situation with respect to visual psychophysics, the choice of the pigeon as a subject is particularly advantageous. The pigeon's vision is good, perhaps comparable to that of man (3, 9, 15); physiological and anatomical studies have been made on its visual apparatus (4, 7, 8, 11); Ferster and Skinner have outlined (6, 14) attributes that make it an excellent subject for closely controlled behavioral investigation.

This paper reports experiments in which the absolute visual thresholds of pigeons were traced during dark adaptation. The method involves behavior control techniques based on the work of Skinner and his associates (6, 14) and a stimulus control technique similar to Békésy's (1) method of human audiometry. The method, together with the reasons for various training and testing procedures, has been described in some detail elsewhere (2, 10). It has two fundamental features: (a) the stimulus controls the bird's responses as a result of differential reinforcement; (b) the bird's responses control the stimulus through an automatic switching circuit. This reciprocal control process is arranged as follows. The pigeon confronts two re-

sponse keys and a small lighted stimulus patch. On a random schedule, pecking key A blacks out the stimulus patch; pecking key B raises a food magazine within reach if the patch is dark. Although only a small proportion of pecks on the two keys is reinforced in this way, the bird gradually learns to peck key A when the patch is visible and key B when the patch is dark. The bird's responses control the stimulus through a separate, automatic switching circuit; pecks on key A reduce the luminance of the stimulus patch, while pecks on key B increase the luminance of the patch. As a result, the stimulus is kept oscillating about the bird's absolute threshold. When the luminance rises above threshold, the bird pecks key A, driving the stimulus dimmer again. When the stimulus disappears, below threshold, the bird pecks key B and the stimulus gets brighter. A record of the stimulus luminance traces the absolute threshold of the pigeon through time.

Method

TRAINING PROCEDURE The pigeon's basic task was to peck key A when the stimulus patch was visible and key B when the patch was dark. Training proceeded in several stages. When the bird became proficient at one stage, the next was introduced; about fifty training hours were needed before experimental data could be collected. The only light in the adaptation box came from the stimulus patch, except in the earliest stages of training, when a supplementary overhead light was used.

First, the hungry bird (70 per cent to 80 per cent of free-feeding cage weight) was trained to peck the two keys at random by the "response differentiation" technique described by Ferster (6). Next, the stimulus patch was illuminated and the control circuit adjusted so that a peck on key A closed the shutter, blacking out the patch. After a peck on key A blacked out

FIGURE 1 *Response chamber of the adaptation box. Left, side view, showing relative positions of pigeon, food magazine, response keys, and stimulus patch. Right, keys and patch seen from the pigeon's position.*

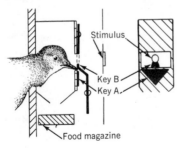

the patch a peck on key B caused the food magazine to be raised within reach for about 5 sec. After most reinforcements, the shutter opened, and the lighted patch reappeared. Continued darkness followed one reinforcement in five; in this case, a peck on key B brought food a second time.

In the next stage of training, several pecks in a row, rather than a single peck, were required on key A to close the shutter and on key B to obtain food. The number of pecks required varied randomly between one and eight. An interval during which no amount of pecking could close the shutter was introduced after each reinforcement. The duration of this interval varied randomly between 0 and 15 sec., with a mean of 7.5 sec. The longest interval was later increased to 30 sec. and the mean to 15 sec.

When training was nearly complete, the luminance of the stimulus patch was put under the control of the bird's responses during the intervals between reinforcements. Each peck on key A reduced the luminance of the patch by .03 log unit, while each peck on key B increased the luminance of the patch by this amount. The pen coupled to the wedge drive recorded these luminance changes continuously. When the patch reappeared following a reinforcement, it always had the same luminance that it had had just before it was blacked out.

TESTING PROCEDURE   In the last stage of the training just described the procedure was such that absolute thresholds were obtained. When these thresholds became stable from day to day, the collection of experimental data began. At about the same time each day, the bird was carried from its home cage and placed in total darkness in the pre-exposure box. After the pigeon had been in the dark at least 1 hr., the pre-exposure light was turned on for a predetermined interval, following which the bird was transferred to the adaptation

box. The transfer, done in dim light, took less than 5 sec. The bird usually began to respond within 1 min. after the box was sealed. If it did not peck within 3 min., the bird was returned to its home cage until the next day.

Results

A sample dark-adaptation curve appears in Figure 2. This curve was produced by bird 192 in a single hour, following a 10-min. pre-exposure at 22 mL. The luminance of the stimulus patch is represented on the ordinate; time in dark is on the abscissa. The curve can readily be separated into two continuous segments, joined at a rather sharp "break." These divisions will be referred to as the "first (or 'cone') segment" and the "second (or 'rod') segment." No threshold is shown for 3 min. at the beginning of the adaptation period. This is due to the fact that each run began with the stimulus at a super-threshold luminance (7.2 log $\mu\mu$L); the first responses were all to key A and served only to reduce the luminance to threshold. Consequently, a record of the luminance in this period was a rapidly falling curve that bore no relation to the threshold.

FIGURE 2   *Sample dark-adaptation curve secured from a bird in a single hour. Pre-exposure was 10 min. at 22 mL. The luminance of the stimulus patch, in log micromicrolamberts, is on the ordinate.*

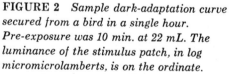
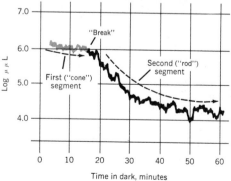

Time in dark, minutes

Discussion

A variety of findings (12) relates the first segment of the human adaptation curve to cone function and photopic sensitivity and relates the second segment to rods and scotopic sensitivity. In man, rods far outnumber cones except in or near the fovea, and unless the test stimulus is restricted to the fovea, the second segment characteristically dominates the dark-adaptation picture.

The pigeon possesses a duplex retina with elements grossly similar to their counterparts in the human retina, except for the fact that the pigeon cones contain red, orange, or yellowish oil droplets. Schultze's diagrams (11) of the pigeon retina show up to 20 of these cones for each rod in the temporal retina, while in the nasal region the proportion falls to about two cones to a rod; the fovea is rod-free. This cone dominance in the pigeon retina appears to be expressed in the bird's dark adaptation; a short, low-luminance pre-exposure suffices to produce an identifiable first segment.

Despite the appearance of familiar features in the pigeon data, it would not do to draw the conclusion that differences between pigeon and human dark adaptation are solely a function of the different distributions of elements on the two retinas. Even at the retinal level other important factors may operate. It has been reported (5) that when the retina of the pigeon is exposed to strong light, considerable pigment migration occurs, and the receptor cells change shape and position. These changes seem to proceed in such a way as to reduce the amount of light reaching the receptors in bright light and to increase it in the dark. The pigmentation of the pigeon's retinal cones may also affect the absolute threshold in ways as yet unclear.

References

1. Békésy, G. von. A new audiometer. *Acta Otolaryngol.*, 1947, 35, 411–422.
2. Blough, D. S. Method for tracing dark adaptation in the pigeon. *Science,* 1955, 121, 703–704.
3. Chard, R. D. Visual acuity in the pigeon. *J. exp. Psychol.*, 1939, 24, 588–608.
4. Chard, R. D., and Grundlach, R. H. The structure of the eye of the homing pigeon. *J. comp. Psychol.*, 1938, 25, 249–272.
5. Detweiler, S. R. *Vertebrate photoreceptors.* New York: Macmillan, 1943.
6. Ferster, C. B. The use of the free operant in the analysis of behavior. *Psychol. Bull.,* 1953, 50, 263–274.
7. Graham, C. H., Kemp, E. H., and Riggs, L. A. An analysis of the electrical retinal responses of a color-discriminating eye to light of different wave-lengths. *J. gen. Psychol.*, 1935, 13, 275–296.
8. Granit, R. The photopic spectrum of the pigeon. *Acta physiol. Scand.*, 1942, 4, 118–124.
9. Hamilton, W. F., and Coleman, T. B. Trichromatic vision in the pigeon as illustrated by the spectral hue discrimination curve. *J. comp. Psychol.*, 1933, 15, 183–191.
10. Ratliff, F., and Blough, D. S. Behavioral studies of visual processes in the pigeon. USN, ONR, Tech. Rep., 1954 (Contract N5 ori–07663, Proj. NR140–072).
11. Schultze, M. Zür Anatomie und Physiologie der Retina. *Arch. f. mikr. Anat.*, 1866, 2, 175.
12. Sheard, C. Dark adaptation: some physical, physiological, clinical, and aeromedical considerations. *J. opt. Soc. Amer.*, 1944, 34, 464–508.
13. Skinner, B. F. *The behavior of organisms.* New York: Appleton-Century-Crofts, 1938.
14. Skinner, B. F. Some contributions of an experimental analysis of behavior to psychology as a whole. *Amer. Psychologist*, 1953, 8, 69–78.
15. Walls, G. L. *The vertebrate eye and its adaptive radiation.* Bloomfield Hills, Mich.: Cranbrook Institute of Science, 1942.

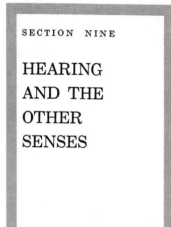

SECTION NINE

HEARING AND THE OTHER SENSES

This authoritative article is the contribution of a man who won a Nobel prize for studies on the function of the ear. The mechanics of the action of the ear have been discovered largely through the efforts of von Békésy.

A POINT TO GUIDE YOUR STUDY   *Note how the author shifts back and forth between practical, everyday examples and the mechanisms responsible for these effects.*

35: THE EAR

Georg von Békésy, Harvard University

Even in our era of technological wonders, the performances of our most amazing machines are still put in the shade by the sense organs of the human body. Consider the accomplishments of the ear. It is so sensitive that it can almost hear the random rain of air molecules bouncing against the eardrum. Yet in spite of its extraordinary sensitivity the ear can withstand the pounding of sound waves strong enough to set the body vibrating. The ear is equipped, moreover, with a truly impressive selectivity. In a room crowded with people talking, it can suppress most of the noise and concentrate on one speaker. From the blended sounds of a symphony orchestra the ear of the conductor can single out the one instrument that is not performing to his satisfaction.

In structure and in operation the ear is extraordinarily delicate. One measure of its fineness is the tiny vibrations to which it will respond. At some sound frequencies the vibrations of the eardrum are as small as one billionth of a centimeter—about one tenth the diameter of the hydrogen atom! And the vibrations of the very fine membrane in the inner ear which transmits this stimulation to the auditory nerve are nearly 100 times smaller in amplitude. This fact alone is enough to explain why hearing has so long been one of the mysteries of physiology. Even today we do not know how these minute vibrations stimulate the nerve endings. But thanks to refined electro-acoustical instruments we

273

do know quite a bit now about how the ear functions.

What are the ear's abilities? We can get a quick picture of the working condition of an ear by taking an audiogram, which is a measure of the threshold of hearing at the various sound frequencies. The hearing is tested with pure tones at various frequencies, and the audiogram tells how much sound pressure on the eardrum (*i.e.*, what intensity of sound) is necessary for the sound at each frequency to be just barely audible. Curiously, the audiogram curve often is very much the same for the various members of a family; possibly this is connected in some way with the similarity in the shape of the face.

The ear is least sensitive at the low fre-

quencies: for instance, its sensitivity for a tone of 100 cycles per second is 1,000 times lower than for one at 1,000 cycles per second. This comparative insensitivity to the slower vibrations is an obvious physical necessity, because otherwise we would hear all the vibrations of our own bodies. If you stick a finger in each ear, closing it to air-borne sounds, you hear a very low, irregular tone, produced by the contractions of the muscles of the arm and finger. It is interesting that the ear is just insensitive enough to low frequencies to avoid the disturbing effect of the noises produced by muscles, bodily movements, etc. If it were any more sensitive to these frequencies than it is, we would even hear the vibrations of the head that are produced by

FIGURE 1 *Audiograms plot the threshold of hearing (in terms of pressure on the tympanic membrane) against the frequency of sound. The first three audiograms show the threshold for three members of the same family; the fourth, the threshold for an unrelated person. The black curves represent the threshold for one ear of the subject; the gray curves, for the other ear of the same subject. The curves indicate that in normal hearing the threshold in both ears, and the threshold in members of the same family, are remarkably similar. (From "The Ear," by G. von Békésy. Copyright © 1957 by Scientific American, Inc. All rights reserved.)*

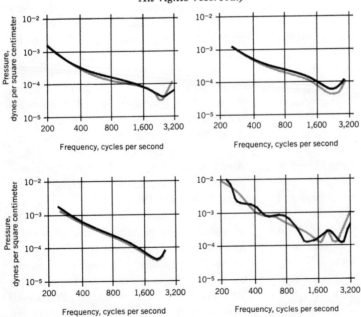

the shock of every step we take when walking.

On the high-frequency side the range that the ear covers is remarkable. In childhood some of us can hear well at frequencies as high as 40,000 cycles per second. But with age our acuteness of hearing in the high-frequency range steadily falls. Normally the drop is almost as regular as clockwork: testing several persons in their 40s with tones at a fixed level of intensity, we found that over a period of five years their upper limit dropped about 80 cycles per second every six months. (The experiment was quite depressing to most of the participants.) The aging of the ear is not difficult to understand if we assume that the elasticity of the tissues in the inner ear declines in the same way as that of the skin: it is well known that the skin becomes less resilient as we grow old—a phenomenon anyone can test by lifting the skin on the back of his hand and measuring the time it takes to fall back.

However, the loss of hearing sensitivity with age may also be due to nerve deterioration. Damage to the auditory nervous system by extremely loud noises, by drugs or by inflammation of the inner ear can impair hearing. Sometimes after such damage the hearing improves with time; sometimes (*e.g.*, when the damaging agent is streptomycin) the loss is permanent. Unfortunately a physician cannot predict the prospects for recovery of hearing loss, because they vary from person to person.

Psychological factors seem to be involved. Occasionally, especially after an ear operation, a patient appears to improve in hearing only to relapse after a short time. Some reports have even suggested that operating on one ear has improved the unoperated ear as well. Since such an interaction between the two ears would be of considerable neurological interest, I have investigated the matter, but I have never found an improvement in the un-

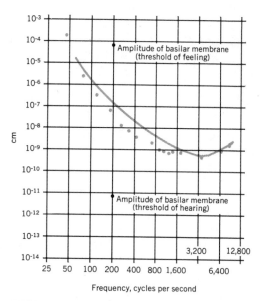

FIGURE 2 *Sensitivity of the ear is indicated by this curve, in which the amplitude of the vibrations of the tympanic membrane in fractions of a centimeter is plotted against the frequency of sound impinging on the membrane. Diameter of hydrogen atom is 10^{-8} centimeter. (From "The Ear," by G. von Békésy. Copyright © 1957 by Scientific American, Inc. All rights reserved.)*

treated ear that could be validated by an objective test.

Structure of the Ear

To understand how the ear achieves its sensitivity, we must take a look at the anatomy of the middle and the inner ear. When sound waves start the eardrum (tympanic membrane) vibrating, the vibrations are transmitted via certain small bones (ossicles) to the fluid of the inner ear. One of the ossicles, the tiny stirrup (weighing only about 1.2 milligrams), acts on the fluid like a piston, driving it back and forth in the rhythm of the sound pressure. These movements of the fluid force into vibration a thin membrane, called the basilar membrane. The latter in turn finally transmits the stimulus to the organ

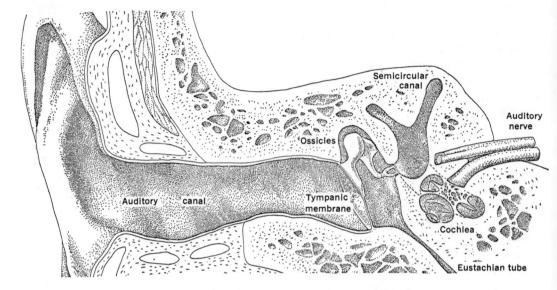

FIGURE 3 *Parts of the ear are illustrated in somewhat simplified cross section. Between the eardrum (tympanic membrane) and the fluid-filled inner ear are the three small bones (ossicles) of the middle ear. The auditory nerve endings are in an organ (not shown) between the plate of bone which spirals up the cochlea and the outer wall of the cochlea. (From "The Ear," by G. von Békésy. Copyright © 1957 by Scientific American, Inc. All rights reserved.)*

of Corti, a complex structure which contains the endings of the auditory nerves. The question immediately comes up: Why is this long and complicated chain of transmission necessary?

The reason is that we have a formidable mechanical problem if we are to extract the utmost energy from the sound waves striking the eardrum. Usually when a sound hits a solid surface, most of its energy is reflected away. The problem the ear has to solve is to absorb this energy. To do so it has to act as a kind of mechanical transformer, converting the large amplitude of the sound pressure waves in the air into more forceful vibrations of smaller amplitude. A hydraulic press is such a transformer: it multiplies the pressure acting on the surface of a piston by concentrating the force of the pressure upon a second piston of smaller area. The middle ear acts exactly like a hydraulic

press: the tiny footplate of the stirrup transforms the small pressure on the surface of the eardrum into a 22-fold greater pressure on the fluid of the inner ear. In this way the ear absorbs the greater part of the sound energy and transmits it to the inner ear without much loss.

But it needs another transformer to amplify the pressure of the fluid into a still larger force upon the tissues to which the nerves are attached. I think the ear's mechanism for this purpose is very ingenious indeed. It is based on the fact that a flat membrane, stretched to cover the opening of a tube, has a lateral tension along its surface. This tension can be increased tremendously if pressure is applied to one side of the membrane. And that is the function of the organ of Corti. It is constructed in such a way that pressure on the basilar membrane is transformed into shearing forces many times larger on the other side of the organ. The enhanced shearing forces rub upon extremely sensitive cells attached to the nerve endings.

The eardrum is not by any means the only avenue through which we hear. We also hear through our skull, which is to say, by bone conduction. When we click our teeth or chew a cracker, the sounds come mainly by way of vibrations of the skull. Some of the vibrations are transmitted directly to the inner ear, by-passing the middle ear. This fact helps in the diagnosis of hearing difficulties. If a person can hear bone-conducted sounds but is comparatively deaf to air-borne sounds, we know that the trouble lies in the middle ear. But if he hears no sound by bone conduction, then his auditory nerves are gone, and there is no cure for his deafness. This is an old test, long used by deaf musicians. If a violin player cannot hear his violin even when he touches his teeth to the vibrating instrument, then he knows he suffers from nerve deafness, and there is no cure.

Speaking and Hearing

Hearing by bone conduction plays an important role in the process of speaking.

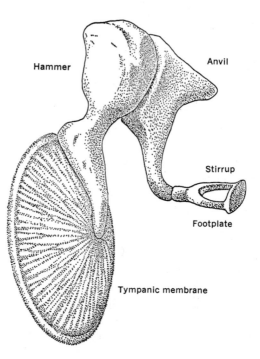

FIGURE 4   *Three ossicles transmit the vibrations of the tympanic membrane to the inner ear. The footplate of stirrup, surrounded by a narrow membrane, presses against inner-ear fluid. (From "The Ear," by G. von Békésy. Copyright © 1957 by Scientific American, Inc. All rights reserved.)*

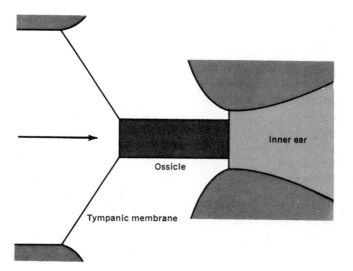
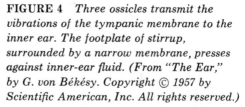

FIGURE 5   *How ossicles act as a piston pressing against the fluid of the inner ear is indicated by this drawing. Pressure of the vibrations of tympanic membrane are amplified 22 times. (From "The Ear," by G. von Békésy. Copyright © 1957 by Scientific American, Inc. All rights reserved.*

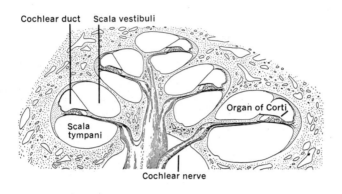

Cochlear duct   Scala vestibuli

Organ of Corti

Scala
tympani

Cochlear nerve

The vibrations of our vocal cords not only produce sounds which go to our ears via the air but also cause the body to vibrate, and the vibration of the jawbone is transmitted to the ear canal. When you hum with closed lips, the sounds you hear are to a large degree heard by bone conduction. (If you stop your ears with your fingers, the hum sounds much louder.) During speaking and singing, therefore, you hear two different sounds—one by bone conduction and the other by air conduction. Of course another listener hears only the air-conducted sounds. In these sounds some of the low-frequency components of the vocal cords' vibrations are lost. This explains why one can hardly recognize his own voice when he listens to a recording of his speech. As we normally hear ourselves, the low-frequency vibrations of our vocal cords, conducted to our own ears by the bones, make our speech sound much more powerful and dynamic than the pure sound waves heard by a second person or through a recording system. Consequently the recording of our voice may strike us as very thin and disappointing. From this point of view we have to admire the astonishing performance of an opera singer. The singer and the audience hear rather different sounds, and it is a miracle to me that they understand each other so well. Perhaps young singers would progress faster if during their training they spent more time studying recordings of their voices.

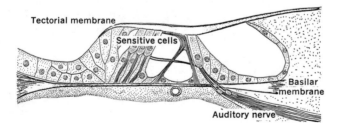

Tectorial membrane

Sensitive cells

Basilar
membrane

Auditory nerve

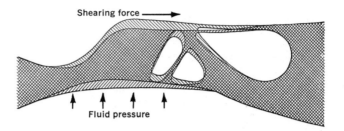

Feedback to the voice

The control of speaking and singing involves a complicated feedback system. Just as feedback between the eyes and the muscles guides the hand when it moves to pick up an object, so feedback continually adjusts and corrects the voice as we speak or sing. When we start to sing, the beginning of the sound tells us the pitch, and we immediately adjust the tension of the vocal cords if the pitch is wrong. This feedback requires an exceedingly elaborate and rapid mechanism. How it works is not yet entirely understood. But it is small wonder that it takes a child years to learn to speak, or that it is almost impossible for an adult to learn to speak a foreign language with the native accents.

Any disturbance in the feedback immediately disturbs the speech. For instance, if, while a person is speaking, his speech is fed back to him with a time delay by means of a microphone and receivers at his ears, his pronunciation and accent will change, and if the delay interval is made long enough, he will find it impossible to speak at all. This phenomenon affords an easy test for exposing pretended deafness. If the subject can continue speaking normally in the face of a delayed feedback through the machine to his ears, we can be sure that he is really deaf.

The same technique can be used to assess the skill of a pianist. A piano player generally adjusts his touch to the acoustics of the room: if the room is very reverberant, so that the music sounds too loud, he uses a lighter touch; if the sound is damped by the walls, he strengthens his touch. We had a number of pianists play in a room where the damping could be varied, and recorded the amplitude of the vibrations of the piano's sounding board while the musicians played various pieces. When they played an easy piece, their adjustment to the acoustics was very clear: as the sound absorption of the room was increased, the pianist played more loudly, and when the damping on the walls was taken away, the pianist's touch became lighter. But when the piece was difficult, many of the pianists concentrated so hard on the problems of the music that they failed to adjust to the feedback of the room. A master musician, however, was not lost to the sound effects. Taking the technical difficulties of the music in stride, he was able to adjust the sound level to the damping of the room with the same accuracy as for an easy piece. Our rating of the pianists by this test closely matched their reputation among musical experts.

Suppressed sounds

In connection with room acoustics, I should like to mention one of the ear's most amazing performances. How is it that we can locate a speaker, even without seeing him, in a bare-walled room where reflections of his voice come at us from every side? This is an almost unbelievable performance by the ear. It is as if, looking into a room completely lined with mirrors, we saw only the real figure and none of the hundreds of reflected images. The eye cannot suppress the reflections, but the ear can. The ear is able to ignore all the sounds except the first that strikes it. It has a built-in inhibitory mechanism.

One of the most important factors that subordinate the reflected sounds is the delay in their arrival; necessarily they come to the ear only after the sound that has traveled directly from the speaker to the listener. The reflected sounds reinforce the loudness and tone volume of the direct sound, and perhaps even modify its localization, but by and large, they are not distinguishable from it. Only when the delay is appreciable does a reflected sound appear as a separate unit—an echo. Echoes often are heard in a large church, where reflections may lag more than half a second behind the direct sound. They are apt to be a problem in a concert hall. Dead walls are not desirable, because the music

would sound weak. For every size of concert room there is an optimal compromise on wall reflectivity which will give amplification to the music but prevent disturbing echoes.

In addition to time delay, there are other factors that act to inhibit some sounds and favor others. Strong sounds generally suppress weaker ones. Sounds in which we are interested take precedence over those that concern us less, as I pointed out in the examples of the speaker in a noisy room and the orchestra conductor detecting an errant instrument. This brings us to the intimate collaboration between the ear and the nervous system.

Auditory messages

Any stimulation of the ear (*e.g.*, any change in pressure) is translated into electrical messages to the brain via the nerves. We can therefore draw information about the ear from an analysis of these electrical impulses, now made possible by electronic instruments. There are two principal types of electric potential that carry the mes-

FIGURE 9 *Electrical potentials of the microphonic type generated by the inner ear of an experimental animal can be detected by this arrangement. At left is a highly schematic diagram of the ear; the cochlea is represented in cross section by the fluid-filled chamber and the organ of Corti by the horizontal line in this chamber. When the vibrations of the eardrum are transmitted to the organ of Corti, its microphonic potentials can be picked up at the round window of the cochlea and displayed on the face of an oscilloscope (right). (From "The Ear," by G. von Békésy. Copyright © 1957 by Scientific American, Inc. All rights reserved.)*

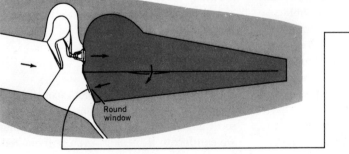
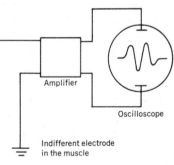

sages. One is a continuous, wavelike potential which has been given the name microphonic. In experimental animals such as guinea pigs and cats the microphonics are large enough to be easily measured (they range up to about half a millivolt). It has turned out that the magnitude of the microphonics produced in the inner ear is directly proportional to the displacements of the stirrup footplate that set the fluid in the inner ear in motion. The microphonics therefore permit us to determine directly to what extent the sound pressure applied to the eardrum is transmitted to the inner ear, and they have become one of the most useful tools for exploring sound transmission in the middle ear. For instance, there used to be endless discussion of the simple question: Just how much does perforation of the eardrum affect hearing? The question has now been answered with mathematical precision by experiments on animals. A hole of precisely measured size is drilled in the eardrum, and the amount of hearing loss is determined by the change in the microphonics. This type of observation on cats has shown that a perforation about one millimeter in diameter destroys hearing at the frequencies below 100 cycles per second but causes almost no impairment of hearing in the range of frequencies above 1,000 cycles per second. From studies of the physical properties of the human ear we can judge that the findings on animals apply fairly closely to man also.

The second type of electric potential takes the form of sharp pulses, which appear as spikes in the recording instrument. The sound of a sharp click produces a series of brief spikes; a pure tone generates volleys of spikes, generally in the rhythm of the period of the tone. We can follow the spikes along the nerve pathways all the way from the inner ear up to the cortex of the brain. And when we do, we find that stimulation of specific spots on the membrane of the inner ear seems to be pro-

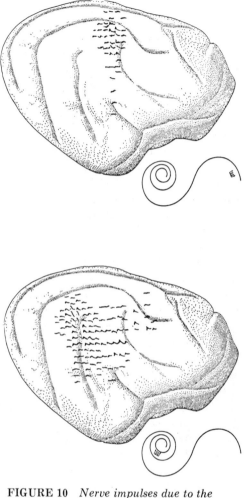

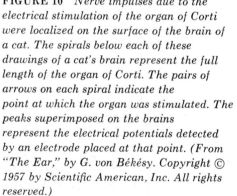

FIGURE 10 *Nerve impulses due to the electrical stimulation of the organ of Corti were localized on the surface of the brain of a cat. The spirals below each of these drawings of a cat's brain represent the full length of the organ of Corti. The pairs of arrows on each spiral indicate the point at which the organ was stimulated. The peaks superimposed on the brains represent the electrical potentials detected by an electrode placed at that point. (From "The Ear," by G. von Békésy. Copyright © 1957 by Scientific American, Inc. All rights reserved.)*

jected to corresponding spots in the auditory area of the cortex. This is reminiscent of the projection of images on the retina of the eye to the visual area of the brain.

But in the case of the ear the situation must be more complex, because there are nerve branches leading to the opposite ear and there seem to be several auditory projection areas on the surface of the brain. At the moment research is going on to find out how the secondary areas function and what their purpose is.

Detecting pitch

The orderly projection of the sensitive area of the inner ear onto the higher brain levels is probably connected with the resolution of pitch. The ear itself can analyze sounds and separate one tone from another. There are limits to this ability, but if the frequencies of the tones presented are not too close together, they are discriminated pretty well. Long ago this raised the question: How is the ear able to discriminate the pitch of a tone? Many theories have been argued, but only within the last decade has it been possible to plan pertinent experiments.

In the low-frequency range up to 60 cycles per second the vibration of the basilar membrane produces in the auditory nerve volleys of electric spikes synchronous with the rhythm of the sound. As the sound pressure increases, the number of spikes packed into each period increases. Thus two variables are transmitted to the cortex: (1) the number of spikes and (2) their rhythm. These two variables alone convey the loudness and the pitch of the sound.

Above 60 cycles per second a new phenomenon comes in. The basilar membrane now begins to vibrate unequally over its area: each tone produces a maximal vibration in a different area of the membrane. Gradually this selectivity takes over the determination of pitch, for the rhythm of the spikes, which indicates the pitch at low frequencies, becomes irregular at the higher ones. Above 4,000 cycles per second pitch is determined entirely by the location of the maximal vibration amplitude along the basilar membrane. Apparently there is an inhibitory mechanism which suppresses the weaker stimuli and thus sharpens considerably the sensation around the maximum. This type of inhibition can also operate in sense organs such as the skin and the eye. In order to see sharply we need not only a sharp image of the object on the retina but also an inhibitory system to suppress stray light entering the eye. Otherwise we would see the object surrounded by a halo. The ear is much the same. Without inhibitory effects a tone would sound like a noise of a certain pitch but not like a pure tone.

We can sum up by saying that the basilar membrane makes a rough, mechanical frequency analysis, and the auditory nervous system sharpens the analysis in some manner not yet understood. It is a part of the general functioning of the higher nerve centers, and it will be understood only when we know more about the functioning of these centers. If the answer is found for the ear, it will probably apply to the other sense organs as well.

Deafness

Now let us run briefly over some of the types of hearing disorders, which have become much more understandable as a result of recent experimental researches.

Infections of the ear used to be responsible for the overwhelming majority of the cases of deafness. Ten years ago in a large city hospital there was a death almost every day from such infections. Thanks to antibiotics, they can now be arrested, and, if treated in time, an ear infection is seldom either fatal or destructive of hearing, though occasionally an operation is necessary to scoop out the diseased part of the mastoid bone.

The two other principal types of deafness are those caused by destruction of the auditory nerves and by otosclerosis (a tumorous bone growth). Nerve deafness cannot be cured; no drug or mechanical manipulation or operation can restore the victim's hearing. But the impairment of hearing caused by otosclerosis can usually be repaired, at least in part.

Otosclerosis is an abnormal but painless growth in a temporal bone (*i.e.*, at the side of the skull, near the middle ear). If it does not invade a part of the ear that participates in the transmission of sound, no harm is done to the hearing. But if the growth happens to involve the stirrup footplate, it will reduce or even completely freeze the footplate's ability to make its piston-like movements; the vibrations of the eardrum then can no longer be transmitted to the inner ear. An otosclerotic growth can occur at any age, may slow down for many years, and may suddenly start up again. It is found more often in women than in men and seems to be accelerated by pregnancy.

Immobilization of the stirrup blocks the hearing of air-borne sound but leaves hearing by bone conduction unimpaired. This fact is used for diagnosis. A patient who has lost part of his hearing ability because of otosclerosis does not find noise disturbing to his understanding of speech; in fact, noise may even improve his discrimination of speech. There is an old story about a somewhat deaf English earl (in France it is a count) who trained his servant to beat a drum whenever someone else spoke, so that he could understand the speaker better. The noise of the drum made the speaker raise his voice to the earl's hearing range. For the hard-of-hearing earl the noise of the drum was tolerable, but for other listeners it masked what the speaker was saying, so that the earl enjoyed exclusive rights to his conversation.

Difficulty in hearing air-borne sound can be corrected by a hearing aid. Theoretically it should be possible to compensate almost any amount of such hearing loss, because techniques for amplifying sound are highly developed, particularly now with the help of the transistor. But there is a physiological limit to the amount of pressure amplification that the ear will stand. Heightening of the pressure eventually produces an unpleasant tickling sensation through its effect on skin tissue in the middle ear. The sensation can be avoided by using a bone-conduction earphone, pressed firmly against the surface of the skull, but this constant pressure is unpleasant to many people.

Operations

As is widely known, there are now operations (*e.g.*, "fenestration") which can cure otosclerotic deafness. In the 19th century physicians realized that if they could somehow dislodge or loosen the immobilized stirrup footplate, they might restore hearing. Experimenters in France found that they could sometimes free the footplate sufficiently merely by pressing a blunt needle against the right spot on the stirrup. Although it works only occasionally, the procedure seems so simple that it has recently had a revival of popularity in the U. S. If the maneuver is successful (and I am told that 30 per cent of these operations are) the hearing improves immediately. But unfortunately the surgeon cannot get a clear look at the scene of the operation and must apply the pushing force at random. This makes the operation something of a gamble, and the patient's hearing may not only fail to be improved but may even be reduced. Moreover, the operation is bound to be ineffectual when a large portion of the footplate is fixed. There are other important objections to the operation. After all, it involves the breaking of bone, to free the adhering part of the stirrup. I do not think that bone-breaking can be improved to a standard procedure. In any case, precision cutting seems to me always superior to breaking, in surgery as in mechanics. This brings us to the operation called fenestration.

For many decades it has been known that drilling a small opening, even the size of a pinhead, in the bony wall of the inner

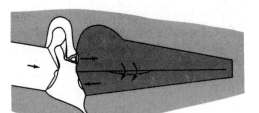

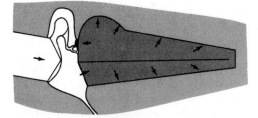

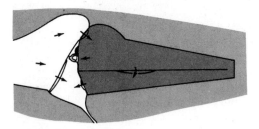

FIGURE 11 *Fenestration operation can alleviate the effects of otosclerosis. The drawing at the top schematically depicts the normal human ear as described in the caption for the illustration on page 280. The pressure on the components of the ear is indicated by the arrows. The drawing in the middle shows an otosclerotic ear; the otosclerotic growth is represented as a black protuberance. Because the stirrup cannot move, the pressure on the tympanic membrane is transmitted to the organ of Corti only through the round window of the cochlea; and because the fluid in the cochlea is incompressible, the organ of Corti cannot vibrate. The drawing at the bottom shows how the fenestration operation makes a new window into the cochlea to permit the organ of Corti to vibrate freely. (From "The Ear," by G. von Békésy. Copyright © 1957 by Scientific American, Inc. All rights reserved.)*

ear on the footplate side can produce a remarkable improvement in hearing. The reason, now well understood, is quite simple. If a hole is made in the bone and then covered again with a flexible membrane, movements of the fluid in, for instance, the lateral canal of the vestibular organ can be transmitted to the fluid of the inner ear, and so vibrations are once again communicable from the middle to the inner ear. In the typical present fenestration operation the surgeon bores a small hole in the canal wall with a dental drill and then covers the hole with a flap of skin. The operation today is a straightforward surgical procedure, and all its steps are under accurate control.

Hazards to hearing

I want to conclude by mentioning the problem of nerve deafness. Many cases of nerve deafness are produced by intense noise, especially noise with high-frequency components. Since there is no cure, it behooves us to look out for such exposures. Nerve deafness creeps up on us slowly, and we are not as careful as we should be to avoid exposure to intense noise. We should also be more vigilant about other hazards capable of producing nerve deafness, notably certain drugs and certain diseases.

We could do much to ameliorate the tragedy of deafness if we changed some of our attitudes toward it. Blindness evokes our instant sympathy, and we go out of our way to help the blind person. But deafness often goes unrecognized. If a deaf person misunderstands what we say, we are apt to attribute it to lack of intelligence instead of to faulty hearing. Very few people have the patience to help the deafened. To a deaf man the outside world appears unfriendly. He tries to hide his deafness, and this only brings on more problems.

Before reading this selection, make sure you have read about sensation in your text. You will get a lot more out of this if you have.

POINTS TO GUIDE YOUR STUDY   *(1) What is the doctrine of the "specific energies of nerves"? How does the article bear on this idea?*
(2) See the notes on the article "Dark Adaptation in the Pigeon" for a discussion of psychophysics. The discussion should help to clarify the statement that "a particular sensory dimension is not isomorphic with a particular physical dimension."

GLOSSARY   **Modality:** *refers to the different types of sensory experience. For instance, visual experience and touch experience are separate modalities.* **Isomorphism:** *literally means "same form." In sensory psychology, it usually refers to the relationship between the pattern of activity in the nervous system, on the one hand, and experience on the other.* **Afferent:** *refers to input to the central nervous system. This term is to be contrasted with* efferent, *which refers to nerve impulses flowing from the central nervous system, often to the muscles or glands.* **Synapse:** *the region where two nerve fibers come together. The fibers do not actually touch, however. The nerve impulse is transmitted across the gap by a combination of electrical and chemical processes.* **Molar (M):** *the measure of the physical stimulus in most taste studies is in terms of the concentration of dissolved material in the solution which is applied to the taste receptor. The unit of measurement is often the "molar" unit. A molar solution is one in which one molecular weight of substance is dissolved in one liter of the solution.* **Nociceptor:** *a receptor which, when stimulated, gives rise to unpleasant experiences. The pain receptors are nociceptors. This term should be contrasted with its opposite, "beneceptor."* **Temporal:** *refers to time.* **Phenomenology:** *in psychology, this term is usually used to refer to a person's immediate experience.* **Reify:** *the tendency to think about concepts, which are not objects, as if they were actual objects which can be seen, heard, touched, or experienced in some other way. In other words, this is the tendency to make* things *out of* abstractions.

36:   THE AFFERENT CODE FOR SENSORY QUALITY

Carl Pfaffmann, Rockefeller University

One of the basic problems in the psychology and physiology of sensation is that of the mechanism by which different sensory qualities are perceived. The classical dictum on this problem was propounded by Johannes Müller in his doctrine of the Specific Energies of Nerves. Actually Charles Bell had enunciated (Carmichael, 1926) the principle somewhat earlier, but Müller's version is better known. This doctrine made clear that "We are aware of the state of our nerves, not of the external stimulus itself." The eye, however stimulated, gives rise to sensations of light; the ear, to sensations of sound; and the taste buds, to sensations of taste.

Presented as part of the Presidential Address to the Division of Experimental Psychology at the APA Annual Convention, September 3, 1957.
  Carl Pfaffmann. The afferent code for sensory quality. *Amer. Psychologist*, 1959, **14**, 226–232. Copyright © 1959 by the American Psychological Association. Reprinted here with permission from the author and the American Psychological Association.

The further extension of the doctrine of Specific Nerve Energies to the different sensation qualities within a single modality was made by Helmholtz. According to his place theory of hearing, the perception of a particular pitch was attributed to the activity at a particular region of the basilar membrane of the inner ear, stimulation of the individual nerve fibers at these specific locations gave rise to unique tonal qualities of pitch. *Pitch* depended upon *which* nerve fiber was activated (Boring, 1950). In the less complex modalities, like the cutaneous or gustatory senses, von Frey and his school propounded the view of "modalities within modalities." The cutaneous sense was said to consist of separate modalities: touch, pressure, warm, cold, and pain, each with their specific receptors. The history of research on cutaneous sensitivity is, in large measure, a history of the search for such receptors. In taste the "BIG FOUR" are familiar to all; the qualities, salty, sour, bitter, and sweet, were each mediated by a specific receptor type.

Implicit in these formulations is an isomorphism between receptor structure and phenomenology. Pure sensation as a basic psychological entity was to be reduced to a physiological entity. Psychology (at least a part thereof) was to be "explained" by the underlying physiology, hence, "Physiological Psychology." This formulation, simple and direct, dominated the field of sensory psychology from the beginning with only an occasional and sporadic dissenting voice. The fact that the psychological entities were only postulated and the question of whether they were, in fact, valid were almost forgotten in the search for the "real thing."

Many of the more recent findings in sensory psychology and physiology derive from the application of electrophysiology to the study of sensory processes. The publication of E. D. Adrian's *The Basis of Sensation* in 1928 opened a new era. The invention of the electronic tube, appropri-ate amplifying circuits, and recording instruments made it possible to study directly the activity of the sense organs and their nerves. Since 1928, the advances in technique and instrumentation have been so dramatic that there is almost no part of the nervous system that cannot be probed by the inquisitive microelectrode. Psychologists have played a significant role in this development. One of their best known early discoveries was that of Wever and Bray (1930), on the cochlea and VIIIth nerve.

This paper will review some experiments with this procedure on another sense, that of taste, and will discuss their general implications for the theory of afferent coding.[1] It should be emphasized that sensation itself is not being studied. Rather the investigator "taps in" on the "basis of sensation" by recording and amplifying the nerve impulse traffic in the sensory fibers "en route" to the brain.

The sense of taste is particularly well suited to this problem because it consists of well defined differentiated structures, the taste buds, which are capable of mediating quite different sensory qualities, but the array of qualities and dimensions is not too complex for interpretation. The afferent message from receptor to brain can be studied directly in the afferent nerve fibers from the tongue, for the primary sensory nerve fibers from the receptive organs are relatively accessible with no synaptic complexities in the direct line from the receptors except for the junction between sense cell and sensory fiber.

The taste stimulus, like all stimuli, acts first upon a receptor cell. Changes in the receptor cell in turn activate or "trigger" impulses in the nerve fiber. Both the sense cell, as well as the nerve fiber, and in fact all living cells are like tiny batteries with a potential difference across the cell membrane. When stimulated, this membrane is

[1] Many of our experiments on taste were supported by a contract with the Office of Naval Research.

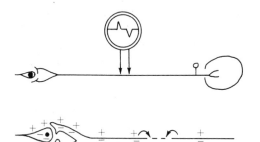

FIGURE 1 *Diagram of electrophysiological recording from a single sensory nerve fiber. Upper diagram shows a single fiber in contact with a single sense cell to the left. A diphasic response on the cathode ray tube is shown as an impulse passes the recording electrodes en route to the central nervous system schematized to the right. The lower figure shows in more detail the positive and negative charges around the cell membranes associated with the passage of the nerve impulse.*

depolarized, and it is this depolarization that can be recorded. Figure 1 schematizes such recording from a single sensory nerve fiber shown in contact with a receptor cell to the left of the figure and entering the central nervous system (CNS) to the right. The recording electrodes on the fiber connect with an appropriate recording device such as a cathode ray oscillograph shown schematically. As the impulse passes the first electrode, there is an upward deflection; as it passes the second electrode, there is a downward deflection. By an appropriate arrangement, a single or monophasic deflection only may be obtained so that at each passage of an impulse there will be a "spike" on the oscillograph tracing. The lower figure shows schematically the electrical activity associated with the passage of a nerve impulse. The message delivered along any single nerve fiber therefore consists of a train of impulses, changes in excitation of the receptor are signaled by changes in the frequency of this train. Thus, changes in strength of solution bathing the tongue change the frequency of impulse discharge

per second. In any one fiber, the size of the impulse is nearly constant. The sensory nerve message, therefore, is a digital process.

Figure 2 shows a typical series of oscillograph tracings obtained from a *single* nerve fiber when different concentrations of sodium chloride are applied to the tongue of the rat. The "spikes" signal the passage of each impulse past the recording electrode. With stronger stimuli there is a higher frequency of discharge. Threshold for this fiber lies at approximately 0.003 M. Other fibers will show similar behavior, but may possess higher thresholds, for the tongue contains a population of taste receptors with thresholds of differing value.

This description applies to the impulse in the single sensory nerve fiber. Actually, the sensory nerve is a cable, made up of many different fibers each connected with one or more receptor cells. The single fiber recordings shown were obtained after the nerve cable had been dissected to a strand containing just one functional unit. Sometimes the same effect is achieved by using microelectrodes.

The nerve fibers subserving taste travel in three nerves from the mouth region: the

FIGURE 2 *A series of oscillograph tracings obtained from a single taste nerve fiber when different concentrations of salt solution are placed on the tongue. Note that water as well as .001 M NaCl will elicit two impulses. A concentration of .003 M NaCl will elicit three impulses and may be considered as threshold. (Reproduced from the* Journal of Neurophysiology.*)*

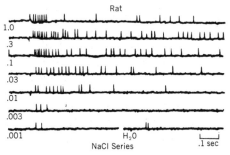

lingual, glossopharyngeal, and vagus nerves which contain touch, temperature, pressure and pain fibers as well as those concerned with taste. The taste fibers from the anterior tongue branch off from the lingual nerve to form the chorda tympani nerve where it is possible to record almost exclusively from taste nerve fibers. This nerve can be exposed by appropriate surgery in the anesthetized animal and placed on the electrodes leading to the recording apparatus.

A block diagram of the apparatus together with sample records is shown in Figure 3. The integrated record is readily adapted to quantitative treatment by measuring the magnitude of the deflection at each response and so provides a measure of the total activity of all the fibers in the nerve. An index of over-all taste sensitivity can be obtained from such recordings. The curves in Figure 4 are such measures for the cat for quinine, hydrochloric acid, sodium chloride, potassium chloride, and sucrose solutions (Pfaffmann, 1955).

The basic taste stimuli can be arranged in order of thresholds from low to high as follows: quinine, hydrochloric acid, sodium chloride, potassium chloride, and sucrose. In this animal, as in man, quinine is effec-

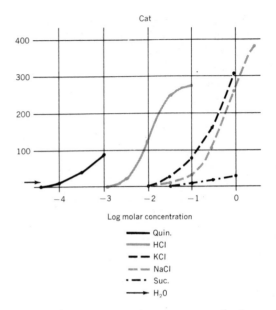

FIGURE 4   *Curves of taste response in the cat to four different taste stimuli as indicated by the integrated response method.*
(Reproduced from the Journal of Neurophysiology.*)*

tive in relatively low concentrations. Sugar at the other end of the scale requires relatively high concentrations, and the electrolytes are intermediate. Sugar produces a nerve response of small magnitude compared with that to other stimuli. Differences in response magnitudes are found from one species to another. In the hamster or guinea pig, for example, sugar will elicit a strong discharge, and other species differences with quinine and the salts have been observed (Beidler, Fishman, and Hardiman, 1955; Pfaffmann, 1953). Recently, Carpenter (1956) has correlated certain of these species differences with behavioral data using the preference method.

The representation in Figure 4 does not show that the animal can distinguish one substance from another. Actually an animal like the rat will avoid quinine and acid, but will show a preference for NaCl and sucrose. To find how the animal can discriminate among different chemicals the single fiber analysis is required.

FIGURE 3   *A block diagram of the recording apparatus showing two types of record. The upper trace shows a typical asynchronus, multifiber discharge from a large number of active fibers; the lower trace shows the integrated record of such activity.*
(Reproduced from the American Journal of Clinical Nutrition.*)*

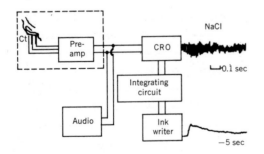

In the early study of the single gustatory fibers in the cat (Pfaffmann, 1941), three different kinds of fiber were found. One was responsive to sodium chloride and acid, another to quinine and acid, and a third to acid alone. Thus, acid stimulated all receptor-neural units found. This established not only that the gustatory endings were differentially sensitive to different chemicals but that the physiological receptor "types" *did not* correspond to the phenomenal categories as reported by man. In view of the more recently demonstrated species difference, this might not appear to be surprising. But, regardless of what the cat "tastes," these findings pointed to an important principle of sensory coding. This is that *the same afferent fiber may convey different information depending upon the amount of activity in another parallel fiber.* To illustrate, suppose A represents an acid-salt unit and C, an acid sensitive unit, then activity in A only would lead to salty; but activity in that same fiber, A, plus discharge in C, would lead to sourness. Recent studies emphasize still another important point, namely, that some stimuli may decrease or inhibit the frequency of sensory discharge. Certain receptors, which can be stimulated by water (as well as other agents), may be inhibited by the application of dilute salt solutions (Liljestrand & Zotterman, 1954). Taste stimuli, therefore, may either increase or decrease, i.e., modulate, the amount of afferent nerve traffic. A diminution in activity may signal, not merely the

withdrawal of a particular stimulus, but the application of a different one.

Table 1 taken from a recent paper from Zotterman's laboratory (Cohen, Hagiwara, & Zotterman, 1955) illustrates the afferent code or pattern which may be described for the cat based on a compilation of the "types" so far discovered for that species.

But the use of the term "fiber type" harks back to some of the errors of classical thinking. Types are defined only by the range of stimuli sampled, the wider the range, the more difficult will it be to define pure "types." "Taste types" may turn out to be as varied and individual as "personality types." Figure 5 shows the variety of response patterns of nine single fiber preparations to the following standard test solutions: .03 N HCl, .1 M KCl, .1 M NaCl, .01 M quinine hydrochloride, and 1.0 M sucrose (Pfaffmann, 1955).

The bar graph shows the magnitude of response in each of the single fiber preparations in impulses per second of discharge. The central crosshatched bar graph shows the relative magnitude of response to these same solutions in the integrated response of the whole nerve. It is apparent that the individual fibers do not all have the same pattern. The sum of the activity of all fibers is shown by the crosshatched diagram. Furthermore, fiber types are not immediately apparent in this array.

The fact that the individual receptor cells possess combined sensitivity as salt plus acid, or salt plus sugar, cannot be dismissed as the result of multiple innerva-

TABLE 1   *Fiber type response in the cat**

STIMULUS	"WATER" FIBER	"SALT" FIBER	"ACID" FIBER	"QUININE" FIBER	SENSATION EVOKED
H₂O (0.03M Salt)	+	0	0	0	→ water
NaCl (0.05 M)	0	+	0	0	→ salt
HCL (*ph* 2.5)	+	+	+	0	→ sour
Quinine	+	0	0	+	→ bitter

* Cf., Cohen, Hagiwara, & Zotterman, 1955.

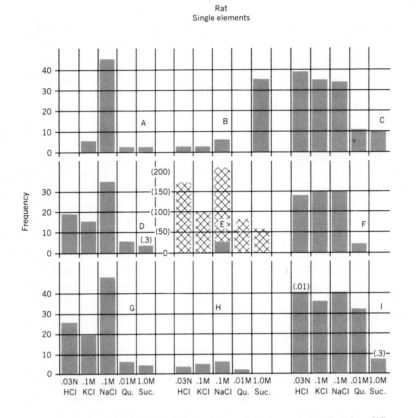

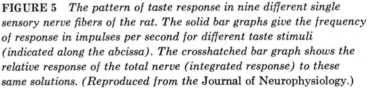

FIGURE 5   *The pattern of taste response in nine different single sensory nerve fibers of the rat. The solid bar graphs give the frequency of response in impulses per second for different taste stimuli (indicated along the abcissa). The crosshatched bar graph shows the relative response of the total nerve (integrated response) to these same solutions. (Reproduced from the* Journal of Neurophysiology.)

tion of more than one receptor cell by a single fiber. Kimura (Beidler, 1957; Kimura & Beidler, 1956) has studied the sensitivity patterns of the individual taste cells by inserting micro-pipette electrodes directly into the sense cells themselves. The pattern of sensitivity found in the individual sensory cells is like that already described for the single afferent fiber. Thus, within the individual sense cell there must be different sites which are selectively sensitive to different taste stimuli. These sites on the membrane may be determined by molecular configuration, the shape and size of pores in the membrane, or some such microcellular feature.

One additional principle must be intro-

duced. This is that the relative rather than the absolute amount of activity in any one set of afferent fibers may determine the quality of sensation. Figure 6 shows frequency of discharge as a function of stimulus intensity for two units labelled A and B. Both are stimulated by both sugar and salt, but it is apparent that A is more sensitive to salt and B to sugar (Pfaffmann, 1955). Once each stimulus intensity exceeds the threshold for a particular receptor unit, the frequency of discharge increases with concentration. Thus the afferent pattern as the code for sensory quality must take account of the changing frequency of discharge with stimulus intensity. The pattern concept may be retained by recognizing that "pattern" is still apparent in the relative amount of activity of different fibers. In the two-fiber example shown in Figure 6, low concentrations of salt will discharge only A, higher concentrations will discharge both A and B, but activity in A will be greater than that in B. Low concentrations of sugar will activate only B, higher concentrations will activate both B and A, but B will be greater than A. Thus the sensory code might read:

Frequency   Code
A > B =   salty
B > A =   sweet

where A or B may go to zero. It is not only the activity in parallel fibers that is important, it is the *relative amount* of such parallel activity.

Studies of the other senses indicate that these principles are not unique to taste. In the cutaneous senses there is a variety of different endings which overlap two or more of the classical skin modalities (Maruhashi, Mizuguchi, & Tasaki, 1952). For example, some pressure receptors in the cat's tongue are activated by cold (Hensel & Zotterman, 1951), and there are several different pressure, temperature, and nociceptor endings, some serving large or small areas, some adapting slowly, others rapidly to give a variety of temporal as well as spatial "discriminanda." These findings are reminiscent of Nafe's (1934) quantitative theory of feeling, and the recent anatomical studies of Weddell (1955) and his group are of similar import.

In audition, selective sensitivity among the individual primary afferent fibers is very broad. Those fibers arising from the basal turn of the cochlea respond to tones of any audible frequency; those arising in the upper part respond only to a band of low frequency tones (Tasaki, 1954). Further, it has been suggested (Wever, 1949) that the temporal patterning of the discharge, especially in the low frequencies, provides a basis for pitch discrimination.

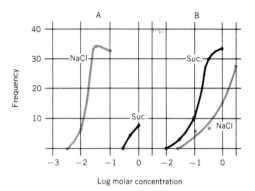
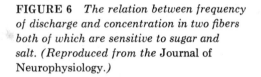

FIGURE 6 *The relation between frequency of discharge and concentration in two fibers both of which are sensitive to sugar and salt. (Reproduced from the* Journal of Neurophysiology.*)*

In vision, Granit (1955) has suggested that different impulse frequencies in the *same* third order neuron from the retina may signal different spectral events at the periphery.

These electrophysiological results should not have been surprising to us. That a particular sensory dimension is not isomorphic with a particular physical dimension is well known. Auditory loudness, functionally dependent upon sound pressure level, is not synonymous with physical intensity. Pitch is not the same as frequency, although the latter is its major determinant (Stevens & Davis, 1938). Visual brightness is not the same as physical luminance. It would, indeed, have been surprising if similar nonidentities had not been found at the physiological level.

And so in attacking Müller's classic problem with modern techniques, we have found, at least, within the modalities, a solution different from that which was first anticipated. Differential sensitivity rather than specificity, patterned discharges rather than a mosaic of sensitivities is the form of our modern view. Müller's principle did not answer a problem so much as it posed one. In the answers that I have attempted to suggest, we see, not only the details of the mechanism for which we have searched, but we can discern broader implications for the principles governing the relation between psychology and physiology. Psychology cannot rest content with a pseudophysiology based solely upon phenomenology. So long as the receptor surface was conceived to be a static mosaic where phenomenal qualities were reified (in some instances in the form of specific anatomical structures), sensory psychology and physiology were reduced to the study of how the "little pictures" were transmitted via the sensory nerves to the "sensorium" located presumably somewhere "inside the head." Such a view is not only out of date, but it diverts our attention from the proper study of the afferent influx, its dynamic properties and interactions and its relevance for all levels of neural integration and behavioral organization.

References

Adrian, E. D. *The basis of sensation.* New York: Norton, 1928.

Beidler, L. M. Facts and theory on the mechanism of taste and odor perception. In *Chemistry of natural food flavors.* Quartermaster Research and Engineering Center, 1957, pp. 7–47.

Beidler, L. M., Fishman, I. Y., and Hardiman, C. W. Species differences in taste responses. *Amer. J. Physiol.,* 1955, **181**, 235–239.

Boring, E. G. *A history of experimental psychology.* New York: Appleton-Century-Crofts, 1950.

Carmichael, L. Sir Charles Bell: A contribution to the history of physiological psychology. *Psychol. Rev.,* 1926, **33**, 188–217.

Carpenter, J. A. Species differences in taste preferences. *J. comp. physiol. Psychol.,* 1956, **49**, 139–144.

Cohen, M. J., Hagiwara, S., and Zotterman, Y. The response spectrum of taste fibers in the cat: A single fiber analysis. *Acta. physiol., Scand.,* 1955, **33**, 316–332.

Granit, R. *Receptors and sensory perception.* New Haven: Yale Univer. Press, 1955.

Hensel, H., and Zotterman, Y. The response of mechanoreceptors to thermal stimulation. *J. Physiol.,* 1951, **115**, 16–24.

Kimura, K., and Beidler, L. M. Microelectrode study of taste bud of the rat. *Amer. J. Physiol.,* 1956, **187**, 610.

Liljestrand, G., and Zotterman, Y. The water taste in mammals. *Acta. physiol., Scand.,* 1954, **32**, 291–303.

Maruhashi, J., Mizuguchi, K. and Tasaki, I. Action currents in single afferent nerve fibers elicited by stimulation of the skin of the toad and the cat. *J. Physiol.,* 1952, **117**, 129–151.

Nafe, J. P. The pressure, pain and temperature senses. In C. Murchison (Ed.), *Handbook of general experimental psychology.* Worcester: Clark Univer. Press, 1934, chap. 20.

Pfaffmann, C. Gustatory afferent impulses. *J. cell. comp. Physiol.,* 1941, **17**, 243–258.

Pfaffmann, C. Species differences in taste sensitivity. *Science,* 1953, **117**, 470.

Pfaffmann, C. Gustatory nerve impulses in rat, cat, and rabbit. *J. Neurophysiol.,* 1955, **18**, 429–440.

Stevens, S. S., and Davis, H. *Hearing.* New York: Wiley, 1938.

Tasaki, I. Nerve impulses in individual auditory nerve fibers of guinea pigs. *J. Neurophysiol.,* 1954, **17**, 97–122.

Weddell, G. Somesthesis and the chemical senses. *Ann. Rev. Psychol.,* 1955, **6**, 119–136.

Wever, E. G. *Theory of hearing.* New York: Wiley, 1949.

Wever, E. G., and Bray, C. W. Action currents in the auditory nerve in response to acoustical stimulation. *Proc. Nat. Acad. Sci.,* 1930, **16**, 344–350.

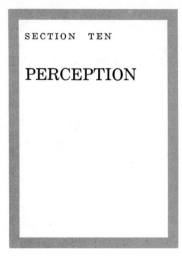

SECTION TEN

PERCEPTION

In recent years, it has become more and more apparent that the nervous system acts in a unified manner. Thus, it is now an accepted fact, based in part upon evidence similar to that presented here, that there is efferent outflow from the central nervous system to the peripheral sense organs. The afferent input to the central nervous system from most of the receptors is modified by the central nervous system itself. When a system acts in this way to regulate its own activity, the principle of negative feedback *is said to be in operation. This article illustrates this important principle of CNS functioning for auditory reception.*

The article also suggests a possible mechanism for the selection of sensory inputs which may be related to attentive behavior.

POINTS TO GUIDE YOUR STUDY *(1) If you have difficulty with your first reading of this article, read it again. Look up words you don't know. (2) The article illustrates an important technique which is much used in neurophysiology and physiological psychology—the implantation of electrodes for stimulation or recording. A stereotaxic instrument, a device for locating certain points inside the skull, is usually used in this implantation process. One works from a map of the brain on which the various structures are numbered by a series of coordinates. These coordinates are usually in terms of so many millimeters anterior or posterior from a certain point of reference, so many millimeters lateral from the midline, and so many millimeters deep. The animal's head is placed in the stereotaxic instrument, which is then set at the posterior-anterior and lateral map coordinates, and the electrode, in an electrode carrier, is then lowered to the proper depth. It is to be hoped that the electrode will then be in the structure indicated on the map. (3) Compare the behavioral and CNS records in Figure 1.*

37: MODIFICATION OF ELECTRIC ACTIVITY IN COCHLEAR NUCLEUS DURING "ATTENTION" IN UNANESTHETIZED CATS

Raúl Hernández-Peón, University of Mexico, Harald Scherrer, University of British Columbia, and Michel Jouvet, University of Lyon

Attention involves the selective awareness of certain sensory messages with the simultaneous suppression of others. Our sense organs are activated by a great variety of sensory stimuli, but relatively few evoke conscious sensation at any given moment. It is common experience that there is a pronounced reduction of extraneous sensory awareness when our attention is concentrated on some particular matter. During the attentive state, it seems as though the brain integrates for consciousness only a limited amount of sensory information, specifically, those impulses concerned with the object of attention.

An interference with impulses initiated by sensory stimuli other than those pertaining to the subject of attention seems to be an obvious possibility. It is clear that this afferent blockade might occur at any point along the classical sensory pathways from receptors to the cortical receiving areas, or else perhaps in the recently disclosed extraclassical sensory paths that traverse the brain-stem reticular system (1).

Recent evidence indicates the existence of central mechanisms that regulate sensory transmission. It has been shown that appropriate stimulation of the brain-stem reticular system will inhibit afferent conduction between the first- and second-order neurons in all three principal somatic paths (2–4). During central anesthesia, the afferent-evoked potentials in the first sensory relays are enhanced. This appears to be due to the release of a tonic descending inhibitory influence that operates during wakefulness and requires the functional integrity of the brain-stem reticular formation.

The possibility that a selective central inhibitory mechanism might operate during attention for filtering sensory impulses was tested by studying (5) afferent transmission in the second- or third-order neurons of the auditory pathway (cochlear nucleus) in unanesthetized, unrestrained cats during experimentally elicited attentive behavior. Bipolar stainless steel electrodes with a total diameter of 0.5 mm were implanted stereotaxically in the dorsal cochlear nucleus through a small hole bored in the skull. The electrode was fixed to the skull with dental cement. A minimum of 1 week elapsed between the operation and the first electroencephalographic recordings. Electric impulses in the form of short bursts of rectangular waves (0.01 to 0.02 sec) at a frequency of 1000 to 5000 cy/sec were delivered to a loudspeaker near the cats at an intensity comfortable to human observers in the same environment.

Three types of sensory modalities were used to attract the animal's attention: visual, olfactory, and somatic. As is illustrated in Figure 1, during presentation of visual stimuli (two mice in a closed bottle), the auditory responses in the cochlear nucleus were greatly reduced in comparison with the control responses; they were practically abolished as long as the visual stimuli elicited behavioral evidence of attention. When the mice were removed, the auditory responses returned to the same order of magnitude as the initial controls. An olfactory stimulus that attracted the animal's attention produced a similar blocking effect. While the cat was

R. Hernández-Peón, H. Scherrer, and M. Jouvet. Modification of electric activity in cochlear nucleus during "attention" in unanesthetized cats. *Science*, 1956, **123**, 331–332. Copyright © 1956 by the American Association for the Advancement of Science. Reprinted here with permission from the senior author, for the authors, and the American Association for the Advancement of Science.

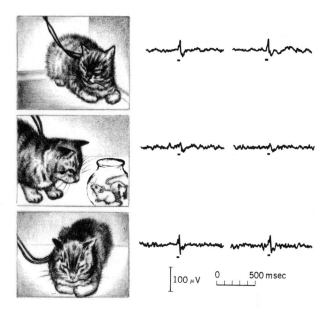

FIGURE 1 *Direct recording of click responses in the cochlear nucleus during three periods: the photographs were taken simultaneously. Top and bottom, cat is relaxed; the click responses are large. Middle, while the cat is visually attentive to the mice in the jar, the click responses are diminished in amplitude.*

attentively sniffing tubing through which fish odors were being delivered, the auditory potential in the cochlear nucleus was practically absent (Figure 2). After the stimulus had been removed and when the cat appeared to be relaxed once more, the auditorily evoked responses in the cochlear nucleus were of the same magnitude as they had been prior to the olfactory stimulation. Similarly, a nociceptive shock delivered to the forepaw of the cat—a shock that apparently distracted the animal's attention—resulted in marked reduction of auditorily evoked responses in the cochlear nucleus.

If this sensory inhibition during attentive behavior, as demonstrated in the auditory pathway, occurs in all other sensory paths except the ones concerned with the object of attention, such an inhibitory mechanism might lead to favoring of the attended object by the selective exclusion of incoming signals. It is conceivable not only that such a selective sensory inhibition might operate simultaneously for various sensory modalities, leaving one or more

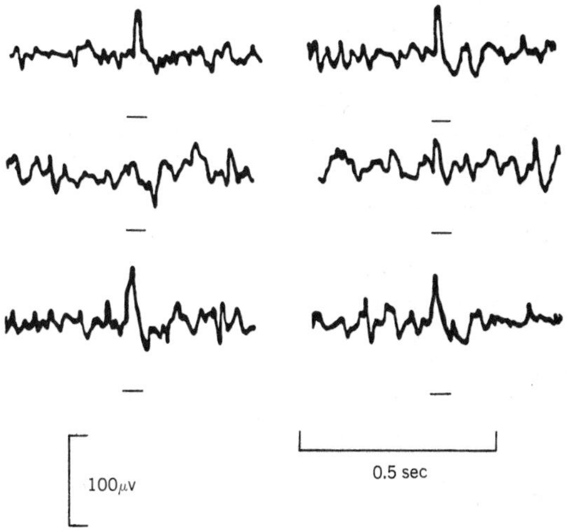

FIGURE 2 *Click responses recorded from the cochlear nucleus of the cat. Top, cat is relaxed; middle, cat is attentively sniffing an olfactory stimulus; bottom, cat is relaxed again. Note the reduced amplitude of the click responses when the animal is sniffing.*

unaffected but that the selectivity could extend to some discriminable aspects of any single modality—for example, to one tone and not to others. This suggestion finds support in the recent demonstration that sensory "habituation" may occur to a particular tone—that is, a slowly developing inhibitory effect on auditorily evoked potentials observed in the cochlear nucleus on prolonged repetition of a given tone, an influence that does not affect other frequencies that are novel to the animal (6). The pathway by which this inhibitory influence acts on incoming auditory impulses remains to be determined, but experiments now in progress have shown that during electric stimulation of the midbrain reticular formation, the auditory potential in the cochlear nucleus is depressed (7).

The present observations suggest that the blocking of afferent impulses in the lower portions of a sensory path may be a mechanism whereby sensory stimuli out of the scope of attention can be markedly reduced while they are still in their trajectory toward higher levels of the central nervous system. This central inhibitory mechanism may, therefore, play an important role in selective exclusion of sensory messages along their passage toward mechanisms of perception and consciousness. In a recent symposium on brain mecha-

nisms and consciousness, Adrian pointed out that "the signals from the sense organs must be treated differently when we attend to them and when we do not, and if we could decide where and how the divergence arises we should be nearer to understanding how the level of consciousness is reached" (8).

References and notes

1. J. D. French, M. Verzeano, H. W. Magoun, *Arch. Neurol. Psychiat.* 69, 505 (1953).
2. K.-E. Hagbarth and D. I. B. Kerr, *J. Neurophysiol.* 17, 295 (1954).
3. R. Hernández-Peón and K.-E. Hagbarth, *ibid.* 18, 44 (1955).
4. H. Scherrer and R. Hernández-Peón, *Federation Proc.* 14, 132 (1955).
5. This work was aided by grants from the Commonwealth Fund, the National Institute for Neurological Diseases and Blindness of the U.S. Public Health Service, and Eli Lilly and Company. This report is based on a paper presented before the American Physiological Society on 12 Apr. 1955.
6. R. Hernández-Peón and H. Scherrer, *Federation Proc.* 14, 71 (1955); R. Hernández-Peón, M. Jouvet, H. Scherrer, in preparation.
7. M. Jouvet, E. Berkowitz, R. Hernández-Peón, in preparation.
8. E. D. Adrian, in *Brain Mechanisms and Consciousness*, J. F. Delafresnaye, Ed. (Blackwell, Oxford, 1954), p. 238.

One of the enduring problems of perception is this: Is the perceptual organization involved in the seeing of visual depth innate (nativistic theory)? Or must this organization be acquired through experience with visual depth (empiricist theory)? This selection describes an ingenious apparatus for testing depth perception in animals, and points toward some answers to these questions.

POINTS TO GUIDE YOUR STUDY   *(1) For depth perception in the rat, what tentative answer do the authors give to the nativist-empiricist question?   (2) Note the control condition. The apparent depth of the two sides of the apparatus was equated to control for factors other than depth which might influence the choice of a particular side. As a general point, one should always try to eliminate factors other*

than the experimental ones which might affect the dependent variable
under study. The most satisfying experiments are the ones which
do this most adequately.   (3) The p values in this experiment have
the same statistical interpretation as they do in other experiments.
(See the article by Braun and Geiselhart in Section Three.)

38: BEHAVIOR OF LIGHT- AND DARK-REARED RATS ON A VISUAL CLIFF

R. D. Walk, George Washington University, E. J. Gibson, Cornell University,
T. J. Tighe, Dartmouth College

From the 18th century to the present the empiricist and the nativist theories of depth perception have been vigorously debated. One experiment aimed at resolving the dispute is Lashley and Russell's (1), in which rats reared in darkness jumped to a platform from a stand placed at a variable distance from it. The force of the jump was found to be graded in accordance with the distance of the platform. This is evidence for nativism. But, since the tests with graduated distances were not given until the rats' third day in the light, and after pretraining, the conclusion was not indubitable. Confirmation by another technique is desirable and has been provided in the experiment described in this report (2).

A technique of testing for visual depth perception which involves no pretraining at all—the "visual cliff"—was developed. It is based on the assumption that, given a choice, an animal will avoid descending over a vertical edge to a surface which appears to be far away (3). The apparatus (Fig. 1) was constructed of two thicknesses of glass (24 in. by 32 in.), parallel to the floor and held by metal supports 53 in. above it. A board (4 in. wide, 24 in. long, and 3 in. high) extended across the glass, dividing it into two equal fields. On one side (the "near" side), patterned wallpaper was inserted between the two sheets of glass. Through the clear glass of the other side (the "far" side) the same pattern was visible on the floor and also on the walls below the glass surface.

Optically speaking, the edge on one side of the board dropped away for a distance of 53 in. (making the simulated cliff), while on the other side the edge dropped away for only 3 in. Thus, two visual fields existed, both filled with patterned wallpaper, but the pattern of the "far" field was optically much smaller and denser than that of the other and elicited more motion parallax. (More binocular parallax

FIGURE 1 *Apparatus for the experimental condition. The larger-checked field is the "near" side, optically; the clear glass field is the "far" or "cliff" side.*

was also possible at one edge than at the other, but the rat is probably insensitive to this cue.) The fields were matched for reflected luminous intensity. The physical space, as distinguished from the optical space, was identical on both sides, since a glass surface was present at a distance of 3 in. The only difference between the two fields, therefore, was a difference in optical stimulation. Other possible cues for safe descent (tactual, olfactory, auditory echolocation, air currents, or temperature differentials) were equalized by the glass.

In addition to the experimental condition described here, a control condition was included, in order to check on the presence of any unknown factors that would make for a preference for one side. A piece of wallpaper was inserted between the glass on both sides (Fig. 2); otherwise, the apparatus was identical to that for the experimental condition. If controls are adequate, animals should show no preference for either side in this case.

Subjects for the experimental condition were 19 dark-reared, hooded rats, 90 days old, and 29 light-reared litter mates.

FIGURE 2 *Apparatus for the control condition.*

Twenty minutes after coming into the light, the dark-reared rats were placed on the apparatus. An animal was placed on the center board in a box, to avoid any handling bias. It was then observed for 5 minutes. Results are summarized in Table 1. The percentage of animals that descended on the near side was not significantly different for light- and dark-reared rats. Of the light-reared rats, 23 descended on the near side, three descended on the far side, and three remained on the board for all 5 minutes. Of the dark-reared rats, 14 descended on the near side, three descended on the far side, and two remained on the board.

But a comparison of descent behavior of the experimental animals with the controls, for whom the visual surface was near on both sides, showed a difference. The control group, all light-reared litter mates of the experimental group, showed no preference in descending from the board; five went to each side. This group differs significantly from the experimental group ($p < 0.02$).

Even more interesting is a comparison of the exploratory behavior of the animals. The light-reared and dark-reared rats of the experimental group again behaved similarly; most of them stayed on the side of the center board that they had first chosen. Of the 43 experimental animals that descended from the board, only one crossed to the other side. But the control animals explored back and forth, often crossing the board to the other side several times. The difference in crossing behavior between experimental and control groups is highly significant ($p < 0.001$). The percentage of time spent on the two sides confirms the other measurements. Both experimental groups spent more than twice as much time on the side with the near optical pattern as on the side with the far optical pattern, while the control animals reversed this trend.

TABLE 1 *Comparison of light- and dark-reared animals on a visual cliff (experimental group) and comparison of both with a no-cliff control group*

| | EXPERIMENTAL GROUP | | CONTROL GROUP |
	LIGHT-REARED ($N = 29$)	DARK-REARED ($N = 19$)	LIGHT-REARED ($N = 10$)
Percentage descending on "near" side	88.5	82.4	50.0
Mean no. crossings	0.00	0.06	1.70
Percentage of time			
On "near"	76.0	57.9	24.1
On "far"*	10.0	16.9	61.5
On board	14.0	25.2	14.4

* The control group had no optically "far" side. Reference is to the same physical side that was "far" for the experimental group.

These results suggest two conclusions. First, hooded rats, 90 days of age, do discriminate visual depth or distance. They avoid a visual cliff as compared with a short visual drop-off, and this preference is eliminated when the visual cliff is eliminated. Second, such discrimination seems to be independent of previous visual experience, since dark-reared adult animals behaved like their light-reared litter mates only 20 minutes after being exposed to the light.

References and notes

1. K. S. Lashley and J. T. Russell, *J. Genet. Psychol.* **45**, 136 (1934).
2. This research was supported, in part, by a grant from the National Science Foundation. We wish to thank J. J. Gibson, for suggestions about apparatus and stimulus conditions.
3. The work of K. T. Waugh [*J. Comp. Neurol.* **20**, 549 (1910)] and J. T. Russell [*J. Genet. Psychol.* **40**, 136 (1932)] makes this assumption seem plausible. Latency of jumping or "disinclination to jump" apparently increased as distance increased.

This will be a good article to read more than once. It is packed with experimental findings which bear on a number of aspects of the problem of perception without awareness.

POINTS TO GUIDE YOUR STUDY *(1)* Research on behavior without awareness. *Try to remember: (a) the method, results, and authors of one of the "zero confidence" experiments; (b) one of the studies on the learning of a subliminal discrimination; and (c) one of the studies showing the strengthening of responses with "unnoticed" rewards.* *(2)* Effects of inner states upon thresholds. *Try to remember the results and the authors of several of these experiments. The influence of needs, values, attitudes, emotions, and motivation on perceptual organization has been called the "new look" in perception.* *(3) If you were an advertiser thinking about using these techniques, what are some of the methodological problems you would want answered?* *(4) Psychology, in common with other*

*professions, has ethical problems. Guidelines have been formulated
and are published in a book,* Ethical Standards of Psychologists. *These
are only guidelines, however, and the particular problems which
arise often require anguished decision by the individual involved.*

39: SUBLIMINAL STIMULATION: AN OVERVIEW

James V. McConnell, Richard L. Cutler, and Elton B. McNeil, University of Michigan

Seldom has anything in psychology caused such an immediate and widespread stir as the recent claim that the presentation of certain stimuli below the level of conscious awareness can influence people's behavior in a significant way. The controversy was precipitated primarily by a commercial firm which claimed that the subliminal presentation of the words "Eat Popcorn" and "Drink Coca-Cola" fantastically stimulated the respective sales of these products among the motion picture audiences who received the stimulation. Despite the fact that detailed reports of the experiment have not been made directly available in any published form, this technique was seized upon as the newest of the "new look" promises of the application of psychology to advertising. While such claims and demonstrations will be considered in greater detail below, it is important to note here that they have given rise to a series of charges and countercharges, the effects of which have reached the United States Congress and the Federal Communications Commission (7, 117).

Rarely does a day pass without a statement in the public press relating to the Utopian promise or the 1984 threat of the technique (8, 17, 29, 37, 42, 45, 118, 132). Since the process of choosing up sides promises to continue unabated, it appears wise to provide the potential combatants with a more factual basis for arriving at their positions than presently seems available. Meanwhile, the present writers have cautiously sought to avoid aligning themselves behind either of the barricades.

Obviously, the notion that one may influence the behavior of another individual without the individual's knowing about it is a fascinating one. It is of extreme interest, not only to psychologists and advertisers, but also to politicians, psychiatrists, passionate young men, and others, whose motives would be considered more or less sacred by the larger society. Equally obvious is the need for a clarification of the issues surrounding the application of subliminal perception. This clarification must involve the assessment of available scientific evidence, the answering of a series of technical questions, and the examination of what, if any, levels of behavior may indeed be influenced. Finally, a series of extremely complex ethical issues need to be explored. It is the purpose of the present paper to undertake this task, in the hope of providing information upon which possible decisions involving its application may be based.

Recent history of the technique

The custom of providing a chronological review of the literature will be violated in this paper, inasmuch as three separate threads of investigation seem worth tracing: (a) the recent demonstrations by advertisers which first aroused large-scale public interest in subliminal perception,

J. V. McConnell, R. L. Cutler, and E. B. McNeil. Subliminal stimulation: an overview. *Amer. Psychologist,* 1958, **13,** 229–242. Copyright © 1958 by the American Psychological Association. Excerpts reprinted here with permission from the authors and the American Psychological Association.

(b) systematic research by psychologists relating directly to the influencing of behavior without the individual's awareness that he is being influenced, and (c) psychological research concerned primarily with the influence of inner states of the organism upon the threshold for conscious recognition of certain stimuli.

RECENT   ADVERTISING   DEMONSTRATIONS
While the advertising possibilities of subliminal stimulation were recognized by Hollingworth (59) as early as 1913, the intensive work in its application to this area has been carried out within the past two years. In 1956, BBC-TV, in conjunction with one of its regular broadcasts, transmitted the message "Pirie Breaks World Record" at a speed assumed to be subliminal (85). At the conclusion of the regular program, viewers were asked to report whether they had noticed "anything unusual" about the program. While no reliable statistical data are available, it seems possible that those few viewers responding to the message possessed sufficiently low thresholds so that for them the message was supraliminal.

A demonstration by the commercial enterprise which has been most vocal in its claims for the advertising promise of the technique consisted of projecting, during alternate periods, the words "Eat Popcorn" and "Drink Coca-Cola" during the regular presentation of a motion picture program. As a result of this stimulation, reports contend,[1] popcorn sales rose more than 50% and Coca-Cola sales 18%, as compared to a "previous period." Despite the likelihood of serious methodological and technical defects (exposure time was reported as 1/3,000 sec., far faster than any previously reported stimulation), this demonstration

has been the one which has caused the most stir in both the fields of advertising and psychology. There were no reports, however, of even the most rudimentary scientific precautions, such as adequate controls, provision for replication, etc., which leaves the skeptical scientist in a poor position to make any judgment about the validity of the study.

In a later demonstration for the press, technical difficulties permitted the viewers to become consciously aware of the fact that they were being stimulated. Although described as a purposeful and prearranged part of the demonstration, it left many of the reporters present unconvinced that the technical difficulties inherent in the technique have been surmounted.

The FCC, turning its attention to the problem, has reported that one TV station (WTWO, Bangor, Maine) has experimented with the transmission of public service announcements at subliminal levels, with "negative results" (117).

The uncontrolled and unsystematic nature of the demonstrations reported above makes very difficult the task of reaching a trustworthy conclusion about the effectiveness of subliminal stimulation in advertising. Whether the technique represents a promising means of communicating with the individual at a level of his unconsciousness or whether it reflects only the hyperenthusiasm of an entrepreneurial group remain unanswered questions.

RESEARCH ON BEHAVIOR WITHOUT AWARENESS In the hope of providing a more substantial foundation upon which to base judgments of the validity of advertising claims for subliminal stimulation, a systematic review of relevant scientific work was undertaken. While we believe that our review was comprehensive, we have decided not to provide an extensive critical discussion of the various studies, choosing instead to present summative statements and conclusions based upon what seems to

---

[1] The essential facts of this study have not been reported in any journal. The discussion of this experiment and the findings reported by the commercial enterprise responsible for the study is based on reports in several general news accounts appearing in the popular press (7, 8, 16, 17, etc.).

be sufficient evidence and consensus in the literature.[2]

The work of experimental psychologists in subliminal stimulation dates from Suslowa (119) in 1863, as reported by Baker (5). Suslowa's experiments concerned the effect of electrical stimulation upon subjects' ability to make two-point threshold discriminations. He found that, even when the intensity of the electrical stimulation was so low that the subjects were not aware of its presence, their ability to discriminate one- from two-point stimulation was somewhat reduced.

In 1884, Peirce and Jastrow (94) were able to show that subjects could discriminate differences between weights significantly better than chance would allow, even though the differences were so small they had no confidence whatsoever in their judgments.

Numerous experimenters have relied upon this criterion of "zero confidence" to establish that discrimination of stimuli presented below the level of conscious awareness is possible. For example, Sidis (107) showed that subjects could reliably distinguish letters from numbers, even when the stimuli were presented at such a distance from them that the subjects thought they were relying on pure guesswork for their judgments.

In what was essentially a replication of Sidis' research, Stroh, Shaw, and Washburn (116) found evidence to support his conclusions. They found similar results when auditory stimuli (whispers) were presented at a distance such that the subjects were not consciously aware that they were hearing anything.

Several experiments have provided further support for Peirce and Jastrow's initial conclusions (44, 127). Baker (5) found subjects able to discriminate diag-

onal from vertical crossed lines, and a dot-dash from a dash-dot auditory pattern. Miller (88) presented five geometric figures at four different levels of intensity below the threshold and found that, while subjects could discriminate which was being presented a significant proportion of the time, their ability to discriminate was reduced as the intensity of stimulation was further reduced. More recently, a series of studies by Blackwell (11) has shown that subjects can reliably identify during which of four time periods a subliminal spot of light is presented upon a homogeneous field. Blackwell, however, stresses that reliability of discrimination decreases as the intensity of the stimulus is further lowered. Several other supporting studies are available (28, 97, 130) which show essentially the same results, namely, that even when subjects have zero confidence in their judgments, they can discriminate reliably (though not perfectly) between stimuli.

In his review, Adams (1) points out certain general weaknesses inherent in studies of this type, but agrees with the present authors that discrimination can occur under certain circumstances. However, it is interesting to note that, in nearly all studies reporting relevant data, the reliability of the subjects' judgment increases directly with the intensity of the stimuli. If a valid extrapolation can be drawn from this finding, it would be that accuracy of perception increases as the stimulation approaches a supraliminal level.

A second series of studies has involved presenting subjects with variations of the Mueller-Lyer illusion, in which the angular lines have differed, subliminally, in hue or brightness from the background. The first of these studies, reported by Dunlap in 1909 (36), gave clear evidence that the subjects were influenced in their judgments of line length, even though they could not "see" the angular lines. Several replications of this study have been carried out, and while at least three have found partial

---

[2] The reader who wishes a more complete technical critique of studies in the field is referred to reviews by Adams (1), Collier (27), Coover (28), Lazarus and McCleary (76), and Miller (90).

support for Dunlap's conclusions (14, 59, 86), others have failed to find the phenomenon (123). In another experiment conducted by Sidis in 1898 (107), subjects asked to fixate on a number series in the center of a card, and then asked to pick a number from this series, systematically chose that number which was written in the periphery of the card, even though they were not consciously aware of its presence. Coover (28) in 1917 showed essentially the same results by asking subjects to pick a number at random while they were fixating on a letter in the upper right portion of a card. He found that subjects tended to pick the number printed in the lower left of the card, even though they did not *usually* know it was there. In similar experiments, Collier (27) and Perky (95) showed that subjects could be made to produce drawings, even though they were not aware that they were being influenced in their actions. While these studies are not unequivocal in their findings, nor generally rigorous in their methodology, they too seem to support the contention that behavior of a sort can be influenced by subliminal means. However, they require cautious interpretation, since the degree of the subject's attention to the stimuli seems clearly to be a factor. Further, as contrasted to those studies where the subject is actually aware in advance of at least the general nature of the stimulation, these studies reveal a somewhat less pronounced effect of subliminal stimulation upon the subject's behavior.

While the studies reported above seem to indicate that discrimination without awareness may occur, it may reasonably be asked whether stimulation below the level of conscious awareness can produce any but the most simple modifications in behavior. A series of studies (24, 26, 73, 109), beginning with Newhall and Sears in 1933 (92), have attempted to show that it is possible to condition subjects to subliminal stimuli. Newhall and Sears found

it possible to establish a weak and unstable conditioned response to light presented subliminally, when the light had been previously paired with shock. Baker (6) in 1938 reported the successful conditioning of the pupillary reflex to a subliminal auditory stimulus, but later experimenters have failed to replicate his results (57, 128). In a now classic experiment, McCleary and Lazarus (79) found that nonsense syllables which had previously been associated with shock produced a greater psychogalvanic reflex when presented tachistoscopically at subliminal speeds than did nonshock syllables. Deiter (34) confirmed the McCleary and Lazarus findings and showed further that, when verbal instructions were substituted for the shock, no such differences were produced. Bach and Klein (4) have recently reported that they were able to influence subjects' judgments of whether the line drawing of a face (essentially neutral in its emotional expression) was "angry" or "happy" by projecting the appropriate words at subliminal speeds upon the drawings.

A series of related studies (58, 65, 89, 99, 105, 121, 122) have shown that, even when the subject is not aware that any cue is being given, certain responses can be learned or strengthened during the experimental process. For example, Cohen, Kalish, Thurston, and Cohen (25) showed that, when the experimenter said "right" to any sentence which the subject started with "I" or "We," the number of such sentences increased significantly. Klein (69) was able to produce both conditioning and extinction without awareness, using the Cohen *et al.* technique.

Several experimenters have used subliminal or "unnoticed" reward-punishment techniques to modify subjects' responses in a variety of situations, including free or chained association tasks, performance on personality tests, and interview-elicited conversation (35, 41, 50, 56, 72, 78, 93, 120, 125, 126). Typical is the work of

Greenspoon (48), who reinforced the use of plural nouns by saying "mm-humm" after each plural mentioned by the subject. He found that, even though none of his subjects could verbalize the relationship between their response and his reinforcement, their use of plural nouns doubled. Sidowski (108) demonstrated essentially the same thing using a light, of which the subject was only peripherally aware, as a reinforcer for the use of plural words. Weiss (129), however, failed to find any increase in the frequency of "living things" responses, using a right-wrong reinforcement to free associations by the subjects.

This evidence suggests that subjects may either (a) "learn" certain subliminally presented stimuli or (b) make use of subliminal reinforcers either to learn or strengthen a previously learned response. Again, the critical observations of Adams (1) and the introduction of other possible explanations by Bricker and Chapanis (15) make necessary a cautious interpretation of these results.

EFFECTS OF INNER STATES UPON THRESH-OLDS Whatever the possibility that subliminal stimulation may significantly alter behavior, there is excellent evidence that certain inner states of the organism, as well as externally induced conditions, may significantly alter the recognition threshold of the individual. This, of course, has important implications for the susceptibility of the individual to the effects of subliminal stimulation. It is well known that physiological factors, such as fatigue, visual acuity, or satiation, may change the threshold of an individual for various kinds of stimuli.

Recent evidence has accumulated to show that, in addition to these physiological factors, certain "psychological states," such as psychological need, value, conflict, and defense, may also significantly influence thresholds, as well as other aspects of the perceptual process. Early work in this area is reported by Sanford (102, 103)

who showed that subjects who had been deprived of food were more prone to produce "food-relevant" responses to a series of ambiguous stimuli. McClelland and Atkinson (80) showed that levels of the hunger drive were systematically related to the ease with which food responses were made when no words were presented on the screen.

While a complete review of the experimental work on "perceptual defense" and "selective vigilance" would take us too far afield, it seems wise to indicate, by example, some of the inner state factors which allegedly produce variations in recognition threshold. Bruner and Postman (19, 20, 21) and Bruner and Goodman (18) were able to show that such factors as symbolic value, need, tension and tension release, and emotional selectivity were important in the perceptual process. Ansbacher (3) had earlier demonstrated that the perception of numerosity was significantly affected by the monetary value of the stimuli. Rees and Israel (101) called attention to the fact that the mental set of the organism was an important factor in the perceptual process. Beams and Thompson (9) showed that emotional factors were important determiners of the perception of the magnitude of need-relevant objects. Other studies bearing upon the issue of inner state determiners of perception are reported by Carter and Schooler (23), Cowen and Beier (31, 32), and Levine, Chein, and Murphy (77).

More specifically related to the issue of altered recognition thresholds is a study by McGinnies (82) in which he demonstrated that emotionally toned words had generally higher thresholds than neutral words. Blum (13) has shown that subjects tend to be less likely to choose conflict-relevant stimuli from a group presented at subliminal speeds than to choose neutral stimuli. Lazarus, Eriksen, and Fonda (75) have shown that personality factors are at least in part determiners of the recognition threshold for classes of auditory stimuli.

Reece (100) showed that the association of shock with certain stimuli had the effect of raising the recognition threshold for those stimuli.

While many writers have contended that the variations in threshold can be accounted for more parsimoniously than by introducing "motivational" factors such as need and value (60, 61, 111), and while the issue of the degree to which need states influence perception is still unresolved (22, 39, 40, 62, 74, 83), it is apparent that the recognition threshold is not a simple matter of intensity nor speed of presentation. Recent work by Postman and others (47, 96, 98), which has sought to illuminate the prerecognition processes operating to produce the apparent changes in threshold, does not alter the fact that individual differences in the perceptual process must be taken into account in any further work on the effects of subliminal stimulation.

Unanswered methodological questions

Having now concluded that, under certain conditions, the phenomenon of subliminal perception does occur, we turn our attention next to the many unanswered questions which this conclusion raises. For example, what kinds of behavior can be influenced by subliminal stimulation? What types of stimuli operate best at sub-threshold intensities? Do all subliminal stimuli operate at the same "level of unconsciousness," or do different stimuli (or modes of stimulation) affect different levels of unconsciousness? What characteristics of the perceiver help determine the effectiveness of subliminal stimulation? All of these questions, as well as many others of a technological nature, will be discussed in the ensuing paragraphs.

A few words of caution concerning the word "subliminal" seem in order, however. It must be remembered that the psychological limen is a statistical concept, a fact overlooked by far too many current textbook writers. The common definition of the limen is "that stimulus value which gives a response exactly half the time" (44, p. 111). One of the difficulties involved in analyzing the many studies on subliminal perception is the fact that many experimenters have assumed that, because the stimuli which they employed were below the statistical limen for a given subject, the stimuli were therefore never consciously perceivable by the subject. This is, of course, not true. Stimuli slightly below the statistical limen might well be consciously perceivable as much as 49% of the time. Not only this, but thresholds vary from moment to moment, as well as from day to day. All this is not to deny that stimuli which are so weak that they are never consciously reportable under any circumstances may indeed influence behavior. We simply wish to make the point that the range of stimulus intensities which are in fact "subliminal" may be smaller than many experimenters in the past have assumed. It has been commonly assumed that the several methods of producing subliminal stimuli, i.e., reducing intensity, duration, size, or clarity, are logically and methodologically equivalent. While this may be true, it remains to be demonstrated conclusively.

TYPES OF BEHAVIOR INFLUENCED BY SUBLIMINAL STIMULATION   One of the first questions that springs to mind concerns the types of response which can be elicited with subliminal stimulation. Let us assume for the moment that the below-threshold advertisements used in commercial demonstrations were the sole cause of increased popcorn buying among the movie audiences subjected to the ads. How did this come about? Did the stimulus "Eat Popcorn" elicit an already established response in some members of the audience? Or did the frequent repetitions of the stimulus message cause a shift in attitude towards popcorn eating which eventually resulted in the purchase of popcorn at the first opportunity the audience had? Did the ads merely raise an already existing, presumably learned, but weak need for popcorn to an above the action-threshold level, or did the ads actually create a need for popcorn where no need had existed beforehand? Did members of the audience rise like automatons during the course of the movie and thus miss part of the feature in order to satisfy a sudden craving for popcorn or in order to respond to a suddenly evoked stimulus-response connection? Or did they wait until a "rest period" to do their purchasing? How many patrons bought popcorn only after they had seen the film and were heading home? How many people purchased popcorn on their way *in* to see the next movie they attended? How many of those who purchased popcorn did so for the first time in their lives, or for the first time in recent memory? What if the message presented had been "Buy Christmas Seals," which are available only in one season? How many people failed to buy popcorn at the theater, but purchased it subsequently at the local supermarket?

Unfortunately, these pertinent questions have yet to be answered. Let us tentatively accept this demonstration that impulse buying of inexpensive items such as popcorn and Coca-Cola can be influenced by subliminal advertising, without yet knowing what the mechanism involved is. It remains to be demonstrated, however, that such ads could make a person of limited means wreck himself financially by purchasing a Cadillac merely because the ads told him to do so. Nor do we know if deep-seated, strongly emotional attitudes or long-established behavior patterns can be shifted one way or another as a result of subliminal stimulation. The answers to these questions must come from further experimentation.

TECHNOLOGICAL PROBLEMS INVOLVED IN STIMULATING SUBJECTS SUBLIMINALLY The paucity of data presented by those dealing with subliminal perception on a commercial basis, as well as the equivocal nature of their results, suggests that there are many technological problems yet to be solved by these and other investigators. For example, during a two-hour movie (or a one-hour television show), how many times should the stimulus be repeated to make sure that the "message" gets across to the largest possible percentage of the audience? Should the stimulus be repeated every second, every five seconds, only once a minute? Is the effect cumulative, or is one presentation really enough? Is there a satiation effect, such that the audience becomes "unconsciously tired" of the stimulation, and "unconsciously blocks" the incoming subliminal sensations? Should the stimuli be presented "between frames" of the movie (that is, when the shutter of the film projector is closed and the screen momentarily blank as it is 24 times each second), or should the message be presented only when the screen already has a picture on it? How close to the threshold (statistical or otherwise) should the stimuli be? How many words long can the message be? If the message must be short, could successive stimulations present sequential parts of a longer advertisement? How much of the screen should the stimuli fill? Should the stimuli be presented only during "happier" moments in the film, in order to gain positive affect? Does any affect transfer at all from the film to the ad? Should one use pictures, or are words best? Must the words be familiar ones? And what about subliminal auditory, cutaneous, and olfactory stimulation?

As we have stated before, there has been so much talk and so little experimentation, and much of what experimentation has been done is so inadequately reported, that we can merely hazard guesses based on related but perhaps not always applicable studies.

To begin with, we can state with some assurance that, the closer to the threshold of awareness the stimuli are, the more effect they are likely to have. Study after study has reported increased effectiveness with increased intensity of stimulation (5, 14, 88, 97, 104). The main difficulty seems to be that thresholds vary so much from subject to subject (112), and from day to day (114), that what is subliminal but effective for one person is likely to be subliminal but ineffective for a second, and supraliminal for a third. As is generally the case, anyone who wishes to use the technique of subliminal stimulation must first experiment upon the specific group of people whom he wishes to influence before he can decide what intensity levels will be most efficacious.

Somewhat the same conclusion holds for the question of how many times the stimuli should be presented. While under some conditions subliminal stimuli which did not influence behavior when presented only once seemed to "summate" when presented many times (10, 66), Bricker and Chapanis (15) found that one presentation of a stimulus slightly below the (statistical) limen was enough to increase the likelihood of its being recognized on subsequent trials. We interpret this to mean that too many presentations may well raise the "subliminal" stimuli above the limen of awareness if the stimuli themselves are not carefully chosen.

As for the physical properties of the message itself, we can but guess what the relevant issues are. Both verbal and pictorial presentations apparently are effective in the visual modality, but no one has tested the relative effectiveness of these two types of stimulation. Quite possibly subsequent experimentation will show that words are best for some situations (such as direct commands), while pictures are best for others.[3] It can be stated unequivo-

cally, however, that advertisers should look to their basic English when writing their subliminal commercials. Several studies have shown that, the more familiar a subject is with the stimulus he is to perceive, the more readily he perceives it (22, 54, 63, 110). We interpret these studies to mean that unfamiliar stimuli may be ineffective when presented subliminally, even though familiar messages may "get through."

The exact length the message should be, its composition, and the background in which it should be presented are variables upon which no work has been done and about which no conclusions can presently be drawn. Suffice it to say, however, that a message which would be short enough to be perceived by one person might be too long for another person to perceive under any conditions.

Which modalities are most useful for subliminal stimulation? While most of the work has been done on the visual modality, Vanderplas and Blake (124) and Kurland (71) have found subthreshold auditory stimuli to be effective, and earlier in this paper we have reported similar studies with cutaneous stimulation. Advertisers who wish to "sneak up on" their patrons by presenting subliminal stimuli in one modality while the patrons are attending to supraliminal stimuli from another modality are probably doomed to failure, however. Collier (27) presented subliminal geometric forms simultaneously to both the visual and the cutaneous modalities and found little, if any, lowering of thresholds. Correspondingly, it should be remembered that Hernández-Peón *et al.* (55) found that some part of the nervous system acts as a kind of gating mechanism, and when an organism is attending strongly to one modality, the other modalities are probably "shut off" to most incoming stimuli.

Even if experimenters succeed in finding answers to many of the questions raised

---

[3] Perhaps much of the work on sensory preconditioning is applicable here. When Ellson (38) presented his subjects with both a light and a buzzer for many trials, then presented the light alone, subjects "heard" the buzzer too.

above concerning the physical characteristics of the stimuli to be employed, it is quite probable that they will have succeeded in discovering the source of only a small part of the variance operant in subliminal perception. For, as always, the major source of variance will come from the perceiver himself.

CHARACTERISTICS OF THE PERCEIVER WHICH AFFECT SUBLIMINAL PERCEPTION   The following section of this paper might well be considered a plea for the recognition that individual differences exist and that they must be taken into account by anyone who wishes to deal with individuals. We know next to nothing about the relationships between such factors as age, sex, social class, etc., and subliminal perception. Perhaps only one study is relevant: Perky (95) found that children were as much influenced by subthreshold visual stimulation as were naïve adults. It is quite likely that many differences in the perception of subliminal stimuli do exist between individuals of differing classes, ages, and sexes. As always, only experimentation can determine what these differences are.

We do have some idea, however, of how what might be called "personality factors" influence subliminal perception. First and foremost, there seems little doubt but that a high need state affects perception. Gilchrist and Nesberg (46) found that the greater the need state, the more their subjects tended to overestimate the brightness of objects relevant to that need. It should be noted that they were dealing with difference limens, not absolute limens, but other studies to be quoted later show the same effect for absolute limens. It should be noted also that Gilchrist and Nesberg apparently overlooked evidence in their own data that a strong need affects judgments of non-need-related objects in the same direction (but not as much) as it does need-related objects. Wispe and Drambarean, dealing with visual duration

thresholds, concluded that "need-related words were recognized more rapidly as need increased" (131, p. 31). McClelland and Lieberman (81) found that subjects with high need achievement scores had lower visual thresholds for "success" words than did subjects not scoring as high on need achievement. Do all of these findings mean that subliminal ads will work only when some fairly strong need (of any kind) is present in the viewers? Only experimentation can answer this question.

What about abnormalities of personality? What effect do they have? Kurland (71) tested auditory recognition thresholds using emotional and neutral words. He found that hospitalized neurotics perceived the emotional words at significantly lower thresholds than did a group of normal subjects. Does this mean that neurotics are more likely to respond to low-intensity subliminal commands than normals? Should advertisers take a "neurotic inventory" of their audiences?

A more pertinent problem is posed by the findings of Krech and Calvin (70). Using a Wechsler Vocabulary Score of 30.5 as their cutting point, they found that almost all college students above this score showed better visual discriminations of patterns presented at close to liminal values than did almost all students scoring below the cutting point. Does this mean that the higher the IQ, the better the subliminal perception? What is the relationship between the value of the absolute limen and intelligence? Will advertisers have to present their messages at such high intensities (in order that the "average man" might perceive the message) that the more intelligent members of the audience will be consciously aware of the advertising?

One further fascinating problem is posed by Huntley's work (64). He surreptitiously obtained photographs of the hands and profiles of his subjects, as well as handwriting samples and recordings of their voices. Six months later each subject was presented with the whole series of samples, among which were his own. Each subject was asked to make preference ratings of the samples. Huntley reports evidence of a significant tendency for subjects to prefer their own forms of expression above all others, even though in most cases they were totally unaware that the samples were their own and even though many subjects were unable to identify their own samples when told they were included in the series. If an advertiser is making a direct appeal to one specific individual, it would seem then that he should make use of the photographs and recordings of that individual's behavior as the subliminal stimuli. If an advertiser is making an appeal to a more general audience, however, it might be that he would find the use of pictures and recordings of Hollywood stars, etc., more efficacious than mere line drawings, printed messages, and unknown voices.

Nor can the advertiser afford to overlook the effects of set and attention. Miller (88), Perky (95), and Blake and Vanderplas (12), among others, discovered that giving the subject the proper set lowered the recognition threshold greatly. In fact, in many cases the stimulus intensity which was subliminal but effective for sophisticated subjects was far too subliminal to have much, if any, effect upon naïve subjects. Thus advertisers might do well to tell their audiences that subliminal messages were being presented to them, in order to bring all members of that audience closer to a uniform threshold. Does this not, however, vitiate some of the effect of subliminal advertising?

As for attentional effects, we have presented evidence earlier (46) that strong needs seem to have an "alerting" effect upon the organism, lowering recognition thresholds for *all* stimuli, not just need-related stimuli. In addition to this, two studies by Hartmann (52, 53), as well as two by Spencer (113, 114), lead us to the belief that subliminal stimuli might best be presented when either the television or movie screen was blank of other pictures. Perhaps, then, subliminal commercials in movie houses should be shown between features; while on television the commercials should consist of an appropriate period of apparent "visual silence," during which the audience would not be aware of the subliminal stimulation presented, but might react to it later.

One fact emerges from all of the above. Anyone who wishes to utilize subliminal stimulation for commercial or other purposes can be likened to a stranger entering into a misty, confused countryside where there are but few landmarks. Before this technique is used in the market place, if it is to be used at all, a tremendous amount of research should be done, and by competent experimenters.

The ethics of subliminal influence

From its beginnings as a purely academic offshoot of philosophy, psychology has, with ever increasing momentum, grown in the public perception as a practical and applied discipline. As psychologists were called upon to communicate and interpret their insights and research findings to lay persons, it was necessary to make decisions about what constituted proper professional behavior, since it was evident that the misuse of such information would reflect directly on the community of psychologists. As a growing number of our research efforts are viewed as useful to society, the problem of effective and honest communication becomes magnified, although its essential nature does not change. Recently, to our dismay, the announcement of a commercial application of long-established psychological principles has assumed nightmarish qualities, and we find ourselves unwillingly cast in the role of invaders of personal privacy and enemies of society. A kind of guilt by association seems to be occurring, and, as future incidents of this kind will, it threatens to undermine the public relations we have built with years of caution and concern for the public welfare. The highly emotional public reaction to the "discovery" of subliminal perception should serve as an object lesson to our profession, for in the bright glare of publicity we can see urgent ethical issues as well as an omen of things to come. When the theoretical notion $E = MC^2$ became the applied reality of an atom bomb, the community of physicists became deeply concerned with social as well as scientific responsibility. Judging from the intensity of the public alarm when confronted with a bare minimum of fact about this subliminal social atom, there exists a clear need for psychologists to examine the ethical problems that are a part of this era of the application of their findings.

The vehemence of the reaction to the proposed use of a device to project subliminal, or from the public's point of view "hidden," messages to viewers indicates that the proposal touches a sensitive area. One of the basic contributors to this reaction seems to be the feeling that a technique which avowedly tampers with the psychological status of the individual ought to be under the regulation or control of a trusted scientific group. As a professional group, psychologists would fit this description, for in the *Ethical Standards of Psychologists* (2) there is a clear statement of their motives and relationship to society:

Principle 1.12–1 The psychologist's ultimate allegiance is to society, and his professional behavior should demonstrate an awareness of his social responsibilities. The welfare of the profession and of the individual psychologist are clearly subordinate to the welfare of the public. . . .

Both this statement and the long record of responsible behavior of the members of the profession would certainly seem to be sufficient to reduce any anxiety the public might have over the possible unscrupulous use of this or any other device. It is precisely the fact that the public *is* aware that decisions about the use of subliminal perception devices rest not with psychologists but with commercial agencies that may be distressing to the public. The aura of open-for-business flamboyance and the sketchily presented percentages in the first public announcement tended to reinforce existing apprehensions rather than allay them.

Although subliminal perception happens now to be the focus of a great deal of reaction, it is merely the most recent in a succession of perturbing events to which the public has been exposed. It has become the focus of, and is likely to become the whipping boy for, a host of techniques which now occupy the twilight zone of infringement of personal psychological freedom. It must be remembered that to the lay person the notion of an unconscious part of the "mind" is eerie, vague, and more than a little mysterious. Unable fully to comprehend the systematic and theoretical aspects of such a concept, he must be content with overly popularized and dramatic versions of it. In every form of mass media the American public has been exposed to convincing images of the bearded hypnotist (with piercing eye) who achieves his nefarious ends by controlling the unconscious of his victim. It has been treated to the spectacle of the seeming reincarnation of Bridey Murphy out of the unconscious of an American housewife and, in *Three Faces of Eve,* to complex multiple personalities hidden in the psychic recesses of a single individual. With such uncanny and disturbing images as an emotional backdrop, the appearance of *The Hidden Persuaders* on the best seller lists formed the indelible impression of the exploitation of the unconscious for purposes of profit and personal gain. In combination, this growth of emotionally charged attitudes toward the unconscious and the suspicions about commercial morality came to be a potentially explosive set of tensions which was triggered off by the first commercial use of subliminal techniques.

What is to be the psychologist's position in regard to future developments with subliminal perception? The apparent discrepancy between the claims being made for the technique and the available research evidence suggests a need for considerable scientific caution as well as extensive investigation. The responsibility of psychologists in this instance is clearly indicated in the code of ethics:

Principle 2.12–1 The psychologist should refuse to suggest, support, or condone unwarranted assumptions, invalid applications, or unjustified conclusions in the use of psychological instruments or techniques.

The flurry of claim and opinion about the effectiveness of subliminal methods seems to be based more on enthusiasm than controlled scientific experimentation, and it is here that psychology can be of service. Until acceptable scientific answers are forthcoming, we believe psychologists should guard against a premature commitment which might jeopardize public respect for them. The course of scientific history is strewn with the desiccated remains of projects pursued with more vigor than wisdom.

Scientific caution is essential, but it falls short of meeting the ethical issue raised by the nature of subliminal perception itself. The most strident public objections have been directed toward the possibility that suggestions or attempts to influence or persuade may be administered without the knowledge or consent of the audience. Assurances that widespread adoption of this technique would provide increased enjoyment through the elimination of commercial intrusions, or that the users will establish an ethical control over the content of the messages presented, can only fail to

be convincing in light of past experience. The suggestion that the public can be taught means of detecting when it is being exposed to a planned subliminal stimulation is far from reassuring since such a suggestion implies that the ability to defend oneself warrants being attacked. A captive audience is not a happy audience, and even the plan to inform the viewers in advance concerning the details of what is to be presented subliminally may not prevent the public from reacting to this technique as a demand that it surrender an additional degree of personal freedom. Fresh from similar encounters, the public may not allow this freedom to be wrested from it.

Finally, the argument that a great deal of our normal perception occurs on the fringe of conscious awareness and that subliminal events are no more effective than weak conscious stimuli rests on opinion and not fact. This seems particularly dangerous clinical ground on which to tread since the effect, on behavior, of stimuli which may possibly be inserted directly into the unconscious has yet to be explored. Assurances that this technique can only "remind" a person of something he already knows or "support" a set of urges already in existence but cannot establish a completely new set of urges or needs are reckless assertions having no evidence to support them. So it seems that the aspect of subliminal projection which is marked by the greatest potential risk to the individual's emotional equilibrium is the aspect about which the least is scientifically known.

The psychologist's ethical quandary, then, stems directly from the inescapable implication of deviousness in the use of such a technique. The appropriate guidelines for conduct are provided in this ethical statement:

Principle 2.62–2 It is unethical to employ psychological techniques for devious purposes, for entertainment, or for other reasons not consonant with the best interests of a client or with the development of psychology as a science.

It is obvious that "devious purposes" and "the best interests . . . of psychology as a science" are not self-defining terms and must be interpreted by the individual psychologist in light of the circumstances of each situation. It is a trying and complex decision to make. If in his mature judgment the intended uses of the principles of subliminal perception do not meet acceptable ethical standards, the psychologist is obligated to disassociate himself from the endeavor and to labor in behalf of the public welfare to which he owes his first allegiance. In this respect, the responsibility of the social scientist must always be that of watchdog over his own actions as well as the actions of those to whom he lends his professional support.

The furor which promises to accompany the further application of a variety of devices involving subliminal perception is certain to embroil psychology in a dispute not of its own choosing. The indiscriminate and uncontrolled application of psychological principles is increasing at a fearsome rate in the form of motivation research, propaganda, public relations, and a host of other "useful" practices based on the work of psychologists. In a very real sense this era of applied psychology will be a test of the workability of the psychologist's code of ethics and promises to stimulate the profession to give further consideration to its responsibility for assisting society to use its findings wisely.

References

1. Adams, J. K. Laboratory studies of behavior without awareness. *Psychol. Bull.,* 1957, 54, 383–405.

2. American Psychological Association, Committee on Ethical Standards for Psychology. *Ethical standards of psychologists.* Washington: APA, 1953.

3. Ansbacher, H. Perception of number as affected by the monetary value of the objects. *Arch. Psychol.,* 1937, 30, No. 215.

4. Bach, S., and Klein, G. S. Conscious effects of prolonged subliminal exposures of words. *Amer. Psychologist,* 1957, 12, 397. (Abstract)

5. Baker, L. E. The influence of subliminal stimuli upon verbal behavior. *J. Exp. Psychol.,* 1937, 20, 84–100.

6. Baker, L. E. The pupillary response conditioned to subliminal auditory stimuli. *Psychol. Monogr.,* 1938, 50, No. 3 (Whole No. 223).

7. Ban on subliminal ads, pending FCC probe, is urged. *Adv. Age,* 1957, 28, No. 45.

8. Battelle, Phyllis. The lady objects to id tampering. *Publishers Auxiliary,* 1957, 92, No. 40.

9. Beams, H. L., and Thompson, G. G. Affectivity as a factor in the perception of the magnitude of food objects. *Amer. Psychologist,* 1952, 7, 323. (Abstract)

10. Beitel, R. J., Jr. Spatial summation of subliminal stimuli in the retina of the human eye. *J. gen. Psychol.,* 1934, 10, 311–327.

11. Blackwell, H. R. Personal communication, 1958.

12. Blake, R. R., and Vanderplas, J. M. The effects of prerecognition hypotheses on veridical recognition thresholds in auditory perception. *J. Pers.,* 1950–1951, 19, 95–115.

13. Blum, G. S. Perceptual defense revisited. *J. abnorm. soc. Psychol.,* 1955, 56, 24–29.

14. Bressler, J. Illusion in the case of subliminal visual stimulation. *J. gen. Psychol.,* 1931, 5, 244–250.

15. Bricker, P. D., and Chapanis, A. Do incorrectly perceived tachistoscopic stimuli convey some information? *Psychol. Rev.,* 1953, 60, 181–188.

16. Britt, S. H. Subliminal advertising—fact or fantasy? *Adv. Age,* 1957, 28, 103.

17. Brooks, J. The little ad that isn't there. *Consumer Rep.,* 1957, 23, No. 1.

18. Bruner, J. S., and Goodman, C. C. Value and need as organizing factors in perception. *J. abnorm. soc. Psychol.,* 1947, 42, 33–44.

19. Bruner, J. S., and Postman, L. Emotional selectivity in perception and action. *J. Pers.,* 1947, 16, 69–77.

20. Bruner, J. S., and Postman, L. Tension and tension-release as organizing factors in perception. *J. Pers.,* 1947, 16, 300–308.

21. Bruner, J. S., and Postman, L. Symbolic value as an organizing factor in perception. *J. soc. Psychol.,* 1948, 27, 203–208.

22. Bruner, J. S., and Postman, L. Perception, cognition, and behavior. *J. Pers.,* 1949, **18,** 14–31.

23. Carter, L. F., and Schooler, K. Value, need, and other factors in perception. *Psychol. Rev.,* 1949, **56,** 200–207.

24. Cason, H., and Katcher, Naomi. An attempt to condition breathing and eyelid responses to a subliminal electric stimulus. *J. exp. Psychol.,* 1934, **16,** 831–842.

25. Cohen, B. D., Kalish, H. I., Thurston, J. R., and Cohen, E. Experimental manipulation of verbal behavior. *J. exp. Psychol.,* 1954, **47,** 106–110.

26. Cohen, L. H., Hilgard, E. R., and Wendt, G. R. Sensitivity to light in a case of hysterical blindness studied by reinforcement-inhibition and conditioning methods. *Yale J. Biol. Med.,* 1933, **6,** 61–67.

27. Collier, R. M. An experimental study of the effects of subliminal stimuli. *Psychol. Monogr.,* 1940, **52,** No. 5 (Whole No. 236).

28. Coover, J. E. Experiments in psychical research. *Psychical Res. Monogr.,* 1917, No. 1.

29. Cousins, N. Smudging the subconscious. *Saturday Rev.,* 1957, **40,** No. 40.

30. Cowen, E. L., and Beier, E. G. The influence of "threat-expectancy" on perception. *J. Pers.,* 1950–1951, **19,** 85–94.

31. Cowen, E. L., and Beier, E. G. A further study of the "threat-expectancy" variable in perception. *Amer. Psychologist,* 1952, **7,** 320–321. (Abstract)

32. Cowen, E. L., and Beier, E. G. Threat-expectancy, word frequencies, and perceptual prerecognition hypotheses. *J. abnorm. soc. Psychol.,* 1954, **49,** 178–182.

33. Culler, E., and Mettler, F. A. Conditioned behavior in a decorticate dog. *J. comp. Psychol.,* 1934, **18,** 291–303.

34. Deiter, J. The nature of subception. Unpublished doctoral dissertation, Univer. of Kansas, 1953.

35. Diven, K. Certain determinants in the conditioning of anxiety reactions. *J. Psychol.,* 1937, **3,** 291–308.

36. Dunlap, K. Effect of imperceptible shadows on the judgments of distance. *Psychol. Rev.,* 1900, **7,** 435–453.

37. DuShane, G. The invisible word, or no thresholds barred. *Science,* 1957, **126,** 681.

38. Ellson, D. G. Hallucinations produced by sensory conditioning. *J. exp. Psychol.,* 1941, **28,** 1–20.

39. Eriksen, C. W. The case for perceptual defense. *Psychol. Rev.,* 1954, **61,** 175–182.

40. Eriksen, C. W. Subception: Fact or artifact? *Psychol. Rev.,* 1956, **63,** 74–80.

41. Eriksen, C. W., and Kuethe, J. L. Avoidance conditioning of verbal behavior without awareness: A paradigm of repression. *J. abnorm. soc. Psychol.,* 1956, **53,** 203–209.

42. Fink, A. A. Questions about subliminal advertising. New York: Author, 1957.

43. Foley, J. P., Jr. The cortical interpretation of conditioning. *J. gen. Psychol.,* 1933, **9,** 228–234.

44. Fullerton, G. S., and Cattell, J. McK. On the perception of small differences. *Univer. Penn. Publ., Philos. Ser.,* 1892, No. 2.

45. "Ghost" ads overrated. *Sci. Newsltr.,* 1957, **72,** No. 17.

46. Gilchrist, J. C., and Nesberg, L. S. Need and perceptual change in need-related objects. *J. exp. Psychol.,* 1952, **44,** 369–376.

47. Goodnow, Jacqueline J., and Postman, L. Probability learning in a problem-solving situation. *J. exp. Psychol.,* 1955, **49,** 16–22.

48. Greenspoon, J. The reinforcing effect of two spoken sounds on the frequency of two responses. *Amer. J. Psychol.,* 1955, **68,** 409–416.

49. Guilford, J. P. *Psychometric methods.* New York: McGraw-Hill, 1936.

50. Haggard, E. A. Experimental studies in affective processes: I. Some effects of cognitive structure and active participation on certain autonomic reactions during and following experimentally induced stress. *J. exp. Psychol.,* 1943, **33,** 257–284.

51. Hankin, H. *Common sense.* New York: Dutton, 1926.

52. Hartmann, G. W. I. The increase of visual acuity in one eye through the illumination of the other. *J. exp. Psychol.,* 1933, **16,** 383–392.

53. Hartmann, G. W. II. Changes in visual acuity through simultaneous stimulation of other sense organs. *J. exp. Psychol.,* 1933, **16,** 393–407.

54. Henle, Mary. An experimental investigation of past experience as a determinant of visual form perception. *J. exp. Psychol.,* 1942, **30,** 1–21.

55. Hernández-Peón, R., Scherrer, H., and Jouvet, M. Modification of electrical activity of cochlear nucleus during "attention" in unanesthetized cats. *Science,* 1955, **123,** 331–332.

56. Hildum, D. C., and Brown, R. W. Verbal reinforcement and interviewer bias. *J. abnorm. soc. Psychol.,* 1956, **53,** 108–111.

57. Hilgard, E. R., Miller, J., and Ohlson, J. A. Three attempts to secure pupillary conditioning to auditory stimuli near the

absolute threshold. *J. exp. Psychol.*, 1941,
29, 89–103.

58. Hilgard, E. R., and Wendt, G. R. The
problem of reflex sensitivity to light studied in a case of hemianopsia. *Yale J.
Biol. Med.*, 1933, 5, 373–385.

59. Hollingworth, H. L. *Advertising and selling*. New York: Appleton, 1913.

60. Howes, D. A statistical theory of the
phenomenon of subception. *Psychol. Rev.*,
1954, **61**, 98–110.

61. Howes, D. On the interpretation of word
frequency as a variable affecting speed of
recognition. *J. exp. Psychol.*, 1954, 48,
106–112.

62. Howes, D., and Solomon, R. L. A note on
McGinnies' "Emotionality and perceptual defense." *Psychol. Rev.*, 1950, 57,
235–240.

63. Howes, D., and Solomon, R. L. Visual
duration threshold as a function of word
probability. *J. exp. Psychol.*, 1951, 41,
401–410.

64. Huntley, C. W. Judgments of self based
upon records of expressive behavior. *J.
abnorm. soc. Psychol.*, 1953, 48, 398–427.

65. Irwin, F. W., Kaufman, K., Prior, G.,
and Weaver, H. B. On "Learning without
awareness of what is being learned." *J.
exp. Psychol.*, 1934, 17, 823–827.

66. Karn, H. W. The function of intensity in
the spatial summation of subliminal stimuli in the retina. *J. gen. Psychol.*, 1935,
12, 95–107.

67. Kennedy, J. L. Experiments on "unconscious whispering." *Psychol. Bull.*, 1938,
35, 526. (Abstract)

68. Kennedy, J. L. A methodological review
of extrasensory perception. *Psychol.
Bull.*, 1939, 36, 59–103.

69. Klein, G. S., Meister, D., and Schlesinger, H. J. The effect of personal values
on perception: An experimental critique.
Amer. Psychologist, 1949, 4, 252–253.
(Abstract)

70. Krech, D., and Calvin, A. Levels of perceptual organization and cognition. *J.
abnorm. soc. Psychol.*, 1953, 48, 394–400.

71. Kurland, S. H. The lack of generality in
defense mechanisms as indicated in auditory perception. *J. abnorm. soc. Psychol.*,
1954, 49, 173–177.

72. Lacey, J. I., and Smith, R. L. Conditioning and generalization of unconscious
anxiety. *Science*, 1954, **120**, 1045–1052.

73. Lacey, J. I., Smith, R. L., and Green, A.
Use of conditioned autonomic responses
in the study of anxiety. *Psychosom.
Med.*, 1955, 17, 208–217.

74. Lazarus, R. S. Subception: Fact or artifact? A reply to Eriksen. *Psychol. Rev.*,
1956, **63**, 343–347.

75. Lazarus, R. S., Eriksen, C. W., and
Fonda, C. P. Personality dynamics and
auditory perceptual recognition. *J. Pers.*,
1950–1951, **19**, 471–482.

76. Lazarus, R. S., and McCleary, R. A. Autonomic discrimination without awareness: A study of subception. *Psychol.
Rev.*, 1951, 58, 113–122.

77. Levine, R., Chein, I., and Murphy, G.
The relation of the intensity of a need to
the amount of perceptual distortion. *J.
Psychol.*, 1942, 13, 283–293.

78. Lysak, W. The effects of punishment
upon syllable recognition thresholds. *J.
exp. Psychol.*, 1954, 47, 343–350.

79. McCleary, R. A., and Lazarus, R. S. Autonomic discrimination without awareness: An interim report. *J. Pers.*, 1949,
18, 171–179.

80. McClelland, D. C., and Atkinson, J. W.
The projective expression of needs: I.
The effect of different intensities of the
hunger drive on perception. *J. Psychol.*,
1948, **25**, 205–222.

81. McClelland, D. C., and Lieberman, A. M.
The effect of need for achievement on
recognition of need-related words. *J.
Pers.*, 1949, 18, 236–251.

82. McGinnies, E. Emotionality and perceptual defense. *Psychol. Rev.*, 1949, 56, 244–
251.

83. McGinnies, E. Discussion of Howes' and
Solomon's note on "Emotionality and
perceptual defense." *Psychol. Rev.*, 1950,
57, 229–234.

84. Mandler, G., and Kaplan, W. K. Subjective evaluation and reinforcing effect of a
verbal stimulus. *Science*, 1956, **124**, 582–
583.

85. Mannes, Marya. Ain't nobody here but
us commercials. *Reporter*, 1957, 17, No.
6.

86. Manro, H. M., and Washburn, M. F.
Effect of imperceptible lines on judgment
of distance. *Amer. J. Psychol.*, 1908, 19,
242–243.

87. Michigan State prof. tells weaknesses of
invisible commercials. *Publishers Auxiliary*, 1957, **92**, No. 40.

88. Miller, J. G. Discrimination without
awareness. *Amer. J. Psychol.*, 1939, **52**,
562–578.

89. Miller, J. G. The role of motivation in
learning without awareness. *Amer. J.
Psychol.*, 1940, 53, 229–239.

90. Miller, J. G. *Unconsciousness*. New
York: Wiley, 1942.

91. Newhall, S. M., and Dodge, R. Colored

after images from unperceived weak chromatic stimulation. *J. exp. Psychol.,* 1927, **10,** 1–17.

92. Newhall, S. M., and Sears, R. R. Conditioning finger retraction to visual stimuli near the absolute threshold. *Comp. psychol. Monogr.,* 1933, 9, No. 43.

93. Nuthmann, Anne M. Conditioning of a response class on a personality test. *J. abnorm. soc. Psychol.,* 1957, 54, 19–23.

94. Peirce, C. S., and Jastrow, J. On small differences of sensation. *Mem. Nat. Acad. Sci.,* 1884, 3, 73–83.

95. Perky, C. W. An experimental study of imagination. *Amer. J. Psychol.,* 1910, **21,** 422–452.

96. Philbrick, E. B., and Postman, L. A further analysis of "learning without awareness." *Amer. J. Psychol.,* 1955, **68,** 417–424.

97. Pillai, R. P. B. K. A study of the threshold in relation to the investigations on subliminal impressions and allied phenomena. *Brit. J. educ. Psychol.,* 1939, 9, 97–98.

98. Postman, L., and Jarrett, R. F. An experimental analysis of "learning without awareness." *Amer. J. Psychol.,* 1952, **65,** 244–255.

99. Razran, G. Stimulus generalization of conditioned responses. *Psychol. Bull.,* 1949, **46,** 337–365.

100. Reece, M. M. The effect of shock on recognition thresholds. *J. abnorm. soc. Psychol.,* 1954, 49, 165–172.

101. Rees, H. J., and Israel, H. E. An investigation of the establishment and operation of mental sets. *Psychol. Monogr.,* 1935, **46,** No. 6 (Whole No. 210).

102. Sanford, R. N. The effects of abstinence from food upon imaginal processes: A preliminary experiment. *J. Psychol.,* 1936, 2, 129–136.

103. Sanford, R. N. The effects of abstinence from food upon imaginal processes: A further experiment. *J. Psychol.,* 1937, 3, 145–159.

104. Schafer, T. H. Influence of the preceding item on units of the noise masked threshold by a modified constant method. *J. exp. Psychol.,* 1950, 40, 365–371.

105. Sears, R. R., and Cohen, L. H. Hysterical anesthesia, analgesia, and astereognosis. *Arch. Neurol. Psychiat.,* 1933, **29,** 260–271.

106. Settlage, T. The effect of sodium amytal on the formation and elicitation of conditioned reflexes. *J. comp. Psychol.,* 1936, **22,** 339–343.

107. Sidis, B. *The psychology of suggestion.* New York: Appleton, 1898.

108. Sidowski, J. B. Influence of awareness of reinforcement on verbal conditioning. *J. exp. Psychol.,* 1954, 48, 355–360.

109. Silverman, A., and Baker, L. E. An attempt to condition various responses to subliminal electrical stimulation. *J. exp. Psychol.,* 1935, 18, 246–254.

110. Smoke, K. L. An objective study of concept formation. *Psychol. Monogr.,* 1932, 42, No. 4 (Whole No. 191).

111. Solomon, R. L., and Howes, D. H. Word frequency, personal values, and visual duration thresholds. *Psychol. Rev.,* 1951, 58, 256–270.

112. Solomon, R. L., and Postman, L. Frequency of usage as a determinant of recognition thresholds for words. *J. exp. Psychol.,* 1952, 43, 195–201.

113. Spencer, L. T. The concept of the threshold and Heymans' law of inhibition: I. Correlation between the visual threshold and Heymans' coefficient of inhibition of binocular vision. *J. exp. Psychol.,* 1928, 11, 88–97.

114. Spencer, L. T., and Cohen, L. H. The concept of the threshold and Heymans' law of inhibition. II. *J. exp. Psychol.,* 1928, 11, 194–201.

115. Sterling, K., and Miller, J. G. Conditioning under anesthesia. *Amer. J. Psychol.,* 1941, 54, 92–101.

116. Stroh, M., Shaw, A. M., and Washburn, M. F. A study in guessing. *Amer. J. Psychol.,* 1908, 19, 243–245.

117. Subliminal ad okay if it sells: Lessler; FCC peers into subliminal picture on TV. *Adv. Age,* 1957, **28,** No. 48.

118. Subliminal ads wash no brains, declare Moore, Becker, developers of precon device. *Adv. Age,* 1957, **28,** No. 48.

119. Suslowa, M. Veranderungen der Hautgefule unter dem Einflusse electrischer Reizung. *Z. Rationelle Med.,* 1863, 18, 155–160.

120. Taffel, C. Anxiety and the conditioning of verbal behavior. *J. abnorm. soc. Psychol.,* 1955, 51, 496–501.

121. Thorndike, E. L. *The fundamentals of learning.* New York: Teachers College, Columbia Univer., 1932.

122. Thorndike, E. L., and Rock, R. T. Learning without awareness of what is being learned or intent to learn it. *J. exp. Psychol.,* 1934, 17, 1–19.

123. Titchner, E. B., and Pyle, W. H. Effect of imperceptible shadows on the judgment of distance. *Proc. Amer. phil. Soc.,* 1907, **46,** 94–109.

124. Vanderplas, J. M., and Blake, R. R. Selective sensitization in auditory perception. *J. Pers.,* 1949, **18**, 252–266.

125. Verplanck, W. S. The control of the content of conversation: Reinforcement of statements of opinion. *J. abnorm. soc. Psychol.,* 1955, **51**, 668–676.

126. Verplanck, W. S. The operant conditioning of human motor behavior. *Psychol. Bull.,* 1956, **53**, 70–83.

127. Vinacke, W. E. The discrimination of color and form at levels of illumination below conscious awareness. *Arch. Psychol.,* 1942, **38**, No. 267.

128. Wedell, C. H., Taylor, F. V., and Skol-

nick, A. An attempt to condition the pupillary response. *J. exp. Psychol.,* 1940, **27**, 517–531.

129. Weiss, R. L. The influence of "set for speed" on "learning without awareness." *Amer. J. Psychol.,* 1955, **68**, 425–431.

130. Williams, A. C. Perception of subliminal visual stimuli. *J. Psychol.,* 1938, **6**, 187–199.

131. Wispe, L. G., and Drambarean, N. C. Physiological need, word frequency, and visual duration thresholds. *J. exp. Psychol.,* 1953, **46**, 25–31.

132. Woolf, J. D. Subliminal perception is nothing new. *Adv. Age,* 1957, **28**, No. 43.

The influence of needs, values, attitudes, emotions, and motivation on perceptual organization has been called the "new look" in perception. Many criticisms have been leveled at the "new look" experiments, but this one seems to have held up.

POINTS TO GUIDE YOUR STUDY   *(1) Can you think of situations in real life in which perceptual organization might be influenced by motivation?   (2) Analysis of variance is a technique for determining whether or not differences in results are probably real or due to chance alone.*

40: REINFORCEMENT AND EXTINCTION AS FACTORS IN SIZE ESTIMATION

William W. Lambert, Cornell University, Richard L. Solomon, University of Pennsylvania, and Peter D. Watson

I. Introduction

In recent experiments on the psychology of perceiving, there has been a noticeable tendency to emphasize determinants which might be classed as motivational in character. The work of Sanford (6, 7) involving the relationship between drive states and 'autistic perceiving,' and the exten-

This research was facilitated by the Laboratory of Social Relations, Harvard University. The authors wish to thank Miss Winifred Lydon, Director of the Harvard Veteran's Nursery School, and Major Gertrude Atkinson, of the Salvation Army Nursery School, Boston, for their indispensable help and cooperation in carrying out this study.

W. W. Lambert, R. L. Solomon, and P. D. Watson. Reinforcement and extinction as factors in size estimation. *J. exp. Psychol.,* 1949, **39**, 637–641. Copyright © 1949 by the American Psychological Association. Reprinted here with permission from the authors and the American Psychological Association. Footnote 2 omitted.

sion of this work by Murphy and his collaborators (3, 5, 8), and by McClelland and Atkinson (4), illustrate this trend. More closely related to the present problem is the work of Bruner, Postman, and their collaborators (1, 2) dealing with the 'selection' and 'accentuation' of perceived objects relative to the 'value systems' of an individual. Two of their experiments in particular illustrate the operation of the conceptualized value dimension. Bruner and Postman (2) found that circles of the same diameter, embossed with (1) a high-valued social symbol, and (2) a low-valued social symbol, were judged to be larger than circles embossed with (3) a neutral symbol. This might indicate that 'perceptual accentuation' is a U-shaped function of a value dimension varying from −1 to +1, with a minimum of accentuation at 'neutrality.' Bruner and Goodman (1) have shown that poor children tend to overestimate the size of coins more than rich children do. These experimenters stated: "The reasonable assumption was made that poor children have a greater subjective need for money than rich ones." (1, p. 39) They further asserted that "the greater the value of the coin, the greater is the deviation of *apparent* size from *actual* size." (1, p. 38)

The multitude of influences correlated with being rich or poor makes it difficult to analyze the specific determinants of size overestimation. It was thought that some light could be shed on this problem by experimentally controlling the life history of children with respect to an initially neutral object. Specifically, we wished to associate a relatively neutral poker chip[1] with candy reward and later extinguish this association by removal of reward and to measure the effects of such procedures on the estimated size of the poker chip. Our hypothesis was that 'value,' as defined by changes in apparent size, is a function of both reinforcement and extinction procedures.

II. Subjects and procedure

In the first study, 32 children from the Harvard Nursery School (ages three to five) were divided into 22 experimental subjects and 10 control subjects. In the second study, 22 children of comparable age from a Salvation Army Nursery School provided 15 experimental subjects and 7 control subjects.

The experimental subjects were individually introduced to a token-reward situation where they turned a crank 18 turns in order to receive a white poker chip which, when put into a slot, led to the automatic delivery of a piece of candy. The control subjects were introduced into the same situation, but candy came directly after work, *without* the mediation of a poker chip. In the first study, both groups worked (and were rewarded) once a day for 10 days; in the second study, the subjects worked (and were rewarded) *five* times a day for 10 days.

Size estimates of the white poker chip token were made by the subjects (1) prior to the experiment; (2) after 10 days of reward; (3) after extinction had occurred (11th day); and (4) after reward had been reinstated (12th day).

Measurements were taken with the equipment designed and used by Bruner and Goodman (1). This equipment was composed of a rectangular wooden box (9 × 9 × 18 in.) with a 5-in. square ground-glass screen in the center of the front panel, and a control knob at the lower right-hand corner. At the center of the ground-glass screen the subject was presented with a circular patch of light (16.2 app. ft. cdls.) the diameter of which was under the control of the knob. The light source was a 60-watt incandescent light shining through an iris diaphragm which could be varied (in terms of the visible light patch) from ⅛ to 2 in. As Bruner and Goodman reported: "The circle was not truly round, containing the familiar nine-elliptoid sides found in the Bausch and Lomb iris diaphragm. It was so close, however, that subjects had no difficulty making the subjective equations required of them." (1, p. 37)

The subjects stood in front of the apparatus with the light patch at or slightly below eye level, and about 12 to 18 in. away. The token, pasted on a 5-in. square gray cardboard, was held by the experimenters so that it was parallel to the circular patch. About 7 in. separated the centers of the two objects to be compared.

The judgment problem was presented to the children of both groups as a game. Each child made his estimates alone. Two judgments starting from the open and two starting from the closed position of the

---

[1] Only one of our children knew what a poker chip was. It was called a circle in our experiment.

iris were obtained from each child at each measurement session; these judgments were made in an order which was counterbalanced for direction of turning of the control knob. The children were not informed of their success in approximating the actual size of the poker chip.

On the 11th day—after 10 days of rewarded trials—extinction was instituted. The children of both groups worked, but no candy was forthcoming. They worked until they met the arbitrary criterion of extinction: three min. during which they did not turn the handle of the work machine. The size estimates were made immediately after the subject had met the extinction criterion.

On the 12th day the subjects were reintroduced to the reward sequence, and the work brought candy to the control group and token plus candy to the experimental group. Size estimates were made immediately after this 12th session.

III. Results

The results for both nursery schools were combined and they are shown graphically in Figure 1. The four size estimation sessions are distributed on the x-axis; the mean estimate of the token size in terms of percent of actual size is shown on the y-axis. The actual size is indicated by the horizontal line parallel to the x-axis. The means for the experimental group are connected by the solid lines, and the means for the control group are connected by the dotted lines. The connecting lines are meant to increase legibility; they do not imply a continuous function of any sort.

It would appear that the control group showed no significant changes with experience. The experimental group, however, showed a rise in the apparent size of the token after ten days of using the token to obtain reward. The estimates dropped to the level of the beginning estimates following the extinction procedure in which the token no longer led to candy reward. The estimates went back in the direction of over-estimation when reward was reinstated on the 12th day.

The mean size estimates in arbitrary units of the comparison-stimulus diameter are given in Table 1, together with the corresponding percent of the actual token diameter, for each of the four points in our experiment. The results for our two studies are combined, since there were no appreciable differences between the 10-reinforcement and the 50-reinforcement experiments.

Analyses of variance were performed on the data which are summarized in Table 1. The following differences are of interest: (1) In the experimental group, the estimated size of the token after 10 days of reinforcement was significantly greater than at the pretest. This difference is reliable at the one percent level of confidence. (2) In the experimental group, the size estimates after extinction were significantly smaller than they were after the 10 days of reinforcement. This difference is reliable at the one percent level of confidence. (3) In the experimental group the rise in estimated size following reinstatement of reward is significant at the one

FIGURE 1 *Effects of the experimental conditions upon children's estimates of the diameter of a token when these estimates are taken as percents of the true diameter.*

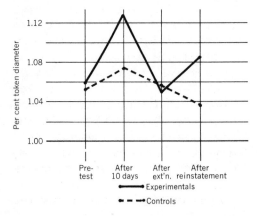

TABLE 1 *The alteration of size estimation with experience in the experimental situation*

	EXPERIMENTAL GROUP			CONTROL GROUP		
	MEAN ESTIMATED SIZE*	σ_m	PERCENT ACTUAL SIZE	MEAN ESTIMATED SIZE*	σ_m	PERCENT ACTUAL SIZE
Pretest	66.8	1.2	1.06	66.4	1.5	1.05
After 10 days	70.9	1.1	1.13	67.7	1.2	1.07
After extinction	66.3	1.3	1.05	66.6	1.2	1.06
After reinstatement	68.5	1.8	1.09	65.4	1.4	1.04

* Actual size of poker chips is 63.0 in arbitrary units of diameter. The error of measurement of diameter by experimenter is ±0.2 units.

percent level of confidence. (4) In the control group, none of the four mean estimates is significantly different from any other. (5) The mean estimates for the experimental and control groups after ten days of reinforcement are significantly different from one another with a reliability between the one and five percent levels of confidence. (6) The mean estimates for the experimental and control groups after reinstatement of reward are not significantly different from one another even though a marked trend seems evident.

IV. Discussion

Several alternative theoretical interpretations for our results could be made. Since experiments are in progress to study further the factors involved, these possibilities will merely be listed at this time. These views are not mutually exclusive, but overlap, as do so many formulations in this field.

1. The estimation changes in the experimental group may be compatible with a generalized pattern of behavior which we would call the 'cookie effect.' That is, the effect may be peculiar to our culture where, for example, a 'bigger cookie is *better* than a little one.' 'Bigness' and 'value,' or 'bigness' and 'goodness,' may be acquired equivalencies for our children, particularly at the ages of the subjects

used here. Experiments have been planned which may provide evidence on whether this phenomenon is 'culture bound' or not.

2. These results may provide a measure reflecting some of the secondary reinforcing characteristics taken on by the token during the reinforced trials. These characteristics become lost when reinforcement is not maintained, as during extinction, but are restored when reward is reinstated. This formulation, if further bulwarked with evidence, could serve to integrate perceptual distortion phenomena with learning theory and possibly provide a valuable indirect measure of secondary reinforcement.

3. It is possible that the size enhancement phenomenon can provide us with inferences about perceptual processes as envisioned by Bruner and his collaborators (1, 2). They hypothesize: "The greater the social value of an object, the more will it be susceptible to organization by behavioral determinants." (1, p. 36) In its learning aspects, however, overestimation of size may reflect either 'expectancy' or 'hypothesis' formation (and decay) or it may, as stated above, reflect learned 'needs' which operate in the workings of this conceptualized perceptual process. The actual mechanism which produces overestimation following reinforcement is, however, entirely obscure at the present stage of our research.

In view of the fact that relatively 'neutral' poker chips were used in the experiment, our data cannot be legitimately compared with the coin size data of Bruner and Goodman (1). In addition, our two nursery school groups do not fulfill the criteria of distinct economic class differences. In no sense can we call one group 'rich children' and the other group 'poor children.'

It is interesting to note the possibility that effects such as those discussed here depend on a 'difficult' or 'ambiguous' judgment situation. Probably, the more ambiguous the stimulus situation, the more strongly can reinforcement and motivational factors operate in determining size judgments.

4. It is interesting to note that, following extinction procedures, the estimates of the experimental group do not increase above the original level, when the chip was 'neutral.' This could mean that the U-shaped function postulated to relate accentuation and value does not apply here. Or it could mean that extinction removes positive value without producing negative value. Perhaps extinction by punishment is necessary for producing negativity and an increase in size estimates at the negative end of the U-shaped function.

V. Summary

We have described the results of an experiment which was designed to investigate the effects of reinforcement and extinction on size estimation. It was found that the establishment of a token reward sequence results in relative overestimation of the token size. Extinction of the sequence removes this overestimation tendency to a great extent. The results are thought to have relevance for both learning and perception theory.

References

1. Bruner, J. S., and Goodman, C. C. Value and need as organizing factors in perception. *J. abnorm. soc. Psychol.*, 1947, **42**, 33–44.
2. Bruner, J. S., and Postman, L. Symbolic value as an organizing factor in perception. *J. soc. Psychol.*, 1948, **27**, 203–208.
3. Levine, R., Chein, I., and Murphy, G. The relation of the intensity of a need to the amount of perceptual distortion: a preliminary report. *J. Psychol.*, 1942, **13**, 283–293.
4. McClelland, D. C., and Atkinson, J. W. The projective expression of needs: I. The effect of different intensities of hunger drive on perception. *J. Psychol.*, 1948, **25**, 205–222.
5. Proshansky, H., and Murphy, G. The effects of reward and punishment on perception. *J. Psychol.*, 1942, **13**, 295–305.
6. Sanford, R. N. The effect of abstinence from food upon imaginal processes: a preliminary experiment. *J. Psychol.*, 1936, **2**, 129–136.
7. Sanford, R. N. The effect of abstinence from food upon imaginal processes: a further experiment. *J. Psychol.*, 1937, **3**, 145–159.
8. Shafer, R., and Murphy, G. The role of autism in a visual figure-ground relationship. *J. exp. Psychol.*, 1943, **32**, 335–343.

SECTION ELEVEN

PSYCHOLOGICAL MEASUREMENT

This is the last chapter of a book entitled How to Lie with Statistics; *this explains the occasional references to earlier parts of the book. The message of the selection is clear and well worth heeding.*

A POINT TO GUIDE YOUR STUDY   *Can you think of any examples in your own experience which illustrate the points made in this selection?*

41:   HOW TO TALK BACK TO A STATISTIC. FROM: HOW TO LIE WITH STATISTICS

Darrell Huff

So far, I have been addressing you rather as if you were a pirate with a yen for instruction in the finer points of cutlass work. In this concluding chapter I'll drop that literary device. I'll face up to the serious purpose that I like to think lurks just beneath the surface of this book: explaining how to look a phony statistic in the eye and face it down; and no less important, how to recognize sound and usable data in that wilderness of fraud to which the previous chapters have been largely devoted.

Not all the statistical information that you may come upon can be tested with the sureness of chemical analysis or of what goes on in an assayer's laboratory. But

Reprinted from *How to Lie with Statistics* by Darrell Huff. Pictures by Irving Geis. By permission of W. W. Norton & Co., Inc. Copyright © 1954 by Darrell Huff and Irving Geis.

you can prod the stuff with five simple questions, and by finding the answers avoid learning a remarkable lot that isn't so.

Who says so?

About the first thing to look for is bias—the laboratory with something to prove for the sake of a theory, a reputation, or a fee; the newspaper whose aim is a good story; labor or management with a wage level at stake.

Look for conscious bias. The method may be direct misstatement or it may be ambiguous statement that serves as well and cannot be convicted. It may be selection of favorable data and suppression of unfavorable. Units of measurement may be shifted, as with the practice of using one year for one comparison and sliding over to a more favorable year for another. An improper measure may be used: a mean where a median would be more informative (perhaps all too informative), with the trickery covered by the unqualified word "average."

Look sharply for unconscious bias. It is often more dangerous. In the charts and predictions of many statisticians and economists in 1928 it operated to produce remarkable things. The cracks in the economic structure were joyously overlooked, and all sorts of evidence was adduced and statistically supported to show that we had no more than entered the stream of prosperity.

It may take at least a second look to find out who-says-so. The who may be hidden by what Stephen Potter, the *Lifemanship* man, would probably call the "O.K. name." Anything smacking of the medical profession is an O.K. name. Scientific laboratories have O.K. names. So do colleges, especially universities, more especially ones eminent in technical work. The writer who proved a few chapters back that

BIG NOSE AND THROAT MAN

higher education jeopardizes a girl's chance to marry made good use of the O.K. name of Cornell. Please note that while the data came from Cornell, the conclusions were entirely the writer's own. But the O.K. name helps you carry away a misimpression of "Cornell University says . . ."

When an O.K. name is cited, make sure that the authority stands behind the information, not merely somewhere alongside it.

You may have read a proud announcement by the Chicago *Journal of Commerce*. That publication had made a survey. Of 169 corporations that replied to a poll on price gouging and hoarding, two-thirds declared that they were absorbing price increases produced by the Korean war. "The survey shows," said the *Journal* (look sharp whenever you meet those words!), "that corporations have done exactly the opposite of what the enemies of the American business system have charged." This is an obvious place to ask, "Who says so?" since the *Journal of Commerce* might be regarded as an interested party. It is also a splendid place to ask our second test question:

How does he know?

It turns out that the *Journal* had begun by sending its questionnaires to 1,200 large companies. Only fourteen per cent had replied. Eighty-six per cent had not cared to say anything in public on whether they were hoarding or price gouging.

The *Journal* had put a remarkably good face on things, but the fact remains that there was little to brag about. It came down to this: Of 1,200 companies polled, nine per cent said they had not raised prices, five per cent said they had, and eighty-six per cent wouldn't say. Those that had replied constituted a sample in which bias might be suspected.

Watch out for evidence of a biased sample, one that has been selected improperly or—as with this one—has selected itself. Ask the question we dealt with in an early chapter: Is the sample large enough to permit any reliable conclusion?

Similarly with a reported correlation: Is it big enough to mean anything? Are there enough cases to add up to any significance? You cannot, as a casual reader, apply tests of significance or come to exact conclusions as to the adequacy of a sample. On a good many of the things you see reported, however, you will be able to tell at a glance —a good long glance, perhaps—that there just weren't enough cases to convince any reasoning person of anything.

What's missing?

You won't always be told how many cases. The absence of such a figure, particularly when the source is an interested one, is enough to throw suspicion on the whole thing. Similarly a correlation given without a measure of reliability (probable error, standard error) is not to be taken very seriously.

Watch out for an average, variety unspecified, in any matter where mean and median might be expected to differ substantially.

Many figures lose meaning because a comparison is missing. An article in *Look* magazine says, in connection with Mongolism, that "one study shows that in 2,800 cases, over half of the mothers were 35 or over." Getting any meaning from this depends upon your knowing something about the ages at which women in general pro-

duce babies. Few of us know things like that.

Here is an extract from the *New Yorker* magazine "Letter from London" of January 31, 1953.

The Ministry of Health's recently published figures showing that in the week of the great fog the death rate for Greater London jumped by twenty-eight hundred were a shock to the public, which is used to regarding Britain's unpleasant climatic effects as nuisances rather than as killers. . . . The extraordinary lethal properties of this winter's prize visitation . . .

But how lethal *was* the visitation? Was it exceptional for the death rate to be that much higher than usual in a week? All such things do vary. And what about ensuing weeks? Did the death rate drop below average, indicating that if the fog killed people they were largely those who would have died shortly anyway? The figure sounds impressive, but the absence of other figures takes away most of its meaning.

Sometimes it is percentages that are given and raw figures that are missing, and this can be deceptive too. Long ago, when Johns Hopkins University had just begun to admit women students, someone not particularly enamored of coeducation reported a real shocker: Thirty-three and one-third per cent of the women at Hopkins had married faculty members! The

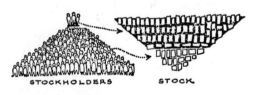

STOCKHOLDERS   STOCK

raw figures gave a clearer picture. There were three women enrolled at the time, and one of them had married a faculty man.

A couple of years ago the Boston Chamber of Commerce chose its American Women of Achievement. Of the sixteen among them who were also in *Who's Who*, it was announced that they had "sixty academic degrees and eighteen children." That sounds like an informative picture of the group until you discover that among the women were Dean Virginia Gildersleeve and Mrs. Lillian M. Gilbreth. Those two had a full third of the degrees between them. And Mrs. Gilbreth, of course, supplied two-thirds of the children.

A corporation was able to announce that its stock was held by 3,003 persons, who had an average of 660 shares each. This was true. It was also true that of the two million shares of stock in the corporation three men held three-quarters and three thousand persons held the other one-fourth among them.

If you are handed an index, you may ask what's missing there. It may be the base, a base chosen to give a distorted picture. A national labor organization once showed that indexes of profits and production had risen much more rapidly after the depression than an index of wages had. As an argument for wage increases this demonstration lost its potency when someone dug out the missing figures. It could be seen then that profits had been almost bound to rise more rapidly in percentage than wages simply because profits had reached a lower point, giving a smaller base.

Sometimes what is missing is the factor that caused a change to occur. This omission leaves the implication that some other, more desired, factor is responsible. Figures published one year attempted to show that business was on the upgrade by pointing out that April retail sales were greater than in the year before. What was missing was the fact that Easter had come in March in the earlier year and in April in the later year.

A report of a great increase in deaths from cancer in the last quarter-century is misleading unless you know how much of it is a product of such extraneous factors as these: Cancer is often listed now where "causes unknown" was formerly used; autopsies are more frequent, giving surer diagnoses; reporting and compiling of medical statistics are more complete; and people more frequently reach the most susceptible ages now. And if you are looking at total deaths rather than the death rate, don't neglect the fact that there are more people now than there used to be.

Did somebody change the subject?

When assaying a statistic, watch out for a switch somewhere between the raw figure and the conclusion. One thing is all too often reported as another.

As just indicated, more reported cases of a disease are not always the same thing as more cases of the disease. A straw-vote victory for a candidate is not always negotiable at the polls. An expressed preference by a "cross section" of a magazine's readers for articles on world affairs is no final proof that they would read the articles if they were published.

Encephalitis cases reported in the central valley of California in 1952 were triple the figure for the worst previous year. Many alarmed residents shipped their children away. But when the reckoning was in, there had been no great increase in deaths from sleeping sickness. What had

happened was that state and federal health people had come in in great numbers to tackle a long-time problem; as a result of their efforts a great many low-grade cases were recorded that in other years would have been overlooked, possibly not even recognized.

It is all reminiscent of the way that Lincoln Steffens and Jacob A. Riis, as New York newspapermen, once created a crime wave. Crime cases in the papers reached such proportions, both in numbers and in space and big type given to them, that the public demanded action. Theodore Roosevelt, as president of the reform Police Board, was seriously embarrassed. He put an end to the crime wave simply by asking Steffens and Riis to lay off. It had all come about simply because the reporters, led by those two, had got into competition as to who could dig up the most burglaries and whatnot. The official police record showed no increase at all.

"The British male over 5 years of age soaks himself in a hot tub on an average of 1.7 times a week in the winter and 2.1 times in the summer," says a newspaper story. "British women average 1.5 baths a week in the winter and 2.0 in the summer." The source is a Ministry of Works hot-water survey of "6,000 representative British homes." The sample was representative, it says, and seems quite adequate in size to justify the conclusion in

Jim in the tub

the San Francisco *Chronicle's* amusing headline: BRITISH HE'S BATHE MORE THAN SHE'S.

The figures would be more informative if there were some indication of whether they are means or medians. However, the major weakness is that the subject has been changed. What the Ministry really found out is how often these people said they bathed, not how often they did so. When a subject is as intimate as this one is, with the British bath-taking tradition involved, saying and doing may not be the same thing at all. British he's may or may not bathe oftener than she's; all that can safely be concluded is that they say they do.

Here are some more varieties of change-of-subject to watch out for.

A back-to-the-farm movement was discerned when a census showed half a million more farms in 1935 than five years earlier. But the two counts were not talking about the same thing. The definition of farm used by the Bureau of the Census had been changed; it took in at least 300,000 farms that would not have been so listed under the 1930 definition.

Strange things crop out when figures are based on what people say—even about things that seem to be objective facts. Census reports have shown more people at thirty-five years of age, for instance, than at either thirty-four or thirty-six. The false picture comes from one family member's reporting the ages of the others and, not being sure of the exact ages, tending to round them off to a familiar multiple of five. One way to get around this: ask birth dates instead.

The "population" of a large area in China was 28 million. Five years later it was 105 million. Very little of that increase was real; the great difference could be explained only by taking into account the purposes of the two enumerations and the way people would be inclined to feel about being counted in each instance. The first

census was for tax and military purposes, the second for famine relief.

Something of the same sort has happened in the United States. The 1950 census found more people in the sixty-five-to-seventy age group than there were in the fifty-five-to-sixty group ten years before. The difference could not be accounted for by immigration. Most of it could be a product of large-scale falsifying of ages by people eager to collect social security. Also possible is that some of the earlier ages were understated out of vanity.

Another kind of change-of-subject is represented by Senator William Langer's cry that "we could take a prisoner from Alcatraz and board him at the Waldorf-Astoria cheaper. . . ." The North Dakotan was referring to earlier statements that it cost eight dollars a day to maintain a prisoner at Alcatraz, "the cost of a room at a good San Francisco hotel." The subject has been changed from total maintenance cost (Alcatraz) to hotel-room rent alone.

The *post hoc* variety of pretentious nonsense is another way of changing the subject without seeming to. The change of something *with* something else is presented as *because of*. The magazine *Electrical World* once offered a composite chart in an editorial on "What Electricity Means to America." You could see from it that as "electrical horsepower in factories" climbed, so did "average wages per hour." At the same time "average hours per week" dropped. All these things are longtime trends, of course, and there is no evidence at all that any one of them has produced any other.

And then there are the firsters. Almost anybody can claim to be first in *something* if he is not too particular what it is. At the end of 1952 two New York newspapers were each insisting on first rank in grocery advertising. Both were right too, in a way. The *World-Telegram* went on to explain that it was first in full-run advertising, the kind that appears in all copies,

which is the only kind it runs. The *Journal-American* insisted that total linage was what counted and that it was first in that. This is the kind of reaching for a superlative that leads the weather reporter on the radio to label a quite normal day "the hottest June second since 1949."

Change-of-subject makes it difficult to compare cost when you contemplate borrowing money either directly or in the form of installment buying. Six per cent sounds like six per cent—but it may not be at all.

If you borrow $100 from a bank at six per cent interest and pay it back in equal monthly installments for a year, the price you pay for the use of the money is about $3. But another six per cent loan, on the basis sometimes called $6 on the $100, will cost you twice as much. That's the way most automobile loans are figured. It is very tricky.

The point is that you don't have the $100 for a year. By the end of six months you have paid back half of it. If you are charged at $6 on the $100, or six per cent of the amount, you really pay interest at nearly twelve per cent.

Even worse was what happened to some careless purchasers of freezer-food plans in 1952 and 1953. They were quoted a figure of anywhere from six to twelve per cent. It sounded like interest, but it was not. It was an on-the-dollar figure and, worst of all, the time was often six months rather than a year. Now $12 on the $100 for money to be paid back regularly over half a year works out to something like forty-eight per cent real interest. It is no wonder that so many customers defaulted and so many food plans blew up.

Sometimes the semantic approach will be used to change the subject. Here is an item from *Business Week* magazine.

Accountants have decided that "surplus" is a nasty word. They propose eliminating it from corporate balance sheets. The Committee on Accounting Procedure of the American Institute of Accountants says: . . . Use such descriptive terms as "retained earnings" or "appreciation of fixed assets."

This one is from a newspaper story reporting Standard Oil's record-breaking revenue and net profit of a million dollars a day.

Possibly the directors may be thinking some time of splitting the stock for there may be an advantage . . . if the profits per share do not look so large. . . .

Does it make sense?

"Does it make sense?" will often cut a statistic down to size when the whole rigmarole is based on an unproved assumption. You may be familiar with the Rudolf Flesch readability formula. It purports to measure how easy a piece of prose is to read, by such simple and objective items as length of words and sentences. Like all devices for reducing the imponderable to a number and substituting arithmetic for judgment, it is an appealing idea. At least it has appealed to people who employ writers, such as newspaper publishers, even if not to many writers themselves. The assumption in the formula is that such things as word length determine readability. This, to be ornery about it, remains to be proved.

A man named Robert A. Dufour put the Flesch formula to trial on some literature that he found handy. It showed "The Legend of Sleepy Hollow" to be half again as hard to read as Plato's *Republic*. The Sinclair Lewis novel *Cass Timberlane* was rated more difficult than an essay by Jacques Maritain, "The Spiritual Value of Art." A likely story.

Many a statistic is false on its face. It gets by only because the magic of numbers brings about a suspension of common sense. Leonard Engel, in a *Harper's* article, has listed a few of the medical variety.

An example is the calculation of a well-known urologist that there are eight million cases of cancer of the prostate gland in the United States—which would be enough to provide 1.1 carcinomatous prostate glands for every male in the susceptible age group! Another is a prominent neurologist's estimate that one American in twelve suffers from migraine; since migraine is responsible for a third of chronic headache cases, this would mean that a quarter of us must suffer from disabling headaches. Still another is the figure of 250,000 often given for the number of multiple sclerosis cases; death data indicate that there can be, happily, no more than thirty to forty thousand cases of this paralytic disease in the country.

Hearings on amendments to the Social Security Act have been haunted by various forms of a statement that makes sense only when not looked at closely. It is an argument that goes like this: Since life expectancy is only about sixty-three years, it is a sham and a fraud to set up a social-security plan with a retirement age of sixty-five, because virtually everybody dies before that.

You can rebut that one by looking around at people you know. The basic fallacy, however, is that the figure refers to expectancy at birth, and so about half the babies born can expect to live longer than that. The figure, incidentally, is from the latest official complete life table and is correct for the 1939-1941 period. An up-to-date estimate corrects it to sixty-five-plus. Maybe that will produce a new and equally silly argument to the effect that practically everybody now lives to be sixty-five.

Postwar planning at a big electrical-appliance company was going great guns a few years ago on the basis of a declining birth rate, something that had been taken for granted for a long time. Plans called for emphasis on small-capacity appliances, apartment-size refrigerators. Then one of the planners had an attack of common sense: He came out of his graphs and charts long enough to notice that he and his co-workers and his friends and his neighbors and his former classmates with few exceptions either had three or four children or planned to. This led to some open-minded investigating and charting— and the company shortly turned its emphasis most profitably to big-family models.

The impressively precise figure is something else that contradicts common sense. A study reported in New York City newspapers announced that a working woman living with her family needed a weekly pay check of $40.13 for adequate support. Anyone who has not suspended all logical processes while reading his paper will realize that the cost of keeping body and soul together cannot be calculated to the last cent. But there is a dreadful temptation; "$40.13" sounds so much more knowing than "about $40."

You are entitled to look with the same suspicion on the report, some years ago, by the American Petroleum Industries Committee that the average yearly tax bill for automobiles is $51.13.

Extrapolations are useful, particularly in that form of soothsaying called forecasting trends. But in looking at the figures or the charts made from them, it is necessary to remember one thing constantly: The trend-to-now may be a fact, but the future trend represents no more than an educated guess. Implicit in it is "everything else being equal" and "present trends continuing." And somehow everything else refuses to remain equal, else life would be dull indeed.

For a sample of the nonsense inherent in uncontrolled extrapolation, consider the trend of television. The number of sets in American homes increased around 10,000% from 1947 to 1952. Project this for the next five years and you find that there'll soon be a couple billion of the things, Heaven forbid, or forty sets per family. If you want to be even sillier, begin with a base year that is earlier in the television scheme of things than 1947 and you can just as well "prove" that each family will soon have not forty but forty thousand sets.

A Government research man, Morris Hansen, called Gallup's 1948 election forecasting "the most publicized statistical error in human history." It was a paragon of accuracy, however, compared with some of our most widely used estimates of future population, which have earned a nationwide horselaugh. As late as 1938 a presi-

dential commission loaded with experts doubted that the U. S. population would ever reach 140 million; it was 12 million more than that just twelve years later. There are textbooks published so recently that they are still in college use that predict a peak population of not more than 150 million and figure it will take until about 1980 to reach it. These fearful underestimates came from assuming that a trend would continue without change. A similar assumption a century ago did as badly in the opposite direction because it assumed continuation of the population-increase rate of 1790 to 1860. In his second message to Congress, Abraham Lincoln predicted the U. S. population would reach 251,689,-914 in 1930.

Not long after that, in 1874, Mark Twain summed up the nonsense side of extrapolation in *Life on the Mississippi:*

In the space of one hundred and seventy-six years the Lower Mississippi has shortened itself two hundred and forty-two miles. That is an average of a trifle over one mile and a third per year. Therefore, any calm person, who is not blind or idiotic, can see that in the Old Oölitic Silurian Period, just a million years ago next November, the Lower Mississippi River was upward of one million three hundred thousand miles long, and stuck out over the Gulf of Mexico like a fishing-rod.

And by the same token any person can see that seven hundred and forty-two years from now the Lower Mississippi will be only a mile and three-quarters long, and Cairo and New Orleans will have joined their streets together, and be plodding comfortably along under a single mayor and a mutual board of aldermen. There is something fascinating about science. One gets such wholesale returns of conjecture out of such a trifling investment of fact.

PSYCHOLOGICAL TESTING

The term "genius" is not necessarily applicable to a person who has an IQ, or intelligence test score, greater than 140—it is generally taken to mean more. For many psychologists, the definition of genius is related to creativity, and the chances of being highly creative increase with intelligence, as measured by performance on an intelligence test. However, "genius is as genius does." Thus, some very intelligent people are geniuses, while others are not. This selection considers the early environment as an especially important factor in the creative capacity that makes for genius.

POINTS TO GUIDE YOUR STUDY *(1) If you are not familiar with the achievements of some of the people mentioned in this article, look them up in an encyclopedia. (2) Note that, under conditions in which the environment is moderately stimulating, the largest contribution to intelligence test scores, or IQs, is probably from inheritance. This article, however, is concerned with the environmental conditions necessary for the development of the creativity which seems to be an essential part of genius.*

42: THE CHILDHOOD PATTERN OF GENIUS

Harold G. McCurdy, University of North Carolina

Genius by any definition is rare. If, following Galton, we make lasting fame one of the requirements, it is very rare indeed, and we are reduced to studying it at a distance through biography. Now, biographies have their limitations; as Havelock

H. G. McCurdy. The Childhood Pattern of Genius. *J. Elisha Mitchell Sci. Society,* 1957, **73,** 448–462. Reprinted here with permission from the author and the Elisha Mitchell Scientific Society.

Ellis noted, one may search through them in vain for the most ordinary vital statistics. Above all, they cannot be expected to yield information on those details of early life, such as nursing and weaning and toilet training, to which psychoanalysis has attached so much importance. When, therefore, one proposes as I do here to explore the question whether there is some pattern of environmental influences operating on children of genius which might help to account for their later achievement, it should be self-evident that the question is necessarily adjusted to something less than microscopic precision. Not only so, but, because the factor of heredity cannot be controlled, any answer whatsoever must be regarded as partial and tentative and ambiguous. Nevertheless, there may be some profit in asking the question, and insofar as it is directed simply toward the discovery of uniformity of environmental pattern there is no inherent reason why it should not be answerable, provided we do not insist on minute detail.

Table I presents the twenty geniuses into whose childhood this paper will inquire. The selection was partly deliberate, on theoretical grounds, and partly random, as will be explained. In Cox's monumental study of great geniuses (7) the main sample consists of 282 men drawn from the list of 1,000 which was compiled by J. McKeen Cattell on the principle that the amount of space allotted to them in biographical dictionaries could be taken as an objective measure of their true eminence. Though one may certainly quarrel with some of Cattell's results, the sifting process applied by Cox was admirable. She arrived at her smaller list by requiring: one, that the attained eminence should clearly depend upon notable personal achievement; and two, that the biographical material available should be sufficient to permit a reliable estimate of early mental ability. Men born before 1450 were eliminated. The chief task of Cox's investigation was to estimate the intelligence level displayed by these rigorously selected geniuses during childhood and youth. For this purpose the appropriate information was extracted from biographical sources and submitted to the judgment of three raters thoroughly experienced in the use of intelligence tests and the valuation of IQ from behavior. Their three independent ratings, expressed as IQs, were combined. Separate estimates

were made for two periods of life: from birth to age 17, and from age 17 to age 26. As might be expected, the reliabilities of the estimates increased in proportion to the amount of biographical information, and, in general, the IQs based on the more adequate material were higher. Consequently, one in search of illumination on the early environment of genius would naturally turn most hopefully to the geniuses in Cox's list who had been assigned the highest childhood IQs. This I did. From her list I chose as my preliminary sample the 27 men whose IQs in childhood had been estimated at 160 or higher. The final sample of 20, as given in Table I, was reached by dropping out those individuals for whom the biographical material in the University of North Carolina Library appeared to be inadequate.[1] As will be observed, the order of listing in the table is from the highest childhood IQ downwards. The reputation of each man is indicated in the column headed "Fame" by his rank number in Cox's sample, as based on Cattell. With respect to fame the sample appears to be a fair cross-section of Cox's larger group; with respect to IQ, as explained, it is highly selected. One sees at a glance that here are individuals who did extraordinary work in science, law, literature, or politics, and who fully deserve to be called geniuses. Their biographies should be relevant to the proposed question.

It should be understood from the outset that Cox did not neglect the problem of environment. Her biographical sketches furnish some very pertinent information, and she states as an important conclusion that, on the whole, youths who achieve eminence have superior advantages in their early days. Though she notes exceptions, she says: "The average opportunity of our young geniuses for superior education and

[1] The seven omitted were Schelling, Haller, Wolsey, Sarpi, Constant, Brougham, Bossuet. In order to retain Leibniz an interlibrary loan was arranged for Guhrauer's biography.

for elevating and inspiring social contacts was unusually high." . . . The extraordinary training for leadership received by Pitt the younger, John Quincy Adams, Niebuhr, and the Humboldt brothers; the specialized instruction of Mozart, Weber, and Michelangelo undoubtedly contributed to the rapid progress of these great men among the great" (7, p. 216). The object of the present study is to push forward in the same direction of inquiry, but with more pointed attention to the social relations and their repercussions.

In Table I, one column briefly summarizes facts concerning order of birth. Considerable theoretical importance is sometimes attached to the chronological position of a child in the family. In particular, Galton, who was not prone to overemphasize environment, thought enough of order of birth to pay some heed to it in his investigation of British scientists; and he comments that "the elder sons have, on the

whole, decided advantages of nurture over the younger sons. They are more likely to become possessed of independent means, and therefore able to follow the pursuits that have most attraction to their tastes; they are treated more as companions by their parents, and have earlier responsibility, both of which would develop independence of character; probably, also, the first-born child of families not well-to-do in the world would generally have more attention in his infancy, more breathing-space, and better nourishment, than his younger brothers and sisters in their several turns" (13, p. 26). There is an intuitive appeal in the argument, but Galton does not support it by any precise analysis of his data. What may be said about the present sample? First, it must be admitted that there are several ways of stating the facts, depending on whether one includes or excludes half-siblings and siblings who died at an early age. The figures given in

TABLE I

	ESTIMATED IQ IN CHILDHOOD	FAME (RANK IN 282)	BIRTH ORDER	AGE AT MARRIAGE
J. S. Mill (1806–1873)	190	103	1 in 9	45
Leibniz (1646–1717)	185	19	Only	—
Grotius (1583–1645)	185	72	1 in 5	25
Goethe (1749–1832)	185	4	1 in 6	39
Pascal (1623–1662)	180	35	2 in 3	—
Macaulay (1800–1859)	180	53	1 in 9	—
Bentham (1748–1832)	180	181	1 in 2	—
Coleridge (1772–1834)	175	157	10 in 10	23
Voltaire (1694–1778)	170	2	5 in 5	—
Leopardi (1798–1837)	170	280	1 in 5	—
Chatterton (1752–1770)	170	163	3 in 3	—
Niebuhr (1776–1831)	165	135	2 in 2	24
Mirabeau (1749–1791)	165	30	9(?) in 11	22
J. Q. Adams (1767–1848)	165	274	2 in 5	30
Wieland (1733–1813)	160	152	1 in ?	32
Tasso (1544–1595)	160	48	3 in 3	—
Pope (1688–1744)	160	50	Only	—
Pitt (1759–1806)	160	9	2 in 5	—
Musset (1810–1857)	160	261	2 in 2	—
Melanchthon (1497–1560)	160	77	1 in 5	23

the table stand for full siblings and include all births. The half-siblings excluded in the three cases involved (Leibniz, Coleridge, Pope) were children by previous wives of their fathers. The impression produced by inspection is that there may be an excess of only and first children among these twenty geniuses. But an analysis of the probabilities does not favor this view very strongly. The average likelihood of being born in first place in the twenty families works out to about ⅓, and the observed frequencies deviate from the theoretically expected only enough to yield a chi square of 2 in support of the hypothesis; since this corresponds to a confidence level of between .2 and .1 for the one degree of freedom, one is left in doubt. Pascal, Niebuhr, and Adams were first sons. If we estimate in terms of first sons, a total of 13, and adjust the probabilities to the expectation that about half the children in multiple birth would be girls, the chi square is 1.8, again too small to support the hypothesis firmly.

Though the figures do not support a birth order hypothesis, there may nevertheless be something about position in the family which is significant. Let us look at the seven who do not rank as first-born children or first-born sons. Coleridge was born in his father's old age and was his "Benjamin"; Voltaire was so sickly during the first year of his life that there was daily concern over his survival, and his mother, an invalid, was incapable of having any more children; Chatterton was a posthumous child, and the previous boy in the family had died in infancy; Mirabeau was the first son to survive after the death of the first and a succession of girls; Tasso was the only surviving son, his older brother having died before he was born; Pitt was in the interesting position of being able to follow his father in a parliamentary career in the House of Commons, as his older brother could not do because of the inherited title; and Musset, the second of

two sons, was younger than the first by a significant span of six years. When we weigh these additional facts, the general notion of some sort of positional effect begins to reassert itself.

One way in which position in the family might favor the development of a child would be by giving it higher attentional value for the parents. Close examination of the biographical data leads to the conclusion that these twenty men of genius, whether because of their position in the family or not, did as children receive a high degree of attention from their parents, as well as from others. In several cases it is clear that the attention exceeded that accorded to their brothers and sisters. Both very decided and very positive parental interest was displayed toward Mill, Leibniz, Grotius, Goethe, Pascal, Macaulay, Bentham, Coleridge, Niebuhr, Adams, Wieland, Pope, Pitt, and Melanchthon. Voltaire and Musset were far from neglected, but the attention bestowed upon them may have lacked some of the intensity of focus notable in the preceding cases. If any of the children suffered comparative neglect or abuse, they would be Leopardi, Chatterton, and Mirabeau. Chatterton had no father from the time of his birth, and the fathers of Leopardi and Mirabeau were lacking in sympathy or worse. On the other hand, Chatterton's mother and sister helped him to learn to read, saw that he went to school, and were good enough to him that the promise he made them when a child to reward them with all kinds of finery when he grew up was fulfilled in the last year of his short life; Leopardi was provided with tutors and had access to his father's rich library; and Mirabeau, cuffed and persecuted as he finally was by his erratic father, was received into the world with an outburst of joy and was always provided for educationally, even though the arrangement may have been savagely disciplinary.

Favorable parental attention may take

the two forms of displays of affection and intellectual stimulation. There is strong evidence for both in most of the cases in our list. Remarkable indeed are the educational programs followed by Mill, Goethe, Pascal, Bentham, Niebuhr, Adams, Wieland, Tasso, and Pitt, under the encouragement, guidance, and powerful insistence of their fathers. Yet it is not the educational program itself which requires our notice so much as it is the intimate and constant association with adults which it entails. Not only were these boys often in the company of adults, as genuine companions; they were to a significant extent cut off from the society of other children. The same statement can be made, on the whole, for others in the list whose educations proceeded less directly, or less strenuously under the guidance of fathers.

Warm attachments to children outside the family circle seem to have been rare, and there are several cases of isolation within the family, too. Yet it is within the family that most of the recorded intimacies between these geniuses and other children developed. Goethe, Pascal, Niebuhr, Macaulay, Voltaire, and Mirabeau experienced some intensity of affection for sisters; Musset for his older brother; Macaulay and Voltaire remained attached to their favorite sisters throughout their lives, becoming devoted uncles to their sisters' children; Goethe's and Pascal's affection for their younger sisters approached passion; and Mirabeau speaks of incestuous relations with his.

The reality and nature of the pattern to which I am pointing—the very great dominance of adults in the lives of these children, and their isolation from contemporaries outside the family and, sometimes, within—can be adequately appreciated only through a more detailed statement about each individual.

Mill, under his father's personal and unremitting tutelage, began hard intellectual work before he was three. From very early

he was given the responsibility of acting as tutor to his brothers and sisters. This did not increase his affection for them. In fact, he came to share some of his father's own antipathy toward them and toward his mother. He explicitly states in his autobiography that his father kept him apart from other boys. "He was earnestly bent upon my escaping not only the ordinary corrupting influence which boys exercise over boys, but the contagion of vulgar modes of thought and feeling; and for this he was willing that I should pay the price of inferiority in the accomplishments which schoolboys in all countries chiefly cultivate" (21, pp. 24f.) And again: "as I had no boy companions, and the animal need of physical activity was satisfied by walking, my amusements, which were mostly solitary, were in general of a quiet, if not a bookish turn, and gave little stimulus to any other kind even of mental activity than that which was already called forth by my studies" (p. 25).

Leibniz, his mother's only child, lost his father, a prominent university professor, when he was six. He retained two vivid memories of him, both of them expressive of the high esteem in which his father held him. His mother, who died when he was eighteen, devoted the remainder of her life to caring for him. He lived at home, free from "the doubtful liberties, the numerous temptations, the barbarous follies of student life" (18, p. 12). Before he was ten his father's carefully guarded library was opened to him, and he plunged into its treasures eagerly. It was conceivably no small thing to Leibniz that his father had regarded his christening as marked by a symbolic movement which seemed to promise that his son, as he wrote in his domestic chronicle, would continue in a spiritual and burning love for God all his life and do wonderful deeds in honor of the Highest (15, p. 4).

Grotius was close to his father. He signed his early poems Hugeianus, thus joining his own name Hugo with his father's name Janus or Joannes. At eight he reacted to the death of a brother by writing his father consolatory Latin verses. He had competent teachers at home, and entered the University of Leiden at eleven; there he dwelt with a devoutly religious man who impressed him deeply. He was famous in the literary world very early, and received high praise from distinguished men. He sought his father's advice when he chose a wife. One would infer from the limited evidence that his association from early childhood was primarily with adults.

Goethe throughout his childhood was carefully and energetically supervised in his varied studies by his father. He associated frequently with numerous skilled and learned and eminent men in Frankfort, among whom was his grandfather Textor. He enjoyed considerable freedom of movement through the city, in the intervals of his studies, and struck up several acquaintances outside the home among boys and girls; but these were certainly far outweighed by his adult contacts, and by his intimacy with his sister, who had much less freedom than he and who became increasingly embittered by the educational discipline of their father. In his autobiography he notes that he was not on friendly terms with a brother, three years younger, who died in childhood, and scarcely retained any memory of the three subsequent children who also died young. How close he and his sister were may be gauged by these words regarding the after-effects of his love-affair with Gretchen, at about fourteen: "my sister consoled me the more earnestly, because she secretly felt the satisfaction of having gotten rid of a rival; and I, too, could not but feel a quiet, half-delicious pleasure, when she did me the justice to assure me that I was the only one who truly loved, understood, and esteemed her" (14, p. 192).

Pascal was so precious in the eyes of his father, after his mother's death when he was three, that, as the older sister tells us,

the father could not bear the thought of leaving his education to others, and accordingly became and remained his only teacher. At eighteen Pascal's health broke down from ceaseless application. He was frequently in the company of the learned men surrounding his father. His primary emotional attachment was to his younger sister, Jacqueline; her religious retirement strongly influenced his own religious development.

Macaulay early became absorbed in books, but his studies were more unobtrusively guided by his father and mother and other relatives than in the cases preceding. He was especially attached to his mother in early childhood, and at home among his brothers and sisters was overflowingly happy and playful. A sister writes: "He hated strangers, and his notion of perfect happiness was to see us all working round him while he read aloud a novel, and then to walk all together on the Common" (30, p. 67). He was reluctant to leave home for school for even a single day, and he was acutely homesick when placed in a boarding school at about twelve; there, though tolerated and even admired by his fellow pupils, he had little to do with them, living almost exclusively among books. The children at home passionately loved him. It should not be overlooked that his father was a deeply religious man of great force of character, energetic in religious and political reform movements of considerable scope.

Bentham's father, ambitious to make a practical lawyer of his first and for nine years his only child, kept him to a rigorous schedule of instruction in everything from dancing and military drill to Greek from a very early age. From seven to twelve he spent the winters at a boarding school, which he did not enjoy; in the vacations at home his schooling, under private tutors, was much more intensive. He was happiest on visits to grandparents in the country, where he could talk to an old gardener or climb up in a tree and read a novel. Too small and weak to win the admiration of his fellows, "he tried to be industrious and honest and noble and dutiful, finding that such a course brought praise from his elders" (10, pp. 20f.). When the death of his warmhearted mother desolated his father and himself, Jeremy "was just turned twelve, and was ready for Oxford, if a frail and undersized boy of twelve could be said to be ready for anything" (10, p. 22).

Coleridge's father, though unambitious in general and not very attentive to the education of his numerous other children, took special pride in him and endeavored from the beginning to prepare him for the Church. Coleridge was the last of fourteen children (ten by his mother), and the extreme fondness of his parents aroused the hostility of the older boys toward him. They drove him from play and tormented him. On one occasion, when he was eight, he ran away from home after a ferocious combat with the brother whom he had displaced as baby of the family; he was found only after a prolonged search, and he remembered all his life the tears of joy on his father's face and his mother's ecstasy when he was recovered. Death of the father, when he was nine, deprived him of his most valued companion. Shortly afterwards he was sent to a charity school in London. Here he made a few friends, notably Lamb, but he lived a great deal in books and in his own imagination.

Voltaire was born five years after the death in infancy of the next preceding child, and his own life was despaired of daily for the first year. His mother was an invalid; his father was a busy lawyer and does not seem to have concentrated any particular attention on him, beyond desiring that the boy should himself be prepared for the law. His education at home proceeded under the guidance of three distinguished and learned men, particularly the Abbé Chateauneuf, his godfather. The two other surviving children were considerably older than he; the brother he dis-

liked, but he was fond of his seven-years-older sister, and, after his mother's death when he was seven, it was she to whom he was chiefly attached in the family. At ten he was quartered in the best Jesuit school in France by his ambitious and wealthy father; here he made the warmest and most lasting friendships in his life, but they were with the teachers rather than with the boys.

Leopardi, the oldest of five children, remained until he was twenty-four, practically immured, in the house of his father, the Count, in a town which he despised. In Leopardi's own words: "Had no teachers except for the first rudiments, which he learned under tutors kept expressly in the house of his father. But had the use of a rich library collected by his father, a great lover of literature. In this library passed the chief portion of his life, while and as much as permitted by his health, ruined by these studies; which he began independently of teachers, at ten years of age, and continued thenceforth without intermission, making them his sole occupation" (29, p. 2). His closest companion was his brother Carlo, a year younger; but he was reticent even with him. With the other children he liked to produce plays in which the tyrant (his father) was worsted by the hero (himself). At a later age he regarded his home as a prison from which he had to break out.

Chatterton, born three months after his talented father's death, was the second surviving child of his very young mother, who had borne her daughter four or five years earlier before her marriage was legalized. Under their instruction, he learned the alphabet from an old illuminated music manuscript of his father's, which his mother had been about to throw away, and learned how to read from an old blackletter Testament. He had been dismissed from his first school as a dullard. Later, he went to the uninspiring charity school which had been attended by his father. A note on his relations with playmates before he was five speaks of him as "presiding over his playmates as their master and they as his hired servants" (20, p. 22). Already at five he was greedy for fame, and asked that a cup which had been presented to him by a relative should have on it "an angel with a trumpet, 'to blow his name about,' as he said" (20, p. 23). He did form friendships at school, one in particular; and the death of this boy plunged him into melancholy. But with none of these, or with his sister, was he intimate enough to share the secret of his Rowley poems, those impressive forgeries which seem to have been written under the inspiration and tutelage of the beautiful church of St. Mary Redcliffe rather than any human preceptor.

Niebuhr's father, who had been a military engineer and explorer, took up residence after his marriage at forty in a retired little town and devoted himself to his wife and family of two children. He liked to entertain his own and other children with stories, games, and music; but he concentrated particularly on the instruction of his son, for whom he also provided tutors from about four or five. A cultured neighbor, Boje, who was editor of a literary periodical, took much interest in the boy; and Boje's wife began his instruction in French. Her death when he was ten overwhelmed him with grief and inclined him even more seriously to his studies. Between fourteen and eighteen he spent most of the day in hard work and general reading. When he was sixteen his father, thinking that his attachment to home was excessive and that he was studying too much alone, sent him off to a school in Hamburg in the hope that he would become more sociable; but he was unhappy, and insisted on coming back. From an early age ill health and his mother's anxiety contributed their share to his inclination to solitude.

Mirabeau, the first surviving son of a family of the nobility, was in the beginning his father's pride. Later, after disfigurement by smallpox at three and displacement from the position of only son by the birth of a brother when he was five, he became increasingly the object of his erratic father's dislike. Intense marital discord made him the more hateful because he resembled his mother's side of the house. He was unfavorably compared with the other children, and repeatedly put under severe disciplinarians as tutors. Eventually his father had him imprisoned more than once. In the face of this persecution, helped partly by the affectionate interest of an uncle, Mirabeau succeeded nevertheless in developing an extraordinarily winning manner in speech and personal contacts, even charming his jailers into relaxing their punishments. Whether or not he was inclined to solitude, it was forced on him by his father; much of his learning and literary production took place in prisons or their equivalents. He was highly erotic, and may have had sexual relations with his younger sister; for so he asserts.

Adams regarded even his name, John Quincy, which was his great-grandfather's, as a perpetual admonition to live nobly. The Revolutionary War and the battle of Bunker Hill, which he witnessed, confirmed a serious habit of mind from early childhood. As his father was absent from home a great deal, he was already as a small boy depended upon by his mother as if he were a man. His education commenced at home under a tutor, and continued in Europe in the company of his father and other men notable in the governmental service. It was not until he entered Harvard that he attended a regular school for any length of time. Both his mother and his father tried to keep him from the corrupting influence of other boys, and it is evident from the nature of his life that his chief contacts were with grown men of serious and intellectual character. He read a great deal under the guidance of his father, whom in his earliest letters he obviously wished to please.

Wieland was educated at home under the eyes of his father, a pastor, in somewhat the same severe manner as was Goethe. He studied hard from three years of age. He says of his childhood: "I was deeply in love with solitude and passed whole days and summer nights in the garden, observing and imitating the beauties of nature" (26, p. 19). He was much more attached to books than to people. Prior to age seventeen, says his biographer, "We encounter not a single friend of his own age, only books and those who helped with them!" (26, p. 24). He was sensitive and unsociable when away at school, and when he returned home he lived alone or associated only with older men. His biographer makes no mention of his relations with his several siblings.

Tasso, whose old father was often compelled to be away from home, lived with his young mother and his sister until he was separated from them forever at ten, to join his father at the court of his patron prince. Even while he remained at home he was being strictly educated, first by an old priest, and then in a Jesuit school, which he loved. His mother, of whom he was passionately fond, died two years after he went to join his father. Of his childhood, Boulting says: "The prolonged absences of his father, the tears of his mother, the straitened circumstances and this sudden death were not healthy influences for a sensitive lad, and there was a great deal too much educational pressure put upon him. Bernardo was proud of Torquato's talents and ambitious as to his future. He forced him on and took scudi from a slender purse to pay for special lessons in Greek. But a cousin came to Rome from Bergamo to share in Torquato's studies. No bookworm was this lad, but full of fun and a thorough boy. Nothing could have been luckier" (3, p. 31). A little later he had as his companion in the study of the graces (horsemanship, jousting, etc.) a boy of eight, son of Duke Guidobaldo. Otherwise he seems to have associated primarily with men, often men of great dignity and learning.

Pope, the only child of his mother (there was a half-sister more than nine years older), was from the earliest period a domestic idol, as Stephen says. His father and mother, both forty-six at his birth, and a nurse, concentrated their affection upon him, which must have been all the more intense because he was sickly, and humpbacked like his father. "The religion of the family made their seclusion from the world the more rigid, and by consequence must have strengthened their mutual adhesiveness. Catholics were then harassed by a legislation which would have been condemned by any modern standard as intolerably tyrannical" (28, p. 2). Most of his education was accomplished at home, with some help from a family priest and his father, who corrected his early rhymes. From twelve he threw himself into his studies so passionately that his frail constitution threatened to break down.

Pitt was born at the high peak of his father's career as Prime Minister of England. When the title of Earl of Chatham was conferred on him, this second son, then seven, exclaimed, "I am glad that I am not the eldest son. I want to speak in the House of Commons like papa." Partly because of his feeble health, the boy was brought up at home under the instruction of his father and a tutor. His father concentrated upon developing his oratorical powers. At fourteen he was sent to Cambridge, where he was placed in the care of a sound scholar, who remained his inseparable companion, and practically his only one, for more than two years. He had no social life there. He read with facility such books as Newton's *Principia* and the obscurest of the Greek poets. "Through his whole boyhood, the House of Commons was never out of his thoughts, or out of the thoughts of his instructors" (17, p. 129).

Musset was the second son in a family devoted to literature, "an infant prodigy on whom the intelligence of his brother, six years his elder, did not fail to exercise a stimulating effect. Alfred developed his mind in the constant companionship of Paul much more rapidly than he would have in the company of children his own age" (5, p. 12). He was notable from early childhood for his sensitivity, charm, emotional ardor, dramatic power, and susceptibility to feminine beauty. At a very tender age he was already disappointed in love. He went to school for a short time with his brother, but sickness and the hostility of the other children toward these Bonapartists soon led to their being tutored at home, by a young man who knew how to combine pleasure with instruction.

Melanchthon always remembered the dying injunction of his father: "I have seen many and great changes in the world, but greater ones are yet to follow, in which may God lead and guide you. Fear God, and do right" (25, p. 6). Before this time (his father died when he was eleven) he was, by his father's express wishes, strictly educated, for a while in a local school, and then by a tutor, a conscientious teacher and stern disciplinarian. Afterwards, he came more directly under the influence of the celebrated scholar Reuchlin, who was his relative. It was Reuchlin, impressed by the scholarship of the little boy, who changed his name from Schwartzerd to its Greek equivalent Melanchthon. Of his earlier childhood it is related that he often gathered his schoolfellows around him to discuss what they had been reading and learning; and his grandfather delighted to engage him in learned disputes with traveling scholars, whom he usually confounded.

The brief sketches preceding tend to confirm the rule, I believe, that children of genius are exposed to significantly great amounts of intellectual stimulation by adults and experience very restricted contacts with other children of their age. Nor should we overlook the fact that books themselves, to which these children are so much attached, are representatives of the adult world. This is true in the superficial sense that they are provided by adults and, more significantly, may be drawn from a father's sacred library (one thinks of Leibniz, Leopardi, even Chatterton); it is true in the profounder sense that they are written by adults, and, in the case of most of the reading done by these children, *for* adults. Books extend the boundaries of the adult empire.

There is an effect of this constant intercourse with the adult world which may be especially important in the development of genius. Not only is there an increase of knowledge, which is the usual aim of the instructors; there is also, in many cases, a profound excitement of imagination. Even John Stuart Mill confesses that he did not perfectly understand such grave works as the more difficult dialogues of Plato when he read them in Greek at seven. What, then, happens to such adult material pouring into the child's mind? Mill does not elucidate his own case; but there is evidence in a number of the biographies before me that the dynamic processes of phantasy go to work on it and richly transform both what is understood and what is not.

Much of Goethe's association with other children was simply an occasion for expressing his vivid phantasy life; he entranced them with stories of imaginary adventures. Musset, also, reveled in a world of make-believe based upon the Arabian Nights and similar literature, and bewitched his enemies by the magic power of imagination. These were to become poets. But Bentham, who was no poet, imagined himself growing up as a hero like Fénelon's Telemachus and was stirred to moral fervor by sentimental novels. And two of the practical politicians in the list, Pitt and Niebuhr, may give us some insight into the process. When Pitt was around thirteen or fourteen he had written a tragedy, of which Macaulay has this to say: "This piece is still preserved at Chevening, and is in some respects highly curious. There is no love. The whole plot is political; and it is remarkable that the interest, such as it is, turns on a contest about a regency. On one side is a faithful servant of the Crown, on the other an ambitious and unprincipled conspirator. At length the King, who had been missing, reappears, resumes his power, and rewards the faithful defender of his rights. A reader who should judge only by the internal evidence, would have no hesitation in pronouncing that the play was written by some Pittite poetaster at the time of the rejoicings for the recovery of George the Third in 1789" (17, pp. 68f.). Out of his learning Pitt had constructed a dream prescient of his own future career. And who can say that the actions of a Prime Minister are not as much the expression of a private drama as they are the realistic application of the sciences and the laws? Niebuhr, who became a practical man of business and politics as well as the historian of Rome, writes explicitly about his own childhood experience, in a letter to Jacobi in 1811: "Our great seclusion from the world, in a quiet little provincial town, the prohibition, from our earliest years, to pass beyond the house and garden, accustomed me to gather the materials for the insatiable requirements of my childish fancy, not from life and nature, but from books, engravings, and conversation. Thus, my imagination laid no hold on the realities around me, but absorbed into her dominions all that I read —and I read without limit and without aim —while the actual world was impenetrable to my gaze; so that I became almost incapable of apprehending anything which had not already been apprehended by another—of forming a mental picture of anything which had not before been shaped into a distinct conception by another. It is true that, in this second-hand world, I was very learned, and could even, at a very early age, pronounce opinions like a grown-up person; but the truth in me and around me was veiled from my eyes—the genuine truth of objective reason. Even when I grew older, and studied antiquity

with intense interest, the chief use I made of my knowledge, for a long time, was to give fresh variety and brilliancy to my world of dreams" (4, p. 354).

My point is that phantasy is probably an important aspect of the development of genius, not only in those cases where the chief avenue to fame is through the production of works of imagination in the ordinary sense, but also in those where the adult accomplishment is of a different sort. Instead of becoming proficient in taking and giving the hard knocks of social relations with his contemporaries, the child of genius is thrown back on the resources of his imagination, and through it becomes aware of his own depth, self-conscious in the fullest sense, and essentially independent. There is danger, however, in the intense cultivation of phantasy. If it does not flow over into the ordinary social relations by some channel, if it has to be dammed up as something socially useless, then it threatens life itself. An expression of what I am referring to is given in that powerful scene in the first part of Goethe's *Faust* where the physician-magician, tampering with incantations, raises a spirit of overwhelming presence and quails before him. Something nearer to an outright demonstration is furnished by the life of Chatterton and his suicide.

Before he was eighteen Chatterton was dead by his own hand. If we examine his life, we see that it breaks apart into two distinct regions: an outer shell of schoolboy, apprentice, pretended antiquarian, and writer of brittle satire; and a core— the serious and deeply emotional 15th century poet Rowley, whose connection with himself he never publicly acknowledged. One must not forget that Chatterton's phantasy existence as Rowley has points of contact with his father, the musician schoolteacher who died before his son was born, but who, in a sense, presided over the boy's education through the music manuscript from which he learned his letters and the blackletter Testament in which he learned to read, and who, by his connection and the connection of his family with the magnificent church of St. Mary Redcliffe, which overshadowed the place of Chatterton's birth and was his favorite resort from the brutalities of Bristol, might surely continue to hold converse with the imaginative boy. The Rowley poems furthermore are related to Chatterton's search for a pedigree. In short, through Rowley, Chatterton established relations with the world of the dead; and since he could not admit that he himself was the author of the Rowley poems, but had to pretend to have found them in his role as antiquary, and was thus rejected as an impostor by Walpole, he could not through Rowley establish contact with the world of the living. The surface which he was able to present to the world was hard, brittle, violent, unreal. Yet even in his relations with the world he appeared to be doing the same thing he was doing through the Rowley phantasies, namely, seeking a father to love and protect him. He evidently placed great hopes in Walpole; but he had also tried and been disappointed in the patronage of men of lower caliber in Bristol. Eventually he came to a dead end in London, where he had no friends even of the quality of Bristol's Catcott. Just before he committed suicide he was Rowley once again in the most beautiful of his poems, the *Balade of Charitie,* which sums up his experience of the world and his yearning for a loving father. If it was Rowley who enabled Chatterton to live, it was also Rowley who opened the door of death for him and ushered him out of a world of constant bitter disappointment into a world of kindly and Christian spirits.

Chatterton is a supreme example of the dangers and costs of genius. Having no father or other appreciative adult to link him to the world, he was swallowed up by his imagination. But it is too often overlooked in the textbooks that genius in less tragic cases is generally a costly gift.

Superficially an enviable piece of luck, it is actually a fatality which exacts tribute from the possessor. Extreme absorption in very hard work is one of the penalties, and sometimes broken health. Isolation from contemporaries, often increasing with the years, is another. Whether we should include heterosexual difficulties as another, I am not sure, but I have indicated some of the facts in the last column of Table I and wish to consider the matter briefly. Fifty-five percent of our sample did not marry at all. There may be no special significance in this, since according to statistics for the United States (11) the marriage rate for the total population of males above fifteen is only about 60 per cent and may have been lower in earlier times. On the other hand, this group, with the exception of Chatterton, ranges in age from 39 to 84 and should be compared with the higher age groups. According to the 1930 census in the United States marriage had been entered into by 86 per cent of men in the age range from 35 to 44, and by age 60, which is about the median for our group of geniuses, it had been entered into by about 90 per cent. I will only note further that some delay or reluctance or dissatisfaction attend the marriages of Mill, Goethe, Coleridge, Mirabeau, Wieland, and perhaps Melanchthon, but it would not be desirable here to go into greater detail because of the impossibility of making appropriate comparisons. It may be that for marriages both freely contracted and happily sustained a rate of 3 in 20 is not out of the ordinary, though I should be inclined to say that here too we have an expression of the costliness of genius.

In summary, the present survey of biographical information on a sample of twenty men of genius suggests that the typical developmental pattern includes as important aspects: (1) a high degree of attention focused upon the child by parents and other adults, expressed in intensive educational measures and, usually, abundant love; (2) isolation from other children, especially outside the family; and (3) a rich efflorescence of phantasy, as a reaction of the two preceding conditions. In stating these conclusions I by no means wish to imply that original endowment is an insignificant variable. On the contrary, Galton's strong arguments on behalf of heredity appear to me to be well-founded; and in this particular sample the early promise of these very distinguished men cannot be dissociated from the unusual intellectual qualities evident in their parents and transmitted, one would suppose, genetically as well as socially to their offspring. It is upon a groundwork of inherited ability that I see the pattern operating. Whether the environmental phase of it summarized under (1) and (2) is actually causally important, and to what extent the environmental factors are related to the blossoming out of phantasy, are questions which could be examined experimentally, though obviously any thorough experiment would require both a great deal of money and a certain degree of audacity. It might be remarked that the mass education of our public school system is, in its way, a vast experiment on the effect of reducing all three of the above factors to minimal values, and should accordingly, tend to suppress the occurrence of genius.

References

1. Adams, C. F. Memoirs of John Quincy Adams. Vol. I. Philadelphia: Lippincott. 1874.
2. Bielschowsky, A. The life of Goethe. Vol. I. New York: Putnam. 1905.
3. Boulting, W. Tasso and his Times. London: Methuen. 1907.
4. Bunsen, C. C. J., J. Brandis, and J. W. Loebell. The Life and Letters of Barthold George Niebuhr. Vol. I. London: Chapman & Hall. 1852.
5. Charpentier, J. La Vie Meurtrie de Alfred de Musset. Paris: Piazza. 1928.
6. Courtney, W. L. Life of John Stuart Mill. London: Walter Scott. 1888.
7. Cox, C. M. The Early Mental Traits of Three Hundred Geniuses. Stanford University Press. 1926.
8. Elliot, H. S. R. The Letters of John Stuart Mill. Vol. I. London: Longmans. 1910.
9. Ellis, H. A Study of British Genius. Boston: Houghton Mifflin. 1926.
10. Everett, C. W. The Education of Jeremy Bentham. New York: Columbia University Press. 1931.
11. Folsom, J. K. The Family and Democratic Society. New York: Wiley. 1943.
12. Galton, F. Hereditary Genius. New York: Appleton. 1871.
13. Galton, F. English Men of Science. New York: Appleton. 1875.
14. Goethe, J. W. von. The Auto-Biography of Goethe. Truth and Poetry: from my own Life. London: Bohn. 1848.
15. Guhrauer, G. E. Gottfried Wilhelm Freiherr von Leibnitz, eine Biographie. Vol. I. Breslau: Hirt. 1842(?).
16. Hanson, L. The Life of S. T. Coleridge: the Early Years. New York: Oxford University Press. 1939.
17. Macaulay, T. B. Life of Pitt. New York: Delisser & Procter. 1859.
18. Merz, J. T. Leibniz. New York: Hacker. 1948.
19. Mesnard, J. Pascal, l'Homme et l'Oeuvre. Paris: Boivin. 1951.
20. Meyerstein, E. H. W. A Life of Thomas Chatterton. London: Ingpen & Grant. 1930.
21. Mill, J. S. Autobiography of John Stuart Mill. New York: Columbia University Press. 1948.
22. Montigny, L. Memoirs of Mirabeau. London: Edward Churton. 1835.
23. Parton, J. Life of Voltaire. Vol. I. Boston: Houghton Mifflin. 1881.
24. Périer, Mme. "Vie de B. Pascal." *In* Pensées de B. Pascal. Paris: Didot. 1854.
25. Richard, J. W. Philip Melanchthon, the Protestant Preceptor of Germany, 1497–1560. New York: Putnam. 1902.
26. Sengle, F. Wieland. Stuttgart: Metzler. 1949.
27. Stanhope, Earl. Life of the Right Honourable William Pitt. Vol. I. London: Murray. 1861.
28. Stephen, L. Alexander Pope. New York: Harper. N.d.
29. Thomson, J. Essays, Dialogues and Thoughts of Giacomo Leopardi. London: Routledge. N.d.
30. Trevelyan, G. O. The Life and Letters of Lord Macaulay. Vol. I. New York: Harper. 1876.
31. Vallentin, A. Mirabeau. New York: Viking. 1948.
32. Vreeland, H. Hugo Grotius, the Father of the Modern Science of International Law. New York: Oxford University Press. 1917.
33. Willert, P. F. Mirabeau. London: Macmillan. 1931.

As tests, and particularly personality tests or inventories, have become more effective, their use has become more widespread. Quite naturally, this increase in use and effectiveness has aroused some apprehension. This selection is a letter written in reply to a question which was raised about some particular items on one personality inventory, the Minnesota Multiphasic Personality Inventory—MMPI. In the course of answering the question about the specific items, the author, one of the developers of the MMPI, discusses the need for such tests, ethical considerations concerning their use, and the rationale behind their construction.

A POINT TO GUIDE YOUR STUDY   *Note the way in which the scales of the MMPI were developed experimentally, or empirically. This is, perhaps, the major strength of this particular personality inventory.*

43: MMPI: PROFESSIONAL USE BY PROFESSIONAL PEOPLE

Starke R. Hathaway, *University of Minnesota*

This long letter was prompted by a courteous inquiry that I received. The inquiry referred to the use of the MMPI as an aid in the selection of policemen from among applicants. It was pointed out that there are laws against inquiry about religious affiliation and the specific issue was the presence in the MMPI of items relating to religion.

Letter to Mr. R.

First I would like to express my appreciation of your reasonably expressed inquiry about the MMPI as possibly offensive in the statements that relate to religious activities and which might provide personal information on which discriminatory acts might be based. Because of sporadic public antagonism to psychological testing, and in view of our mutual concern for our civil liberties, I am going to answer you at considerable length and with unusual care. I shall send copies of this answer to the Psychological Corporation and to others

who may be concerned. Let me assure you at the outset that I believe I am proceeding from a considered position rather than from a defensive attitude that could lead me to irrationally protect the MMPI, other such tests, or psychologists in general. I believe that I would be among the first to criticize some of the uses to which tests are put, and some of those who use them improperly. I must also immediately make it clear that I am antagonistic to ignorant attacks upon tests. Tests are not offensive elements; the offensive elements, if any, come with the misuse of tests. To attack tests is, to a certain extent, comparable to an attack upon knives. Both good and bad use of knives occurs because they are sharp instruments. To eliminate knives would, of course, have a limiting effect upon the occurrence of certain hostile acts, but it would also greatly limit the activities of surgeons. I simply discriminate between the instrument and the objectives and applications of the persons who wield it. I am calling attention to the difference between a switchblade knife, which is good for nothing but attack, and a scalpel knife, good for healing purposes but which can also be used as a weapon. I

S. R. Hathaway. MMPI: Professional use by professional people. *Amer. Psychologist*, 1964, 19, 204–210. Copyright © 1964 by the American Psychological Association. Reprinted here with permission from the author and the American Psychological Association.

hope that no one will think that any test was devised in the same spirit that switchblade knives were devised. It is absurd if someone holds the belief that psychologists malignantly developed instruments such as the MMPI for use against the welfare of man, including of course man's personal liberties and rights. But if the MMPI and such tests have origins analogous to the scalpel, and are really perversely used to man's disadvantage, we are properly concerned. Let me turn to a history of the MMPI items about which you have inquired.

I should begin with an account of the origin of the MMPI itself. I believe I am competent to do this, and I hope you will see that its origins were motivated toward virtue as I have suggested above. In about 1937, J. C. McKinley, then head of the Department of Neuropsychiatry of the Medical School at the University of Minnesota, supported me in a venture which grew out of a current problem in our psychopathic hospital. The problem lay in the fact that insulin therapy as a treatment method for certain forms of mental disease had just become a widespread method of treatment. Different clinics were finding highly varied values. Some reported the treatment to be exceedingly effective; others said it was ineffective. The treatment was somewhat dangerous to patients, and it was exceedingly expensive in terms of hospitalization and nursing care. McKinley happened to be one of the neuropsychiatrists of the time who felt that more careful investigation should be undertaken before such treatments were applied, and in particular before we used them on our patients.

It occurred to us that the difficulty in evaluation of insulin treatment lay largely in the fact that there was no good way to be assured that the patients treated by this method in one clinic were like those treated in another clinic. This was due to the fact that the estimations of the nature of a person's mental illness and of its severity were based upon professional judgment, and could vary with the training background of the particular psychiatrist as well as with his personal experiences. Obviously, if the patients treated at one center were not like those treated at another center, the outcome of treatment might be different. At that time there was no psychological test available that would have helped to remove the diagnostic decisions on the patients in two clinics from the personal biases of the local staffs. There was no way that our hospital staff could select a group of patients for the new treatment who would be surely comparable in diagnosis and severity of illness to those from some other setting. It became an obvious possibility that one might devise a personality test which, like intelligence tests, would somewhat stabilize the identification of the illness and provide an estimate of its severity. Toward this problem the MMPI research was initiated.

I have established that decisions about the kind and severity of mental illness depend upon the psychological examinations of the psychiatrists and other professional persons. The items upon which the judgments are based constitute the symptoms of mental maladjustment or illness. Such symptoms have for many, many years been listed in the textbooks of psychiatry and clinical psychology that treat with mental disorder. These symptoms are verbal statements from or about the patient. The simplest and most obvious form of these symptoms are statements that confess feelings of unhappiness, depression, and the like. The statements may also be less personal, as in complaints about one's lot in life and about the inability to find employment or the mistreatment by others.

In summary, the symptoms of mental illness and unhappiness are represented in verbal complaints or statements that relate to personal feelings or personal experiences or reactions to job and home. It should be immediately apparent that unlike most physical illnesses, these verbally presented complaints or symptoms usually do not permit direct observation by others. If a patient reports a painful nodule or abdominal pain, the reported pain can usually be observed by some physical or nonverbal means that lends credence to the complaint. Many symptoms of mental illness are contrastingly difficult to observe by nonverbal means. It is almost impossible to establish that the person presenting the symptom is actualy suffering from a distortion of his psychologically healthy mental state by some psychological complex. There is much arbitrariness even in the statement "I am unhappy." Frequently no physical observation can be brought to bear upon the statement. The complainant may look unhappy and may even add that he is suicidal, yet friends and the examiner can agree that he is, "just asking for sympathy, is no worse off than the average." There is no way of solidly deciding what the words really mean. This point is crucial to what I am writing. If it is not clear at this point, reference books on semantics should be consulted. S. I. Hayakawa would be a good source.

I know of no method which will permit us to absolutely assess unhappiness or mental illness, either as to kind or severity, unless we start from inescapable symptoms that are verbally expressed and subject to the vagaries in the personal connotations of words and phrases. In initiating the research upon what was to produce the MMPI, we collected as many as we could find of the symptomatic statements recognized by authorities as indicative of unhappiness and mental illness. There were hundreds of these statements. We had at one time well over a thousand of them. Every one of these symptomatic statements had already been written into the literature or had been used as a practical

bit of clinical evidence in the attempt to understand patients. I repeat this because I want to thoroughly emphasize that every item in the MMPI came from assumed relationships to the assessment of human beings for better diagnosis and treatment of possible mental illness.

Now with all this preamble I am prepared to discuss the particular items that you have highlighted in your letter. It happens that, among the many items collected and finally selected to make up the MMPI, there were at least 19 relating to religion in one way or another. I have listed these items [on p. 347] to remind you again of the ones you cited, and I have added others that may further illustrate what I am saying. Now you have asked why we included these statements on religion among the possible symptoms of psychological maladjustment. Why should these items still appear in the MMPI?

In the first instance, the subject matter evidenced in the symptoms of depressed or otherwise mentally disturbed persons often largely centers in religion. There is a well-recognized pattern of psychological distortion to which we apply the term religiosity. When we use the word "religiosity," we indicate a symptomatic pattern wherein the process of an intercurrent psychological maladjustment is evidenced by extremes of religious expression that are out of the usual context for even the deeply religious person. A bishop friend of mine once illustrated the problem he sometimes had in this connection by his account of a parishioner who had routinely given a tithe as his offering toward support of the church, but who, within a few weeks, had increased the amount he gave until it was necessary for him to embezzle money for his weekly offering. Surely, my friend said, there is more here than ordinary devotion; there is something which should be considered from another frame of reference. In this anecdote there is an element of the symptomatic pattern,

	MALE		FEMALE	
	TRUE	NO ANSWER	TRUE	NO ANSWER
I am very religious (more than most people).	8*	9	11	9
Religion gives me no worry.	83	4	70	4
I go to church almost every week.	42	3	52	4
I pray several times every week.	50	3	83	2
I read in the Bible several times a week.	21	5	30	3
I feel sure that there is only one true religion.	49	8	51	11
I have no patience with people who believe there is only one true religion.	56	4	47	10
I believe there is a God.	92	5	96	2
I believe there is a devil and a hell in afterlife.	63	14	67	14
I believe in a life hereafter.	76	12	87	7
I believe in the second coming of Christ.	57	18	68	12
Christ performed miracles such as changing water into wine.	69	16	77	15
The only miracles I know of are simply tricks that people play on one another.	37	10	27	14
A minister can cure disease by praying and putting his hand on your head.	4	10	5	11
Everything is turning out just like the prophets of the Bible said it would.	52	29	54	32
My soul sometimes leaves my body.	8	18	5	12
I am a special agent of God.	14	13	16	21
I have had some very unusual religious experiences.	20	5	13	2
I have been inspired to a program of life based on duty which I have since carefully followed.	42	14	50	15

* Numbers in this table are percentages (*Ed.*).

religiosity. But, as is true of nearly every other aspect of human personality to which the MMPI refers, no one item will ordinarily establish this distortion of the ordinarily meaningful position of religion. And no one item can be used to detect the problem as it occurs in various persons. Two persons rarely express even their usual religious feelings in identical ways.

It never occurred to us in selecting these items for the MMPI that we were asking anything relative to the particular religion of our patients. It obviously did not occur to us that there were other than the Christian orientation wherein religiosity might be observed. Because of this oversight on our part, several of our MMPI symptoms that we assumed were indicative of religi-

osity happen to be obviously related to the Christian religion, although we find that most persons simply translate to their own orientation if it is different. I should hasten to add that although these symptoms were hoped to be specific to persons who suffer from religiosity, they have not all turned out that way. Not every aspect of religion is at times a symptom of mental illness. Certainly it is obvious that there is nothing symptomatic in admitting to one's personal acceptance or rejection of several of the items. The point at which a group of items becomes consistent in suggesting symptoms is subtle to distinguish. As my bishop friend's story illustrated, it is not unusual that one contributes to religious work even though there exists a doubtful extreme. As

I will show below, all these items are en-
dorsed or rejected by some ordinary,
normal people. If any of the items have
value toward clinical assessment, the value
comes in combination with other items
which probably will not seem to relate to
religion.

The MMPI, which started out so small
and inconspicuously, has become a world-
known and -used instrument. We did not
expect this outcome. If I were to select
new items, I would again include items
that related to religiosity. I would this
time, of course, try to avoid the implication that the religiosity occurred only
among adherents to the Christian faith. I
am obviously unhappy about the limited
applicability of these items, but I am, in
the same sense, unhappy about other items
in the MMPI. A considerable number of
the items have been challenged by other
groups from other standpoints. By this I
mean only to remind those concerned
about these religiosity items that there
are frankly stated items on sex, there are
items on body functions, there are items on
certain occupations; in fact, there are items
on most every aspect of psychological life
that can be symptomatic of maladjustment
and unhappiness. If the psychologist cannot use these personal items to aid in the
assessment of people, he suffers as did the
Victorian physician who had to examine
his female patients by feeling the pulse in
the delicate hand thrust from behind a
screen. I shall come back to this point
later, but it is obvious that if we were making a new MMPI, we would again be faced
either with being offensive to subgroupings
of people by personal items they object to
or, if we did not include personal items
and were inoffensive, we would have lost
the aim of the instrument.

One may protest that the MMPI is intended for the patient, the mentally ill
person, not applicants to schools, high-
school children, or to those being considered for jobs. I cannot give a general

defense of every such use, but this is a
time when preventive health is being
emphasized. We urge everyone to get chest
X rays and to take immunizing shots. We
are now beginning to advocate general sur-
veys with such psychological instruments
as the MMPI. The basic justification is
the same. We hope to identify potential
mental breakdown or delinquency in the
school child before he must be dragged
before us by desperate parents or by other
authority. We hope to hire police, who
are given great power over us, with assurance that those we put on the rolls should
have good personal qualities for the job.
This is not merely to protect us, this also
is preventive mental health, since modern
job stability can trap unwary workers into
placements that leave them increasingly
unhappy and otherwise maladjusted. If the
personality of an applicant is not appropriate to the job, neither employer nor
applicant should go ahead. We have always recognized the employer's use of this
principle in his right to personal interview
with applicants. Since the items and responses are on record, the MMPI and such
devices could be considered to be a more
fair method of estimation than the personal interview, and, when they are machine scored, they make possible much
greater protection from arbitrary personal
judgments and the open ended questions
that are standard for personal interviews.

It seems to me that the MMPI examination can be rather comparable to the
physical examination for selection of persons. One would not wish to hire a person
with a bad heart when the job required
behavior that was dangerous to him. I
think it would be equally bad to hire a
person as a policeman whose psychological
traits were inappropriate and then expect
him to do dangerous things or shoot to kill
as a policeman is expected to do. There is,
from physical and psychological examinations, a protection to the person being
hired as well as to those hiring him. This

is not meant as an argument for the use of the MMPI in every placement that requires special skills or special personality traits. I am arguing a general point.

I would next like to take up MMPI items to bring out a new line of evidence which, I am sorry to say, is not familiar to some psychologists, but which is of importance in giving you an answer to your questions. Turn again to the above items, particularly to the "True" response frequencies. We will look at implications about the people taking the MMPI as we interpret the True frequencies of response for these items.

Before we do so, we should consider the source of the frequency figures. The males and females who provided these standard data, which are the basis for all MMPI standards, were persons who came to the University Hospitals bringing patients or who were around the hospitals at the time when we were collecting data. Only those were tested who were not under a doctor's care and who could be reasonably assumed to be normal in mind and body. These persons, whom we call the normal adult cross-section group, came from all over Minnesota, from every socioeconomic and educational level; there is reason to believe that they are a proper representation of the rank and file people of Minnesota. It is probably well known that, in the main, Minnesota population was drawn from North European stock, is largely Christian in background, and has a rather small number in the several minority groups. Certainly, it can hardly be said that this population is unduly weighted with extremists in the direction of overemphasis upon religion or in atheism or in other belief characteristics. Probably one would expect this population to be rather more religious than the average for all the states. Finally, the majority of the persons who provided these basic norms were married persons and most were parents. Data given in the table can be found in the fundamental book on the MMPI, *An MMPI Handbook* by Dahlstrom and Welsh (1960).

But now consider the items. Let us assume, as is often naively assumed, that when one answers an item one tells the truth about oneself. Of course, there is no requirement that those who take the MMPI should tell the truth, and this is a very important point. Also, I have tried to establish that truth is a very complicated semantic concept. But let us assume for the moment that people do tell the truth as they see it. Take the item, "I go to church almost every week." According to the data given, 42% of the men and 52% of the women go to church almost every week. Now these data are representative of the whole state. I am sure that ministers of the state would be gratified if all these people were reporting accurately. Parenthetically, I suppose that "church" was read as "synagogue" or "temple" without much trouble. But I do not know what percentage of people are actually estimated to go to some church almost every week. At any rate I cannot conceive that 42% of the men of the state of Minnesota are in church nearly every week even if 52% of the women are. I even cannot conceive that half of the men in Minnesota and 83% of the women actually pray several times a week. I might imagine that 21% of the men and 30% of the women would read in the Bible several times a week. This would represent about one-fifth of all the men and about one-third of all the women. My real impression is that people simply do not know that much about the Bible. However, take the next item. Here it says that one feels sure there is only one true religion. To this about half of the men and half of the women answered True. Perhaps these might be considered bigoted, but what of the ones who have obviously answered false? There seems to be a great deal of religious tolerance here; about half of the persons of

Minnesota do not even express a belief that there is only one true religion.

It is true that a high percentage say they believe there is a God. This seems to be a noncommittal item, since most people are aware that God has many meanings. The item which follows it, however, which permits denying or accepting a belief in a devil and hell in afterlife, is quite interesting. Twenty-three percent of men and 19% of women reject this belief. By contrast, a life hereafter is denied by 24% of men and by 13% of women. The second coming of Christ is expected by only 57% of men and 68% of women if we accept what these figures seem to say. Again, with reversal, Christ as a miracle worker is doubted by 31% of men and by 23% of women. Stated more directly, 37% of men and 27% of women come straight out and say that miracles were not performed. The item apparently includes Old and New Testament sources among others. On down in the list, one finds that only 14% of men and 16% of women believe themselves to be special agents of God.

I think I have gone over enough of these items to provide a suggestion of what I am going to next point out. But I would like to add two more MMPI items in sharper illustration of the point. These two additional items have nothing obvious to do with religion. The first of them is, "I almost never dream," and the second is, "I dream frequently." One of the first things we found in the early studies of MMPI items was that the same person frequently answered True to both these items. When asked about the seeming contradiction, such a person would respond, among other possibilities, by saying to the first item that surely he had very few dreams. But, coming to the next item, he changed his viewpoint to say that he dreamed frequently as compared to some of the people he knew. This shift of emphasis led us to recognize that, in addition to the general semantic problem developed above, when

people respond to items, they also do not usually respond with the connotations we expect. Apparently even if the people are telling a truth of some kind, one would need an interview with them to know what they really intend to report by answering True or False. I suppose this is similar to the problem of the oath of allegiance over which some people are so concerned. One may state that he is loyal to the United States, for example, yet really mean that he is deeply convinced that its government should be overthrown and that, with great loyalty to his country, he believes revolution to be the only salvation for the country. However much we might object to it, this belief would permit a person to swear to his loyalty in complete honesty. I think most everyone is aware of this problem about oaths, and it is a routine one with MMPI item responses.

In summary of all this, if one wished to persecute those who by their answers to these items seemed inconsistent with some religious or atheistic pattern of beliefs, there would be an embarrassingly large number of ordinary people in Minnesota who would be open to suspicion both ways. In reality, the responses made to these items have many variations in truth and meaning. And it would betray considerable ignorance of the practical psychology of communication if any absolute reliance were placed on responses.

As a final but most significant point relative to these items, I should point out that administration of the MMPI requires that those who are taking the test be clearly informed that they may omit any item they do not wish to answer for whatever purpose. I have never seen any studies that have drawn conclusions from the omission of particular items by a particular person. We found that items among these that are being considered were unusually frequently omitted. You may notice this in the No Answer columns. One-third of all the respondents failed to answer the item relative to the Bible and the prophets, for example. This is a basic fact about the MMPI and such tests, and I cannot see why this freedom will not permit to each person the latitude to preserve his privacy if he is afraid. Still again I would add that, in many settings, possibly nearly every setting, where the MMPI is used in group administration, those who take it are permitted to refuse the whole test. I admit that this might seem prejudicial, and I suspect that if any one chooses to protect himself, he will do it by omitting items rather than by not taking the test at all. Is refusal to take the test any different from refusing to subject oneself to an employment or admission interview by a skilled interviewer? I think that some people who have been writing about the dangers of testing must have an almost magical belief in tests. Sometimes, when I feel so at a loss in attempting to help someone with a psychological problem, I wish that personality tests were really that subtle and powerful.

Groups of items called scales, formed into patterns called profiles, are the useful product of tests like the MMPI. I note that in your inquiry you show an awareness that the MMPI is usually scored by computers. The scales that are used for most interpretation include 10 "clinical" scales. These are the ones that carry most of the information. Several other scales indicate whether the subject understood and followed the directions. No one of these main scales has less than 30 items in it and most of them have many more than 30. The scores from the machine come back not only anonymously indicating the number of items answered in a way that counts on the scale, but the scores are usually already transformed into what we call T or standard scores. These T scores are still more remote from the particular items that make up a scale. The graphic array of T scores for the scales are finally printed into the profile.

In this connection, there is a very pretty possibility offered by the development of computer scoring. If we wish to take advantage of the presumed advantages of the use of tests, yet be assured that particular item responses shall not be considered, then we only need to be assured that those using the test do not score it, must send it straightway to the computer center, and, in the end, receive back only the profiles which are all that should be used in any case. The original test may be destroyed.

The scales of the profile were not arbitrarily set up. The MMPI is an experimentally derived instrument. If an item counts on a scale, I want to make it very clear that that item counts, not because some clinician or somebody thought that the item was significant for measuring something about human personality, but it counts because in the final analysis well-diagnosed groups of maladjusted, sometimes mentally ill persons answered the item with an average frequency differing from the average frequency of the normative group that I have used for the above illustrative data. This is an exceedingly significant point and is probably least often understood by those who have not had psychometric training. No one read or composed these items to decide what it meant if one of them were answered True or False. The meanings of the items came from the fact that persons with a certain kind of difficulty answered in an average way different from the "normal" standard. For example, the item "I go to church almost every week" is counted on a scale for estimating the amount of depression. We did not just decide that going to church was related to depression. We had the response frequencies from men who complained that they were depressed. They answered True with a frequency of only 20%. You will note that the normals answered True with a frequency of 42%— 22% more often. Now this difference also turned up for women who were depressed.

We adopted a False response to this item as a count on the depression scale of the MMPI. We do not even now know why depressed people say they go to church less often. Note that you are not depressed if you say False to this one item. Actually, 55% of the normals answered False. Use of the item for an MMPI scale depended on the fact that even more of the depressed persons answered False and so if you say False you have added one item more in common with depressed people than with the normals despite the fact that more than half the normals answered as you did.

Even psychologists very familiar with the MMPI cannot tell to which scale or scales an item belongs without looking it up. People often ask for a copy of a test so they can cite their objections to items they think objectionable, and they assume that the meaning of the item is obvious and that they can tell how it is interpreted. I am often asked what specified items mean. I do not know because the scoring of the scales has become so abstracted that I have no contact with items.

One more point along this line. Only 6 of the above 19 items are counted on one of the regular scales that are mostly used for personality evaluation. Four more are used on a measure that is only interpreted in estimation of the ability of the subject to follow directions and to read well enough. In fact, about 200 of the whole set of items did not end up on any one of the regularly used scales. But, of course, many of these 200 other items occur on one or another of the many experimental MMPI scales that have been published.

We cannot change or leave out any items or we lose an invaluable heritage of research in mental health. To change even a comma in an item may change its meaning. I would change the words of some items, omit some, and add new ones if I could. A new test should be devised, but its cost would be on the order a $100,000 and we are not at this time advanced

enough so that the new one would be enough better to compensate for the loss of the research and diagnostic value of the present MMPI even in view of its manifest weaknesses.

The subject of professional training brings me to my next line of response. It is appropriate that the public should be aware of the uses of such tests as the MMPI, but I have repeatedly pointed out that it is far more important that the public should be aware of the persons who are using the test and of the uses to which it is put. In this context, the distributor of the MMPI, the Psychological Corporation of New York City, accepts and practices the ethical principles for test distributors that have been promulgated by the American Psychological Association. These rules prohibit the sale of tests to untrained or incompetent persons. Use or possession of the MMPI by others is prohibited but, since this carries no present penalty, the distributor is helpless except for his control of the supply. Tests, as I have said above, are not like switchblade knives, designed to be used against people; they offer potential contributions to happiness. And I cannot believe that a properly accredited clinical psychologist or psychiatrist or physician who may use the MMPI would under any circumstances use it to the disadvantage of the persons being tested. If he does so, he is subject to the intraprofessional ethical-practice controls that are explicit and carry sanctions against those of us who transgress. The MMPI provides data which, like certain medical data, are considered by many to be helpful in guidance and analysis and understanding of people. Of course, in the making of this point, I am aware that there is no absolute meaning to what is ethical. What one group may think should be done about a certain medical-examination disclosure may be considered by another group to be against the patient's interest. I cannot do more than extend this ubiquitous ethical dilemma to the use of the personality test.

The essential point is that such tests should not be used except in professional circles by professional people and that the data it provides should be held confidential and be protected within the lawful practice of ethics. When these requirements are not met, there is reason for complaint. I hope I have made it clear that it is also my conviction that the MMPI will hurt no one, adult or child, in the taking of it. Without defending all uses of it, I surely defend it, and instruments like it, when they are in proper hands and for proper purposes. Monachesi and I have tested 15,000 ninth-grade school children with the MMPI. This took us into public schools all over the state, even into some parochial schools. In all of this testing, we had no difficulties with children, parents, or teachers except for a few courteous inquiries. We are now publishing what we hope will be significant data from this work, data bearing on delinquency and school dropout. We believe that this work demonstrates that properly administered, properly explained, and properly protected tests are acceptable to the public.

At the beginning of this statement I warned that I was going to make it quite long because I felt deeply on the matter. I hope I have not sounded as though I were merely being defensive, protecting us from those who would burn tests and who for good reasons are exceedingly sensitive about psychological testing. I am apologetic if I have sounded too much like the professional scientist and have seemed to talk down to the issue or to be too minutely explicit. I have not meant to insult by being unduly simple, but I have felt that I had to expand adequately on the points. As for psychologists who are those most widely applying such tests, I am aware that the public will look with increasing seriousness upon those who are entrusted with problems of mental health and the assessment of human actions.

I will end with a repetition of my feeling that, while it is desirable for the public to require ethical practices of those using tests, the public may be reassured that the psychologists, physicians, and others who use these new tests will be even more alert to apply the intraprofessional controls that are a requisite to professional responsibility. But I must emphasize that it is not to public advantage to so limit these professional judgments that we fail to progress in mental-health research and applications from lack of freedom to use the best instruments we have and to develop better ones.

Reference

Dahlstrom, W. G., & Welsh, G. S. *An MMPI handbook: A guide to use in clinical practice and research.* Minneapolis: Univer. Minnesota Press, 1960.

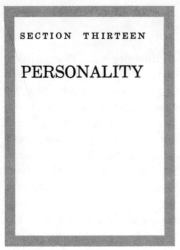

An interesting approach to the measurement and description of two important personality configurations is presented in this article.

POINTS TO GUIDE YOUR STUDY   *(1) The meaning of p values and levels of significance, e.g., .05, has been explained in previous introductions. (See the selection by Braun and Geiselhart in Section Three). (2) Note that the author is apparently tapping configurations which have widespread ramification.   (3) Note that the author is describing the most typical members of each group. In most of us, mixtures of the configurations exist.*

44: PERSONALITY STYLE AND PERCEPTUAL CHOICE

Frank Barron, University of California, Berkeley

The experimental investigation to be reported here is part of a comprehensive study of personality functioning in the highly effective, well-integrated American man whose life work is to be in the sciences or professions. The results of this particular subproject, however, are relevant not only to the aims of the larger study, but to the general question of the

relationship of perceptual attitude to personality. It is in the context of this latter area of psychological investigation that the findings seem most significant.

History of the research

In 1947 Welsh (8) constructed a test consisting of 200 ruled and freehand line drawings in black on 3-by-5-inch white cards. It was intended as an aid in the detection and diagnosis of psychiatric abnormality. Subjects were asked to indicate for each drawing whether they liked it or did not like it. The test was given to large groups of psychiatric patients as well as to persons who were not then, and had never been, psychiatric patients.

This study was carried on at the Institute of Personality Assessment and Research, University of California, and was supported financially by the grant of the Rockefeller Foundation to that Institute. The writer owes a special debt of gratitude to the Director of the Institute, Dr. Donald W. MacKinnon, for his unfailing encouragement and generous criticism of this portion of the Institute's program.

Frank Barron. Personality style and perceptual choice. *J. Pers.*, 1952, **20**, 385–401. Copyright © 1952 by the Duke University Press. Reprinted here with permission from the author and the Duke University Press.

From a factor analysis of the preferences of these subjects there emerged two factors: an acceptance-rejection factor (expressing the general tendency of the subject either to like or to dislike the figures), and a second, bipolar factor, orthogonal to the first, whose poles, as determined by inspection of the figures, seemed to be simplicity-symmetry and complexity-asymmetry.

Welsh noted that normal subjects who had very high positive scores on this bipolar factor differed markedly in personality style from those who had high negative scores. The consensus of a group of psychologists who were acquainted with the subjects was that the high positives (who preferred simple and symmetrical figures) were extremely conservative and conventional, while the high negatives tended to be dissident, cynical, and somewhat eccentric and deviant.

The possibility suggested itself, however, that the polar opposition evident in the factor was due more to good and poor artistic discrimination than to personality style. Some weight was lent to this view by the fact that the few artists in the normal sample all clustered together at the negative end of the factor. On the other hand, artists have sometimes been known to be dissident, cynical, deviant, and so on. A comparison of the figure preferences of a large sample of artists and nonartists seemed indicated, as a preliminary to the systematic exploration of the possibilities which had suggested themselves.

Accordingly, the set of figures, expanded now to 400 items, was given for sorting, with the same directions, to a sample of 37 artists and art students, and an item analysis was carried out to determine what figures were preferred in a significantly greater frequency by artists, on the one hand, and on the other by people in general. (The latter group consisted of 75 men and 75 women, covering a wide range of age, education, occupation, and geographical location.)

A scale was thus derived (1) consisting of 40 items disliked by artists significantly (p less than .01) more often than by people in general, and 25 items liked by artists significantly (p less than .05) more often. The items disliked by artists proved to be of the simple-symmetrical sort, while the items they liked were complex-asymmetrical. When tested on new groups of artists and nonartists, the scale proved highly effective in differentiating the groups. (This scale will hereafter be referred to as the Barron-Welsh Art Scale.)

It was now clear that artists differed from people in general in liking complex and asymmetrical figures, and in disliking the simple and symmetrical. It remained to be seen whether differences in personality style exist between artists and nonartists, as well as between nonartists who like simple and symmetrical figures as opposed to those who like complex and asymmetrical ones.

The present study

As we pointed out earlier, the present investigation was originally incidental to a study of personal effectiveness in the sciences and professions. A rather unusual sample was drawn for that study; its unique character in some respects restricts the generality of these findings, while at the same time lending them special meaning in other respects.

The sample, in brief, consisted of 40 male university students who were within one year of obtaining their final higher degrees (generally the doctorate) in a variety of departments. Twenty of these forty students had been rated by the faculties of their departments as possessing in high degree such qualities as originality and personal soundness, and were in addition judged to be outstanding in terms of promise and potential success in the fields of their choice. The other 20 students, while they all performed above the minimum required for obtaining the highest degree the department offered, nevertheless were judged, comparatively, to be low in originality, personal soundness, and potential success.

One research hypothesis was that the Highs would prove to differ from the Lows in being better able to discriminate the good from the poor (as judged by experts) in artistic productions. The Barron-Welsh Art Scale of the Welsh Figure Preference test, since it so clearly separated artists from nonartists, strongly recommended itself for partial test of this hypothesis (on the presumption that artists have better taste in such matters than do nonartists). In addition, since the design of the larger investigation called for intensive personality study of the subjects, some light might thereby be shed upon the relationship, if any, between personality style and kinds of figures preferred. The scale was therefore included in the extremely comprehensive battery of tests and techniques being used to study effective functioning.

In this new sample of 40 male graduate students, the scores on the test proved to be distributed bimodally, so much so that there were two distinct groups defined by these figure preferences. When the four middlemost cases of the distribution were excluded, there was an interval of 20 points on the 65-unit scale which was not occupied by any case, 18 cases falling on each side of this interval.

It was evident from an inspection of how scores were arrived at that one of these groups preferred, as did the artists, those figures which were asymmetrical, highly complex, freehand rather than ruled, and rather restless and moving in their general effect. (Several artists, in reacting to them, had described them as "organic.") The other group preferred the symmetrical, relatively simple, and decidedly "balanced" figures.

The symmetrical figures might also be described as "regularly predictable," following some cardinal principle which could be educed at a glance. This is in strong contrast to the asymmetrical figures, which give the impression of being unpredictable, irregular, and a product of the artist's momentary whim.

The 18 subjects who preferred the symmetrical and regularly predictable figures will hereafter be referred to as Group S, and the 18 who preferred the asymmetrical, irregular, and unpredictable figures as Group A.

Comparisons of the groups thus defined will be limited in the present paper to the results of a few fairly clear-cut techniques, involving little specialized psychological knowledge. A later report will deal with group performances on standardized personality tests.

Preferences for paintings

The subjects in this study had been asked to indicate the degree of their liking for each of 105 postcard-size reproductions in color of paintings by a large number of European artists, widely varied both as to time and place of origin, and representing many styles of painting as well as different choices of subject matter. Each painting was to be placed in one of four groups: Like Best of All, Like Much, Like Just Moderately, and Like Least of All. The subjects were asked to place approximately twice as many items in each of the two middle categories as in each of the two extreme ones.

An item was now defined to be a characteristic preference of a group if that item was placed in a given category significantly (.05 level of confidence) more often by that group than by the other. When this sort of analysis was carried out, it was found that no item was "characteristic" of a group in more than one category. It did happen, however, that some items appeared as characteristic of one group in the category "Like Best of All" while appearing as characteristic of the other group in the category "Like Least of All." Such extreme discordances in aesthetic prefer-

ences between Groups A and S are of special interest; in the lists below, they are
set off from the rest of the paintings in
the "Liked Best of All" and "Least of All"
categories for the two groups.

Liked best of all by Group S

Veneziano	Portrait of a Young Lady
Botticelli	Virgin and Child
Corot	The Woman with the Pearl
Fra Lippo Lippi	The Adoration
Leonardo da Vinci	John the Baptist
École Française, 16th century	Elizabeth of Austria
Gainsborough	Blue Boy
Raeburn	Boy with a Rabbit
Clouet	Portrait of Francis I
École Francaise, 16th century	Francis I

Paintings above were "liked least" by Group A

Rembrandt	Portrait of Hendriche Stoffels
Rembrandt	Portrait of Himself in Old Age
Sanzio	Portrait of Balthazar Castiglione
Rembrandt	His Portrait by Himself
Utrillo	A View of Anse
Rembrandt	The Syndics
Gauguin	The Seine at Paris

DISCUSSION The first thing that strikes the
eye about this set of paintings is that it
consists largely of portraits. Of seventeen
paintings in the group, twelve are portraits, three are religious scenes, and two
are landscapes.

Considering how portraits usually get to
be painted, one is not surprised to note in
addition that the subjects are generally of
aristocratic bearing and mien, richly and
fashionably clothed. The ladies portrayed
are pure and noble—not by character only,
but by birth. The gentlemen are clearly
persons of substance, accustomed to hom-
age and given to command. (The imperi-
ous Francis I is represented twice, the
portraits being by different artists.)

The paintings with a religious theme are
of the Virgin and Child, the Adoration of
the Infant, and Leonardo's St. John the
Baptist. The landscapes are tranquil and
pleasant ones, somewhat formal and "cul-
tivated."

The dominant note in this set of paintings is one of religion, authority, and
aristocracy, personified in the courtly,
high-born, and holy personages depicted.

Liked least of all by Group S

Picasso	The Bust before the Window
Picasso	Still-life by Candle-light
Modigliani	The Woman from Burgundy
Gris	The Breakfast
Modigliani	Marcelle
Gris	Woman with a Book
Toulouse-Lautrec	The Clowness
Vuillard	In Bed

Paintings above were "liked best" by Group A

Cézanne	Women bathing
Cézanne	The Black Marble Clock
Léger	Composition in 3 Profiles
Renoir	Woman with the Veil
Cézanne	Onions and Bottle
Lautrec	Jeanne Avril

DISCUSSION Now, let us examine the
paintings which are placed at the opposite
pole by Group S.

First, we note that all of the "abstractions" (five in a group of 105) are placed
by these subjects in the Like Least of All
category. (Four of these same five abstractions are liked "Best" by Group A.) In
addition, the Modigliani women (who
clearly are not faithful representations of
"real" women) are similarly liked "Least"
by Group S but "Best" by Group A.

What seems to be expressed here is a
strong rejection of the esoteric, the radically experimental, and the "unnatural."
(Supernatural themes, however, win approval if naturally represented and peopled
by recognizably human beings.)

Rejected along with the unnatural and
the radically experimental are ladies of
low birth and ignoble pursuits. In this
group we find the prostitute painted by
Toulouse-Lautrec, the nudes in the Ce-
zanne painting, "Women Bathing," Re-
noir's "Woman with the Veil" (an impressionistic suggestion of intrigue, assignation,
and so on), and Vuillard's young woman
"In Bed."

In summary, Group S approves good breeding, religion, and authority, and rejects the daring, the esoteric, the "unnatural," and the frankly sensual.

Liked best of all by Group A

Picasso	The bust before the window
Picasso	Still-life by candle-light
Modigliani	The Woman from Burgundy
Gris	The Breakfast
Modigliani	Marcelle
Gris	Woman with a Book
Toulouse-Lautrec	The Clowness
Vuillard	In Bed

Paintings above were "liked least" by Group S

Renoir	Bathing woman
Van Gogh	The Bridge
Vlaminck	The House with the Weatherboard
Daumier	The Amateur of Etchings
Dunoyer de Segonzac	Staddle
Toulouse-Lautrec	Two Walzes
Gauguin	Women of Tahiti
Gauguin	And the Gold of Their Bodies
Degas	The Ironers

DISCUSSION We note immediately that in this set are represented the products of such "modern" art movements as Primitivism, Expressionism, Impressionism, and Cubism. These were revolts against traditional ways in art, expressed in radical experimentation in design, a search for the primitive and the naïve, a rejection of the directly representational in favor of the derivative and the abstract, and a choice of subject matter which affirmed the importance of the commonplace. Here sensuality and the instinctual life receive, to say the least, their due. Like many revolutionary movements, these delighted in being extreme, and one senses at times a certain histrionic and theatrical element accompanying the honest quest for new ways of expressing reality (and new realities to express).

Liked least of all by Group A

Veneziano	Portrait of a Young Lady
Botticelli	Virgin and Child
Fra Lippo Lippi	The Adoration

Corot	The Woman with the Pearl
da Vinci	John the Baptist
École Francaise, 16th century	Elizabeth of Austria
Gainsborough	Blue Boy
Raeburn	Boy with a Rabbit
Clouet	Portrait of Francis I
École Française	Francis I

Paintings above were "liked best" by Group S

da Vinci	The Virgin, Child, and St. Anne
Redon	Flowers
Lucientes	Lady with the Fan
Whistler	Mother
Grunewald	The Annunciation
da Vinci	Portrait of Lucrezia Crivelli
Holbein	Portrait of Ann of Cleves
Watteau	Embarkment for Cythera
Goya y Lucientes	The Manikin
Ingres	The Odalisque
Corot	Landscape
École Française	Francis I
Angelico	The Anunciation

DISCUSSION It is evident that the members of Group A do not like religious themes in paintings. Of the eight religious scenes in the 105 paintings, six are placed in the Like Least category: Leonardo, Botticelli, Angelico, Grunewald, and Fra Lippo Lippi alike fall before this categorical rejection of the religious.

Further, the members of Group A do not like portraits of lords and ladies. Three different portraits of Francis I are relegated to the "Like Least" category, in company with Lucrezia Crivelli, Ann of Cleves, Elizabeth of Austria, the young aristocrat who served as the model for Blue Boy, and Whistler's Mother. (It is ironic that the eccentric and self-consciously nonconformist Whistler should be remembered to common fame, largely by courtesy of the American commercialization of Mother's Day, for a painting which he intended as an innovation in design, and which he titled "Arrangement in Grey and Black.")

The women in the portraits disliked by Group A have in common that they are rather aloof and distant. Even the odalisque in Ingres' painting is remarkably unsensual in appearance. This is in strong contrast to the women in the paintings liked best by Group A, who are considerably more informal and relaxed, and whose sexual role receives more emphasis.

In summary, Group A approves the modern, the radically experimental, the primitive and the sensual, while disliking what is religious, aristocratic, traditional, and emotionally controlled.

Group differences in self-description

We have seen that the two groups defined by figure preferences show consistently different preferences in paintings as well, and that the two sets of preferences taken together seem to suggest quite different perceptual attitudes bearing on (1) predictability, stability, balance, symmetry, and governance by a simple general principle; and (2) acceptance or rejection of tradition, religion, authority, and sensuality. How do persons with such different attitudes differ in seeing themselves?

A partial answer to this question is provided by an item analysis of the Gough Adjective Check-List, which was used in the study. Each subject had been asked to indicate (by a check mark) what adjectives in the list were, in his opinion, descriptive of himself. There were 279 adjectives in all.

Here are the adjectives which differentiated the groups, listed in the order of their discriminating power [see right column, above]:

In these self-descripions, as in the characteristic art preferences, these two groups clearly separate themselves from one another. It seems not too much to say that they hold different views of themselves and of the world. The origins and consequences of such divergent perspectives on self and universe will be explored, necessarily somewhat speculatively, in the concluding section of this paper. Before embarking on

	GROUP S	GROUP A
At the .05 level:	contented	gloomy
	gentle	loud
	conservative	unstable
	unaffected	bitter
	patient	cool
	peaceable	dissatisfied
		pessimistic
		emotional
		irritable
		pleasure-seeking
At the .10 level:	serious	aloof
	individualistic	sarcastic
	stable	spendthrift
	worrying	distractible
	timid	demanding
	thrifty	indifferent
At the .15 level:	dreamy	anxious
	deliberate	opinionated
	moderate	temperamental
	modest	quick
	responsible	
	foresighted	
At the .2 level:	conscientious	

that further inquiry, however, we should note immediately that both types, A and S, are represented with about equal frequency among the Highs and the Lows of our sample of graduate students. Neither one nor the other view is significantly related to the total constellation of factors which make for personal effectiveness and success in graduate school. One may be both contented and original, gloomy and personally sound. There is more than one path to personal integrity, and more than one way in which to contribute meaningfully to scientific and professional life.

Relevant work of other psychologists

WILLIAM JAMES   Although we have come

upon these facts largely incidentally while in search of others, it is quite understandable in the light of the facts themselves that they have been anticipated by someone who proceeded more by reason than by experiment. For in his lectures on pragmatism, William James set forth quite clearly the very opposition between "types of mental make-up" which these experimental data have made evident. Consider the respective traits of these two types, as he lists them in "The Present Dilemma in Philosophy" (6):

Rationalistic (going by "principles")	Empiricist (going by "facts")
Intellectualistic	Sensationalistic
Idealistic	Materialistic
Optimistic	Pessimistic
Religious	Irreligious
Free-willist	Fatalistic
Monistic	Pluralistic
Dogmatical	Skeptical

Now compare them with these experimentally found characteristics of Groups S and A [see right column above]:

James set forth these "contrasted mixtures" by way of making more particular his thesis that "the history of philosophy is to a great extent that of a certain clash of human temperaments." He remarks that "nature seems to combine most frequently with intellectualism an idealistic and optimistic tendency. Empiricists on the other hand are not uncommonly materialistic, and their optimism is apt to be decidedly conditional and tremulous. Rationalism is always monistic. It starts from wholes and universals, and makes much of the unity of things. Empiricism starts from the parts, and makes of the whole a collection—is not averse therefore to calling itself pluralistic. Rationalism usually considers itself more religious than empiricism, but there is much to say about this claim; so I merely mention it. It is a true claim when the individual rationalist is what is called a man of feeling, and when the individual

GROUP S	GROUP A
In figure preferences: Preferring what is simple, regularly predictable, following some cardinal principle which can be educed at a glance.	In figure preferences: Preferring what is complex, irregular, whimsical.
In art preferences: Preferring themes involving religion, authority, and aristocracy.	In art preferences: Preferring what is radically experimental, sensational, esoteric, primitive, and naïve.
In adjective self-checks: Contented, gentle, conservative, patient, peaceable, etc.	In adjective self-checks: Gloomy, pessimistic, bitter, dissatisfied, emotional, pleasure-seeking, etc.

empiricist prides himself on being hard-headed. In that case the rationalist will usually also be in favor of what is called free-will, and the empiricist will be a fatalist—I use the terms most popularly current. The rationalist finally will be of dogmatic temper in his affirmations, while the empiricist may be more skeptical and open to discussion." (6, pp. 10f.)

Now it happens that these essays in pragmatism were not known to the present writer at the time this research was carried out. The writer's somewhat similar views, however, led to the inclusion in the research program of an interview with each subject on his philosophy of life, the interview centering generally around the freedom-determinism question and the problem of evil. The results of this interview will be reported in a later paper, and will be discussed both in the context of the types here delineated and in terms of the childhood events which seemed determinative of such basic attitudes towards the world.

BURT AND EYSENCK   There are two significant lines of experimental investigation in aesthetic choice and personality style which are relevant to the present findings. While both have used primarily the technique of factor analysis, they have been marked by somewhat different approaches to the same subject matter. One point of origin was the search for temperamental factors, while the other was the search for factors present in aesthetic preferences.

The first of these lines of investigation, comprising a series of studies by Cyril Burt and his students, and summarized by him in (2), was centered upon the discovery and description of factors in personality. He distinguished four temperamental types: (1) the unstable extravert; (2) the stable extravert; (3) the unstable introvert; (4) the stable introvert. Tendencies towards these types, when measured by a regression equation or some similar device, prove to be approximately normally distributed; Burt therefore selected the extreme 10 per cent of the distributions as more or less "pure" representatives of the type. In samples thus selected, he found these characteristic aesthetic preferences:

1. The Unstable Extravert likes dramatic and romantic art, and prefers color to form and line in paintings. In music he likes chromatic rather than diatonic harmony, and prefers rhythm to melody. His penchant is for dramatic events, emotionally or even sensationally treated. Pictures in which a human figure is conspicuous are preferred to landscapes, interiors, or still life. The unstable extravert likes vivid colors, strong contrasts, and vigorous and flowing curves. There is strong empathy for "restless movement" in art and architecture.

2. The Stable Extravert differs in emphasizing the cognitive rather than the emotional aspects of external reality. He is strongly representational and practical, and sets more store by solidity and mass than by decoration and flowing curves. He likes historical subject matter, realistically treated.

3. The Unstable Introvert prefers impressionistic art, with emphasis on the supernatural and the mystical—a sort of romanticism, but without the element of adventure in the real world which characterizes the unstable extravert. The unstable introvert prefers landscapes, especially if "mystically" treated, to portraits; he likes the work of such artists as El Greco, Blake, Corot, Durer, Monet, Botticelli, and Rossetti. In literature, his preferences are for Spenser, Shelley, Yeats, Coleridge, De Quincy.

4. The Stable Introvert has a strongly intellectual attitude, and attends to the picture as an object in itself. The chief appeal is in "the significant form." Pattern rather than content is important. Good drawing, clean lines, and chiaroscuro appeal more than colors. There is a strong repugnance for the sentimental and the theatrical. Tranquil landscapes and formal, closed-in scenes are preferred. The stable introvert has little interest in portraiture, except that of Rembrandt and Van Eyck. He prefers unity and repetition to diversity and variegation, likes economy rather than exuberance, and prefers the conventional to the obtrusively original.

While the findings reported by Burt cannnot be unequivocally assimilated to the results of the present research, there are certainly many points of contact. In general, Unstable Extraverts would seem to belong to our Group A, while "stable" people, both extraverts and introverts, would probably be classed with Group S. Where the Unstable Introvert would fit is not entirely clear, although the tendency would probably be towards Group A rather than Group S. Indeed, since "stable" is one of the adjectives with which Group S characterizes itself, while Group A describes itself as "unstable," perhaps we can do no better than to take the subjects' own word on the matter, using stability-instability as the most relevant principle of classification.

The second line of investigation, no doubt deriving historically from the first, but conceptually somewhat different, is that carried on by Eysenck. Rather than working from personality factors to their correlates in aesthetic preferences, he began by establishing factors in the latter realm of behavior, and then sought their correlates in personality.

Eysenck demonstrated for a number of stimulus classes (colors, odors, paintings, polygons, poetry, etc.) the existence of a general factor of aesthetic appreciation, and in addition showed that when the influence of this factor is eliminated a secondary, bipolar factor can be found (3, 4, 5). This latter factor, which he named "K," generally has positive and negative saturations in about equal numbers in the populations studied. One of its poles seems to be represented by preference for the simple polygon, the strong, obvious odor, the poem with the obvious rhyming scheme and the definite, unvarying, simple rhythm, and the simple, highly unified picture. At the other pole is preference for the more complex polygon, the more subtle odors, the poem with a less obvious rhythm and a more variable and loose rhyming scheme, and the complex, more diversified picture.

Eysenck's description of this bipolar factor fits quite well the factor found by Welsh in his original study. As a result both of Eysenck's further work and of our own investigations, we now know a great deal more about the relationship of this factor to personality variables. Eysenck himself showed that the K-factor (as measured anew by a "K-test" consisting of 100 pairs of pictures) correlated significantly with both extraversion-introversion and radicalism-conservatism. Subjects who preferred the modern, impressionistic paintings were extraverted and radical, while those who preferred the older, more conventional paintings were introverted and conservative. Taken in conjunction with Burt's findings, this would point to the members of Group S as being predominantly stable introverts, while the members of Group A would be best classed as unstable extraverts. There is perhaps little point, however, in attempting to reconcile these different classifications in the absence of data collected specifically to resolve the issue.

Conclusions and discussion

The findings which require explanation, then, are these:

1. We are dealing with two types of perceptual preferences, one of them being a choice of what is stable, regular, balanced, predictable, clear-cut, traditional, and following some general abstract principle, which in human affairs is personified as authority; the other a choice of what is unstable, asymmetrical, unbalanced, whimsical, rebellious against tradition, and at times seemingly irrational, disordered, and chaotic.

2. These two types occur with equal frequency in the two classes of subjects defined by ratings as low or high in a constellation of factors making for personal effectiveness.

We suggest that the types of perceptual preference we have observed are related basically to a *choice of what to attend to* in the complex of phenomena which make up the world we experience; for the world *is* both stable and unstable, predictable and unpredictable, ordered and chaotic. To see it predominantly as one or the other is a sort of *perceptual decision;* one may attend to its ordered aspect, to regular sequences of events, to a stable center of the universe (the sun, the church, the state, the home, the parent, God, eternity, etc.) or one may instead attend primarily to the eccentric, the relative, and the arbitrary aspect of the world (the briefness of the individual life, the blind uncaringness of matter, the sometime hypocrisy of authority, accidents of circumstance, the presence of evil, tragic fate, the impossibility of freedom for the only organism capable of conceiving freedom, and so on).

Either of these alternative perceptual decisions may be associated with a high degree of personal effectiveness. It is as though there is an effective and an ineffective aspect of each alternative. Our thinking about these various aspects is as yet based only upon clinical impressions of our subjects, but it is perhaps worth recording while we go on with the business of gathering more objective evidence.

At its best, the decision in favor of order makes for personal stability and balance, a sort of easy-going optimism combined with religious faith, a friendliness towards tradition, custom, and ceremony, and respect for authority without subservience to it. This sort of decision will be made by persons who from an early age had good reason to trust the stability and equilibrium of the world and who derived an inner sense of comfort and balance from their perception of an outer certainty.

At its worst, the decision in favor of order makes for categorical rejection of all that threatens disorder, a fear of anything which might bring disequilibrium. Optimism becomes a matter of policy, religion a prescription and a ritual. Such a decision is associated with stereotyped thinking, rigid and compulsive morality, and hatred of instinctual aggressive and erotic forces which might upset the precariously maintained balance. Equilibrium depends essentially upon exclusion, a kind of perceptual distortion which consists in refusing to see parts of reality which cannot be assimilated to some preconceived system.

The decision in favor of complexity, at its best, makes for originality and creativeness, a greater tolerance for unusual ideas and formulations. The sometimes disordered and unstable world has its counterpart in the person's inner discord, but the crucial ameliorative factor is a constant effort to integrate the inner and outer complexity in a higher-order synthesis. The goal is to achieve the psychological analogue of mathematical elegance; to allow into the perceptual system the greatest possible richness of experience, while yet finding in this complexity some over-all pattern. Such a person is not immobilized by anxiety in the face of great uncertainty, but is at once perturbed and challenged. For such an individual, optimism is impossible, but pessimism is lifted from the personal to the tragic level, resulting not in apathy but in participation in the business of life.

At its worst, such a perceptual attitude leads to grossly disorganized behavior, to a surrender to chaos. It results in nihilism, despair, and disintegration. The personal life itself becomes simply an acting out of the meaninglessness of the universe, a bitter joke directed against its own maker. The individual is overwhelmed by the apparent insolubility of the problem, and finds the disorder of life disgusting and hateful. His essential world-view is thus depreciative and hostile.

We have not hesitated to refer here to perceptual *decision,* to an act of choice on the part of the individual. That is to say, we conceive this as a matter not simply of capacity, but of preference. Such a choice does of course involve perceptual capacity, but beyond capacity it is a matter of orientation towards experience; in a sense, perceptual attitude. In their important theoretical article (in search of the perceiver in perceptual theory) Klein and Schlesinger (7) have emphasized that their empirically found patterns of modes of perceptual response (to which they give the name syndrome) are to be thought of as *"preferred* styles of expression rather than *required* ones" (italics theirs). In search of the perceiver, they came inevitably upon *choice* rather than capacity or necessity as the determiner of observed response.

This very perceptual decision, of course, is itself determined; and it is to the search for the determinants that the next step in this line of research will be devoted.

References

1. Barron, F., and Welsh, G. S. Artistic perception as a possible factor in personality style: its measurement by a figure preference test. (To appear.)
2. Burt, C. The factorial analysis of emotional traits, Parts I and II. *Charact. & Pers.,* 1939, 7, pp. 238–254, 275–299.
3. Eysenck, H. J. The general factor in aesthetic judgments. *Brit. J. Psychol.,* 1940, 31, 94–102.
4. Eysenck, H. J. Some factors in the appreciation of poetry, and their relation to temperamental qualities. *Charact. & Pers.,* 1940–41, 9, 160–167.
5. Eysenck, H. J. "Type" factors in aesthetic judgments. *Brit. J. Psychol.,* 1941, 31, 262–270.
6. James, W. The present dilemma in philosophy, Lecture I in *Pragmatism,* New York: Longmans, Green & Co., 1907.
7. Klein, G., and Schlesinger, H. Where is the perceiver in perceptual theory?, *J. Pers.,* 1949, 18, 32–47.
8. Welsh, G. S. A projective figure-preference test for diagnosis of psychopathology: 1. A preliminary investigation. Unpublished Ph.D. thesis, University of Minnesota, 1949.

The analysis of conflict situations has been quite useful in psychology. What follows is one of the first accounts of approach-approach, approach-avoidance, and avoidance-avoidance conflicts.

K. Lewin placed much emphasis on field forces in psychology, both in Germany and later in the United States. The individual was viewed as being acted upon by psychological forces, having both direction and strength, of various kinds. These psychological forces should not be confused with physical forces. Their strength and direction is determined by the individual's perception of his environment.

A POINT TO GUIDE YOUR STUDY   *Think of the last time you experienced a conflict and make a Lewinian diagram of it.*

GLOSSARY   **Valence:** *Lewin's term for attraction to, or repulsion from, a goal.* **Vector:** *represents the strength (by arrow length) and the direction of a force.*

45: SELECTION FROM: A DYNAMIC THEORY OF PERSONALITY

Kurt Lewin

Constellations of forces

CONFLICT The ways in which different valences may interact in a situation are

Kurt Lewin. *A dynamic theory of personality.* New York: McGraw-Hill, 1935. Trans. by D. K. Adams and K. Zener. Copyright © 1935 by the McGraw-Hill Book Company, Inc. Excerpt reprinted here with permission from the McGraw-Hill Book Company, Inc. Footnotes omitted and figures renumbered.

naturally very numerous. I select for discussion the case of conflict because of its special significance.

Conflict is defined psychologically as the opposition of approximately equally strong field forces. There are three basic cases of conflict, so far as driving forces are concerned.

1. The child stands between two posi-

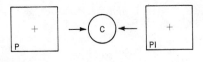

FIGURE 1.

tive valences (Figure 1). He has to choose
perhaps between going on a picnic (P)
and playing (Pl) with his comrades. In
this type of conflict situation decision is
usually relatively easy. As a result of the
fact that after the choice is made the goal
chosen often seems inferior (for reasons to
be described later), oscillation does sometimes occur.

2. The child faces something that has
simultaneously both a positive and a negative valence (Figure 2). He wants, for

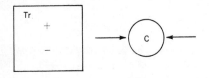

FIGURE 2.

example, to climb a tree (Tr), but is
afraid. This constellation of forces plays
an important part in cases in which a
reward is offered for an activity (e.g., a
school task) which the child does not want
to execute.

Conflict situations of this type usually
develop rather quickly also in the detour
experiments mentioned above, in the experiments of Fajans, or in other situations
in which the attainment of the goal is impeded by some barrier. At first the child
sees a difficult barrier (B) between him-

FIGURE 3.

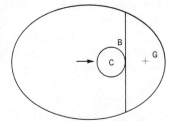

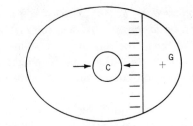

FIGURE 4.

self and his goal (G), which hinders the
completion of actions in the direction of
the field forces (Figure 3). But after the
child has run against the barrier several
times and perhaps hurt himself, or had the
wounding experience of failure, the barrier
itself acquires a negative valence (Figure 4). Besides the positive, there comes
into existence a negative vector, and we
have the Type 2 conflict situation. The
negative vector usually increases gradually
in strength and finally becomes stronger
than the positive. Accordingly, the child
goes out of the field.

This withdrawal [*Aus-dem-Felde-Ge-
hen*] either may be physical, as when the
child retreats, turns away, or possibly
leaves the room or place, or may be an
inward going out of the field, as when the
child begins to play or to occupy himself
with something else.

It not infrequently occurs, for example
in embarrassment, that the child makes
certain bodily movements toward the goal
but at the same time is mentally occupied
with something else. In such cases the
bodily act has the character of a more or
less set gesture.

In such situations the withdrawal is at
first almost always merely temporary. The
child turns away, only to return after a
while for another try at the barrier. A final
and permanent withdrawal usually occurs
only after several temporary withdrawals,
the duration of which increases until finally
the child does not return.

Unusual persistence in such a situation

is not necessarily an indication of activity. On the contrary, active children usually go out of the field earlier than passive children. It is not the duration but the kind of approach that is significant for activity.

Related to this is the fact that under certain circumstances the single actions in such a conflict situation are longer with the infant than with the young child, although in general the duration of action unities increases with the age of the child.

3. The third type of conflict situation occurs when the child stands between two negative valences, for example, when it is sought by threat of punishment (P) to move a child to do a task (T) he does not want to do (Figure 5).

There is an essential difference between this and the conflict situation described under 1. This becomes clear when one proceeds to represent the total distribution of forces in the field of force.

FIELD OF FORCE   The field of force indicates which force would exist at each point in the field if the individual involved were at that point. To a positive valence there corresponds a convergent field (Figure 6).

As a simple example of the structure of the field of force in a conflict situation of

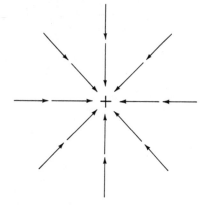

FIGURE 6.

Type 2, a case from one of my films may be adduced: a three-year-old boy wants to fetch a rubber swan out of the water to the beach, but is afraid of the water. To the swan (S) as positive valence there corresponds a convergent field (Figure 7). This field is overlaid by a second field which corresponds to the negative valence of the waves. It is important that here, as frequently in such cases, the strength of the field forces which correspond to the negative valence diminishes much more rapidly with increasing spatial distance than do the field forces corresponding to the positive valence. From the direction and strength of the field forces at the various points of the field it can be deduced

FIGURE 5.

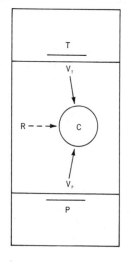

FIGURE 7.

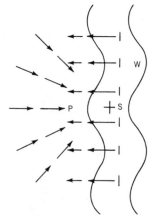

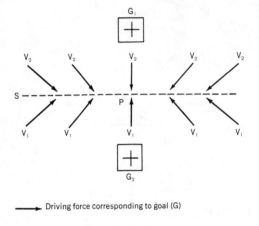

Driving force corresponding to goal (G)

- - - - - Line of equilibrium

FIGURE 8   *(From K. Lewin, Vectors, Cognitive Processes, and Mr. Tolman's Criticism,* Jour. general Psychol., *1933, 8, 323)*

that the child must move to the point P where equilibrium occurs. (At all other points there exists a resultant which finally leads to P.) Corresponding to the momentary oscillations of the situation, above all to the more or less threatening aspect of the waves, this point of equilibrium ap-

FIGURE 9   *(From K. Lewin, Vectors, Cognitive Processes, and Mr. Tolman's Criticism,* Jour. general Psychol., *1933, 8, 323)*

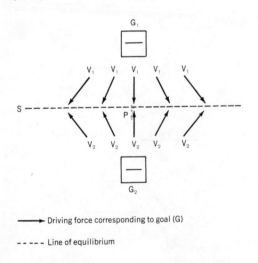

Driving force corresponding to goal (G)

- - - - - Line of equilibrium

proaches and retreats from the water. Indeed, this oscillation is reflected in the child's approaches to and retreats from the water.

If we return now to Type 3 of the conflict situation and compare it with Type 1, the chief difference is shown in Figures 8 and 9: in both cases two central fields overlap. But while in Type 1 a stable equilibrium exists at the point P (Figure 8) so far as sidewise movements (on line S) are concerned, in Type 3 this equilibrium is labile (Figure 9). That is, there exists in the case of threat of punishment (Figure 5) a situation which evokes a tendency to break out toward the side, in accordance with the strong sidewise resultant (R) of the two vectors (V_p and V_t). Consequently the child always goes out of the field unless other circumstances prevent it. Hence, if the threat of punishment is to be effective, the child must be so inclosed by a barrier that escape is possible only by way of the punishment or by way of doing the disagreeable task. That is, in addition to requiring the execution of the task, it is necessary to limit the child's freedom of movement, thus creating (by physical or social means) a more or less constrained situation.

With the young child, the opposition of two approximately equal field forces in the conflict situation leads typically (so far as it is not an unstable equilibrium) to a relatively rapid alternation of actions in the direction of each of the two field forces in turn. It is a characteristic indication of greater self-control when, instead of this oscillation of action, the child displays a relatively calm type of behavior while the conflict remains unresolved.

Ability to endure such unresolved conflict situations is an important aim of the education of the will. Of course, the occurrence of such conflict situations presupposes that the two opposed field forces are of approximately equal strength. If threats of punishment, pressure from the adult,

FIGURE 10.

FIGURE 11.

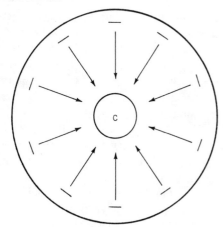

or other restrictions leave the child little enough freedom, no real conflict situation can develop.

If a situation becomes *hopeless,* that is, if it becomes as a whole inescapably disagreeable, the child, despairing, *contracts,* physically and psychically, under the vectors coming from all sides and usually attempts to build a wall between himself and the situation. This is expressed both in the typical bodily gestures of despair (crumpling up, covering the eyes with the arms, etc.) (see Figure 10), and by a sort of encysting (Figure 11) of the self: the child becomes obdurate.

Frustration occurs when there is interference with goal-directed behavior and goal attainment. Conflict is considered one of the most important causes of frustration because, in conflicts, motives interfere with each other. Most psychologists think that frustration has many outcomes, including such important ones as the ego-defense mechanisms and, perhaps, some neurotic symptoms.

This article presents data in an attempt to set up a model of the outcome of an approach-avoidance conflict. The model was developed with rats, and the details were not expected to transfer to humans. However, it was hoped that the outcome of the experiment would give ideas about, that is, would serve as a model for, human approach-avoidance conflict. Although it has some disadvantages, the main advantage of such a method is that it allows for quantification and control.

POINTS TO GUIDE YOUR STUDY   *(1) Were the assumptions (hypotheses) in the introduction upheld? For each assumption, state the evidence which supports or fails to support it.   (2) Note that the approach and avoidance gradients were obtained from separate groups.   (3) The t values and probabilities have the same meaning as in other studies in these readings. See "Points to guide your study" under the articles where these are discussed more fully (for example, the selection by Braun and Geiselhart in Section Three).*

46: GRADIENTS OF APPROACH AND AVOIDANCE RESPONSES AND THEIR RELATION TO LEVEL OF MOTIVATION

Judson S. Brown, University of Iowa

The present experiment stemmed originally from a series of studies of conflict behavior by N. E. Miller and the writer. In the first experiment of that series[1] an investigation was made of the conflict behavior exhibited by rats in a narrow straight alley when tendencies both to approach and avoid one end of the alley were simultaneously present. In developing a theoretical interpretation of the observed behavior, it was found expedient to make a number of explicit assumptions regarding the manner in which the excitatory tendencies varied with distance from the region of reinforcement and with variations in strength of drive and strength of punishment. These assumptions were:

1. When a motivated organism is suitably reinforced for approaching a given region in space, a gradient in the strength of its excitatory tendency to approach that region will be established, the strength of the tendency increasing with nearness to the goal.

2. When an organism has escaped from a noxious stimulus located at a given region in space, a gradient in the strength of its excitatory tendency to avoid that region will be set up, the strength of the tendency decreasing with distance from that region.

3. Other things equal, gradients in the strength of excitatory tendencies to avoid are steeper than gradients of excitatory tendencies to approach.

4. The heights of the approach and avoidance gradients vary directly with strength of drive and intensity of the noxious stimulus, respectively.

The general procedure employed in testing the four assumptions was as follows. One group of hunger-motivated rats was thoroughly trained to approach one end of a short straight alley for food. A second group was trained to avoid one end of the alley by the use of strong electric shocks. The strengths of the resulting approach and avoidance responses were then tested by measuring (at different points in the alley) the force with which the animals would pull either toward or away from the region of reinforcement. The approach and avoidance responses of other groups, whose

A portion of a dissertation submitted to the faculty of Yale University in partial fulfillment of the requirements for the Ph.D. degree. The author is indebted to Dr. N. E. Miller for extensive aid in planning and conducting the study. The research was supported in part by funds from the Institute of Human Relations.

J. S. Brown. Gradients of approach and avoidance responses and their relation to level of motivation. *J. comp. physiol. Psychol.*, 1948, 41, 450–465. Copyright © 1948 by the American Psychological Association. Excerpts reprinted here with permission from the author and the American Psychological Association.

[1] By N. E. Miller, H. Lipofsky, and J. S. Brown. Reported in part by the writer at the 1938 meetings of the Eastern Psychological Association and summarized by Miller (15).

hunger motivation was weak or who had received weaker shocks, were also tested by the same method at different positions in the alley.

Apparatus

A schematic diagram of the apparatus used in this study is shown in Figure 1. Only the essential features are indicated and the distances are not drawn to scale. The alley at the right was 200 cm. long, 12 cm. wide and 10 cm. deep (inside measurements). The cover of the alley, made of celluloid tacked to a wooden frame, was hinged at the back and is not shown in the figure. The bottom of the alley was formed of a grid of stainless-steel wire (#20) stretched tightly across a bakelite-and-wood spreader at intervals of 8 mm. A gap of 20 mm. was provided below the grid so that feces and urine might drop through freely. The spreader and the wires were coated with paraffin at points of mutual contact to decrease surface leakage in moist weather.

The endless loop of cord (fish line) shown at the right passed through slots in the ends of the alley and ran along about 2.5 cm. below the cover. Outside the alley this cord passed around an idler pulley at one end and around the larger diameter of a 10:1 reduction pulley at the other. The smaller section of this pulley was coupled by a second endless loop to the lower of the two sliding markers shown at the left. This marker served to provide detailed records of the movements of the rat along the alley and was employed in a previous study for the purpose of recording the locomotor components of conflict behavior.

At the center of the alley is shown the harness by which a rat was attached to the endless belt. A light aluminum T with a swivel hook at its lower end was tied into the main loop of cord. Two sturdy rubber bands passed through the swivel hook and

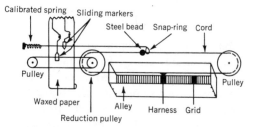

FIGURE 1 *Schematic diagram of apparatus for measuring the force exerted by rats when restrained at various distances from a region of reinforcement.*

around the rat, one around the thorax and the other in front of the forelegs around the neck. These bands, though tight enough to prevent the rat's escape even when it was pulling against the restraining spring, did not interfere with its normal movements in the alley.

The mechanism for measuring strength-of-pull functioned as follows. The force exerted by the rat against the harness was transmitted through the T to the endless loop of cord. A small steel bead was fastened to the portion of the loop which passed along the outside of the alley. This bead engaged a smaller snap-ring attached to a string running to the upper one of the two sliding markers shown at the left. This marker was in turn attached to one end of a calibrated spring. Before the bead engaged the snap-ring and took up the slack in the string, the main loop could be moved freely, being opposed only by a slight friction from the pulleys. After the rat had progressed down the alley (toward the left in Figure 1) to the point where the bead engaged the snap-ring and took up the slack in the string, further movements were impeded by the force of the spring. In this way, the force of a rat's surges against the resistance of the spring was recorded on the waxed paper by movements of the upper marker. By changing the length of the cord between this marker and the snap-ring, measurements of strength of pull could be made at any desired point in the alley.

Training and testing procedure

Four basic experimental groups were employed in this study. In groups I and II the animals were trained under a strong hunger drive to approach the lighted end of the alley for food. In order to test the assumption that the approach tendencies should be weaker the farther the subject is from the region of reinforcement, the pull of the animals in Group I was measured at a point near the goal and at a point near the start. These animals were tested under strong hunger motivation. In order to test the assumption that the strength of approach tendencies should vary with strength of drive, the pull of the animals in Group II was measured at only one point in the alley, near the goal, under two degrees of hunger: 1 hour and 46 hours of food deprivation.

The animals in Groups III and IV were trained to avoid the lighted end of the alley. In order to test the assumption that

FIGURE 2 *The approach gradient represents the mean force exerted by 46-hour motivated rats when restrained at two points in the alley. The avoidance gradient reveals the force exerted by rats in their efforts to avoid a region where strong shock has been given. Although the experimental points in this figure and in Figure 3 have been joined by straight lines, no assumption is intended with respect to the linearity of the gradients.*

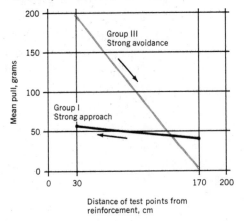

strength of avoidance varies with the intensity of a noxious stimulus, the animals in Group III were trained with strong shock and those in Group IV with weak shock. As a test of the assumption that the avoidance tendencies should be weaker the farther the subject is from the point of reinforcement, the pull of the animals in both groups was measured at different distances from the point at which the shock was administered.

Results

APPROACH AND AVOIDANCE GRADIENTS   The results of the strength-of-pull tests administered to Group I (strong approach) and to Group III (strong avoidance) are summarized in Table 1. The basic data underlying these statistics were obtained by first measuring (planimetrically) the areas under the curves made on the waxed-paper records by the strength-of-pull marker. The average height of each curve was then computed by dividing its area by a standard baseline of 17.5 mm., the distance travelled by the paper during the 5-sec. interval. These average heights were finally converted into mean pull in grams by multiplying each by a constant derived from the calibration of the spring[2] against which the animals pulled. An average strength-of-pull value was obtained for each animal at each test point and the values in Table 1 were calculated from the distributions of these individual mean values.

EFFECTS OF STRENGTH OF DRIVE AND STRENGTH OF SHOCK   In Table 2 and in Figure 3 the results of the tests made on Group II (strong-weak approach) and Group IV (weak avoidance) are presented. For purposes of comparison, the avoidance

[2] The spring was made by winding 0.020-in. music wire on a 0.25-in. mandrel. The relation of elongation to applied force was roughly linear, with approximately 10 gm. being required for each millimeter of elongation.

TABLE 1 *Means, medians, and standard deviations computed from average strength-of-pull measurements made on Groups I and III at points near to, and remote from, the point of reinforcement*

	NEAR POINT			FAR POINT		
	M	Md	SD	M	Md	SD
Group I (Strong approach)	56.5	47.5	33.7	40.9	36.1	26.3
Group III (Strong avoidance)	198.4	191.9	109.7	2.1	0	*

* No SD is given here, since 16 of the animals failed to reach the pull point within the criterion time of one minute and hence received zero scores.

TABLE 2 *Statistics computed from measurements of average strength of pull exhibited by animals in Group II when tested under two degrees of food deprivation and by animals in Group IV when tested near the shock point and at the center of the alley. (No standard deviations are presented for Group IV because of the presence of zero scores at both points.)*

	46-HOUR DRIVE			1-HOUR DRIVE		
	M	Md	SD	M	Md	SD
Group II (strong-weak approach)	48.7	41.8	30.9	16.5	11.4	19.33

	NEAR POINT		CENTER POINT	
	M	Md	M	Md
Group IV (weak avoidance)	141.2	146.3	51.7	19.0

gradient from Figure 2 has been replotted in Figure 3. It is apparent from this figure that reducing the strength of the drive or of the shock reduces the heights of both approach and avoidance gradients, a result that accords well with the fourth assumption. In the case of Group IV, the difference between the means at the two points cannot be evaluated by the *t* test since five animals failed to pull at the far point and two failed to pull at either point. However, if one of the two no-pull animals is assigned to a favorable category and the other to an unfavorable category, then 19 of the 20 animals fall in the favorable category of pulling harder at the near point or else pulling at the near point and failing to reach the center point. If there were no real difference, the probabil-

FIGURE 3 *This figure summarizes the results of tests made on Groups II, III, and IV, and illustrates the effect of reduced shock and reduced drive upon the strengths of the avoidance and approach responses, respectively.*

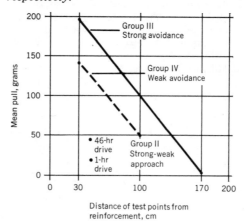

ity of obtaining a 19-to-1 split by chance would be substantially less than 0.01 according to the binomial theorem. No attempt has been made to determine the significance of the difference between the two avoidance gradients because of the presence of zero scores and the lack of a far test point common to the two groups.

For the animals of Group II the difference between the mean pulls exerted under the 46- and 1-hour drives can be evaluated by the t test. This gives a value of 3.2 (d.f. = 11), leading to the rejection of the null hypothesis at slightly better than the 1 per cent level. Some indication of the reliability of the strength-of-pull technique is perhaps afforded by the fact that the mean force exerted by the 12 animals in Group II is almost exactly the same as that exerted by the 20 animals in Group I tested under comparable conditions.

References

1. Browman, L. G. Light in its relation to activity and oestrous rhythm in the albino rat. *J. exp. Zool.*, 1937, 75, 375–388.
2. Brown, J. S. The generalization of approach responses as a function of stimulus intensity and strength of motivation. *J. comp. Psychol.*, 1942, 33, 209–226.
3. Bugelski, R., and Miller, N. E. A spatial gradient in the strength of avoidance responses. *J. exp. Psychol.*, 1938, 23, 494–505.
4. Drew, G. C. The speed of locomotion gradient and its relation to the goal gradient. *J. comp. Psychol.*, 1939, 27, 333–372.
5. Grice, G. R. The relation of secondary reinforcement to delayed reward in visual discrimination learning. *J. exp. Psychol.*, 1948, 38, 1–16.
6. Hilgard, E. R., and Marquis, D. G. *Condi-*

7. *tioning and learning.* New York: Appleton-Century, 1940.
7. Hill, C. G. Goal gradient, anticipation, and perseveration in compound trial-and-error learning. *J. exp. Psychol.*, 1939, 25, 566–585.
8. Hull, C. L. The goal-gradient hypothesis and maze learning. *Psychol. Rev.*, 1932, 39, 25–43.
9. ———. The rat's speed-of-locomotion gradient in the approach to food. *J. comp. Psychol.*, 1934, 17, 393–422.
10. ———. The goal-gradient hypothesis applied to some "field-force" problems in the behavior of young children. *Psychol. Rev.*, 1938, 45, 271–299.
11. ———. *Principles of behavior.* New York: Appleton-Century, 1943.
12. Hunt, J. McV., and Schlosberg, H. The influence of illumination upon general activity in normal, blinded and castrated male white rats. *J. comp. Psychol.*, 1939, 28, 285–298.
13. Lewin, K. Environmental forces. In C. Murchison (Ed.), *A handbook of child psychology.* (2nd ed.). Worcester: Clark Univ. Press, 1933.
14. Miller, N. E., and Miles, W. R. Effect of caffeine on the running speed of hungry, satiated, and frustrated rats. *J. comp. Psychol.*, 1935, 20, 397–412.
15. Miller, N. E. Experimental studies in conflict. In J. McV. Hunt (Ed.), *Personality and the behavior disorders.* New York: Ronald Press, 1944.
16. Morgan, C. T., and Fields, P. E. The effect of variable preliminary feeding upon the rat's speed-of-locomotion. *J. comp. Psychol.*, 1938, 26, 331–348.
17. Muenzinger, K. F., and Walz, F. C. An examination of electrical-current-stabilizing devices for psychological experiments. *J. gen. Psychol.*, 1934, 10, 477–482.
18. Spence, K. W. The order of eliminating blinds in maze learning by the rat. *J. comp. Psychol.*, 1932, 14, 9–27.
19. ———. The role of secondary reinforcement in delayed reward learning. *Psychol. Rev.*, 1947, 54, 1–8.

In this brief excerpt from one of his later books, Freud describes some of his ideas about personality structure. In addition to providing descriptions of id, ego, and superego, the selection illustrates clearly the style and type of argument favored by Freud.

A POINT TO GUIDE YOUR STUDY *One is mistaken if he thinks of the id, ego, and superego as representing "parts of the personality."*

> *Rather, these concepts are convenient abstractions which are meant to*
> *summarize many behavioral observations. For example, there is no*
> *"id deep within the personality"; but there are behaviors which may*
> *be grouped together because they seem to have similar characteristics.*
> *The term "id" may be applied to these behaviors if it seems useful.*

47: SELECTION FROM: AN OUTLINE OF PSYCHOANALYSIS.
THE PSYCHICAL APPARATUS

Sigmund Freud

Psycho-analysis makes a basic assumption, the discussion of which is reserved to philosophical thought but the justification for which lies in its results. We know two kinds of things about what we call our psyche (or mental life); firstly, its bodily organ and scene of action, the brain (or nervous system) and, on the other hand, our acts of consciousness, which are immediate data and cannot be further explained by any sort of description. Everything that lies between is unknown to us, and the data do not include any direct relation between these two terminal points of our knowledge. If it existed, it would at the most afford an exact localization of the processes of consciousness and would give us no help towards understanding them.

Our two hypotheses start out from these ends or beginnings of our knowledge. The first is concerned with localization. We assume that mental life is the function of an apparatus to which we ascribe the characteristics of being extended in space and of being made up of several portions—which we imagine, that is, as resembling a telescope or microscope or something of

the kind. Notwithstanding some earlier attempts in the same direction, the consistent working-out of a conception such as this is a scientific novelty.

We have arrived at our knowledge of this psychical apparatus by studying the individual development of human beings. To the oldest of these psychical provinces or agencies we give the name of *id*. It contains everything that is inherited, that is present at birth, that is laid down in the constitution—above all, therefore, the instincts, which originate from the somatic organization and which find a first psychical expression here [in the id] in forms unknown to us.

Under the influence of the real external world around us, one portion of the id has undergone a special development. From what was originally a cortical layer, equipped with the organs for receiving stimuli and with arrangements for acting as a protective shield against stimuli, a special organization has arisen which henceforward acts as an intermediary between the id and the external world. To this region of our mind we have given the name of *ego*.

Here are the principal characteristics of the ego. In consequence of the pre-established connection between sense perception and muscular action, the ego has voluntary movement at its command. It has the task of self-preservation. As regards *external* events, it performs that task by becoming aware of stimuli, by storing up experiences about them (in the memory), by avoiding excessively strong stimuli (through flight), by dealing with moderate stimuli (through adaptation) and finally by learning to bring about expedient changes in the external world to its own advantage (through activity). As regards *internal* events, in relation to the id, it performs that task by gaining control over the demands of the instincts, by deciding whether they are to be allowed satisfaction, by postponing that satisfaction to times and circumstances favourable in the external world or by suppressing their excitations entirely. It is guided in its activity by consideration of the tensions produced by stimuli, whether these tensions are present in it or introduced into it. The raising of these tensions is in general felt as *unpleasure* and their lowering as *pleasure*. It is probable, however, that what is felt as pleasure or unpleasure is not the *absolute* height of this tension but something in the rhythm of the changes in them. The ego strives after pleasure and seeks to avoid unpleasure. An increase in unpleasure that is expected and foreseen is met by a *signal of anxiety;* the occasion of such an increase, whether it threatens from without or within, is known as a *danger*. From time to time the ego gives up its connection with the external world and withdraws into the state of sleep, in which it makes far-reaching changes in its organization. It is to be inferred from the state of sleep that this organization consists in a particular distribution of mental energy.

The long period of childhood, during which the growing human being lives in dependence on his parents, leaves behind it as a precipitate the formation in his ego of a special agency in which this parental influence is prolonged. It has received the name of *super-ego*. In so far as this super-ego is differentiated from the ego or is opposed to it, it constitutes a third power which the ego must take into account.

An action by the ego is as it should be if it satisfies simultaneously the demands of the id, of the super-ego and of reality— that is to say, if it is able to reconcile their demands with one another. The details of the relation between the ego and the super-ego become completely intelligible when they are traced back to the child's attitude to its parents. This parental influence of course includes in its operation not only the personalities of the actual parents but also the family, racial and national traditions handed on through them, as well as the demands of the immediate social *milieu* which they represent. In the same way, the super-ego, in the course of an individual's development, receives contributions from later successors and substitutes of his parents, such as teachers and models in public life of admired social ideals. It will be observed that, for all their fundamental difference, the id and the super-ego have one thing in common: they both represent the influences of the past—the id the influence of heredity, the super-ego the influence, essentially, of what is taken over from other people—whereas the ego is principally determined by the individual's own experience, that is by accidental and contemporary events.

This general schematic picture of a psychical apparatus may be supposed to apply as well to the higher animals which resemble man mentally. A super-ego must be presumed to be present wherever, as is the case with man, there is a long period of dependence in childhood. A distinction between ego and id is an unavoidable assumption. Animal psychology has not yet taken in hand the interesting problem which is here presented.

Psychoanalysis is both theory and therapy. The following excerpts are concerned with the theoretical aspects of psychoanalysis although they give only a sketchy account of the broad aspects of psychoanalytic theories. Many good books, and, unfortunately, some poor books, are available. Among the better ones are those by Freud himself. A number of good summaries, which elaborate on different points of view, are available. Among them are:

S. Freud. An Outline of Psychoanalysis. *W. W. Norton, 1949.*
G. S. Blum, Psychoanalytic theories of personality. *McGraw-Hill, 1953.*
Charles Brenner, Elementary textbook of psychoanalysis. *Anchor, 1955. (Paperback.)*
C. S. Hall, A primer of Freudian psychology. *Mentor, 1954. (Paperback.)*

Notice that there is more than one psychoanalytic theory. The orthodox psychoanalytic school, founded by Freud, was soon split by the divergent theories of Adler and Jung. More recently, orthodox theory has been reevaluated. Some, Fenichel and Klein, for instance, have tended to reemphasize the orthodox libido theory. Others, Fromm, Horney, and Sullivan, for instance, the so-called neo-Freudians, have put emphasis on the importance of social rather than biological factors in personality development.

POINTS TO GUIDE YOUR STUDY   *(1) These excerpts will seem a little epigrammatic. A great deal is packed into each paragraph. Therefore, it is especially important to read this selection very carefully.*
(2) A major disadvantage of this method of presenting psychoanalytic theory is that the data on which the theory is based are not presented. This tends to make many of the statements seem quite arbitrary.
(3) One point of this selection is well-taken. Psychoanalytic theories, while extremely fruitful, lack the rigor which is characteristic of other scientific theories. The final paragraphs of this selection reveal this view quite clearly.

48: PSYCHOANALYTIC THEORIES OF PERSONALITY

Gerald S. Blum, University of Michigan

THE NEONATE'S PERSONALITY POTENTIAL Orthodox psychoanalytic theory explains mental phenomena as the result of a dynamic interaction between urging forces or instincts within the organism and counterforces set up by the external environment. Instincts, described as psychic representatives of stimuli originating in the soma, already exist for the newborn child.

G. S. Blum. *Psychoanalytic theories of personality.* New York: McGraw-Hill, 1953. Copyright © 1953 by the McGraw-Hill Book Company. Excerpts reprinted here with permission from the author and the McGraw-Hill Book Company. References omitted. Some sections retitled.

Each instinct has its aim, object, and source. Fenichel classifies instincts generally into the simple physical needs and the sexual urges. The former, such as hunger, breathing, and thirst, are said to be less important for personality development since they require quick satisfaction and thus allow for very little variability among individuals. Sexual urges, conceived in the broadest sense, operate from birth onward so that adult forms of sexuality are continuations of the infantile ones. The energy of the sexual instincts is termed "libido," fixed quantities of which are presumed to be present in the neonate. Jung defines libido more broadly as a primal energy underlying all mental life, not merely the sexual. The neo-Freudians, on the other hand, reject the notions of instinct and libido, though Sullivan does speak of a "power motive."

Freud in his later writings also postulated an innate death instinct to account for aggression and self-destructive urges. However, Fenichel takes issue with this notion and prefers to explain aggression as a mode of response to frustration, growing like the sexual instincts out of a need for tension reduction. Similarly the neo-Freudians offer interpersonal difficulties as a better explanation than the death instinct for aggression and suicide.

Another major element in the personality potential of the neonate is the unconscious, a cornerstone of psychoanalytic theory. Its influence is purported to be far more powerful than that of the conscious mind, for unconscious impulses continually strive in a very active fashion for conscious expression. Processes in the unconscious are timeless and bear little relation to external reality. Incompatible wishes can exist side by side, and there are no considerations of doubt, negation, or uncertainty. The term "id" was added later to designate that portion of the unconscious which functions as a source of instinctual energy, forming a reservoir of libido. Freud's own view on the origin of content in the unconscious is phylogenetic, that is, through some form of racial inheritance. The latter resembles to some extent Jung's formulation of the collective unconscious, a product of the racial inheritance of significant memories or germs of ideas. Transmitted in the collective unconscious are primordial images or archetypes which, according to Jung, become known through the symbolic interpretation of dreams. Examples are the mother and father archetypes, dealing, respectively, with nourishment and strength. In addition to the collective unconscious each individual is said to possess a personal unconscious—forgotten memories which are a consequence, not so much of repression, but of one-sided development. Neo-Freudians accept the principle of unconscious function but criticize Freud's connotation of the unconscious as a place, where, for example, repressed experiences and id forces can combine with each other.

Finally orthodox theory ascribes to the neonate a condition known as "primary narcissism." The infant is unable to differentiate himself from external objects, so that sexual aims are autoerotic and libido is turned inward. Because of the magical gratification of his needs, the infant soon develops a feeling of omnipotence which later in life he may wishfully seek to regain. For Greenacre primary narcissism connotes more than this "oceanic feeling." She considers that narcissism, catalyzed by the birth processes, contains the beginnings of a propulsive drive based on the biological need for survival. An increase in anxiety is said to cause a corresponding defensive increase in narcissism. Fromm quarrels with the fixed-amount-of-libido notion and criticizes Freud's formulation of narcissism on the grounds that a person capable of genuinely loving himself is actually more capable of loving others.

THE FIRST YEAR OF LIFE According to orthodox psychoanalytic theory, the newborn child has no awareness of the outside world and can experience only changes in his own tension state. The beginnings of ego functioning appear when he longs for something to be done by the external world to satisfy his wants. This distinction between self and environment is said to occur in the context of indulgence and deprivation, with some amount of the latter essential for development. Self-esteem, one of the properties of the ego, is first regulated by the supply of nourishment from the outside, a magical source which leads the

infant to feel omnipotent. Later there follows a period of passive-receptive mastery,
in which he shares in the newly discovered
omnipotence of adults and passively induces them to deliver the desired supplies.
As the child grows, the earliest forms of
pure pleasure seeking are gradually replaced by the reality principle—the ability to substitute future for immediate gratification.

Melanie Klein deviates from orthodox
theory by postulating the active functioning of both ego and superego during the
first year of life. Her theories are predi-
cated upon the assumption of powerful unconscious fantasies at this time. Sullivan,
in the neo-Freudian school, describes the
first year as belonging to the prototaxic
mode of experience. At first the infant
knows only momentary states, with no distinctions of time and place. After a while
he perceives or "prehends" the mother,
mainly in terms of good and bad.

With respect to psychosexual development, the orthodox theory of infantile
sexuality portrays the child as "poly-
morphous perverse." The beginning expression of the sexual instinct is said to be
the act of sucking in the early oral-passive
stage. Pleasure from this activity is soon
discovered apart from the feeding situation, so that the first aim is autoerotic
stimulation of the membranes of the
mouth. Later the desire to incorporate persons and things is added. Individuals are
looked upon primarily as food or providers
of food in terms of these fantasies of incorporation, which are often accompanied
by oral fears like the fear of being eaten.
The second aspect of the oral stage, com-
mencing with the eruption of teeth, is the
sadistic, during which the child seeks to
retaliate for frustration by biting.

Klein describes a wide array of sexual
and aggressive fantasies in the first year,
including oedipal impulses, the desire to
incorporate the father's penis, the wish to
destroy the mother's body, and so on. For

Jung the earliest phase is characterized
almost exclusively by nutrition and growth.
The link between these nutritive functions
and later sexuality is presumed to be
rhythmic activity. The neo-Freudians also
minimize the erotic element and stress instead cultural and developmental manifestations of orality. Erikson, closer to the
orthodox position, adds the concepts of
zones and modes, in this case the oral zone
and incorporative mode.

In the area of relationships to people,
orthodox theory traces a gradual transition from the infant's missing of things
which bring satisfaction, to his differentiation of trusted and strange impressions,
and finally to his recognition of the mother
as a whole object. The notion of ambivalence is introduced in the oral-sadistic
stage, at which period he longs for pleasurable union with the mother and yet in
times of frustration wishes to attack her.
Klein states that the mother probably
exists as a whole object from the very
beginning, but in vague outline. She tends
to emphasize the child's fear of losing the
love object. Sullivan concentrates his description of early relationships on the process of empathy—a peculiar nonverbal,
emotional communication between parent
and child, said to be strongest between the
ages of six and twenty-seven months.

Mechanisms used in the first year include introjection, projection, denial, fixation, and regression. Introjection, based on
swallowing or taking in food, is aimed first
at instinctual satisfaction, later at regain-
ing omnipotence, and still later at destroying the hated object by oral incorporation.
Projection, stemming from spitting out the
unpleasant, involves the attribution of
painful stimuli to the outside world.
Denial, also a very primitive mechanism,
means the avoidance of unpleasant reality
simply by closing one's eyes to it and
pretending it does not exist. Fixation and
regression refer to the retention of an abnormal number of characteristics of an

earlier stage, to which the individual is predisposed to return if difficulties arise. All
the preceding mechanisms, as they operate in the first year, are considered fore-
runners of the later defense mechanisms.

AGES ONE TO THREE YEARS   In his discussion of ego formation at this age level
Fenichel traces the development of active
mastery and the handling of anxiety. As
a result of both newly acquired control
over his motor apparatus and the growth
of the function of judgment (reality testing), the young child learns to cope actively with the environment. His ego becomes capable of judging potentially traumatic situations, so that anxiety serves as
a protective warning signal. Common
sources of anxiety at this time derive from
the talion principle—the fear that others
may do to him what he fantasies doing to
them—and fear over the loss of love and
protection. When anxiety-provoking situations have been experienced, the child
through a process of belated mastery attempts to reduce tension by reliving the
trauma over and over in games and
dreams. The acquisition of speech and the
advances in thinking contribute heavily to
a new feeling of power. Thinking in this
period is said to contain many prelogical
and symbolic elements. Superego forerun-
ners are also prominent in the form of
internalized parental prohibitions.

Sullivan speaks of the parataxic mode,
in which experience is undergone as momentary, unconnected organismic states.
The earlier prototaxic undifferentiated
wholeness is now broken down into parts,
but these have no logical relation to one
another. Dreams and the transference reaction in psychotherapy are given as illustrations of parataxic distortion. Communication in ages one to three involves the use
of autistic language, words having a personal, private meaning. Anxiety is described as a further development of the

loss of euphoria and arises from rewards
and punishments in the socialization of the
child. It serves to make him focus his alert-
ness on performances which bring approval
or disapproval, and out of this focusing the
self-dynamism is evolved. Three personifi-
cations of self gradually emerge: the "good
me," "bad me," and "not me."

Psychosexual development in the orthodox system witnesses the anal-sadistic
stage. Two trends are distinguished—the
earlier expulsive and the later retentive.
Expulsiveness is expressed in the physiological pleasure of excretion but can also
serve aggressive purposes by defying the
parents in their insistence on toilet training. The retentive phase derives from both
stimulation of the mucous membrane and
the social values placed upon conformity.
The neo-Freudians maintain that the emphasis should be placed, not on the pleasure obtained from expelling and retaining
feces, but rather on the struggle with
parents. Erikson occupies an intermediate
position with his stress upon the social
modalities of "letting go" and "holding
on."

Concomitant relationships, according to
orthodox sources, entail ambivalence, bi-
sexuality, sadism, and masochism. Anal
ambivalence is said to arise from the contradictory attitude toward feces; bisexu-
ality from the fact that the rectum is an
excretory hollow organ; sadism from frustration in the toilet-training situation; and
masochism from the erotic stimulation of
the buttocks in spankings. Sullivan approaches interpersonal relationships from
another angle. He describes the operation
of "reflected appraisals," in which the
child forms an opinion of himself mainly
from the reactions of significant adults to
him; and also multiple "me-you patterns,"
which refer to incongruent attitudes toward
others.

Two new mechanisms at these ages include Anna Freud's "denial in word and

act," a later counterpart of denial in fantasy, and Sullivan's "consensual validation," a process in which the individual tries to correct his parataxic distortions by evaluating his own thoughts and feelings against those of others.

AGES THREE TO FIVE   At ages three to five the orthodox scene shifts to the phallic stage of psychosexual development. Early in this period urethral preoccupations appear, first in the form of pleasurable auto-eroticism and later in association with sadistic fantasies of urinating on others. Interest in the genitals increases, along with masturbation and exhibitionism. The extreme narcissistic value placed upon the penis by boys leads them to fear damage to that organ—castration anxiety—in retaliation for guilt-laden oedipal fantasies. In girls penis envy, arising from observation of differences in male and female genitals, is said to predominate. The lack of a penis is presumably felt as a punishment for some wrongdoing.

Among the neo-Freudians, Thompson questions whether observation of the genitals is sufficient to elicit castration anxiety unless reinforced by parental threats. Horney objects to the notion of primary penis envy in girls. She attributes envy in women to the desire for masculine qualities prized by the culture rather than to sexual experiences in early childhood. In his system Erikson stresses the "intrusive" features of the phallic-locomotor stage, such as aggressiveness. competition, curiosity, and the pleasure of conquest.

Relationships to others revolve around the Oedipus complex, defined as sexual love for the parent of the opposite sex accompanied by hatred for the parent of the same sex. In the case of the boy the transition is relatively simple, for the preoedipal object, the mother, continues to be the preferred parent. The girl, however, has to undergo a complicated switch in her affec-

tions from mother to father. The particular form which the Oedipus complex takes is said by Fenichel to be a product of family influence.

Other theorists offer a variety of explanations. Adler emphasizes pampering by the mother and the child's subsequent lust for power over her. Jung considers the Oedipus to be really a possession complex, with the mother seen as the source of protection, nourishment, and love. For Rank it represents an unsuccessful attempt to overcome the birth trauma. He also stresses the importance of the family situation and the child's struggle for individuality. Likewise family attachments are pointed up by Horney, based mainly on two conditions: sexual stimulation by the parents and anxiety aroused by conflict between dependency needs and hostile impulses toward the mother and father. Fromm minimizes the sexual tie and prefers to ascribe the difficulties between father and son to the effects of authoritarian patriarchal society. Sullivan's interpretation is in terms of familiarity and strangeness between parent and child, and Thompson also emphasizes interpersonal relationships beyond the erotic reactions.

In the orthodox framework the heir of the Oedipus complex is the superego. Psychosexual frustrations are said to cause a regression from object choice to identification, so that sexual longing for the object is replaced by an asexual alteration within the ego. The child identifies with his own idealized version of the parents, and being on good or bad terms with his superego becomes as important as being on good or bad terms with the parents previously was. Whereas the ego holds an executive position mediating between id, superego, and outside world, the superego functions center about moral demands and thereby represent the incorporated standards of society.

Rank traces the growth of the superego

genetically from inhibited sadism, with the real nucleus being the strict mother as sadistically conceived by the child. Fromm attempts to distinguish authoritarian from humanistic conscience, the relative strengths of which depend upon the individual's experiences. The authoritarian conscience is described as the voice of internalized external authority, corresponding to Freud's supergo. In contrast the humanistic is the voice of the person himself, the expression of man's self-interest and integrity.

With respect to mechanisms, Fenichel draws a distinction between successful defenses, which bring a cessation of the blocked impulses, and unsuccessful defenses, which necessitate a continuing repetition of the warding-off process. Included in the former are various types of sublimation, involving the desexualized expression of impulses via an artificial route. Among the latter are the previously discussed mechanisms of denial, projection, introjection, and regression, along with repression, reaction formation, undoing, isolation, and displacement. Sullivan adds his concepts of selective inattention and disassociation; and Fromm offers three mechanisms of escape from the feeling of isolation engendered by our society: sado-masochism, destructiveness, and automaton conformity.

THE LATENCY PERIOD (AGE FIVE TO PRE-PUBERTY) During the latency period, says Anna Freud, the ego becomes much stronger in relation to the outside world. Along with a decline in strength of the instincts, the ego has a new ally, the superego, in its struggle to master impulses. The superego tends to be overly rigid at first but gradually adjusts and grows more pliable. There is said to be a relative drop in infantile sexual interests. Energy for the new activities, interests, and attitudes still derives from the sexual but operates mainly through the mechanisms of partial sublimation and reaction formation.

Thompson doubts whether sexual latency even takes place. She maintains that the child, because of his expanded relationships, tends to share his thoughts and actions with those his own age.

Libidinal desires for the parental love object are replaced by sublimated expressions of affection. Hostile reactions seem to drop out and there are beginnings of reaching out toward others in the environment for friendly relations. Sullivan, coining the term "juvenile era," stresses the importance of school experiences and the need to interact with other children in the same age range. One's reputation becomes crucial and fears of ostracism by others are prominent. The introduction of the chum is another characteristic of this period.

ADULT CHARACTER STRUCTURE In the orthodox system character is defined as "the ego's habitual modes of adjustment to the external world, the id and the supergo, and the characteristic types of combining these modes with one another." It includes in addition to defense mechanisms the positive, organizing functions of the ego. Fenichel classifies character traits into two broad categories: sublimation and reactive. In the former the original instinctual energy is discharged freely as a result of an alteration in aim. The genital character belongs here. In the latter instinctual energy is constantly held in check by countercathexes. The various reactive types are the oral, anal, urethral, and phallic, in which psychosexual fixations predominate.

Among the early deviants, Adler also stresses the importance of early childhood for the molding of character but places his emphasis upon universal feelings of inferiority. The latter are accompanied by a compensatory struggle for power and "masculine protest" behavior. Jung focuses upon four basic psychological functions: thinking, feeling, sensation, and intuition.

The conscious aspects of men are said to be thinking and sensation, whereas feeling and intuition are repressed. The opposite is true of women. The four functions are further classified into two general ways of looking at the world, extraverted and introverted. In addition each individual plays a prescribed role in society—the concept of "persona." Rank's characterology hinges upon his theory of will. The average man, the neurotic, and the creative man each correspond to stages in the development of will.

Neo-Freudian theorists like Horney and Fromm discount any causal connections between libidinal manifestations in childhood and later personality traits. Instead they stress the sum total of parent-child interactions in the early environment. Horney distinguishes the compliant type who "moves toward" people; the aggressive type who "moves against"; and the detached who "moves away" from others. Fromm speaks of the "social character," a core common to most members of a social class, on which are superimposed individual variations due to specific parental influences. His typology includes five different orientations: receptive, exploitative, hoarding, marketing, and productive. In applying psychoanalytic principles to the field of anthropology, Kardiner evolved the formulation of "basic personality structure," which refers to the personality configuration shared by the bulk of a society's members as a result of common early experiences. The vehicles through which the specific influences are brought to bear on the growing individual are the institutions, or practices and customs of the society.

A somewhat different approach to character structure is offered by Alexander, who points out the psychological correlates of the physiological life process of intaking, retaining, and elimination. An individual's character is said to reflect the relative participation of these three elementary attitudes in his dealings with other people. Erikson on his part emphasizes the concept of "ego identity," by which a person feels that he belongs to his group and knows where he is going. The development of this feeling arises from an integration of the various identifications experienced in childhood, culminating in late adolescence.

Post-mortem

By rights the last chapter in a book dealing with, in this instance, the eight ages of man should be read softly, accompanied by a few fading strains of organ music. However, our mission in this concluding note is neither to bury nor to praise, but instead to sum up and exhort.

If one may venture a guess as to the reader's (and author's) state of mind upon finishing this effort, the most appropriate word is probably "confused." It seems as though a large number of psychoanalysts through many years of observing patients, discussing cases, and borrowing from their own unconscious ideas have contributed to a massive, vague, yet potent personality theory. Encompassed are many controversial issues and many sharp disagreements. As if this were not enough, we have complicated the picture still further by introducing a curious assortment of bits of evidence. Obviously none of these factors makes for a feeling of closure.

But perhaps some degree of comfort can be gained by looking to the future rather than the past. The scientist typically achieves contentment first by selecting what for him is a meaningful area in which to work; next he sets up hypotheses which he considers to be worth investigating; and finally he puts them to the test. His security and peace of mind derive at least in part from the knowledge that he can apply methods adequate to his task, even though the final answers may be a long way off.

We can reason similarly with respect to psychoanalysis. The importance of its domain has been clearly established. Its assertions continue to enjoy wide application. If these assertions can be viewed, not as indestructible facts, but as hypotheses subject to verification or disproof, we have the makings of a theory. From the preceding pages there is ample justification for the belief that psychoanalytic concepts *can* be put to independent test in settings other than the traditional couch. Herein lies the exhortation. A combined and concerted research approach—through the experimental laboratory, the interview situation, the projective technique, the field study, etc.—holds real promise for the development of a sound theory of personality. With such an approach we can hope to chart, not the "future of an illusion," but the future of a science.

BEHAVIOR
DISORDERS

Many psychologists would agree with the description of neurosis presented here. If you have already studied conflict and motivation, you will see that it fits quite well with what has been said.

Although this analysis uses some psychoanalytic terms, e.g., repression and conflict, it is based on a view quite different from that of psycholanalysis in that it stresses learning. Some of the less orthodox psychoanalysts place substantial emphasis on learning, but the orthodox ones have little place for it in their systems.

A POINT TO GUIDE YOUR STUDY *With a learning orientation toward neuroses, what would the therapist concentrate upon in the treatment?*

49: SELECTION FROM: PERSONALITY AND PSYCHOTHERAPY. WHAT IS A NEUROSIS?

John Dollard, Yale University, and Neal E. Miller, Rockefeller University

Most people, even scientists, are vague about neurosis. Neither the neurotic victim nor those who know him seem able to state precisely what is involved. The victim feels a mysterious malady. The witness observes inexplicable behavior. The neurotic is mysterious because he is *capable* of acting and yet he is *unable* to act and enjoy. Though physically capable of attaining sex rewards, he is anesthetic; though capable of aggression, he is meek; though capable of

John Dollard and N. E. Miller. *Personality and psychotherapy*. New York: McGraw-Hill, 1950. Copyright © 1950 by the McGraw-Hill Book Company. Excerpt reprinted here with permission from the authors and McGraw-Hill Book Company.

affection, he is cold and unresponsive. As seen by the outside witness, the neurotic does not make use of the obvious opportunities for satisfaction which life offers him.

To be explained:
misery, stupidity, symptoms

The therapist confronts a person who is miserable, stupid (in some ways), and who has symptoms. These are the three major factors to be accounted for. Why is he miserable, in what curious way is he stupid, and whence arise the symptoms?

The waiting room of every psychiatric clinic is crowded with patients showing these common signs.

NEUROTIC MISERY IS REAL   Neurotic misery is real—not imaginary. Observers, not understanding the neurotic conflict, often belittle the suffering of neurotics and confuse neurosis with malingering. Neurotic habits are forced upon an individual by peculiar conditions of life and are not cheap attempts to escape duty and responsibility. In most cases the misery is attested by many specific complaints. These complaints or symptoms differ with each category of neurosis but sleeplessness, restlessness, irritability, sexual inhibitions, distaste for life, lack of clear personal goals, phobias, headaches, and irrational fears are among the more common ones.

At times the depth of the misery of the neurotic is concealed by his symptoms. Only when they are withdrawn does his true anguish appear. Occasionally the misery will be private, not easily visible to outside observers because friends and relatives are ringed around the neurotic person and prevent observation of his pain. In still other cases, the neurotic person is miserable but apathetic. He has lost even the hope that complaining and attracting attention will be helpful. However this may be, *if the neurotic takes the usual risks of life* he is miserable. He suffers if he attempts to love, marry, and be a parent. He fails if he tries to work responsibly and independently. His social relations tend to be invaded by peculiar demands and conditions. Neurotic misery is thus often masked by the protective conditions of life (as in childhood) and appears only when the individual has to "go it on his own."

CONFLICT PRODUCES MISERY   Suffering so intense as that shown by neurotics must have powerful causes, and it does. The neurotic is miserable because he is in conflict. As a usual thing two or more strong drives are operating in him and producing incompatible responses. Strongly driven to approach and as strongly to flee, he is not able to act to reduce either of the conflicting drives. These drives therefore remain dammed up, active, and nagging.

Where such a drive conflict is conscious there is no problem in convincing anyone why it should produce misery. If we picture a very hungry man confronting food which he knows to be poisoned, we can understand that he is driven on the one hand by hunger and on the other by fear. He oscillates at some distance from the tempting food, fearing to grasp but unable to leave. Everyone understands immediately the turmoil produced by such a conflict of hunger and fear.

Many people remember from their adolescence the tension of a strong sex conflict. Primary sex responses heightened by imaginative elaboration are met by intense fear. Though usually not allowed to talk about such matters, children sometimes can, and the misery they reveal is one of the most serious prices exacted of adolescents in our culture. That this conflict is acquired and not innate was shown by Margaret Mead in her brilliant book, "Coming of Age in Samoa" (1928). It is also agonizingly depicted in a novel by Vardis Fisher (1932).

Our third example of conscious conflict shows anger pitted against fear. In the early part of the war, an officer, newly commissioned from civilian life and without the habits of the professional soldier, was sent to an Army post. There he met a superior officer who decided to make an example of some minor mistake. The ranking officer lectured and berated the subordinate, refusing to let him speak and explain his behavior. He made him stand at attention against the wall for half an hour while this lecture was going on. The new-made officer quaked in fearful conflict. He detected the sadistic satisfaction which his superior got in dressing him down. He had never so much wanted to kill anyone. On the other hand, the junior officer felt the strong pressure of his own conscience to be a competent soldier and some real fear about what the consequence of assault might be. We met him shortly after this episode, and he still shook with rage when he described the experience. There was no doubt in his mind but that bearing strong, conflicting drives is one of the most severe causes of misery.

REPRESSION CAUSES STUPIDITY In each of the above cases, however, the individual could eventually solve his conflict. The hungry man could find nourishing food; the sex-tortured adolescent could eventually marry; the new officer could and did avoid his punishing superior.

With the neurotic this is not the case. He is not able to solve his conflict even with the passage of time. Though obviously intelligent in some ways, he is stupid in-so-far as his neurotic conflict is concerned. This stupidity is not an over-all affair, however. It is really a stupid area in the mind of a person who is quite intelligent in other respects. For some reason he cannot use his head on his neurotic conflicts.

Though the neurotic is sure he is miserable and is vocal about his symptoms, he is vague about what it is within him that could produce such painful effects. The fact that the neurotic cannot describe his own conflicts has been the source of great confusion in dealing with him either in terms of scientific theory or in terms of clinical practice. Nor can the therapist immediately spot these areas of stupidity. Only after extensive study of the patient's life can the areas of repression be clearly identified. Then the surprising fact emerges that the competing drives which afflict the neurotic person are not labeled. He has no language to describe the conflicting forces within him.

Without language and adequate labeling the higher mental processes cannot function. When these processes are knocked out by repression, the person cannot guide himself by mental means to a resolution of his conflict. Since the neurotic cannot help himself, he must have the help of others if he is to be helped at all—though millions today live out their lives in strong neurotic pain and never get help. The neurotic, therefore, is, or appears to be, stupid because he is unable to use his mind in dealing with certain of his problems. He feels that someone should help him, but he does not know how to ask for help since he does not know what his problem is. He may feel aggrieved that he is suffering, but he cannot explain his case.

SYMPTOMS SLIGHTLY REDUCE CONFLICT Although in many ways superficial, the symptoms of the neurotic are the most obvious aspects of his problems. These are what the patient is familiar with and feels he should be rid of. The phobias, inhibitions, avoidances, compulsions, rationalizations, and psychosomatic symptoms of the neurotic are experienced as a nuisance by him and by all who have to deal with him. The symptoms cannot be integrated into the texture of sensible social relations. The patient, however, believes that the symptoms *are* his disorder. It is these he wishes to be rid of and, not knowing that a serious conflict underlies them, he would like to confine the therapeutic discussion to getting rid of the symptoms.

The symptoms do not solve the basic conflict in which the neurotic person is plunged, but they mitigate it. They are responses which tend to reduce the conflict, and in part they succeed. When a successful symptom occurs it is reinforced because it reduces neurotic misery. The symptom is thus learned as a habit. One very common function of symptoms is to keep the neurotic person away from those stimuli which would activate and intensify his neurotic conflict. Thus, the combat pilot with a harrowing military disaster behind him may "walk away" from the sight of any airplane. As he walks toward the plane his anxiety goes up; as he walks away it goes down. "Walking away" is thus reinforced. It is this phobic walking away which constitutes his symptom. If the whole situation is not understood, such behavior seems bizarre to the casual witness.

CONFLICT, REPRESSION, AND SYMPTOMS CLOSELY RELATED   In the foregoing discussion we have "taken apart" the most conspicuous factors which define the neurosis and have separately discussed conflict, stupidity, and misery. We hope that the discussion has clarified the problem even at the expense of slightly distorting the actual relationships. In every human case of neurosis the three basic factors are closely and dynamically interrelated. The conflict could not be unconscious and insoluble were it not for the repressive factors involved. The symptoms could not exist did they not somewhat relieve the pressure of conflict. The mental paralysis of repression has been created by the very same forces which originally imposed the emotional conflict on the neurotic person.

The case of Mrs. A[1]

We are presenting the facts about Mrs. A for two reasons: (1) as background material on a case from which we will draw many concrete examples throughout the book; (2) as a set of facts from which we can illustrate the relationships between misery and conflict, stupidity and repression, symptoms and reinforcement. The reader will understand, of course, that the sole function of this case material is to give a clear exposition of principles by

[1] We are allowed to present and analyze the material on Mrs. A through the kindness of a New York colleague, a man so remarkable as to provide this laboriously gathered material and yet be willing to remain anonymous to aid in the complete disguise of the case.

means of concrete illustrations; it is *not* presented as evidence or proof.

THE FACTS   Mrs. A was an unusually pretty twenty-three-year-old married woman. Her husband worked in the offices of an insurance company. When she came to the therapist she was exceedingly upset. She had a number of fears. One of the strongest of these was that her heart would stop beating if she did not concentrate on counting the beats.

The therapist, who saw Mrs. A twice a week over a three-month period, took careful notes. The life-history data that we present were pieced together from the patient's statements during a total of 26 hours. The scope of the material is necessarily limited by the brevity of the treatment. The treatment had to end when a change in the husband's work forced her to move to another city.

Her first neurotic symptoms had appeared five months before she came to the psychiatrist. While she was shopping in a New York store, she felt faint and became afraid that something would happen to her and "no one would know where I was." She telephoned her husband's office and asked him to come and get her. Thereafter she was afraid to go out alone. Shortly after this time, she talked with an aunt who had a neurotic fear of heart trouble. After a conversation with this aunt, Mrs. A's fears changed from a fear of fainting to a concern about her heart.

Mrs. A was an orphan, born of unknown parents in a city in the upper South. She spent the first few months of life in an orphanage, then was placed in a foster home, where she lived, except for a year when she was doing war work in Washington, until her marriage at the age of twenty.

The foster parents belonged to the working class, had three children of their own, two girls and a boy, all of them older than the patient. The foster mother, who dominated the family, was cruel, strict, and miserly toward all the children. She had a coarse and vulgar demeanor, swore continually, and punished the foster child for the least offense. Mrs. A recalls: "She whipped me all the time—whether I'd done anything or not."

The foster mother had imposed a very repressive sex training on the patient, making her feel that sex was dirty and wrong. Moreover, the foster mother never let the patient think independently. She discouraged the patient's striving for an education, taking her out of school at sixteen when the family could have afforded to let her go on.

Despite the repressive sex training she received, Mrs. A had developed strong sexual appetites. In early childhood she had overheard parental intercourse, had masturbated, and had witnessed animal copulation. When she was ten or twelve, her foster brother seduced her. During the years before her marriage a dozen men tried to seduce her and most of them succeeded.

Nevertheless, sex was to her a dirty, loathsome thing that was painful for her to discuss or think about. She found sexual relations with her husband disgusting and was morbidly shy in her relations with him.

The patient had met her husband-to-be while she was working as a typist in Washington during the war. He was an Army officer and a college graduate. Her beauty enabled the patient to make a marriage that improved her social position; her husband's family were middle-class people. At the time of treatment Mrs. A had not yet learned all the habits of middle-class life. She was still somewhat awkward about entertaining or being entertained and made glaring errors in grammar and pronunciation. She was dominated, socially subordinated, and partly rejected by her husband's family.

When they were first married, Mr. and Mrs. A lived with his parents in a small town north of New York City and commuted to the city for work. Mrs. A had an office job there. Later, they were able to get an apartment in New York, but they stayed with the in-laws every week end. Although she described her mother-in-law in glowing terms at the beginning of the treatment, Mrs. A later came to express considerable hostility toward her.

When she came to the psychiatrist, Mrs. A was in great distress. She had to pay continual attention to her heart lest it stop beating. She lived under a burden of vague anxiety and had a number of specific phobias that prevented her from enjoying many of the normal pleasures of her life, such as going to the movies. She felt helpless to cope with her problems. Her constant complaints had tired out and alienated her friends. Her husband was fed up with her troubles and had threatened to divorce her. She could not get along with her foster mother and her mother-in-law had rejected her. She had no one left to talk to. She was hurt, baffled, and terrified by the thought that she might be going crazy.

ANALYSIS IN TERMS OF CONFLICT, REPRESSION, REINFORCEMENT   We have described Mrs. A as of the moment when she came to treatment. The analysis of the case, however, presents the facts as they were afterward ordered and clarified by study.

Misery. Mrs. A's misery was obvious to her family, her therapist, and herself. She suffered from a strong, vague, unremitting fear. She was tantalized by a mysterious temptation. The phobic limitations on her life prevented her from having much ordinary fun, as by shopping or going to the movies. Her husband and mother-in-law criticized her painfully. She feared that her husband would carry out his threat and divorce her. She feared that her heart would stop. She feared to be left all alone, sick and rejected. Her friends and relatives pitied her at first, then became put out with her when her condition persisted despite well-meant advice. Her misery, though baffling, was recognized as entirely real.

Conflict. Mrs. A suffered from two conflicts which produced her misery. The first might be described as a sex-fear conflict. Thanks to childhood circumstances she had developed strong sex appetites. At the same time strong anxieties were created in her and attached to the cues produced by sex excitement. However, she saw no connection between these remembered circumstances and the miserable life she was leading. The connective thoughts had been knocked out and the conflict was thus unconscious. The presence of the sexual appetites showed up in a kind of driven behavior in which she seemed to court seduction. Her fear was exhibited in her revulsion from sexual acts and thoughts and in her inability to take responsibility for a reasonable sexual expressiveness with her husband. The conflict was greatly intensified after her marriage because of her wish to be a dutiful wife. Guilt about the prospect of adultery was added to fear about sex motives.

Mrs. A was involved in a second, though less severe, conflict between aggression and fear. She was a gentle person who had been very badly treated by her mother-in-law. Resentful tendencies arose in her but they were quickly inhibited by fear. She attempted to escape the anger-fear conflict by exceptionally submissive behavior, putting up meekly with slights and subordination and protesting her fondness for the mother-in-law. She was tormented by it nevertheless, especially by feelings of worthlessness and helplessness. She felt much better, late in therapy, when she was able to state her resentment and begin to put it into effect in a measured way. (After all, she had the husband and his love, and if the mother-in-law wanted to see her son and prospective grandchildren she would have to take a decent attitude toward Mrs. A.)

Stupidity. Mrs. A's mind was certainly of little use to her in solving her problem. She tried the usual medical help with no result. She took a trip, as advised, and got no help. Her symptoms waxed and waned in unpredictable ways. She knew that she was helpless. At the time she came for therapy she had no plans for dealing with her problem and no hope of solving it. In addition to being unable to deal with her basic problems, Mrs. A did many things that were quite unintelligent and maladaptive. For example, in spite of the fact that she wanted very much to make a success of her marriage and was consciously trying to live a proper married life, she frequently exposed herself to danger of seduction. She went out on drinking parties with single girls. She hitchhiked rides with truck drivers. She was completely unaware of the motivation for this behavior and often unable to foresee its consequences until it was too late. While her behavior seems stupid in the light of a knowledge of the actual state of affairs, there were many ways in which Mrs. A did not seem at all stupid—for example, when debating with the therapist to protect herself against fear-producing thoughts. She then gave hopeful evidence of what she could do with her mind when she had available all the necessary units to think with.

Repression. Mrs. A gave abundant evidence of the laming effects of repression. At the outset she thought she had no sex feelings or appetites. She described behavior obviously motivated by fear but could not label the fear itself. The closest she came was to express the idea that she was going insane. Further, Mrs. A thought she had an organic disease and clung desperately to this idea, inviting any kind of treatment so long as it did not force her to think about matters which would produce fear. Such mental gaps and distortions are a characteristic result of repression. They are what produce the stupidity.

Symptoms. Mrs. A's chief symptoms were the spreading phobia which drove her out of theaters and stores and the compulsive counting of breaths and heartbeats. These symptoms almost incapacitated her. She had lost her freedom to think and to move.

Reinforcement of symptoms. An analysis of the phobia revealed the following events. When on the streets alone, her fear of sex temptation was increased. Someone might speak to her, wink at her, make an approach to her. Such an approach would increase her sex desire and make her more vulnerable to seduction. Increased sex desire, however, touched off both anxiety and guilt, and this intensified her conflict when she was on the street. When she "escaped home," the temptation stimuli were lessened, along with a reduction of the fear which they elicited. Going home and, later, avoiding the temptation situation by anticipation were reinforced. Naturally, the basic sex-anxiety conflict was not resolved by the defensive measure of the symptom. The conflict persisted but was not so keen.

The counting of heartbeats can be analytically taken apart in a similar way. When sexy thoughts came to mind or other sex stimuli tended to occur, these stimuli elicited anxiety. It is clear that these stimuli were occurring frequently because Mrs. A was responding with anxiety much of the time. Since counting is a highly preoccupying kind of response, no other thoughts could enter her mind during this time. While counting, the sexy thoughts which excited fear dropped out. Mrs. A "felt better" immediately when she started counting, and the counting habit was reinforced by the drop in anxiety. Occasionally, Mrs. A would forget to count and then her intense anxiety would recur. In this case, as in that of the phobia, the counting symptom does not resolve the basic conflict—it only avoids exacerbating it.

Thus Mrs. A's case illustrates the analysis of neurotic mechanisms made in the earlier part of the chapter. Conflict produced high drives experienced as misery; repression interfered with higher mental processes and so with the intelligent solution of the conflict; the symptoms were learned responses which were reinforced by producing some reduction in the strength of drive. We will discuss later how higher mental life can be restored and how actions which *will* resolve the poisonous conflict can be made to occur.

SECTION FIFTEEN

MENTAL
HEALTH
AND
PSYCHOTHERAPY

*Since this article was published in 1946, the client-centered method
has become especially prominent in guidance and counseling with
people who are not severely disturbed. The method is most successful
with those who are able to make use of their own creative and
integrative abilities—the not-so-severely disturbed.*

POINTS TO GUIDE YOUR STUDY *(1) Contrast this technique with
psychoanalysis. (2) Pay special attention to the elements of the
client-centered therapy situation. (3) How might client-centered
counseling help a person decide for himself on a career?*

50: SIGNIFICANT ASPECTS OF CLIENT-CENTERED THERAPY

Carl R. Rogers, Western Behavioral Sciences Institute

In planning to address this group, I have
considered and discarded several possible
topics. I was tempted to describe the process of nondirective therapy and the counselor techniques and procedures which
seem most useful in bringing about this
process. But much of this material is now
in writing. My own book on counseling and
psychotherapy contains much of the basic
material, and my recent more popular book
on counseling with returning servicemen

tends to supplement it. The philosophy of
the client-centered approach and its application to work with children is per-
suasively presented by Allen. The application to counseling of industrial employees
is discussed in the volume by Cantor. Curran has now published in book form one
of the several research studies which are
throwing new light on both process and
procedure. Axline is publishing a book on
play and group therapy. Snyder is bringing out a book of cases. So it seems unnecessary to come a long distance to summarize material which is, or soon will be,
obtainable in written form.

Another tempting possibility, particularly in this setting, was to discuss some

Paper given at a seminar of the staffs of the Menninger Clinic and the Topeka Veteran's Hospital,
Topeka, Kansas, May 15, 1946.

C. R. Rogers. Significant aspects of client-centered
therapy. *Amer. Psychologist*, 1946, **1**, 415–422. Copyright
© 1946 by the American Psychological Association. Reprinted here with permission from the author and the
American Psychological Association.

of the roots from which the client-centered approach has sprung. It would have been interesting to show how in its concepts of repression and release, in its stress upon catharsis and insight, it has many roots in Freudian thinking, and to acknowledge that indebtedness. Such an analysis could also have shown that in its concept of the individual's ability to organize his own experience there is an even deeper indebtedness to the work of Rank, Taft, and Allen. In its stress upon objective research, the subjecting of fluid attitudes to scientific investigation, the willingness to submit all hypotheses to a verification or disproof by research methods, the debt is obviously to the whole field of American psychology, with its genius for scientific methodology. It could also have been pointed out that although everyone in the clinical field has been heavily exposed to the eclectic "team" approach to therapy of the child guidance movement, and the somewhat similar eclecticism of the Adolf Myers-Hopkins school of thought, these eclectic viewpoints have perhaps not been so fruitful in therapy and that little from these sources has been retained in the nondirective approach. It might also have been pointed out that in its basic trend away from guiding and directing the client, the nondirective approach is deeply rooted in practical clinical experience, and is in accord with the experience of most clinical workers, so much so that one of the commonest reactions of experienced therapists is that "You have crystallized and put into words something that I have been groping toward in my own experience for a long time."

Such an analysis, such a tracing of root ideas, needs to be made, but I doubt my own ability to make it. I am also doubtful that anyone who is deeply concerned with a new development knows with any degree of accuracy where his ideas came from.

Consequently I am, in this presentation, adopting a third pathway. While I shall bring in a brief description of process and procedure, and while I shall acknowledge in a general way our indebtedness to many root sources, and shall recognize the many common elements shared by client-centered therapy and other approaches, I believe it will be to our mutual advantage if I stress primarily those aspects in which nondirective therapy differs most sharply and deeply from other therapeutic procedures. I hope to point out some of the basically significant ways in which the client-centered viewpoint differs from others, not only in its present principles, but in the wider divergencies which are implied by the projection of its central principles.

The predictable process of client-centered therapy

The first of the three distinctive elements of client-centered therapy to which I wish to call your attention is the predictability of the therapeutic process in this approach. We find, both clinically and statistically, that a predictable pattern of therapeutic development takes place. The assurance which we feel about this was brought home to me recently when I played a recorded first interview for the graduate students in our practicum immediately after it was recorded, pointing out the characteristic aspects, and agreeing to play later interviews for them to let them see the later phases of the counseling process. The fact that I knew with assurance what the later pattern would be before it had occurred only struck me as I thought about the incident. We have become clinically so accustomed to this predictable quality that we take it for granted. Perhaps a brief summarized description of this therapeutic process will indicate those elements of which we feel sure.

It may be said that we now know how to initiate a complex and predictable chain of events in dealing with the maladjusted individual, a chain of events which is therapeutic, and which operates effectively in problem situations of the most diverse type. This predictable chain of events may come about through the use of language, as in counseling, through symbolic language, as in play therapy, through disguised language as in drama or puppet therapy. It is effective in dealing with individual situations, and also in small group situations.

It is possible to state with some exactness the conditions which must be met in order to initiate and carry through this releasing therapeutic experience. Below are listed in brief form the conditions which seem to be necessary, and the therapeutic results which occur.

This experience which releases the growth forces within the individual will come about in most cases if the following elements are present.

1. If the counselor operates on the principle that the individual is basically responsible for himself, and is willing for the individual to keep that responsibility.

2. If the counselor operates on the principle that the client has a strong drive to become mature, socially adjusted, independent, productive, and relies on this force, not on his own powers, for therapeutic change.

3. If the counselor creates a warm and permissive atmosphere in which the individual is free to bring out any attitudes and feelings which he may have, no matter how unconventional, absurd, or contradictory these attitudes may be. The client is as free to withhold expression as he is to give expression to his feelings.

4. If the limits which are set are simple limits set on behavior, and not limits set on attitudes. (This applies mostly to children. The child may not be permitted to break a window or leave the room, but he is free to feel like breaking a window, and the feeling is fully accepted. The adult client may not be permitted more than an hour for an interview, but there is full acceptance of his desire to claim more time.)

5. If the therapist uses only those procedures and techniques in the interview which convey his deep understanding of the emotionalized attitudes expressed and his acceptance of them. This understanding is perhaps best conveyed by a sensitive reflection and clarification of the client's attitudes. The counselor's acceptance involves neither approval nor disapproval.

6. If the counselor refrains from any expression or action which is contrary to the preceding principles. This means refraining from questioning, probing, blame, interpretation, advice, suggestion, persuasion, reassurance.

If these conditions are met, then it may be said with assurance that in the great majority of cases the following results will take place.

1. The client will express deep and motivating attitudes.

2. The client will explore his own attitudes and reactions more fully than he has previously done and will come to be aware of aspects of his attitudes which he has previously denied.

3. He will arrive at a clearer conscious realization of his motivating attitudes and will accept himself more completely. This realization and this acceptance will include attitudes previously denied. He may or may not verbalize this clearer conscious understanding of himself and his behavior.

4. In the light of his clearer perception of himself he will choose, on his own initiative and on his own responsibility, new goals which are more satisfying than his maladjusted goals.

5. He will choose to behave in a different fashion in order to reach these goals, and this new behavior will be in the direction of greater psychological growth and maturity. It will also be more spontaneous and less tense, more in harmony with social needs of others, will represent a more realistic and more comfortable ad-

justment to life. It will be more integrated than his former behavior. It will be a step forward in the life of the individual.

The best scientific description of this process is that supplied by Snyder. Analyzing a number of cases with strictly objective research techniques, Snyder has discovered that the development in these cases is roughly parallel, that the initial phase of catharsis is replaced by a phase in which insight becomes the most significant element, and this in turn by a phase marked by the increase in positive choice and action.

Clinically we know that sometimes this process is relatively shallow, involving primarily a fresh reorientation to an immediate problem, and in other instances so deep as to involve a complete reorientation of personality. It is recognizably the same process whether it involves a girl who is unhappy in a dormitory and is able in three interviews to see something of her childishness and dependence, and to take steps in a mature direction, or whether it involves a young man who is on the edge of a schizophrenic break, and who in thirty interviews works out deep insights in relation to his desire for his father's death, and his possessive and incestuous impulses toward his mother, and who not only takes new steps but rebuilds his whole personality in the process. Whether shallow or deep, it is basically the same.

We are coming to recognize with assurance characteristic aspects of each phase of the process. We know that the catharsis involves a gradual and more complete expression of emotionalized attitudes. We know that characteristically the conversation goes from superficial problems and attitudes to deeper problems and attitudes. We know that this process of exploration gradually unearths relevant attitudes which have been denied to consciousness.

We recognize too that the process of achieving insight is likely to involve more adequate facing of reality as it exists within the self, as well as external reality; that it involves the relating of problems to each other, the perception of patterns of behavior; that it involves the acceptance of hitherto denied elements of the self, and a reformulating of the self-concept; and that it involves the making of new plans.

In the final phase we know that the choice of new ways of behaving will be in conformity with the newly organized concept of the self; that first steps in putting these plans into action will be small but symbolic; that the individual will feel only a minimum degree of confidence that he can put his plans into effect; that later steps implement more and more completely the new concept of self, and that this process continues beyond the conclusion of the therapeutic interviews.

If these statements seem to contain too much assurance, to sound "too good to be true," I can only say that for many of them we now have research backing, and that as rapidly as possible we are developing our research to bring all phases of the process under objective scrutiny. Those of us working clinically with client-centered therapy regard this predictability as a settled characteristic, even though we recognize that additional research will be necessary to fill out the picture more completely.

It is the implication of this predictability which is startling. Whenever, in science, a predictable process has been discovered, it has been found possible to use it as a starting point for a whole chain of discoveries. We regard this as not only entirely possible, but inevitable, with regard to this predictable process in therapy. Hence, we regard this orderly and predictable nature of nondirective therapy as one of its most distinctive and significant points of difference from other approaches. Its importance lies not only in the fact that it is a present difference, but in the fact that it points toward a sharply different future, in which scientific exploration of this known chain of events should lead to many new discoveries, developments, and applications.

The discovery of the capacity of the client

Naturally the question is raised, what is the reason for this predictability in a type of therapeutic procedure in which the therapist serves only a catalytic function? Basically the reason for the predictability of the therapeutic process lies in the discovery—and I use that word intentionally—that within the client reside constructive forces whose strength and uniformity have been either entirely unrecognized or grossly underestimated. It is the clearcut and disciplined reliance by the therapist upon those forces within the client, which seems to account for the orderliness of the therapeutic process, and its consistency from one client to the next.

I mentioned that I regarded this as a discovery. I would like to amplify that statement. We have known for centuries that catharsis and emotional release were helpful. Many new methods have been and are being developed to bring about release, but the principle is not new. Likewise, we have known since Freud's time that insight, if it is accepted and assimilated by the client, is therapeutic. The principle is not new. Likewise we have realized that revised action patterns, new ways of behaving, may come about as a result of insight. The principle is not new.

But we have not known or recognized that in most if not all individuals there exist growth forces, tendencies toward self-actualization, which may act as the sole motivation for therapy. We have not realized that under suitable psychological conditions these forces bring about emotional release in those areas and at those rates which are most beneficial to the individual. These forces drive the individual to explore his own attitudes and his relationship to

reality, and to explore these areas effectively. We have not realized that the individual is capable of exploring his attitudes and feelings, including those which have been denied to consciousness, at a rate which does not cause panic, and to the depth required for comfortable adjustment. The individual is capable of discovering and perceiving, truly and spontaneously, the interrelationships between his own attitudes, and the relationship of himself to reality. The individual has the capacity and the strength to devise, quite unguided, the steps which will lead him to a more mature and more comfortable relationship to his reality. It is the gradual and increasing recognition of these capacities within the individual by the client-centered therapist that rates, I believe, the term discovery. All of these capacities I have described are released in the individual if a suitable psychological atmosphere is provided.

There has, of course, been lip service paid to the strength of the client, and the need of utilizing the urge toward independence which exists in the client. Psychiatrists, analysts, and especially social case workers have stressed this point. Yet it is clear from what is said, and even more clear from the case material cited, that this confidence is a very limited confidence. It is a confidence that the client can take over, if guided by the expert, a confidence that the client can assimilate insight if it is first given to him by the expert, can make choices providing guidance is given at crucial points. It is, in short, the same sort of attitude which the mother has toward the adolescent, that she believes in his capacity to make his own decisions and guide his own life, providing he takes the directions of which she approves.

This is very evident in the latest book on psychoanalysis by Alexander and French. Although many of the former views and practices of psychoanalysis are discarded, and the procedures are far more nearly in line with those of nondirective therapy, it is still the therapist who is definitely in control. He gives the insights, he is ready to guide at crucial points. Thus while the authors state that the aim of the therapist is to free the patient to develop his capacities, and to increase his ability to satisfy his needs in ways acceptable to himself and society; and while they speak of the basic conflict between competition and cooperation as one which the individual must settle for himself; and speak of the integration of new insight as a normal function of the ego, it is clear when they speak of procedures that they have no confidence that the client has the capacity to do any of these things. For in practice, "As soon as the therapist takes the more active role we advocate, systematic planning becomes imperative. In addition to the original decision as to the particular sort of strategy to be employed in the treatment of any case, we recommend the conscious use of various techniques in a flexible manner, shifting tactics to fit the particular needs of the moment. Among these modifications of the standard technique are: using not only the method of free association but interviews of a more direct character, manipulating the frequency of the interviews, giving directives to the patient concerning his daily life, employing interruptions of long or short duration in preparation for ending the treatment, regulating the transference relationship to meet the specific needs of the case, and making use of real-life experiences as an integral part of therapy" (1). At least this leaves no doubt as to whether it is the client's or the therapist's hour; it is clearly the latter. The capacities which the client is to develop are clearly not to be developed in the therapeutic sessions.

The client-centered therapist stands at an opposite pole, both theoretically and practically. He has learned that the constructive forces in the individual can be trusted, and that the more deeply they are relied upon, the more deeply they are released. He has come to build his procedures upon these hypotheses, which are rapidly becoming established as facts: that the client knows the areas of concern which he is ready to explore; that the client is the best judge as to the most desirable frequency of interviews; that the client can lead the way more efficiently than the therapist into deeper concerns; that the client will protect himself from panic by ceasing to explore an area which is becoming too painful; that the client can and will uncover all the repressed elements which it is necessary to uncover in order to build a comfortable adjustment; that the client can achieve for himself far truer and more sensitive and accurate insights than can possibly be given to him; that the client is capable of translating these insights into constructive behavior which weighs his own needs and desires realistically against the demands of society; that the client knows when therapy is completed and he is ready to cope with life independently. Only one condition is necessary for all these forces to be released, and that is the proper psychological atmosphere between client and therapist.

Our case records and increasingly our research bear out these statements. One might suppose that there would be a generally favorable reaction to this discovery, since it amounts in effect to tapping great reservoirs of hitherto little-used energy. Quite the contrary is true, however, in professional groups. There is no other aspect of client-centered therapy which comes under such vigorous attack. It seems to be genuinely disturbing to many professional people to entertain the thought that this client upon whom they have been exercising their professional skill actually knows more about his inner psychological self than they can possibly know, and that he possesses constructive strengths which make the constructive push by the therapist seem puny indeed by comparison.

The willingness fully to accept this strength of the client, with all the reorientation of therapeutic procedure which it implies, is one of the ways in which client-centered therapy differs most sharply from other therapeutic approaches.

The client-centered nature of the therapeutic relationship

The third distinctive feature of this type of therapy is the character of the relationship between therapist and client. Unlike other therapies in which the skills of the therapist are to be exercised upon the client, in this approach the skills of the therapist are focused upon creating a psychological atmosphere in which the client can work. If the counselor can create a relationship permeated by warmth, understanding, safety from any type of attack, no matter how trivial, and basic acceptance of the person as he is, then the client will drop his natural defensiveness and use the situation. As we have puzzled over the characteristics of a successful therapeutic relationship, we have come to feel that the sense of communication is very important. If the client feels that he is actually communicating his present attitudes, superficial, confused, or conflicted as they may be, and that his communication is understood rather than evaluated in any way, then he is freed to communicate more deeply. A relationship in which the client thus feels that he is communicating is almost certain to be fruitful.

All of this means a drastic reorganization in the counselor's thinking, particularly if he has previously utilized other approaches. He gradually learns that the statement that the time is to be "the client's hour" means just that, and that his biggest task is to make it more and more deeply true.

Perhaps something of the characteristics of the relationship may be suggested by excerpts from a paper written by a young minister who has spent several months learning client-centered counseling procedures.

Because the client-centered, nondirective counseling approach has been rather carefully defined and clearly illustrated, it gives the *"Illusion of Simplicity."* The technique seems deceptively easy to master. Then you begin to practice. A word is wrong here and there. You don't quite reflect feeling, but reflect content instead. It is difficult to handle questions; you are tempted to interpret. Nothing seems so serious that further practice won't correct it. Perhaps you are having trouble playing two roles—that of minister and that of counselor. Bring up the question in class and the matter is solved again with a deceptive ease. But these apparently minor errors and a certain woodenness of response seem exceedingly persistent.

Only gradually does it dawn that if the technique is true it demands a feeling of warmth. You begin to feel that the attitude is the thing. Every little word is not so important if you have the correct accepting and permissive attitude toward the client. So you bear down on the permissiveness and acceptance. You *will* permiss and accept and reflect the client, if it kills you!

But you still have those troublesome questions from the client. He simply doesn't know the next step. He asks you to give him a hint, some possibilities, after all you are expected to know something, else why is he here? As a minister, you ought to have some convictions about what people should believe, how they should act. As a counselor, you should know something about removing this obstacle—you ought to have the equivalent of the surgeon's knife and use it. Then you begin to wonder. The technique is good, *but . . .* does it go *far* enough? does it really work on clients? is it *right* to leave a person helpless, when you might show him the way out?

Here it seems to me is the crucial point. "Narrow is the gate" and hard the path from here on. No one else can give satisfying answers and even the instructors seem frustrating because they appear not to be helpful in your specific case. For here is demanded of you what no other person can do or point out

—and that is to rigorously scrutinize yourself and your attitudes towards others. Do you believe that all people truly have a creative potential in them? That each person is a unique individual and that he alone can work out his own individuality? Or do you really believe that some persons are of "negative value" and others are weak and must be led and taught by "wiser," "stronger" people.

You begin to see that there is nothing compartmentalized about this method of counseling. It is not just counseling, because it demands the most exhaustive, penetrating, and comprehensive consistency. In other methods you can shape tools, pick them up for use when you will. But when genuine acceptance and permissiveness are your tools it requires nothing less than the whole complete personality. And to grow oneself is the most demanding of all.

He goes on to discuss the notion that the counselor must be restrained and "self-denying." He concludes that this is a mistaken notion.

Instead of demanding less of the counselor's personality in the situation, client-centered counseling in some ways demands more. It demands discipline, not restraint. It calls for the utmost in sensitivity, appreciative awareness, channeled and disciplined. It demands that the counselor put all he has of these precious qualities into the situation, but in a disciplined, refined manner. It is restraint only in the sense that the counselor does not express himself in certain areas that he may use himself in others.

Even this is deceptive, however. It is not so much restraint in any area as it is a focusing, sensitizing one's energies and personality in the direction of an appreciative and understanding attitude.

As time has gone by we have come to put increasing stress upon the "client-centeredness" of the relationship, because it is more effective the more completely the counselor concentrates upon trying to understand the client *as the client seems to himself*. As I look back upon some of our earlier published cases—the case of Her-

bert Bryan in my book, or Snyder's case of Mr. M.—I realize that we have gradually dropped the vestiges of subtle directiveness which are all too evident in those cases. We have come to recognize that if we can provide understanding of the way the client seems to himself at this moment, he can do the rest. The therapist must lay aside his preoccupation with diagnosis and his diagnostic shrewdness, must discard his tendency to make professional evaluations, must cease his endeavors to formulate an accurate prognosis, must give up the temptation subtly to guide the individual, and must concentrate on one purpose only; that of providing deep understanding and acceptance of the attitudes consciously held at this moment by the client as he explores step by step into the dangerous areas which he has been denying to consciousness.

I trust it is evident from this description that this type of relationship can exist only if the counselor is deeply and genuinely able to adopt these attitudes. Client-centered counseling, if it is to be effective, cannot be a trick or a tool. It is not a subtle way of guiding the client while pretending to let him guide himself. To be effective, it must be genuine. It is this sensitive and sincere "client-centeredness" in the therapeutic relationship that I regard as the third characteristic of nondirective therapy which sets it distinctively apart from other approaches.

Some implications

Although the client-centered approach had its origin purely within the limits of the psychological clinic, it is proving to have implications, often of a startling nature, for very diverse fields of effort. I should like to suggest a few of these present and potential implications.

In the field of psychotherapy itself, it leads to conclusions that seem distinctly heretical. It appears evident that training and practice in therapy should probably precede training in the field of diagnosis. Diagnostic knowledge and skill is not necessary for good therapy, a statement which sounds like blasphemy to many, and if the professional worker, whether psychiatrist, psychologist or caseworker, received training in therapy first he would learn psychological dynamics in a truly dynamic fashion, and would acquire a professional humility and willingness to learn from his client which is today all too rare.

The viewpoint appears to have implications for medicine. It has fascinated me to observe that when a prominent allergist began to use client-centered therapy for the treatment of nonspecific allergies, he found not only very good therapeutic results, but the experience began to affect his whole medical practice. It has gradually meant the reorganization of his office procedure. He has given his nurses a new type of training in understanding the patient. He has decided to have all medical histories taken by a nonmedical person trained in nondirective techniques, in order to get a true picture of the client's feelings and attitudes toward himself and his health, uncluttered by the bias and diagnostic evaluation which is almost inevitable when a medical person takes the history and unintentionally distorts the material by his premature judgments. He has found these histories much more helpful to the physicians than those taken by physicians.

The client-centered viewpoint has already been shown to have significant implications for the field of survey interviewing and public opinion study. Use of such techniques by Likert, Lazarsfeld, and others has meant the elimination of much of the factor of bias in such studies.

This approach has also, we believe, deep implications for the handling of social and group conflicts, as I have pointed out in another paper (9). Our work in applying a client-centered viewpoint to group therapy situations, while still in its early stages, leads us to feel that a significant clue to the constructive solution of interpersonal and intercultural frictions in the group may be in our hands. Application of these procedures to staff groups, to inter-racial groups, to groups with personal problems and tensions, is under way.

In the field of education, too, the client-centered approach is finding significant application. The work of Cantor, a description of which will soon be published, is outstanding in this connection, but a number of teachers are finding that these methods, designed for therapy, produce a new type of educational process, an independent learning which is highly desirable, and even a reorientation of individual direction which is very similar to the results of individual or group therapy.

Even in the realm of our philosophical orientation, the client-centered approach has its deep implications. I should like to indicate this by quoting briefly from a previous paper.

As we examine and try to evaluate our clinical experience with client-centered therapy, the phenomenon of the reorganization of attitudes and the redirection of behavior by the individual assumes greater and greater importance. This phenomenon seems to find inadequate explanation in terms of the determinism which is the predominant philosophical background of most psychological work. The capacity of the individual to reorganize his attitudes and behavior in ways not determined by external factors nor by previous elements in his own experience, but determined by his own insight into those factors, is an impressive capacity. It involves a basic spontaneity which we have been loath to admit into our scientific thinking.

The clinical experience could be summarized by saying that the behavior of the human organism may be determined by the influences to which it has been exposed, *but it may also be determined by the creative and integrative insight of the organism itself.* This ability of the person to discover new meaning in the forces which impinge upon him and in the past experiences which have been controlling him, and the ability to alter consciously his behavior in the light of this new meaning, has a profound significance for our thinking which has not been fully realized. We need to revise the philosophical basis of our work to a point where it can admit that forces exist within the individual which can exercise a spontaneous and significant influence upon behavior which is not predictable through knowledge of prior influences and conditionings. The forces released through a catalytic process of therapy are not adequately accounted for by a knowledge of the individual's previous conditionings, but only if we grant the presence of a spontaneous force within the organism which has the capacity of integration and redirection. This capacity for volitional control is a force which we must take into account in any psychological equation (9).

So we find an approach which began merely as a way of dealing with problems of human maladjustment forcing us into a revaluation of our basic philosophical concepts.

Summary

I hope that throughout this paper I have managed to convey what is my own conviction, that what we now know or think we know about a client-centered approach is only a beginning, only the opening of a door beyond which we are beginning to see some very challenging roads, some fields rich with opportunity. It is the facts of our clinical and research experience which keep pointing forward into new and exciting possibilities. Yet whatever the future may hold, it appears already clear that we are dealing with materials of a new and significant nature, which demand the most open-minded and thorough exploration. If our present formulations of those facts are correct, then we would say that some important elements already stand out; that certain basic attitudes and skills can create a psychological atmosphere which releases, frees, and utilizes deep strengths in the client; that these strengths and capacities are more sensitive and more rugged than hitherto supposed; and that they are released in an orderly and predictable process which may prove as significant a basic fact in social science as some of the laws and predictable processes in the physical sciences.

Selected references

1. Alexander, F., and French, T. *Psychoanalytic Therapy.* New York: Ronald Press, 1946.
2. Allen, F. *Psychotherapy with Children.* New York: Norton, 1942.
3. Cantor, N. *Employee Counseling.* New York: McGraw-Hill Book Company.
4. Cantor, N. The Dynamics of Learning. (unpublished mss.) University of Buffalo, 1943.
5. Curran, C. A. *Personality Factors in Counseling.* New York: Grune and Stratton, 1945.
6. Rank, O. *Will Therapy.* New York: Alfred A. Knopf, 1936.
7. Rogers, C. R. "Counselling," *Review of Educational Research,* April 1945 (Vol. 15), pp. 155–163.
8. Rogers, C. R. *Counseling and Psychotherapy.* New York: Houghton Mifflin Co., 1942.
9. Rogers, C. R. *The implications of nondirective therapy for the handling of social conflicts.* Paper given to a seminar of the Bureau of Intercultural Education, New York City, Feb. 18, 1946.
10. Rogers, C. R., and Wallen, J. L. *Counseling with Returned Servicemen.* New York: McGraw-Hill, 1946.
11. Snyder, W. U. "An Investigation of the Nature of Non-Directive Psychotherapy," *Journal of General Psychology.* Vol. 33, 1945. pp. 193–223.
12. Taft, J. *The Dynamics of Therapy in a Controlled Relationship.* New York: Macmillan, 1933.

This selection illustrates what has been called behavior therapy, a technique especially useful in cases in which a troublesome behavior pattern creates difficulties for a person. The focus, then, is on eliminating undesirable behaviors. Some might call this type of therapy "symptomatic" in that it changes superficial behavior without attacking "the underlying causes of the behavior." But when it is the bizarre, impulsive, or intrusive behavior itself which is the problem, it makes sense to try to change it by behavioral techniques. Besides, therapies aimed at the "underlying causes" are ineffective in many cases—especially since the "underlying causes" are not readily known.

POINTS TO GUIDE YOUR STUDY *(1) Note that the techniques here were derived from animal studies that depended upon what may loosely be called operant, or Skinnerian, techniques. (Review operant behavior, or instrumental conditioning, in your text.) Other types of behavior therapy use classical conditioning techniques. (2) Since this paper was published in England, the English spelling of* behavior *is retained.*

51: INTENSIVE TREATMENT OF PSYCHOTIC BEHAVIOUR BY STIMULUS SATIATION AND FOOD REINFORCEMENT

T. Ayllon, Anna State Hospital, Anna, Illinois

SUMMARY   *This investigation demonstrates that extensive and effective behavioural modification is feasible without costly and lengthy psychotherapeutic treatment. In addition, the often heard notion that another undesirable type of behaviour will replace the original problem behaviour is not supported by the findings to date.*

Introduction

Until recently, the effective control of behaviour was limited to the animal laboratory. The extension of this control to human behaviour was made when Lindsley successfully adapted the methodology of operant conditioning to the study of psychotic behaviour (Lindsley, 1956). Following Lindsley's point of departure other investigators have shown that, in its essentials, the behaviour of mental defective individuals (Orlando and Bijou, 1960), stutterers (Flanagan, Goldiamond and Azrin, 1958), mental patients (Hutchinson and Azrin, 1961), autistic (Ferster and DeMyer, 1961), and normal children (Bijou, 1961; Azrin and Lindsley, 1956) is subject to the same controls.

Despite the obvious implications of this research for applied settings there has been a conspicuous lag between the research findings and their application. The greatest limitation to the direct application of laboratory principles has been the absence of control over the subjects' environment. Recently, however, a series of applications in a regulated psychiatric setting has clearly demonstrated the possiblities of behavioural modification (Ayllon and Michael, 1959; Ayllon and Haughton, 1962). Some of the behaviour studied has

This report is based, in part, on a two-year research project (1959–1961), conducted by the author at the Saskatchewan Hospital, Weyburn, Saskatchewan, Canada, and supported by a grant from the Commonwealth Fund. Grateful acknowledgment is due to H. Osmond and I. Clancey of the Saskatchewan Hospital. The author also thanks E. Haughton who assisted in the conduct of this investigation, and N. Azrin and W. Holtz for their critical reading of the manuscript.
  T. Ayllon. Intensive treatment of psychotic behaviour by stimulus satiation and food reinforcement. *Behav. Res. Ther.*, 1963, 1, 53–61. Copyright © 1963 by Pergamon Press, Ltd. Reprinted with permission from the author and Pergamon Press. Figure 7 slightly different from that in the article as originally published.

included repetitive and highly stereotyped responses such as complaining, pacing, refusal to eat, hoarding and many others.

What follows is a demonstration of behaviour techniques for the intensive individual treatment of psychotic behaviour. Specific pathological behaviour patterns of a single patient were treated by manipulating the patient's environment.

THE EXPERIMENTAL WARD AND CONTROL OVER THE REINFORCEMENT This investigation was conducted in a mental hospital ward, the characteristics of which have been described elsewhere (Ayllon and Haughton, 1962). Briefly, this was a female ward to which only authorized personnel were allowed access. The ward staff was made up of psychiatric nurses and untrained aides who carried out the environmental manipulations under the direction of the experimenter. Using a time-sample technique, patients were observed daily every 30 minutes from 7.00 a.m. to 11.00 p.m.

The dining room was the only place where food was available and entrance to the dining room could be regulated. Water was freely available at a drinking fountain on the ward. None of the patients had ground passes or jobs outside the ward.

SUBJECT The patient was a 47-year-old female patient diagnosed as a chronic schizophrenic. The patient had been hospitalized for 9 years. Upon studying the patient's behaviour on the ward, it became apparent that the nursing staff[1] spent considerable time caring for her. In particular, there were three aspects of her behaviour which seemed to defy solution. The first was stealing food. The second was the hoarding of the ward's towels in her room. The third undesirable aspect of her behaviour consisted in her wearing

[1] As used in this paper, 'nurse' is a generic term including all those who actually work on the ward (attendants, aides, psychiatric and registered nurses).

excessive clothing, e.g. a half-dozen dresses, several pairs of stockings, sweaters, and so on.

In order to modify the patient's behaviour systematically, each of these three types of behaviour (stealing food, hoarding, and excessive dressing) was treated separately.

Experiment I

CONTROL OF STEALING FOOD BY FOOD WITHDRAWAL The patient had weighed over 250 pounds for many years. She ate the usual tray of food served to all patients, but, in addition, she stole food from the food counter and from other patients. Because the medical staff regarded her excessive weight as detrimental to her health, a special diet had been prescribed for her. However, the patient refused to diet and continued stealing food. In an effort to discourage the patient from stealing, the ward nurses had spent considerable time trying to persuade her to stop stealing food. As a last resort, the nurses would force her to return the stolen food.

To determine the extent of food stealing, nurses were instructed to record all behaviour associated with eating in the dining room. This record, taken for nearly a month, showed that the patient stole food during two thirds of all meals.

PROCEDURE The traditional methods previously used to stop the patient from stealing food were discontinued. No longer were persuasion, coaxing, or coercion used.

The patient was assigned to a table in the dining room, and no other patients were allowed to sit with her. Nurses removed the patient from the dining room when she approached a table other than her own, or when she picked up unauthorized food from the dining room counter. In effect, this procedure resulted in the patient missing a meal whenever she attempted to steal food.

RESULTS   Figure 1 shows that when withdrawal of positive reinforcement (i.e.
meal) was made dependent upon the
patient's stealing, this response was eliminated in two weeks. Because the patient no
longer stole food, she ate only the diet prescribed for her. The effective control of the
stealing response is also indicated by the
gradual reduction in the patient's body
weight. At no time during the patient's 9
years of hospitalization had she weighed
less than 230 pounds. Figure 2 shows that
at the conclusion of this treatment her
weight stabilized at 180 pounds or 17 per
cent loss from her original weight. At this
time, the patient's physical condition was
regarded as excellent.

DISCUSSION   A principle used in the laboratory shows that the strength of a response may be weakened by the removal
of positive reinforcement following the
response (Ferster, 1958). In this case, the
response was food-stealing and the reinforcer was access to meals. When the
patient stole food she was removed from
the dining room and missed her meal.

  After one year of this treatment, two
occasions of food stealing occurred. The

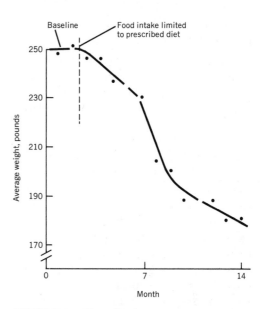

FIGURE 2   *The effective control of food
stealing results in a notable reduction in body
weight. As the patient's food intake is limited
to the prescribed diet, her weight decreases
gradually.*

first occasion, occurring after one year of
not stealing food, took the nurses by surprise and, therefore the patient 'got away'
with it. The second occasion occurred
shortly thereafter. This time, however, the
controlling consequences were in force.
The patient missed that meal and did not
steal again to the conclusion of this investigation.

  Because the patient was not informed
or warned of the consequences that followed stealing, the nurses regarded the
procedure as unlikely to have much effect
on the patient's behaviour. The implicit
belief that verbal instructions are indispensable for learning is part of present day
psychiatric lore. In keeping with this
notion, prior to this behaviour treatment,
the nurses had tried to persuade the patient to co-operate in dieting. Because
there were strong medical reasons for her
losing weight, the patient's refusal to follow a prescribed diet was regarded as
further evidence of her mental illness.

FIGURE 1   *A response, food stealing, is
eliminated when it results in the withdrawal
of food reinforcement. The arrows
indicate the rare occasions when food stealing
occurred. For purposes of presentation, a
segment comprising 20 weeks during which
no stealing occurred is not included.*

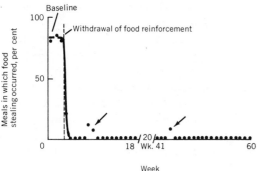

Experiment II

CONTROL OF ONE FORM OF HOARDING BE-
HAVIOUR THROUGH STIMULUS SATIATION
During the 9 years of hospitalization, the
patient collected large numbers of towels
and stored them in her room. Although
many efforts had been made to discourage
hoarding, this behaviour continued un-
altered. The only recourse for the nursing
staff was to take away the patient's towels
about twice a week.

To determine the degree of hoarding
behaviour, the towels in her room were
counted three times a week, when the
patient was not in her room. This count
showed that the number of towels kept in
her room ranged from 19 to 29 despite the
fact that during this time the nurses continued recovering their towel supply from
the patient's room.

FIGURE 4   *The early stages of satiation.
As the patient received the towels she folded
them properly and stacked them around her
bed. Notice that the towels on her bed are
also kept neatly.*

FIGURE 3   *A response, towel hoarding, is
eliminated when the patient is given towels
in excess. When the number of towels reaches
625 the patient starts to discard them. She
continues to do so until the number found
in her room averages 1.5 compared to the
previous 20 towels per week.*

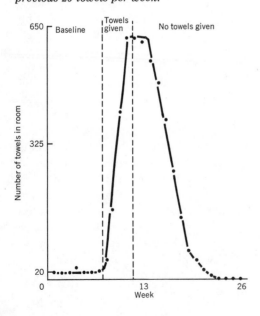

PROCEDURE   The routine removal of the
towels from the patient's room was discontinued. Instead, a programme of stimulus satiation was carried out by the nurses.
Intermittently, throughout the day, the
nurses took a towel to the patient when
she was in her room and simply handed
it to her without any comment. The first
week she was given an average of 7 towels
daily, and by the third week this number
was increased to 60.

RESULTS   The technique of satiation eliminated the towel hoarding. Figure 3 shows
the mean number of towels per count
found in the patient's room. When the
number of towels kept in her room reached
the 625 mark, she started taking a few of
them out. Thereafter, no more towels were
given to her. During the next 12 months
the mean number of towels found in her
room was 1.5 per week. Two photographs
are included to illustrate this procedure
(Figs. 4 and 5).

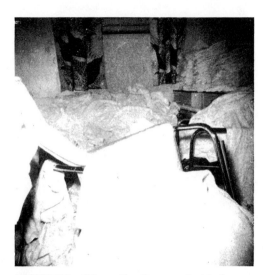

FIGURE 5   *The patient's room just before she started to rid herself of the towels. Notice that there are still a few stacks of folded towels, but now the chairs, bed and floor are literally covered with them.*

DISCUSSION   The procedure used to reduce the amount of towel hoarding bears resemblance to satiation of a reinforcer. A reinforcer loses its effect when an excessive amount of that reinforcer is made available. Accordingly, the response maintained by that reinforcer is weakened. In this application, the towels constituted the reinforcing stimuli. When the number of towels in her room reached 625, continuing to give her towels seemed to make their collection aversive. The patient then proceeded to rid herself of the towels until she had virtually none.

During the first few weeks of satiation, the patient was observed patting her cheeks with a few towels, apparently enjoying them. Later, the patient was observed spending much of her time folding and stacking the approximately 600 towels in her room. A variety of remarks were made by the patient regarding receipt of towels. All verbal statements made by the patient were recorded by the nurse. The following represent typical remarks made during this experiment. First week: As the nurse entered the patient's room carrying a towel, the patient would smile and say, "Oh, you found it for me, thank you." Second week: When the number of towels given to patient increased rapidly, she told the nurses, "Don't give me no more towels. I've got enough." Third week: "Take them towels away. . . . I can't sit here all night and fold towels." Fourth and fifth weeks: "Get these dirty towels out of here." Sixth week: After she had started taking the towels out of her room, she remarked to the nurse, "I can't drag any more of these towels, I just can't do it."

The quality of these remarks suggests that the initial effect of giving towels to the patient was reinforcing. However, as the towels increased they ceased to be reinforcing, and presumably became aversive.

The ward nurses, who had undergone a three year training in psychiatric nursing, found it difficult to reconcile the procedure in this experiment with their psychiatric orientation. Most nurses subscribed to the popular psychiatric view which regards hoarding behaviour as a reflection of a deep 'need' for love and security. Presumably no 'real' behavioural change was possible without meeting the patient's 'needs' first. Even after the patient discontinued hoarding towels in her room, some nurses predicted that the change would not last and that worse behaviour would replace it. Using a time-sampling techinque the patient was under continuous observation for over a year after the termination of the satiation programme. Not once during this period did the patient return to hoarding towels. Furthermore, no other behaviour problem replaced hoarding.

Experiment III

CONTROL OF AN ADDITIONAL FORM OF HOARDING THROUGH FOOD REINFORCEMENT Shortly after the patient had been admitted to the hospital she wore an excessive amount of clothing which included

several sweaters, shawls, dresses, undergarments and stockings. The clothing also
included sheets and towels wrapped around
her body, and a turban-like head-dress
made up of several towels. In addition, the
patient carried two to three cups in one
hand while holding a bundle of miscel-
laneous clothing, and a large purse in the
other.

To determine the amount of clothing
worn by the patient, she was weighed
before each meal over a period of two
weeks. By subtracting her actual body
weight from that recorded when she was
dressed, the weight of her clothing was
obtained.

PROCEDURE   The response required for reinforcement was stepping on a scale and
meeting a predetermined weight. The
requirement for reinforcement consisted of
meeting a single weight (i.e. her body
weight plus a specified number of pounds
of clothing). Initially she was given an
allowance of 23 pounds over her current
body weight. This allowance represented a
2 pound reduction from her usual clothing
weight. When the patient exceeded the
weight requirement, the nurse stated in a
matter-of-fact manner, "Sorry, you weigh
too much, you'll have to weigh less." Failure to meet the required weight resulted
in the patient missing the meal at which
she was being weighed. Sometimes, in an
effort to meet the requirement, the patient
discarded more clothing than she was required. When this occurred the requirement was adjusted at the next weighing-
time to correspond to the limit set by the
patient on the preceding occasion.

RESULTS   When food reinforcement is
made dependent upon the removal of
superfluous clothing the response increases
in frequency. Figure 6 shows that the
patient gradually shed her clothing to meet
the more demanding weight requirement
until she dressed normally. At the con-

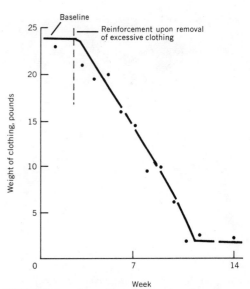

FIGURE 6   *A response, excessive dressing,
is eliminated when food reinforcement is
made dependent upon removal of superfluous
clothing. Once the weight of the clothing
worn by the patient drops to 3 pounds, it
remains stable.*

clusion of this experiment her clothes
weighed 3 pounds compared to the 25
pounds she wore before this treatment.

Some verbal shaping was done in order
to encourage the patient to leave the cups
and bundles she carried with her. Nurses
stopped her at the dining room and said,
"Sorry, no things are allowed in the dining
room." No mention of clothing or specific
items was made to avoid focusing undue
attention upon them. Within a week, the
patient typically stepped on the scale without her bundle and assorted objects. When
her weight was over the limit, the patient
was informed that she weighed "too
much." She then proceeded to take off a
few clothes, stepped on the scale again,
and upon meeting the weight requirement,
gained access to the dining room. A few
pictures are shown to illustrate this behavioural modification (Figs. 7, 8, 9 and 10).

DISCUSSION   According to the principle of
reinforcement a class of responses is

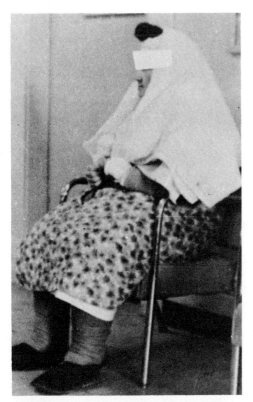

FIGURE 7   *The patient as she appeared before the start of Experiment III. The thickness of her legs is enhanced by approximately 2 dozen pairs of stockings that she wore. Notice the bandages she wears on her wrists as well as the cup beside her.*

FIGURE 8   *The patient eating in the dining room in the initial stages of Experiment III.*

strengthened when it is followed by reinforcement. A reinforcer is such when it results in a response increase. In this application the removal of excessive clothing constituted the response and the reinforcer was food (i.e. access to meals). When the patient met the weight requirement she was reinforced by being given access to meals.

At the start of this experiment, the patient missed a few meals because she failed to meet the weight requirement, but soon thereafter she gradually discarded her superfluous clothing. First, she left behind odd items she had carried in her arms, such as bundles, cups and handbags. Next she took off the elaborate headgear

and assorted "capes" or shawls she had worn over her shoulders. Although she had worn 18 pairs of stockings at one time, she eventually shed these also.

During the initial part of this experiment, the patient showed some emotional behaviour, e.g. crying, shouting and throwing chairs around. Because nurses were instructed to "ignore" this emotional behaviour, the patient obtained no sympathy or attention from them. The withholding of social reinforcement for emotional behaviour quickly led to its elimination.

At the conclusion of this behaviour treatment, the patient typically stepped on

FIGURE 9   *The patient after she started to discard a few items of clothing.*

FIGURE 10 *The patient during the final stages of the experiment.*

the scale wearing a dress, undergarments, a pair of stockings and a pair of light shoes. One of the behavioural changes concomitant with the current environmental manipulation was that as the patient began dressing normally she started to participate in small social events in the hospital. This was particularly new to the patient as she had previously remained seclusive, spending most of the time in her room.

About this time the patient's parents came to visit her and insisted on taking her home for a visit. This was the first time during the patient's 9 years of hospitalization that her parents had asked to take her out. They remarked that previously they had not been interested in taking her out because the patient's excessive dressing in addition to her weight made her look like a "circus freak."

Conclusions

The research presented here was conducted under nearly ideal conditions. The variables manipulated (i.e. towels and food) were under full experimental control. Using a time-sample technique the patient was observed daily every 30 minutes from 7:00 a.m. to 11:00 p.m. Nurses and aides carried out these observations which were later analysed in terms of gross behaviour categories. These observations were in force for over a year during which time these three experiments were conducted. The results of these observations indicate that none of the three pathological behaviour patterns (i.e. food stealing, hoarding and excessive dressing) exhibited by the patient were replaced by any undesirable behaviour.

The patient displayed some emotional behaviour in each experiment, but each time it subsided when social reinforcement (i.e. attention) was not forthcoming. The patient did not become violent or seclusive as a consequence of these experiments. Instead, she became socially more accessible to patients and staff. She did not achieve a great deal of social success but she did begin to participate actively in social functions.

A frequent problem encountered in mental hospitals is overeating. In general this problem is solved by prescribing a reduction diet. Many patients, however, refuse to take a reduction diet and continue overeating. When confronted with this behaviour, psychiatric workers generally resort to two types of explanations.

One explanation of overeating points out that only with the active and sincere co-operation of the patient can weight reduction be accomplished. When the patient refuses to co-operate he is regarded as showing more signs of mental illness and all hopes of eliminating overeating come to an end.

Another type of explanation holds that overeating is not the behaviour to be concerned with. Instead, attention is focused on the psychological 'needs' of the patient. These 'needs' are said to be the cause of the observable behaviour, overeating. Therefore the emphasis is on the removal of the cause and not on the symptom or behaviour itself. Whatever theoretical merit these explanations may have, it is unfortunate that they fail to suggest practical ways of treating the behaviour itself.

As a consequence, the patient continues to overeat often to the detriment of his health.

The current psychiatric emphasis on the resolution of the mental conflict that is presumably at the basis of the symptoms, is perhaps misplaced. What seems to have been forgotten is that behaviour problems such as those reported here, prevent the patient from being considered for discharge not only by the hospital personnel but also by the patient's relatives. Indeed, as far as the patient's relatives are concerned, the index of improvement or deterioration is the readily observable behaviour and not a detailed account of the mechanics of the mental apparatus.

Many individuals are admitted to mental hospitals because of one or more specific behaviour difficulties and not always because of a generalized 'mental' disturbance. For example, an individual may go into a mental hospital because he has refused to eat for several days, or because he talks to himself incessantly. If the goal of therapy were behavioural rehabilitation, these problems would be treated and normal eating and normal talking reinstated. However, the current emphasis in psychotherapy is on 'mental-conflict resolution' and little or no attention is given to dealing directly with the behavioural problems which prevent the patient from returning to the community.

References

Ayllon, T. and Michael, J. (1959) The psychiatric nurse as a behavioural engineer. *J. exp. anal. Behav.* **2**, 323–334.

Ayllon, T. and Haughton, E. (1962) Control of the behaviour of schizophrenic patients by food. *J. exp. anal. Behav.* **5**, 343–352.

Azrin, N. and Lindsley, O. (1956) The reinforcement of cooperation between children. *J. abnorm. soc. Psychol.* **52**, 100–102.

Bijou, S. (1961) Discrimination performance as a baseline for individual analysis of young children. *Child Develpm.* **32**, 153–160.

Ferster, C. B. (1958) Control of behavior in chimpanzees and pigeons by time out from positive reinforcement. *Psychol. Monogr.* **72**, 1–38.

Ferster, C. and DeMyer, M. (1961) The development of performances in autistic children in an automatically controlled environment. *J. chron. Dis.* **13**, 312–345.

Flanagan, B., Goldiamond, I. and Azrin, N. (1958) Operant stuttering: The control of stuttering behaviour through response-contingent consequences. *J. exp. anal. Behav.* **1**, 49–56.

Hutchinson, R. R. and Azrin, N. H. (1961) Conditioning of mental hospital patients to fixed-ratio schedules of reinforcement. *J. exp. anal. Behav.* **4**, 87–95.

Lindsley, O. R. (1956) Operant conditioning methods applied to research in chronic schizophrenia. *Psychiat. Res. Rep.* **5**, 118–139.

Orlando, R. and Bijou, S. (1960) Single and multiple schedules of reinforcement in developmentally retarded children. *J. exp. anal. Behav.* **3**, 339–348.

SOCIAL INFLUENCES ON BEHAVIOR

Conflicting results have been obtained from experiments in which performance in groups is compared with performance alone. Sometimes group membership facilitates performance; sometimes it hinders performance. The author brings data to bear from many diverse sources to support an hypothesis about the reason for these apparently conflicting results. In the course of doing this, he also gives a good summary of much of the work done on the effects of group membership on performance.

A POINT TO GUIDE YOUR STUDY *What resolution of the problem is reached by the author?*

52: SOCIAL FACILITATION

Robert B. Zajonc, University of Michigan

Most textbook definitions of social psychology involve considerations about the influence of man upon man, or, more generally, of individual upon individual. And most of them, explicitly or implicitly, commit the main efforts of social psychology to the problem of how and why the *behavior* of one individual affects the behavior of another. The influences of individuals on each others' behavior which are of interest to social psychologists today take on very complex forms. Often they involve vast networks of interindividual effects, such

as one finds in studying the process of group decision-making, competition, or conformity to a group norm. But the fundamental forms of interindividual influence are represented by the oldest experimental paradigm of social psychology: social facilitation. This paradigm, dating back to Triplett's original experiments on pacing and competition, carried out in 1897 (1), examines the consequences upon behavior which derive from the sheer presence of other individuals.

Until the late 1930's, interest in social facilitation was quite active, but with the outbreak of World War II it suddenly died. And it is truly regrettable that it died, because the basic questions about

R. B. Zajonc. Social facilitation. *Science*, 1965, **149**, 269–274. Copyright © 1965 by the American Association for the Advancement of Science. Reprinted here with permission from the author and the American Association for the Advancement of Science.

social facilitation—its dynamics and its causes—which are in effect the basic questions of social psychology, were never solved. It is with these questions that this article is concerned. I first examine past results in this nearly completely abandoned area of research and then suggest a general hypothesis which might explain them.

Research in the area of social facilitation may be classified in terms of two experimental paradigms: audience effects and co-action effects. The first experimental paradigm involves the observation of behavior when it occurs in the presence of passive spectators. The second examines behavior when it occurs in the presence of other individuals also engaged in the same activity. We shall consider past literature in these two areas separately.

Audience effects

Simple motor responses are particularly sensitive to social facilitation effects. In 1925 Travis (2) obtained such effects in a study in which he used the pursuit-rotor task. In this task the subject is required to follow a small revolving target by means of a stylus which he holds in his hand. If the stylus is even momentarily off target during a revolution, the revolution counts as an error. First each subject was trained for several consecutive days until his performance reached a stable level. One day after the conclusion of the training the subject was called to the laboratory, given five trials alone, and then ten trials in the presence of from four to eight upperclassmen and graduate students. They had been asked by the experimenter to watch the subject quietly and attentively. Travis found a clear improvement in performance when his subjects were confronted with an audience. Their accuracy on the ten trials before an audience was greater than on any ten previous

trials, including those on which they had scored highest.

A considerably greater improvement in performance was recently obtained in a somewhat different setting and on a different task (3). Each subject (all were National Guard trainees) was placed in a separate booth. He was seated in front of a panel outfitted with 20 red lamps in a circle. The lamps on this panel light in a clockwise sequence at 12 revolutions per minute. At random intervals one or another light fails to go on in its proper sequence. On the average there are 24 such failures per hour. The subject's task is to signal whenever a light fails to go on. After 20 minutes of intensive training, followed by a short rest, the National Guard trainees monitored the light panels for 135 minutes. Subjects in one group performed their task alone. Subjects in another group were told that from time to time a lieutenant colonel or a master sergeant would visit them in the booth to observe their performance. These visits actually took place about four times during the experimental session. There was no doubt about the results. The accuracy of the supervised subjects was on the average 34 percent higher than the accuracy of the trainees working in isolation, and toward the end of the experimental session the accuracy of the supervised subjects was more than twice as high as that of the subjects working in isolation. Those expecting to be visited by a superior missed, during the last experimental period, 20 percent of the light failures, while those expecting no such visits missed 64 percent of the failures.

Dashiell, who, in the early 1930's, carried out an extensive program of research on social facilitation, also found considerable improvement in performance due to audience effects on such tasks as simple multiplication or word association (4). But, as is the case in many other areas, negative audience effects were also found. In 1933 Pessin asked college students to learn lists of nonsense syllables under two conditions, alone and in the presence of several spectators (5). When confronted with an audience, his subjects required an average of 11.27 trials to learn a seven-item list. When working alone they needed only 9.85 trials. The average number of errors made in the "audience" condition was considerably higher than the number in the "alone" condition. In 1931 Husband found that the presence of spectators interferes with the learning of a finger maze (6), and in 1933 Pessin and Husband (7) confirmed Husband's results. The number of trials which the isolated subjects required for learning the finger maze was 17.1. Subjects confronted with spectators, however, required 19.1 trials. The average number of errors for the isolated subjects was 33.7; the number for those working in the presence of an audience was 40.5.

The results thus far reviewed seem to contradict one another. On a pursuit-rotor task Travis found that the presence of an audience improves performance. The learning of nonsense syllables and maze learning, however, seem to be inhibited by the presence of an audience, as shown by Pessin's experiment. The picture is further complicated by the fact that when Pessin's subjects were asked, several days later, to recall the nonsense syllables they had learned, a reversal was found. The subjects who tried to recall the lists in the presence of spectators did considerably better than those who tried to recall them alone. Why are the learning of nonsense syllables and maze learning inhibited by the presence of spectators? And why, on the other hand, does performance on a pursuit-rotor, word-association, multiplication, or a vigilance task improve in the presence of others?

There is just one, rather subtle, consistency in the above results. It would appear that the emission of well-learned responses is facilitated by the presence of spectators, while the acquisition of new responses is impaired. To put the statement in conventional psychological language, performance is facilitated and learning is impaired by the presence of spectators.

This tentative generalization can be reformulated so that different features of the problem are placed into focus. During the early stages of learning, especially of the type involved in social facilitation studies, the subject's responses are mostly the wrong ones. A person learning a finger maze, or a person learning a list of nonsense syllables, emits more wrong responses than right ones in the early stages of training. Most learning experiments continue until he ceases to make mistakes —until his performance is perfect. It may be said, therefore, that during training it is primarily the wrong responses which are dominant and strong; they are the ones which have the highest probability of occurrence. But after the individual has mastered the task, correct responses necessarily gain ascendency in his task-relevant behavioral repertoire. Now they are the ones which are more probable—in other words, dominant. Our tentative generalization may now be simplified: audience enhances the emission of dominant responses. If the dominant responses are the correct ones, as is the case upon achieving mastery, the presence of an audience will be of benefit to the individual. But if they are mostly wrong, as is the case in the early stages of learning, then these wrong responses will be enhanced in the presence of an audience, and the emission of correct responses will be postponed or prevented.

There is a class of psychological processes which are known to enhance the emission of dominant responses. They are subsumed under the concepts of drive, arousal, and activation (8). If we could show that the presence of an audience has arousal consequences for the subject, we would be a step further along in trying to arrange the results of social-facilitation experiments into a neater package. But let us first consider another set of experimental findings.

Co-action effects

The experimental paradigm of co-action is somewhat more complex than the paradigm involved in the study of audience effects. Here we observe individuals all simultaneously engaged in the same activity and in full view of each other. One of the clearest effects of such simultaneous action, or co-action, is found in eating behavior. It is well known that animals simply eat more in the presence of others. For instance, Bayer had chickens eat from a pile of wheat to their full satisfaction (9). He waited some time to be absolutely sure that his subject would eat no more, and then brought in a companion chicken who had not eaten for 24 hours. Upon the introduction of the hungry co-actor, the apparently sated chicken ate two-thirds again as much grain as it had already eaten. Recent work by Tolman and Wilson fully substantiates these results (10). In an extensive study of social-facilitation effects among albino rats, Harlow found

FIGURE 1 *Data on feeding of isolated and paired rats.* [*Harlow (11).*]

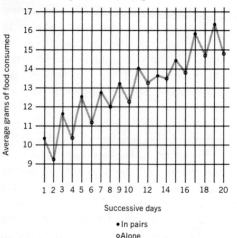

dramatic increases in eating (11). In one of his experiments, for instance, the rats, shortly after weaning, were matched in pairs for weight. They were then fed alone and in pairs on alternate days. Figure 1 shows his results. It is clear that considerably more food was consumed by the animals when they were in pairs than when they were fed alone. James (12), too, found very clear evidence of increased eating among puppies fed in groups.

Perhaps the most dramatic effect of co-action is reported by Chen (13). Chen observed groups of ants working alone, in groups of two, and in groups of three. Each ant was observed under various conditions. In the first experimental session each ant was placed in a bottle half filled with sandy soil. The ant was observed for 6 hours. The time at which nest-building began was noted, and the earth excavated by the insect was carefully weighed. Two days afterward the same ants were placed in freshly filled bottles in pairs, and the same observations were made. A few days later the ants were placed in the bottles in groups of three, again for 6 hours. Finally, a few days after the test in groups of three, nest-building of the ants in isolation was observed. Figure 2 shows some of Chen's data.

There is absolutely no question that the amount of work an ant accomplishes increases markedly in the presence of another ant. In all pairs except one, the presence of a companion increased output by a factor of at least 2. The effect of co-action on the latency of the nest-building behavior was equally dramatic. The solitary ants of session 1 and the final session began working on the nest in 192 minutes, on the average. The latency period for ants in groups of two was only 28 minutes. The effects observed by Chen were limited to the immediate situation and seemed to have no lasting consequences for the ants. There were no differences in the results of session 1, during which the ants worked in

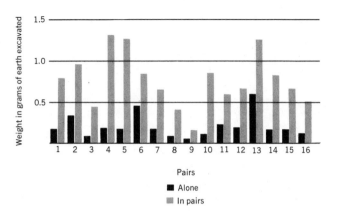

FIGURE 2 *Data on nest-building behavior of isolated and paired ants.* [*Chen. (13)*.]

■ Alone
■ In pairs

isolation, and of the last experimental session, where they again worked in solitude.

If one assumes that under the conditions of Chen's experiment nest-building *is* the dominant response, then there is no reason why his findings could not be embraced by the generalization just proposed. Nest-building is a response which Chen's ants have fully mastered. Certainly, it is something that a mature ant need not learn. And this is simply an instance where the generalization that the presence of others enhances the emission of dominant and well-developed responses holds.

If the process involved in audience effects is also involved in co-action effects, then learning should be inhibited in the presence of other learners. Let us examine some literature in this field. Klopfer (14) observed greenfinches—in isolation and in heterosexual pairs—which were learning to discriminate between sources of palatable and of unpalatable food. And, as one would by now expect, his birds learned this discrimination task considerably more efficiently when working alone. I hasten to add that the subjects' sexual interests cannot be held responsible for the inhibition of learning in the paired birds. Allee and Masure, using Australian parakeets, obtained the same result for homosexual pairs as well (15). The speed of learning was considerably greater for the isolated birds than for the paired birds, regardless

of whether the birds were of the same sex or of the opposite sex.

Similar results are found with cockroaches. Gates and Allee (16) compared data for cockroaches learning a maze in isolation, in groups of two, and in groups of three. They used an E-shaped maze. Its three runways, made of galvanized sheet metal, were suspended in a pan of water. At the end of the center runway was a dark bottle into which the photophobic cockroaches could escape from the noxious light. The results, in terms of time required to reach the bottle, are shown in Fig. 3. It is clear from the data that the solitary cockroaches required considerably less time to learn the maze than the grouped animals. Gates and Allee believe that the group situation produced inhibition. They add, however (16, p. 357): "The nature of these inhibiting forces is speculative, but the fact of some sort of group interference is obvious. The presence of other roaches did not operate to change greatly the movements to different parts of the maze, but did result in increased time per trial. The roaches tended to go to the corner or end of the runway and remain there a longer time when another roach was present than when alone; the other roach was a distracting stimulus."

The experiments on social facilitation performed by Floyd Allport in 1920 and continued by Dashiell in 1930 (4, 17),

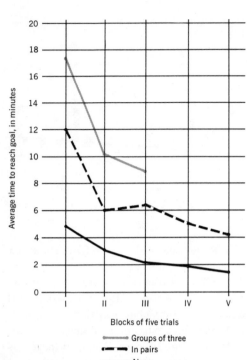

FIGURE 3   *Data on maze learning in isolated and grouped cockroaches. [Gates and Allee (16).]*

both of whom used human subjects, are the ones best known. Allport's subjects worked either in separate cubicles or sitting around a common table. When working in isolation they did the various tasks at the same time and were monitored by common time signals. Allport did everything possible to reduce the tendency to compete. The subjects were told that the results of their tests would not be compared and would not be shown to other staff members, and that they themselves should refrain from making any such comparisons.

Among the tasks used were the following: chain word association, vowel cancellation, reversible perspective, multiplication, problem solving, and judgments of odors and weights. The results of Allport's experiments are well known: in all but the problem-solving and judgments test, performance was better in groups than in the "alone" condition. How do these results fit

our generalization? Word association, multiplication, the cancellation of vowels, and the reversal of the perceived orientation of an ambiguous figure all involve responses which are well established. They are responses which are either very well learned or under a very strong influence of the stimulus, as in the word-association task or the reversible-perspective test. The problem-solving test consists of disproving arguments of ancient philosophers. In contrast to the other tests, it does not involve well-learned responses. On the contrary, the probability of wrong (that is, logically incorrect) responses on tasks of this sort is rather high; in other words, wrong responses are dominant. Of interest, however, is the finding that while intellectual work suffered in the group situation, sheer output of words was increased. When working together, Allport's subjects tended consistently to write more. Therefore, the generalization proposed in the previous section can again be applied: if the presence of others raises the probability of dominant responses, and if strong (and many) incorrect response tendencies prevail, then the presence of others can only be detrimental to performance. The results of the judgment tests have little bearing on the present argument, since Allport gives no accuracy figures for evaluating performance. The data reported only show that the presence of others was associated with the avoidance of extreme judgments.

In 1928 Travis (18), whose work on the pursuit rotor I have already noted, repeated Allport's chain-word-association experiment. In contrast to Allport's results, Travis found that the presence of others decreased performance. The number of associations given by his subjects was greater when they worked in isolation. It is very significant, however, that Travis used stutterers as his subjects. In a way, stuttering is a manifestation of a struggle between conflicting response tendencies, all of which are strong and all of which compete for expression. The stutterer, momentarily hung up in the middle of a sentence, waits for the correct response to reach full ascendancy. He stammers because other competing tendencies are dominant at that moment. It is reasonable to assume that, to the extent that the verbal habits of a stutterer are characterized by conflicting response tendencies, the presence of others, by enhancing each of these response tendencies, simply heightens his conflict. Performance is thus impaired.

Avoidance learning

In two experiments on the learning of avoidance responses the performances of solitary and grouped subjects were compared. In one, rats were used; in the other humans.

Let us first consider the results of the rat experiment, by Rasmussen (19). A number of albino rats, all litter mates, were deprived of water for 48 hours. The apparatus consisted of a box containing a dish of drinking water. The floor of the box was made of a metal grille wired to one pole of an electric circuit. A wire inserted in the water in the dish was connected to the other pole of the circuit. Thirsty rats were placed in the box alone and in groups of three. They were allowed to drink for 5 seconds with the circuit open. Following this period the shock circuit remained closed, and each time the rat touched the water he received a painful shock. Observations were made on the number of times the rats approached the water dish. The results of this experiment showed that the solitary rats learned to avoid the dish considerably sooner than the grouped animals did. The rats that were in groups of three attempted to drink twice as often as the solitary rats did, and suffered considerably more shock than the solitary subjects.

Let us examine Rasmussen's results somewhat more closely. For purposes of analysis let us assume that there are just two critical responses involved: drinking, and avoidance of contact with the water.

They are clearly incompatible. But drinking, we may further assume, is the dominant response, and, like eating or any other dominant response, it is enhanced by the presence of others. The animal is therefore prevented, by the facilitation of drinking which derives from the presence of others, from acquiring the appropriate avoidance response.

The second of the two studies is quite recent and was carried out by Ader and Tatum (20). They devised the following situation with which they confronted their subjects, all medical students. Each subject is told on arrival that he will be taken to another room and seated in a chair, and that electrodes will be attached to his leg. He is instructed not to get up from the chair and not to touch the electrodes. He is also told not to smoke or vocalize, and is told that the experimenter will be in the next room. That is all he is told. The subjects are observed either alone or in pairs. In the former case the subject is brought to the room and seated at a table equipped with a red button which is connected to an electric circuit. Electrodes, by means of which electric shock can be administered, are attached to the calf of one leg. After the electrodes are attached, the experimenter leaves the room. From now on the subject will receive $\frac{1}{2}$ second of electric shock every 10 seconds unless he presses the red button. Each press of the button delays the shock by 10 seconds. Thus, if he is to avoid shock, he must press the button at least once every 10 seconds. It should be noted that no information was given him about the function of the button, or about the purpose of the experiment. No essential differences are introduced when subjects are brought to the room in pairs. Both are seated at the table and both become part of the shock circuit. The response of either subject delays the shock for both.

The avoidance response is considered to have been acquired when the subject (or pair of subjects) receives less than six shocks in a period of 5 minutes. Ader and Tatum report that the isolated students required, on the average, 11 minutes, 35 seconds to reach this criterion of learning. Of the 12 pairs which participated in the experiment, only two reached this criterion. One of them required 46 minutes, 40 seconds; the other, 68 minutes, 40 seconds! Ader and Tatum offer no explanation for their curious results. But there is no reason why we should not treat them in terms of the generalization proposed above. We are dealing here with a learning task, and the fact that the subjects are learning to avoid shock by pressing a red button does not introduce particular problems. They are confronted with an ambiguous task, and told nothing about the button. Pressing the button is simply not the dominant response in this situation. However, escaping is. Ader and Tatum report that eight of the 36 subjects walked out in the middle of the experiment.

One aspect of Ader and Tatum's results is especially worth noting. Once having learned the appropriate avoidance response, the individual subjects responded at considerably lower rates than the paired subjects. When we consider only those subjects who achieved the learning criterion and only those responses which occurred *after* criterion had been reached, we find that the response rates of the individual subjects were in all but one case lower than the response rates of the grouped subjects. This result further confirms the generalization that, while learning is impaired by the presence of others, the performance of learned responses is enhanced.

There are experiments which show that learning is enhanced by the presence of other learners (21), but in all these experiments, as far as I can tell, it was possible for the subject to *observe* the critical responses of other subjects, and to determine when he was correct and when incorrect. In none, therefore, has the co-action paradigm been employed in its pure form. That paradigm involves the presence of others, and nothing else. It requires that these others not be able to provide the subject with cues or information as to appropriate behavior. If other learners can supply the critical individual with such cues, we are dealing not with the problem of co-action but with the problem of imitation or vicarious learning.

The presence of others as a source of arousal

The results I have discussed thus far lead to one generalization and to one hypothesis. The generalization which organizes these results is that the presence of others, as spectators or as co-actors, enhances the emission of dominant responses. We also know from extensive research literature that arousal, activation, or drive all have as a consequence the enhancement of dominant responses (22). We now need to examine the hypothesis that the presence of others increases the individual's general arousal or drive level.

The evidence which bears on the relationship between the presence of others and arousal is, unfortunately, only indirect. But there is some very suggestive evidence in one area of research. One of the more reliable indicators of arousal and drive is the activity of the endocrine systems in general, and of the adrenal cortex in particular. Adrenocortical functions are extremely sensitive to changes in emotional arousal, and it has been known for some time that organisms subjected to prolonged stress are likely to manifest substantial adrenocortical hypertrophy (23). Recent work (24) has shown that the main biochemical component of the adrenocortical output is hydrocortisone (17-hydroxycorticosterone). Psychiatric patients characterized by anxiety states, for instance, show elevated plasma levels of hydrocortisone (25). Mason, Brady, and Sidman (26) have recently trained monkeys to press a lever for food and have given these animals unavoidable electric shocks, all preceded by warning signals. This procedure led to elevated hydrocortisone levels; the levels returned to normal within 1 hour after the end of the experimental session. This "anxiety" reaction can apparently be attenuated if the animal is given repeated doses of reserpine 1 day before the experimental session (27). Sidman's conditioned avoidance schedule also results in raising the hydrocortisone levels by a factor of 2 to 4 (26). In this schedule the animal receives an electric shock every 20 seconds without warning, unless he presses a lever. Each press delays the shock for 20 seconds.

While there is a fair amount of evidence that adrenocortical activity is a reliable symptom of arousal, similar endocrine manifestations were found to be associated with increased population density (28). Crowded mice, for instance, show increased amphetamine toxicity—that is, susceptibility to the excitatory effects of amphetamine—against which they can be protected by the administration of phenobarbital, chlorpromazine, or reserpine (29). Mason and Brady (30) have recently reported that monkeys caged together had considerably higher plasma levels of hydrocortisone than monkeys housed in individual cages. Thiessen (31) found increases in adrenal weights in mice housed in groups of 10 and 20 as compared with mice housed alone. The mere presence of other animals in the same room, but in separate cages, was also found to produce elevated levels of hydrocortisone. Table 1, taken from a report by Mason and Brady (30), shows plasma

TABLE 1 *Basal plasma concentrations of 17-hydroxycorticosterone in monkeys housed alone (cages in separate rooms), then in a room with other monkeys (cages in same room).*

| SUBJECT | TIME | CONC. OF 17-HYDROXYCORTICOSTERONE IN CAGED MONKEYS (μg PER 100 ml OF PLASMA) | |
		IN SEPARATE ROOMS	IN SAME ROOM
M-1	9 a.m.	23	34
M-1	3 p.m.	16	27
M-2	9 a.m.	28	34
M-2	3 p.m.	19	23
M-3	9 a.m.	32	38
M-3	3 p.m.	23	31
Mean	9 a.m.	28	35
Mean	3 p.m.	19	27

Leiderman and Shapiro (*35*, p. 7).

levels of hydrocortisone for three animals which lived at one time in cages that afforded them the possibility of visual and tactile contact and, at another time, in separate rooms.

Mason and Brady also report urinary levels of hydrocortisone, by days of the week, for five monkeys from their laboratory and for one human hospital patient. These very suggestive figures are reproduced in Table 2 (30). In the monkeys, the low weekend traffic and activity in the laboratory seem to be associated with a clear decrease in hydrocortisone. As for

TABLE 2 *Variations in urinary concentration of hydrocortisone over a 9-day period for five laboratory monkeys and one human hospital patient*

| SUBJECTS | AMOUNTS EXCRETED (mg/24 hr) | | | | | | | | |
	MON.	TUES.	WED.	THURS.	FRI.	SAT.	SUN.	MON.	TUES.
Monkeys	1.88	1.71	1.60	1.52	1.70	1.16	1.17	1.88	
Patient		5.9	6.5	4.5	5.7	3.3	3.9	6.0	5.2

Leiderman and Shapiro (*35*, p. 8).

the hospital patient, Mason and Brady report (30, p. 8), "he was confined to a thoracic surgery ward that bustled with activity during the weekdays when surgery and admissions occurred. On the weekends the patient retired to the nearby Red Cross building, with its quieter and more pleasant environment."

Admittedly, the evidence that the mere presence of others raises the arousal level is indirect and scanty. And, as a matter of fact, some work seems to suggest that there are conditions, such as stress, under which the presence of others may lower the animal's arousal level. Bovard (32), for instance, hypothesized that the presence of another member of the same species may protect the individual under stress by inhibiting the activity of the posterior hypothalamic centers which trigger the pituitary adrenal cortical and sympathetico-adrenal medullary responses to stress. Evidence for Bovard's hypothesis, however, is as indirect as evidence for the one which predicts arousal as a consequence of the presence of others, and even more scanty.

Summary and conclusion

If one were to draw one practical suggestion from the review of the social-facilitation effects which are summarized in this article he would advise the student to study all alone, preferably in an isolated cubicle, and to arrange to take his examinations in the company of many other students, on stage, and in the presence of a large audience. The results of his examination would be beyond his wildest expectations, provided, of course, he had learned his material quite thoroughly.

I have tried in this article to pull together the early, almost forgotten work on social facilitation, and to explain the seemingly conflicting results. This explanation is, of course, tentative, and it has never been put to a direct experimental test. It is, moreover, not far removed from the one originally proposed by Allport. He theorized (33, p. 261) that "the sights and sounds of others doing the same thing" augment ongoing responses. Allport, however, proposed this effect only for *overt* motor responses, assuming (33, p. 274) that *"intellectual* or *implicit responses* of thought are hampered rather than facilitated" by the presence of others. This latter conclusion was probably suggested to him by the negative results he observed in his research on the effects of co-action on problem solving.

Needless to say, the presence of others may have effects considerably more complex than that of increasing the individual's arousal level. The presence of others may provide cues as to appropriate or inappropriate responses, as in the case of imitation or vicarious learning. Or it may supply the individual with cues as to the measure of danger in an ambiguous or stressful situation. Davitz and Mason (34), for instance, have shown that the presence of an unafraid rat reduces the fear of another rat in stress. Bovard (32) believes that the calming of the rat in stress which is in the presence of an unafraid companion is mediated by inhibition of activity of the posterior hypothalamus. But in their experimental situations (that is, the open field test) the possibility that cues for appropriate escape or avoidance responses are provided by the co-actor is not ruled out. We might therefore be dealing not with the effects of the mere presence of others but with the considerably more complex case of imitation. The animal may not be calming *because* of his companion's presence. He may be calming *after* having copied his companion's attempted escape responses. The paradigm which I have examined in this article pertains only to the effects of the mere presence of others, and to the consequences for the arousal level. The exact parameters involved in social facilitation still must be specified.

References and notes

1. N. Triplett, *Amer. J. Psychol.* **9**, 507 (1897).

2. L. E. Travis, *J. Abnormal Soc. Psychol.* **20**, 142 (1925).

3. B. O. Bergum and D. J. Lehr, *J. Appl. Psychol.* **47**, 75 (1963).

4. J. F. Dashiell, *J. Abnormal Soc. Psychol.* **25**, 190 (1930).

5. J. Pessin, *Amer. J. Psychol.* **45**, 263 (1933).

6. R. W. Husband, *J. Genet. Psychol.* **39**, 258 (1931). In this task the blindfolded subject traces a maze with his finger.

7. J. Pessin and R. W. Husband, *J. Abnormal Soc. Psychol.* **28**, 148 (1933).

8. See, for instance, E. Dufy, *Activation and Behavior* (Wiley, New York, 1962); K. W. Spence, *Behavior Theory and Conditioning* (Yale Univ. Press, New Haven, 1956); R. B. Zajonc and B. Nieuwenhuyse, *J. Exp. Psychol.* **67**, 276 (1964).

9. E. Bayer, *Z. Psychol.* **112**, 1 (1929).

10. C. W. Tolman and G. T. Wilson, *Animal Behavior* **13**, 134 (1965).

11. H. F. Harlow, *J. Genet. Psychol.* **43**, 211 (1932).

12. W. T. James, *J. Comp. Physiol. Psychol.* **46**, 427 (1953); *J. Genet. Psychol.* **96**, 123 (1960); W. T. James and D. J. Cannon, *ibid.* **87**, 225 (1956).

13. S. C. Chen, *Physiol. Zool.* **10**, 420 (1937).

14. P. H. Klopfer, *Science* **128**, 903 (1958).

15. W. C. Allee and R. H. Masure, *Physiol. Zool.* **22**, 131 (1936).

16. M. J. Gates and W. C. Allee, *J. Comp. Psychol.* **15**, 331 (1933).

17. F. H. Allport, *J. Exp. Psychol.* **3**, 159 (1920).

18. L. E. Travis, *J. Abnormal Soc. Psychol.* **23**, 45 (1928).

19. E. Rasmussen, *Acta Psychol.* **4**, 275 (1939).

20. R. Ader and R. Tatum, *J. Exp. Anal. Behavior* **6**, 357 (1963).

21. H. Gurnee, *J. Abnormal Soc. Psychol.* **34**, 529 (1939); J. C. Welty, *Physiol. Zool.* **7**, 85 (1934).

22. See K. W. Spence, *Behavior Theory and Conditioning* (Yale Univ. Press, New Haven, 1956).

23. H. Selyé, *J. Clin. Endocrin.* **6**, 117 (1946).

24. D. H. Nelson and L. T. Samuels, *ibid.* **12**, 519 (1952).

25. E. L. Bliss, A. A. Sandberg, D. H. Nelson, *J. Clin. Invest.* **32**, 9 (1953); F. Board, H. Persky, D. A. Hamburg, *Psychosom. Med.* **18**, 324 (1956).

26. J. W. Mason, J. V. Brady, M. Sidman, *Endocrinology* **60**, 741 (1957).

27. J. W. Mason and J. V. Brady, *Science* **124**, 983 (1956).

28. D. D. Thiessen, *Texas Rep. Biol. Med.* **22**, 266 (1964).

29. L. Lasagna and W. P. McCann, *Science* **125**, 1241 (1957).

30. J. W. Mason and J. V. Brady, in *Psychobiological Approaches to Social Behavior,* P. H. Leiderman and D. Shapiro, Eds. (Stanford Univ. Press, Stanford, Calif., 1964).

31. D. D. Thiessen, *J. Comp. Physiol. Psychol.* **57**, 412 (1964).

32. E. W. Bovard, *Psychol. Rev.* **66**, 267 (1959).

33. F. H. Allport, *Social Psychology* (Houghton Mifflin, Boston, 1924).

34. J. R. Davitz and D. J. Mason, *J. Comp. Physiol. Psychol.* **48**, 149 (1955).

35. P. H. Leiderman and D. Shapiro, Eds., *Psychobiological Approaches to Social Behavior* (Stanford Univ. Press, Stanford, Calif., 1964).

36. The preparation of this article was supported in part by grants Nonr-1224(34) from the Office of Naval Research and GS-629 from the National Science Foundation.

Living together in social groups requires a good deal of adjustment, or give and take, between groups and between members within groups. Bargaining is essential in this adjustment process. Marriage partners bargain with each other, labor union representatives and business representatives bargain with each other, diplomats bargain with each other. Understanding of the bargaining process is therefore quite important, practical, and useful.

One good way of finding out about the bargaining process is through experiment. In such experiments, one sets up a simple model of a

*"real" social situation and then introduces variables to see how they
will affect bargaining behavior in the model situation. In the
experiments discussed in this selection, the influence of threat on
bargaining is studied.*

POINTS TO GUIDE YOUR STUDY   *(1) Make sure you understand the
model situation and the game which is played. You must grasp this
before you can understand the article.   (2) Put yourself in the place
of Acme or Bolt. Do you think you would behave typically under
the three conditions—no threat, unilateral threat, or bilateral
threat—of the experiment?*

GLOSSARY   **Cognitive:** *refers to thinking or thought.*
p < .01 etc.: *means that the odds of obtaining a difference, by chance
alone, as large as the one obtained are less than one in a hundred.
(See the article by Braun and Geiselhart, Section Three.)*

53: THE EFFECT OF THREAT UPON INTERPERSONAL BARGAINING

*Morton Deutsch, Columbia University, and Robert M. Krauss,
Bell Telephone Laboratories, Murray Hill, New Jersey*

A bargain is defined in Webster's Unabridged Dictionary as "an agreement between parties settling what each shall give and receive in a transaction between them"; it is further specified that a bargain is "an agreement or compact viewed as advantageous or the reverse." When the term "agreement" is broadened to include tacit, informal agreements as well as explicit agreements, it is evident that bargains and the processes involved in arriving at bargains ("bargaining") are pervasive characteristics of social life.

The definition of bargain fits under sociological definitions of the term "social norm." In this light, the experimental study of the bargaining process and of bargaining outcomes provides a means for the laboratory study of the development of certain types of social norms. But unlike many other types of social situations, bargaining situations have certain distinctive features that make it relevant to consider the conditions that determine whether or not a social norm will develop as well as those that determine the nature of the social norm if it develops. Bargaining situations high-light the possibility that, even where cooperation would be mutually advantageous, shared purposes may not develop, agreement may not be reached, and interaction may be regulated antagonistically rather than normatively.

The essential features of a bargaining situation exist when:

1. Both parties perceive that there is the possibility of reaching an agreement in which each party would be better off, or no worse off, than if no agreement were reached.

2. Both parties perceive that there is more than one such agreement that could be reached.

3. Both parties perceive each other to have conflicting preferences or opposed interests with regard to the different agreements that might be reached.

Everyday examples of bargaining include such situations as: the buyer-seller relationship when the price is not fixed, the husband and wife who want to spend

Morton Deutsch and R. M. Krauss. The effect of threat
upon interpersonal bargaining. *J. abnorm. soc. Psychol.*,
1960, **61**, 181–189. Copyright © 1960 by the American
Psychological Association. Reprinted here with permission from the authors and the American Psychological Association.

an evening out together but have conflicting preferences about where to go, union-management negotiations, drivers who meet at an intersection when there is no clear right of way, disarmament negotiations.

In terms of our prior conceptualization of cooperation and competition (Deutsch, 1949) bargaining is thus a situation in which the participants have mixed motives toward one another: on the one hand, each has interest in cooperating so that they reach an agreement; on the other hand, they have competitive interests concerning the nature of the agreement they reach. In effect, to reach agreement the cooperative interest of the bargainers must be strong enough to overcome their competitive interests. However, agreement is not only contingent upon the *motivational* balances of cooperative to competitive interests but also upon the situational and *cognitive* factors which facilitate or hinder the recognition or invention of a bargaining agreement that reduces the opposition of interest and enhances the mutuality of interests.[1]

These considerations lead to the formulation of two general, closely related propositions about the likelihood that a bargaining agreement will be reached.

1. Bargainers are more likely to reach an agreement, the stronger are their cooperative interests in comparison with their competitive interests.

2. Bargainers are more likely to reach an agreement, the more resources they have available for recognizing or inventing potential bargaining agreements and for communicating to one another once a potential agreement has been recognized or invented.

From these two basic propositions and additional hypotheses concerning conditions that determine the strengths of the cooperative and competitive interests and the amount of available resources, we believe it is possible to explain the ease or difficulty of arriving at a bargaining agreement. We shall not present a full statement of these hypotheses here but turn instead to a description of an experiment that relates to Proposition 1.

The experiment was concerned with the effect of the availability of threat upon bargaining in a two-person experimental bargaining game.[2] Threat is defined as the expression of an intention to do something detrimental to the interests of another. Our experiment was guided by two assumptions about threat:

1. If there is a conflict of interest and one person is able to threaten the other, he will tend to use the threat in an attempt to force the other person to yield. This tendency should be stronger, the more irreconcilable the conflict is perceived to be.

2. If a person uses threat in an attempt to intimidate another, the threatened person (if he considers himself to be of equal or superior status) would feel hostility toward the threatener and tend to respond with counterthreat and/or increased resistance to yielding. We qualify this assumption by stating that the tendency to resist should be greater, the greater the perceived probability and magnitude of detriment to the other and the less the perceived probability and magnitude of detriment to the potential resister from the anticipated resistance to yielding.

The second assumption is based upon the view that when resistance is not seen to be suicidal or useless, to allow oneself to be intimidated, particularly by someone who does not have the right to expect deferential behavior, is to suffer a loss of social face and, hence, of self-esteem; and that the culturally defined way of maintaining self-esteem in the face of attempted intimidation is to engage in a contest for

[1] Schelling in a series of stimulating papers on bargaining (1957, 1958) has also stressed the "mixed motive" character of bargaining situations and has analyzed some of the cognitive factors which determine agreements.

[2] The game was conceived and originated by M. Deutsch; R. M. Krauss designed and constructed the apparatus employed in the experiment.

supremacy vis-à-vis the power to intimidate or, minimally, to resist intimidation. Thus, in effect, the use of threat (and if it is available to be used, there will be a tendency to use it) should strengthen the competitive interests of the bargainers in relationship to one another by introducing or enhancing the competitive struggle for self-esteem. Hence, from Proposition 1, it follows that the availability of a means of threat should make it more difficult for the bargainers to reach agreement (providing that the threatened person has some means of resisting the threat). The preceding statement is relevant to the comparison of both of our experimental conditions of threat, bilateral and unilateral (described below), with our experimental condition of nonthreat. We hypothesize that a bargaining agreement is more likely to be achieved when neither party can threaten the other, than when one or both parties can threaten the other.

Consider now the situations of bilateral threat and unilateral threat. For several reasons, a situation of bilateral threat is probably less conducive to agreement than is a condition of unilateral threat. First, the sheer likelihood that a threat will be made is greater when two people rather than one have the means of making the threat. Secondly, once a threat is made in the bilateral case it is likely to evoke counterthreat. Withdrawal of threat in the

face of counterthreat probably involves more loss of face (for reasons analogous to those discussed in relation to yielding to intimidation) than does withdrawal of threat in the face of resistance to threat. Finally, in the unilateral case, although the person without the threat potential can resist and not yield to the threat, his position vis-à-vis the other is not so strong as the position of the threatened person in the bilateral case. In the unilateral case, the threatened person may have a worse outcome than the other whether he resists or yields; while in the bilateral case, the threatened person is sure to have a worse outcome if he yields but he may insure that he does not have a worse outcome if he does not yield.

Method

PROCEDURE Subjects (Ss) were asked to imagine that they were in charge of a trucking company, carrying merchandise over a road to a destination. For each trip completed they made $.60, minus their operating expenses. Operating expenses were calculated at the rate of one cent per second. So, for example, if it took 37 seconds to complete a particular trip, the player's profit would be $.60 − $.37 or a net profit of $.23 for that particular trip.

Each S was assigned a name, Acme or Bolt. As the "road map" (see Figure 1)

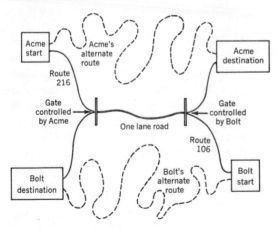

FIGURE 1 *Subject's road map.*

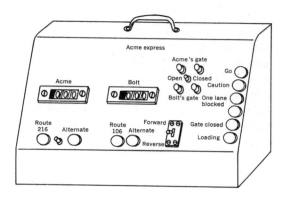

FIGURE 2   *Subject's control panel.*

indicates, both players start from separate points and go to separate destinations. At one point their paths cross. This is the section of road labeled "one-lane road," which is only one lane wide, so that two trucks, heading in opposite directions, could not pass each other. If one backs up the other can go forward, or both can back up, or both can sit there head-on without moving.

There is another way for each S to reach the destination on the map, labeled the "alternate route." The two players' paths do not cross on this route, but the alternate is 56% longer than the main route. Ss were told that they could expect to lose at least $.10 each time they used the alternate route.

At either end of the one-lane section there is a gate that is under the control of the players to whose starting point it is closest. By closing the gate, one player can prevent the other from traveling over that section of the main route. The use of the gate provides the threat potential in this game. In the bilateral threat potential condition (Two Gates) both players had gates under their control. In a second condition of unilateral threat (One Gate) Acme had control of a gate but Bolt did not. In a third condition (No Gates) neither player controlled a gate.

Ss played the game seated in separate booths placed so that they could not see each other but could see the experimenter (*E*). Each S had a "control panel"

mounted on a 12″ × 18″ × 12″ sloping-front cabinet (see Figure 2). The apparatus consisted essentially of a reversible impulse counter that was pulsed by a recycling timer. When the S wanted to move her truck forward she threw a key that closed a circuit pulsing the "add" coil of the impulse counter mounted on her control panel. As the counter cumulated, S was able to determine her "position" by relating the number on her counter to reference numbers that had been written in on her road map. Similarly, when she wished to reverse, she would throw a switch that activated the "subtract" coil of her counter, thus subtracting from the total on the counter each time the timer cycled.

S's counter was connected in parallel to counters on the other S's panel and on E's panel. Thus each player had two counters on her panel, one representing her own position and the other representing the other player's. Provision was made in construction of the apparatus to permit cutting the other player's counter out of the circuit, so that each S knew only the position of her own truck. This was done in the present experiment. Experiments now in progress are studying the effects of knowledge of the other person's position and other aspects of interpersonal communication upon the bargaining process.

The only time one player definitely knew the other player's position was when they had met head-on on the one-way section of road. This was indicated by a traffic light mounted on the panel. When this light was on, neither player could move forward unless the other moved back. The gates were controlled by toggle switches and panel-mounted indicator lights showed, for both Ss, whether each gate was open or closed.

The following "rules of the game" were stated to the Ss:

1. A player who started out on one route and wished to switch to the other route could only do so after first reversing and going back to the start position. Direct transfer from one route to the other was not permitted except at the start position.

2. In the conditions where Ss had gates, they were permitted to close the gates no matter where they were on the main route, so long as they were on the main route (i.e., they were not permitted to close the gate while on the alternate route or after having reached their destinations). However, Ss were permitted to open their gates at any point in the game.

Ss were taken through a number of practice exercises to familiarize them with the game. In the first trial they were made to meet head-on on the one-lane path; Acme was then told to back up until she was just off the one-lane path and Bolt was told to go forward. After Bolt had gone through the one-lane path, Acme was told to go forward. Each continued going forward until each arrived at her destination. The second practice trial was the same as the first except that Bolt rather than Acme backed up after meeting head-on. In the next practice trial, one of the players was made to wait just before the one-way path while the other traversed it and then was allowed to continue. In the next practice trial, one player was made to take the alternate route and the other was made to take the main route. Finally, in the bilateral and unilateral threat conditions the use of the gate was illustrated (by having the player get on the main route, close the

gate, and then go back and take the alternate route). The Ss were told explicitly, with emphasis, that they did not have to use the gate. Before each trial in the game the gate or gates were in the open position.

The instructions stressed an individualistic motivational orientation. Ss were told to try to earn as much money for themselves as possible and to have no interest in whether the other player made money or lost money. They were given $4.00 in poker chips to represent their working capital and told that after each trial they would be given "money" if they made a profit or that "money" would be taken from them if they lost (i.e., took more than 60 seconds to complete their trip). The profit or loss of each S was announced so that both Ss could hear the announcement after each trial. Each pair of Ss played a total of 20 trials; on all trials, they started off together. In other words each trial presented a repetition of the same bargaining problem. In cases where Ss lost their working capital before the 20 trials were completed, additional chips were given them. Ss were aware that their monetary winnings and losses were to be imaginary and that no money would change hands as a result of the experiment.

SUBJECTS   Sixteen pairs of Ss were used in each of the three experimental conditions. The Ss were female clerical and supervisory personnel of the New Jersey Bell Telephone Company who volunteered to participate during their working day.[3] Their ages ranged from 20 to 39, with a mean of 26.2. All were naïve to the purpose of the experiment. By staggering the arrival times and choosing girls from different locations, we were able to insure that the Ss did not know with whom they were playing.

[3] We are indebted to the New Jersey Bell Telephone Company for their cooperation in providing Ss and facilities for the experiment.

DATA RECORDED Several types of data were collected. We obtained a record of the profit or loss of each S on each trial. We also obtained a detailed recording of the actions taken by each S during the course of a trial. For this purpose, we used an Esterline-Angus model AW Operations Recorder which enabled us to obtain a "log" of each move each S made during the game (e.g., whether and when she took the main or alternate route; when she went forward, backward, or remained still; when she closed and opened the gate; when she arrived at her destination).

Results[4]

The best single measure of the difficulty experienced by the bargainers in reaching an agreement is the sum of each pair's profits (or losses) on a given trial. The higher the sum of the payoffs to the two players on a given trial, the less time it took them to arrive at a procedure for sharing the one-lane path of the main route. (It was, of course, possible for one or both of the players to decide to take the alternate route so as to avoid a protracted stalemate during the process of bargaining. This, however, always resulted in at least a $.20 smaller joint payoff if only one player took the alternate route, than an optimally arrived at agreement concerning the use of the one-way path.) Figure 3 presents the medians of the summed payoffs (i.e., Acme's plus Bolt's) for all pairs in each of the three experimental conditions over the 20 trials.[5] These striking results indicate that agreement was least difficult to arrive at in the no threat condition, was more difficult to arrive at in the unilateral threat condition, and exceedingly difficult or impossible to arrive at in the bilateral threat condition (see also Table 1).

[4] We are indebted to M. J. R. Healy for suggestions concerning the statistical analysis of our data.
[5] Medians are used in graphic presentation of our results because the wide variability of means makes inspection cumbersome.

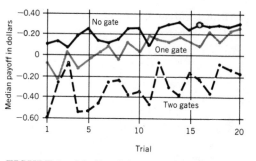

FIGURE 3   *Median joint payoff (Acme + Bolt) over trials.*

Examination of Figure 3 suggests that learning occurred during the 20 trials: the summed payoffs for pairs of Ss tend to improve as the number of trials increases. This suggestion is confirmed by an analysis of variance of the slopes for the summed payoffs[6] over the 20 trials for each of the 16 pairs in each of the 3 experimental treatments. The results of this analysis indicate that the slopes are significantly greater than zero for the unilateral threat ($p < .01$) and the no threat ($p < .02$) conditions; for the bilateral threat condition, the slope does not reach statistical significance ($.10 < p < .20$). The data indicate that the pairs in the no threat condition started off at a fairly high level but, even so, showed some improvement over the 20 trials; the pairs in the

[6] A logarithmic transformation of the summed payoffs on each trial for each pair was made before computing the slopes for a given pair.

FIGURE 4   *Acme's median payoff.*

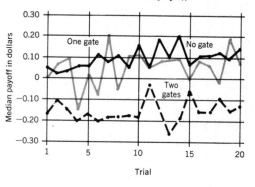

TABLE 1 *Mean payoffs summated over the twenty trials*

	MEANS				STATISTICAL COMPARISONS: p VALUES*		
VARIABLE	(1) NO THREAT	(2) UNILATERAL THREAT	(3) BILATERAL THREAT	OVER-ALL	1 vs 2	1 vs 3	2 vs 3
Summed payoffs (Acme + Bolt)	203.31	−405.88	−875.12	.01	.01	.01	.05
Acme's payoff	122.44	−118.56	−406.56	.01	.10	.01	.05
Bolt's payoff	80.88	−287.31	−468.56	.01	.01	.01	.20
Absolute differences in payoff (A − B)	125.94	294.75	315.25	.05	.05	.01	ns

* Evaluation of the significance of over-all variation between conditions is based on an F test with 2 and 45 df. Comparisons between treatments are based on a two-tailed t test.

unilateral threat condition started off low and, having considerable opportunity for improvement used their opportunity; the pairs in the bilateral threat condition, on the other hand, did not benefit markedly from repeated trials.

Figure 4 compares Acme's median profit in the three experimental conditions over the 20 trials; while Figure 5 compares Bolt's profit in the three conditions. (In the unilateral threat condition, it was Acme who controlled a gate and Bolt who did not.) Bolt's as well as Acme's outcome is somewhat better in the no threat condition than in the unilateral threat condition; Acme's, as well as Bolt's, outcome is clearly worst in the bilateral threat condition (see Table 1 also). However, Figure 6 reveals that Acme does somewhat better than Bolt in the unilateral condition. Thus, if threat-potential exists within a bargaining relationship it is better to possess it oneself than to have the other party possess it. However, it is even better for neither party to possess it. Moreover, Figure 5 shows that Bolt is better off not having than having a gate even when Acme has a gate: Bolt tends to do better in the unilateral threat condition than in the bilateral threat condition.

The size of the absolute discrepancy between the payoffs of the players in each pair provides a measure of the confusion or difficulty in predicting what the other player is going to do. Thus, a large absolute discrepancy might indicate that after

FIGURE 5 *Bolt's median payoff.*

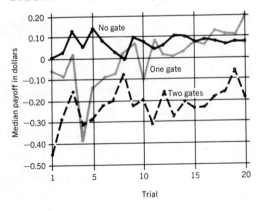

FIGURE 6 *Acme's and Bolt's median payoffs in unilateral threat condition.*

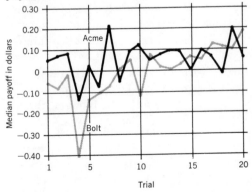

one player had gone through the one-way path and left it open, the other player continued to wait; or it might indicate that one player continued to wait at a closed gate hoping the other player would open it quickly but the other player did not; etc. Figure 7 indicates that the discrepancy between players in the no threat condition is initially small and remains small for the 20 trials. For the players in both the bilateral and unilateral threat conditions, the discrepancy is initially relatively larger; but it decreases more noticeably in the unilateral threat condition by the tenth trial and, therefore, is consistently smaller than in the bilateral condition.

By way of concrete illustration, we present a synopsis of the game for one pair in each of three experimental treatments.

NO THREAT CONDITION   *Trial 1.* The players met in the center of the one-way section. After some back-and-forth movement Bolt reversed to the end of the one-way section, allowing Acme to pass through, and then proceeded forward herself.

Trial 2. They again met at the center of the one-way path. This time, after moving back and forth deadlocked for some time, Bolt reversed to "start" and took the alternate route to her destination, thus leaving Acme free to go through on the main route.

Trial 3. The players again met at the center of the one-way path. This time, however, Acme reversed to the beginning of the path, allowing Bolt to go through to her destination. Then Acme was able to proceed forward on the main route.

Trial 5. Both players elected to take the alternate route to their destinations.

Trial 7. Both players took the main route and met in the center. They waited, deadlocked, for a considerable time. Then Acme reversed to the end of the one-way path allowing Bolt to go through, then proceeded through to her destination.

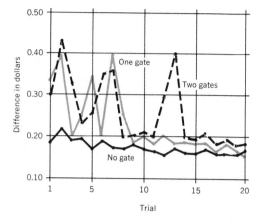

FIGURE 7   *Median absolute differences in payoff.*

Trials 10–20. Acme and Bolt fall into a pattern of alternating who is to go first on the one-way section. There is no deviation from this pattern.

The only other pattern that emerges in this condition is one in which one player dominates the other. That is, one player consistently goes first on the one-way section and the other player consistently yields.

UNILATERAL THREAT CONDITION   *Trial 1.* Both players took the main route and met in the center of it. Acme immediately closed the gate, reversed to "start," and took the alternate route to her destination. Bolt waited for a few seconds, at the closed gate, then reversed and took the alternate route.

Trial 2. Both players took the main route and met in the center. After moving back and forth deadlocked for about 15 seconds, Bolt reversed to the beginning of the one-way path, allowed Acme to pass, and then proceeded forward to her destination.

Trial 3. Both players started out on the main route, meeting in the center. After moving back and forth deadlocked for a while, Acme closed her gate, reversed to "start," and took the alternate route.

Bolt, meanwhile, waited at the closed gate. When Acme arrived at her destination she opened the gate, and Bolt went through to complete her trip.

Trial 5. Both players took the main route, meeting at the center of the one-way section. Acme immediately closed her gate, reversed, and took the alternate route. Bolt waited at the gate for about 10 seconds, then reversed and took the alternate route to her destination.

Trial 10. Both players took the main route and met in the center. Acme closed her gate, reversed, and took the alternate route. Bolt remained waiting at the closed gate. After Acme arrived at her destination, she opened the gate and Bolt completed her trip.

Trial 15. Acme took the main route to her destination and Bolt took the alternate route.

Trials 17–20. Both players took the main route and met in the center. Bolt waited a few seconds, then reversed to the end of the one-way section allowing Acme to go through. Then Bolt proceeded forward to her destination.

Other typical patterns that developed in this experimental condition included an alternating pattern similar to that described in the no threat condition, a dominating pattern in which Bolt would select the alternate route leaving Acme free to use the main route unobstructed and a pattern in which Acme would close her gate and then take the alternate route, also forcing Bolt to take the alternate route.

BILATERAL THREAT CONDITION   *Trial 1.* Acme took the main route and Bolt took the alternate route.

Trial 2. Both players took the main route and met head-on. Bolt closed her gate. Acme waited a few seconds, then closed her gate, reversed to "start," then went forward again to the closed gate. Acme reversed and took the alternate route. Bolt again reversed, then started on the alternate route. Acme opened her gate and Bolt reversed to "start" and went to her destination on the main route.

Trial 3. Acme took the alternate route to her destination. Bolt took the main route and closed her gate before entering the one-way section.

Trial 5. Both players took the main route and met head-on. After about 10 seconds spent backing up and going forward, Acme closed her gate, reversed, and took the alternate route. After waiting a few seconds, Bolt did the same.

Trials 8–10. Both players started out on the main route, immediately closed their gates, reversed to "start," and took the alternate route to their destinations.

Trial 15. Both players started out on the main route and met head-on. After some jockeying for position, Acme closed her gate, reversed, and took the alternate route to her destination. After waiting at the gate for a few seconds, Bolt reversed to "start" and took the alternate route to her destination.

Trials 19–20. Both players started out on the main route, immediately closed their gates, reversed to "start," and took the alternate routes to their destinations.

Other patterns that emerged in the bilateral threat condition included alternating first use of the one-way section, one player dominating the other on first use of the one-way section, and another dominating pattern in which one player consistently took the main route while the other consistently took the alternate route.

Discussion

From our view of bargaining as a situation in which both cooperative and competitive tendencies are present and acting upon the individual, it is relevant to inquire as to the conditions under which a stable agreement of any form develops. However, implicit in most economic models of bargaining (e.g., Stone, 1958; Zeuthen, 1930) is the assumption that the cooperative interests of the bargainers are sufficiently strong to insure that some form of mutually satisfactory agreement will be reached. For this reason, such models have focused upon the form of the agreement reached by the bargainers. Siegel and Fouraker (1960) report a series of bargaining experiments, quite different in structure from ours, in which only one of many pairs of Ss were unable to reach agreement. Siegel and Fouraker explain this rather startling result as follows:

Apparently the disruptive forces which lead to the rupture of some negotiations were at least partially controlled in our sessions. . . .

Some negotiations collapse when one party becomes incensed at the other, and henceforth strives to maximize his opponent's displeasure rather than his own satisfaction . . . Since it is difficult to transmit insults by means of quantitative bids, such disequilibrating behavior was not induced in the present studies. If subjects were allowed more latitude in their communications and interactions, the possibility of an affront-offense-punitive behavior sequence might be increased (p. 100). (Quoted by permission of McGraw-Hill.)

In our experimental bargaining situation, the availability of threat clearly made it more difficult for bargainers to reach a mutually profitable agreement. These results, we believe, reflect psychological tendencies that are not confined to our bargaining situation: the tendency to use threat (if the means for threatening is available) in an attempt to force the other person to yield, when the other is seen as obstructing one's path; the tendency to respond with counterthreat or increased resistance to attempts at intimidation. How general are these tendencies? What conditions are likely to elicit them? Answers to these questions are necessary before our results can be generalized to other situations.

Dollard, Doob, Miller, Mowrer, and Sears (1939) have cited a variety of evidence to support the view that aggression (i.e., the use of threat) is a common reaction to a person who is seen as the agent of frustration. There seems to be little reason to doubt that the use of threat is a frequent reaction to interpersonal impasses. However, everyday observation indicates that threat does not inevitably occur when there is an interpersonal impasse. We would speculate that it is most likely to occur: when the threatener has no positive interest in the other person's welfare (he is either egocentrically or competitively related to the other); when the threatener believes that the other has no positive interest in his welfare; and when the threatener anticipates either that his threat will be effective or, if ineffective, will not worsen his situation because he expects the worst to happen if he does not use his threat. We suggest that these conditions were operative in our experiment; Ss were either egocentrically or competitively oriented to one another[7] and they felt that they would not be worse off by the use of threat.

Everyday observation suggests that the tendency to respond with counterthreat or increased resistance to attempts at intimidation is also a common occurrence. We believe that introducing threat into a bargaining situation affects the meaning of yielding. Although we have no data to support this interpretation directly, we will attempt to justify it on the basis of some additional assumptions.

Goffman (1955) has pointed out the pervasive significance of "face" in the maintenance of the social order. In this view, self-esteem is a socially validated system that grows out of the acceptance by others of the claim for deference, prestige, and recognition that a person pre-

---

[7] A post-experimental questionnaire indicated that, in all three experimental conditions, the Ss were most strongly motivated to win money, next most strongly motivated to do better than the other player, next most motivated to "have fun," and were very little or not at all motivated to help the other player.

sents in his behavior toward others. Since the rejection of such a claim would be perceived (by the recipient) as directed against his self-esteem, he must react against it rather than accept it in order to maintain the integrity of his self-esteem system.

One may view the behavior of our Ss as an attempt to make claims upon the other, an attempt to develop a set of shared expectations as to what each was entitled to. Why then did the Ss' reactions differ so markedly as a function of the availability of threat? The explanation lies, we believe, in the cultural interpretation of yielding (to a peer or subordinate) under duress, as compared to giving in without duress. The former, we believe, is perceived as a negatively valued form of behavior, with negative implications for the self-image of the person who so behaves. At least partly, this is so because the locus of causality is perceived to be outside the person's voluntary control. No such evaluation, however, need be placed on the behavior of one who "gives in" in a situation where no threat or duress is a factor. Rather we should expect the culturally defined evaluation of such a person's behavior to be one of "reasonableness" or "maturity," because the source of the individual's behavior is perceived to lie within his own control.

Our discussion so far has suggested that the psychological factors which operate in our experimental bargaining situation are to be found in many real-life bargaining situations. However, it is well to recognize some unique features of our experimental game. First, the bargainers had no opportunity to communicate verbally with one another. Prior research on the role of communication in trust (Deutsch 1958, 1960; Loomis, 1959) suggests that the opportunity for communication would have made reaching an agreement easier for individualistically-oriented bargainers. This same research (Deutsch, 1960) indicates, however, that communication may not be effective between competitively oriented bargainers. This possibility was expressed spontaneously by a number of our Ss in a post-game interview.

Another characteristic of our bargaining game is that the passage of time, without coming to an agreement, is costly to the players. There are, of course, bargaining situations in which lack of agreement may simply preserve the *status quo* without any worsening of the bargainers' respective situations. This is the case in the typical bilateral monopoly case, where the buyer and seller are unable to agree upon a price (e.g., see Siegel & Fouraker, 1960). In other sorts of bargaining situations, however, (e.g., labor-management negotiations during a strike, international negotiations during an expensive cold war) the passage of time may play an important role. In our experiment, we received the impression that the meaning of time changed as time passed without the bargainers reaching an agreement. Initially, the passage of time seemed to place the players under pressure to come to an agreement before their costs mounted sufficiently to destroy their profit. With the continued passage of time, however, their mounting losses strengthened their resolution not to yield to the other player. They comment: "I've lost so much, I'll be damned if I give in now. At least I'll have the satisfaction of doing better than she does." The mounting losses and continued deadlock seemed to change the game from a mixed motive into a predominantly competitive situation.

It is, of course, hazardous to generalize from a laboratory experiment to the complex problems of the real world. But our experiment and the theoretical ideas underlying it can perhaps serve to emphasize some notions which, otherwise, have an intrinsic plausibility. In brief, these are that there is more safety in cooperative than in competitive coexistence, that it is dangerous for bargainers to have weapons, and that it is possibly even more dangerous for a bargainer to have the capacity to retaliate in kind than not to have this capacity when the other bargainer has a weapon. This last statement assumes that the one who yields has more of his values preserved by accepting the agreement preferred by the other than by extended conflict. Of course, in some bargaining situations in the real world, the loss incurred by yielding may exceed the losses due to extended conflict.

Summary

The nature of bargaining situations was discussed. Two general propositions about the conditions affecting the likelihood of a bargaining agreement were presented. The effects of the availability of threat upon interpersonal bargaining were investigated experimentally in a two-person bargaining game. Three experimental conditions were employed: no threat (neither player could threaten the other), unilateral threat (only one of the players had a means of threat available to her), and bilateral threat (both players could threaten each other). The results indicated that the difficulty in reaching an agreement and the amount of (imaginary) money lost, individually as well as collectively, was greatest in the bilateral and next greatest in the unilateral threat condition. Only in the no threat condition did the players make an overall profit. In the unilateral threat condition,

the player with the threat capability did better than the player without the threat capability. However, comparing the bilateral and unilateral threat conditions, the results also indicate that when facing a player who had threat capability one was better off *not* having than having the capacity to retaliate in kind.

References

Deutsch, M. A theory of cooperation and competition. *Hum. Relat.,* 1949, **2**, 129–152.

Deutsch, M. Trust and suspicion. *J. conflict Resolut.,* 1958, **2**, 265–279.

Deutsch, M. The effect of motivational orientation upon trust and suspicion. *Hum. Relat.,* 1960, 13, 123–140.

Dollard, J., Doob, L. W., Miller, N. E., Mowrer, O. H., and Sears, R. H. *Frustration and aggression.* New Haven: Yale Univer. Press, 1939.

Goffman, E. On face-work. *Psychiatry,* 1955, 18, 213–231.

Loomis, J. L. Communication, the development of trust and cooperative behavior. *Hum. Relat.,* 1959, **12**, 305–315.

Schelling, T. C. Bargaining, communication and limited war. *J. conflict Resolut.,* 1957, 1, 19–38.

Schelling, T. C. The strategy of conflict: Prospectus for the reorientation of game theory. *J. conflict Resolut.,* 1958, **2**, 203–264.

Siegel, S., and Fouraker, L. E. *Bargaining and group decision making.* New York: McGraw-Hill, 1960.

Stone, J. J. An experiment in bargain games. *Econometrica,* 1958, **26**, 286–296.

Zeuthen, F. *Problems of monopoly and economic warfare.* London: Routledge, 1930.

The influence of group membership upon behavior is strikingly illustrated in this article. Some of the variables which determine the degree of yielding are even more interesting. The yielding situation provides a model in which the influence of many variables may be explored.

A POINT TO GUIDE YOUR STUDY ·*Compare the personality descriptions of the yielders and nonyielders with those in the selection by Barron in Section Thirteen. Which of Barron's configurations would you expect to show the greatest amount of yielding?*

54: CONFORMITY AND CHARACTER

Richard S. Crutchfield, University of California, Berkeley

During the Spring of 1953, one hundred men visited the Institute of Personality Assessment and Research at the University of California, Berkeley, to participate in an intensive three-day assessment of those qualities related to superior functioning in their profession.

As one of the procedures on the final day of assessment, the men were seated in groups of five in front of an apparatus consisting of five adjacent electrical panels. Each panel had side wings, forming an open cubicle, so that the person, though sitting side by side with his fellow subjects, was unable to see their panels. The experimenter explained that the apparatus was so wired that information could be sent by each man to all the others by closing any of eleven switches at the bottom of his panel. This information would appear on the other panels in the form of signal lights, among five rows of eleven lights, each row corresponding to one of the five panels. After a warm-up task to acquaint the men with the workings of the apparatus, the actual procedure commenced.

Slides were projected on a wall directly facing the men. Each slide presented a question calling for a judgment by the person. He indicated his choice of one of several multiple-alternative answers by closing the appropriately numbered switch on his panel. Moreover, he responded *in order*, that is, as designated by one of five

Adapted from the address of the retiring president of the Division of Personality and Social Psychology, American Psychological Association, New York City, September 4, 1954. The principal study reported here owes much to the collaboration of Dr. Donald W. MacKinnon, director of the Institute of Personality Assessment and Research, and of his staff. Mr. Donald G. Woodworth has contributed especially to the statistical analysis of data.
    R. S. Crutchfield. Conformity and character. *Amer. Psychologist*, 1955, **10**, 191–198. Copyright © 1955 by the American Psychological Association. Reprinted here with permission from the author and the American Psychological Association. One reference completed; was in press (*Ed.*).

red lights lettered A, B, C, D, E, on his panel. If he were A, he responded first, if B, second, and so on. The designations, A, B, C, D, and E, were rotated by the experimenter from time to time, thus permitting each person to give his judgments in all the different serial positions. No further explanation about the purpose of this procedure was offered.

It may help to convey the nature of the men's typical experiences by giving an illustrative description of what happens concretely to one of the men. The first slide calls for a simple judgment of which of two geometrical figures is larger in area. Since his red light C is on, he waits for A and B to respond before making his response. And, as he is able to observe on the panel, his own judgment coincides with the judgments of A and B who preceded him, and of D and E who follow him. After judgments on several further slides in position C, he is then shifted to position D for more slides, then to A.

The slides call for various kinds of judgments—lengths of lines, areas of figures, logical completion of number series, vocabulary items, estimates of the opinions of others, expression of his own attitudes on issues, expression of his personal preferences for line drawings, etc. He is not surprised to observe a perfectly sensible relationship between his judgments and those of the other four men. Where clear-cut perceptual or logical judgments are involved, he finds that his judgments are in perfect agreement with those of the other four. Where matters of opinion are involved, and some differences in opinion to be expected, his judgments and those of the other four men are sometimes in agreement and sometimes not.

Eventually the man finds himself for the first time in position E, where he is to respond last. The next slide shows a standard line and five comparison lines, of which he is to pick the one equal in length to the standard. Among the previous slides he has already encountered this kind of perceptual judgment and has found it easy. On looking at this slide it is immediately clear to him that line number 4 is the correct one. But as he waits his turn to respond, he sees light number 5 in row A go on, indicating that that person has judged line number 5 to be correct. And in fairly quick succession light 5 goes on also in rows B, C, and D.

At this point the man is faced with an obvious conflict between his own clear perception and a unanimous contradictory consensus of the other four men. What does he do? Does he rely on the evidence of his own senses and respond independently? Or does he defer to the judgment of the group, complying with their perceptions rather than his own?

We will postpone for a moment the answer as to what he does, and revert to the description of our apparatus.

We have been describing the situation as if seen from the perspective of one of the men. Actually his understanding of the situation is wrong. He has been deceived. For the apparatus is *not* really wired in the way that he was informed. There actually is no connection among the five panels. Instead, they are all wired in an identical manner to a control panel where the experimenter sits behind the men. It is the experimenter who sends all the information which appears on the panels, and the wiring is in parallel in such a way that whatever signals are sent by the experimenter appear simultaneously and identically on all five panels. Moreover, the designations of serial order of responding —A through E—are identical at all times for the five panels, so that at a given moment, for instance, all five men believe themselves to be A, or at another time, E. As we have just said, the responses actu-

ally made by the five men do not affect in any way the panels of the others. They do get registered individually on one part of the experimenter's control panel. The *latency* of each individual response to one tenth of a second is also recorded by timers on the control panel.

Hence, the situation as we have described it for our one illustrative man is actually the situation simultaneously experienced by all five men. They all commence in position C, and all shift at the same time to position D, and to A, and finally E. They all see the same simulated group judgments.

The entire situation is, in a word, contrived, and contrived so as to expose each individual to a standardized and prearranged series of group judgments. By this means the simulated group judgments can be made to appear sensible and in agreement with the individual, or, at chosen critical points, in conflict with his judgments.

Most of you will recognize at once the basic similarity of our situation to that invented by Asch (2) in his extremely important work of recent years on independence of individual judgment under opposing group pressure. In his method, ten subjects announced aloud and in succession their judgments of the relative length of stimulus lines exposed before the group. The first nine subjects were actually confederates of the experimenter, and gave uniformly false answers at pre-established points, thus placing pressure on the single naïve subject.

For extensive research use, for instance in personality assessment, Asch's technique is handicapped by the severely unfavorable ratio of confederates to true subjects. The present technique, utilizing the electrical network described above, avoids this difficulty. There are no confederates required; all five subjects are tested simultaneously in a thoroughly standardized situation. The experimenter exercises highly flexible control of the simulated group judgments, and of the serial order of responding. Stimulus material to be judged can be varied as widely as desired by use of different slides.

Now at last come back to our man still sitting before his panel, still confronted with the spurious group consensus, still torn between a force toward independent judgment and a force toward conformity to the group. How he is likely to behave in the situation can best be described by summarizing the results for our study of 50 of the 100 men in assessment.

Effects of consensus

All of these men were engaged in a profession in which leadership is one of the salient expected qualifications. Their average age was 34 years. Their educational levels were heterogeneous, but most had had some college training.

Fifty of the men were tested in the procedure as described. Another 40 served as *control* subjects; they simply gave individual judgments of the slides without using the apparatus, and hence without knowledge of the judgments of others. The distribution of judgments of these control subjects on each slide was subsequently used as a baseline for evaluating the amount of group pressure influence on the experimental subjects.

Now as to results. When faced with the dilemma posed by this first critical slide, 15 of the 50 men, or 30 per cent, conformed to the obviously false group consensus. The remaining 70 per cent of the men maintained independence of judgment in face of the contradictory group consensus.

The first critical slide was followed by 20 others, all with the subjects responding in position E. The 20 slides involved a broad sampling of judgmental materials, exploring the question of what would happen to other kinds of perceptions, to matters of factual appraisal and of logic, of

opinion and attitude, of personal preference—all under the same conditions of group pressure. Interpolated among them were occasional neutral slides, in which the group consensus was simulated as correct or sensible, in order to help maintain the subjects' acceptance of the genuineness of the apparatus and situation.

The results on several more of the critical slides will give a representative picture of what happens under group pressure. First, take another kind of perceptual judgment. A circle and a star are exposed side by side, the circle being about one-third larger in area than the star. The false group consensus is on the *star* as the larger, and 46 per cent of the men express agreement with this false judgment.

On a simple logical judgment of completion of a number series, as found in standard mental tests, 30 per cent of the men conform to an obviously illogical group answer, whereas not a single control subject gives an incorrect answer.

As striking as these influence effects are, they are overshadowed by the even higher degree of influence exhibited on another set of items. These pertain to perceptual, factual, and logical judgments which are designed to maximize the *ambiguity* of the stimulus. There are three such examples: (a) two actually equal circles are to be judged for relative size; (b) a pair of words are to be judged as either synonyms or antonyms, though actually entirely unrelated in meaning and unfamiliar to all subjects; (c) a number series is to be completed which is actually insoluble, that is, for which there is no logically correct completion.

To take the third example, which gives the most pronounced influence effect of all 21 critical items, 79 per cent of the men conform to a spurious group consensus upon an arbitrarily chosen and irrational answer.

Influence effects are found, we see, on both well-structured and poorly-structured stimuli, with markedly greater effects on the latter.

Turning from perceptual and factual judgments to opinions and attitudes, it is clearly evident that here, too, the judgments of many of the men are markedly dependent upon a spurious group consensus which violates their own inner convictions. For example, among control subjects virtually no one expresses disagreement with the statement: "I believe we are made better by the trials and hardships of life." But among the experimental subjects exposed to a group consensus toward disagreement, 31 per cent of the men shift to expressing disagreement.

It can be demonstrated that the conformity behavior is not found solely for attitudes on issues like the foregoing, which may be of rather abstract and remote significance for the person. Among the control sample of men, not a single one expresses agreement with the statement: "I doubt whether I would make a good leader," whereas 37 per cent of the men subjected to group pressure toward agreement succumb to it. Here is an issue relating to appraisal of the self and hence likely to be of some importance to the person, especially in light of the fact already mentioned that one of the salient expected qualifications of men in this particular profession is that of leadership.

The set of 21 critical items ranges from factual to attitudinal, from structured to ambiguous, from impersonal to personal. With only two exceptions, all these items yield significant group pressure influence effects in our sample of 50 men. The very existence of the two exceptional items is in itself an important finding, for it demonstrates that the observed influences are not simply evidence of indiscriminate readiness to conform to group pressure regardless of the specific nature of the judgment involved. The character of the two exceptional items is significant, for they are the two most extremely personal and subjec-

tive judgments, namely, those in which the individual is asked which one of two simple line drawings *he prefers.* On these slides there is virtually no effective result of group pressure. Not more than one man of the 50 expresses agreement with the spurious group consensus on the nonpreferred drawing. Such personal preferences, being most isolated from the relevance of group standards, thus seem to be most immune to group pressure.

Individual differences

To what extent do the fifty men differ among themselves in their general degree of conformity to group pressure?

A total "conformity score" is readily obtainable for each individual by counting the number of the 21 critical items on which he exhibits influence to the group pressure. The threshold for influence for each item is arbitrarily fixed on the basis of the distribution of judgments by control subjects on that item.

Considering that we are dealing with a fairly homogeneous sample of limited size, the range of individual differences that we obtain is astonishingly large, covering virtually the entire possible scope of our measure. At the lower extreme, several of the men showed conformity on no more than one or two of the critical items. At the upper extreme, one man was influenced on 17 of the 21 items. The rest of the scores are well distributed between these extremes, with a mean score of about eight items and a tendency for greater concentration of scores toward the lower conformity end.

The reliability of the total score, as a measure of generalized conformity in the situation, is obtained by correlating scores on two matched halves of the items. The correlation is found to be .82, which when corrected for the combined halves gives a reliability estimate for the entire 21-item scale of .90.

To recapitulate, we find large and reliable differences among the 50 men in the amount of conformity behavior exhibited, and there appears to be considerable generality of this conformity behavior with respect to widely varied judgmental materials. Whether such conformity tendencies also generalize to other, quite different behavioral situations is a question for future research.

Relations to personality variables

Assuming that we are, indeed, measuring conformity tendencies which are fundamental in the person, the question is what traits of character distinguish between those men exhibiting much conformity behavior in our test and those exhibiting little conformity. The assessment setting within which these men were studied provides an unusually fertile opportunity to explore this question, in light of the wide range of personality measurements available.

Correlational study of the conformity scores with these other variables of personality provides some picture of the independent and of the conforming person. As contrasted with the high conformist, the independent man shows more intellectual effectiveness, ego strength, leadership ability and maturity of social relations, together with a conspicuous absence of inferiority feelings, rigid and excessive self-control, and authoritarian attitudes.

A few correlations will illustrate. The assessment staff rating on "intellectual competence" correlates −.63 with conformity score, this being the highest relationship of any found. The *Concept Mastery Test*,[1] a measure of superior mental functioning, correlates −.51 with conformity. An "ego strength" scale, independently derived by Barron (3), correlates −.33, and a staff rating on "leadership ability," −.30

[1] Used with the kind permission of Dr. Lewis M. Terman.

with conformity. Scales of Gough's *California Psychological Inventory* (6), pertaining to such dimensions as "tolerance," "social participation," and "responsibility," range in correlation from −.30 to −.41 with conformity.

And as for some of the positive correlates, the F scale (1), a measure of authoritarian attitudes, correlates +.39 with conformity, and a staff rating on amount of authoritarian behavior manifested in a standard psychodrama situation correlates +.35 with conformity.

The general appraisal of each man by the assessment staff in the form of descriptive Q sorts further enriches this picture. Those men exhibiting extreme independence in the situation as contrasted with those at the high conformity end are described more often in the following terms by the assessment staff, which was entirely ignorant of the actual behavior of the men in the group pressure procedure:

Is an effective leader.
Takes an ascendant role in his relations with others.
Is persuasive; tends to win other people over to his point of view.
Is turned to for advice and reassurance.
Is efficient, capable, able to mobilize resources easily and effectively.
Is active and vigorous.
Is an expressive, ebullient person.
Seeks and enjoys aesthetic and sensuous impressions.
Is natural; free from pretense, unaffected.
Is self-reliant; independent in judgment; able to think for himself.

In sharp contrast to this picture of the independent men is the following description of those high in conformity behavior:

With respect to authority, is submissive, compliant and overly accepting.
Is conforming; tends to do the things that are prescribed.

Has a narrow range of interests.

Overcontrols his impulses; is inhibited; needlessly delays or denies gratification.

Is unable to make decisions without vacillation or delay.

Becomes confused, disorganized, and unadaptive under stress.

Lacks insight into his own motives and behavior.

Is suggestible; overly responsive to other people's evaluations rather than his own.

Further evidence is found in some of the specific items of personality inventories on which the answers of the high and low conformers are significantly different. Here are some illustrative items more frequently answered "True" by the independent subjects than by the conforming subjects:

Sometimes I rather enjoy going against the rules and doing things I'm not supposed to.

I like to fool around with new ideas, even if they turn out later to be a total waste of time.

A person needs to "show off" a little now and then.

At times I have been so entertained by the cleverness of a crook that I have hoped he would get by with it.

It is unusual for me to express strong approval or disapproval of the actions of others.

I am often so annoyed when someone tries to get ahead of me in a line of people that I speak to him about it.

Compared to your own self-respect, the respect of others means very little.

This pattern of expressed attitudes seems to reflect freedom from compulsion about rules, adventurousness (perhaps tinged with exhibitionism), self-assertiveness, and self-respect.

Turning to the opposite side of the picture, here are some illustrative items more frequently answered "True" by the extreme conformists, which reflect a rather rigid, externally sanctioned, and inconsistent, moralistic attitude.

I am in favor of very strict enforcement of all laws, no matter what the consequences.

It is all right to get around the law if you don't actually break it.

Most people are honest chiefly through fear of being caught.

Another set of items reveals a desire for clarity, symmetry, certainty, or, in presently popular phraseology, "an intolerance of ambiguity."

I don't like to work on a problem unless there is a possibility of coming out with a clear-cut and unambiguous answer.

Once I have made up my mind I seldom change it.

Perfect balance is the essence of all good composition.

Other items express conventionality of values:

I always follow the rule: business before pleasure.

The trouble with many people is that they don't take things seriously enough.

I am very careful about my manner of dress.

Anxiety is revealed in numerous items:

I am afraid when I look down from a high place.

I am often bothered by useless thoughts which keep running through my head.

I often think, "I wish I were a child again."

I often feel as though I have done something wrong or wicked.

And, finally, there are various expressions of disturbed, dejected, and distrustful attitudes toward other people:

When I meet a stranger I often think that he is better than I am.

Sometimes I am sure that other people can tell what I am thinking.

I wish that I could get over worrying about things I have said that may have injured other people's feelings.

I commonly wonder what hidden reason another person may have for doing something nice for me.

People pretend to care more about one another than they really do.

Although there is an unmistakable neurotic tone to many of the foregoing statements, one must be chary of inferring that those high on conformity are measurably more neurotic than the others. There does not in fact appear to be any significant correlation of the conformity scores with obvious standard measures of neuroticism as found, for instance, in scales of the Minnesota Multiphasic Personality Inventory. A similar negative finding has been reported by Barron (4) in his study of the personality correlates of independence of judgment in Asch's subjects.

In another area, attitudes concerning parents and children, differences between those high and low on conformity are especially interesting. The extreme conformists describe their parents in highly idealized terms, unrelieved by any semblance of criticism. The independents, on the other hand, offer a more balanced picture of praise and criticism.

Most of the men in the sample are fathers, and it is instructive to see that in their view of child-rearing practices, the conformers are distinctly more "restrictive" in their attitudes, and the independents distinctively more "permissive" (5).

Finally, there appears to be a marked difference in the early home background of the conformists and independents. The high conformers in this sample come almost without exception from stable homes; the independents much more frequently report broken homes and unstable home environments.

Previous theoretical and empirical studies seem to converge, though imperfectly, on a picture of the overconformist as having less ego strength, less ability to tolerate his own impulses and to tolerate ambiguity, less ability to accept responsibility, less self-insight, less spontaneity and productive originality, and as having more prejudice and authoritarian attitudes, more idealization of parents, and greater emphasis on external and socially approved values.

All of these elements gain at least some substantiation in the present study of conformity behavior, as objectively measured in our test situation. The decisive influence of intelligence in resisting conformity pressures is perhaps given even fuller weight in the present findings.

Conformity behavior in different populations

Two further studies have been made. The first was with 59 college undergraduates, mostly sophomores. Forty were females, 19 males. An additional 40 students served as control subjects.

Using the same procedures and the same items for judgment, the conformity results for this student sample were highly similar to those already reported for the adult men. Here again extensive group pressure effects are found on almost all items. And here again there are wide individual differences, covering virtually the entire score range.

The male students on the average exhibit just about the same level of conformity as do the adult men. The female students, on the other hand, exhibit significantly *higher* amounts of conformity than the male groups. This greater conformity among females is evident across the entire range of items tested. Interpretation of this sex difference in conformity will require further research.

But before male egos swell overly, let me hasten to report the results of a third study, just completed. Fifty women, all college alumnae in their early forties, were tested in the same group pressure procedure, again as part of a larger assessment setting, and under the auspices of the Mary Conover Mellon Foundation.[2] As in the previous populations, virtually the entire range of individual differences in conformity is exhibited by these women. Some of them show no effect at all; others are influenced on almost all items. But the average conformity score for these 50 women is significantly *lower* than that found in the previous populations.

Thus we find our sample of adult women to be more independent in judgment than our adult men. The interpretation is difficult. The two groups differ in many particulars, other than sex. The women are highly selected for educational and socioeconomic status, are persons active in their community affairs, and would be characterized as relatively stable in personality and free of psychopathology. The adult men in our professional group are less advantageously selected in all these respects. Differences in intellectual level alone might be sufficient to account for the observed differences in conformity scores.

Psychological processes

Turn now to questions concerning the nature of the psychological processes involved in these expressions of conformity to group pressure. How, for instance, is the situation perceived by the individual? The most striking thing is that almost never do the individuals under this pressure of a false group consensus come to suspect the deception practiced upon them. Of the total of 159 persons already tested in the

apparatus, and questioned immediately afterwards, only a small handful expressed doubt of the genuineness of the situation. Of these not more than two or three really seem to have developed this suspicion while in the actual situation.

Yet all the subjects are acutely aware of the sometimes gross discrepancies between their own inner judgments and those expressed by the rest of the group. How do they account for these discrepancies?

Intensive individual questioning of the subjects immediately following the procedure elicits evidence of two quite different tendencies. First, for many persons the discrepancies tend to be resolved through self-blame. They express doubt of their own accuracy of perception or judgment, confessing that they had probably misread or misperceived the slides. Second, for many other persons the main tendency is to blame the rest of the group, expressing doubt that they had perceived or read the slides correctly. This is not a neat dichotomy, of course. Most persons express something of a mixture of these explanations, which is not surprising in view of the fact that some slides may tend to favor one interpretation of the difficulty and other slides the opposite interpretation.

As might be predicted, there is a substantial relationship between conformity score and tendency to self-blame; or, putting it the other way, those who remain relatively independent of the group pressure are more likely to blame the discrepancies on poor judgments by the rest of the group.

But this is by no means a perfect relationship. There are many persons who, though retrospectively expressing doubt of the correctness of the group's judgment, did in fact conform heavily while in the situation. And what is even more striking is that a substantial number of the subjects —between 25 and 30 per cent—freely admit on later questioning that there were times when they responded the way the

[2] The assessment was under the direction of Dr. R. Nevitt Sanford.

group did *even when they thought this not the proper answer*. It seems evident, therefore, that along with various forms of cognitive rationalization of the discrepancies, there occurred a considerable amount of what might be called deliberate conforming, that is, choosing to express outward agreement with the group consensus even when believing the group to be wrong.

Another noteworthy effect was the sense of increased psychological distance induced between the person himself and the rest of the group. He felt himself to be queer or different, or felt the group to be quite unlike what he had thought. With this went an arousal of considerable anxiety in most subjects; for some, manifest anxiety was acute.

The existence of these tensions within and between the subjects became dramatically manifest when, shortly after the end of the procedure, the experimenter confessed the deception he had practiced and explained the real situation. There were obvious and audible signs of relaxation and relief, and a shift from an atmosphere of constraint to one of animated discussion.

This is an appropriate point to comment on ethics. No persons when questioned after explanation of the deception expressed feelings that they had been ethically maltreated in the experiment. The most common reaction was a positive one of having engaged in an unusual and significant experience, together with much joking about having been taken in.

Undeniably there are serious ethical issues involved in the experimental use of such deception techniques, especially inasmuch as they appear to penetrate rather deeply into the person. My view is that such deception methods ethically require that great care be taken immediately afterwards to explain the situation fully to the subject.

These remarks on ethics of the method are especially pertinent as we move from study of judgmental materials which are noncontroversial to those which are controversial. In the studies of college students and of mature women, many new critical items were introduced and subjected to the pressure. They were intended to explore more deeply the conformity tendencies in matters of opinion and attitude. And they were so chosen as to pertain to socially important and controversial issues involving civil liberties, political philosophy, crime and punishment, ethical values, and the like.

Here are two salient examples. An expression of agreement or disagreement was called for on the following statement: "Free speech being a privilege rather than a right, it is proper for a society to suspend free speech whenever it feels itself threatened." Among control subjects, only 19 per cent express agreement. But among the experimental subjects confronted with a unanimous group consensus agreeing with the statement, 58 per cent express agreement.

Another item was phrased as follows: "Which one of the following do you feel is the most important problem facing our country today?" And these five alternatives were offered.

Economic recession
Educational facilities
Subversive activities
Mental health
Crime and corruption

Among control subjects, only 12 per cent chose "Subversive activities" as the most important. But when exposed to a spurious group consensus which unanimously selected "Subversive activities" as the most important, 48 per cent of the experimental subjects expressed this same choice.

I think that no one would wish to deny that here we have evidence of the operation of powerful conformity influences in the expression of opinion on matters of critical social controversy.

Reinforcement of conformity

There is one final point upon which I should like to touch briefly. That is the question of whether there are circumstances under which the power of the group to influence the judgments of the individual may be even more greatly reinforced, and if so, how far such power may extend.

One method has been tried as part of the study of college students. With half of the subjects, a further instruction was introduced by the experimenter. They were told that in order to see how well they were doing during the procedure, the experimenter would inform the group immediately after the judgments on each slide what the correct answer was. This was to be done, of course, only for those slides for which there was a correct answer, namely, perceptual judgments, logical solutions, vocabulary, etc. No announcement would be made after slides having to do with opinions and attitudes.

The experimenter here again deceived the subjects, for the answers he announced as correct were deliberately chosen so as to agree with the false group consensus. In short, the external authority of the experimenter was later added on as reinforcement to the group consensus.

The effect of this so-called "correction" method is striking. As the series of judgments goes on, these individuals express greater and greater conformity to the group pressure on slides which are of the same character as those for which earlier in the series the false group consensus was thus reinforced by the false announcement by the experimenter.

But the more critical issue is whether this enhanced power of the group generalizes also to judgments of an entirely unrelated sort, namely, matters of opinion and attitude, rather than of fact. In other words, will the group, through having the rightness of its judgment supported by the experimenter on matters of perception, logic, and the like, thereby come to be regarded by the individual as more right, or more to be complied with, on entirely extraneous matters, such as social issues?

The answer is absolutely clear. The enhanced power of the group does *not* carry over to increase the effective influence on expression of opinions and attitudes. The subjects exposed to this "correction" method do not exhibit greater conformity to group pressure on opinions and attitudes than that found in other subjects.

This crucial finding throws some light on the nature of the psychological processes involved in the conformity situation. For it seems to imply that conformity behavior under such group pressure, rather than being sheerly an indiscriminate and irrational tendency to defer to the authority of the group, has in it important rational elements. There is something of a reasonable differentiation made by the individual in his manner of reliance upon the group. He may be led to accept the superiority of the group judgment on matters where there is an objective frame of reference against which the group can be checked. But he does not, thereby, automatically accept the authority of the group on matters of a less objective sort.

Conclusion

The social psychologist is concerned with the character of conformity, the personologist with conformity of character. Between them they raise many research questions: the comparative incidence of conformity tendencies in various populations; the influence of group structure and the individual's role in the group on the nature and amount of conformity behavior; the effects of reward or punishment for conforming on habits of conformity; the genesis and change of conformity behavior in the individual personality; the determinants of extreme *anti*conformity tendencies.

Contributing to such questions we have what appears to be a powerful new research technique, enabling the study of conformity behavior within a setting which effectively simulates genuine group interaction, yet preserves the essential requirements of objective measurement.

References

1. Adorno, T. W., Frenkel-Brunswik, Else, Levinson, D., and Sanford, R. N. *The authoritarian personality.* New York: Harper, 1950.

2. Asch, S. E. *Social psychology.* New York: Prentice-Hall, 1952.

3. Barron, F. An ego-strength scale which predicts response to psychotherapy. *J. consult. Psychol.,* 1953, 17, 327–333.

4. Barron, F. Some personality correlates of independence of judgment. *J. Pers.,* 1953, 21, 287–297.

5. Block, J. Personality characteristics associated with fathers' attitudes toward child-rearing. *Child Develpm.,* 1955, 26, 41–48.

6. Gough, H. G. *A preliminary guide for the use and interpretation of the California Psychological Inventory.* Privately distributed by the Institute of Personality Assessment and Research, Univer. of California, Berkeley, 1954. (Mimeo.)

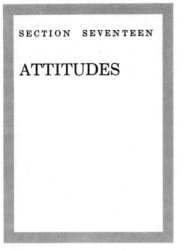

SECTION SEVENTEEN

ATTITUDES

*In addition to the presentation of a good deal of interesting
information about the attitude-change program of the Chinese and
the reactions of prisoners to it, this article makes the point that
"brainwashing" can be understood best as a concerted effort to change
attitudes by the techniques familiar to all propagandists. The
Chinese program was different from most such attitude-change
programs in its intensiveness, its use of many techniques
simultaneously, and its use of absolute control of the environment to
produce results. Thus, "brainwashing" seems to be a social-
psychological phenomenon and not due to the diabolical use of
classical conditioning, hypnosis, and drugs to produce human
automata.*

POINTS TO GUIDE YOUR STUDY   *(1) Stay alert to the social-psychological
techniques used in the "brainwashing" attempts.   (2) How do you
think you would react to the stresses and pressures mentioned in this
article? Would you be likely to yield?   (3) Why was the
"brainwashing" not more effective? How might the armed forces
protect—or innoculate—their members against attitude-change
attempts of the sort mentioned in this selection?*

55: THE CHINESE INDOCTRINATION PROGRAM FOR PRISONERS OF WAR: A STUDY OF ATTEMPTED "BRAINWASHING"

Edgar H. Schein, Massachusetts Institute of Technology

In this paper I shall try to present an
account of the 'typical' experiences of
United Nations prisoners of war in Chinese Communist hands, and to interpret
these experiences in a social-psychological
framework. Before the return of United
Nations prisoners, the "confessions" of
such prominent men as Cardinal Minds-
zenty and William Oatis had already
aroused considerable interest in so-called
brainwashing. This interest was heightened

E. H. Schein. The Chinese indoctrination program for
prisoners of war. A study of attempted "brainwashing."
Psychiatry, 1956, **19**, 149–172. Copyright © 1956 by the
William Alanson White Psychiatric Foundation, Inc.
Reprinted by special permission of The William Alanson White Psychiatric Foundation, Inc. The author has
also given permission.

The views expressed in this paper are those of the
author and do not necessarily reflect the official opinion
of the Department of the Army.

by the widespread rumors of collaboration among United Nations prisoners of war in Korea. Following their repatriation in August 1953, a rash of testimonial articles appeared in the weekly magazines, some attempting to show that the Chinese Communist techniques were so terrifying that no one could withstand them, others roundly condemning the collaborative activities of the so-called "progressives"[1] as having been selfishly motivated under conditions in which resistance was possible. These various accounts fall short because they are too emotionally charged to be objective, and because they fail to have any generality, since they are usually based on the personal experiences of only one man.

The data upon which this paper is based were gathered in an attempt to form a generalized picture of what happened to the average man from the time he was captured until the time he was repatriated. The data were collected during August 1953 at Inchon, Korea, where the repatriates were being processed, and on board the U.S.N.S. General Black in transit to the United States from September 1 to September 16.

The method of collecting the data was, in the main, by intensive interviews conducted in Inchon, where the author was a member of one of the processing teams.[2] In the course of the processing, relatively objective tests and projective tests were also given the men;[3] but intensive interviewing was felt to be preferable for gathering the data presented here, because the material to be obtained was highly novel, and because the men had been

through a highly traumatic situation which might make the eliciting of *any* information very difficult. It was also recognized that the men might find it difficult to remember, might be reluctant to relate certain of their experiences, and might retrospectively falsify many events.

Of approximately 20 repatriates selected at random at different stages of the repatriation, each was asked to tell in chronological order and in as great detail as possible what had happened to him during his captivity. Emphasis was placed on what the Chinese or North Koreans *did* in their handling of the prisoners and how the men reacted. The men were particularly encouraged to relate the reactions of *others,* in order to avoid arousing anxiety or guilt over their own behavior and thereby blocking the flow of memories. The interviews varied in length from two to four hours.

From these interviews a picture emerged which was recorded in the form of a composite or typical account of the capture and imprisonment experience. This account was then given to three psychiatrists[4] who together had interviewed 300 men assigned to them at random. It was their job to delete material which, on the basis of their information, was false and to add details which had not been revealed in my 20 interviews.

On board ship I was present at a large number of psychiatric interviews and group therapy sessions, and engaged in many informal discussions with repatriates. Extended late evening "bull sessions" with repatriates were particularly informative.[5]

Many of the traumatic prison-camp experiences could probably not be fully communicated through verbal interviews. How-

---

[1] Commonly called *pro's* by their fellow prisoners.
[2] As part of the processing, psychiatric interviews were initiated at Inchon during the two or three days that the men were there. The procedure of processing has been described in detail by Henry A. Segal in "Initial Psychiatric Findings of Recently Repatriated Prisoners of War," *Amer. J. Psychiatry* (1954) 111:358–363.
[3] The results of this testing will be reported on in part by H. D. Strassman, Margaret Thaler, and E. H. Schein in "A Prisoner of War Syndrome: Apathy as a Reaction to Severe Stress," *Amer. J. Psychiatry* (1956) 112:998–1003.

[4] These were Dr. Harvey Strassman, Dr. Patrick Israel, and Dr. Clinton Tempereau; their assistance in reading and commenting on the manuscript was extremely valuable.
[5] The reliability of the material was further checked against the complete Army files on the total group of repatriates.

ever, I believe that the data are sufficiently inclusive and reliable to provide a reasonably accurate account of prisoner-of-war experiences. The picture presented is not to be viewed as the experience of any single person, nor as the experience of all the men. Rather, it represents a composite or typical account which, in all its details, may or may not have been true for any one prisoner.

The prisoner-of-war experience

CAPTURE, THE MARCH, AND TEMPORARY CAMPS   United Nations soldiers were captured by the Chinese and North Koreans at all stages of the Korean conflict, although particularly large groups were captured during November and December, 1950. The conditions under which men were captured varied widely. Some men were captured by having their positions overrun or surrounded; others ran into road blocks and were cut off; still others fought for many days on a shifting front before they succumbed. The situation in the front lines was highly fluid, and there was a good deal of confusion on both sides. When a position was overrun, the men often scattered and became disorganized.

While the initial treatment of prisoners by the North Koreans was typically harsh and brutal—they often took the prisoner's clothing, gave him little if any food, and met any resistance with immediate severe punishment or death—the Chinese, in line with their over-all indoctrination policy, often tried to create an atmosphere of friendliness and leniency. Some men reported that their Chinese captors approached them with outstretched hands saying, "Congratulations! You've been liberated." It was made clear to the man that he could now join forces with other "fighters for peace." Often the Chinese soldiers pointed out to their captives how lucky they were not to have been captured by the North Koreans. Some men reported

incidents of Chinese beating off North Koreans who were "trying to hurt" American prisoners, or of punishing their own guards for being too rough or inconsiderate. The men were usually allowed to keep their clothing, and some consideration was given to the sick and wounded. However, the food and medical attention were only slightly better than that provided by the North Koreans.

For the first six to twenty-four hours after capture, a man was usually in a state of dazed shock, unable to take any kind of integrated action and, later, unable to report any kind of feeling he had had during this period. Following this, he expected death or torture at the hands of his captors, for rumors that this would happen had been widely circulated in the front lines, often based on stories of men who had fallen into North Korean hands. These fears were, however, quickly dispelled by the friendly attitude of the Chinese soldiers; and this friendly attitude and the emphasis on "peace" was the first and perhaps most significant step in making the prisoner receptive to the more formal indoctrination which was to come later.

In the next weeks or months the prisoner was exposed to great physical hardship and to a series of psychological pressures which amounted to a cyclical reactivation of fears and their relief by actual events or by extravagant promises. Implicit in most of what the Chinese said and did was the suggestion that these stresses could be brought to an end by the adoption of a "cooperative" attitude by the prisoner, although at first it was not clear just what this meant.

The men were collected behind the lines and were marched north in groups of varying sizes. The men marched only at night, averaging about 20 miles, and were kept under strict cover in the daytime. Conditions on the march were very hard. Most men reported having great difficulty eating strange and badly prepared foods; however, they were often reminded, whether true on not, that they were getting essentially the same rations as the average Chinese foot soldier. Medical care was almost nonexistent, but this too was depicted as being equally true for Chinese soldiers because of supply shortages. Almost all the men had diarrhea, many had dysentery, and most of them suffered from exposure. Every day would find a few more dead.

Although the columns were not well guarded, few escapes were attempted because the men were too weak, did not know the terrain, were on the whole poorly organized, and were afraid of the North Koreans. The few who did escape were almost always returned to the group within a short time.

During these one- to two-week marches the men became increasingly disorganized and apathetic. They developed a slow plodding gait, called by one man a "prisoner's shuffle." Lines of authority tended to break down, and the prevailing attitude was "every man for himself." Open competition for food, clothing, and shelter made the maintenance of group ties almost impossible. Everything that happened tended to be frustrating and depriving, yet there was no ready outlet for hostility, and no opportunity for constructive resistance. The only *realistic* goal was to get to prison camp where, it was hoped, conditions would be better.[6]

Uppermost in the men's minds were fantasies of food—memories of all the good meals they had had in the past, or plans for elaborate menus in the future. The only competing fantasies concerned loved ones at home, or cars, which seemed symboli-

cally to represent the return to their homes and to freedom.

Arrival at one of the temporary camps was usually a severe disappointment. Many men reported that the only thing that had kept them going on the march was the hope of improved conditions in the camp; but they found the food as bad as ever, living conditions more crowded than before, and a continued lack of consideration for the sick and wounded. Moreover, there was now nothing to do but sit and wait. The news given the men was mostly false, playing up Communist military victories, and was, of course, particularly demoralizing. Many of the men became extremely apathetic and withdrawn, and according to some reports these apathy states sometimes became so severe as to result in death.[7]

The Chinese continually promised improvements in conditions or early repatriation, and failures of these promises to materialize were blamed on obstructions created by United Nations air activity or lack of "cooperation" among the prisoners. It was always made clear that only certain prisoners could hope to get a break: those who "did well," "cooperated," "learned the truth," and so on. The Chinese distributed propaganda leaflets and required the men to sing Communist songs. Apparently even guards were sensitized to finding potential collaborators among the prisoners by observing their reactions to such activities. Outright indoctrination was not attempted on the marches and in the temporary camps, but those men who finally reached one of the permanent camps were ill-prepared physically and psychologically for the indoctrination pressures they were about to face.

LIFE IN THE PERMANENT PRISONER-OF-WAR CAMP   Most of the permanent camps were parts of small Korean villages, often split

[6] Not all of the men participated in such severe marches. Those captured in 1951 and 1952 were sometimes taken north by truck or under less severe conditions. The sick and wounded were given somewhat more consideration, although never much in the way of medical aid. Numerous incidents were reported of Chinese guards helping men, occasionally even carrying them.

It should also be mentioned that the North Korean civilians seemed ambivalent toward the prisoners. Many of them were sadistic, but many others helped the Americans by hiding them or giving them food and clothing.

[7] For a more complete description of these apathy reactions, see reference footnote 3.

into several compounds in different parts of the village. The camps were sometimes surrounded by a fence, by barbed wire, or by natural barriers, although sometimes not enclosed at all. While guards were posted at key places, they were not sufficiently plentiful to prevent escapes or excursions to other parts of the village. The camp usually consisted of a series of mud huts in which the men slept on the floor or on straw matting, and a schoolhouse or other permanent building which was used as administrative headquarters, for lectures, and for recreation. The various Chinese officer and enlisted billets were usually scattered through the village. Mess and latrine facilities were very inadequate, and conditions were crowded, but far better than in the temporary camps.

In camp the men were segregated by race, nationality, and rank, and were organized into companies, platoons, and squads. The squads varied in size from 10 to 15 men, who usually shared the same living area. No formal organization was permitted among the prisoners; thus, the Chinese put their own personnel in charge of the platoons and companies, and appointed certain prisoners as squad leaders without consideration of rank.

Although the daily routine in camp varied, the average prisoner arose at dawn, was required to do calisthenics for an hour or more, was assigned to various details—such as gathering wood, carrying water, cooking, repairing roads, burying other prisoners, and general maintenance of the camp—and then was given a breakfast of potato soup or some form of cereal at around eight o'clock. The rest of the morning and afternoon was usually spent on indoctrination or details. Whether there was a midday meal depended on the attitude of the prisoner, the supply of food, and the general state of the political situation. The main meal was served around five o'clock and usually consisted of vegetables, grains, rice, and occasional bits of

pork fat or fish. For men on such a meager diet, details involving many miles of walking or very hard work were especially exhausting.

Recreation varied with the camp and with the political situation. During the first year or so, a heavy emphasis was placed on indoctrination, and recreation was restricted to reading Communist literature, seeing propaganda films, and playing such games as checkers and chess. As the truce talks progressed and repatriation became a possibility, conditions in the camps improved generally. Less emphasis was placed on indoctrination and more leeway was given to the prisoners to engage in recreation of their own choice. The improvement in living conditions made physical recreation more feasible, and the men were permitted to devise athletic fields and equipment. Intercamp "Olympics" conducted by the Chinese—and used by them for their own propaganda purposes—drew wide participation among the more athletically inclined, regardless of their political sentiments.

There are few data available concerning the sexual activities of the prisoners. There were Korean women available in the villages, but men seldom visited them. Reports of homosexuality were very infrequent.

The indoctrination program

All of these conditions in the permanent camp were, in actual practice, interlocked with the indoctrination program. This program cannot be viewed as a collection of specific techniques routinely applied, but rather as the creation of a whole set of social conditions within which certain techniques operated. Whether the Chinese manipulation of the social setting to create certain effects was intentional can only be conjectured; intentional or not, it was an important factor in such success as the indoctrination program achieved.

THE REMOVAL OF SUPPORTS TO BELIEFS,
ATTITUDES, AND VALUES On matters of
opinion, people tend to rely primarily on
the opinions of others for determination of
whether they themselves are "right" or
"wrong"—whether these opinions of others
are obtained through mass media of communication or through personal interaction. All of the prisoners' accustomed
sources of information concerning daily
events on a local, national, or international
level were cut off by the Chinese, who
substituted their own usually heavily
biased newspapers, radio broadcasts, and
magazines. *The Daily Worker* from various cities was available in the camp libraries, as were numerous magazines and
journals from China, Poland, Russia, and
Czechoslovakia. The radio news broadcasts heard usually originated in China.
And the camp headquarters had no
scruples concerning accuracy in the news
announcements made over the camp pub-
lic-address system.

The delivery of mail from home was
systematically manipulated; the evidence
indicates that all mail which contained information about the war or the truce talks,
or which contained favorable personal
news, was withheld, while letters containing no general information, or bad personal
news, were usually delivered.

Personal contact with visitors from outside the camps was very limited, mainly
restricted to Communist news correspond-
ents. For most prisoners, there was simply
no way to find out accurately what was
going on in the world.

The Chinese also attempted to weaken
the means of consensual validation by undermining personal contacts among the
men. First of all, the men were segregated
by race, apparently in order to put special
indoctrination pressure on members of certain minorities, especially Negroes. The
men were also segregated by rank, in what
appeared to be a systematic attempt to
undermine the internal structure of the

group by removing its leaders. Thus the
noncommissioned officers, who were at first
in the enlisted camps, were put into a
special camp when the Chinese found out
that they were quite effective in keeping
the other men from various kinds of collaboration. It was reported that this segregation was often followed by a considerable
increase in collaboration, particularly
among the younger enlisted men.

The Chinese emphasized that rank was
no longer of any significance; the entire
group was now part of a wider "brother-
hood"—the earlier mentioned "fighters for
peace"—in which, under communism,
everyone was to be equal. The Chinese
sometimes put particularly young or inept
prisoners in command of the squads to
remind the men that former bases of organization no longer counted. While such
a procedure aroused only resistance and
hostility in most of the prisoners, undoubtedly a few malcontents welcomed the opportunity to gain occupancy of the favored
positions that had never been available to
them before.

There was also persistent emphasis on
undermining all friendships, emotional
bonds, and group activities. For instance,
the Chinese prohibited all forms of religious expression and ruthlessly persecuted
the few chaplains or others who tried to
organize or conduct religious services.
Bonds to loved ones at home were weakened by the withholding of mail, as the
Chinese frequently pointed out to the men
that the lack of mail meant that their
friends and relatives no longer cared for
them.

The systematic use of Chinese spies and
also informers from prisoner ranks made
it possible for the Chinese to obtain detailed information about almost all activities going on in camp. The men reported
that the Chinese were forever sneaking
around their quarters and listening to conversations or observing activities from hidden posts, and they also knew that some

of their number were acting as informers. These circumstances helped to create a feeling of general distrust, and the only fully safe course was to withdraw from all intimate interaction with other prisoners.

When any semblance of effective organization appeared spontaneously among the men, the Chinese would usually immediately remove and segregate the leaders or key figures; and informal groups which might have supported resistance activities were also usually systematically broken up. The few that were not broken up either were not effective or died because of lack of internal support, thus indicating that this system of social control was highly effective. Usually groups were formed for one of three purposes—to plan for and aid in escapes, to prevent men from collaborating, or for social reasons. According to most reports, the groups organized around escape were highly ineffective. Usually such groups were quickly liquidated by being physically broken up. A few poorly planned escapes were attempted, but the marginal diet, the strangeness of the surrounding terrain, and the carefully built-up fear of the North Koreans all served to minimize escapes. When an escape did occur, the Chinese usually recovered the man easily by offering a bag of rice to anyone turning him in. The groups organized to keep men from collaborating, or to retaliate against them if they did, were usually composed of some of the more outspoken and violent resisters. One such group, labelled the "Ku Klux Klan" by the Chinese because of its militant policy, appeared to be composed mainly of men who had served some time in prison for various infractions of camp rules. They threatened potential collaborators through anonymous notes, but the number of incidents in which they followed through was relatively small. Usually the Chinese discovered their plans and, whenever they became dangerous, disrupted their activities. The third type of group consisted of

prisoners who were solely interested in each other's company; one such group, made up primarily of older prisoners, was called "The Old Soldiers' Home."

A few groups remained intact even though the Chinese knew about them, perhaps because the Chinese did not consider them very dangerous, or because their leaders, as spokesmen for the prisoners, provided a valuable sounding board whenever the Chinese wanted to know how the group would react to certain changes in policy. The latter, in fact, gave such groups some power, but if this power was ever misused—that is, if the group supported an escape attempt or a theft of food, for instance—the group was quickly liquidated and its leaders were imprisoned or moved to another camp.

Various other groupings of men existed, some, such as the squad, for administrative reasons, others to support various Chinese enterprises. Soon after capture, the Chinese made a concerted effort to recruit men for a number of "peace committees" whose purpose it was to aid in the indoctrination by conducting personal interviews with resistant prisoners and to deter any resistance activity. They also were charged with such propaganda missions as the preparation of leaflets, peace petitions, and scripts for radio broadcasts—all under the guise of running such innocuous camp activities as recreation. An intercamp peace organization was also formed to draw up peace appeals and petitions to be submitted to the United Nations, carrying, of course, the endorsement of a large number of prisoners.

The members of the camp peace committees and the delegates to intercamp peace rallies were usually selected by a pseudo-democratic method. However, the men who ended up in the key positions were usually those the Chinese wanted, or, in any case, approved of—that is, men who were willing to cooperate with the Chinese, and who had sincerely or falsely convinced their captors that they were sympathetic to the Communist cause. Sometimes the election was held over and over again until the right man was chosen. At other times the men resigned themselves to the fact that all would go more smoothly if they selected at the beginning the man the Chinese wanted, for the group could be dissolved at will anyway.

Each camp also had a number of other committees operating under the peace committee. They were responsible for the daily routine affairs of the camp, such as sanitation, food, recreation, study, and entertainment. The number of noncollaborators who were allowed to be members appeared to depend on the mood of the Chinese and the degree to which they wanted to keep in touch with prisoner opinions. It is likely that with the general improvement in camp conditions in 1952 and 1953, the membership of the various committees became more representative. The peace committees were, by then, largely defunct; they had been exploited as much as possible by the Chinese and no longer served any function in their propaganda campaigns.

Various social groups formed by pro's were left intact—perhaps as a reminder to other prisoners that one way to enter into meaningful relationships with others was through common political activities for the Communists.

One of the most significant facts about the few types of groups that did exist in camp is that they were highly unstable from an internal point of view because of the possible presence of informers and spies. Mutual distrust existed especially in the peace committees and in groups sanctioned by the Chinese, because no member was ever sure whether any other member was really a pro or was just pretending to "go along." If a man was pretending, he had to hide this carefully lest a real pro turn him in to the Chinese. Yet a man who sincerely believed in the Chinese peace effort had to hide this fact from others who

might be pretenders, for fear they might harm him directly or blacklist him for the future, at the same time convincing other pro's that he really was sincere.

The members of resistance groups and social groups also had to be wary of each other, because they never knew whether the group had been infiltrated by spies and informers. Furthermore, the fact that the group might be broken up at any time tended to keep any member from becoming too dependent on, or close to, another.[8]

From the point of view of this analysis, the most important effect of the social isolation which existed was the consequent emotional isolation which prevented a man from validating any of his beliefs, attitudes, and values through meaningful interaction with other men at a time when these were under heavy attack from many sources, and when no accurate information was available.

DIRECT ATTACKS ON BELIEFS, ATTITUDES, AND VALUES   The chief method of direct indoctrination was a series of lectures that all prisoners had to attend at some time during their imprisonment. These lectures were given daily and lasted from two to three hours. Each camp had one or more political instructors who read the lectures from a prepared text. Often one instructor read while another seemed to follow a second copy of the text, as if to make sure that the right material was being presented. The lectures were direct, simple, black-and-white propaganda. They attacked the United Nations and particularly the United States on various political, social, and economic issues, at the same time glorifying the achievements of the Communist countries, and making strong appeals for "peace."

Most men reported that the anti-American material was naïve and seldom based on adequate or correct information about

---

[8] Segal (reference footnote 2) has aptly described such prisoner groups as "groups of isolates."

the United States. Even the pro-Communist arguments were sometimes weak and susceptible to attack. Occasionally a well-educated prisoner debated points on communism successfully with instructors who had little knowledge of the classical works of communism. Usually the instructors presented the neo-Communist views of writers such as Mao Tse-tung and were unable to counter the arguments of prisoners who knew Marx and Lenin. The number of prisoners with sufficient education to engage in such arguments was, however, extremely small.

The constant hammering at certain points, combined with all the other techniques used—and in a situation where the prisoners had no access to other information—made it likely that many of the Chinese arguments did filter through enough to make many of the men question some of their former points of view. It is also likely that any appeal for "peace," no matter how false, found a receptive audience among combat-weary troops, especially when it was pointed out that they were fighting on foreign soil and were intervening in a civil war which was "none of their business." Both lectures and didactic "interrogations" emphasized detailed predictions of what would happen to the prisoners upon repatriation, some of which turned out to be accurate.[9] The Chinese implied that certain problems which would arise would be the result of the "weakness" or "unfairness" of the democratic ideology.

Another direct technique was the distribution of propaganda leaflets and the showing of Communist films glorifying the accomplishments of the Communist regime in Russia and China, and pointing out how much more had been done by communism for the peasant and laborer than by the capitalist system. While such films

might have been highly ineffectual under ordinary circumstances, they assumed considerable importance because of the sheer lack of any other audio-visual material.

Perhaps the most effective attack on existing values, beliefs, and attitudes was the use of testimonials from prisoners who were ostensibly supporting Communist enterprises. These included peace petitions, radio appeals, speeches, and confessions. The use of such testimonials had a double effect in that it further weakened group ties while presenting pro-Communist arguments. As long as the men unanimously rejected the propaganda, each of them could firmly hold to the position that his beliefs must be right, even if he could not defend them logically. However, *if even one other man became convinced, it was no longer possible to hold this position.* Each man was then required to begin examining his beliefs and was vulnerable to the highly one-sided arguments that were repeatedly presented.

Of particular importance were the germ-warfare confessions which were extracted from a number of Air Force officers and enlisted men. The Chinese made a movie of one or two of the officers giving their testimony to the "international" commission which they had set up to investigate the problem, and showed this movie in all the camps. Furthermore, one or two of the officers personally went from camp to camp and explained how United Nations forces had used these bombs; this made a powerful impression on many men who had, until then, dismissed the whole matter as a Chinese propaganda project. The great detail of the accounts, the sincerity of the officers, the fact that they were freely going from camp to camp and did not look as if they were then or had previously been under any duress made it difficult for some men to believe that the accounts could be anything but true.

While it is difficult to determine how many men were convinced that the United

[9] The various problems that faced repatriates have been discussed by Segal, reference footnote 2, and by Robert J. Lifton in "Home by Ship: Reaction Patterns of American Prisoners of War Repatriated from North Korea," *Amer. J. Psychiatry* (1954) **110**:732–739.

Nations forces had used germ bombs, it is evident that serious doubts arose in the minds of many, and some admitted being still in doubt even some weeks after their repatriation. Unquestionably, personal testimonials were on the whole a far more effective propaganda weapon than any amount of direct lecturing, although they both played a part in the over-all indoctrination. In general, the older and more experienced prisoners were less susceptible to this kind of propaganda. One sergeant stated that the following kinds of reasons prevented him and others from falling for germ-warfare charges: first, germ bombs are tactically impractical and ineffective; second, the United States would probably not abandon its ethics, and germ bombs would not be consistent with those ethics; and third, even if the United States were to use weapons previously not considered ethical, it would use atom bombs in preference to germ bombs.

The Chinese also used Koreans to give testimonials concerning the barbarity of the United Nations; in one instance women and children told one of the peace committees how United Nations planes had dropped toys which exploded when children tried to pick them up. It is difficult to evaluate the effects of such propaganda, but it not likely that many prisoners believed stories of such extremity.

INDIRECT ATTACKS ON BELIEFS, ATTITUDES, AND VALUES   In the direct attacks which I have been discussing, the source of propaganda was external. In the indirect attacks, a set of conditions was created in which each prisoner of war was encouraged to participate in a way that would make it more possible for him to accept some of the new points of view. One attempt to accomplish this was by means of group discussions following lectures.

Most lectures ended with a series of conclusions—for example, "The South Koreans started the war by invading North Korea," or "The aim of the capitalist

nations is world domination." The men were then required to break up into squads, go to their quarters, and discuss the material for periods of two hours or more. At the end of the discussion each squad had to provide written answers to questions handed out during the lecture—the answers, obviously, which had already been provided in the lecture. To "discuss" the lecture thus meant, in effect, to rationalize the predetermined conclusions.[10]

A monitor was assigned to each squad to "aid" the men in the discussion, to make sure that they stayed on the proper topic, and to collect the answers and make sure that they were the "right" ones. Initially, the monitor for most squads was an English-speaking Chinese, but whenever possible the Chinese turned the job over to one of the squad members, usually the one who was most cooperative or sympathetic to the Communist point of view. If one or more members of the squad turned in "wrong" answers—for example, saying that the North Koreans had invaded South Korea—the entire squad had to listen to the lecture again and repeat the group discussion. This procedure might go on for days. The Chinese never tired of repeating the procedure over and over again, apparently believing that group discussion had a better chance of success in converting men to their point of view than individual indoctrination.

The success of such discussions often depended on the degree of supervision. If the monitor was lax, the groups would talk about anything but the required material. But a prisoner-of-war monitor who was actively pro-Communist or a Chinese who had a good understanding of English idiom might obtain considerable discussion. Even when an issue was actively discussed, in

[10] During the last year or so of imprisonment, many of the features of indoctrination which earlier had been compulsory were put on a voluntary basis. Any prisoners who were interested in learning more about communism could attend special lectures and group discussions. The men who participated in such voluntary programs were known as "self-study pro's" and were given many privileges not accorded to other prisoners.

many cases it probably reinforced the United Nations position by providing an opportunity for the men to obtain some consensual validation. But in other cases, the deliberation on points of view other than the one they had always held caused them to question certain beliefs and values which in the past had not led to satisfactory conditions for them.

A second means of indirect attack was interrogation. Interrogations were carried on during all stages of internment, but their apparent function and the techniques utilized varied from time to time. Almost all men went through lengthy and repetitive military interrogations, but failure to answer questions seldom led to severe physical punishment. Instead, various psychological pressures were applied. For instance, all information supplied was cross-checked against earlier interrogations and against the information from other men. If an answer did not tally with other information, the respondent had to explain the discrepancy. Continuous pressure to resolve contrary answers often forced a man to tell the truth.

The Chinese tried to create the impression that they could obtain *any* information from *anyone* by the following interrogation technique: If a man continued to refuse to answer a question, despite great fatigue and continued repetition of the question, the interrogator would suddenly pull out a notebook and point out to the man the complete answer to the question, sometimes in astonishingly accurate detail. The interrogation would then move on to a new topic and the same procedure would be repeated, until the man could not assess whether there was indeed *anything* that the Chinese did *not* know. In most cases the man was told that others had already given information or "confessed," so why should he hold back and suffer?[11]

A further technique was to have the man write out the question and then the answer. If he refused to write it voluntarily, he was asked to copy it from the notebooks, which must have seemed like a harmless enough concession. But the information which he had copied could then be shown to another man as evidence that he had given information of his own volition. Furthermore, it could be used to blackmail him, because he would have a hard time proving that he had merely copied the material.

Another type of interrogation to which almost all men were subjected involved primarily nonmilitary information. The Chinese were very curious about all aspects of life in the Western world and asked many questions about it, often in great detail. They also endeavored, by means of printed forms, to obtain a complete personal history from each prisoner, with particular emphasis on his social-cultural background, his class status, his and his parents' occupational histories, and so on. The purpose was apparently to determine which prisoners' histories might predispose them toward the Communist philosophy and thus make them apt subjects for special indoctrination.

Most men did not give accurate information. Usually the prisoner filled out the form in terms of fictitious characters. But later he would be required to repeat the entire procedure and would usually be unable to remember his earlier answers. He would then be confronted with the discrepancies and would be forced into the fatiguing activity of having to invent justification after justification to resolve them.

If and when the Chinese felt that they had obtained a relatively true account, it was used in discussion between the interrogator and the prisoner to undermine the prisoner's beliefs and values. Various points in the life history were used to show a man the "errors" of his past life—for example, that he or his parents had been ruthless capitalists exploiting workers, yet had really received only meager benefits

---

[11] Many men reported that they felt the Chinese were boasting when they told what they knew—that they were very proud of their ability as interrogators and felt a need to show off to their captors.

from such exploitation. The Chinese were particularly interested in any inconsistencies in the life histories and would focus discussion on them in order to bring to light the motivations involved. Whenever possible, any setbacks that a man had experienced economically or socially were searchingly analyzed, and the blame was laid on the capitalistic system.

The fact that many men were unclear about why they were fighting in Korea was a good lever for such discussions. The interrogator or instructor could point out the basic injustices of foreign intervention in a civil war, and simultaneously could arouse longings for home and the wish that the United Nations had never taken up the fight in the first place. It was not difficult to convince some men that being in Korea was unfair to the Koreans, to themselves, and to their families who wanted them home.

Interrogations might last for hours, days, or even weeks. In some cases the interrogator lived with his subject and tried to create an atmosphere of warmth and friendliness. The main point seemed to be to get the prisoner talking, no matter what he was talking about. The discussions sometimes became effective didactic sessions because of the friendly relationship which the interrogator built up. If there were any weaknesses or inconsistencies in a man's belief systems, once he lowered his guard and began to examine them critically, he was in danger of being overwhelmed by the arguments of the instructor. This did not, of course, occur typically. For many men such critical self-evaluation served as a reinforcement to their own beliefs and actually enabled them to expose weaknesses in the Communist arguments.

Another effective technique for getting the men to question their own beliefs and values was to make them confess publicly to wrongdoings and to "criticize" themselves. Throughout the time that the men

were in camp they were required to go through these rituals over and over again, no matter how trivial the offense. These offenses usually were infractions of camp rules. Soon after the men had arrived in permanent camp they were given copies of the camp rules and were required to sign a statement that they would abide by them. Most of the men were far too hungry and cold to read several pages of script covering every aspect of camp life in such minute detail that it was practically impossible not to break one of the rules from time to time. For example, an elaborate set of rules governed where in camp a man was allowed to expectorate.

Sooner or later a minor or major infraction of the rules would occur. The man would be immediately brought up before the camp commander, where his offense would be condemned as a serious crime—one for which he, the commander would point out, could be severely punished, if it were not for the lenient Chinese policy. In line with the great show which the Chinese made of treating the prisoner as a responsible person, the fact that he had agreed in writing to abide by the rules would be emphasized. The prisoner could not now say that he had not read the rules, for this would expose him to further embarrassment. The camp commander would then ask whether the man would admit that he had broken the rule, whether he was sorry that he had done so, and whether he would promise not to behave in such a "criminal" manner in the future. If the offender agreed, which seemed at the time to be harmless enough and an easy way to get off, he would be asked to write out a confession.

Sometimes this ended the matter. But frequently the man was required to read his confession to a group of prisoners and to follow it by "self-criticism," which meant that the description of the wrong deed had to be analyzed in terms of the wrong *idea* that lay behind it, that the self had to be "deeply and sincerely" criticized in terms of a number of reasons why the idea and deed were "wrong," and that an elaborate set of promises about future conduct had to be made, along with apologies for the past. Such public self-effacement was a humiliating and degrading experience, and it set a bad precedent for other men who had been attempting to resist getting caught in this net.

Writing out confessions, reading them, and criticizing oneself for minor misconduct in camp did not seem too great a concession at first when viewed against the possibility of physical punishment, torture, or imprisonment. However, these techniques could become a psychological torture once the initial concession had been made. A man who had broken a rule and had gone through the whole ritual of criticism would shortly afterward break another rule, which would arouse increased hostility on the part of the Chinese and lead to correspondingly greater demands for confession and self-criticism. Men who had confessed at first to trivial offenses soon found themselves having to answer for relatively major ones.[12]

It should be pointed out, however, that the prisoners found numerous ways to obey the letter but not the spirit of the Chinese demands. For example, during public self-criticism sessions they would often emphasize the wrong words in the sentence, thus making the whole ritual ridiculous: "I am sorry I called Comrade Wong *a no-good son-of-a-bitch.*" Another favorite device was to promise never to "get caught" committing a certain crime in the future. Such devices were effective because even those Chinese who knew En-

glish were not sufficiently acquainted with idiom and slang to detect subtle ridicule.

There is also some evidence that the Chinese used enforced idleness or solitary confinement to encourage prisoners to consider the Communist point of view. One of the few activities available, in such circumstances, was to read Communist literature and books by Western authors who directly or indirectly attacked capitalism. The camp libraries were wholly made up of such literature. Those who did not have the strength or inclination to go on physically taxing details found themselves with no alternative but to spend their time reading pro-Communist material. In addition, some read because they felt so emotionally isolated from other prisoners that they could enjoy only solitary activities.

THE ELICITING OF COLLABORATION BY REWARDS AND PUNISHMENTS   For a number of propaganda purposes the Chinese seemed to want certain men to cooperate in specific ways, without caring whether they accepted communism or not. These men did not seem to enjoy as much status as other pro's and were cast off by the Chinese as soon as they had ceased to be useful. Such collaboration was elicited directly by a system of rewards and incentives on the one hand, and threats and punishments on the other.

While it is dangerous to relate complex human behavior to a simple pattern of rewards and punishments, the repatriates' accounts of life in the prisoner-of-war camps make possible a considerable number of inferences concerning the 'positive' and 'negative' aspects of the social environment, which were important in eliciting the kind of behavior the Chinese wanted. It was made clear to all prisoners, from the time of their capture on, that cooperation with the Chinese would produce a more comfortable state of affairs, while noncooperation or open resistance would produce a continuing marginal existence.

---

[12] It can be seen that such a technique of "training" a man to confess can ultimately lead to the demand that he confess not only to misdeeds and the "wrong" ideas which lay behind them, but also to "wrong" thoughts and feelings which had not even resulted in action. In conjunction with public self-appraisal, prisoners were also often encouraged to keep diaries of their activities and thoughts. Usually only those prisoners who seriously studied Communism kept diaries.

Which rewards were of primary importance to the men varied with their current condition. On the marches and in the temporary camps physical conditions were so bad that more food, any medication, any clothing or fuel, better and less crowded living conditions, and the like constituted a powerful reward. Promises of early repatriation, or at least of marked improvement of conditions in the permanent camps, were powerful incentives which were chronically exploited.

In the permanent camps there was some improvement in the physical conditions, so that basic necessities became less effective incentives. The promise of early repatriation continued to be a great incentive, however, despite the fact that it had been promised many times before without result. Communicating with the outside world now became a major concern. To let those at home know they were alive, some prisoners began to collaborate by making slanted radio broadcasts or filling their letters with propaganda or peace appeals in order to make sure that they were sent.

As conditions continued to improve, some of the luxury items and smaller accessories to living assumed greater significance. Cigarettes, combs, soap, candy, small items of clothing, a cup of hot tea, a drink of liquor, fresh fruit, and other items of this kind were sought avidly by some men.[13] Obtaining such items from the Chinese was inextricably linked with the degree to which the prisoner was willing to "cooperate." Any tendency toward "cooperation" was quickly followed by an increase in material rewards and promises for the future.

In some cases rewards were cleverly linked with participation in the indoctrination. For example, highly valued prizes

such as cigarettes or fresh fruit were offered for essays dealing with certain aspects of world politics. The winning entries were published in the camp newspaper or magazine. Usually the winning entry was selected on the basis of its agreement with a Communist point of view and the winner was usually someone well on the road to collaboration anyway, but the whole competition succeeded in getting the men to participate—to consider the various sides of an issue and to examine their previous views critically.

The Chinese also used rewards and punishments to undermine group organization. For example, shortly after capture, a number of men were led to believe that if they made radio broadcasts to the United Nations lines they would be repatriated early. The content of the broadcasts was not specified, but the men agreed to make them in the hope of letting their relatives know that they were alive. These men were then conspicuously assembled in front of other prisoners and were taken to a special location some distance away, where the broadcasts were to be made. In the meantime, other prisoners were encouraged to believe that these men were obtaining special privileges because they were "cooperating" in bringing "peace" to Korea.

The actual content of the radio messages turned out to be a peace appeal which tacitly condemned the United Nations, and a statement that the prisoners were being well treated by the Chinese. When the men saw the messages that they were to read, some of them refused to make the broadcast, despite threats of severe punishment. Other men agreed to make the broadcast but tried to code a message into the prescribed text, and still others hoped that the recipients of the broadcasts would somehow know that they were under duress. At least their families would know that they were alive if they broadcasted something.

---

[13] A number of men reported that black-market activities flourished among the prisoners. Those items of value which men did not wish to use themselves were bartered or sold to other men. Even valuable medicines could sometimes be obtained only by bartering with pro's who had obtained them from the Chinese.

When these men rejoined the other prisoners, they found that they had aroused the suspicion and hostility of many, especially since the Chinese showed their "appreciation" by ostentatiously bestowing favors on them. In order to retain these special privileges—and having in any case incurred the hostility or even ostracism of their own group—some of these men continued to broadcast, rationalizing that they were not really harming the United Nations cause. They became self-appointed secret agents and attempted to infiltrate the Chinese hierarchy to gather "intelligence information," in which capacity they felt that they could actually aid the United Nations cause.

Among the most effective rewards used by the Chinese were special privileges and certain symbolic rewards, such as rank and status in the prison hierarchy. Perhaps the most important of the privileges was freedom of movement; the pro's had free access to the Chinese headquarters and could go into town or wherever they wished at any time of the day or night. They were given certain preferred jobs, such as writing for the camp newspaper, and were excused from the more unpleasant chores around the camp. They were often consulted by the Chinese in various policy matters. They received as a status symbol a little peace dove to be worn in the lapel or a Mao Tse-tung button which served as an identification badge. And many rewards were promised them for the future; they were told that they were playing a vital role in the world-wide movement for "peace," and that they could enjoy positions of high rank in this movement if they stayed and continued to work for it.

If one asks why men "fell" for this kind of line—why they were able to believe this kind of promise—one must look to the circumstances described earlier. These men had no sources of contrary information to rely on, and once they had collaborated even a little they were ostracized by their buddies, thus losing the support of the group which might have kept them from collaborating further.

Just as the probability of collaborative behavior could be increased through the use of rewards, the probability of resistance could be decreased through negative or painful stimulation. Usually threats of punishment were used when prisoners refused to "cooperate," and actual punishment was meted out for more aggressive resistance. Threats of death, nonrepatriation, torture, reprisals against families, reduction in food and medication, and imprisonment were all used. While the only one of these threats which was carried out with any degree of consistency was imprisonment, which sometimes involved long periods of solitary confinement, the other threats were nevertheless very effective and the possibility that they might be carried out seemed very real. Especially frightening was the prospect of nonrepatriation, which seemed a likely possibility before the prisoner lists were exchanged at Panmunjom. The threat of death was also effective, for the men knew that they could be killed and listed officially as having died of heart failure or the like.[14] With regard to food and medication, the men could not determine whether they were actually being punished by having these withheld, or whether the meager supply was merely being reserved for "deserving" prisoners.

An effective threat with officers was that of punishing the whole group for which the officer was responsible if he personally did not "cooperate." The incidence of such group punishment was not revealed in the accounts, but it is clear that if an officer did "cooperate" with the Chinese, he was able both to relieve his own fears and to

---

[14] There is evidence that the Chinese sometimes staged "executions" in order to elicit cooperation. A prisoner might be marched out into a field, an empty gun placed to his head, and the trigger actually pulled. This procedure first created a state of high anxiety and then a state of grateful relief when it was discovered by the prisoner that he would not be executed after all.

rationalize his cooperation as being the only means of saving the men for whom he was responsible.

Reinforcing all these threats was the vague but powerful fear of the unknown; the men did not know what they were up against in dealing with the Chinese and could not predict the reactions of their captors with any degree of reliability. The only course that led to a consistent reduction in such tension was participation in Chinese enterprises.

Overt punishment varied with the offense, with the political situation, and with the person administering it. Shortly after capture there were numerous incidents of brutality, most of them committed by North Koreans. During early interrogations the Chinese frequently resorted to minor physical punishment such as face-slapping or kicking when answers were not forthcoming, but a prisoner who continued to be silent was usually dismissed without further physical punishment.

Physical punishments in permanent camps had the effect of weakening rather than injuring the men. They varied from severe work details to such ordeals as standing at attention for long periods; being exposed to bright lights or excessive cold; standing on tiptoe with a noose around the neck; being confined in the "cage," a room too small to allow standing, sitting, or lying down; being thrown in the "hole," a particularly uncomfortable form of solitary confinement; or being kept in filthy surroundings and denied certain essentials for keeping clean. Those who were *chronically* uncooperative were permanently segregated from the rest of the group and put into special camps where more severe forms of discipline backed by harsher punishments were in effect. Basically, the "lenient policy" applied only to those men whom the Chinese hoped they could use.

More common forms of punishment for minor infractions were social in character,

intended to degrade or embarrass the prisoner in front of his fellows. Public confessions and self-criticisms were the outstanding forms of such punishment, with blackmail being frequently used if a prisoner had once collaborated to any extent. There is *no* evidence that the Chinese used any drugs or hypnotic methods, or offered sexual objects to elicit information, confessions, or collaborative behavior. Some cases of severe physical torture were reported, but their incidence is difficult to estimate.

GENERAL PRINCIPLES IN ALL TECHNIQUES
Several general principles underlay the various phases of the Chinese indoctrination, which may be worth summing up at this point. The first of these was *repetition*. One of the chief characteristics of the Chinese was their immense patience in whatever they were doing; whether they were conducting interrogation, giving a lecture, chiding a prisoner, or trying to obtain a confession, they were always willing to make their demand or assertion over and over again. Many men pointed out that most of the techniques used gained their effectiveness by being used in this repetitive way until the prisoner could no longer sustain his resistance. A second characteristic was the *pacing of demands*. In the various kinds of responses that were demanded of the prisoners, the Chinese always started with trivial, innocuous ones and, as the habit of responding became established, gradually worked up to more important ones. Thus after a prisoner had once been "trained" to speak or write out trivia, statements on more important issues were demanded of him. This was particularly effective in eliciting confessions, self-criticism, and information during interrogation.

Closely connected with the principle of pacing was the principle of constant *participation* from the prisoner. It was never enough for the prisoner to listen and absorb; some kind of verbal or written response was always demanded. Thus if a man would not give original material in question-and-answer sessions, he was asked to copy something. Likewise, group discussions, autobiographical statements, self-criticisms, and public confessions all demanded an active participation by the prisoner.[15]

In their propaganda campaign the Chinese made a considerable effort *to insert their new ideas into old and meaningful contexts.* In general this was not very successful, but it did work for certain prisoners who were in some way not content with their lot in the United States. The obtaining of autobiographies enabled each interrogator to determine what would be a significant context for the particular person he was dealing with, and any misfortune or setback that the person had suffered served as an ideal starting place for undermining democratic attitudes and instilling communistic ones.

No matter which technique the Chinese were using, they always structured the situation in such a way that the correct response was followed by some form of *reward,* while an incorrect response was immediately followed by *threats* or *punishment.* The fact that the Chinese had complete control over material resources and had a monopoly of power made it possible for them to manipulate hunger and some other motives at will, thereby giving rewards and punishments their meaning.

Among the various propaganda techniques employed by the Chinese, their use of *prestige suggestion* was outstanding. The average prisoner had no way of disputing the germ-warfare confessions and testimonials of Air Force officers, or the conclusions of an investigation of the germ-warfare charges by ostensibly impartial scientists from many nations.

Among the positive propaganda appeals made, the most effective was probably the *plea for peace.* The Chinese presented an antiwar and laissez-faire ideology which strongly appealed to the war-weary combat soldier.

In addition, the Chinese used a number of *manipulative tricks,* which were usually successful only if the prisoner was not alert because of fatigue or hunger. One such trick was to require signatures, photographs, or personal information for a purpose which sounded legitimate, then using them for another purpose. Some prisoners reported that they were asked to sign "camp rosters" when they first arrived in camp and later found that they had actually signed a peace petition.

In essence, the prisoner-of-war experience in camp can be viewed as a series of problems which each man had to solve in order to remain alive and well integrated. Foremost was the problem of physical privation, which powerfully motivated each man to improve his living conditions. A second problem was to overcome the fears of nonrepatriation, death, torture, or reprisals. A third problem was to maintain some kind of cognitive integration, a consistent outlook on life, under a set of conditions where basic values and beliefs were strongly undermined and where systematic confusion about each man's role in life was created. A fourth problem was to maintain a valid position in a group, to maintain friendship ties and concern for others under conditions of mutual distrust, lack of leadership, and systematically created social disorganization. The Chinese had created a set of conditions in which col-

[15] The Chinese apparently believed that if they could once get a man to participate he was likely to continue, and that eventually he would accept the attitudes which the participation expressed. However, it may have also been true that the interrogators, for instance, were in danger of losing face with their own group if they could not produce concrete evidence that they had obtained some information; at times they seemed to want any kind of answers, so long as they had something to show to headquarters as proof that they had done their job. Similarly, the material obtained at the end of the group discussions was perhaps used as evidence that the instructors were doing their jobs properly. Thus it is possible that part of the aim was a check by the Chinese on each other.

laboration and the acceptance of communism led to a resolution of conflicts in all these areas.

Reactions to the indoctrination

It is very difficult to determine after the fact what happened in his highly complex and novel situation—what it was really like for the men who had to spend several years in the Chinese prisoner-of-war camps. Each set of experiences had a highly personal and unique flavor to it, making generalized conclusions difficult.

I may illustrate the problem by discussing *ideological change* and *collaboration*. Both of these were responses to the indoctrination, broadly conceived, *but neither necessarily implies the other*. It was possible for a man to collaborate with the enemy without altering his beliefs, and it was equally possible for a man to be converted to communism to some degree without collaborating.

Obviously, it is necessary to define these responses, even though any precise definition will to some degree distort the actual events. *Collaboration* may be defined as any kind of behavior which helped the enemy: signing peace petitions, soliciting signatures for peace petitions, making radio appeals, writing radio scripts, writing false information home concerning conditions in the camps (or recording statements to this effect), writing essays on communism or working for the Communist-controlled newspaper, allowing oneself to be photographed in "rigged" situations, participating in peace rallies or on peace committees, being friendly with the enemy, asking others to cooperate with the enemy, running errands for the enemy, accepting special privileges or favors, making false confessions or pro-enemy speeches, informing on fellow prisoners, divulging military information, and so on.

Nothing about ideological conversion is implied in this definition. A man who engaged in any of these collaborative behaviors because he wanted an extra cigarette was just as much a collaborator as one who did so because he wanted to further the Communist cause. Moreover, the definition does not take into account the temporal pattern of such behavior. Many men collaborated at one time during their imprisonment when one set of conditions existed, but did not collaborate at other times under other conditions. The man who moved from collaboration to resistance was obviously different from the man who moved from resistance to collaboration. Perhaps most important of all, this definition says nothing about the particular pattern of motivations or circumstances that drove a man to the first collaborative act and subsequently into a situation in which it was difficult to stop collaborating.

Yet such a concept of collaboration has an advantage in its reference to *overt* behavior. It was such behavior which the other men in camp reacted to and which often formed the basis for later judgments of a man by his government, family, and friends, although different motives were often imputed by different sources for such behavior. The motives that lay behind the behavior are of obvious importance and must be understood, but it should also be recognized that conjectures of motives are more precarious than analyses of behavior.

Ideological change may be defined as a reorganization of political beliefs, which could vary from acquiring mild doubts concerning some aspects of the democratic ideology to the complete abandonment of this ideology and a total embracing of communism. The latter I shall label *conversion*. The problem of measuring the degree of ideological change is complicated by the lack of good behavioral criteria for measuring such a process of reorganization of beliefs. One might be tempted to say that anyone could be termed a convert who actively attempted to convince others of the worth of communism, who took all the advanced courses in camp, and who was able to demonstrate in his overt behavior a disregard for democratic values. But such behavior might also characterize a relatively intelligent man who had begun to read Communist literature out of boredom, only to find that both his friends and the Chinese took this as evidence of his genuine interest in communism. He might then be ostracized by his friends and pressed into collaboration by the Chinese, who, it was rumored, severely punished anyone who deceived them.

Of all the prisoners, 21 refused repatriation; one might assume that these represent the total number of converts, but such a criterion is inadequate on at least two grounds. On the one hand, some converts would undoubtedly have been sent back to the United States to spread Communism and form a potential fifth column. On the other hand, some collaborators who had not changed ideologically might have been afraid to return, knowing that court-martial proceedings and personal degradation probably awaited them.

One might think that the identification of such men could be made successfully by others who were collaborators and possibly converts. However, anyone who had been and remained a convert would *not* identify other converts. On the other hand, a collaborator who had repudiated communism and his own collaborative activities would be likely to implicate as many others as possible in order to make his own behavior look better. Allegations from known collaborators are therefore very unreliable.

Thus it is more difficult to determine how the prisoners responded to indoctrination techniques ideologically than it is to determine what overt collaboration occurred. What the prisoners *did* is, relatively speaking, a matter of fact; why they did it is a matter of conjecture. In presenting a classification of types of reactions and the motivation patterns or situations that elicited them, one must rely primarily on the *consensus* of the accounts of the

repatriates and must recognize the possible biases that can arise in such an analysis after the fact. I am not implying that each prisoner could be placed into one of the categories to be presented below; it is more likely that each man fell into several categories at any given time, and, moreover, that his motivation-situation complex shifted as different sets of circumstances presented themselves.

THE "GET-ALONGERS" The predominant reaction of prisoners was to establish a complex compromise between the demands of the Chinese and the demands of their own ideology. This kind of behavior was labeled "playing it cool" by the men, and consisted primarily in a physical and emotional withdrawal from all situations which might arouse basic conflict. Men who reacted in this way were unwilling to do anything that did not have to be done, and learned after some months to 'suspend' their feelings about most events, no matter how provoking they might be. This was not an easy adjustment to maintain, since the prisoner had to make some concessions to the Chinese to avoid the more severe physical or psychological pressures, at the same time avoiding cooperating to such an extent as to arouse the suspicion and hostility of his fellow prisoners. The safest course was to withdraw emotionally both from the Chinese and from the rest of the prisoner group; this withdrawal was made easier by the apathy and physical weakness induced by life under marginal conditions.[16]

Most of the men who achieved this kind of compromise successfully without too

---

[16] For Puerto Ricans and other foreign nationals whose knowledge of English was very shaky, the problem was easily solved. These men conveniently forgot what little English they knew, and, because the Chinese did not have instructors who could speak their languages, they were permitted to withdraw to a relatively comfortable existence of doing details or routine chores. A few others successfully convinced the Chinese that they were illiterate or in some other way incapacitated for study. Some men resolved the conflict by volunteering for all the heavy or unpleasant details, but obviously such a solution was available only to the physically strong and healthy.

great a toll on their personality were well integrated and retained secure and stable group identifications from before their prisoner-of-war experience. Their judgment concerning the extent to which they could collaborate safely had to be relatively unimpaired, and they had to be able to evaluate objectively and dispassionately threats made by the Chinese.

At the beginning, while the noncommissioned officers were still in the enlisted camps, many of them were able—partly because of their strong identification with the Army, and partly because of their wider experience—to help the other men carry out such a compromise solution. In many situations they were able to give advice that appears to have been sound from all points of view; thus they would help the other men compose answers to questions that would be sufficiently pro-Communist to satisfy the Chinese but not extreme enough to arouse the suspicion of other prisoners or to be called treasonable. They would also advise the other men on the wisdom of cooperating in the lectures, of trying to escape, and so on.

THE RESISTERS A number of men developed chronic resistance as their main mode of behavior in camp, refusing to go along with even the most trivial of Chinese requests. This lack of cooperation varied from passive resistance to active, organized obstructionism. Such men were a great trial to the Chinese, who labeled them "reactionaries" and either imprisoned them, if they felt they had some justification, or segregated them in special camps. According to the dynamics involved, these men seem to have fallen into four somewhat separate classes.

The obstructionist. These men were characterized by a life-long pattern of indiscriminate resistance to all forms of authority,[17] and had histories of inability to get along in the United Nations Army just

as they were unable to get along with the Chinese. They openly defied any attempt to get them to conform, and performed deeds which other prisoners considered heroic, such as withstanding severe torture. Usually these men spent a major part of their internment in the camp prison, in solitary confinement, or in the "hole."

The idealist or martyr. These men had unusually powerful identifications with groups whose ideology demanded that they actively resist all forms of pressure from the Chinese. The best example would be the man who was deeply religious and whose faith demanded absolute noncooperation with a "Godless enterprise" of the type the Chinese represented.

The anxious guilt-ridden person. This was the man who was afraid of his own inclination to be tempted by the positive rewards that the Chinese offered for collaboration, and who could handle these impulses only by denying them and overreacting in the other direction. He was chronically guilt-ridden over his unpatriotic and antisocial impulses and absolved himself by indulging in exaggerated forms of resistance.

The well-integrated resistance leader. Probably the majority of resisters fell into this class, although there is no way to estimate their number. Because of extensive experience in difficult situations and a thorough understanding of the military, they were able systematically to organize other men and to set important precedents for resistance. Most of the commissioned and noncommissioned officers fell into this group.[18] The chief characteristic of these men seemed to be their ability to make valid judgments concerning possible courses of action in a situation in which there was little information on which to

---

[17] This pattern has been well described by Lifton, reference footnote 9.

[18] I have already mentioned the role of noncommissioned officers in helping the "get-alongers" to maintain a compromise role; my mention of them here is an illustration of the fact that this is not a classification of the men, as such, but a classification of behavior. Thus, just as the noncommissioned officers displayed leadership in many instances in compromise, so they also functioned as resistance leaders whenever possible.

base such judgments. They had to be able to guess what Chinese reactions would be, what United Nations reactions would be, and most important, how to handle the other prisoners.

THE COOPERATORS   This group is the most difficult to delineate, since I am attempting to include not only those whom the Chinese considered progressives but all those who collaborated to any significant extent. The accounts of prisoners concerning men who collaborated make possible the discrimination of six somewhat separate patterns of motivation for such behaviors.

The weakling.   This was the man who was chronically unable to resist any form of authority, and who was unable to withstand any degree of physical or psychological discomfort. Such men probably became collaborators very soon after their internment, with a minimum of ideological involvement, because it was the easiest way. They often found that the more they collaborated, the more collaboration was demanded of them. They were highly susceptible to threats of blackmail by the Chinese, who could exhibit the evidence of their collaboration to the other prisoners or the United Nations authorities. From the point of view of these men, collaboration was an acceptable adjustment under the physical strains of internment, and they developed elaborate rationalizations to justify their behavior and to convince themselves that they would not suffer for it in the future.

The opportunist.   These men exploited the role of pro for all its material benefits, again without any ideological involvement, and with little consideration for the future welfare of themselves or others. They were characterized chiefly by their lack of stable group identifications either inside or outside the Army. They met all situations as they arose and tried to make the most out of them for themselves.

The misguided leader.   A minority of commissioned and noncommissioned offi-

cers engaged in various types of collaborative activities under the firm impression that they were furthering the United Nations cause and resisting the enemy: Their primary error was one of judgment. They reasoned that the best way to resist indoctrination was to go along with it, to find out what the Chinese were up to, to get into the inner circle so as to better plan resistance. In most cases, they managed merely to set a bad precedent for other prisoners, who felt that if their superiors were getting special privileges they should be getting them as well. These officers, like others, found that once they had begun to collaborate it was difficult to stop. Some of these men were probably weakling types who personally preferred the path of least resistance, but who, because of their responsible positions, had to develop adequate rationalizations. They could not see that their course of action was highly inappropriate; they saw only a justification which met their own needs.

The bored or curious intellectual.   Of the very small number of men who had superior education, some turned to Communist literature out of boredom or curiosity, and then found that they had aroused both the hostility of their own group and the expectations of the Chinese that they would collaborate. Only a few managed to interest themselves in the Communist literature without falling into this dilemma. More often, material rewards for the intellectual's interest resulted in his ostracism from his own group, and drove him in the direction of collaboration. Some of these men were fooled by the promise of early repatriation in return for collaboration, and they felt that their collaboration would be sufficiently minor not to damage their own futures. These men, like those previously described, seldom became ideologically confused or converted. Essentially they used bad judgment in an ambiguous situation.

The 'low-status' person.   The man who was most vulnerable *ideologically* was one who had never enjoyed any kind of secure or rewarding status position either in his home community or in the Army. This type included the younger and less intelligent, the malcontent, and the man whose social reference groups made the attainment of status difficult—that is, the member of various racial, religious, national, or economic minority groups. These men had little realization of the benefits of democracy because they had never experienced them in a meaningful way. They felt that the society was more to blame for their failures than they were. Such men were ready to give serious consideration to an ideology that offered remedies for their misfortunes. As pro's within the Communist hierarchy they could, for the first time, enjoy some measure of status and privilege, and the Chinese wisely promised them important roles in the future of the "peace movement." Some of these men were probably among those who declined repatriation—perhaps out of fear, when they realized how seriously they had jeopardized their position in the Army and at home, perhaps in order to stay with the cause which had for the first time allowed them to be important. It is difficult to determine whether such men underwent a complete ideological conversion, but there is no doubt that they gave serious consideration to the Communist cause, at least to the limit of their intellectual capacity.[19]

The accounts of the repatriates were unclear regarding the reactions of members of the various minority groups, especially the Negroes. The Communist technique of segregating the Negroes and giving them special indoctrination was probably

a tactical error. Many Negroes felt that if they were going to be segregated they might as well be segregated in the United States—that there was nothing new or better about communism in this respect. Moreover, the propaganda given them was too extreme; even the very low-status Negro knew that his circumstances in the United States was not as bad as the Communists painted them.

However, because of the low-status category of most of the Negroes, the positive appeals made to them must have struck responsive chords in some. They had an opportunity to be leaders and to enjoy fully equal status if they became pro's, and they could rationalize that they would be able to improve the position of their race by participating in Communist peace movements which advocated equality. It is not possible to determine to what extent these positive appeals outweighed the deterrents, and thus to estimate the degree to which ideological change occurred among the Negroes. In any case, the Chinese probably could have persuaded more Negroes to collaborate and to embrace communism had they not made the fundamental errors of segregation and poor propaganda.

The Communist sympathizer. This was the man who, even before he had joined the Army, was sympathetic to the Communist cause and who, therefore, felt no conflict about his course of action in the prisoner-of-war camp. However, if there were loyal Communists in the camps, it is unlikely that the Chinese divulged their identity by calling them pro's, since they would be of far more use as undercover agents.

ATTITUDES TOWARD PROGRESSIVES The reaction of most men toward the pro's was one of perplexity, fear, and hostility. They could not understand how anyone could "swallow the junk" the Chinese were presenting, yet they were afraid that they too

---

[19] The men who were most vulnerable to ideological appeals were not necessarily the ones the Chinese encouraged to become pro's. There is considerable evidence that the Chinese were quite selective in giving important jobs to prisoners and that they favored more mature and stable ones. Thus the younger, less intelligent, and less stable person was exploited by the Chinese in the same manner as he had probably been exploited before. The Chinese made what use they could of such men and then rejected them when they ceased to be useful.

might be swayed, for among the pro's were many men like themselves. If the pro was a "weak-minded guy" or a man who did not have the stamina to resist the physical pressures, other men felt some sympathy for him, but at the same time they resented the extra privileges that his weakness gained for him. If the pro was perceived to be an opportunist, he was hated and threatened with retaliation during internment or following repatriation. If the pro was a person who had status or rank, the men felt perplexed and afraid; they could not decide what they themselves should do, especially if such a pro tried to convince them that it was acceptable to collaborate.

The pro's were very conspicuous in camp by their identification symbols, by their special privileges—which they did not hesitate to flaunt—and by the fact that they usually congregated around camp headquarters. This made them ideal scapegoats and targets for hostility.

They were ostracized by the other prisoners who often refused even to carry on conversations with each other when a pro was present, forcing the pro's into interaction with each other. Thus they tended to form tightly knit groups, which continued even after the end of their internment. The men accused the pro's of informing, imputed to them many motives about which they themselves felt guilty, and attributed any punishment they suffered to some report by a pro. They threatened the pro's with physical violence, but were usually prevented by the Chinese from carrying out such threats. Later, on board ship, the men frequently said that they would now "get even," but the low rate of incidents suggests that no realistic plans underlay the threats. Perhaps most men felt too guilty about their own actual or fantasied collaboration to be comfortable about retaliating against those who had succumbed to the temptations.

The attitudes of the pro's varied with their motivations. Those who had been tricked or "seduced" into collaborating before they could fully realize the consequences remained aloof from other prisoners because they felt guilty and afraid. The opportunists or low-status prisoners felt their collaboration to be entirely justified by the prison-camp situation and viewed noncollaborators as "fools who don't know a good thing when they see it." They tried to persuade others to collaborate—in some cases because they sincerely believed part of the Chinese propaganda, and in other cases because they knew that the Chinese would reward them still further if they succeeded. Many pro's tried hard to remain liked both by the Chinese and by the other prisoners, but few succeeded. Since the Chinese presented themselves as benevolent captors, the pro's were the only group in camp who could consistently be used as an outlet for all the hostility engendered by the prison-camp situation.

The effectiveness of the indoctrination techniques

By disrupting social organization and by the systematic use of reward and punishment, the Chinese were able to elicit a considerable amount of collaboration. This is not surprising when one considers the tremendous effort the Chinese made to discover the weak points in individual prisoners, and the unscrupulousness with which they manipulated the environment. Only a few men were able to avoid collaboration altogether—those who adopted a completely negativistic position from the moment of capture without considering the consequences for themselves or their fellow prisoners. At the same time the number of men who collaborated to a sufficient extent to be detrimental to the United Nations cause was also very small. The majority collaborated at one time or another by doing things which seemed to them trivial, but which the Chinese were able to turn to their own advantage. Such behavior did not necessarily reflect any defection from democratic values or ideology, nor did it necessarily imply that these men were opportunists or neurotics. Often it merely represented poor judgment in evaluating a situation about which they had little information, and poor foresight regarding the reactions of the Chinese, other prisoners, and people back home.

The extent to which the Chinese succeeded in converting prisoners of war to the Communist ideology is difficult to evaluate because of the previously mentioned hazards in measuring ideological change, and because of the impossibility of determining the *latent* effects of the indoctrination. In terms of *overt* criteria of conversion or ideological change, one can only conclude that, considering the effort devoted to it, the Chinese program was a failure. Only a small number of men decided to refuse repatriation—possibly for reasons other than ideological change[20]— and it was the almost unanimous opinion of the prisoners that most of the pro's were opportunists or weaklings. One can only conjecture, of course, the extent to which prisoners who began to believe in communism managed to conceal their sympathies from their fellows and the degree to which repatriates are now, as a result of their experience, predisposed to find fault with a democratic society if they cannot make a go of it.

It is difficult to determine whether to attribute this relative failure of the Chinese program to the inadequacy of their principles of indoctrination, to their technical inefficiency in running the program, or to both these factors. In actual practice the direct techniques used were usually ineffective because many of the Chinese

instructors were deficient in their knowledge of Western culture and the English language. Many of their facts about America were false, making it impossible for them to obtain a sympathetic audience, and many of their attempts to teach by means of group discussion failed because they were not sensitive to the subtle ways in which prisoners managed to ridicule them by sarcasm or other language devices. The various intensive pressures brought to bear on single prisoners and the fostering of close personal relationships between prisoner and instructor were far more effective in producing ideological change, but the Chinese did not have nearly enough trained personnel to indoctrinate more than a handful of men in this intensive manner.

The technique of breaking up both formal and spontaneous organization was effective in creating feelings of social and emotional isolation, but it was never sufficiently extended to make the prisoners completely dependent on the Chinese. As long as the men lived and "studied" together, there remained opportunities for consensual validation and thus for resisting indoctrination. However, as a means of social control this technique was highly effective, in that it was virtually impossible for the prisoners to develop any program of organized resistance or to engineer successful communication with the outside by means of escapes or clandestine sending out of information.

The most powerful argument against the intellectual appeal of communism was the low standard of living which the men observed in the Korean villages in which they lived. The repatriates reported that they were unable to believe in a system of values whch sounded attractive on paper but which was not practiced, and they were not impressed by the excuse that such conditions were only temporary.

Most men returned from prison camp expressing a strong anti-Communist feeling and a conviction that their eyes had,

---

[20] A discussion of some background factors in the lives of these men is presented by Virginia Pasley in *21 Stayed*; New York, Farrar, Strauss & Cudahy, 1955. Unfortunately her study is inconclusive because she did not investigate the background factors in a control group of men who decided to be repatriated.

for the first time, been opened to the real dangers of communism. Many men who had taken little interest in politics before returned with the feeling that they now knew what the United States was fighting for in Korea, and expressed a willingness to continue the fight wherever necessary. Hostility toward the Communists was expressed in such violent proposals as blowing up the *Daily Worker* building or deporting all registered Communists to Korea so that they could see the system in operation firsthand. The repatriates' attitude implied that anything labeled "Communist" had to be destroyed, and anything or anyone against communism had to be supported to the greatest possible extent; types of communism or types of approaches in dealing with communism were not evaluated separately.

It was, of course, difficult to determine the strength and stability of sentiments expressed a few days or weeks after repatriation. In some men these feelings undoubtedly represented an attempt to overcome the guilt that they felt for having collaborated or wavered in their beliefs. In other men they represented simply the accumulated hostility of two to three years of unrelieved frustration and deprivation. But, curiously, this hostility was seldom verbalized against the Chinese as such; it was always the Communists or the pro's who were the targets. The men were confused about the Chinese because they were so inconsistent; they never felt that they could understand or predict the Chinese reaction to anything.

In summary, it can be said that the Chinese were successful in eliciting and controlling certain kinds of behavior in the prisoner population. They were less successful in changing the beliefs of the prisoners. Yet this lack of success might have been due to the inefficiency of a program of indoctrination which could have been highly effective had it been better supported by adequate information and adequately trained personnel.

Collaboration with the enemy occurs to a greater or lesser extent in any captive population. It occurred in the Japanese and German prisoner-of-war camps during World War II. But never before have captured American soldiers faced a *systematic effort* to make them collaborate and to convert them to an alien political ideology. The only precedent in recent history was the handling of political prisoners by the Nazis, described by Bettelheim.[21] By means of extreme and degrading physical and psychological torture the Nazis attempted to reduce the prison population to an "infantile" state in which the jailer would be viewed with the same awe as the child views his father. Under these conditions, the prisoners tended, in time, to identify with the punitive authority figures and to incorporate many of the values they held, especially with respect to proper behavior in camp. They would curry the favor of the guards, would imitate their style of dress and speech, and would attempt to make other prisoners follow camp rules strictly.

It is possible that such a mechanism also operated in the Chinese prison camps. However, the Nazis attempted, by brutal measures, to reduce their prisoners to docile slave laborers, while the Chinese attempted, by using a "lenient policy" and by treating the prisoners as men in need of "education," to obtain converts who would actively support the Communist point of view. Only those prisoners who showed themselves to be "backward" or "reactionary" by their inability to see the fundamental "truths" of communism were treated punitively.

The essence of this novel approach is to gain complete control over those parts of the physical and social environment which sustain attitudes, beliefs, and values, breaking down interactions and emotional bonds which support the old beliefs and

[21] Bruno Bettelheim, "Individual and Mass Behavior in Extreme Situations," *J. abnormal and social Psychol.* (1943) 38:417–452.

values, and building up new interactions which will increase the probability of the adoption of new beliefs and values. If the only contacts a person is permitted are with persons who *unanimously* have beliefs different from his own, it is very likely that he will find at least some among them with whom, because of growing emotional bonds, he will identify and whose beliefs he will subsequently adopt.

Is the eliciting of collaborative behavior in itself sufficient to initiate the process of ideological change? One might assume that a person who had committed acts consonant with a new ideology might be forced to adopt this ideology in order to rationalize his behavior. This might happen especially if the number of possible rationalizations were limited. The situation in the prison camps, however, allowed the men to develop rationalizations which did not necessarily involve Communist premises. Furthermore, it is likely that whatever rationalizations are adopted, they will not acquire the permanence of beliefs unless supported by social reinforcements. When the prisoners re-entered the democratic setting, most of them gave up whatever Communist premises they might have been using to rationalize their collaboration and found new rationalizations that attempted to explain, from the standpoint of democratic premises, why they had collaborated. Apart from the technical difficulties the Chinese experienced in running their indoctrination program, they were never able to control social interactions to a sufficient extent to reinforce in meaningful social relationships the Communist rationalizations for collaboration.

Taken singly, there is nothing new or terrifying about the specific techniques used by the Chinese; they invented no mysterious devices for dealing with people. Their method of controlling information by controlling the mass media of communication has been a well-known technique of totalitarian governments throughout history. Their system of propagandizing by means of lectures, movies, reading materials, and testimonials has its counterparts in education and in advertising. Group discussions and other methods requiring participation have their counterparts in education and in psychiatry. The possibility that group discussion may be fundamentally superior to lectures in obtaining stable decisions by participants has been the subject of extensive research in American social psychology. The Chinese methods of interrogation have been widely used in other armies, by the police, by newspaper reporters, and by others interested in aggressively eliciting information. Forced confessions and self-criticism have been widely used techniques in religious movements as a basis for conversion or as a device to perpetuate a given faith. The control of behavior by the manipulation of reward and punishment is obviously the least novel of all the techniques, for men have controlled each other in this way since the beginning of history.

Thus the only novelty in the Chinese methods was the attempt *to use a combination of all these techniques and to apply them simultaneously* in order to gain complete control over significant portions of the physical and social environment of a group of people. Such an ambitious effort applied on such a large scale is probably unique in the Communist movement, and perhaps in the *Chinese* Communist movement. In order to understand and evaluate this attempt to create ideological uniformity, it is necessary to view the techniques cited in terms of a social-psychological model which does justice to the complexity of this combination. Attempts such as Meerloo's[22] or Winokur's[23] to conceptualize the process of brainwashing in terms of a simple conditioning or learning model seem not only to be premature, but to

[22] Joost A. M. Meerloo, "Pavlovian Strategy as a Weapon of Menticide," *Amer. J. Psychiatry* (1954) 110:809–813.
[23] George Winokur, " 'Brainwashing'—A Social Phenomenon of Our Time," *Human Organization* (1955) 13:16–18.

ignore the most important factor—the simultaneous application of many techniques of social and behavioral control.

Before brainwashing can be properly understood, far more information must be gathered on its operation within China and within the Communist party as a whole; factors which the Chinese have succeeded in manipulating must be built into social-psychological researches on social conformity and attitude change; theoretical models must be constructed which will give a properly weighted emphasis to the variety of factors which probably operate

in brainwashing; and personality concepts must be developed which can be used convincingly to categorize the behavior of people subjected to an attack on their most fundamental beliefs and values.

And most important, those who are attempting to understand brainwashing must look at the facts objectively, and not be carried away by hysteria when another country with a different ideology and with different ultimate ends succeeds in eliciting from a small group of Americans behavior that is not consonant with the democratic ideology.

The theory of cognitive dissonance is an important one in contemporary social psychology although the predictions made from this theory sometimes seem counter to "common sense." Perhaps this is one of its attractions. But, more important, the theory of cognitive dissonance makes it possible to predict some of the conditions under which attitudes may change; it also makes possible the prediction of the direction of attitude change. Generally, attitudes will change in a direction such that any discrepancies which arise between overt actions and attitudes, or between different attitudes, are minimized. The tendency is toward consonance by reduction of dissonance.

POINTS TO GUIDE YOUR STUDY   *(1) The t tests and P values have been explained in previous introductions. (See the article by Braun and Geiselhart in Section Three.)   (2) In the experiment discussed in this selection, attitudes about a group are manipulated by the creation of cognitive dissonance.*

56: THE EFFECT OF SEVERITY OF INITIATION ON LIKING FOR A GROUP

Elliot Aronson, University of Minnesota, and Judson Mills, University of Missouri

It is a frequent observation that persons who go through a great deal of trouble or

This research was partially supported by a grant from the National Science Foundation, administered by Leon Festinger. The authors are grateful to Leon Festinger for his help and encouragement during the planning and execution of the study.

Elliot Aronson and Judson Mills. The effect of severity of initiation on liking for a group. *J. abnorm. soc. Psychol.*, 1959, **59**, 177–181. Copyright © 1959 by the American Psychological Association. Reprinted here with permission from the authors and the American Psychological Association.

pain to attain something tend to value it more highly than persons who attain the same thing with a minimum of effort. For example, one would expect persons who travel a great distance to see a motion picture to be more impressed with it than those who see the same picture at a neighborhood theater. By the same token, individuals who go through a severe initiation to gain admission to a club or organization should tend to think more highly of that organization than those who do not go through the severe initiation to gain admission.

Two questions are relevant here: (1) Is this "common observation" valid, that is, does it hold true when tested under controlled conditions? (2) If the observation is valid, how can it be accounted for? The relationship might be simply a result of differences in initial motivation. To take the case of initiations, persons who initially have a strong desire to join a particular club should be more willing to undergo unpleasantness to gain admission to it than persons who are low in initial interest. Therefore, a club that requires a severe initiation for admission should be joined only by those people with a strong desire to become members. On the other hand, a club that does not require a severe initiation should be joined by some individuals who like it very much, and by others who are relatively uninterested. Because of this self-selection, one would expect persons who are members of clubs with severe initiations to think more highly of their club, on the average, than members of clubs without severe initiations.

But is there something in the initiation itself that might account for this relationship? Is severity of initiation positively related to group preference when motivation for admission is held constant? Such a relationship is strongly implied by Festinger's (1957) theory of cognitive dissonance. The theory of cognitive dissonance predicts this relationship in the following manner. No matter how attractive a group is to a person it is rarely completely positive, i.e., usually there are some aspects of the group that the individual does not like. If he has undergone an unpleasant initiation to gain admission to the group, his cognition that he has gone through an unpleasant experience for the sake of membership is dissonant with his cognition that there are things about

the group that he does not like. He can reduce this dissonance in two ways. He can convince himself that the initiation was not very unpleasant, or he can exaggerate the positive characteristics of the group and minimize its negative aspects. With increasing severity of initiation it becomes more and more difficult to believe that the initiation was not very bad. Thus, a person who has gone through a painful initiation to become a member of a group should tend to reduce his dissonance by overestimating the attractiveness of the group. The specific hypothesis tested in the present study is that individuals who undergo an unpleasant initiation to become members of a group increase their liking for the group; that is, they find the group more attractive than do persons who become members without going through a severe initiation.

Method

In designing the experiment it was necessary to have people join groups that were similar in every respect except for the severity of the initiation required for admission—and then to measure each individual's evaluation of the group. It was also necessary to randomize the initial motivation of subjects (Ss) to gain admission to the various groups in order to eliminate systematic effects of differences in motivation. These requirements were met in the following manner: Volunteers were obtained to participate in group discussions. They were assigned randomly to one of three experimental conditions: A *Severe* initiation condition, a *Mild* initiation condition, and a *Control* condition. In the Severe condition, Ss were required to read some embarrassing material before joining the group; in the Mild condition the material they read in order to join the group was not very embarrassing; in the Control condition, Ss were not required to read any material before becoming group members. Each *S* listened to the same tape recording which was ostensibly an ongoing discussion by the members of the group that he had just joined. *S*s then evaluated the discussion.

The *S*s were 63 college women. Thirty-three of them volunteered to participate in a series of group discussions on the psychology of sex. The remaining 30, tested at a somewhat later date, were "captive volunteers" from a psychology course who elected to participate in the group discussions on the psychology of sex in preference to several other experiments. Since the results obtained from these two samples were very similar, they were combined in the analysis presented here.

Each *S* was individually scheduled to "meet with a group." When she arrived at the experimental room, she was told by the experimenter (*E*) that he was conducting several group discussions on the psychology of sex. *E* informed her that she was joining a group that had been meeting for several weeks and that she was taking the place of a girl who had to leave the group because of scheduling difficulties. *E* stated that the discussion had just begun and that she would join the other members of the group after he had explained the nature of the experiment to her. The purpose of the foregoing instructions was to confront *S* with an ongoing group and thus make plausible the recorded discussion to which she was to be exposed.

E then "explained" the purpose of the experiment. He said that he was interested in investigating the "dynamics of the group discussion process." Sex was chosen as the topic for the groups to discuss in order to provide interesting subject matter so that volunteers for the discussion groups could be obtained without much difficulty. *E* continued as follows:

But the fact that the discussions are concerned with sex has one major drawback. Although most people are interested in sex,

they tend to be a little shy when it comes to discussing it. This is very bad from the point of view of the experiment; if one or two people in a group do not participate as much as they usually do in group discussion because they are embarrassed about sex, the picture we get of the group discussion process is distorted. Therefore, it is extremely important to arrange things so that the members of the discussion group can talk as freely and frankly as possible. We found that the major inhibiting factor in the discussions was the presence of the other people in the room. Somehow, it's easier to talk about embarrassing things if other people aren't staring at you. To get around this, we hit upon an idea which has proved very successful. Each member of the group is placed in a separate room, and the participants communicate through an intercom system using headphones and a microphone. In this way, we've helped people relax, and have succeeded in bringing about an increase in individual participation.

The foregoing explanation set the stage for the tape recording, which could now be presented to the *S* as a live discussion conducted by three people in separate rooms.

E then mentioned that, in spite of this precaution, occasionally some persons were still too embarrassed to engage in the discussions and had to be asked to withdraw from the discussion group. *S* was asked if she thought she could discuss sex freely. She invariably answered affirmatively. In the Control condition *S* was told, at this point, that she would be a member of the group.

In the other two conditions, *E* went on to say that it was difficult for him to ask people to leave the group once they had become members. Therefore, he had recently decided to screen new people before admitting them to the discussion groups. The screening device was described as an "embarrassment test" which consists of reading aloud some sexually oriented material in the presence of *E*. *S* was told that *E* would make a clinical judgment of her degree of embarrassment, based upon hesitation, blushing, etc., and would determine whether or not she would be capable of participating in the discussion group. He stressed that she was not obligated to take this test, but that she could not become a member unless she did. Only one S declined to take the test. She was excluded from the experiment. It was also emphasized, at this point, that the "embarrassment test" was a recent innovation and that the other members had joined the group before it was required for admission. These instructions were included in order to counteract any tendency to identify more strongly with the group as a result of feelings of having shared a common unpleasant experience. Such a process could conceivably bring about a greater preference for the discussion group on the part of Ss in the Severe condition, introducing ambiguity in the interpretation of the results.

In the Severe condition, the "embarrassment test" consisted of having Ss read aloud, from 3 × 5 cards, 12 obscene words, e.g., fuck, cock, and screw. Ss also read aloud two vivid descriptions of sexual activity from contemporary novels. In the Mild conditions, Ss read aloud five words that were related to sex but not obscene, e.g., prostitute, virgin, and petting. In both the Severe and the Mild conditions, after each S finished reading the material, she was told that she had performed satisfactorily and was, therefore, a member of the group and could join the meeting that was now in progress.

It was of the utmost importance to prevent the S from attempting to participate in the discussion, for if she did, she would soon find that no one was responding to her statements and she would probably infer that the discussion was recorded. To insure their silence, all Ss were told that, in preparation for each meeting, the group reads an assignment which serves as the focal point of the discussion; for this meeting, the group read parts of the book, *Sexual Behavior in Animals*. After the S had indicated that she had never read this book, E told her that she would be at a disadvantage and would, consequently, not be able to participate as fully in this discussion as she would had she done the reading. He continued, "Because the presence of a participant who isn't contributing optimally would result in an inaccurate picture of the dynamics of the group discussion process, it would be best if you wouldn't participate at all today, so that we may get an undistorted picture of the dynamics of the other three members of this group. Meanwhile, you can simply listen to the discussion, and get an idea of how the group operates. For the next meeting, you can do the reading and join in the discussion." Ss were invariably more than willing to comply with this suggestion. The above instructions not only prevented S from attempting to participate in the discussion but also served to orient her toward the actual content of discussion.

Under the guise of connecting the S's headphones and microphone, E went into the next room and turned on the tape recorder. He then returned to the experimental room, put on the headphones, picked up the microphone, and pretended to break into the discussion which supposedly was in progress. After holding a brief conversation with the "members of the group," he introduced the S to them. Then he handed the headphones to her. The tape was timed so that at the precise moment that S donned her headphones, the "group members" introduced themselves and then continued their discussion.

The use of a tape recording presented all Ss with an identical group experience. The recording was a discussion by three female undergraduates. It was deliberately designed to be as dull and banal as possible in order to maximize the dissonance of the Ss in the Severe condition. The participants spoke dryly and haltingly on secondary sex behavior in the lower animals, "inadvertently" contradicted themselves and one another, mumbled several *non sequiturs,* started sentences that they never finished, hemmed, hawed, and in general conducted one of the most worthless and uninteresting discussions imaginable.

At the conclusion of the recording, *E* returned and explained that after each meeting every member of the group fills out a questionnaire expressing her reactions to the discussion. The questionnaire asked the *S* to rate the discussion and the group members on 14 different evaluative scales, e.g., dull–interesting, intelligent–unintelligent, by circling a number from 0 to 15. After completing the questionnaire, *S* made three additional ratings, orally, in response to questions from *E.* Nine of the scales concerned the *S*'s reactions to the discussion, while the other eight concerned her reactions to the participants.

At the close of the experiment, *E* engaged each *S* in conversation to determine whether or not she was suspicious of the procedure. Only one *S* entertained definite suspicions; her results were discarded.

Finally, the true nature of the experiment was explained in detail. None of the *S*s expressed any resentment or annoyance at having been misled. In fact, the majority were intrigued by the experiment and several returned at the end of the academic quarter to ascertain the results.

Results and discussion

The sum of the ratings for the 17 different scales provides an index of each *S*'s liking for the discussion group. The means and *SD*s for the three experimental conditions for this measure are presented in Table 1. Means and *SD*s are also presented in Table 1 separately for the nine scales which tapped the *S*s' attitudes toward the discussion and the eight scales which

TABLE 1   *Means of the sum of ratings for the different experimental conditions*

	EXPERIMENTAL CONDITIONS		
RATING SCALES	CONTROL ($N = 21$)	MILD ($N = 21$)	SEVERE ($N = 21$)
Discussion [9]			
M	80.2	81.8	97.6
SD	13.2	21.0	16.6
Participants [8]			
M	89.9	89.3	97.7
SD	10.9	14.1	13.2
Total [17]			
M	170.1	171.1	195.3
SD	21.6	34.0	31.9

tapped their attitudes toward the participants. The significance of the differences between the means for the different conditions were determined by *t* tests. The *t* values and significance levels are presented in Table 2.

Examination of Table 1 shows that *S*s in the Severe condition rated both the discussion and the participants higher than did those in the Control and Mild conditions. The over-all difference between the ratings by *S*s in the Severe condition and *S*s in the Control condition reaches the .01 level of significance. The over-all difference between the ratings by *S*s in the Severe initiation condition and *S*s in the

TABLE 2   *Significance levels of the differences between experimental conditions*

	DIFFERENCES BETWEEN CONDITIONS		
RATING SCALES	CONTROL-SEVERE	MILD-SEVERE	CONTROL-MILD
Discussion [9]	$t = 3.66$ $P < .001^*$	$t = 2.62$ $P < .02$	$t = .29$ N.S.
Participants [8]	$t = 2.03$ $P < .05$	$t = 1.97$ $P < .10$	$t = .15$ N.S.
Total [17]	$t = 2.92$ $P < .01$	$t = 2.33$ $P < .05$	$t = .49$ N.S.

* The *P* values given are based on both tails of the *t* distribution.

Mild initiation condition reaches the .05 level.

These differences cannnot be explained by differences in initial motivation to become members of the group, since Ss (with varying degrees of motivation) were randomly assigned to the three experimental conditions. The differences in liking for the group must be considered a consequence of the unpleasant experience. The results clearly substantiate the hypothesis: persons who undergo a severe initiation to attain membership in a group increase their liking for the group. This hypothesis follows directly from Festinger's theory of cognitive dissonance. According to the theory, Ss in the Severe initiation condition held the cognition that they had undergone a painful experience to become members of the discussion group. Then they listened to a dull, banal discussion. Negative cognitions about the discussion which they formed from listening to it were dissonant with the cognition that they had undergone a painful experience to gain membership in this group. The presence of dissonance leads to pressure to reduce it. Ss in this condition could reduce their dissonance either by denying the severity of the initiation or by distorting their cognitions concerning the group discussion in a positive direction. The initiation of the Ss in the Severe condition was apparently too painful for them to deny—hence, they reduced their dissonance by overestimating the attractiveness of the group.

There was no appreciable difference between the ratings made by Ss in the Control condition and those made by Ss in the Mild condition. It would seem that the Mild condition was so devoid of unpleasantness as to constitute little investment in the group. Hence, little dissonance was created. If any dissonance did occur in this situation it would be more realistic for the S to reduce it by minimizing the pain of the initiation, than by distorting her cogni-

tions concerning the discussion. Thus, it is not an initiation per se that leads to increase in liking for a group. The initiation must be severe enough to constitute a genuine investment and to render it difficult to reduce dissonance by playing down the extent of the pain involved.

An examination of Table 1 shows that the rating scales concerning the discussion show greater differences between the conditions than the scales dealing with the evaluations of the participants in the discussion. There are at least two possible explanations for this result: (a) It may be easier for people to express negative criticism about an impersonal discussion than about the people involved. Thus, Ss in the Control and Mild conditions may have inflated their ratings of the participants to avoid making negative statements about fellow college students. (b) It is possible that Ss in the Severe condition had less need to distort their perception of the participants than of the discussion itself. The dissonance of the Ss in the Severe condition resulted from the actual discussion: they experienced dissonance between going through an unpleasant experience and taking part in worthless uninteresting discussions. The most direct way for them to reduce this dissonance would be to change their perceptions of the discussion in a positive direction. The participants in the discussion were peripheral to the cause of dissonance. If Ss in the Severe condition had less need to distort their perceptions of the participants than their perception of the discussion, their evaluations of the participants could be expected to be closer to the evaluations of the participants made by Ss in the Control and Mild conditions.

Summary and conclusions

An experiment was conducted to test the hypothesis that persons who undergo an unpleasant initiation to become members of a group increase their liking for the group; that is, they find the group more attractive than do persons who become members without going through a severe initiation. This hypothesis was derived from Festinger's theory of cognitive dissonance.

College women who volunteered to participate in discussion groups were randomly assigned to one of three experimental conditions: A *Severe* initiation condition, a *Mild* initiation condition, and a *Control* condition. In the Severe condition, subjects were required to read some embarrassing material before joining the group; in the Mild condition the material they read in order to join the group was not very embarrassing; in the Control condition, subjects were not required to read any material before becoming group members. Each subject listened to a recording that appeared to be an ongoing discussion being conducted by the group which she had just joined. Afterwards, subjects filled out a questionnaire evaluating the discussion and the participants. The results clearly verified the hypothesis. Subjects who underwent a severe initiation perceived the group as being significantly more attractive than did those who underwent a mild initiation or no initiation. There was no appreciable difference between ratings by subjects who underwent a Mild initiation and those by subjects who underwent no initiation.

Reference

Festinger, L. *A theory of cognitive dissonance.* Evanston: Row, Peterson, 1957.

PSYCHOLOGY IN INDUSTRY

Two contrasting ideas about human motivation are presented. "Theory X" states that people have to be driven to work and that they work to satisfy their physiological and safety needs; "Theory Y" states that people will work hard if the work is arranged so that it meets their needs for fulfillment—or self-actualization.

If we accept the hierarchy of needs proposed by Maslow— physiological needs, safety needs, belongingness and love needs, esteem needs, and the need for self-actualization—it would seem that Theory X fails to take into account the human strivings toward the higher goals—esteem and status, and self-actualization, or, loosely speaking, creative accomplishment. As industrialized societies become more and more affluent, it seems likely that lower-order needs will more readily be satisfied, and management would be wise to begin to turn toward the satisfaction of the higher-order needs in order to motivate and retain employees. To some extent, this has happened in the United States.

A POINT TO GUIDE YOUR STUDY *In most managerial situations, action based on Theory Y seems most appropriate; but can you think of some situations in which action based on Theory X might be best? Which assumption about motivation seems to motivate your teachers? Do they differ?*

57: SELECTIONS FROM THE HUMAN SIDE OF ENTERPRISE

Douglas McGregor

Theory X: the traditional view of direction and control

Behind every managerial decision or action are assumptions about human nature and human behavior. A few of these are remarkably pervasive. They are implicit in most of the literature of organization and in much current managerial policy and practice:

1. *The average human being has an inherent dislike of work and will avoid it if he can.* This assumption has deep roots.

The punishment of Adam and Eve for eating the fruit of the Tree of Knowledge was to be banished from Eden into a world where they had to work for a living. The stress that management places on productivity, on the concept of "a fair day's work," on the evils of featherbedding and restriction of output, on rewards for performance—while it has a logic in terms of the objectives of enterprise—reflects an underlying belief that management must counteract an inherent human tendency to avoid work. The evidence for the correctness of this assumption would seem to most managers to be incontrovertible.

2. *Because of this human characteristic of dislike of work, most people must be coerced, controlled, directed, threatened with punishment to get them to put forth adequate effort toward the achievement of organizational objectives.* The dislike of work is so strong that even the promise of rewards is not generally enough to overcome it. People will accept the rewards and demand continually higher ones, but these alone will not produce the necessary effort. Only the threat of punishment will do the trick.

The current wave of criticism of "human relations," the derogatory comments about "permissiveness" and "democracy" in industry, the trends in some companies toward recentralization after the postwar wave of decentralization—all these are assertions of the underlying assumption that people will only work under external coercion and control. The recession of 1957–1958 ended a decade of experimentation with the "soft" managerial approach, and this assumption (which never really was abandoned) is being openly espoused once more.

3. *The average human being prefers to be directed, wishes to avoid responsibility, has relatively little ambition, wants security above all.* This assumption of the "mediocrity of the masses" is rarely expressed so bluntly. In fact, a good deal of

lip service is given to the ideal of the worth of the average human being. Our political and social values demand such public expressions. Nevertheless, a great many managers will give private support to this assumption, and it is easy to see it reflected in policy and practice. Paternalism has become a nasty word, but it is by no means a defunct managerial philosophy.

I have suggested elsewhere the name Theory X for this set of assumptions. In later chapters of this book I will attempt to show that Theory X is not a straw man for purposes of demolition, but is in fact a theory which materially influences managerial strategy in a wide sector of American industry today. Moreover, the principles of organization which comprise the bulk of the literature of management *could only have been derived from assumptions such as those of Theory X*. Other beliefs about human nature would have led inevitably to quite different organizational principles.

Theory X provides an explanation of some human behavior in industry. These assumptions would not have persisted if there were not a considerable body of evidence to support them. Nevertheless, there are many readily observable phenomena in industry and elsewhere which are not consistent with this view of human nature.

Such a state of affairs is not uncommon. The history of science provides many examples of theoretical explanations which persist over long periods despite the fact that they are only partially adequate. Newton's laws of motion are a case in point. It was not until the development of the theory of relativity during the present century that important inconsistencies and inadequacies in Newtonian theory could be understood and corrected.

The growth of knowledge in the social sciences during the past quarter century has made it possible to reformulate some assumptions about human nature and human behavior in the organizational setting which resolve certain of the inconsistencies inherent in Theory X. While this reformulation is, of course, tentative, it provides an improved basis for prediction and control of human behavior in industry.

SOME ASSUMPTIONS ABOUT MOTIVATION   At the core of any theory of the management of human resources are assumptions about human motivation. This has been a confusing subject because there have been so many conflicting points of view even among social scientists. In recent years, however, there has been a convergence of research findings and a growing acceptance of a few rather basic ideas about motivation. These ideas appear to have considerable power. They help to explain the inadequacies of Theory X as well as the limited sense in which it is correct. In addition, they provide the basis for an entirely different theory of management.

The following generalizations about motivation are somewhat oversimplified. If all of the qualifications which would be required by a truly adequate treatment were introduced, the gross essentials which are particularly significant for management would be obscured. These generalizations do not misrepresent the facts, but they do ignore some complexities of human behavior which are relatively unimportant for our purposes.

Man is a wanting animal—as soon as one of his needs is satisfied, another appears in its place. This process is unending. It continues from birth to death. Man continuously puts forth effort—works, if you please—to satisfy his needs.

Human needs are organized in a series of levels—a hierarchy of importance. At the lowest level, but preeminent in importance when they are thwarted, are the physiological needs. Man lives by bread alone, when there is no bread. Unless the circumstances are unusual, his needs for love, for status, for recognition are inopera-

tive when his stomach has been empty for a while. But when he eats regularly and adequately, hunger ceases to be an important need. The sated man has hunger only in the sense that a full bottle has emptiness. The same is true of the other physiological needs of man—for rest, exercise, shelter, protection from the elements.

A satisfied need is not a motivator of behavior! This is a fact of profound significance. It is a fact which is unrecognized in Theory X and is, therefore, ignored in the conventional approach to the management of people. I shall return to it later. For the moment, an example will make the point. Consider your own need for air. Except as you are deprived of it, it has no appreciable motivating effect upon your behavior.

When the physiological needs are reasonably satisfied, needs at the next higher level begin to dominate man's behavior—to motivate him. These are the safety needs, for protection against danger, threat, deprivation. Some people mistakenly refer to these as needs for security. However, unless man is in a dependent relationship where he fears arbitrary deprivation, he does not demand security. The need is for the "fairest possible break." When he is confident of this, he is more than willing to take risks. But when he feels threatened or dependent, his greatest need is for protection, for security.

The fact needs little emphasis that since every industrial employee is in at least a partially dependent relationship, safety needs may assume considerable importance. Arbitrary management actions, behavior which arouses uncertainty with respect to continued employment or which reflects favoritism or discrimination, unpredictable administration of policy—these can be powerful motivators of the safety needs in the employment relationship at every level from worker to vice president. In addition, the safety needs of managers are often aroused by their dependence downward or laterally. This is a major reason for emphasis on management prerogatives and clear assignments of authority.

When man's physiological needs are satisfied and he is no longer fearful about his physical welfare, his social needs become important motivators of his behavior. These are such needs as those for belonging, for association, for acceptance by one's fellows, for giving and receiving friendship and love.

Management knows today of the existence of these needs, but it is often assumed quite wrongly that they represent a threat to the organization. Many studies have demonstrated that the tightly knit, cohesive work group may, under proper conditions, be far more effective than an equal number of separate individuals in achieving organizational goals. Yet management, fearing group hostility to its own objectives, often goes to considerable lengths to control and direct human efforts in ways that are inimical to the natural "groupiness" of human beings. When man's social needs—and perhaps his safety needs, too—are thus thwarted, he behaves in ways which tend to defeat organizational objectives. He becomes resistant, antagonistic, uncooperative. But this behavior is a consequence, not a cause.

Above the social needs—in the sense that they do not usually become motivators until lower needs are reasonably satisfied—are the needs of greatest significance to management and to man himself. They are the egoistic needs, and they are of two kinds:

1. Those that relate to one's self-esteem: needs for self-respect and self-confidence, for autonomy, for achievement, for competence, for knowledge
2. Those that relate to one's reputation: needs for status, for recognition, for appreciation, for the deserved respect of one's fellows

Unlike the lower needs, these are rarely satisfied; man seeks indefinitely for more satisfaction of these needs once they have become important to him. However, they do not usually appear in any significant way until physiological, safety, and social needs are reasonably satisfied. Exceptions to this generalization are to be observed, particularly under circumstances where, in addition to severe deprivation of physiological needs, human dignity is trampled upon. Political revolutions often grow out of thwarted social and ego, as well as physiological, needs.

The typical industrial organization offers only limited opportunities for the satisfaction of egoistic needs to people at lower levels in the hierarchy. The conventional methods of organizing work, particularly in mass production industries, give little heed to these aspects of human motivation. If the practices of "scientific management" were deliberately calculated to thwart these needs—which, of course, they are not—they could hardly accomplish this purpose better than they do.

Finally—a capstone, as it were, on the hierarchy—there are the needs for self-fulfillment. These are the needs for realizing one's own potentialities, for continued self-development, for being creative in the broadest sense of that term.

The conditions of modern industrial life give only limited opportunity for these relatively dormant human needs to find expression. The deprivation most people experience with respect to other lower-level needs diverts their energies into the struggle to satisfy *those* needs, and the needs for self-fulfillment remain below the level of consciousness.

Now, briefly, a few general comments about motivation:

We recognize readily enough that a man suffering from a severe dietary deficiency is sick. The deprivation of physiological needs has behavioral consequences. The same is true, although less well recognized, of the deprivation of higher-level needs. The man whose needs for safety, association, independence, or status are thwarted is sick, just as surely as is he who has rickets. And his sickness will have behavioral consequences. We will be mistaken if we attribute his resultant passivity, or his hostility, or his refusal to accept responsibility to his inherent "human nature." These forms of behavior are *symptoms* of illness—of deprivation of his social and egoistic needs.

The man whose lower-level needs are satisfied is not motivated to satisfy *those* needs. For practical purposes they exist no longer. (Remember my point about your need for air.) Management often asks, "Why aren't people more productive? We pay good wages, provide good working conditions, have excellent fringe benefits and steady employment. Yet people do not seem to be willing to put forth more than minimum effort." It is unnecessary to look far for the reasons.

Consideration of the rewards typically provided the worker for satisfying his needs through his employment leads to the interesting conclusion that most of these rewards can be used for satisfying his needs *only when he leaves the job.* Wages, for example, cannot be spent at work. The only contribution they can make to his satisfaction on the job is in terms of status differences resulting from wage differentials. (This, incidentally, is one of the reasons why small and apparently unimportant differences in wage rates can be the subject of so much heated dispute. The issue is not the pennies involved, but the fact that the status differences which they reflect are one of the few ways in which wages can result in need satisfaction in the job situation itself.)

Most fringe benefits—overtime pay, shift differentials, vacations, health and medical benefits, annuities, and the proceeds from stock purchase plans or profit-sharing plans—yield needed satisfaction

only when the individual leaves the job. Yet these, along with wages, are among the major rewards provided by management for effort. It is not surprising, therefore, that for many wage earners *work is perceived as a form of punishment* which is the price to be paid for various kinds of satisfaction away from the job. To the extent that this is their perception, we would hardly expect them to undergo more of this punishment than is necessary.

Under today's conditions management has provided relatively well for the satisfaction of physiological and safety needs. The standard of living in our country is high; people do not suffer major deprivation of their physiological needs except during periods of severe unemployment. Even then, the social legislation developed since the thirties cushions the shock.

But the fact that management has provided for these physiological and safety needs has shifted the motivational emphasis to the social and the egoistic needs. Unless there are opportunities *at work* to satisfy these higher-level needs, people will be deprived; and their behavior will reflect this deprivation. Under such conditions, if management continues to focus its attention on physiological needs, the mere provision of rewards is bound to be ineffective, and reliance on the threat of punishment will be inevitable. Thus one of the assumptions of Theory X will appear to be validated, but only because we have mistaken effects for causes.

People *will* make insistent demands for more money under these conditions. It becomes more important than ever to buy the material goods and services which can provide limited satisfaction of the thwarted needs. Although money has only limited value in satisfying many higher-level needs, it can become the focus of interest if it is the only means available.

The "carrot and stick" theory of motivation which goes along with Theory X works reasonably well under certain circumstances. The *means* for satisfying man's physiological and (within limits) safety needs can be provided or withheld by management. Employment itself is such a means, and so are wages, working conditions, and benefits. By these means the individual can be controlled so long as he is struggling for subsistence. Man tends to live for bread alone when there is little bread.

But the "carrot and stick" theory does not work at all once man has reached an adequate subsistence level and is motivated primarily by higher needs. Management cannot provide a man with self-respect, or with the respect of his fellows, or with the satisfaction of needs for self-fulfillment. We can create conditions such that he is encouraged and enabled to seek such satisfactions for himself, or we can thwart him by failing to create those conditions.

But this creation of conditions is not "control" in the usual sense; it does not seem to be a particularly good device for directing behavior. And so management finds itself in an odd position. The high standard of living created by our modern technological know-how provides quite adequately for the satisfaction of physiological and safety needs. The only significant exception is where management practices have not created confidence in a "fair break"—and thus where safety needs are thwarted. But by making possible the satisfaction of lower-level needs, management has deprived itself of the ability to use the control devices on which the conventional assumptions of Theory X has taught it to rely: rewards, promises, incentives, or threats and other coercive devices.

The philosophy of management by direction and control—*regardless of whether it is hard or soft*—is inadequate to motivate because the human needs on which this approach relies are relatively unimportant motivators of behavior in our society today. Direction and control are of limited value in motivating people whose important needs are social and egoistic.

People, deprived of opportunities to satisfy at work the needs which are now important to them, behave exactly as we might predict—with indolence, passivity, unwillingness to accept responsibility, resistance to change, willingness to follow the demagogue, unreasonable demands for economic benefits. It would seem that we may be caught in a web of our own weaving.

Theory X explains the *consequences* of a particular managerial strategy; it neither explains nor describes human nature although it purports to. Because its assumptions are so unnecessarily limiting, it prevents our seeing the possibilities inherent in other managerial strategies. What sometimes appear to be new strategies—decentralization, management by objectives, consultative supervision, "democratic" leadership—are usually but old wine in new bottles because the procedures developed to implement them are derived from the same inadequate assumptions about human nature. Management is constantly becoming disillusioned with widely touted and expertly merchandized "new approaches" to the human side of enterprise. The real difficulty is that these new approaches are no more than different tactics—programs, procedures, gadgets—within an unchanged strategy based on Theory X.

In child rearing, it is recognized that parental strategies of control must be progressively modified to adapt to the changed capabilities and characteristics of the human individual as he develops from infancy to adulthood. To some extent industrial management recognizes that the human *adult* possesses capabilities for continued learning and growth. Witness the many current activities in the fields of training and management development. In its *basic* conceptions of managing human resources, however, management appears to have concluded that the average human being is permanently arrested in his development in early adolescence. Theory X is built on the least common human denominator: the factory "hand" of the past. As Chris Argyris has shown dramatically in his *Personality and Organization,* conventional managerial strategies for the organization, direction, and control of the human resources of enterprise are admirably suited to the capacities and characteristics of the child rather than the adult.

In one limited area—that of research administration—there has been some recent recognition of the need for selective adaptation in managerial strategy. This, however, has been perceived as a unique problem, and its broader implications have not been recognized. As pointed out in this and the previous chapter, changes in the population at large—in educational level, attitudes and values, motivation, degree of dependence—have created both the opportunity and the need for other forms of selective adaptation. However, so long as the assumptions of Theory X continue to influence managerial strategy, we will fail to discover, let alone utilize, the potentialities of the average human being.

References

Allen, Louis A., *Management and Organization.* New York: McGraw-Hill Book Company, Inc., 1958.

Bendix, Reinhard, *Work and Authority in Industry.* New York: John Wiley & Sons, Inc., 1956.

Brown, Alvin, *Organization of Industry.* Englewood Cliffs, N.J.: Prentice-Hall, Inc., 1947.

Fayol, Henri, *General and Industrial Administration.* New York: Pitman Publishing Corporation, 1949.

Gouldner, Alvin W., *Patterns of Industrial Bureaucracy.* Glencoe, Ill.: Free Press, 1954.

Koontz, Harold, and Cyril O'Donnell, *Principles of Management.* New York: McGraw-Hill Book Company, Inc., 1955.

Maslow, A. H., *Motivation and Personality.* New York: Harper & Brothers, 1954.

Urwick, Lyndall, *The Elements of Administration.* New York: Harper & Brothers, 1944.

Walker, Charles R., *Toward the Automatic Factory.* New Haven, Conn.: Yale University Press, 1957.

Whyte, William F., *Money and Motivation.* New York: Harper & Brothers, 1955.

Zaleznik, A., C. R. Christensen, and F. J. Roethlisberger, *The Motivation, Productivity, and Satisfaction of Workers: A Prediction Study.* Boston: Division of Research, The Graduate School of Business Administration, Harvard University, 1958.

Theory Y: the integration of individual and organizational goals

To some, the preceding analysis will appear unduly harsh. Have we not made major modifications in the management of the human resources of industry during the past quarter century? Have we not recognized the importance of people and made vitally significant changes in managerial strategy as a consequence? Do the developments since the twenties in personnel administration and labor relations add up to nothing?

There is no question that important progress has been made in the past two or three decades. During this period the human side of enterprise has become a major preoccupation of management. A tremendous number of policies, programs, and practices which were virtually unknown thirty years ago have become commonplace. The lot of the industrial employee—be he worker, professional, or executive—has improved to a degree which could hardly have been imagined by his counterpart of the nineteen twenties. Management has adopted generally a far more humanitarian set of values; it has successfully striven to give more equitable and more generous treatment to its employees. It has significantly reduced economic hardships, eliminated the more extreme forms of industrial warfare, provided a generally safe and pleasant working environment, *but it has done all these things without changing its fundamental theory of management*. There are exceptions here and there, and they are important; nevertheless, the assumptions of Theory X remain predominant throughout our economy.

Management was subjected to severe pressures during the Great Depression of the thirties. The wave of public antagonism, the open warfare accompanying the unionization of the mass production industries, the general reaction against authoritarianism, the legislation of the New Deal produced a wide "pendulum swing." However, the changes in policy and practice which took place during that and the next decade were primarily adjustments to the increased power of organized labor and to the pressures of public opinion.

Some of the movement was away from "hard" and toward "soft" management, but it was short-lived, and for good reasons. It has become clear that many of the initial strategic interpretations accompanying the "human relations approach" were as naïve as those which characterized the early stages of progressive education. We have now discovered that there is no answer in the simple removal of control— that abdication is not a workable alternative to authoritarianism. We have learned that there is no direct correlation between employee satisfaction and productivity. We recognize today that "industrial democracy" cannot consist in permitting everyone to decide everything, that industrial health does not flow automatically from the elimination of dissatisfaction, disagreement, or even open conflict. Peace is not synonymous with organizational health; socially responsible management is not coextensive with permissive management.

Now that management has regained its earlier prestige and power, it has become obvious that the trend toward "soft" management was a temporary and relatively superficial reaction rather than a general modification of fundamental assumptions or basic strategy. Moreover, while the progress we have made in the past quarter century is substantial, it has reached the point of diminishing returns. The tactical possibilities within conventional managerial strategies have been pretty completely exploited, and significant new developments will be unlikely without major modifications in theory.

THE ASSUMPTIONS OF THEORY Y   There have been few dramatic break-throughs in social science theory like those which have occurred in the physical sciences during the past half century. Nevertheless, the accumulation of knowledge about human behavior in many specialized fields has made possible the formulation of a number of generalizations which provide a modest beginning for new theory with respect to the management of human resources. Some of these assumptions were outlined in the discussion of motivation [in the first section of this selection—Theory X: The Traditional View of Direction and Control]. Some others, which will hereafter be referred to as Theory Y, are as follows:

1. *The expenditure of physical and mental effort in work is as natural as play or rest.* The average human being does not inherently dislike work. Depending upon controllable conditions, work may be a source of satisfaction (and will be voluntarily performed) or a source of punishment (and will be avoided if possible).

2. *External control and the threat of punishment are not the only means for bringing about effort toward organizational objectives. Man will exercise self-direction and self-control in the service of objectives to which he is committed.*

3. *Commitment to objectives is a function of the rewards associated with their achievement.* The most significant of such rewards, e.g., the satisfaction of ego and self-actualization needs, can be direct products of effort directed toward organizational objectives.

4. *The average human being learns, under proper conditions, not only to accept but to seek responsibility.* Avoidance of responsibility, lack of ambition, and emphasis on security are generally consequences of experience, not inherent human characteristics.

5. *The capacity to exercise a relatively high degree of imagination, ingenuity, and creativity in the solution of organizational problems is widely, not narrowly, distributed in the population.*

6. *Under the conditions of modern industrial life, the intellectual potentialities of the average human being are only partially utilized.*

These assumptions involve sharply different implications for managerial strategy than do those of Theory X. They are dynamic rather than static: They indicate the possibility of human growth and development; they stress the necessity for selective adaptation rather than for a single absolute form of control. They are not framed in terms of the least common denominator of the factory hand, but in terms of a resource which has substantial potentialities.

Above all, the assumptions of Theory Y point up the fact that the limits on human collaboration in the organizational setting are not limits of human nature but of management's ingenuity in discovering how to realize the potential represented by its human resources. Theory X offers management an easy rationalization for ineffective organizational performance: It is due to the nature of the human resources with which we must work. Theory Y, on the other hand, places the problems squarely in the lap of management. If employees are lazy, indifferent, unwilling to take responsibility, intransigent, uncreative, uncooperative, Theory Y implies that the causes lie in management's methods of organization and control.

The assumptions of Theory Y are not

finally validated. Nevertheless, they are far more consistent with existing knowledge in the social sciences than are the assumptions of Theory X. They will undoubtedly be refined, elaborated, modified as further research accumulates, but they are unlikely to be completely contradicted.

On the surface, these assumptions may not seem particularly difficult to accept. Carrying their implications into practice, however, is not easy. They challenge a number of deeply ingrained managerial habits of thought and action.

THE PRINCIPLE OF INTEGRATION   The central principle of organization which derives from Theory X is that of direction and control through the exercise of authority— what has been called "the scalar principle." The central principle which derives from Theory Y is that of integration: the creation of conditions such that the members of the organization can achieve their own goals *best* by directing their efforts toward the success of the enterprise. These two principles have profoundly different implications with respect to the task of managing human resources, but the scalar principle is so firmly built into managerial attitudes that the implications of the principle of integration are not easy to perceive.

Someone once said that fish discover water last. The "psychological environment" of industrial management—like water for fish—is so much a part of organizational life that we are unaware of it. Certain characteristics of our society, and of organizational life within it, are so completely established, so pervasive, that we cannot conceive of their being otherwise. As a result, a great many policies and practices and decisions and relationships could only be—it seems—what they are.

Among these pervasive characteristics of organizational life in the United States today is a managerial attitude (stemming from Theory X) toward membership in the industrial organization. It is assumed almost without question that organizational requirements take precedence over the needs of individual members. Basically, the employment agreement is that in return for the rewards which are offered, the individual will accept external direction and control. The very idea of integration and self-control is foreign to our way of thinking about the employment relationship. The tendency, therefore, is either to reject it out of hand (as socialistic, or anarchistic, or inconsistent with human nature) or to twist it unconsciously until it fits existing conceptions.

The concept of integration and self-control carries the implication that the organization will be more effective in achieving its economic objectives if adjustments are made, in significant ways, to the needs and goals of its members.

A district manager in a large, geographically decentralized company is notified that he is being promoted to a policy level position at headquarters. It is a big promotion with a large salary increase. His role in the organization will be a much more powerful one, and he will be associated with the major executives of the firm.

The headquarters group who selected him for this position have carefully considered a number of possible candidates. This man stands out among them in a way which makes him the natural choice. His performance has been under observation for some time, and there is little question that he possesses the necessary qualifications, not only for this opening but for an even higher position. There is genuine satisfaction that such an outstanding candidate is available.

The man is appalled. He doesn't want the job. His goal, as he expresses it, is to be the "best damned district manager in the company." He enjoys his direct associations with operating people in the field, and he doesn't want a policy level job. He and his wife enjoy the kind of life they have created in a small city, and they dislike actively both the living conditions and the social obligations of the headquarters city.

He expresses his feelings as strongly as he can, but his objections are brushed aside. The organization's needs are such that his refusal to accept the promotion would be unthinkable. His superiors say to themselves that of course when he has settled into the new job, he will recognize that it was the right thing. And so he makes the move.

Two years later he is in an even higher position in the company's headquarters organization, and there is talk that he will probably be the executive vice-president before long. Privately he expresses considerable unhappiness and dissatisfaction. He (and his wife) would "give anything" to be back in the situation he left two years ago.

Within the context of the pervasive assumptions of Theory X, promotions and transfers in large numbers are made by unilateral decision. The requirements of the organization are given priority automatically and almost without question. If the individual's personal goals are considered at all, it is assumed that the rewards of salary and position will satisfy him. Should an individual actually refuse such a move without a compelling reason, such as health or a severe family crisis, he would be considered to have jeopardized his future because of this "selfish" attitude. It is rare indeed for management to give the individual the opportunity to be a genuine and active partner in such a decision, even though it may affect his most important personal goals. Yet the implications following from Theory Y are that the organization is likely to suffer if it ignores these personal needs and goals. In making unilateral decisions with respect to promotion, management is failing to utilize its human resources in the most effective way.

The principle of integration demands that both the organization's and the individual's needs be recognized. Of course, when there is a sincere joint effort to find it, an integrative solution which meets the needs of the individual *and* the organization is a frequent outcome. But not always

—and this is the point at which Theory Y begins to appear unrealistic. It collides head on with pervasive attitudes associated with management by direction and control.

The assumptions of Theory Y imply that unless integration is achieved *the organization will suffer*. The objectives of the organization are *not* achieved best by the unilateral administration of promotions, because this form of management by direction and control will not create the commitment which would make available the full resources of those affected. The lesser motivation, the lesser resulting degree of self-direction and self-control are costs which, when added up for many instances over time, will more than offset the gains obtained by unilateral decisions "for the good of the organization."

One other example will perhaps clarify further the sharply different implications of Theory X and Theory Y.

It could be argued that management is already giving a great deal of attention to the principle of integration through its efforts in the field of economic education. Many millions of dollars and much ingenuity have been expended in attempts to persuade employees that their welfare is intimately connected with the success of the free enterprise system and of their own companies. The idea that they can achieve their own goals best by directing their effort toward the objectives of the organization has been explored and developed and communicated in every possible way. Is this not evidence that management is already committed to the principle of integration?

The answer is a definite no. These managerial efforts, with rare exceptions, reflect clearly the influence of the assumptions of Theory X. The central message is an exhortation to the industrial employee to work hard and follow orders in order to protect his job and his standard of living. Much has been achieved, it says, by our established way of running industry, and much more could be achieved if employees would adapt themselves *to management's definition* of what is required. Behind these exhortations lies the expectation that of course the requirements of the organization and its economic success must have priority over the needs of the individual.

Naturally, integration means working together for the success of the enterprise so we all may share in the resulting rewards. But management's implicit assumption is that working together means adjusting to the requirements of the organization *as management perceives them*. In terms of existing views, it seems inconceivable that individuals, seeking their own goals, would further the ends of the enterprise. On the contrary, this would lead to anarchy, chaos, irreconcilable conflicts of self-interest, lack of responsibility, inability to make decisions, and failure to carry out those that were made.

All these consequences, and other worse ones, *would* be inevitable unless conditions could be created such that the members of the organization perceived that they could achieve their own goals *best* by directing their efforts toward the success of the enterprise. If the assumptions of Theory Y are valid, the practical question is whether, and to what extent, such conditions can be created. To that question the balance of this volume is addressed.

THE APPLICATION OF THEORY Y In the physical sciences there are many theoretical phenomena which cannot be achieved in practice. Absolute zero and a perfect vacuum are examples. Others, such as nuclear power, jet aircraft, and human space flight, are recognized theoretically to be possible long before they become feasible. This fact does not make theory less useful. If it were not for our theoretical convictions, we would not even be attempting to develop the means for human flight into space today. In fact, were it not for the development of physical science theory during the past century and a half, we would still be depending upon the horse and buggy and the sailing vessel for transportation. Virtually all significant technological developments wait on the formulation of relevant theory.

Similarly, in the management of the human resources of industry, the assumptions and theories about human nature at any given time limit innovation. Possibilities are not recognized, innovating efforts are not undertaken, until theoretical conceptions lay a groundwork for them. Assumptions like those of Theory X permit us to conceive of certain possible ways of organizing and directing human effort, *but not others*. Assumptions like those of Theory Y open up a range of possibilities for new managerial policies and practices. As in the case of the development of new physical science theory, some of these possibilities are not immediately feasible, and others may forever remain unattainable. They may be too costly, or it may be that we simply cannot discover how to create the necessary "hardware."

There is substantial evidence for the statement that the potentialities of the average human being are far above those which we typically realize in industry today. If our assumptions are like those of Theory X, we will not even recognize the existence of these potentialities and there will be no reason to devote time, effort, or money to discovering how to realize them. If, however, we accept assumptions like those of Theory Y, we will be challenged to innovate, to discover new ways of organizing and directing human effort, even though we recognize that the perfect organization, like the perfect vacuum, is practically out of reach.

We need not be overwhelmed by the dimensions of the managerial task implied by Theory Y. To be sure, a large mass production operation in which the workers have been organized by a militant and hostile union faces management with problems which appear at present to be insurmountable with respect to the application of the principle of integration. It may be

decades before sufficient knowledge will have accumulated to make such an application feasible. Applications of Theory Y will have to be tested initially in more limited ways and under more favorable circumstances. However, a number of applications of Theory Y *in managing managers and professional people* are possible today. Within the managerial hierarchy, the assumptions can be tested and refined, techniques can be invented and skill acquired in their use. As knowledge accumulates, some of the problems of application at the worker level in large organizations may appear less baffling than they do at present.

Perfect integration of organizational requirements and individual goals and needs is, of course, not a realistic objective. In adopting this principle, we seek that degree of integration in which the individual can achieve his goals *best* by directing his efforts toward the success of the organization. "Best" means that this alternative will be more attractive than the many others available to him: indifference, irresponsibility, minimal compliance, hostility, sabotage. It means that he will continuously be encouraged to develop and utilize voluntarily his capacities, his knowledge, his skill, his ingenuity in ways which contribute to the success of the enterprise.[1]

Acceptance of Theory Y does not imply abdication, or "soft" management, or "permissiveness." As was indicated above, such

---

[1] A recent, highly significant study of the sources of job satisfaction and dissatisfaction among managerial and professional people suggests that these opportunities for "self-actualization" are the essential requirements of both job satisfaction and high performance. The researchers find that "the wants of employees divide into two groups. One group revolves around the need to develop in one's occupation as a source of personal growth. The second group operates as an essential base to the first and is associated with fair treatment in compensation, supervision, working conditions, and administrative practices. *The fulfillment of the needs of the second group does not motivate the individual to high levels of job satisfaction and . . . to extra performance on the job.* All we can expect from satisfying [this second group of needs] is the prevention of dissatisfaction and poor job perormance." Frederick Herzberg, Bernard Mausner, and Barbara Bloch Snyderman, *The Motivation to Work*. New York: John Wiley & Sons, Inc., 1959, pp. 114–115. (Italics mine.)

notions stem from the acceptance of authority as the *single* means of managerial control, and from attempts to minimize its negative consequences. Theory Y assumes that people will exercise self-direction and self-control in the achievement of organizational objectives *to the degree that they are committed to those objectives.* If that commitment is small, only a slight degree of self-direction and self-control will be likely, and a substantial amount of external influence will be necessary. If it is large, many conventional external controls will be relatively superfluous, and to some extent self-defeating. Managerial policies and practices materially affect this degree of commitment.

Authority is an inappropriate means for obtaining commitment to objectives. Other forms of influence—help in achieving integration, for example—are required for this purpose. Theory Y points to the possibility of lessening the emphasis on external forms of control to the degree that commitment to organizational objectives can be achieved. Its underlying assumptions emphasize the capacity of human beings for self-control, and the consequent possibility of greater managerial reliance on other means of influence. Nevertheless, it is clear that authority *is* an appropriate means for control under certain circumstances—particularly where genuine commitment to objectives cannot be achieved. The assumptions of Theory Y do not deny the appropriateness of authority, but they do deny that it is appropriate for all purposes and under all circumstances.

Many statements have been made to the effect that we have acquired today the know-how to cope with virtually any technological problems which may arise, and that the major industrial advances of the next half century will occur on the human side of enterprise. Such advances, however, are improbable so long as management continues to organize and direct and control its human resources on the basis of assumptions—tacit or explicit—like those of Theory X. Genuine innovation, in contrast to a refurbishing and patching of present managerial strategies, requires first the acceptance of less limiting assumptions about the nature of the human resources we seek to control, and second the readiness to adapt selectively to the implications contained in those new assumptions. Theory Y is an invitation to innovation.

References

Brown, J. A. C., *The Social Psychology of Industry.* Baltimore: Penguin Books, Inc., 1954.

Cordiner, Ralph J., *New Frontiers for Professional Managers.* New York: McGraw-Hill Book Company, Inc., 1956.

Dubin, Robert, *The World of Work: Industrial Society and Human Relations.* Englewood Cliffs, N.J.: Prentice-Hall, Inc., 1958.

Friedmann, Georges, *Industrial Society: The Emergence of the Human Problems of Automation.* Glencoe, Ill.: Free Press, 1955.

Herzberg, Frederick, Bernard Mausner, and Barbara Bloch Snyderman, *The Motivation to Work.* New York: John Wiley & Sons, Inc., 1959.

Krech, David, and Richard S. Crutchfield, *Theory and Problems of Social Psychology.* New York: McGraw-Hill Book Company, Inc., 1948.

Leavitt, Harold J., *Managerial Psychology.* Chicago: University of Chicago Press, 1958.

McMurry, Robert N., "The Case for Benevolent Autocracy," *Harvard Business Review,* vol. 36, no. 1 (January–February), 1958.

Rice, A. K., *Productivity and Social Organizations: The Ahmedabad Experiment.* London: Tavistock Publications, Ltd., 1958.

Stagner, Ross, *The Psychology of Industrial Conflict.* New York: John Wiley & Sons, Inc., 1956.

NERVOUS SYSTEM AND INTERNAL ENVIRONMENT

Many techniques for the investigation of the relationship of the brain to behavior—especially motivated behavior, in this case—are discussed here. Among these are lesions, or damage to selected portions of the nervous system, electrical stimulation of selected portions of the central nervous system through permanently implanted electrodes, the systemic injection of drugs, the stimulation of the brain itself by substances which are placed directly into selected portions of the brain, and electrical recording of the activity of the central nervous system. Note that one of the main points of this article is to suggest that many techniques should be applied to the understanding of the brain as a basis for behavioral events.

GLOSSARY   **Electrolytic lesions:** *lesions made by electric currents, usually direct (DC) currents, although other types of current are sometimes used. Note that the brain may also be stimulated by electrical currents. The characteristics of the current are the important determiners of whether it results in stimulation or a lesion.* **Hypothalamus:** *a region of the brain at the base of the third ventricle which seems important in the control of feeding, drinking, sexual, and emotional behavior. (See your text for a more exact anatomical localization.)* **Amygdala:** *several nuclei, or collections of nerve cells, of the forebrain lateral to the hypothalamus. (See your text for a more exact anatomical localization.)* **Curare:** *a paralyzing drug.*

58: CENTRAL STIMULATION AND OTHER NEW APPROACHES TO MOTIVATION AND REWARD

Neal E. Miller, Rockefeller University

Combination of behavioral and physiological techniques

The recent spurt of fruitful research on the mechanisms of motivations has emerged as a result of the convergence of two lines of development. Physiologists, pharmacologists, and biochemists have been developing new and subtler tools for radically affecting and measuring organic processes. At the same time, experimental psychologists have been developing a variety of more effective techniques for measuring drives. The combination of techniques from these two sources is beginning to yield results which have exciting potentialities.

In this brief presentation I can only sample a few of these results. I shall include some pictures to give you a firsthand impression of the work.

AN EARLY STUDY OF HUNGER   Using the improved electrolytic technique for making lesions deep in the more primitive structures of the brain, Hetherington and Ranson (12) found that lesions in the region of the ventromedial nuclei of the hypothalamus would cause albino rats to overeat enormously so that, as Fig. 1 shows, they became very fat. But Bailey, Stevenson, and I (25) used behavioral tests to show that these lesions do not necessarily always potentiate hunger. Although our rats would eat more, they would not work as hard for food. Further-

more, they were stopped by smaller doses of quinine. Thus the additional behavioral tests did not support the original inference of increased hunger drawn from the measure of amount of food consumed. It seemed more reasonable to assume that the lesion interfered with complete satiation.

In the foregoing study, the single test of amount of food consumed disagreed with the rate of bar pressing and a number of other behavioral measures. Other studies, summarized elsewhere (18), show that certain circumstances can affect the rate of bar pressing, so the results of this test will disagree with those of a number of different tests. Discrepancies among tests purporting to measure the same thing raise important problems which the aptitude testers have long since explored: namely, problems of general versus specific factors, and of the purity of various measures of such factors.[1] But our main point for the moment is that it is prudent and extremely fruitful to use a variety of behavioral tests in studying a drive such as hunger. We are just beginning to cash in on the potentialities of these tests; to date most studies of the physiological mechanisms of hunger are still limited to the single measure of the amount of food consumed (17).

SAMPLE OF OTHER BRAIN-LESION STUDIES   Lesions in the same general region as those producing overeating can markedly change the temperament of the rat. Anand and Brobeck (1) found that such lesions in the hypothalamus could make rats far more aggressive (a finding which Bailey, Stevenson, and I confirmed on our fingers) and that lesions in the region of the

---

The preparation of this paper, as well as most of the author's studies cited in it, was supported by a research grant M 647 from the National Institute of Mental Health, United States Public Health Service.

[1] For a discussion of the design required, but seldom used, to test for the unity and generality of intervening variables such as drives, see (20).

amygdala could abolish this hyperaggressiveness. Similarly, Brady and Nauta (6) have shown that lesions in the septal region can produce heightened startle responses and, with the interesting exception of conditioned suppression (CER), a variety of other indications of increased emotionality. An abstract by King (13) indicates that his paper shows that such emotionality can also be counteracted by lesions in the amygdaloid complex.

In addition to making the animals much tamer, lesions in the region of the amygdala can also produce marked hypersexuality. This is part of the classical Klüver-Bucy (14) syndrome which has been one of the points of departure for many excellent studies of the effects of brain lesions on motivation (e.g., 28, 30, 31, 33).

In the past, the combination of the ablation technique with behavioral tests has been found to be a powerful method for studying sensory, perceptual, and motor functions of the brain. The same combination is becoming a powerful technique for studying also the motivational and emotional functions of the brain. I have cited only a small sample out of the increasingly impressive population of sophisticated studies by able men in this field.

DRIVE ELICITED BY ELECTRICAL STIMULATION
Electrical stimulation of specific points has been another classical technique for studying brain function. Originally, this technique was used to study motor effects on anaesthetized animals. In his classic work, Hess (11) refined this technique by permanently implanting electrodes in the brains of cats so that they could be stimulated in the normal unanaesthetized state. In addition to eliciting complex motor and postural responses, which were less like reflexes and more like acts, Hess discovered that stimulation in the hypothalamus produced a variety of apparently motivational effects such as rage, flight, and eat-

FIGURE 1   *Effects of overeating produced by lesions in the region of the ventromedial nuclei of the hyothalamus. (Picture by J. A. F. Stevenson.)*

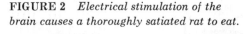

FIGURE 2   *Electrical stimulation of the brain causes a thoroughly satiated rat to eat.*

FIGURE 3 *Since the brain stimulation can also cause the rat to bite inedible objects, one wonders whether it elicits true hunger or only responses of gnawing.*

ing. His trail-blazing results, which were limited to naturalistic observation, have provided an excellent point of departure for recent studies using a variety of more rigorous behavioral tests.

Let me illustrate by brief excerpts from a film joined together by pieces of black leader to form a series of animated slides. First we see a cat with electrodes permanently implanted in his brain. As soon as he is stimulated, he lowers his head and starts lapping up water. This cat has Delgado-type electrodes ending in subminiature radio sockets so that the wires can be plugged into his head. The demonstration of drinking is very effective. But when the dish is moved a few inches to one side, the cat lowers his head and licks the floor. This simple test shows that we obviously are not eliciting normal thirst, but only a reflex licking response. Other less extreme examples require considerably more subtle tests.

Turning now to some work in collaboration with E. E. Coons, we see in Fig. 2 a rat with electrodes placed in a region where stimulation elicits eating. This rat has been thoroughly satiated on food. Soon after stimulation is turned on, the rat starts to eat; soon after it is turned off, he stops. Again, the demonstration is very effective.

But Fig. 3 shows that these rats, like

FIGURE 4 *In a critical test, electrical stimulation of the brain causes a moderately thirsty rat to stop drinking at a water spout and go to a different place to perform a learned response, pushing back a hinged door to get food.*

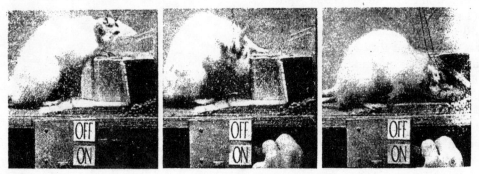

Hess's cats will sometimes also gnaw at inedible objects such as pieces of wood. Therefore, we wonder whether the centrally elicited eating has the properties of normal hunger or is mere reflex gnawing. As a test, we thoroughly trained rats, when thirsty, to get water from a spout above; and, when hungry, to get food by pushing aside a little hinged door below. Then, after thorough satiation, we tested the effects of electrical stimulation. In Fig. 4 you can see that the stimulation can cause a moderately thirsty rat to leave the water spout where he has been drinking and go to a different place to perform the instrumental response of pushing back the hinged door which he has learned as a means of getting food. The fact that the rat stops drinking shows that the effects of stimulation are not mere indiscriminate activation. The fact that the stimulation elicits the learned response of pushing aside the hinged door shows that it has at least some of the more general motivating properties of normal hunger.

In order to make the results completely official, we also trained the rats, when hungry, to secure food by pressing a Skinner bar which delivered small pellets on a variable-interval schedule. Fig. 5 shows the effects of brain stimulation on a thoroughly satiated rat. (Each time the rat presses the bar, the recording lever moves upwards slightly. Each time a bar press actually delivers food, the pen draws a downward spike.) Horizontal sections of the cumulative record show that the satiated rat did relatively little work at the bar during two-minute periods of non-stimulation. The upward steps show that, during the two minutes when the stimulation was on, the rat worked at the bar which occasionally delivered food. Thus we have further evidence that electrical stimulation in the areas that induce eating will also motivate the performance of learned instrumental responses that have been reinforced by food. The results are

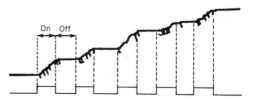

FIGURE 5   *Stimulation in the hypothalamus elicits the learned response of bar pressing in a satiated rat. Each bar press moves the pen up a little. The rat has been trained on a variable-interval schedule; each spike below the record indicates when a bar press actually delivers food.*

convincing pictorially; they also are statistically reliable.

Continuing our program of testing point-by-point whether the motivation elicited by the electrical stimulation of the brain has all of the properties of normal hunger, Coons and I found that its effects were not limited to the gnawing of solid foods; it caused a satiated rat to drink milk. In control tests the stimulation did not elicit similar sustained drinking of water. Furthermore, the stimulation could be used to motivate the rat to run a T maze with the termination of the stimulation serving as a reward to produce highly reliable choice of the endbox in which the stimulation was turned off. In short, the termination of centrally stimulated "hunger" by turning off the switch seems to have the same rewarding effects as the eating of food which ordinarily terminates normally elicited hunger.

Let us turn now to a different type of motivation: a pain-fear–like emotional disturbance which can be elicited by electrical stimulation in a number of regions deep in the brain (8). Does this emotional reaction have all of the functional properties of normally aroused pain and fear? Some of these properties are: (*a*) Pain and fear can motivate, and their termination reinforce, trial-and-error learning. (*b*) They can be used to establish a conditioned response. (*c*) They can serve as a punishment to establish an approach-avoidance conflict so that a hungry animal will avoid food.

The purpose of the experiments is to demonstrate point-by-point that central stimulation of the critical places in the brain has all of the foregoing properties.

Figure 6 illustrates the first of these experiments. It shows a cat with chronic Delgado-type electrodes ending in subminiature tube sockets into which are plugged the wires bearing the stimulation. This cat first learned to rotate a paddle wheel to turn off electric shock. Then he was tested with brain stimulation. As soon as the stimulation was delivered, the cat became active and, after a few irrelevant responses, rotated the wheel which turned off the stimulation and thus rewarded the response of rotating the wheel. After a few trials, facilitated by transfer from the previous training, the cat learned to rotate the wheel as soon as the stimulation was turned on. Fig. 6 shows him performing this habit motivated by electrical stimulation of the brain.

In the next experiment, preliminary tests showed that a tone was a neutral stimulus which produced no obvious response. Then for a number of trials the tone was immediately followed by the brain stimulation which elicited wheel turning. After a few such trials, the wheel turning was conditioned: the tone alone, without brain stimulation, caused the cat to turn the wheel.

In the final experiment, we found that stimulation in the sensorimotor area of a hungry control cat, which was eating, produced a violent withdrawal from food; but even after repeated stimulation, the control animals promptly returned to eat. By contrast, experimental cats, stimulated once or twice with a lower voltage in the critical area of the brain, learned to avoid the food.

These experiments have shown that brain stimulation at critical points can have a number of the significant properties of normally elicited pain and fear. In addition to illustrating a general approach to the problem of investigating motivational factors elicited by electrical stimulation of the brain, experiments of the foregoing type may yield information which will help us in knowing where to place lesions in order to relieve certain hitherto hopeless patients from the acute misery of intractable pain.

Similar experiments on centrally aroused aggression have elicited a spectacular and relatively well-integrated cluster of symptoms of rage—hissing, spitting, clawing, etc.—which suggest that rage contains some integrated motor components differ-

FIGURE 6 *Electrical stimulation of a pain-fear area in a cat's brain elicits a learned response: rotating a wheel which turns off the stimulation. Stimulation is turned on between the first and second pictures. (From a motion picture by Miller, Delgado, and Roberts, shown by the author at the 1953 meeting of the APA.)*

ent from fear (24). So far, however, Warren Roberts and I have confirmed Masserman's results (16) in that we have not been able to condition such responses. This raises an interesting question. Is anger a distinctive drive whose mechanisms we have simply failed to date to locate, or are the motor components involved in rage organized without any separate, distinctive drive so that they must be motivated by other drives such as fear, hunger, or sex?

The results of these experiments are enough to illustrate that the combination of the physiological technique of electrical stimulation with various behavioral techniques for measuring the effects of such stimulation is turning out to be a powerful new tool for investigating the motivational functions of the brain.

REWARD EFFECTS OF ELECTRICAL STIMULATION   The combination of the techniques for stimulating the brains of unanaesthetized animals with those of exact behavioral testing led Olds and Milner (27) to a completely unexpected discovery. They found that electrical stimulation of certain areas of the brain would act as a powerful reward. This reward could be used to cause animals to choose the correct side of a T maze or to press a bar in a Skinner box. Often in the history of science, the unexpected discovery of a novel phenomenon, such as X-rays or radioactivity, has forced drastic revisions in current theory and ultimately led to important practical developments. While it is too early to be certain exactly how important will be the effects of this unexpected discovery by Olds and Milner, I suspect they will be considerable.

On the theoretical front, the rewarding effect of central stimulation tends to revive hedonistic theories of reinforcement. As I have pointed out elsewhere, however, the results known to date can be fitted in fairly well with any of the current theories of reinforcement, and the drive-reduction

hypothesis suggests a number of interesting lines of investigation in the area of centrally rewarding effects (22). The important thing is that we have here a genuinely novel phenomenon and a completely new technique for investigating the mechanism of reward and its relationship to various drives.

This new discovery has touched off a flurry of research which is still mounting with positive acceleration. Olds (26) has shown that there are certain regions of the hypothalamus where the rate of bar pressing increases with hunger much as it would if the animals were receiving a food reward. In a slightly different area, the rate of bar pressing varies positively with sex—being reduced by castration and increased by androgen therapy. Furthermore, different drugs, such as tranquilizers, seem to have differential effects on the reward phenomenon elicited by stimulation in different parts of the brain. Thus, we probably have here a technique for learning more about how drugs affect different parts of the brain and also for screening drugs in order to discover ones that have more specific psychological effects.

PARADOXICAL DUAL EFFECTS   The experiments which I performed in collaboration with Delgado and Roberts (8) showed that stimulation of certain points in the brain can serve as a punishment. The experiments by Olds and Milner (27) showed that stimulation at other points of the brain can serve as a reward. One of my students, Roberts (29), has recently shown that stimulation in other places may paradoxically function first as a reward and then as a punishment. Bower and I (5) have described further work along this line.

Figure 7 shows pictures of a rat with electrodes at a point in the anterior portion of the medial forebrain bundle which elicits these paradoxical dual effects. Pressing the bar turns the stimulation on. As you can see, immediately after having

FIGURE 7 *Paradoxical reward-aversion effect illustrated by a rat which presses a bar to turn the stimulation on, runs to the opposite end of the apparatus and rotates a wheel to turn it off, and then returns to press the bar, continuing to repeat this sequence. (Photographed in the author's laboratory by Martin Iger for Harcourt, Brace and Company.)*

pressed the bar the rat turns away and goes to rotate a wheel which terminates the stimulation, then he returns to press the bar again, continuing to repeat the sequence. I believe that this phenomenon may conceivably give us a technique for studying drugs that accentuate the positive rewarding function of the brain and minimize the negative punishing ones.

MOTIVATIONAL EFFECTS OF DRUGS One of my students, Robert Kirschner, used an apparatus much like the one illustrated in Fig. 7 except that the bar and wheel were replaced by two bars diagonally across a corner from each other in order to equalize the skill and effort required to turn the stimulation on or off. Studying the effects of methamphetamine and chlorpromazine, he found that 2 mg/kg of the former and 4 mg/kg of the latter produced roughly equivalent reductions in the total number of bar presses.

But, when the rewarding and aversive effects were analyzed separately, these two drugs had strikingly different effects. The methamphetamine increased the time to turn the stimulation off while decreasing the time to turn it on. By contrast, the chlorpromazine produced a great increase in the time to turn the stimulation on and also some increase in the time to turn it off. One interpretation of these results is that methamphetamine was accentuating the positive rewarding effects and minimizing the negative punishing ones—a result congruent with its clinical euphoric effects. Chlorpromazine seemed to be reducing reward more than the aversion—a result congruent with the fact that it sometimes causes patients to feel depressed.

The organic chemists are turning out thousands of new compounds and are able to produce at will slight modifications in known drugs. Similarly, the biochemists are learning more about vital hormones, enzymes, enzyme inhibitors, and other powerful agents of metabolism. But one of the chief bottlenecks to the discovery of superior psychotropic drugs is the difficulty in efficiently and safely testing for the psychological effects of all these new compounds. Perhaps this test, along with many other ingenious ones recently devised by experimental psychologists, will help us in finding drugs which have more potent therapeutic effects with fewer harmful side effects. Although the current enthusiasm for the tranquilizing drugs may have the same rocketing rise and frustrating fall as other "wonder cures" for schizophrenia, I believe that the recent signs of vigorous growth of a new infant science of psychopharmacology afford a reasonable ground for eventual hope.

For the rapid growth of psychopharmacology to be healthy, however, I believe that it should soon advance beyond the stage where a single test is widely used for screening merely on the basis of its face validity. The standards and methods of modern aptitude testing should be adapted to this new area. Batteries of tests should be tried out and validated, first by the criterion of internal consistency and eventually by the criterion of predicting clinically useful effects. Both screening tests and drugs might eventually be factor analyzed. At the same time that we are refining our screening instruments, we should also be conducting pure-science studies to analyze how well-known drugs achieve their psychological effects. We need to discover fundamental laws to develop a basic science of psychopharmacology. Such a science should provide a rational basis for practical applications to mental hygiene in the same way that organic chemistry provides a basis for the analysis and synthesis of new compounds (21).

In connection with the problem of drugs, let me emphasize that there is no necessary incompatibility between organic and functional approaches to the problem of mental disease.[2] As you know, I find it useful to describe neurosis and psychotherapy in terms of learning theory. But the book (9) which Dollard and I wrote on this topic contains a chapter on drugs and brain lesions. It is entirely possible that people differ, for example, in the strength of the innate mechanisms for fear, guilt, and anxiety just as they vary in

physical size and strength. A person with unusually strong emotional mechanisms of this kind would be especially susceptible to learning strong fears and guilts by traumatic incidents. These unusually strong fears and guilts might directly elicit certain psychosomatic symptoms, produce strong conflicts, or motivate the learning of functional symptoms. It is quite conceivable that chronic medication by suitable drugs could reduce this special susceptibility to irrationally strong fears and guilts much as insulin enables the diabetic to tolerate a diet containing more carbohydrates.

Furthermore, drug effects have the great advantage over certain other forms of organic intervention in that they are reversible. Some interesting results have already been secured by combining the use of barbiturates with psychotherapy. It is conceivable that a superior drug will be produced which will be a much more effective aid to emotional re-education. Indeed, it is conceivable that radically improved results with certain forms of mental disease may be achieved by an unconventional combination of drug therapy, individual therapy, group therapy, training in social skills, and temporary manipulation of the environment.

BIOCHEMICAL STIMULATION   In addition to electrical techniques of stimulation, new biochemical techniques (which obviously have implications also for psychopharmacology) have recently been exploited. For example, Andersson (2) has shown that minute injections of salt solution into the region of the third ventricle can cause excessive drinking in goats. Conversely our group has shown that minute injections of water into the brain can cause a thirsty cat to stop drinking. Furthermore, we have shown that the minute salt injections increase, while the water ones decrease, the rate of performing a learned response to get water. Therefore, these minute injec-

[2] For a more detailed discussion, see (19).

tions into the brain have some of the more general effects of normal increases or reductions of thirst (23).

Similarly, Alan Fisher (10) has shown that a minute injection of male hormone into a specific site in the brain can induce complex sexual, and in some instances maternal, behavior as though it had a motivating effect. Since similar effects were not produced by electrical stimulation of the same sites, there is reason to believe that, in some instances at least, the chemical stimulation may be more effective and selective than the electrical technique. Here again, we have a powerful new tool, the potentialities of which are just beginning to be explored.

ELECTRICAL RECORDING OF BRAIN ACTIVITY
The converse of the stimulation technique is that of recording electrical activity of the brain and other parts of the nervous system. This technique has been used with great success in tracing sensory systems and has recently produced some quite exciting results which may help to explain the mechanism for the relationship between motivation and attention. For example, it has been found that stimulation of the reticular system in the brain can actually reduce the transmission of sensory impulses from the end organs and through lower relay centers, thus partially shielding the brain from certain sources of stimulation. As Livingston (15) has pointed out, this finding produces a radical change in our previous notions of sensory neurophysiology.

Can these new techniques be applied to other motivational phenomena? For example, Pavlov reports that, when a somewhat painful stimulus is made the conditioned stimulus for food, all of the obvious emotional responses to pain seem to drop out. By using suitable recording techniques, could we demonstrate that the pain impulses themselves are reduced before they reach the highest centers? Would we have an experimental method for pro-

ducing and studying a phenomenon analogous to hysterical anaesthesia?

Although techniques for recording the electrical activity of the nervous system have been used very successfully in the study of sensory mechanisms, they have not been used much in the study of drive and reward. Here seems a promising new area of application, although there are technical difficulties to overcome. For example, if an animal's motor responses (which disturb electrical recording) were eliminated by one of the improved curare derivatives, such as flaxidil, would we find that the electrical activity in different tracts and centers of the brain is altered when the animal is hungry, thirsty, or suffering painful stimulation? What would be the effects of rewards such as water injected directly into the blood stream of a thirsty animal, if indeed it can be demonstrated that such injections function as a reward? Would there be any effects specific to stimulation of the brain at points where such stimulation is rewarding and different from those at points where it is neutral or aversive? Any such differences are likely to give us significant clues to the basic mechanisms of motivation and reward (22).

Other promising approaches

Now fasten your seat belts for a final spurt through a number of different approaches for which the brevity of listing does not mean any inferiority in merit.

Recently Roger Russell's group has been studying the effects of what might be called biochemical lesions of the brain, while David Krech and Mark Rosenzweig have been pursuing the relationships among brain chemistry, heredity, and behavior. While these new lines of work have been aimed chiefly at cognitive functions, they could easily turn up facts which would lead directly into problems of motivation and reward.

Most of the studies I have sampled thus

far have involved relatively direct approaches to the brain. The combination of exact behavioral tests with various "intermediate" techniques has also proved fruitful. Some of the techniques used in this way have been a fistula into the stomach, a cannula into a vein, a subcutaneous saline injection, enzyme inhibitors, and unusual substances which are similar to a metabolite in one respect but different in others. Programs involving such work are well under way in Mayer's laboratory at Harvard (3), Stellar's (32) at Pennsylvania, and our own laboratory at Yale (24). Similarly, Beach (4) and his students are introducing a greater variety of behavioral techniques into the study of sex.

Thus far, various approaches usually have been used in relative isolation. Additional advances may be expected when more use is made of systematic combinations of these approaches. For example, appropriately placed lesions might be used in the analysis of the systems involved in the drive or reward effect of brain stimulation or of the different effects of distending the stomach with either food or a balloon.

Finally, a completely different and highly promising development has been the use of behavioral techniques to bring new drives into the laboratory: first fear, then curiosity, and most recently social deprivation. We can and should extend the range of drives experimentally studied. But that is another story (20).

References

1. Anand, B. K., & Brobeck, J. R. Food intake and spontaneous activity of rats with lesions in the amygdaloid nuclei. *J. Neurophysiol.,* 1952, **15,** 421–430.

2. Andersson, B. The effect of injections of hypertonic NaCl solutions into different parts of the hypothalamus of goats. *Acta Physiol., Scand.,* 1953, **28,** 188–201.

3. Anliker, J., & Mayer, J. The regulation of food intake: Some experiments relating behavioral, metabolic and morphologic aspects. *Amer. J. clin. Nutr.,* 1957, **5,** 148–153.

4. Beach, F. A. Characteristics of masculine "sex drive." In M. R. Jones (Ed.), *Nebraska symposium on motivation.* Lincoln: Univer. Nebraska Press, 1956.

5. Bower, G., & Miller, N. E. Paradoxical rewarding and aversive effects from stimulating the same place in a rat's brain. *Amer. Psychologist,* 1957, **12,** 464. (Abstract)

6. Brady, J. V., & Nauta, W. J. H. Subcortical mechanisms in emotional behavior: The duration of affective changes following septal and habenular lesions in the albino rat. *J. comp. physiol. Psychol.,* 1955, **48,** 412–420.

7. Brown, J. The generalization of approach responses as a function of stimulus intensity and strength of motivation. *J. comp. Psychol.,* 1942, **33,** 209–226.

8. Delgado, J. M. R., Roberts, W. W., & Miller, N. E. Learning motivated by electrical stimulation of the brain. *Amer. J. Physiol.,* 1954, **179,** 587–593.

9. Dollard, J., & Miller, N. E. *Personality and psychotherapy: An analysis in terms of learning, thinking, and culture.* New York: McGraw-Hill, 1950.

10. Fisher, A. Maternal and sexual behavior induced by intracranial chemical stimulation. *Science,* 1956, **124,** 228–229.

11. Hess, W. R. *Das Zwischenhirn: Syndrome, Lokalisationen, Functionen.* (2nd ed.) Basel: Schwabe, 1954.

12. Hetherington, A. W., & Ranson, S. W. The relation of various hypothalamic lesions to adiposity in the rat. *J. comp. Neurol.,* 1942, **76,** 475–499.

13. King, F. A. Effects of amygdaloid lesions upon septal hyperemotionality in the rat. *Amer. Psychologist,* 1957, **12,** 466. (Abstract)

14. Klüver, H., & Bucy, P. C. Preliminary analysis of functions of the temporal lobes in monkeys. *Arch. Neurol. Psychiat.,* 1939, **42,** 979–1000.

15. Livingston, R. B. Central control of afferent activity. In H. H. Jasper, et al. (Ed.), *Henry Ford hospital international symposium: Reticular formation of the brain.* Boston: Brown, in press.*

16. Masserman, J. H. Is the hypothalamus a center of emotion? *Psychosom. Med.,* 1941, **3,** 3–25.

17. Miller, N. E. Shortcomings of food consumption as a measure of hunger: Results from other behavioral techniques. *Ann. N.Y. Acad. Sci.,* 1955, **63,** 141–143.

18. Miller, N. E. Effects of drugs on motivation: The value of using a variety of measures. *Ann. N.Y. Acad. Sci.,* 1956, **65,** 318–333.

* Since published (*Ed.*).

19. Miller, N. E. A psychologist speaks. In H. D. Kruse (Ed.), *Integrating the approaches to mental disease.* New York: Paul B. Hoeber, 1957.

20. Miller, N. E. Liberalization of basic S-R concepts: Extensions to conflict behavior and social learning. In S. Koch (Ed.), *Psychology: A study of a science. Vol. II. General systematic formulations, learning and special processes.* New York: McGraw-Hill, in press.**

21. Miller, N. E. Objective techniques for studying motivational effects of drugs on animals. In S. Garatini & V. Ghetti Eds.), *Psychotropic drugs.* Amsterdam: Elsevier; New York: Van Nostrand, 1957.

22. Miller, N. E. Comments on the implications of the Olds reward effect for theories of reinforcement. In D. E. Sheer (Ed.), *Electrical stimulation of the brain: Subcortical integrative systems.* Houston: Univer. Texas Press, in press.†

23. Miller, N. E. Learning and performance motivated by direct stimulation of the brain. In D. E. Sheer (Ed.), *Electrical stimulation of the brain: Subcortical integrative systems.* Houston: Univer. Texas Press, in press.‡

24. Miller, N. E. Experiments on motivation: Studies combining psychological, physiological, and pharmacological techniques. *Science,* 1957, **126,** 1271–1278.

25. Miller, N. E., Bailey, C. J., & Stevenson, J. A. F. Decreased "hunger" but increased food intake resulting from hypothalamic lesions. *Science,* 1950, **112,** 256–259.

26. Olds, J. Self-stimulation of the brain: Used to study local effects of hunger, sex and drugs. *Science,* in press.¶

27. Olds, J., & Milner, P. Positive reinforcement produced by electrical stimulation of septal area and other regions of rat brain. *J. comp. physiol. Psychol.,* 1954, 47, 419–427.

28. Pribram, K. H., & Weiskrantz, L. A comparison of the effects of medial and lateral cerebral resections on conditioned avoidance behavior in monkeys. *J. comp. physiol. Psychol.,* 1957, 50, 77–80.

29. Roberts, W. W. Both rewarding and punishing defects from stimulation of posterior hypothalamus with same electrodes at same intensity. *J. comp. physiol. Psychol.,* in press.§

30. Rosvold, H. E., Mirsky, A. F., & Pribram, K. H. Influence of amygdalectomy on social behavior in monkeys. *J. comp. physiol. Psychol.,* 1954, 47, 173–178.

31. Schreiner, L., & Kling, A. Rhinencephalon and behavior. *Amer. J. Physiol.,* 1956, 184, 486–490.

32. Stellar, E. Physiological psychology. In P. R. Farnsworth (Ed.), *Annual review of psychology.* Vol. 8. Palo Alto, Calif.: Annual Reviews Inc., 1957.

33. Waterhouse, I. K. Effects of prefrontal lobotomy on conditioned fear and food responses in monkeys. *J. comp. physiol. Psychol.,* 1957, 50, 81–88.

** Since published, 1959 *(Ed.).*
† Since published, 1961 *(Ed.).*
‡ Since published, 1961 *(Ed.).*

¶ Since published, 1958 *(Ed.).*
§ Since published, 1958 *(Ed.).*

In addition to electrical stimulation, the more usual type of brain stimulation, chemical stimulation, has certain advantages in attempts to discover brain-behavior relationships. In this experiment, small hollow tubes—cannulas—were permanently implanted in rats' skulls and into the lateral region of the hypothalamus. Thus chemical substances could be injected directly into the brain.

Work with lesions in the lateral region of the hypothalamus has indicated that this is an area concerned with the regulation of eating and drinking behavior. From studies with chemical stimulation, it seems that the hypothalamic systems controlling these behaviors can be separated on the basis of the substances which trigger the neural circuits in them. Thus, eating is adrenergic—that is, substances such as adrenaline will, when injected into the lateral hypothalamus, set off eating behavior. Drinking is cholinergic—that is, substances such as acetylcholine will, when injected into the lateral hypothalamus, set off

*drinking behavior. These adrenergic and cholinergic substances may
be effective because the synaptic transmissions of the eating and
drinking systems depend, respectively, upon adrenergic and
cholinergic substances.*

A POINT TO GUIDE YOUR STUDY   *The p values, p < .01 for instance,
have the same meaning as in the other articles where they are used.
(See the selection by Braun and Geiselhart in Section Three.)*

GLOSSARY   **Antidromic:** *the conduction of nerve impulses in a direction
opposite to the usual, "normal," direction.* **Stereotaxic instrument:** *a
device for accurately placing electrodes, cannulas, and so forth,
inside the skull, in the brain. (See the description in the article by
Hernández-Peón et al. in Section Ten.)* **Synapse:** *the gap between
neurons; a point of functional, not anatomical, connection; one nerve
fiber can excite another across the synaptic gap by means of*
transmitter substances. Adrenergic: *stimulated by substances such as
adrenaline and noradrenaline.* **Cholinergic:** *stimulated by substances
such as acetylcholine and carbachol.*

59:   EATING OR DRINKING ELICITED BY DIRECT ADRENERGIC OR CHOLINERGIC STIMULATION OF HYPOTHALAMUS

S. P. Grossman, *The University of Chicago*

ABSTRACT   A double cannula system, allowing repeated stimulation of central structures with crystalline chemicals, was developed. This technique was employed to study the effects of adrenergic and cholinergic stimulation of the lateral hypothalamus of rats. Drug-specific effects on the feeding and drinking mechanisms, respectively, were observed.

The exploration of the central nervous system by means of electrical stimulation has provided a wealth of information of great interest to physiologists and psychologists alike. The usefulness of this technique is limited, however, because the effects of stimulation are not restricted to synaptic junctions but affect fibers of passage, causing conduction in both normal and antidromic directions.

S. P. Grossman. Eating or drinking elicited by direct adrenergic or cholinergic stimulation of hypothalamus. *Science*, 1960, **132**, 301–302. Copyright © 1960 by the American Association for the Advancement of Science. Reprinted with permission from the author and the American Association for the Advancement of Science.

It has long been recognized that chemical stimulation avoids these problems, but the technique has in the past been plagued by the problem of uncontrolled spread, which raises a serious objection to the injection of chemicals in solution. Attempts to control for this factor by minimizing the injected quantities have apparently not been completely successful in preventing the escape of the fluid along the shank of the needle, following the path of least resistance.

Depositing chemicals in solid form has been shown to reduce this problem greatly (1), but this method has not allowed repeated stimulation of a selected locus. In the present study, a technique was developed which avoids this objection.

A double cannula system, consisting of two modified syringe needles, was permanently implanted unilaterally, by means of a stereotaxic instrument, into the lateral hypothalamus of each of 12 albino rats. Histological verification of the intended placements showed the tip of the cannula

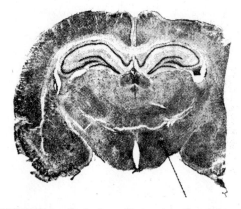

FIGURE 1   *End of needle tract in the right perifornical region of the rat brain.*
Stimulation at this point, as well as at loci slightly more medial and ventral, produced the effects described in the text.

to be located in a circumscribed periforni-cal region at the same rostrocaudal coordinate as the ventro-medial nucleus (see Fig. 1), an area corresponding to the ventral portion of Anand and Brobeck's "feeding area" of the lateral hypothalamus (2).

After 5 days of postoperative recuperation, the inner cannula was removed and minute amounts (1 to 5 μg) of crystalline chemicals were tapped into its tip before it was returned to its usual position. Successive treatments were administered to all animals in a counterbalanced order, with a minimum of 3 days between injections. Both food and water were freely available

throughout the experiment. The food and water consumption of satiated rats was recorded for 1 hour immediately following stimulation and compared with the consumption in a comparable period immediately preceding the injection. Daily food and water consumption records were maintained.

None of the animals ever consumed food or water in measurable quantities during the prestimulation period. The injection of epinephrine or norepinephrine resulted in highly significant ($p < .01$) food consumption beginning 5 to 10 minutes after stimulation and persisting with variable intensity for 20 to 40 minutes. Food consumption averaged 3.0 gm under epinephrine and 4.3 gm under norepinephrine.

The injection of acetylcholine (capped by physostigmine) or carbachol into the identical loci in the same animals resulted in highly significant drinking ($p < .01$), the latency, duration, and magnitude of the effect being comparable to those obtained for eating after the injection of adrenergic substances. Water consumption averaged 7.4 ml after the injection of acetylcholine and 12.8 ml after the injection of carbachol, this difference being highly significant ($p < .01$). There was no significant food consumption after cholinergic stimulation (see Fig. 2).

The injection of adrenergic substances

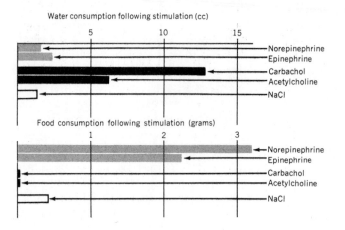

FIGURE 2   *Food and water intake during 1 hour following stimulation. (The intake during a comparable control period was zero in all cases and is not shown.)*

resulted in significantly less water intake than cholinergic stimulation ($p < .01$). Since in all but one animal the drinking occurred only after a considerable amount of dry food had been consumed, water consumption seemed to be secondary to the food intake rather than a direct consequence of stimulation. To establish further the specificity of the adrenergic effect, norepinephrine was deposited in the lateral hypothalamus of six food- and water-satiated animals, which were then placed in observation cages containing only water. For 30 minutes after the injection none of the animals consumed measurable quantities of water, though four of them repeatedly sampled the drinking tube very briefly. Food was then introduced, and all animals ate almost immediately, though total food consumption was lower than that normally observed, since the food was introduced only toward the end of the period previously established as the duration of the adrenergic effect.

In order to control for the effect of osmotic stimulation, comparable amounts of NaCl were deposited in all the animals. No significant food or water intake was observed. In order to control for general excitation effects, strychnine in comparable quantities was deposited in six animals which also showed the above-described effects of adrenergic and cholinergic stimulation. No consumatory behavior was observed following this stimulation.

The daily consumption records indicate that the amount of food or water consumed during the 1-hour period after stimulation, totaling as much as 40 percent of the animal's normal daily intake, appeared to be consumed above and beyond the normal daily intake. Because of the variability of these records, no statistical evaluation of this effect can be presented, but the conclusion is supported, at least for eating, by the consistent weight gain observed on the day following adrenergic stimulation.

A control for the specificity of the localization of the observed effects was obtained in a preliminary study designed to yield optimal stereotaxic coordinates for the study reported here. It was found that very small deviations from the optimal position, shown in Fig. 1, sufficed to eliminate the effects completely.

The results of this investigation indicate that (i) cell concentrations active in the regulation of both food and water intake are present in the lateral hypothalamus; (ii) cell concentrations exerting this control appear to be highly localized but not clearly separate from each other, since stimulation of "identical" loci in the same animal can evoke both forms of behavior; and (iii) the feeding mechanism appears to be selectively activated by adrenergic stimulation, while the drinking mechanisms appear to respond selectively to cholinergic stimulation (3).

References and notes

1. P. D. MacLean, *A.M.A. Arch. Neurol. Psychiat.* 78, 113 (1957).
2. B. K. Anand and J. R. Brobeck, *Proc. Soc. Exptl. Biol. Med.* 77, 323 (1951).
3. This investigation was supported by a Public Health Service research fellowship (MF-10, 597), as well as by funds from Dr. Neal E. Miller's grant (M647) from the National Institute of Mental Health, U.S. Public Health Service.

PHYSIOLOGICAL
BASIS
OF
BEHAVIOR

In this introduction to a reprinting of an important book in physiological psychology, Brain Mechanisms and Intelligence, *by K. S. Lashley, D. O. Hebb attempts to evaluate the impact of Lashley's work on the history of recent psychology. He gives a short biography of Lashley and then summarizes some of Lashley's most important contributions. Much of Lashley's work called into question the speculative physiological theories of behavior which were prevalent in the psychology of the first part of the twentieth century. One reaction to this was a weakening of interest in the physiological, or biological, explanations of behavior in the decades of the Thirties and Forties. Physiological speculations were supplanted by behavioral theories—positivistic theories—based on stimulus and response, input and output. For the most part, the influential psychological theories of this time paid little attention to happenings in the "black box" of the nervous system. However, in the past 10 to 15 years, with new techniques, new discoveries, and a growing dissatisfaction with the stimulus-response theories, a new physiological, or biological, psychology has come into being.*

A POINT TO GUIDE YOUR STUDY   *The chapters referred to in this selection are those in the book* Brain Mechanisms and Intelligence.

GLOSSARY **Maze I** *and* **Maze III:** *simple mazes for rats with differing numbers of blind alleys; maze III has the most blind alleys and is the most difficult.* **Golgi stain:** *a silver stain of neurons which shows individual cell bodies and fibers in great detail.* **Mass action:** *the idea that the severity of the deficit in certain functions is proportional to the amount of brain tissue removed; the brain tissue is supposed to act as a whole—or mass—for the particular function under investigation.* **Equipotentiality:** *the idea that different regions of the brain can act equivalently with respect to certain psychological functions; for instance, the brain is said to function equipotentially for some types of learning.*

60: INTRODUCTION TO DOVER EDITION OF: BRAIN MECHANISMS AND INTELLIGENCE, BY K. S. LASHLEY

D. O. Hebb, McGill University, Montreal, Canada

It is not far-fetched to date the beginning of the modern period in psychology from the publication of this book in 1929. Its importance for physiological psychology, of course, is obvious. In it Lashley developed methods, formulated problems, and established critical standards of analysis that have affected all subsequent studies using brain operation as a method. But the influence extended through a much wider field, unacknowledged and perhaps unrealized by psychologists who nevertheless spoke and experimented differently from what they would have if it had not been written. The student who wants to understand the course of psychology in the past thirty years, and certain peculiarities of psychology today, should have some knowledge of this book and the circumstances in which it appeared.

The behavior theory that existed before its publication was mostly cast in neurological terms, and concerned ideas that could never be the same again. Lashley's critique had been building up in a brilliant series of studies begun about 1920, but examination of the contemporary literature suggests that the full weight of the critique was not felt until the appearance of his book (together with his presidential address to the American Psychological Association in the same year). In the preceding decades it was possible to debate the question seriously, whether consciousness was due to an impulse passing high resistance at the synapse, or low resistance. It was still possible to put single memories into single brain cells, like little jewel cases, each with its own jewel. It was pos-

sible to take as an axiom that "conscious" means "cortical" and "cortical" means "conscious" (so if a habit becomes automatic and needs no thought, a cortical pathway has been short-circuited and is now subcortical). None of this carefree neurologizing was possible after 1930, at least not for a psychologist.

Instead there was a conspicuous avoidance. In the perspective of time one can see an extraordinary change of theoretical climate between, say, 1928 and 1938. From Wundt onward psychology had been predominantly physiological psychology, however fanciful. Now psychology became anti-physiological or a-physiological, a theme most effectively presented in the work of B. F. Skinner and E. C. Tolman. Both these men argued that talking about the nervous system is unnecessary, even a positive hindrance, in behavioral analysis. C. L. Hull seems to have taken a less extreme position, but the fact that his highly influential theorizing made no real use of neurological conceptions was a vote cast on the same side. (It is said that Hull was rather inclined to take cognizance of the nervous system except after a visit from K. W. Spence, who was opposed, and that Spence visited Yale often enough to keep him on the strait and narrow.)

Now the positivistic views of Skinner and Tolman are really extreme—they go much farther than merely saying that physiology is not essential for a psychologist—and they represent a sharp break from the main tradition of psychological thought. Persuasive as the supporting arguments were, it is astonishing that they could have been so successful in so short a period of time, allowing for the conservativeness of scientific thought—except for one thing.

The traditionalist, the man who might

have argued the opposing case, found himself all at once without arguments. The stock-in-trade of physiological behavior theory had been synaptic resistances, detailed localizations of cortical function, and new paths from point to point in the cortex for new habits. Now, suddenly, it appeared from Lashley's work that such ideas were fantasy, not science. In these circumstances the positivistic *coup d'état* becomes more intelligible. Neither of the main movers, Tolman and Skinner, adopted his position because of Lashley, but one hardly doubts that their success in carrying others along with them owed much to work that made the ideas of physiological theory more than slightly ridiculous.

The literature of the day does not directly reveal the impact made by this book and the research papers that led up to it, evident as the impact was in the bars and hotel corridors at the time. It can be seen however in what was *not* said after 1930, what people *stopped* writing. The last major formulation of the pre-Lashley type, with synaptic resistances and receptor-effector connections all complete to account for all behavior, is to be found in E. B. Holt's *Animal Drive and the Learning Process*. Its publication was as late as 1931, but the writing must have been done earlier, and the book was an anachronism before it was published. Tolman's *Purposive Behavior in Animals and Men* took over in 1932, to be followed by Skinner's *The Behavior of Organisms* in 1938, with hardly a murmur from the defenders of physiological psychology. The defenders had in fact become few in number. Positivism is still with us in the 1960's and if the student is (as he might well be) puzzled by some of its manifestations he should look to the historical background of which this book is such a significant part.

It is of some interest to see how the book came to be written. Karl Spencer Lashley (1890–1958) was born in Davis, West Virginia. At the University of West Virginia

at the age of 15 he meant to major in Latin or English, but an accidental encounter with John Black Johnston, the neurologist, discovered for him the world of biological science, with which he promptly fell in love; and, by his own account, another accidental encounter the next year with a set of Golgi slides of the frog brain determined that this love would take the form of the study of behavior.

His conversion to neurological problems and psychology seems not to have really been so complete and immediate, for he took his M.S. at Pittsburgh in bacteriology and then went on to zoology at Johns Hopkins, where he took his Ph.D. with H. S. Jennings in 1914. It seems clear, however, that he was deeply involved with psychology by this time, and the earlier contact with the frog brain, in his sophomore year, had something to do with it. Finding the abandoned set of slides, he went to his instructor and proposed, in his innocence (he was only 16 or 17 years old), to work out all the connections: "Then we should know how the frog worked." It was a sharp disappointment to learn that not even the Golgi stain allows one to work out all the connections of the brain, but as Lashley himself said, he spent the rest of his life trying to find out "how the frog worked": frog, rat, monkey or man.

At Johns Hopkins he came into contact with John B. Watson in the period when Watson was preparing the Behaviorist manifesto, in 1912, and collaborated closely with him in a number of studies over the next six years. One collaboration is of special interest here: Lashley wrote a chapter on learning for Watson's *Behavior: an Introduction to Comparative Psychology* (1914), developing in it just those "Watsonian" notions that, later, he spent most of his professional life refuting.

It was during the period at Johns Hopkins that Lashley also encountered Shepherd Ivory Franz and made his first use of the brain-operation method. Franz at this time was working on psychiatric problems at St. Elizabeth's Hospital in Washington, D.C., and apparently had his own methods for selecting a junior collaborator. At any rate, Lashley's story was that Franz first set him to photographing naked female patients. This was to find out whether he was a reliable worker. Satisfied on that point, or else concluding that a young man would do better with other material, he undertook with Lashley two studies of the effect of cortical extirpations on habit in the rat. Thus began the line of work that was the chief basis of the present book.

It was at the University of Minnesota that Lashley followed up in earnest the work begun with Franz. He has told us (cf. p. 14) that he began with the simple aim of demonstrating the soundness of Watson's ideas of synaptic modification and the formation of stimulus-response connections through the cortex. But every experiment he did came out wrong, and at some time during this period (1920–1926) it is evident that he abandoned the theory, though he never abandoned Watson's real aim of achieving a completely monistic and objective explanation of behavior. For the rest of his life Lashley was proud of a remark Watson made to him once, that he was the only thoroughgoing behaviorist that Watson knew.

Then in 1926 Lashley moved to the Institute for Juvenile Research, Chicago, where he undertook the experiments that are reported in this book. It is important for the student of behavior, in reading it, to observe that it is not merely a report of brain operations in the rat. Brain operation was a method, and the rat a convenient subject; what Lashley was interested in was understanding behavior, especially (but not exclusively) human behavior. Unlike some other behaviorists, he was not afraid to use the word *mind*, and it was the problem of mind that he wanted to solve. The rat was a convenient subject for the investigation because a more accurate measurement of the size of brain lesions can be made with a smooth-

brained animal, adequate methods of testing were available, and such methods could be applied to large groups of subjects. All these considerations make for reliable results, in marked contrast to the clinical data of human brain damage. It can be seen from his discussion that his results are nevertheless relevant to problems of the clinic, and in fact, this book has had a continuing influence on neurological thought.

It should also be observed that Lashley's incidental observations were almost as important as his formal data. There was a good deal of talk in the twenties about random behavior, unguided "trial and error," followed by "accidental success." When Lashley observed that

one does not realize the meaning of "random" behavior until he has compared a normal animal with one having extensive cerebral destruction. The normal animal almost never re-enters a cul-de-sac [immediately]. An animal with severe lesions may repeat a single error as many as two hundred times before passing to other parts of the maze (p. 138),

he was telling us that there is a kind of order and system in the *normal* animal's behavior that is missed in making facile assumptions about randomness. In the same context—discussion of the qualitative changes in the rat's behavior following brain damage—he made the radical suggestion (radical indeed for a behavioristically minded psychologist in 1929) that in learning a light-darkness discrimination the rat shows order and *purpose* in the pre-solution period, and that his *attention* is a factor in learning:

. . . responses to position, to alternation, or to cues from the experimenter's movements usually precede the reactions to the light and represent attempted solutions which are within the rat's customary range of activity (p. 135).

And again, in problem-box learning:

. . . the animal which has run across the platform many times without pause, stops and explores the platform thoroughly. The door is opened during this exploration, and there-after all activity . . . centers about the plat-form and door (p. 135).

This was a level of analysis that had mostly been absent in experiments on rat behavior. The discussion led directly to I. Krechevsky's studies of "hypotheses" in the rat, and thus to the continuity-noncontinuity controversy of the thirties and forties—another example of the influ-ence the book has had upon psychological theory and experiment.

The general plan of the work is as fol-lows. Lashley first set out to examine the effect of brain damage on the ability to acquire habits, the rats being operated on before training was begun. Tests of con-tinued retention and habit reversal make a total of ten measures, reported on in Chap-ters III, IV and V.

Chapter VI presents a second main ex-periment, in which the rats were trained before operation. Here Lashley used one test situation only (Maze III) but with a larger number of animals in the experi-mental group. The question is whether brain damage affects the retention of habits already established in the same way as it affects the acquisition of a new one. One might say, roughly, that the question is whether *memory* is affected in the same way as learning ability, and the answer is yes for this test.

Chapter VII then raises the special question of the extent to which the impair-ment of acquisition and retention can be explained by interference with sensory or motor processes rather than learning abil-ity and memory *per se.* Here Lashley first made the brilliant observation that cortical blindness produces a greater deterioration of performance than peripheral blinding by removal of the eyes (pp. 110–112). Even in blind animals, loss of visual cortex produces a disturbance of maze learning. From this it must be concluded that visual cortex has some further function in addi-tion to a sensory one. It is not a mere transmitter of sensory information. Subse-

quently Lashley's interpretation of the data, or the adequacy of the data, was challenged, and he returned to the topic in a later paper[1] in which the point was established beyond dispute.

On the motor side, similarly, the animal with an intact cortex but a gross distur-bance of normal motor control, because of a spinal or cerebellar lesion, can out-perform the cortically-injured rat with nor-mal coordination of the limbs,

although the manner of progression may be almost completely altered. One drags himself through with his forepaws; another falls at every step but gets through by a series of lunges; a third rolls over completely in making each turn, yet manages to avoid roll-ing into a cul-de-sac and makes an errorless run (p. 137).

This, with the observation that what the normal rat learns first is a general orien-tation in the maze rather than specific movements, struck directly at the chained-reflex conception of serial learning in the maze. In fact, simple-minded chaining theory soon disappeared, whether because of Lashley or not, and was replaced by "cog-nitive maps" on the one hand and modern "learning theory" on the other. Neither of these more or less positivistic formulations acknowledges any great debt to physio-logical psychology or, more specifically, to brain-operation experiments, but it hardly seems that the fundamental relevance of Lashley's analysis to their problems can be doubted by the impartial reader.

The fact seems to be that Lashley's data were so overwhelming, both in complexity and in their detailed, extensive denial of the central tenets of the learning theory of the twenties, that they were largely forgot-ten, simplified in memory to a point at which they no longer represented any problem for the theorist. Skinner has pointed out, rightly, that "CNS" often stands for "conceptual nervous system," rather than the complexities of the real

---

[1] "Studies of cerebral function in learning. XII. Loss of the maze habit after occipital lesions in blind rats," *J. comp. Neurol.,* 1943, **79,** 431–462.

central nervous system. To this, however, it must be added that psychological theory, and especially learning theory, mostly deals with a very conceptual animal, shorn of much of the trouble-making complexity of real behavior. Lashley's book, similarly, is remembered only as reporting that there is no localization of function in the rat's cortex, and that large lesions affect learning more than small lesions. "Equipotentiality," and "mass action." Full stop. If this were a true picture, the positivistic learning theorist obviously need not consult the book, and the clinical neurologist who knows that there *is* localization of function in the human brain can say, That's all very well for the rat, but it doesn't apply to man.

But this, of course, is not a true picture of Lashley's research. The qualitative analysis, so relevant to any theory of rat behavior, has already been stressed in the preceding pages. It remains to consider what Lashley did say about brain function and equipotentiality and mass action. In the first place, he did not deny, but rather emphasized, the existence of cortical localizations of function, in rat as well as in man. What he did deny was that localization is all that it has been thought to be. When the double-latch box has been learned by normal animals, lesions in the frontal region produce a loss of retention, but not other lesions. When a brightness discrimination has been acquired, lesions in posterior cortex disrupt it, but not anterior lesions.[2] This is localization of function, if in broad terms. But in either case, if the *same* lesions are made first, the rate of learning is unaffected: a result that is still hard to understand. One result clearly shows localization, the other seems to rule it out.

Lashley concluded, in general, that equi-

potentiality and mass action may both hold over the whole cortex for one function, such as learning a complex alley maze; but that in another situation, such as the elevated maze, vision becomes more important and equipotentiality disappears or is diminished. When he reports that large lesions, up to 50 per cent of neocortex in extent, do not retard learning in the double-latch-box problem, he is saying that mass is not a factor' in such learning. For different situations, different relations. In general, his opinion was that mass action and equipotentiality are most evident in complex problems—in Maze III, for example, as compared with Maze I.

As for man, Lashley's view was that specialization of cortical function has increased with phylogenesis (p. 154), but that the principles of brain function that are evident in the rat, where adequate experimental controls can be made, may still be applied with profit. The effects of functional differentiation of the speech area, for example, mean that the principle of mass action cannot be applied to cortex in general, when one is considering the effects of brain damage on speech; but it can be applied within the limits of speech-area cortex.

The thirty-odd years that have elapsed since the publication of this book have taken away some of its impact—its argument is no longer new—and subsequent research (by Lashley himself as well as others) has qualified its conclusions in some respects. On the other hand, that passage of time has confirmed the importance of Lashley's approach to the problems of behavior. In the perspective of time it can be seen that this is indeed one of the important books of psychology. It brought psychological theory down to earth in a way that had not been done before, with lasting effect; and the quality of its analyses of behavior, quite apart from its neurological and physiological data, gives it a continuing relevance and importance today.

[2] It is repeatedly stated in the book that the loss of the brightness habit obeys the law of mass action, being proportional to the size of the lesion. Lashley later discovered that this was an artifact, and reported the correction in his paper, "The mechanism of vision. XII. Nervous structures concerned in habits based on reactions to light," *Comp. Psychol. Monog.*, 1935, 11, 43–79.

The task of finding how the cerebral cortex of the brain participates in behavior is not an easy one. This selection summarizes many ablation experiments which have been done in an attempt to analyze the functions of the temporal cortex in monkeys. It is relatively easy to show that lesions of this region produce deficits in the ability to learn visual discriminations; but this is just the first step. From this discovery, analysis has proceeded along two lines—anatomical and behavioral. The anatomical analysis indicates that the connections of the temporal cortex with other parts of the cortex—cortical-cortical connections—are crucial for the proper visual function of the temporal cortex. The behavioral analysis is more complex. It has been shown, for instance, that monkeys with the crucial areas of the temporal cortex removed, although they cannot perform visual discriminations, are probably not blind; it has also been shown that the inability to solve visual problems is not due to a general deficit in learning ability. Other complexities have emerged, and the question of "What's wrong with the monkey?" after these temporal lesions has not yet really been settled to anyone's satisfaction. The important thing to notice about this selection is the analysis of the behavioral deficit after certain temporal lesions; much of physiological, or biological, psychology is concerned with such analysis of the behaviors—whatever they are—under study.

A POINT TO GUIDE YOUR STUDY   *For the anatomical position of the temporal lobe, see your text.*

GLOSSARY   **Pulvinar:** *the nucleus, or collection of nerve cells, in the thalamus which projects fibers to the parts of the temporal lobe under discussion in this selection.* **Learning set:** *"learning to learn," or the learning of a "general principle" through exposure to many similar situations. (See the selection by Harlow in Section Three.)*

61: SELECTION FROM: BIOLOGICAL PSYCHOLOGY. TEMPORAL LOBE VISUAL FUNCTION

I. T. Diamond, Duke University, and K. L. Chow, Stanford University

The loss of learned visual discrimination following ablation of the temporal lobe in monkeys

One line of research was initiated by Klüver's discovery that bilateral removal of the temporal lobe produced amnesia for learned visual tasks (12). Many experiments have since been done to determine the nature of the visual deficit and to define the limits of the temporal cortical lesion

I. T. Diamond and K. L. Chow. Excerpt from: Biological Psychology. From *Psychology: a Study of a Science,* Vol. 4. Edited by S. Koch. Copyright © 1962. McGraw-Hill Book Company. Used by permission. References renumbered.

which produces the loss. The first group of studies attempted to discover whether habits other than visual ones were affected by the lesion and whether lesions in areas other than temporal cortex could duplicate the syndrome. The attempt to establish the unique function of a part of the nervous system can be considered as the first goal of the ablation method.

The reasoning underlying the deficit method for establishing structure-function relations has been analyzed by Teuber (24). Teuber's own studies may be used to illustrate the ablation method. It was found that lesions of the visual cortex in man produce a defect in visual perception. However, one cannot conclude from this relationship that the unique function of visual cortex involves visual perception. Perhaps the same deficit will result from a lesion in cortical areas other than visual— an alternative which turned out to be the correct one. When a deficit has been shown to be the result of a specific lesion, the question of the nature of the deficit must be faced. Ablation of somatic cortex, for example, may disturb roughness discrimination because the operated animal has lost sensitivity to touch stimuli or because the operated animal no longer understands the test situation. The second alternative could be eliminated by showing that a discrimination of visual patterns was not disturbed by the same operation. The aim of the investigator is, then, to demonstrate that lesion A will affect task a but not b, while lesion B will affect task b but not a. The term *double dissociation* was invented by Teuber to describe this goal of ablation studies.

In most of the early studies of the temporal lobe the following procedures were used: The monkeys were first trained on two-choice simultaneous visual discriminations. In a two-choice visual discrimination, an animal is shown a pair of objects, such as a red plaque and a green plaque, or a black disk and a black diamond. Food is always placed under one stimulus of the pair, and the animal's task is to select this positive stimulus each time the pair of stimuli is presented. The trials are continued until some learning criterion is reached, usually 90 per cent correct in 30, 60, or 100 trials. Each monkey, prior to the surgery, was trained on a number of such visual discriminations. Selected cortical areas were then ablated bilaterally in one stage, and the animals were tested on the same tasks after the postoperative recovery period. The results showed, in general, that following ablation of the middle and inferior temporal gyri the ani-

mals forgot the preoperatively learned visual habits, but they could relearn these habits with further training (2, 16). Lesions in other regions—the preoccipital cortex, the frontal cortex, the parietal cortex, and the cortex on the medial surface of the temporal lobe—had no such effect (14, 5, 26). Chow and Hutt (9) have discussed what may appear to be exceptions to the conclusion that visual habits are uniquely affected by lesions of temporal neocortex (18).

The deficit produced by temporal cortical injury appears to be specific to visual tasks. At least other behavioral tasks, such as delayed response and somesthetic discriminations, were unaffected by the ablation of temporal cortex (20, 26). Furthermore, the visual deficit was apparent whether the stimuli were presented successively or simultaneously (21). In the method of successive presentation, only one of two stimuli is presented in any given trial. The monkey is required to respond to the positive stimulus and to withhold response to the negative stimulus. Thus further experiments could accept as a starting point that learned visual discriminations are uniquely affected by lesions of the temporal neocortex, and that the deficit from this lesion is specific to visual habits.

Further experimental analysis proceeded along two lines. One problem was to determine the role of anatomical pathways to the temporal cortex either from visual cortex or from subcortical nuclei. The only known cortico-cortical fibers from the visual area are short axon fibers that connect the visual area with the adjacent preoccipital cortex. Monkeys subjected to a partial ablation of preoccipital cortex still retained the learned visual tasks (5, 13). The anterior temporal cortex receives fibers from the medial pulvinar nucleus and sends corticofugal fibers back to this thalamic area (2, 25). Bilateral, partial lesions of the medial pulvinar nucleus did not affect the monkey's retention of visual tasks (7). A lesion which combined a part of the preoccipital cortex and a part of the medial pulvinar similarly failed to duplicate the effect of bilateral removal of the temporal cortex.

Since in none of these cases was there a complete lesion of the preoccipital cortex or a complete lesion of the medial pulvinar, two other types of surgical intervention were attempted (8). It is possible to eliminate all of the fibers from the pulvinar and still preserve cortico-cortical connections by undercutting the temporal cortex. After such a lesion, monkeys retained habits based on visual discrimination. It is possible to disrupt all cortico-cortical fibers and still preserve thalamocortical fibers by crosshatching the temporal cortex. After such a lesion, monkeys failed to retain habits based on visual discrimination. As far as we know, this visual deficit is the same as that produced by ablation of temporal cortex. Thus, whatever the role of impulses from visual centers in the temporal cortex syndrome, the path taken by such impulses must be via cortico-cortical fibers.

These results may resolve the apparent contradiction in experiments reported by Ades (1), Lashley (13), and Chow (5). In contrast to the latter two experiments, Ades found that monkeys with preoccipital lesions failed to retain visual discriminations. If the lesions made by Ades were complete and had interrupted all cortico-cortical fibers, while lesions made by Chow and Lashley spared some of these connections, then the reported difference in the behavioral effects of the lesions is understandable.

Another line of studies deals with the nature of the visual deficit following bilateral temporal removals. The first question asked was whether the deficit in visual discrimination was caused by a reduction in visual acuity or a scotoma. To test for a scotoma, animals were presented with a horizontal row of small pieces of food. It is known that in cases of scotoma, monkeys will miss some pieces in the defective region of their visual field. Animals with temporal lesions showed no such defect. Also temporal animals were able to locate thin threads. The performance on these visual tasks suggests that the animals did not suffer from some change in visual acuity. The effects of temporal lesions on visual discriminations do not then appear to be an expression of a sensory deficiency.

Pasik and others, however, disputed this interpretation (19). They found that monkeys with temporal lesions could learn a form discrimination at a normal rate, provided the visual stimuli were large in size. Furthermore, some of their monkeys showed difficulty in learning a tactile problem. Thus, they felt that the effect of temporal lesion may be accounted for by visual-field defects, such as amblyopia, plus a general disturbance of learning and memory.

The conclusions of Pasik and others were not supported by a recent study of Wilson and Mishkin (27). These authors designed an experiment to demonstrate the dissociation of visual-sensory defects following lesions of visual areas, and visual-learning defects following lesions of the temporal cortex. They found that monkeys with lateral occipital lesions had difficulty in learning string-pattern problems and colored-pattern discrimination. Monkeys with temporal lesions were deficient in acquiring form-discrimination and object-learning set. The string-pattern problem was considered a measure of visual-field defects. Both the form-discrimination and learning-set problems were considered to be tests of learning ability. The form-discrimination test, however, can be interpreted as a measure of perceptual organization, not necessarily dependent on learning as that term has been used in connection with agnosia.

The level of performance on the learning-set problem has been shown to be positively correlated with phylogenetic level (22, 23). In this task the animals are

not required to remember specific discriminations but to arrive at a general rule. The
animal must discover that whatever member of a pair is correct on the first trial will
be correct thereafter. Hundreds of pairs of
visual stimuli were presented to the animals,
each for only a few trials. The animals must
use the first trial to find out which of the two
visual stimuli contains food reward, and
to react appropriately on the very next
trial. After training on two or three hundred problems, a normal monkey will
select the correct stimulus 80 to 90 per cent
of the time on the second trial. Monkeys
with temporal lesions performed at a significantly lower level than did normal animals (22). Thus, the separation of visual-
sensory and learning functions appears to
correspond with the distinction between
visual-sensory cortex and temporal-asso-
ciation cortex. However, the temporal-lobe
deficit does not fit precisely the traditional
agnosia. Clearly, learning set cannot be
equated with perception as that term was
employed by Wundt, James, and Titchener.

Accepting the conclusion that the syndrome of the temporal neocortex cannot
be explained by some sensory disturbance,
further studies were undertaken to explore
the behavioral mechanisms underlying the
symptom of amnesia. One study asked
whether the postoperative memory deficit
may be due to a lack of comprehension of
the testing procedure (6). Monkeys were
trained preoperatively to form learning
sets with pairs of three-dimensional objects and with pairs of forms painted on
cards. After temporal-cortical ablation,
they retained the former but lost and could
not relearn the latter. As stated earlier, the
learning-set task requires the animal to
understand the general principle that determines which member of a pair is correct.
The retention of the learning set under
some conditions indicates that the animals
understood what they were supposed to do
in the testing situation. They were not
deficient in the capacity to form a learning

set. Why then did they lose the learning
set when the stimuli were painted forms?
This puzzling finding may be related to the
more abstract character of painted forms.
In any event, the form-discrimination
learning set is a more difficult problem if
difficulty is defined as the percentage of
correct responses in a certain number of
trials.

Further studies designed to test whether
the temporal lesions cause monkeys to fail
on difficult tasks yielded conflicting results.
Mishkin and Hall (15) found that normal
monkeys made more errors in learning to
discriminate between two circles when the
difference in the size of the circles was
small than when the difference in size was
large. Thus the degree of difficulty in this
discrimination is correlated with size differences. After temporal ablation the animals retained a discrimination between
circles of different sizes when the difference was large. However, they failed when
the difference in size was small. The study
of Pasik and others (19), cited earlier, reported a similar role of size differences in
the temporal-lobe deficit. In another study,
difficulty of the task as defined by the
percentage of correct responses was not a
crucial factor in the amnesia for visual
habits. Chow and Orbach (10) trained monkeys with pairs of stimuli, such as a black
cross versus a black disk. Each pair was
exposed for different durations. The percentage of correct responses made by normal monkeys decreased as the exposure
time was shortened. A gradient of difficulty
is clearly correlated with exposure time.
Monkeys with temporal lesions performed
this task as well as normal animals, regardless of the duration of the stimulus exposure.

The question of whether the postoperative transient loss of learned visual discriminations indicates a loss of particular memory traces was also studied. When monkeys
were given new visual discriminations to
learn during their recovery from the opera-

tion, they sometimes retained visual discriminations originally learned before removal of temporal cortex. In other words, the postoperative recovery of a habit did not depend on practicing that specific habit. The finding of spontaneous recovery without practice is reminiscent of the arguments raised by the opponents of the memory-image theory of aphasia. In other studies, a monkey was given several visual discriminations preoperatively. On some of these discriminations, training continued only until the animal attained a criterion level of 90 per cent correct in 30 trials. But with other discriminations, several hundred additional trials were given after the criterion was reached. Following bilateral temporal ablation, the same animal forgot a discrimination learned just to criterion, but retained one on which additional training had been given (11, 17).

Further experiments have explored the neural basis for relearning following removal of temporal cortex. After animals had relearned visual discriminations, they were subjected to a second cortical ablation. In some cases, but not in all, ablation of frontal and parietal association cortex produced a second loss of the visual habits.

Results from these studies show that the visual defect following the removal of temporal cortex in monkeys cannot be attributed to a sensory change. Further, it is not the result of the animal's failure to comprehend the testing procedure. Nor can the loss be attributed to a complete disappearance of specific memory traces corresponding to specific visual habits. What actually happens to the monkey's visually guided behavior after surgery remains a challenging question.

It is apparent that these attempts to discover the mechanisms underlying the visual defects following temporal neocortical ablation fall short of an explanation at the neuronal level. This review serves to indicate, however, the type of experiments that are currently in progress, and the complexity of the findings. At present, further analytic studies along the lines illustrated above offer the only feasible approach to the temporal-lobe problem. It is hoped that such lines of study will eventually lead to an explanation of the visual defect at a neuronal level. However, this long-run goal need not be the immediate concern of the investigator.

References

1. Ades, H. W. Effect of extirpation of parastriate cortex on learned visual discriminations in monkeys. *J. Neuropath. exp. Neurol.*, 1946, 5, 60–65.

2. Chow, K. L. A retrograde cell degeneration study of the cortical projection field of the pulvinar in the monkey. *J. comp. Neurol.*, 1950, 93, 313–340.

3. Chow, K. L. Effects of partial extirpations of the posterior association cortex on visually mediated behavior in monkeys. *Comp. Psychol. Monogr.*, 1951, 20, 187–217.

4. Chow, K. L. Conditions influencing the recovery of visual discriminative habits in monkeys following temporal neocortical ablations. *J. comp. physiol. Psychol.*, 1952, 45, 430–437.

5. Chow, K. L. Further studies on selective ablation of associative cortex in relation to visually mediated behavior. *J. comp. physiol. Psychol.*, 1952, 45, 109–118.

6. Chow, K. L. Effects of temporal neocortical ablation on visual discrimination learning sets in monkeys. *J. comp. physiol. Psychol.*, 1954, 47, 194–198.

7. Chow, K. L. Lack of behavioral effects following destruction of some thalamic association nuclei in monkeys. *Arch. Neurol. Psychiat.*, 1954, 71, 762–771.

8. Chow, K. L. Anatomical and electrographical analysis of temporal neocortex in relation to visual discrimination learning in monkey. In J. F. Delafresnaye (Ed.), *Brain mechanisms and learning.* Oxford: Blackwell, 1961.

9. Chow, K. L., & Hutt, P. J. The "association cortex" of *Macaca mulatta:* a review of recent contributions to its anatomy and functions. *Brain,* 1953, 76, 625–677.

10. Chow, K. L., & Orbach, J. Performance of visual discriminations presented tachistoscopically in monkeys with temporal neocortical ablations. *J. comp. physiol. Psychol.*, 1957, 50, 636–640.

11. Chow, K. L., & Survis, J. Retention of overlearned visual habit after cortical ablation in monkey. *Arch. Neurol. Psychiat.*, 1958, 79, 640–646.

12. Klüver, H., & Bucy, P. C. An analysis of certain effects of bilateral temporal lobectomy in the rhesus monkey, with special reference to "psychic blindness." *J. Psychol.*, 1938, 5, 33–54.

13. Lashley, K. S. The mechanism of vision. XVIII. Effects of destroying the visual "associative areas" of the monkey. *Genet. psychol. Monogr.*, 1948, 37, 107–166.

14. Mishkin, M. Visual discrimination performance following partial ablations of the temporal lobe. II. Ventral surface vs. hippocampus. *J. comp. physiol. Psychol.*, 1954, 47, 187–193.

15. Mishkin, M., & Hall, M. Discrimination along a size continuum following ablation of the inferior temporal convexity in monkeys. *J. comp. physiol. Psychol.*, 1955, 48, 97–101.

16. Mishkin, M., & Pribram, K. H. Visual discrimination performance following partial ablations of the temporal lobe. I. Ventral vs. lateral. *J. comp. physiol. Psychol.*, 1954, 47, 14–20.

17. Orbach, J., & Fantz, R. L. Differential effects of temporal neo-cortical resections on overtrained and non-overtrained visual habits in monkeys. *J. comp. physiol. Psychol.*, 1958, 51, 126–129.

18. Orbach, J., & Fisher, G. J. Bilateral resections of frontal granular cortex, factors influencing delayed response and discrimination performance in monkeys. *AMA Arch. Neurol.*, 1959, 1, 78–86.

19. Pasik, P., Pasik, T., Battersby, W. S., & Bender, M. B. Visual and tactual discriminations by macaques with serial temporal and parietal lesions. *J. comp. physiol. Psychol.*, 1958, 51, 427–436.

20. Pribram, H. B., & Barry, J. Further behavioral analysis of parieto-temporo-pre-occipital cortex. *J. Neurophysiol.*, 1956, 19, 99–106.

21. Pribram, K. H., & Mishkin, M. Simultaneous and successive visual discrimination by monkeys with inferotemporal lesions. *J. comp. physiol. Psychol.*, 1955, 48, 198–202.

22. Riopelle, A. J., Alper, R. G., Strong, P. N., & Ades, H. W. Multiple discrimination and patterned string performance of normal and temporal-lobectomized monkeys. *J. comp. physiol. Psychol.*, 1953, 46, 145–149.

23. Shell, W. F., & Riopelle, A. J. Progressive discrimination learning in platyrrhine monkeys. *J. comp. physiol. Psychol.*, 1958, 51, 467–470.

24. Teuber, H.-L. Physiological psychology. *Annu. Rev. Psychol.*, 1955, 6, 267–296.

25. Whitlock, D. G., & Nauta, W. J. H. Subcortical projections from the temporal neocortex in *Macaca mulatta*. *J. comp. Neurol.*, 1956, 106, 183–212.

26. Wilson, M. Effects of circumscribed cortical lesions upon somesthetic and visual discrimination in the monkey. *J. comp. physiol. Psychol.*, 1957, 50, 630–635.

27. Wilson, W. A., & Mishkin, M. Comparison of the effects of infero-temporal and lateral occipital lesions on visually guided behavior in monkeys. *J. comp. physiol. Psychol.*, 1959, 52, 10–17.

This summary article brings together much of the evidence for the hypothalamus as a motivational center.

When the motor system is considered, the concept of the "final common path" is often used. Many excitatory and inhibitory influences act upon the motor cells in the spinal cord. The transmission of impulses to muscles depends upon what happens in this last link in the chain, "the final common path." Thus, many influences from elsewhere in the nervous system are integrated in this final link. By analogy, although it may be somewhat strained, one may think of the hypothalamus as containing neurons which are "the final common path" for the physiological motives.

The author also criticizes his own theory. Much of this criticism has been omitted.

POINTS TO GUIDE YOUR STUDY   *(1) Figure 1 is a good summary of the theory. Can you summarize this theory of physiological motivation in your own words?   (2) Review the chapter on motivation in your text.*

62: THE PHYSIOLOGY OF MOTIVATION

Eliot Stellar, University of Pennsylvania

In the last twenty years motivation has become a central concept in psychology. Indeed, it is fair to say that today it is one of the basic ingredients of most modern theories of learning, personality, and social behavior. There is one stumbling-block in this noteworthy development, however, for the particular conception of motivation which most psychologists employ is based upon the outmoded model implied by Cannon in his classical statement of the local theories of hunger and thirst (23). Cannon's theories were good in their day, but the new facts available on the physiological basis of motivation demand that we abandon the older conceptualizations and follow new theories, not only in the study of motivation itself, but also in the application of motivational concepts to other areas of psychology.

This argument for a new theory of motivation has been made before by Lashley (42) and Morgan (47). But it is more impelling than ever today because so much of the recent evidence is beginning to fit into the general theoretical framework which these men suggested. Both Lashley and Morgan pointed out that the local factors proposed by Cannon (e.g., stomach contractions or dryness of the throat) are not necessary conditions for the arousal of motivated behavior. Instead, they offered the more inclusive view that a number of

sensory, chemical, and neural factors cooperate in a complicated physiological mechanism that regulates motivation. The crux of their theory was described most recently by Morgan as a *central motive state (c.m.s.)* built up in the organism by the combined influences of the sensory, humoral, and neural factors. Presumably, the amount of motivated behavior is determined by the level of the *c.m.s.*

Beach (8, 11), in his extensive work on the specific case of sexual motivation, has amply supported the views of Lashley and Morgan. But the important question still remains: Do other kinds of motivated behavior fit the same general theory? As you will see shortly, a review of the literature makes it clear that they do. As a matter of fact, there is enough evidence today to confirm and extend the views of Lashley, Morgan, and Beach and to propose, in some detail, a more complete physiological theory of motivation.

There are a number of ways to present a theoretical physiological mechanism like the one offered here. Perhaps the best approach is to start with an overview and summarize, in a schematic way, the major factors at work in the mechanism. Then we can fill in the details by reviewing the literature relevant to the operation of each factor. Some advantage is lost by not taking up the literature according to behavioral topics, that is, different kinds of motivation. But the procedure adopted here lets us focus attention directly on the theory itself and permits us to make some very useful comparisons among the various kinds of motivation. Once the theoretical

E. Stellar. The Physiology of Motivation. *Psychol. Rev.*, 1954, **61**, 5–22. Copyright © 1954 by the American Psychological Association. Excerpts reprinted here with permission from the author and the American Psychological Association. In shortening this article, some interesting data have been omitted. The interested reader is referred to the original.

mechanism and the evidence bearing on it are presented, the final step will be to evaluate the theory and show what experiments must be done to check it and extend it.

Theoretical scheme

A schematic diagram of the physiological mechanism believed to be in control of motivated behavior is shown in Figure 1. The basic assumption in this scheme is that *the amount of motivated behavior is a direct function of the amount of activity in certain excitatory centers of the hypothalamus.* The activity of these excitatory centers, in turn, is determined by a large number of factors which can be grouped in four general classes: (a) *inhibitory hypothalamic centers* which serve only to depress the activity of the excitatory centers, (b) *sensory stimuli* which control hypothalamic activity through the afferent impulses they can set up, (c) *the internal environment* which can influence the hypothalamus through its rich vascular supply and the cerebrospinal fluid, and (d) *cortical and thalamic centers* which can exert

FIGURE 1 *Scheme of the physiological factors contributing to the control of motivated behavior. (See text.)*

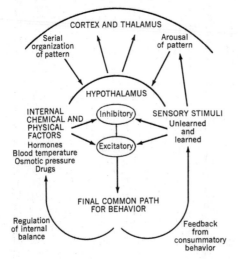

excitatory and inhibitory influences on the hypothalamus.

As can be seen, the present theory holds that the hypothalamus is the seat of Morgan's *c.m.s.* and is the "central nervous mechanism" Lashley claimed was responsible for "drive." Identifying the hypothalamus as the main integrating mechanism in motivation makes the experimental problem we face more specific and more concrete than ever before. But it also makes it more complicated, for the physiological control of the hypothalamus is exceedingly complex. The influence of the internal environment on the hypothalamus is changing continuously according to natural physiological cycles, and of course it may often be changed directly by the chemical and physical consequences of consummatory behavior (see Figure 1). Sensory stimuli may also have varied effects on the hypothalamic mechanism, depending upon their particular pattern, previous stimulation, previous learning, sensory feedback from the consummatory behavior itself, and the influence the internal environment has already exerted on the hypothalamus. Similarly, the influence of the cortex and thalamus will add to the hypothalamic activity already produced by sensory stimuli and the internal evironment. Presumably, these cortical and thalamic influences may result directly or indirectly from sensory stimulation, but they may also be controlled partly by the "upward drive" of the hypothalamus itself (43). Then, to complicate the picture even more, there are the inhibitory centers of the hypothalamus which are also controlled by the various internal changes, sensory stimuli, and cortical and thalamic influences. These centers, presumably, depress the activity of the excitatory centers and, therefore, attenuate their output.

Fortunately, this mechanism is not as formidable against experimental attack as it might appear. The basic experimental approach is to isolate the controlling factors in any type of motivation and determine their relative contributions to hypothalamic activity. As you will see, a number of experimental techniques like sensory deprivation, hormone and drug administration, cortical ablation, and the production of subcortical lesions may be used fruitfully to isolate these factors. But that is only half the problem. Obviously, the factors controlling hypothalamic activity and motivation do not operate in isolation. In fact, it is quite clear that their influences interact. Therefore, it becomes an equally important problem to determine the relative contribution of each factor while the others are operating over a wide range of variation.

Experimental evidence

HYPOTHALAMIC CENTERS   Review of the literature on the role of the hypothalamus in motivation brings out three general conclusions. (a) Damage to restricted regions of the hypothalamus leads to striking changes in certain kinds of motivated behavior. (b) Different parts of the hypothalamus are critical in different kinds of motivation. (c) There are both excitatory and inhibitory centers controlling motivation in the hypothalamus; that is, damage to the hypothalamus can sometimes lead to an increase in motivation and sometimes a marked decrease.

The evidence bearing on these three points can be summarized briefly. Many experiments have shown that restricted bilateral lesions of the hypothalamus will make tremendous changes in basic biological motivations like hunger (16, 22), sleep (49, 50, 53), and sex (6, 18, 20). Less complete evidence strongly suggests that the same kinds of hypothalamic integration are also true in the cases of thirst (61), activity (35), and emotions (5, 62). We have only suggestive evidence in the case of specific hungers (59).

It is clear that there is some kind of localization of function within the hypothalamus although it is not always possible to specify precisely the anatomical nuclei subserving these functions. The centers for hunger are in the region of the ventromedial nucleus which lies in the middle third of the ventral hypothalamus, in the tuberal region (16). (See Figure 2.) Sleep is controlled by centers in the extreme posterior (mammillary bodies) and extreme anterior parts of the hypothalamus (49, 50). The critical region for sexual behavior is in the anterior hypothalamus, between the optic chiasm and the stalk of the pituitary gland (18, 20). The center for activity is not clearly established, but seems to be adjacent with or overlapping the centers for hunger (35). Finally, the centers for emotion are also in the vicinity of the ventromedial nucleus, perhaps somewhat posterior to the hunger centers and overlapping the posterior sleep center (50, 62).

In at least two cases it is clear that there must be both excitatory and inhibitory centers controlling motivated behavior. In the case of hunger, bilateral lesions in the ventromedial nucleus near the midline produce a tremendous amount of overeating (3, 16). Such a center is presumably an inhibitory one since removing it leads directly to an increase in eating behavior. On the other hand, lesions $1\frac{1}{2}$ to 2 millimeters off the midline at the level of the ventromedial nucleus completely eliminate hunger behavior (3, 4). After such lesions animals never eat again, so we can call such centers excitatory centers. Supporting this interpretation is the fact, recently reported, that stimulating these lateral centers in the waking cat through implanted electrodes results in vast overeating (27). The same sort of mechanism turns up in the case of sleep. In the posterior hypothalamus, in the region of the mammillary bodies, there are excitatory centers or "waking" centers which operate to keep the organism awake (49, 50). When they

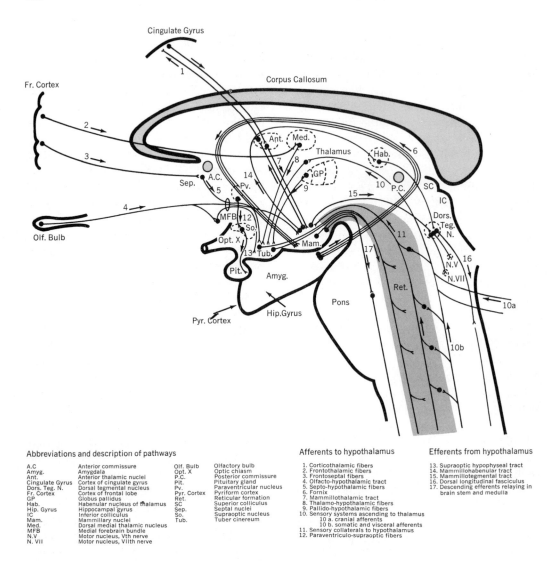

FIGURE 2 *Schematic drawing of the hypothalamus and its major neural connections. Adapted from W. R. Ingram's diagram in Gellhorn (30) and D. B. Lindsley's Figure 9 (43).*

Abbreviations and description of pathways					Afferents to hypothalamus	Efferents from hypothalamus

Abbreviations and description of pathways

A.C	Anterior commissure	Olf. Bulb	Olfactory bulb
Amyg.	Amygdala	Opt. X	Optic chiasm
Ant.	Anterior thalamic nuclei	P.C.	Posterior commissure
Cingulate Gyrus	Cortex of cingulate gyrus	Pit.	Pituitary gland
Dors. Teg. N.	Dorsal tegmental nucleus	Pv.	Paraventricular nucleus
Fr. Cortex	Cortex of frontal lobe	Pyr. Cortex	Pyriform cortex
GP	Globus pallidus	Ret.	Reticular formation
Hab.	Habenular nucleus of thalamus	SC	Superior colliculus
Hip. Gyrus	Hippocampal gyrus	Sep.	Septal nuclei
IC	Inferior colliculus	So.	Supraoptic nucleus
Mam.	Mammillary nuclei	Tub.	Tuber cinereum
Med.	Dorsal medial thalamic nucleus		
MFB	Medial forebrain bundle		
N.V	Motor nucleus, Vth nerve		
N. VII	Motor nucleus, VIIth nerve		

Afferents to hypothalamus

1. Corticothalamic fibers
2. Frontothalamic fibers
3. Frontoseptal fibers
4. Olfacto-hypothalamic tract
5. Septo-hypothalamic fibers
6. Fornix
7. Mammillothalamic tract
8. Thalamo-hypothalamic fibers
9. Pallido-hypothalamic fibers
10. Sensory systems ascending to thalamus
    10 a. cranial afferents
    10 b. somatic and visceral afferents
11. Sensory collaterals to hypothalamus
12. Paraventriculo-supraoptic fibers

Efferents from hypothalamus

13. Supraoptic hypophyseal tract
14. Mammillohabenular tract
15. Mammillotegmental tract
16. Dorsal longitudinal fasciculus
17. Descending efferents relaying in
    brain stem and medulla

are removed, the animal becomes somnolent and cannot stay awake. In the anterior hypothalamus, around the preoptic nucleus, there is an inhibitory center (49). When that is removed, the animal is constantly wakeful.

So far, only an excitatory center has been found in the case of sexual behavior. Bilateral lesions anterior to the pituitary stalk eliminate all mating behavior (18, 20), but no lesion of the hypothalamus has ever been reported that resulted in an exaggeration of sexual motivation. What little we know about the center for activity near the ventromedial nucleus suggests that it is also an excitatory center since lesions there produce only inactivity and not hyperactivity (35). In the case of emotions, the picture is not yet clear. Lesions near the ventromedial nucleus make cats highly emotional (62), and therefore this center must be inhibitory. But the lateral regions of the posterior hypothalamus seem to be excitatory, for lesions there make animals placid (50). Furthermore, direct stimulation of these posterior regions produces many of the signs of rage reactions (52).

There is some evidence that sheds light on how the excitatory and inhibitory hypothalamic centers may cooperate in the regulation of motivation. In the clear-cut cases of sleep and hunger it appears that the inhibitory centers operate mainly through their effects on the excitatory centers. At least we know that when both centers are removed simultaneously the effect is indistinguishable from what happens when only the excitatory centers are removed (3, 49). So it is convenient for present theoretical purposes to think of the inhibitory center as one of the factors which influences the level of activity of the excitatory center. In fact, to speculate one step further, it is worth suggesting that the inhibitory centers may constitute the primary neural mechanism regulating the satiation of motivation.

SENSORY STIMULI   What effects do sensory stimuli have upon the hypothalamus and how important are such stimuli in the control of motivation? Some answer to the first part of this question is given by the schematic outline of hypothalamic connections shown in Figure 2. Clearly the hypothalamus has a rich supply of afferents coming directly or indirectly from all the various sense organs. In fact the diagram is really an understatement of hypothalamic connections because it is an oversimplified and conservative representation. Physiological evidence shows, for example, that there must be connections from the taste receptors via the solitary nucleus of the medulla (36). Also there is evidence of rich connections from the visual system via the lateral geniculate of the thalamus (36). There is no doubt about the fact that the hypothalamus is under very extensive sensory control.

What we know about hunger and thirst suggests that the amount of motivated be-

havior in these cases should be a joint function of sensory impulses arising from gastric contractions or dryness of the throat and taste, tactile, and temperature receptors in the mouth. Unfortunately we have no sensory deprivation experiments that are a good test of this point. But all the evidence on the acceptability of foods and fluids of different temperatures, consistencies, and flavoring suggests the joint operation of many stimuli in the control of these types of motivation.

So far, we have mentioned only stimuli which arouse motivation. What stimulus changes could reduce motivation and perhaps lead to satiation? There are three general possibilities: (a) a reduction in excitatory stimuli, (b) interfering or distracting stimuli that elicit competing behavior, and (c) "inhibitory" stimuli. It is easy to find examples of the first two types of stimulus changes and to guess their mechanisms of operation in terms of the present theory. In the case of "inhibitory" stimuli, however, all we have is suggestive evidence. For example, the fact that dogs with esophageal fistulas eat (37) and drink (1, 13) amounts proportional to the severity of deprivation suggests that the stimuli which feed back from consummatory behavior might have a net inhibitory effect on motivation (see Figure 1). Furthermore, some of the experiments on artificially loading the stomach suggest that a full gut may result in stimuli which inhibit further eating (37) or drinking (2, 13) over and above the possibility that there might be no room left in the stomach or that gastric contractions are reduced.

INTERNAL ENVIRONMENT   That the internal environment plays an important role in certain kinds of motivated behavior is a well-established fact. Two basic questions must be asked, however, before we can understand much about how the internal environment does its work. What kinds of changes that can occur in the internal environment are the important ones in motivation? How do changes in the internal environment influence the nervous system and, therefore, motivated behavior?

A very similar mechanism seems to be involved in the case of motivated behavior dependent upon the organism's defenses against temperature extremes (activity, nesting, hoarding, selection of high-calorie diets). We know, for example, that reactions regulating body temperature in the face of heat and cold are integrated in two separate centers in the hypothalamus (15, 51). Lesions in the anterior hypothalamus destroy the ability to lose heat and, therefore, to survive in high temperatures. Posterior hypothalamic lesions, conversely, result in a loss of heat production mechanisms so that the animal succumbs to cold. Furthermore, artificially raising the temperature of the anterior hypothalamus will quickly induce heat loss, suggesting that normally the temperature of the blood may be important in activating the hypothalamic mechanisms (15, 44). Unfortunately our information stops here. There are no direct physiological studies on the role of these temperature-regulating mechanisms in the control of motivated behavior like activity, hoarding, nesting, or food selection. But it seems clear that the temperature of the blood may be one of the kinds of changes in the internal environment that can affect the hypothalamus, and it may be important in motivated behavior.

Ample evidence demonstrates that there are important changes in the internal environment involved in other kinds of motivated behavior. In hunger it has been shown that chemicals like insulin (32, 33, 48) and d-amphetamine (57) influence the rate of eating. It is clear that these chemicals do not operate primarily through their effects on gastric contractions, but it is only by a process of elimination that we can guess that their sites of action are in the hypothalamus. Supporting this possibility is the evidence that there are chemoreceptors in the hypothalamus which are sensitive to variations in blood sugar and

important in the regulation of hunger (45). In the case of specific hungers, much evidence shows that food preference and diet selection depend upon changes in the internal environment produced by such things as pregnancy, dietary deficiencies, or disturbances of endocrine glands (54). Furthermore there are some preliminary experimental data, in the case of salt and sugar appetites, to suggest that there are separate regulatory centers in the hypothalamus which are responsive to changes in salt and sugar balance (59). Finally, in the case of thirst we know that a change in osmotic pressure, resulting from cellular dehydration, is the important internal change leading to drinking behavior (31). We know further that in the hypothalamus there are nerve cells, called "osmoreceptors," which are extremely sensitive to minute changes in osmotic pressure (61). But the direct experiment has not been done to check whether or not it is these nerve cells which are mainly responsible for the control of thirst.[1]

It is clear from the foregoing that many types of motivated behavior are dependent upon changes in the internal environment. Several points are worth emphasizing. (a) A variety of kinds of changes in the internal environment can play a role in the regulation of motivation: variation in the concentration of certain chemicals, especially hormones, changes in osmotic pressure, and changes in blood temperature. (b) The best hypothesis at present is that these internal changes operate by contributing to the activity of excitatory hypothalamic centers controlling motivation. (c) An equally important but less well-supported hypothesis is that internal changes, normally produced by consummatory behavior, operate in the production of

---

[1] In a recent publication, Andersson of Stockholm has shown that injection of small quantities of hypertonic NaCl directly into restricted regions along the midline of the hypothalamus produces immediate and extensive drinking in water-satiated goats. (B. Andersson. The effect of injections of hypertonic NaCl-solutions into different parts of the hypothalamus of goats. *Acta Physiol. Scand.*, 1953, 28, 188–201.)

satiation by depressing excitatory centers or arousing inhibitory centers of the hypothalamus.

CORTICAL AND THALAMIC CENTERS   The case of emotions offers the best example of how the cortex may operate in motivation. According to the early work of Bard and his co-workers on the production of "sham rage" by decortication, it looked as though the entire cortex might normally play an inhibitory role in emotions (5). More recent work, however, shows that cortical control of emotion is more complicated than this. Bard and Mountcastle (7), for example, have found that removal of certain parts of the old cortex (particularly amygdala and transitional cortex of the midline) produced a tremendous increase in rage reactions in cats. On the other hand, removing only new cortex resulted in extremely placid cats. Results of work with monkeys (40) and some very recent experiments with cats disagree somewhat with these findings in showing that similar old cortex removals lead to placidity rather than ferocity. The disagreement is yet to be resolved, but at least it is clear that different parts of the cortex may play different roles in the control of emotion, certain parts being inhibitory and others excitatory.

In the case of sleep, it appears so far that the cortex and thalamus play excitatory roles, perhaps having the effect of maintaining the activity of the waking center in the posterior hypothalamus. Decortication in dogs, for example, results in an inability to postpone sleep and remain awake for very long, or, as Kleitman puts it, a return to polyphasic sleep and waking rhythms (38, 39). Studies of humans, moreover, show that even restricted lesions of the cortex or thalamus alone can result in an inability to stay awake normally (25, 26). But no inhibitory effects of the cortex in sleep have yet been uncovered.

In sexual behavior it has been found that lesions of the new cortex may interfere directly with the arousal of sexual behavior (9, 11). Large lesions are much more effective than small lesions, as you might expect. Furthermore, cortical damage is much more serious in male animals than in females and is much more important in the sexual behavior of primates than it is in the case of lower mammals. On the other hand, in connection with studies of the cortex in emotions, it has been found that lesions of the amygdala and transitional cortex of the midline can lead to heightened sexuality in cats and monkeys (7, 40). So it looks as though the cortex may exert both excitatory and inhibitory influences in sexual motivation.

Evidence from other types of motivated behavior is only fragmentary, but it fits into the same general picture. In the case of hunger, it has been reported that certain lesions of the frontal lobes will lead to exaggerated eating behavior (41, 55). Hyperactivity may follow similar frontal lobe lesions and is particularly marked after damage to the orbital surface of the frontal lobe (56). The frontal areas may also be involved in what might be called pain avoidance. Clinical studies of man show that lobotomies may be used for the relief of intractable pain (29). The curious thing about these cases is that they still report the same amount of pain after operation but they say that it no longer bothers them. Presumably the frontal cortex normally plays an excitatory role in the motivation to avoid pain.

In all the cases cited so far, the anatomical and physiological evidence available suggests strongly that the main influence of the cortex and thalamus in motivation is mediated by the hypothalamus. But we do not yet have direct proof of this point and need experiments to check it.

Summary and conclusions

A physiological theory of motivated behavior is presented. The basic assumption in this theory is that the amount of motivated behavior is a function of the amount of activity in certain excitatory centers of the hypothalamus. The level of activity of the critical hypothalamic centers, in turn, is governed by the operation of four factors.

1. Inhibitory centers in the hypothalamus directly depress the activity of the excitatory centers and may be responsible for the production of satiation.

2. Sensory stimuli set up afferent impulses which naturally contribute to the excitability of the hypothalamus or come to do so through a process of learning.

3. Changes in the internal environment exert both excitatory and inhibitory effects on the hypothalamus.

4. Cortical and thalamic influences increase and decrease the excitability of hypothalamic centers.

Detailed experimental evidence is brought forward to show how these various factors operate in the management of different kinds of motivated behavior. The over-all scheme is shown diagrammatically in Figure 1.

Out of consideration of this evidence a number of hypotheses are generated to fill in the gaps in experimental knowledge. All these hypotheses are experimentally testable. The ones of major importance can be given here as a summary of what the theory states and a partial list of the experiments it suggests.

1. There are different centers in the hypothalamus responsible for the control of different kinds of basic motivation.

2. In each case of motivation, there is one main excitatory center and one inhibitory center which operates to depress the activity of the excitatory center.

There is already much experimental evidence supporting these two general hypotheses, but it is not certain that they apply fully to all types of basic biological motivation. The hypotheses should be checked further by determining whether changes in all types of motivation can be produced by local hypothalamic lesions and whether both increases and decreases in motivation can always be produced.

3. The activity of hypothalamic centers is, in part, controlled by the excitatory effects of afferent impulses generated by internal and external stimuli.

4. Different stimuli contribute different relative amounts to hypothalamic activity but no one avenue of sensory stimulation is indispensable.

5. It is the sum total of afferent impulses arriving at the hypothalamus that determines the level of excitability and, therefore, the amount of motivation.

The neuroanatomical and neurophysiological evidence shows that the hypothalamus is richly supplied with afferents coming directly and indirectly from all the sense organs (Figure 2). The behavioral evidence, furthermore, strongly suggests that motivation is never controlled, in mammals at least, by one sensory system, but rather is the combination of contributions of several sensory systems. Sensory control and sensory deprivation experiments are needed to check this point in the case of most kinds of biological motivation, particularly hunger, thirst, and specific hungers.

6. A variety of kinds of physical and chemical changes in the internal environment influences the excitability of hypothalamic centers and, therefore, contributes to the control of motivation.

The evidence shows that the hypothalamus is the most richly vascularized region of the central nervous system and is most directly under the influence of the cerebrospinal fluid. Furthermore, it is clear that changes in the internal environment produced by temperature of the blood, osmotic pressure, hormones, and a variety of other chemicals are important in motivation and most likely operate through their influence on the hypothalamus. Direct studies are still needed in many cases, however, to show that the particular change that is important in motivation actually does operate through the hypothalamus and vice versa.

7. The cerebral cortex and thalamus are directly important in the temporal and spatial organization of motivated behavior.

8. Different parts of the cortex and thalamus also operate selectively in the control of motivation by exerting excitatory or inhibitory influences on the hypothalamus.

Tests of these hypotheses can be carried out by total decortication, partial cortical ablations, and local thalamic lesions. It should be especially instructive to see what effects cortical and thalamic lesions have after significant changes in motivation have been produced by hypothalamic lesions.

9. Learning contributes along with other factors to the control of motivation, probably through direct influence on the hypothalamus.

10. The relative contribution of learning should increase in animals higher and higher on the phylogenetic scale.

A whole series of experiments is needed here. Particularly, there should be comparisons of naïve and experienced animals to determine the relative effects of sensory deprivation, cortical and thalamic damage, and hypothalamic lesions. Presumably animals that have learned to be aroused to motivated behavior by previously inadequate stimuli should require more sensory deprivation but less cortical and thalamic damage than naïve animals before motivation is significantly impaired .

11. The various factors controlling motivation combine their influences at the hypothalamus by the addition of all excitatory influences and the subtraction of all inhibitory influences.

Some experiments have already been done in the study of sexual motivation to show that motivation reduced by the elimination of one factor (cortical lesions) can be restored by increasing the contribution of other factors (hormone therapy). Many combinations of this kind of experiment should be carried out with different kinds of motivated behavior.

A number of the limitations and some of the advantages of the present theoretical approach to the physiology of motivation are discussed.

References

1. Adolph, E. F. The internal environment and behavior. Part III. Water content. *Amer. J. Psychiat.,* 1941, 97, 1365–1373.
2. Adolph, E. F. Thirst and its inhibition in the stomach. *Amer. J. Physiol.,* 1950, 161, 374–386.
3. Anand, B. K., and Brobeck, J. R. Hypothalamic control of food intake in rats and cats. *Yale J. Biol. Med.,* 1951, 24, 123–140.
4. Anand, B. K., and Brobeck, J. R. Localization of a "feeding center" in the hypothalamus of the rat. *Proc. Soc. exp. Biol. Med.,* 1951, 77, 323–324.
5. Bard, P. Central nervous mechanisms for emotional behavior patterns in animals. *Res. Publ. Ass. nerv. ment. Dis.,* 1939, 19, 190–218.
6. Bard, P. The hypothalamus and sexual behavior. *Res. Publ. Ass. nerv. ment. Dis.,* 1940, 20, 551–579.
7. Bard, P., and Mountcastle, V. B. Some forebrain mechanisms involved in the expression of rage with special reference to the suppression of angry behavior. *Res. Publ. Ass. nerv. ment. Dis.,* 1947, 27, 362–404.
8. Beach, F. A. Analysis of factors involved in the arousal, maintenance and manifestation of sexual excitement in male animals. *Psychosom. Med.,* 1942, 4, 173–198.
9. Beach, F. A. Central nervous mechanisms involved in the reproductive behavior of vertebrates. *Psychol. Bull.,* 1942, 39, 200–206.
10. Beach, F. A. Relative effect of androgen upon the mating behavior of male rats subjected to forebrain injury or castration. *J. exp. Zool.,* 1944, 97, 249–295.
11. Beach, F. A. A review of physiological and psychological studies of sexual behavior in mammals. *Physiol. Rev.,* 1947, 27, 240–307.
12. Beach, F. A. Evolutionary changes in the physiological control of mating behavior in mammals. *Psychol. Rev.,* 1947, 54, 297–315.
13. Bellows, R. T. Time factors in water drinking in dogs. *Amer. J. Physiol.,* 1939, 125, 87–97.
14. Bremer, F. Etude oscillographique des activités sensorielles du cortex cérébral. *C. R. Soc. Biol.,* 1937, 124, 842–846.
15. Brobeck, J. R. Regulation of energy exchange. In J. F. Fulton (Ed.), *A textbook*

of physiology. Philadelphia: Saunders, 1950. Pp. 1069–1090.

16. Brobeck, J. R., Tepperman, J., and Long, C. N. H. Experimental hypothalamic hyperphagia in the albino rat. *Yale J. Biol. Med.,* 1943, **15**, 831–853.

17. Bromiley, R. B., and Bard, P. A study of the effect of estrin on the responses to genital stimulation shown by decapitate and decerebrate female cats. *Amer. J. Physiol.,* 1940, **129**, 318–319.

18. Brookhart, J. M., and Dey, F. L. Reduction of sexual behavior in male guinea pigs by hypothalamic lesions. *Amer. J. Physiol,* 1941, **133**, 551–554.

19. Brookhart, J. M., Dey, F., and Ranson, S. W. Failure of ovarian hormones to cause mating reactions in spayed guinea pigs with hypothalamic lesions. *Proc. Soc. exp. Biol. Med.,* 1940, 44, 61–64.

20. Brookhart, J. M., Dey, F. L., and Ranson, S. W. The abolition of mating behavior by hypothalamic lesions in guinea pigs. *Endocrinology,* 1941, **28**, 561–565.

21. Brooks, C. M. The role of the cerebral cortex and of various sense organs in the excitation and execution of mating activity in the rabbit. *Amer. J. Physiol.,* 1937, **120**, 544–553.

22. Brooks, C. M. Appetite and obesity. *N. Z. med. J.,* 1947, **46**, 243–254.

23. Cannon, W. B. Hunger and thirst. In C. Murchison (Ed.), *A handbook of general experimental psychology.* Worcester, Mass.: Clark Univer. Press, 1934. Pp. 247–263.

24. Craigie, E. H. Measurements of vascularity in some hypothalamic nuclei of the albino rat. *Res. Publ. Ass. nerv. ment. Dis.,* 1940, **20**, 310–319.

25. Davison, C., and Demuth, E. L. Disturbances in sleep mechanism: a clinico-pathologic study. I. Lesions at the cortical level. *Arch. Neurol. Psychiat., Chicago,* 1945, **53**, 399–406.

26. Davison, C., and Demuth, E. L. Disturbances in sleep mechanism: a clinico-pathologic study. II. Lesions at the corticodiencephalic level. *Arch. Neurol. Psychiat., Chicago,* 1945, 54, 241–255.

27. Delgado, J. M. R., and Anand, B. K. Increase of food intake induced by electrical stimulation of the lateral hypothalamus. *Amer. J. Physiol.,* 1953, **172**, 162–168.

28. Dempsey, E. W., and Rioch, D. McK. The localization in the brain stem of the oestrous responses of the female guinea pig. *J. Neurophysiol.,* 1939, **2**, 9–18.

29. Freeman, W., and Watts, J. W. *Psychosurgery.* (2nd Ed.) Springfield, Ill.: Charles C Thomas, 1950.

30. Gellhorn, E. *Autonomic regulations.* New York: Interscience, 1943.

31. Gilman, A. The relation between blood osmotic pressure, fluid distribution and voluntary water intake. *Amer. J. Physiol.,* 1937, **120**, 323–328.

32. Grossman, M. I., Cummins, G. M., and Ivy, A. C. The effect of insulin on food intake after vagotomy and sympathectomy. *Amer. J. Physiol.,* 1947, **149**, 100–102.

33. Grossman, M. I., and Stein, I. F. Vagotomy and the hunger producing action of insulin in man. *J. appl. Physiol.,* 1948, **1**, 263–269.

34. Harris, L. J., Clay, J., Hargreaves, F. J., and Ward, A. Appetite and choice of diet. The ability of the Vitamin B deficient rat to discriminate between diets containing and lacking the vitamin. *Proc. roy. Soc.,* 1933, **113**, 161–190.

35. Hetherington, A. W., and Ranson, S. W. The spontaneous activity and food intake of rats with hypothalamic lesions. *Amer. J. Physiol.,* 1942, **136**, 609–617.

36. Ingram, W. R. Nuclear organization and chief connections of the primate hypothalamus. *Res. Publ. Ass. nerv. ment. Dis.,* 1940, **20**, 195–244.

37. Janowitz, H. D., and Grossman, M. I. Some factors affecting the food intake of normal dogs and dogs with esophagostomy and gastric fistula. *Amer. J. Physiol.,* 1949, **159**, 143–148.

38. Kleitman, N. *Sleep and wakefulness.* Chicago: Univer. of Chicago Press, 1939.

39. Kleitman, N., and Camille, N. Studies on the physiology of sleep. VI. Behavior of decorticated dogs. *Amer. J. Physiol.,* 1932, **100**, 474–480.

40. Klüver, H., and Bucy, P. C. Preliminary analysis of functions of the temporal lobes in monkeys. *Arch. Neurol. Psychiat., Chicago,* 1939, **42**, 979–1000.

41. Langworthy, O. R., and Richter, C. P. Increased spontaneous activity produced by frontal lobe lesions in cats. *Amer. J. Physiol.,* 1939, **126**, 158–161.

42. Lashley, K. S. Experimental analysis of instinctive behavior. *Psychol. Rev.,* 1938, 45, 445–471.

43. Lindsley, D. B. Emotion. In S. S. Stevens (Ed.), *Handbook of experimental psychology.* New York: Wiley, 1951. Pp. 473–516.

44. Magoun, H. W., Harrison, F., Brobeck, J. R., and Ranson, S. W. Activation of heat loss mechanisms by local heating of the brain. *J. Neurophysiol.,* 1938, **1**, 101–114.

45. Mayer, J., Vitale, J. J., and Bates, M. W. Mechanism of the regulation of food intake. *Nature, Lond.,* 1951, **167**, 562–563.

46. Miller, N. E., Bailey, C. J., and Stevenson, J. A. F. Decreased "hunger" but increased food intake resulting from hypothalamic lesions. *Science,* 1950, **112,** 256–259.

47. Morgan, C. T. *Physiological psychology.* (1st Ed.) New York: McGraw-Hill, 1943.

48. Morgan, C. T., and Morgan, J. D. Studies in hunger. 1. The effects of insulin upon the rat's rate of eating. *J. genet. Psychol.,* 1940, **56,** 137–147.

49. Nauta, W. J. H. Hypothalamic regulation of sleep in rats; an experimental study. *J. Neurophysiol.,* 1946, **9,** 285–316.

50. Ranson, S. W. Somnolence caused by hypothalamic lesions in the monkey. *Arch. Neurol. Psychiat.,* 1939, **41,** 1–23.

51. Ranson, S. W. Regulation of body temperature. *Res. Publ. Ass. nerv. ment. Dis.,* 1940, **20,** 342–399.

52. Ranson, S. W., Kabat, H., and Magoun, H. W. Autonomic responses to electrical stimulation of hypothalamus, preoptic region and septum. *Arch. Neurol. Psychiat., Chicago,* 1935, **33,** 467–477.

53. Ranström, S. *The hypothalamus and sleep regulation.* Uppsala: Almquist and Wiksells, 1947.

54. Richter, C. P. Total self regulatory functions in animals and human beings. *Harvey Lect.,* 1942–43, **38,** 63–103.

55. Richter, C. P., and Hawkes, C. D. In- creased spontaneous activity and food intake produced in rats by removal of the frontal poles of the brain. *J. Neurol. Psychiat.,* 1939, **2,** 231–242.

56. Ruch, T. C., and Shenkin, H. A. The relation of area 13 of the orbital surface of the frontal lobe to hyperactivity and hyperphagia in monkeys. *J. Neurophysiol.,* 1943, **6,** 349–360.

57. Sangster, W., Grossman, M. I., and Ivy, A. C. Effect of d-amphetamine on gastric hunger contractions and food intake in the dog. *Amer. J. Physiol.,* 1948, **153,** 259–263.

58. Scott, E. M., and Verney, E. L. Self selection of diet. VI. The nature of appetites for B vitamins. *J. Nutrit.,* 1947, **34,** 471–480.

59. Soulairac, A. La physiologie d'un comportement: L'appétit glucidique et sa régulation neuro-endocrinienne chez les rongeurs. *Bull. Biol.,* 1947, **81,** 1–160.

60. Tinbergen, N. *The study of instinct.* London: Oxford Univer. Press, 1951.

61. Verney, E. B. The antidiuretic hormone and the factors which determine its release. *Proc. roy. Soc., London,* 1947, **135,** 24–106.

62. Wheatley, M. D. The hypothalamus and affective behavior in cats. *Arch. Neurol. Psychiat.,* 1944, **52,** 296–316.

The two cerebral hemispheres of many higher mammals, cats, monkeys, and man, for instance, are connected by a wide band of fibers—the corpus callosum. *One of the major functions of this connection is to serve as a communication link between the hemispheres. Thus, learning restricted to one hemisphere is relayed to the other hemisphere when the corpus callosum is intact. Testing would then show that, although input was restricted to one hemisphere, the other hemisphere had also learned. However, if the corpus callosum is cut, learning in one cerebral hemisphere is not manifested when the other hemisphere is tested. That is what happened in this experiment.*

The animal with the corpus callosum cut is sometimes known as a "split-brain" animal. Note that it provides an excellent way of controlling certain experiments. One side of the brain has learned something, while the other side is still naïve. In the same animal, then, we have an "experimental" side of the brain and a "control" side of the brain.

A POINT TO GUIDE YOUR STUDY *Note that the experiment involved two operative procedures: The optic chiasma (see your text) was cut to restrict visual input to one cerebral hemisphere when one eye was covered during training and testing; the corpus callosum was also cut.*

The cats were then trained with one eye covered and visual input was thus restricted to one cerebral hemisphere. Then they were tested with the other eye covered and visual input restricted to the "untrained" cerebral hemisphere. Under these conditions, with the corpus callosum cut, the training did not transfer to the "untrained" hemisphere.

63: FUNCTION OF CORPUS CALLOSUM IN INTEROCULAR TRANSFER

Ronald E. Myers, Laboratory of Perinatal Physiology, San Juan, Puerto Rico

The crossed optic fibres may be destroyed in the cat by mid-line section of the optic chiasma. The two eyes then discharge separately into opposite halves of the brain over the surviving uncrossed fibres. Such cats are able to perform with one eye simple pattern discriminations learned with the other eye (Myers, 1955). This interocular transfer in the absence of the crossed optic fibres requires a neural interaction across the mid-line.

The fibre pathways mediating this effect are unknown. From anatomical considerations one would suspect the corpus callosum of subserving an integrative function of this nature and the present investigation was designed to explore this possibility by extending the transfer tests to cats with destruction of both the corpus callosum and the crossed optic fibres.

Methods

SURGICAL TECHNIQUES Section of the optic chiasma was effected through a transbuccal approach as previously described (Myers, 1955). For division of the corpus callosum a large unilateral bone flap was removed by the use of a dental crown saw and the bone overlying the superior sagittal sinus was chipped away with bone forceps. The dura was opened to the mid-line and one or two cortical veins were ligated at their

entrance into the superior sagittal sinus. With the exposed hemisphere retracted laterally the corpus callosum was carefully divided with the aid of a binocular dissecting microscope. The hemisphere was then gently restored to its former position and the dura laid over the cortical surface. The bone flap was replaced and the muscle and skin layers reapposed with catgut sutures. Post-operative course in all cases was uneventful.

Training and testing procedures. Transfer of four different discrimination problems was studied. The test patterns used are illustrated in Fig. 1. The same training box and procedures were used as described earlier (Myers, 1955). In establishing a discrimination, the two patterns of a pair were presented side by side, and the cat was trained to choose one of the two. The patterns were alternated from side to side according to a chance sequence. During the periods of training light was excluded from one eye by the use of a black rubber mask held snugly in place by ties to a leather collar. After a cat attained a performance of 34 trials or more correct out of 40 the response was stabilized by giving approximately 400 overtraining trials run in sessions of 40 per day. An exception was *Brd* who was run 920 overtraining trials on problem I-ab. Following the overtraining, tests for interocular transfer of the discrimination were made by shifting the mask to the trained eye for 40 test runs with the untrained eye.

Six cats were used. Four of them were

R. E. Myers. Function of corpus callosum in interocular transfer. *Brain*, 1956, 79, 358–369. Copyright © 1956 by Brain. Reprinted here with permission from the author and *Brain*.

taught two discriminations, one to each eye, and, in these instances, overtraining was carried out with both of the discriminations before any tests were made for transfer. The problems learned by each cat and the eye initially trained on all discriminations are shown in Table I. In all, transfer tests were made on a total of ten discrimination habits.

Observations and comment

The results obtained on the 40 transfer trials run with the untrained eye are listed in the last column of Table I. It may be seen that the performances dropped from the high level attained on the overtraining trials (40 correct out of 40) to a near chance level on the transfer trials (20 correct out of 40). In two instances, however, the performance was significantly above chance, and, in a third, it was significantly under chance. These exceptions are discussed separately below. Among the remaining seven discriminations, deviations from chance were unexpectedly small. This may be attributed to the strong tendency of the cats to revert to a position preference on the transfer trials. Such position

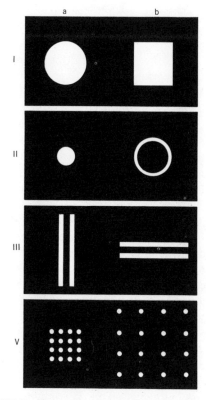

FIGURE 1 *Pairs of test patterns used. The discrimination tasks are listed with the positive pattern first. For example, in discrimination I-ab, the positive pattern would be a circle and the negative a square.*

TABLE I *Interocular transfer in cats with optic chiasma and corpus callosum sectioned*

CAT	EYE TRAINED	DISCRIMINATION	NUMBER CORRECT ON FINAL 40 OVERTRAINING TRIALS	NUMBER CORRECT ON 40 TEST TRIALS WITH UNTRAINED EYE
Slv	R	I-ab	40	20
Mmm	R	III-ba	40	20
	L	III-ab	38	19
Brd	R	I-ab	40	13
	L	III-ba	40	20
Knt	R	II-ab	35	19
	L	III-ab	40	20
Bgw*	L	V-ab	40	34
Hnr	R	V-ab	40	28
	L	III-ab	40	20

* Prior experience with discrimination II-ab.

preferences are also commonly exhibited when a cat is first presented with a new problem.

Brd, the first of the three exceptional cases, performed only 13 correct out of the 40 test runs with discrimination I-ab. This indicates not only lack of transfer but reveals also a definite preference for the negative pattern. This preference was likely due to some resemblance between this pattern and those of discrimination III-ba previously established with the same eye.

Bgw transferred discrimination V-ab. However, this cat had already been taught discrimination II-ab as part of another investigation. The positive transfer in this case may have been due in like manner to generalization effects arising from an unsuspected similarity between the patterns of the two discrimination tasks. This interpretation was strongly supported when subsequent work with another cat showed a 100 per cent generalization from discrimination II-ab to discrimination V-ab. The cats were presumably responding to some general feature of these patterns like smallness versus largeness or concentration versus diffuseness.

Though *Hnr* performed at a chance level on one discrimination (III-ab), on the second (V-ab) his performance was better than chance (28/40). Figural equivalence effects may again have accounted for the partial transfer although these figures have not been actually tested in this respect. That the transfer was due to effects other than a central neural interaction is strongly indicated, however, by the great ease with which *Hnr* was thereafter taught the inverse discrimination, V-ba, with the untrained left eye. Furthermore, this learning of inverse discrimination V-ba by the left eye resulted in absolutely no disruption of performance on discrimination V-ab with the right eye, contrary to what is seen under the same circumstances in cats with intact corpus callosum. Cat *Mmm* also showed no interference effect when the two

eyes were taught inverse discriminations (III-ab and III-ba).

In view of the foregoing it was concluded that the above-chance performances obtained with cats *Bgw* and *Hnr* were a result of irrelevant stimulus generalization effects and did not constitute true exceptions to the lack of interocular transfer seen in the other cases.

The brains of the 6 animals used in this study were examined following formalin fixation. Division of the corpus callosum was found to vary from complete section exclusive of the anterior commissure in *Brd* to section of the posterior two-thirds (12 mm.) in *Mmm.* Varying fragments of the hippocampal commissure were sectioned along with the corpus callosum posteriorly where the two structures lie in close apposition. The mid-line section of the optic chiasma was complete in each case as determined by gross or microscopic examination.

Discussion

Clinical studies have failed to reveal clear-cut alterations in patients with surgical section or pure agenesis of the corpus callosum.[1] Specifically, practic and graphic employment of the two sides of the body is well preserved or normally developed. Visual and tactile gnosis seems also to be unaffected as tested bilaterally, though Maspes (1948) has reported imperfect symbolic recognition in the left homonymous visual fields. Deficits seem to develop only with pathological involvement of one or the other hemisphere. (*See* the reports of Akelaitis, 1941; Akelaitis, 1943; Bruce, 1890; Bunts and Chaffee, 1944; Cameron, 1917; Dandy, 1936; and Smith, 1947.)

Our results in the cat appear, on the other hand, to demonstrate an important integrative function for the corpus callosum. After callosal section there was fail-

[1] An integrative function of the corpus callosum in humans has been shown since the original publication of this paper. (*Ed.*)

ure to transfer simple visual problems. Furthermore, completely conflicting problems could be learned with the two eyes without indication of interference implying independent functioning of the two hemispheres in visual learning and recall. These results are in direct contrast with the results obtained in cats with intact corpus callosum (Myers, 1955).

Destruction of the corpus callosum results in a similar disruption of interhemispheric interaction in the cutaneous (Bikov, 1924) and auditory (Stewart and Ades, 1951) spheres. These results with the three most highly developed of the exteroceptive senses suggest a general participation of the corpus callosum in integrating the activity of the two hemispheres in perceptual or cognitive functions.

This raises the problem as to why deficiencies in perception and cognition were not found in the human subjects lacking the corpus callosum if this structure serves such a seemingly important correlative function. Evidence has been presented which indicates that the visual mechanisms on the two sides of the brain are competent although independent in these capacities in the absence of the corpus callosum. Preservation of visual (and tactile) gnosis in the two half-fields following callosal section may then be related to bilateral establishment of experiential effects such as might occur through the corpus callosum prior to section, or, alternatively, through the bilateral projection of the senory data as occurs with the shifting of the gaze, examination with the hands, and the like. A crucial test of this interpretation has yet to be made in the human. Such a test would involve presentation of novel objects or perceptual problems to one half-field with testing of recognition of the same in the other half-field.

The status of the findings relative to co-ordination within the motor sphere and the transfer of motor learning seems at variance with the findings on perceptual transfer. Bilateral participation in skilled motor performance is unaffected by callosal section (Hartmann and Trendelenburg, 1927). Personal observations of numerous cats and monkeys with total callosal section has also failed to reveal any apparent immediate or long-term deficits in eye-hand co-ordination, skilled manipulatory movements or the like. Ades and Raab (1946) studying reorganization of neuronal mechanisms on the two sides of the brain of the monkey following unilateral removal of the motor area found that the contralateral rearrangement occurred with or without the corpus callosum. Smith (1947) found transfer of non-visual stylus-maze performances from one hand to the other in both the normal and the epileptic with callosal section. Such evidence suggests bilateral integration of these activities through commissural systems at levels below the corpus callosum.

Summary

The efferent connexions from the two eyes were restricted to the ipsilateral brain-halves in 6 cats by surgical section of the crossing fibres in the optic chiasma. This was followed by sagittal transection of the corpus callosum. These cats were then trained to perform pattern discriminations with a mask covering one or the other eye. When a consistently high level of performance had been attained, the mask was shifted to the other previously unmasked eye whereupon the performance dropped abruptly to a chance level with seven of the ten discriminations tested. The three deviant results were attributable to irrelevant generalization effects between the several discriminations taught the separate eyes. These present findings are in marked contrast with the high level transfer obtained with the corpus callosum intact.

Two of the cats were subsequently taught completely conflicting discriminations with the two eyes. The learning with the second eye occurred with relative ease and resulted in no disturbance in performance with the first eye. This also contrasts with the performances of cats with intact corpus callosum. These results demonstrate the importance of the corpus callosum in the integration of the two hemispheres in visual learning and transfer.

Acknowledgments

The author wishes to express thanks to Professor R. W. Sperry for proposal of this study and for helpful suggestions during the course of the work. This investigation was supported by grants from The Abbott Memorial Fund of The University of Chicago and the Frank P. Hixon Fund of the California Institute of Technology.

References

Ades, H. W., and Raab, D. H. (1946) *J. Neurophysiol.*, 9, 55.

Akelaitis, A. J. (1941) *Arch. Neurol. Psychiat., Chicago*, 45, 788.

———— (1943) *J. Neuropath.*, 2, 226.

Bikov, K. (1924–25) *Zbl. ges. Neurol.*, 39, 199.

Bruce, A. (1890) *Brain*, 12, 171.

Bunts, A. T., and Chaffee, J. S. (1944) *Arch. Neurol. Psychiat., Chicago*, 51, 35.

Cameron, J. (1917) *Canad. med. Ass. J.*, 7, 609.

Dandy, W. E. (1936) *Arch. Surg., Chicago*, 33, 19.

Hartmann, F., Jr., and Trendelenburg, W. (1927) *Z. ges. exp. Med.*, 54, 578.

Maspes, P. E. (1948) *Rev. Neurol.*, 80, 100.

Myers, R. E. (1955) *J. comp. physiol. Psychol.*, 48, 470.

Smith, K. U. (1947) *J. exp. Psychol.*, 37, 367.

Stewart, J. W., and Ades, H. W. (1951) *J. comp. physiol. Psychol.*, 44, 479.

This selection summarizes much of the modern work on "the search for the engram," or the memory trace.

POINTS TO GUIDE YOUR STUDY *(1) Much of the experimental data of this article can be organized around a two-factor theory of memory. The first factor, according to this theory, consists of relatively temporary physiological activity; this activity produces a permanent change—a relatively long-lasting memory trace. (2) The evidence for the temporary first factor comes from studies with electroconvulsive shock, or ECS (see the selection by Cronholm and Molander in Section Four), some of the experiments with drugs, and experiments with cooling of animals. The evidence from studies with RNA— ribonucleic acid—inhibitors bears on the second, relatively permanent, factor. The studies with postural asymmetries bear on both aspects of the two-factor theory of memory.*

64: THE MATERIAL BASIS OF MEMORY

R. W. Gerard, University of California, Irvine

Any system—and I shall not define system more closely than as a group of somehow

R. W. Gerard. The material basis of memory. *J. verb. Learning and verb. Behavior*, 1963, 2, 22–33. Copyright © by Academic Press, Inc. Reprinted here with permission from the author and the Academic Press, Inc. Two references completed; were in press. (*Ed.*)

integrated subordinate units that forms an entity of its own—must have a certain architecture, structure, or morphology, which is reasonably constant in time. The way the system is put together, I like to call its "being." This system interacts with its environment, responding to stimuli—whether at the more complex level of organisms giving behavioral responses or simply a rubber band yielding to a weight—and most of these responses are in effect ephemeral, reversible changes in time. The system yields and restores itself, and this I like to call its "behaving." But under certain conditions the interaction of the system and its environment leads to irreversible changes; the system has altered as a result of its experience. It fixes its experience and so becomes something different, and this I like to call "becoming." So this addiction to alliteration gives us architecture or being, functioning or behaving, and development or becoming.

Becoming subsumes, of course, development of the individual, evolution of the species, history of the particular society or social group of any kind, and learning in the individual. And learning may include, if you accept a broad definition, changes as varied as: the hypertrophy of a muscle with exercise; the horny hands of a laborer; and the many other material changes that record the past—as in that lovely couplet on weatherbeaten trees:

Is it as plainly in our living shown,
By slant and twist, which way the wind hath
 blown?

That is memory in trees. I would like, then, to approach the problem of fixation of experience, which is the basis of becoming and which includes in it memory, from the point of view of the interaction of the organism and its environment.

This occurs ordinarily, of course, at the interface. Start with some kind of a system; it is acted upon by the environment, probably mostly reversibly. Sooner or later, however, there are irreversible changes and there is a different system than before. The environment continues to act upon and interact with it to give a still different system. And there is a steady flow through time of the system plus its past, as influenced by all the things that have happened to it. At any one stage, the new system is some product of what was in it at that time, which might be called its inheritance or heredity, plus what was done to it, its environment. This progressive specification or alteration with time is, in the broadest sense, fixation of experience. This process is operating, of course, from the very start. We ordinarily think of organisms as having a fixed genetic past, carried in what happens to the gene complement of a particular individual; but, more profoundly, the kinds of genes that are present represent the influence of the environment on ancestors of that organism —by selection or any other mechanisms that happen to be valid. The environment starts, then, ordinarily with a heterogenous system and does things to it.

In principle, however, even a homogenous system, able to respond differentially to differences in the environment, will develop heterogeneity. Recall the dramatic experiments with frog eggs early in this century. The fertilized egg divides into two, and the two blastomeres become the left and the right sides of the body. From their medial portions come the backbone and the spinal cord and other midline structures. But if these two half-embryos are separated they do not die; they continue to develop and produce identical twins. The left side of the left cell becomes a left side, as it did before; and the right side of the right cell develops as before. But the right side of the left cell no longer becomes a center; it now forms a right side —and the left side of the right cell becomes a left side. This was so mysterious that Driesch, who first was concerned with this, gave up mechanism and said this was obviously vitalistic; that some kind of guiding spirit or entelechy determines which way these cells develop.

Then the zoologist Child got the clue to the explanation in terms of concentration gradients. With the two cells stuck together at the central plane, to form a sphere, oxygen must diffuse from the surface to the center and its concentration would be lowest at the midline. Carbon dioxide, formed in the cells, would have the reverse concentration gradient. If a low oxygen concentration (or a high one of carbon dioxide) favors differentiation of protoplasm into midline structures and the reverse favors lateral structures, each cell will become a side of the embryo and, eventually, of the adult. But with the two cells separated, the same gradients will form between surface and center of each cell—and two complete bilateral individuals will result. So the environment imposes structure on homogeneity by virtue of such a simple mechanism as the concentration gradient!

As the embryo develops further, with many cells, the position of one cell relative to another has certain structural consequences. Where a piece of central nervous system nears the skin, the skin turns in and forms a lens. Where the endoderm adjoins the heart it develops into liver, otherwise into gut. Such relationships have been worked out in great detail. At each stage of development there is further and further differentiation, with more loss of totipotency, and commitment to a particular path from which there is no return. Moreover, the period of flexibility between successive stages of differentiation may be very brief in the life of the embryo; until there is an endoderm no possibility exists to become gut or liver, a few minutes later the path to one or the other has been taken.

Comparably, at a later stage when a nervous system is established, it is possible to rotate a piece of the neuroaxis, the spinal cord and medulla, so that the dorsal side is ventral or so that the caudal end is rostral, and the neurons reorganize to form the normal shapes and connections—they were still totipotent as to general neural structure. Later, this does not work; but

the number and size of the nerve fibers growing out at one segment or another can still be altered by moving the developing limb bud. If this is shifted from the normal shoulder region down to the rib region, the normally small intercostal nerves become the great brachial plexus and the normally great cervical ones remain small. Chemical specification may occur without obvious structural change, as when a nerve artificially attached to some atypical muscle comes to carry messages to it from the spinal cord whenever a reflex activates the normal muscle of the same type. There is even evidence that sex differentiation is carried from the chromosomes—XX for female and XY for male—by differences in the hypothalamus of the developing nervous system. If the hypothalamus of the early male embryo is transplanted into a female embryo, the latter develops as a male, and vice versa; whereas if the pituitary is transplanted at the same stage of development, the embryo retains its own genetic sex—which indicates that the hypothalamus determines the pituitary which, in turn, determines the somatic sex characteristics.

Moving on from the embryo to postnatal stages, the comparable phenomena are more easily recognized as learning and memory. Imprinting, despite some question of precise interpretation, determines which object a chick or duckling adopts as its mother—a further step in neural differentiation, now indicated by behavior. In mammals comparable phenomena have long been recognized. A newborn kid, taken from its mother for only half an hour after birth, is no longer accepted by the mother as her offspring. Some interaction that should have taken place between these two systems does not take place, the kid fails to get the proper label; and ever after is rejected. If it survives at all it becomes an undersized miserable creature with clearly disturbed behavior. The more recent work, raising baby monkeys with surrogate mothers, has given comparable results; if the young grow up at all, they turn out to be bad mates and mothers.

In man, a study of responses to frustration supplied evidence that childhood experience determined whether norepinephrine was liberated, and anger outwardly expressed, or epinephrine was liberated, and anger turned in as self-criticism. With a weak or absent father or a social milieu that frowned on exhibiting feelings, as in brahmin Boston society, the "anger turned in" reaction was likely; with a dominant father and an expressive milieu, as in Brooklyn gangs, "anger turned out" was the norm. These reactions are pretty irreversible; many experiments on conditioned visceral reflexes in animals—vascular or respiratory responses to a shock—show these to remain stable after months or years of inactivity.

I still like to tell of a case that came to my attention many years ago at the University of Chicago. Freshmen, undergoing routine medical examination, came down the line with their chests bared, and the physician slapped his stethoscope over the heart of each. One student fainted, so my friend brought him back for examination and finally spent quite a bit of time with him. The long and short of it was that, with the student in front of a fluoroscope and the doctor as far away as the room permitted, the student's heart could be seen to stop whenever he could recognize as a stethoscope some object gradually being brought into view. This is clearly a conditioned response, and the conditioning must have happened early in childhood; unfortunately, no psychiatric study was made so I have no idea what the traumatic experience was.

The fixations last considered involve the nervous system quite specifically; let us move on to more ordinary kinds of behavior. What we can perceive depends on our early experience. Recall the dramatic ex-periments on newborn chimps, kept in darkness or in unpatterned light for some weeks, and unable later to distinguish visual patterns and jump about in trees. In humans, similarly, a clouded cornea at birth may be replaced in later years by an optically perfect transplant, without bestowing pattern vision. One might think that seeing a circle or a square is a simple business; but it is not. The central nervous system has to learn such discriminations with bitter, hard, carefully built up experience; and, without such perceptual experience in infancy, these people are quite unable to recognize a circle from a square by sight, although making the identification by touch immediately. They may learn this in time but mostly never achieve the fine visual discriminations required for adequate reading.

On the motor side, the same learning of patterns by use occurs in the nervous system. The great athletic champions have practically all, I believe, started to learn their skill very early in life. For top level performance, patterns must be built into the nervous system when it is most plastic; later in life plasticity is largely lost—perhaps it falls off exponentially from the zygote stage. An adult Japanese cannot learn to distinguish r and l, not distinct phonemes in their language; I saw on a fine piece of electrophysiological apparatus built and labeled in Japan, the word Stim-urator. Nor can an adult occidental learn to squat comfortably, for any time, on his haunches with his legs crossed under him, as a Japanese can. A Frenchman, in adult life, cannot learn the English *th;* nor can an English-speaking adult learn the French *r.* These are learned habits, to be sure, but they are actually built into the structure of the developing nervous system.

Some structuring by experience of course continues in adulthood. We lay down new engrams, if I may call them that, throughout life. A striking demonstration of this can be made in the rat. If both occipital lobes are removed simultaneously, pattern vision is entirely lost; if one lobe is removed first and the other two weeks later, pattern vision remains; but if, during that two weeks, the rat is kept in the dark and so denied any further visual experience, pattern vision is again entirely lost. This evidence suggests that existing engrams, built into the brain by visual experience, constitute some sort of scaffolding on which new experience can, so to speak, crystallize itself. Both the nucleus on which to build and the experience to do the building are necessary.

So much for the general behavioral level; it is time to move into the nervous system for a more precise look at the laying down of engrams. First, if a system gives a different performance than before under otherwise similar conditions, and this difference is maintained, it can only mean that the system has undergone a material change of some sort. It is entirely comparable to the change in an hypertrophied muscle or the change in a membrane that makes a cell permeable or not. Whether or not we are as yet able actually to see the structural alteration is of some interest and importance; but whether we see these material changes or not, they are there and they are real. A dynamic, rather than structural, change in the nervous system will not do (this is the question that first interested me in memory problems). One could argue that a memory was something that had been set spinning, like nerve impulses reverberating in closed neuron loops, and that the spinning constituted a dynamic memory. If this were the case, then stopping neural activity should lead to irreversible loss of the memory. To be sure, going to sleep or being under anesthesia does not cause forgetting, but physiological activity of the nervous system is not stopped under those conditions.

We took advantage of the fact that hamsters can be made to hibernate: we taught them a fairly simple maze, cooled them down to 5° C, at which temperature extensive soundings revealed no electrical activity in the brain, warmed them up, and retested on the maze. As expected, they remembered it perfectly well. This was, perhaps, the first clear-cut demonstration that memory does not depend on a dynamic process going on in the brain, but on some change that had become structural. Later we thought of an easier way of stopping neural activity—not by "freezing" it in its tracks but, just the reverse, by activating all neurons simultaneously by electroconvulsive shock. This would stop any messages that depended on sequential activation of neurons in chains or in loops, since all would become refractory. Again, the hamsters remembered.

So there is a material change. Further, this change is localized. There is much work along these lines, the most dramatic perhaps being on split-brain cat preparations. The optic chiasm is divided, so that the left eye remains connected only to the left brain, the right eye to the right, and a pattern discrimination is learned through, say, the left eye. On testing through the right eye, performance is then perfectly good while the corpus callosum remains intact but collapses after this connection between the hemispheres is cut. Left eye performance remains intact. This offers pretty strong evidence that the engram had been formed in the left brain (occipital lobe) and that the right brain had access to it through connecting fibers. Another imaginative experiment, along the same line, took advantage of the spreading depression, produced by concentrated potassium ion, to block one hemisphere in the rat, say the left one, while the animal was given massed learning experiences. Later, with the right hemisphere blocked, even though the left one was now functional, the rat could not perform; when the block of the right hemisphere passed off, performance returned. So learning with the left hemisphere blocked left the engram only in the right hemisphere; again, a clear example of a localized change having been left behind by the learning experience.

How is it brought about? Our experiments with hamsters, and later with rats, were almost not performed, we were so sure of the answer. But a graduate student finally undertook them and turned up a large unexpected dividend. Instead of first having the animal learn and then determining whether it remembered after cold or shock, it was given spaced learning experiences, with interspersed shocks. Every day, at the same time, the animal made massed maze runs and, at another fixed time, was then given an electroconvulsive shock through the head. Comparable foot shocks, incidentally, were ineffective. When several hours elapsed between maze runs and shock, the learning curve was essentially the same as in controls without shock; but as the interval between runs and shock was decreased below an hour, the learning curve fell off until, at some fifteen minutes, no learning occurred. Repeated shocks can produce minor damage, but that could have no relation to this timing phenomenon. Clearly, some process must continue in the nervous system after having an experience before an enduring memory is established; rather as if, after exposing a film, one had to wait a while before developing it or no picture would remain. A certain time is required for the fixation of experience and we have called it the "fixation time." This was a new and exciting discovery for us but we later found others had run into the phenomenon, and by now it is familiar and well studied.

Granted a fixation time, what is going on during that interval; what is the mechanism of fixation? Has the experience started some kind of chemical process in the neuron which then goes on more or less automatically, as light starts progressive changes in a photographic emulsion, or must there be some kind of maintained physiological activity? I think there is good

reason to believe that fixation depends on a continuing physiological activity. Hebb and I suggested independently in 1949 that during fixation there is a continuing reverberation of nerve impulses in neuron loops. In 15 minutes, if one assumes reverberation at 50 a second, there would be some 100,000 repetitions. This is the kind of repetitious impact of an experience that is likely to fix it. It is the old story of one drop of water on the ground disappearing, but a million drops digging a channel, an irreversible material change.

The fact that blocking activity by an electric shock permanently stops the fixation fits better with the notion of some kind of continuing physiological activity as its basis rather than some continuing chemical reaction. There is no a priori reason for an electric shock to stop a chemical reaction and keep it from resuming, but making neurons refractory should end reverberation. Further, we determined the temperature coefficient of the fixation time by combining the electroshock and the cooling techniques. Hamsters were given the learning experience, then cooled down to a low temperature, kept there for a certain time, warmed up again, and then given electroshock. If kept cool during the learning-shock interval, a shock after an hour or two was still effective in blocking fixation. The fixation time was, thus, prolonged at low temperatures; in fact, the temperature coefficient came out at 2.9. This happens to be the temperature coefficient for conduction velocity of the nerve impulse, which well fits the reverberation idea but should not be given too great quantitative weight. Another thing, certain drugs act upon fixation time about as one would expect from their effect on thresholds. Some depressant drugs would tend to prolong fixation time, by making synapses harder and slower to excite and so permitting fewer reverberations per unit time. This has been found by us and others. Conversely, strychnine, which lowers thresholds and speeds excitation, shortens fixation time. Finally, the reverberation suggestion makes physiological sense because there are many changes in nerve fibers, and even more dramatic ones in nerve cells, produced by repeated activity. Changes in potential, in threshold, in chemical and thermal responses may greatly increase in magnitude and, even more (by 1000-fold), in duration as a result of repeated activity; and altered reflex responsiveness, as in post-tetanic potentiation, can last for hours. All these items favor the view that continued physiological activity—and the easiest one to assume is reverberating circuits—lays down the irreversible change.

What sort of a change is it? We are dealing here with storage of information, in contradistinction to transmission of information; and, whereas the latter depends on all-or-none messages going along nerve fibers at fast rates, the storage depends essentially on threshold changes of the neurons and on how these respond to the messages when they arrive. The threshold change may depend on a shift in membrane potential on the dendrites, on altered neurohumor liberation, on many other factors; but it most probably involves changes at the receptive component of the synaptic mechanism. And the change might further involve simple inhibitory connections, or chemical action (epinephrine can both raise and lower thresholds), or the diffuse nervous system, the reticular formation and other deeper structures, which plays upon cortical neurons. All these mechanisms could well be involved, but they are only part of the story; sooner or later the issue comes down to a molecular mechanism. Neurons change spatially, they throw out pseudopods and pull them back again, at least in tissue culture, and may increase connections, as by swelling of terminal knobs; and they turn over chemically. Some kind of molecular continuity seems essential and many have guessed as to what kind of change this might be.

Almost necessarily it has to be at the macromolecular level, ions and simple metabolites are too evanescent, so attention falls on proteins or polynucleotides or perhaps lipids, although not many take the last seriously. Proteins are formed under the influence of nucleotides, and RNA is a likely candidate. Hyden first, I think, explicitly published such a notion and, as have others, has reported that RNA, also seen as Nissl substance in the cytoplasm of neurons, increases under moderate activity, decreases in fatigue.

Many of you know the evidence from planaria studies. If a flatworm is conditioned and then cut in two, the head end regenerates a tail, the tail end renegerates a head, and both worms retain what was learned. If the regenerative process occurs in the presence of ribonuclease, the head end remains educated, the tail end does not. This suggests that RNA is involved in carrying on memories during the generation of new neurons, as in regeneration of the tail but not the head. There has been other evidence that RNA is involved in memory and our recent work has been directed rather specifically to this point.

Given an engram, it should be possible to identify it more precisely. An ingenious experiment by Morrell involved producing an epileptogenic focus by placing alumina cream on one spot in the motor cortex, mainly in rabbits. If this spot were excised after a week or ten days, epileptic convulsions still continued, because the mirror spot on the other hemisphere had also become epileptogenic. If the corpus callosum had been cut, this mirror focus never formed, so this was clearly a result of physiological activation, able progressively to build up changes which then endured on their own. Here was a nice localized engram of a sort; and it contained an increased amount of RNA.

We took advantage of a comparable phenomenon, first studied some decades ago by DiGiorgio. A unilateral lesion in the cerebellum produces a postural asymmetry in the legs, clearly due to an asymmetrical barrage of impulses coming down the two sides of the cord. Therefore, cutting the cord, which abolishes this asymmetrical discharge, should abolish the asymmetry. Such is, indeed, the case, unless the asymmetry has endured for some time; then it may remain after the spinal section. We explored the phenomenon in some detail, for it offered a means of again coming to grips with fixation time. Chamberlain, especially, standardized the preparation in the rat and did careful timing. The fixation time emerged embarrassingly sharply; if the cord is cut within 45 minutes of the time the asymmetry has begun, it will disappear; if after 45 minutes, the asymmetry will remain indefinitely. Figure 1 shows the discontinuity.

The next step was to try and alter the fixation time by modifying the rate of synthesis of ribonucleic acid. Others have tried this kind of experiment on learning rates, using RNA antimetabolites, and have obtained slowing. In our animals, 8-azaguanine prolonged the fixation time from 45 minutes to 70 minutes, still with a surprisingly sharp break (Fig. 2). This was encouraging, but a depression could easily result from nonspecific damage, even though the doses used did not alter the rats' behavior in an exercise wheel nor affect their weight, nor seem to bother them in any way. Nonetheless, a shortened fixation time with a drug that increases formation of RNA would be far more convincing. For over a year we fussed with a malonitrile dimer reported by Grinnell to speed up RNA formation in neurons and made available by Upjohn (U-9189). In time, Chamberlain worked out satisfactory conditions and found the fixation time shortened to 25 minutes (Fig. 3). Finally, Rothschild has shown a comparable improvement in avoidance-conditioning by U-9189. The rat is put in a vertical cylinder, jumps up and receives a strong shock,

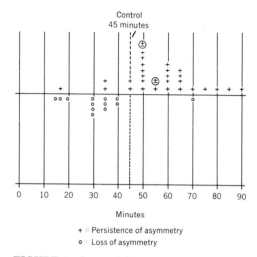

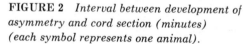

FIGURE 1   *Interval between development of asymmetry and cord section (minutes) (each symbol represents one animal).*

and is taken out. Next day, when put in the cylinder, many animals do not jump, indicating learning, or the latency of jumping is longer. On both counts, U-9189 favors learning.

Even if we accept a role of RNA in establishing the memory trace, some of the most important problems still remain, even in connection with the nature of the engram. For one thing, even though poly-

FIGURE 2   *Interval between development of asymmetry and cord section (minutes) (each symbol represents one animal).*

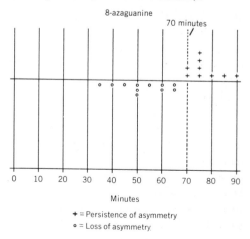

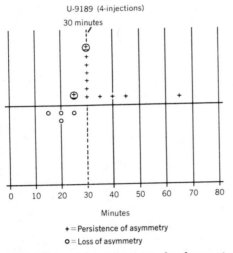

U-9189 (4-injections)

30 minutes

0   10   20   30   40   50   60   70   80

Minutes

+ = Persistence of asymmetry
o = Loss of asymmetry

FIGURE 3   *Interval between development of*
asymmetry and cord section (minutes)
(each symbol represents one animal).

nucleotides might be involved in the process, stored protein molecules, formed by
RNA, might actually constitute the enduring material code. Or, different or additional mechanisms might be involved: (a)
in the very short dynamic memory that
lasts seconds or perhaps a very few minutes (e.g., remembering a telephone number to call) but then vanishes without real
fixation; (b) in the fixed memories that
we have been considering; and (c) in the
really ancient memories, that seem even
more enduring under conditions of aphasia
or other serious memory losses. It may be
that additional mechanisms in the latter
case give it the extra stability—as a nut
left screwed up tightly on a bolt for many
years will rust in place. The sharp end-
point in our cord fixation experiments
would suggest that temporary memory is,
indeed, different in kind rather than in
degree; were it not for the fact that, when
the amount of asymmetry is plotted rather
than its simple presence at criterion level,
there is a rather more continuous curve
across the end of the fixation time (Chamberlain, Haleck, and Gerard, 1963a; Chamberlain, Rothschild and Gerard, 1963b).

The really difficult question as to engram
formation—it will not be possible even to
touch upon the other unsolved one of the
specificity of recall—has to do with the
transduction mechanism of event to structure to event congruent with the initial
one or, in terms of information, of flow to
storage to congruent flow. As discussed
elsewhere (Gerard, 1963), this raises the
same difficulties as does adaptation in evolution. In biological evolution, the answer
seems clear that a selective process, as
postulated by Darwin, is operating; in
social evolution, an instructive process, as
proposed by Lamarck, seems equally established. Individual learning and memory
share some aspects of both kinds of evolution, and the exciting question is, therefore,
whether particular changes in RNA induced by experience are simply a case of
selecting out one type from many possible
ones or of actively modifying a given one
in a certain direction. In either event, much
additional understanding and evidence will
be required before the material engram is
understood sufficiently to translate molecular and cellular changes into patterns of
nerve impulses and organismic behavior.

The functioning of collectivities of neurons, always involved in normal behavior,
brings us to another major area of physiology, which demands at least passing attention in any treatment of memory.
Wherever molecular and cellular changes
may be located, and however specific or
nonspecific, it must still be true that many
neurons are involved in each engram and,
equally, that every such neuron is involved
in many engrams. It is impossible quantitatively that one memory be in one spot
(there just are not enough such spots even
in the human brain to cover a life span of
recallable memories), and extensive destruction of brain regions does not lead to
memory scotomata, but to either no impairment or quite general impairment.
That localization of some sort occurs has
already been evidenced; and one might

add the well-known findings of temporal lobe stimulation in the unanesthetized human, in which different memories were evoked from nearby cortical regions. But these are still a long cry from the position of one input, one memory. Nerve nets or assemblies are required for reverberating circuits of physiological activity; nerve masses or sheets are necessary for somatic or steady potentials and for the transmission of excitation waves of the sort examined by Beurle. These latter are especially interesting in that they may cross one another in a cortical sheet and leave, at the locus of intersection, a sensitized region with physiological properties that would permit recall and association of those particular waves. (Moreover, only groups of neurons can exhibit the extremely general and important phenomenon of lateral, or reciprocal, inhibition.)

There is good electrical evidence that in the course of learning activity at first occurs over much of the cerebrum, but that the paths of activity then become neatly channeled. While an animal is learning a problem, and making frequent mistakes, electric responses can be picked up in widely separated regions; when it is performing with skill and correctness, activity is very sharply circumscribed—only to flare out widely again when uncertainty or confusion returns during a trial. This channeling of activity is probably one instance of the action of a type of lateral or feedback inhibition, which is more obviously seen in perceptual and motor control, and equally clearly present although not yet located and worked out in the sudden, almost all-or-none, shift from one mood to another, or from one idea to a different one, or as one plan after another commands attention.

A muscle or a limb is normally thrown into a clean pattern of action in connection with any reflex or other act. Certain fibers in a muscle and certain muscles in a limb contract, while others may remain or become relaxed, under the precisely patterned messages from the motor neuron nuclei or pools in the spinal cord. Activity reaches such a pool from many sources, yet the delimitation between the active and the inactive neurons is always sharp in each case although it shifts from case to case. Small neurons have been shown to be activated by discharges in the motor fiber from a large motor neuron, and to send their own message to neighboring motor neurons, which are inhibited, thus trimming the edges of the active group. The receptor elements in the eye, similarly, send collaterals to neighboring elements, which they also inhibit. This has the same influence in dissecting out a perceptual entity, for it serves to markedly accentuate the edge between two continuous patches of illumination. On the bright side, all receptors are stimulated to fire rapidly but are inhibiting each other considerably—except that those near the edge, having only slight inhibition from one direction, are considerably more active than their fellows deeper in the patch. An equivalent effect takes place on the dim side; none is firing rapidly because of light nor is being much inhibited by its fellows— except those near the bright edge, which are being strongly inhibited from the bright side. At the edge, therefore, the bright receptors are firing more and the dim receptors less than their fellows in the evenly illuminated patches.

These neural mechanisms for dissecting out entities are largely the product of racial experience and genetic mechanisms, but individual experience, left in material changes which subsume functional ones, are also strongly involved. Such building of the engram by activity on an existing structural scaffolding was discussed above in connection with pattern vision development, and the motor story is comparable. The nervous system starts with primitive units of organization and puts these together in ever larger constellations. Simple acts, essentially reflex patterns, are combined into more complicated ones and these into still more elaborate performance patterns; as someone put it, the motor cortex plays upon the spinal units as a typist on the keys of her typewriter. Old studies in learning revealed the same progressive groupings; an operator learning Morse code telegraphy was found to improve rapidly at first until a plateau was reached at a rather low speed of message reading. Then, often after a surprisingly long time, a further rapid improvement set in, to reach a new asymptote; and in time a third step of improvement would be superimposed. It was recognized that the first learning curve represented the recognition of letters, the second one the recognition of words as units, and the third one the recognition of phrases and sentences. This is an early demonstration of the recent formulation of perception by grouping "bits" into "chunks."

It is obvious that the motor neurons which are active in one motion are not entirely different from those active in another motion; intersecting sets of neurons are involved, with some common to many acts, others different in each. In exactly the same way, integrations at higher functional levels, playing upon the subordinate units, also engage these in individual but overlapping patterns. There is, thus, competition and interaction of neurons in progressive organizations or assemblies and, to the extent that a given memory is itself represented by the grouping or pattern of neurons which operate together, memories gain some of their interesting properties from this. I suspect that the phenomena of association, of interference, of proactive and retroactive inhibition, of the gradual shift in recall over time, and many of the other particular facets of memory of especial interest to psychologists, are more dependent on these interlocking neuron systems than they are on the particular chemical or physical change in any particular neuron or neuron group. Perhaps, even, there is a similar physiological explanation for the fact that older and more frequently used memory patterns are prepotent in determining behavior and in emerging into conscious memory and are best retained under various insults to the organism. If two different perceptions reaching consciousness, or plans leading to action, engage neuron pools which partly overlap; then, by the various inhibitory and other integrative mechanisms, one will come through in toto and the other be entirely suppressed. The one that will take precedence will be that which captures the moot interneuron group and so completes its full complement of active neurons. A stronger input through one set than another will normally lead that one to prevail. But, other things being reasonably equal, the grouping with the best established connections—the junctions with the best transmitting properties—will be the one to capture the interneurons and complete the system. If the firmness of fixation continues to increase, even a little, on repeated use (which should be greater in older than in newer acquisitions), then ancient or rehearsed learned patterns will tend to prevail.

This symposium is concerned with memory as a scientific problem, but I cannot close without drawing an important practical conclusion from this knowledge of how experience writes itself into the structure and performance of the human brain. Clearly, it is of the greatest importance to expose the young individual to as much relevant experience as possible. It is now pretty obvious (and becoming rather widely accepted) that many of the more complex intellectual functions can be enhanced by early exercise, just as pattern vision is developed by looking at visual patterns. Man's great biological virtue is in his malleability, in which he clearly is the present culmination of the major sweep of evolution. A nervous system increased the malleability of organisms, and man's overstuffed brain, with twice as many un-committed neurons, perhaps, as other brains (the functional neuron reserve), has given him the learning capacity of the group as well as of the individual. Man possesses collective and transmitted learn-ing, culture, to a unique degree; the use of symbols, language, science, and, just upon us, computers and automata, makes possible a richness and complexity of inter-action unmatched by any other system that we know. The problems of human in-teraction have mounted with its intensity; it seems obvious that it will be necessary to exploit man's potential intellectual capa-bilities to the fullest—by vastly improved educational methods—for him to keep up with his own machines and to avoid tech-nological obsolescence, if not biological elimination.

References

Chamberlain, T., Haleck, P., and Gerard, R. W. *J. Neurophysiol.*, 1963, **26**, 662–673 (*a*).

Chamberlain, T., Rothschild, G., and Gerard, R. W., *Proc. Nat'l. Acad. Sci. U.S.*, 1963, **49**, 918–924 (*b*).

W. S. Fields and W. Abbott (Eds.) *Information storage and neural control.* Springfield, Illinois: Thomas, 1963.

NAME INDEX

SUBJECT INDEX